AMERICAN GUITARS

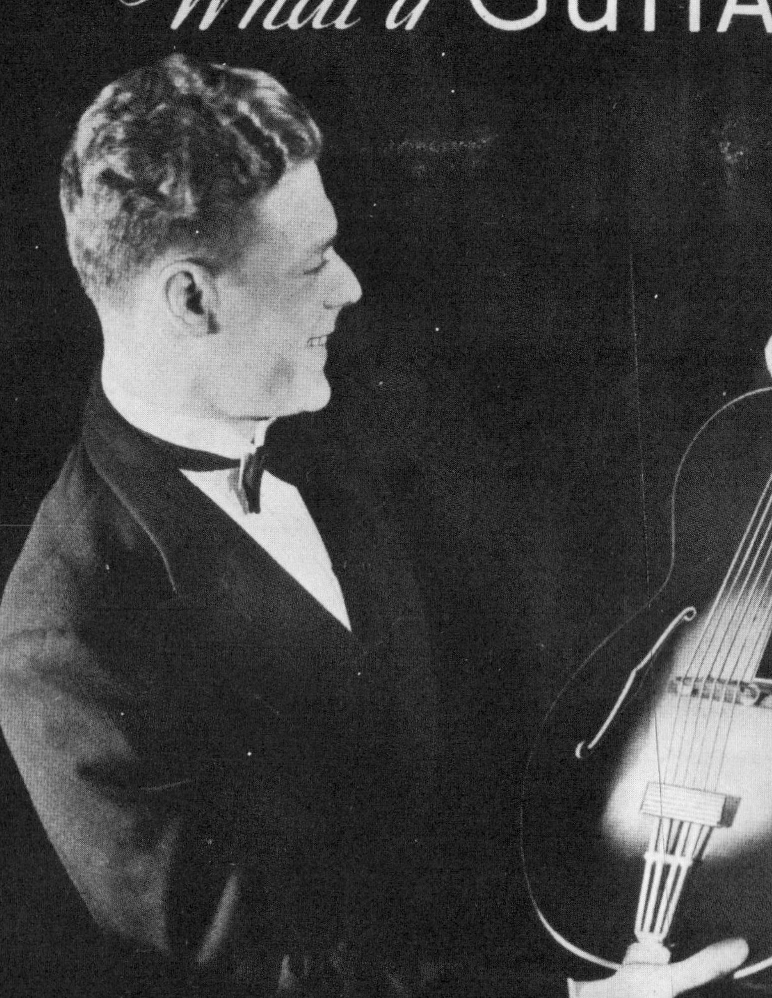

Oh, Man!
What a GUITAR!

AMERICAN GUITARS

AN ILLUSTRATED HISTORY

revised and updated edition

TOM WHEELER

HarperPerennial
A Division of HarperCollins*Publishers*

For inspirational friends
Bob Bassett,
Steve Fishell, and Don Menn

AMERICAN GUITARS. *(Revised and updated edition)*. Copyright © 1992 by Tom Wheeler. All rights reserved. Printed in the United States of America. No part of this book may be used or reproduced in any manner whatsoever without written permission except in the case of brief quotations embodied in critical articles and reviews. For information address HarperCollins Publishers, 10 East 53rd Street, New York, NY 10022.

HarperCollins books may be purchased for educational, business, or sales promotional use. For information, please call or write: Special Markets Department, HarperCollins Publishers, Inc., 10 East 53rd Street, New York, NY 10022. Telephone: (212) 207-7528; Fax: (212) 207-7222.

LIBRARY OF CONGRESS CATALOGING-IN-PUBLICATION DATA
Wheeler, Tom (Thomas Hutchin)
American guitars : an illustrated history / Tom Wheeler. — Rev. and updated ed.
p. cm.
ISBN 0-06-273154-8 (pbk.)
1. Guitar—History. I. Title.
ML1015.G9W5 1992
787.87'1973—dc20 91-58288

---

92 93 94 95 96 MPC 10 9 8 7 6 5 4 3 2 1

FOREWORD

by Les Paul

You should see my place. Guitars all over. Old solidbody prototypes, arch-tops, Epiphones, Gibsons, boxes of pickups and electronics, and just about every kind of recording gear you can think of. You could throw a grenade in here and straighten it up. I just can't imagine my home without guitars everywhere.

I'm so identified with the Les Paul electrics that sometimes a kid'll come up and say, "Hey! You're a real person, not a guitar!" But like a lot of players, I started out on acoustic, and one of my earliest instruments was a Troubador flat-top from Sears. I had a book called *The E-Z Guitar Method.* Sound familiar? On my first radio shows I was known as Rhubarb Red, and I played country music. I hit Chicago in the early 1930s and started playing jazz under my own name on WIND radio, and a lot of people never knew that Rhubarb Red and Les Paul were the same guy.

I can't count the guitars I've owned since that Sears flat-top, and modifying them has been a big thing with me ever since the late 1920s. Once I jammed my mother's phonograph needle right into the top of a guitar and hooked it up. It worked! I had my first electric. The Larson brothers in Chicago made me an experimental model in 1934 with a half-inch maple top and no soundholes. "You're crazy," they said. "It won't vibrate." I said, "I *know* it won't vibrate. That's the whole idea." I was on my way to my first solidbodies. In 1936 Paul Barth at National built me another one, with a half-inch solid maple top and no f-holes. I also built one out of a railroad rail, and another one out of aluminum.

I bought an inexpensive Gibson arch-top in 1937, and John D'Angelico built me a solid wood section to go inside it. It was another step toward a solidbody. Gibson was going crazy because I was playing this cheap model. They kept bringing me their top guitars to try out, and they built some special ones for me, but none sounded as good as the cheapie that John D'Angelico and I had rigged up. Epi Stathopoulo was another friend. In 1941 I went to his Epiphone factory and built a solidbody out of a 4″ x 4″ board. I stuck on a regular guitar body for looks and called it "the Log." The following year I bought an Epiphone from a guy who'd injured his hand and couldn't play anymore. I stuck a Gibson decal and a Gibson fingerboard on it and put in some movable pickups that could slide along the string length for different sounds. It had the solid interior contraption like the one D'Angelico had made me, and it was my favorite guitar at the time.

I moved to Los Angeles in '43 and worked for Bing Crosby, who was interested in my work with electronics and sound. He encouraged me to build my own studio. I went hog-wild out in the garage and built a recording lathe from a Cadillac flywheel. See, I'd built my first crystal set when I was nine, and some radio broadcasting equipment when I was thirteen. I was always taking apart microphones and phonograph pickups to see what made them tick. I used to read a lot of books on that stuff. Still do.

I had a bad car accident in February 1948 and was out of commission for two years. The docs rigged up my body cast so that I could still play guitar with my right thumb, and while I was in the cast I put the final tracks on some records I'd been working on.

I've been experimenting with recording techniques and special effects all along—echo, reverb, overdubbing, speeded-up guitars, and so on. I was doing disc multiples in '46 and sound-on-sound with tape in '49. I built the first multitrack recorder, the kind that's used on just about every record you hear nowadays. On a lot of my hits with my wife, Mary Ford, I played all the parts myself. In concert I'll pre-record the other parts on tape and then play along, controlling the recorder with the Les Paulverizer, a remote-control unit mounted right on the guitar. I'm wired, I'm self-contained. And I was doing phase shifting with discs ten years before anyone tried it with tape. The idea came to me after hearing a disc jockey try to play two copies of the same record simultaneously.

I was working out in my back yard with all this equipment, and a lot of people dropped by—Merle Travis, Paul Bigsby, Leo Fender, and others. They saw me using either the Log or the modified Epiphone. I rigged up a Gibson for Mary. It was a copy of my Epiphone with the solid core. Mary's guitar served as the test model for Gibson. They wanted me to endorse them, and so I told them that they had to match that sound. I wanted a low action, high output, and a lot of treble, and they could only get it with a complete solidbody. I drove 'em crazy up there. We finally got together in about 1950, and that's how the Les Paul guitars came about.

So I've been involved with guitars for half a century, one way or another. It's about time someone put all the modern guitar history into one place, and Tom Wheeler's done it right. I've had his first book for years, right on my library shelf. In fact, I've got a bunch of them. Guys keep giving them to me as presents. I always say, "Gee, just what I wanted!"

This new book covers the history of all the major manufacturers, plus a lot of little guys you probably never heard of, and it's fabulous. I learned a lot from it—facts, dates, serial numbers, how the guitars were built, how they changed from year to year, and how different inventors and companies made the guitar what it is today.

And there are a lot of fun things. I mean, I built some crazy stuff, but some of the inventions in this book are way out in space. There's both humor and seriousness in the text, and a lot of warmth and affection for the guitar. Everybody from Leo Fender and Adolph Rickenbacker and Fred Gretsch up to Hartley Peavey and Travis Bean—they're all here, telling their stories. And the pictures—there's nearly a thousand of them: production guitars, prototypes, goofy inventions, rare collectors' guitars, custom models, people, factories, workshops, advertisements. It's a real slice of American culture. Some of the things in here go back to the Civil War, and some look like the instruments of the future.

I think you'll like *American Guitars*. It's the guitar bible, the best book yet by the world's foremost chronicler of the modern guitar. Take it from Rhubarb Red.

Les Paul

ACKNOWLEDGMENTS

For the first year of this project I did little but write letters, and the response was inspiring. Scores of collectors and retailers answered my questionnaires, adhered to my photo guidelines, photographed their collections (sometimes repeatedly), and provided information. Though there is insufficient room to specify all of their contributions in detail, I must mention a few kind people who gave many hours of their time. Chief among them is George Gruhn of Gruhn Guitars in Nashville. One of America's foremost collectors, he provided many photos, stacks of literature, and sound counsel at several stages of my research. Other members of *American Guitars'* brain trust include Tom Wittrock of Third Eye Music, Springfield, MO; Steve Evans of Jacksonville Guitar Center, Jacksonville, AR; Julius Bellson; Forrest White; and Jim Werner. Thanks, friends.

Every photo credit is an acknowledgment. The following collectors made especially large contributions of illustrations; their corresponding photographers are listed in parentheses. In my view, their work comprises the highlights of this book. They are Norm Harris of Norm's Rare Guitars, Los Angeles (Jon Sievert); Charley Wirz of Charley's Guitars, Dallas (Bill Crump); Matt Spitzer of Spitzer's Music, Hayward, CA (Jon Sievert); Jimmy Wallace (Mike Perla); Pete Wagener of LaVonne Wagener Music, Burnsville, MN (Ed Beaty); Dave deForrest of Guitar Trader, Red Bank, NJ (Photography Unlimited); Jim Beach of Wooden Music, Chicago (Anne Margaret Goodman); Matt Umanov of Matt Umanov Guitars, New York (John Peden); Bruce Berman; Steve Soest of Soest's Guitar Repair, Santa Ana, CA (Thel Rountree); Pearl Jones of The Music Shop, Grant's Pass, OR (Rick Madsen); and David Colburn of Vin-

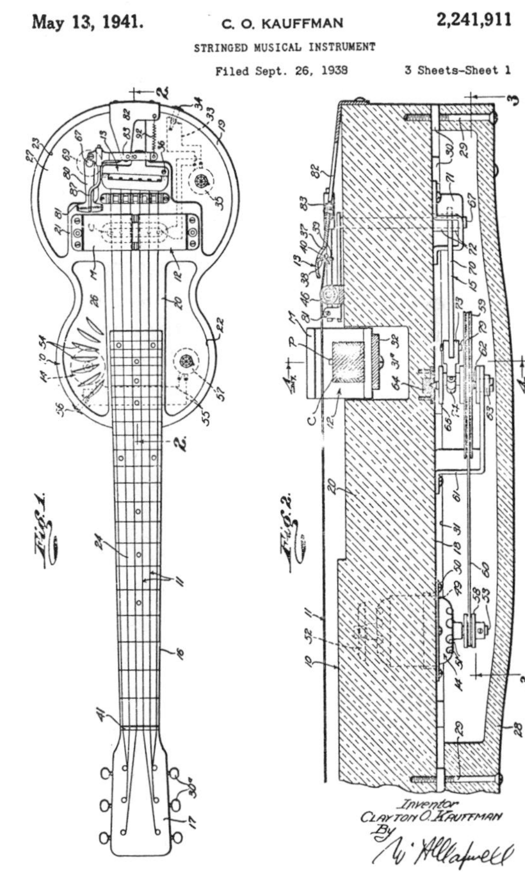

Doc Kauffman's motor-driven vibrato patent (1938) was assigned to Electro.

tage Fret Shop, Ashland, NH (Allen Caswell). Scott Baxendale took several shots of George Gruhn's guitars. Bob Perine, Bill Carson, and Leo Fender provided the early Fender factory pictures and promo material. Some of the Gibson factory photos were taken by Art Boguse. Thanks to Brian Brock for the front cover photograph. *Guitar Player* magazine publisher Jim Crockett freely opened *GP*'s files, which I freely ransacked for pictures. Thanks again, Jim.

I am especially appreciative of the assistance of the interviewees and sources named in the text, as well as that of my proofreaders: Jim Hatlo, who also researched and drafted the Guild chapter, Rani Cochran, Bob Bassett, Connie Bassett, John Brosh, and Joy Clemens. Thanks also to the transcribers: Judie Eremo, Lucienne O'Connor, Sally Schwartz, and especially Ellayn Evans; and to researchers Don Clark, John Quarterman (Dobro), Jeff Tripp (Stromberg), Robert Hartman (Maurer), Rex Herder (Gibson SGs), and especially Don Menn (Travis Bean, Peavey, Ernie Ball, Dean).

Among the many other contributors were Bob Alford, Dick Allen, Ernie Ball, Donna Bennett-Brosh, Fred Bernardo, Bruce Bolen, Brian Brock, Tut Campbell, Louis Catello, Country Music Hall of Fame, John Dopyera, Seymour Duncan, John Entwistle, Leo Fender, *Frets* magazine, George Fullerton, Fred Gretsch, Mike Gerchak, Larry Henrikson of Ax-In-Hand (DeKalb, IL), James Hilligoss, *Mugwumps* publisher Mike Holmes, Wayne Johnson, Chris Kondrath, Dan Lambert, Robb Lawrence, Mike Leonard of Saratoga Camera (San Jose, CA), the Library of Congress, Neil Lilien, Ron Lira of Honest Ron's Guitars (Oklahoma City), Frank Lucido (California Guitar, Santa Barbara), Charlie Malyszka, Dominic Milano, Rick Nielsen, Les Paul, Phil Petillo, Harold Pollock, Alan Rogan, Jim Sallis, Jim Schwartz, Ed Seelig of Silver Strings (St. Louis, MO), Tim Shaw, Smithsonian Institution, Thomas Stevenson, Phil Taylor, Don Teeter, Peter Tenney, Lachland Throndson, Peter Townshend, Merle Travis, the U.S. Patent Office, Dirk Vogel, William Walz, Alan Wolf, Allen Woody, André Duchossoir, Roger Siminoff, and Tom Van Hoose.

Finally, thanks to Karolina Harris, who designed the layout for *American Guitars,* and to my editors, Hal Grove and Buddy Skydell, for believing in the project and making it work.

An elegant 1943 Epiphone Emperor, natural finish. ***Wagener/ Beaty***

INTRODUCTION

In *The Barber of Seville* an alarmed Figaro exclaims to the Count, "I have forgotten my guitar! I am losing my wits!" To this day people often value their guitars above other possessions, never forgetting that red-ribboned Harmony on a Christmas morning, and relating to their Silvertones and herringbones with an uncommon urgency. These legions of devotees continue to swell decade after decade, probably because of their chosen instrument's many textures and moods, musical accessibility and challenges, and romantic associations and sex appeal (its literature steams with both masculine and feminine allusions).

Each of the guitar family's sister instruments is so distinctive and appealing that the listener encounters a whole gallery of characters to enjoy, while the player can explore a hundred modes of expression, from the sublime delicacy of a Segovian harmonic to the feedback brain-fry of a Les Paul plugged through a Marshall stack cranked up to 8. For sheer variety in construction, the guitar is unsurpassed. Revealing a broad spectrum of tastes among makers and owners, guitars range from pristine classics sparingly adorned with Moorish rosettes, inlays of mother of pearl, or marquetries of dyed woods, to baroque wedding cakes whose aesthetics fall just shy of Webb Pierce's silver-dollar-encrusted Pontiac. Each instrument is unique, asserting its personality through a host of character traits. There is the look of metal, from worn gold hardware's muted sheen to the cold chrome glint. There are the sounds of aged, hand-tuned acoustic chambers and souped-up electronics, the colors of deep-shaded French polishes and glossy rainbow enamels, and the smells of seasoned woods, leather cases, glues, oils, and varnishes. And apart from all this there is some radiant guitar

The short-lived Martin F-7 appeared in 1935, and 187 were made before its discontinuance in 1942. Details: large (16 by 20 inch) rosewood body, hexagon markers, Style 45 multicolor back strip.

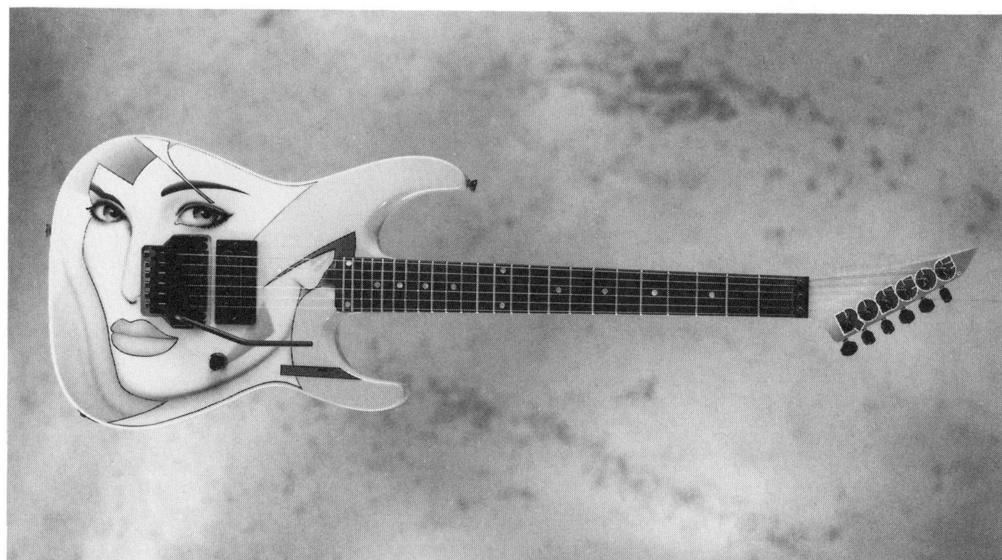

Keith Roscoe opened The Guitar Shop in Greensboro, North Carolina in 1971. From a small workshop crafting four or five guitars a year, it evolved into a modest production factory producing 20 to 30 guitars a month. By 1990, Roscoe had turned out over 900 guitars. Over 75 percent of Roscoe's guitars feature either custom airbrushing or textured finishes. The original Guitar Shop site houses the finishing, assembly, and office facilities.

sensuousness that for centuries has bridged cultural gaps and linked people who may have little else in common.

Steeped in mystery, history, hogwash, and pop voodoo, guitars have become period pieces of almost totemic significance—some timeless, others dated as a crewcut; some spiffy as a showroom Bugatti, others funky as a Studebaker up on blocks. The understated grace of a Martin flat-top is the whisper of a company tradition that was already three decades old when Kit Carson reached Fort Defiance. The Emperors and L-5s are ever-stately veterans of the Jazz and Swing eras, while the lightning bolt in the K&F logo recalls America's early infatuation with radio and progress. A tailfinned Flying V is the '57 Chevy of guitars, while the *G* cattle brand on an old orange Gretsch asserts its electrified cowpoke persona in no uncertain terms.

A young Elmer Stromberg and his wife Mary, circa 1924. With his father Charles, a Swedish immigrant to Boston in 1887, Elmer Stromberg produced big, powerful-sounding guitars, much prized by top jazz musicians of the 1930s, 1940s, and 1950s. With their cutting power, Strombergs were perfect rhythm voices to complement the melodies and harmonies of horns in the big band era.

The guitar was brought to the New World before the union of the colonies, and over the years it has threaded its way through the tapestry of Americana, accompanying Yankee and Confederate soldiers into battle, cowboys into the sunset, and protesters into the streets. There are a hundred indelible guitar images: blues wailers and juke joint jumpers, vagabond poets and Nashville cats, mountain stompers and moonlight crooners, rednecks and bluebloods, big band swingers and combo beboppers, sequin-studded Texas troubadors, rockabilly rebels, electrified corkscrew-haired crazies, campfire comrades, and teen idols. The guitar emerges as one of twentieth-century America's foremost cultural icons.

With vampiric lust, guitar buffs devour whatever printed materials they can scrounge—price lists, Sears catalogues, instruction leaflets, album jacket notes, everything. But with a few exceptions the people who made guitar history were concerned with the guitars, not the history, and most of the instrument's literature is retrospective. For years the only documentation

Left: **Thousands of colorfully painted beginner's models like this one were sold under scores of brand names during the 1930s, 1940s, and 1950s. Note "mother-of-plastic" fingerboard.** *Dan Erlewine/Tom Erlewine* *Right:* **Roy Rogers Signature guitar, made by Harmony circa 1950 and sold through Sears.**
Len Kapushion/Bill Gunter

was found in fairly inaccurate company promo materials and in lists of often erratic serial numbers. Rumors took root and yielded jungles of contradictory stories. Out of the mists of superstitious reverence came the legends of Lloyd Loar and tales of the White Penguin. The passion for old guitars spawned small industries in replacement parts, catalogue reprints, reissue guitars, finish restorations, and even counterfeit instruments. Small-time traders dealing out of their station wagons at bluegrass festivals evolved into vintage instrument retailers with international clienteles, and it was they and the private collectors—more than the manufacturers—who coined today's guitar jargon of "P bass" and "gold-top," "stack-knob" and "dot-neck."

Authors waded into this pool of opportunity, some emerging clean, some muddy. Books and articles derived primarily from catalogue-skimming have unfortunately clouded the already murky waters, while others based on diligent research (for example, Mike Longworth's *Martin Guitars* and André Duchossoir's *Gibson Electrics,* vol. 1) have made permanent contributions.

There are several broad aspects of American guitar history, and with the exception of actual how-to construction, this book

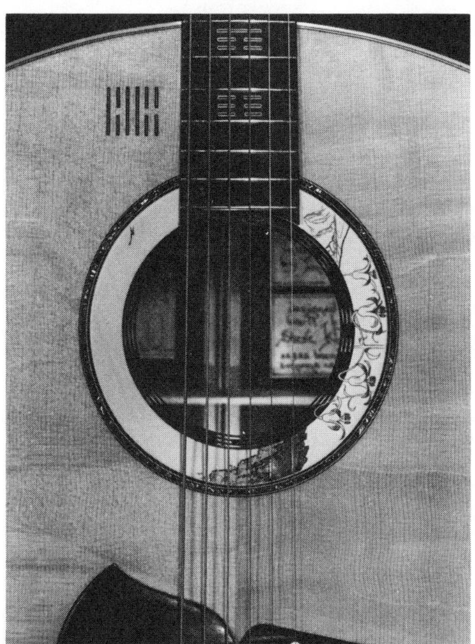

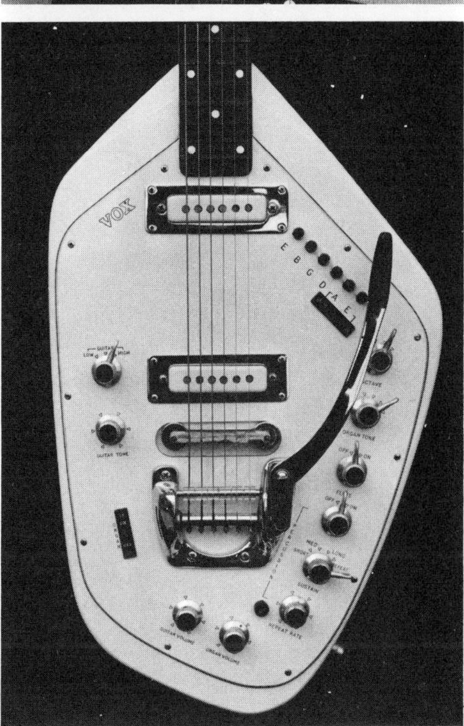

Top: **Rosette detail on a steel-string made by California luthier Steve Klein for Joni Mitchell. The slots in the innermost ebony soundhole ring are I Ching symbols, as are the body and fretboard markings. Note the radically shaped bridge, which provides more contact on the top's bass side.** *Jerome Knill* *Bottom:* **Everything but curb feelers. Though not an American-made guitar, this Vox perfectly illustrates a late-1960s American guitar phenomenon: gadgets.**

Rickenbacker Model 59 Student lap steel with baked ivory finish. The companion amp is a little larger than a lunchbox. *Art Streib*

attempts in varying degrees to explore all of them, including cultural influences, commercial statistics, and particularly chronology, personalities, and structural evolution. Regardless of perspective and given various companies' incomplete records and relentlessly inconsistent manufacturing, one should avoid unqualified conclusions. Since several men figure prominently in the stories of more than one firm, and since there have been numerous acquisitions and mergers, grasping one company's history may require reading another's. For example, understanding the establishment of Rickenbacker necessitates a familiarization with National and Dobro. Other recommended crosschecking: Gibson/Epiphone, Epiphone/Guild, Kay/Valco, Lyon & Healy/Regal, Regal/Dobro, and Dobro/Mosrite.

You won't find the whole story of American guitars in any one book, including this one, but major pieces of puzzles are here—John Dopyera in the mid 1920s experimenting with various metals for his National resonators; Vålco namesake Victor Smith in 1931, studying the elliptical patterns of magnetized iron particles dancing on a piece of paper; and Gibson president Ted McCarty on a rainy-night drive up to Delaware Water Gap to exhibit the Les Paul prototype to Les Paul.

Students of American guitars who set out to chart some continuous river of history will instead encounter crosscurrents and intersecting tributaries. Even when all relevant facts are known, a company's story can be dizzyingly complex. One example: Dobro split off from National (which had figured in the establishment of Rickenbacker). Then the two merged, later

In 1939 John William Gallagher established a furniture-making business in Wartrace, Tennessee, 60 miles southeast of Nashville. He converted to guitar manufacture in the 1960s, and he and his son Don built 24 guitars their first year. Don Gallagher took over management of the business in 1976, prior to his father's death in 1979. By 1982, four full-time employees were helping Don produce three to four instruments per week.

Though Gallaghers are modern instruments, one might conclude from a conversation with Don Gallagher that, around Wartrace, few things have changed over the years: "My family settled here in the late 1820s. My grandfather, my father, and I were all born in the same house. The buildings that my father bought in 1959 were constructed out of bricks made by my grandfather. You might say that we are a part of Wartrace, and Wartrace is a part of us. It's not a big town, and that suits us."

The late J.W. Gallagher examined a guitar under construction in his Wartrace, Tennessee workshop. With the exception of perhaps a dozen classical guitars, all J.W. Gallagher & Son instruments are steel-strings. There are four different body sizes, and all models feature the company's distinctive French-curve headstock. One of the most popular models is the mahogany Doc Watson dreadnought.

moved from L.A. to Chicago, and still later evolved into Valco. A typical Valco guitar might have a Silvertone logo, a Harmony body, a Kluson tailpiece, a National neck, and a Sears, Roebuck catalogue listing. Then Valco got tied up with Kay. OMI, another successor to Dobro, was bought by one of several incarnations of Mosrite (which joined forces with Kustom, which was bought out by Baldwin, which imported Burns, which was associated with Ampeg, some of whose guitars bore the name of Dan Armstrong, who bought Danelectro, which, like National, made guitars for Sears, which owned Harmony). There are many other stories—the guitars that were built by Harmony,

Les Paul and Mary Ford, circa 1961, with modified Gibson SG-style Les Paul models.

Early 1950s Fender promo photo.

Steve Klein's solidbody appeared in 1990, featuring a Steinberger neck and bridge system, EMG pickups, and an ergonomically designed body that balances the guitar in an ideal playing position whether it is played sitting or standing.

labeled Regal, and sold by Fender; veteran Epiphone craftsmen staffing the first Guild plant; CMI's acquisition of Gibson; Gibson's acquisition of Epiphone; and on and on.

Some questions remain unanswered and certain details are obscured by the conflicting memories of eyewitnesses, but here are first-person accounts of most of American guitar's legendary figures—Leo Fender, Les Paul, Fred Gretsch, Joe Maphis, Chet Atkins, John Dopyera, Adolph Rickenbacker, Merle Travis, and others. Their companies' histories, the guitars they built, and their crossed paths are the subject matter of this book.

1958 National Glenwood. Slightly fancier than the Town & Country, it was at one time the top of the solidbody line. ***Wagener/Beaty***

The materials are generally organized alphabetically, according to the brand name's most common usage. Thus John D'Angelico is under *D* and Chas. Stromberg is under *S*, while Ernie Ball is under *E*, and Oscar Schmidt under *O*. A single company's story may well embrace several brand names, so it's not unusual for two or more brands to be covered in a single section. Examples include the section on National, Dobro, and Valco, and the one on Lyon & Healy and Washburn. Cross references are provided throughout the listings.

Following the alphabetical section is the "Gallery," a selection of limited-production but noteworthy guitars.

Incidentally, a manufacturer's significance is not always proportional to the space afforded it in this volume, for companies vary widely in how much documentation they have produced and preserved. The once gigantic Lyon & Healy, for instance, is hardly ever discussed today except by a few vintage guitar buffs. There are more electric guitars here than acoustics for a couple of reasons: manufacturers who make both types tend to offer more electric models; and the features of electrics often change regularly, as opposed to a Martin D-45, for example, whose entire structural evolution could be depicted in just a few photos. Except where otherwise noted, first-person quotes are from interviews conducted by the author in 1979 and 1980.

Guitar aficionados have a special attraction to the unusual instrument, the rare bird, and I'm no exception. Here you'll find some fabulously off-the-wall pieces, such as a left-handed White Falcon, John Entwistle's White Penguin, the first Citation ever made, the first D-76, and the first Dobro, plus several factory original one-of-a-kinds, including the Lucite Stratocaster, the Futura, and the paisley Strat. But the Maltese Falcons and the odd ducks are only a part of the story. Let us not overlook the Sears Silvertone with the amp in the case, the three-dollar mail-order guitar with painted cowboys, the almost forgotten Maurers and Bauers, the TV Pal, the Davy Crockett, and the My Buddy.

American Guitars: An Illustrated History is one person's impression, a celebration of the history of a most compelling instrument, dedicated to flatcar riders and crosstie walkers, to tuxedoed slick-hair gentleman jazzers, to garage rockers who play too loud, and to music store window daydreamers everywhere.

Tom Wheeler

INTRODUCTION TO THE REVISED EDITION

Although the original *American Guitars* covered the mid-1800s to the early 1980s, much of it focused on the 1940s, 1950s, and 1960s, due to the golden-age status of instruments from that period, the guitar's post-war prominence in jazz, blues, country, and rock, and the guitar boom of the 1960s, whose repercussions echo to this day.

Since the book's first appearance, many innovative builders and companies have gained prominence—Ned Steinberger, Paul Reed Smith, Philip Kubicki, Valley Arts, Mike Tobias, Grover Jackson, Tom Anderson, and dozens of others. A few familiar companies, including Fender, Rickenbacker, and Martin, have in recent years turned out some of their best guitars since the 1960s. This excitement was offset during the "Strat mania" of the 1980s, when cookie-cutter clones were cranked out under various brand names, and when many "new" designs were merely rehashed concepts from decades past. In any case, few recent instruments have shown much potential for rivaling classic Gibsons, Epiphones, Fenders, and others as the vintage guitars of the 21st century. One more development: during the 1980s, manufacturers churned out mounds of literature, leaving little need for elaboration here.

For all these reasons, this revision ignores many models of the 1970s and 1980s, includes some noteworthy exceptions, updates some of the previously covered companies, presents several dozen newcomers, and preserves intact the vast majority of the original edition. (Although they produce some of the world's finest guitars, classical builders are not included here because their traditions, aesthetics, and clientele all exist somewhat apart from the world of steel-strings and electric guitars and basses.)

New entries: Benedetto, Benedict, Borys, Bunker, Carl Thompson, Collings, Erlewine, Fodera, Fritz Bros., G & L, Heritage, Jackson/Charvel, Jerry Jones, Ken Smith, Steve Klein, Kubicki, Modulus Graphite, Monroe, Monteleone, Nova, Paul Reed Smith, Pedulla, Pensa-Suhr, Premier, Ripley, Robin, Roscoe, Rose, Santa Cruz, Schecter, Schoenberg, Spector, Steinberger, Tobias, Tom Anderson, Turner, Valley Arts, Zion, and Zon.

The updated companies include Alembic, B.C. Rich, Carvin, Fender, Gibson, Gretsch, Guild, Hamer, Martin, Melobar, Mosrite, Music Man, OMI/Dobro, Ovation, Peavey, Rickenbacker, and Taylor.

Special thanks to the luthiers and manufacturers for their cooperation, to Lonni Gause for handling the correspondence, and to Richard Smith, *Guitar Player*'s fine Rare Bird columnist and author of the excellent *The History of Rickenbacker Guitars*, for his help in updating the Rickenbacker and Fender chapters.

Tom Wheeler, 1992

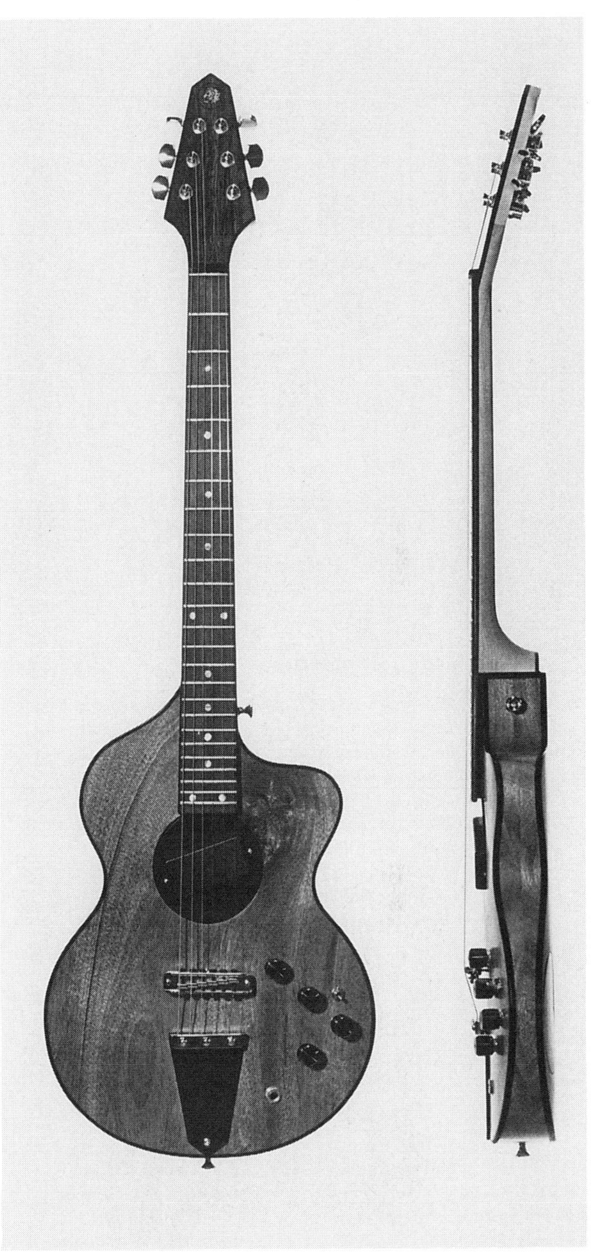

Turner: Rick Turner was an Alembic cofounder and an original partner at Modulus Graphite; the graphite neck patent was issued in his name. His innovative post-Alembic guitars came to be favored by Lindsey Buckingham, among others. (Necks were made from Alembic neck scrap, bodies from stock used as center laminations of Alembics.) In 1979 Rick set up shop in Novato, near San Francisco, eventually hiring five workers. About 200 guitars were built (serial numbers are stamped on the tops of the pegheads, the year indicated on one side). The business failed, and in 1981 Turner called it quits. As we go to press, however, he is again building guitars on a limited basis in Los Angeles. The Turner shown here is distinguished by its shape, rotating Bartolini humbucker, and black binding.

Rose Guitars of Hendersonville, Tennessee, was founded in 1981 by Jonathan Rose. Shown here: a Tele-style solidbody with EMG pickups, active electronics, distinctive "R" carving at the end of the fingerboard, custom wiring and inlay, and extended rear neck cutaway for greater fretboard access. Known for their great feel, Rose's excellent custom guitars have been played by several of Nashville's best-known pickers.

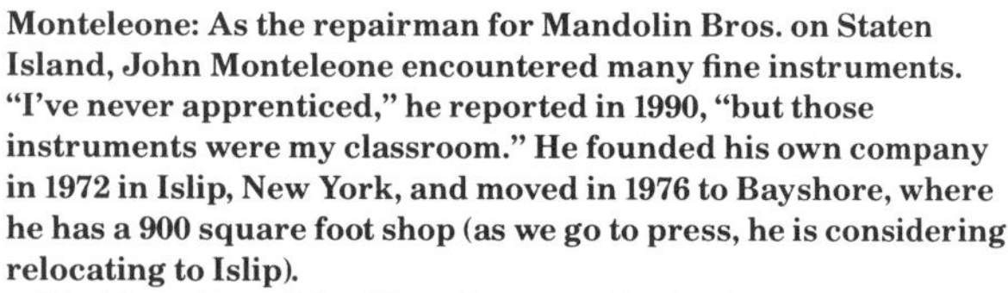

Monteleone: As the repairman for Mandolin Bros. on Staten Island, John Monteleone encountered many fine instruments. "I've never apprenticed," he reported in 1990, "but those instruments were my classroom." He founded his own company in 1972 in Islip, New York, and moved in 1976 to Bayshore, where he has a 900 square foot shop (as we go to press, he is considering relocating to Islip).

Working alone, John Monteleone crafts about two instruments per month, each stunning in its own right. He is shown here with a curly-maple Eclipse arch-top, an elegant masterpiece that recalls various American classics while at the same time clearly departing from them. Details: a top of "bear-claw" Alaskan Sitka spruce, back and sides of fiddleback and quilted big-leaf maple, and ebony binding and trim. Such guitars place John Monteleone among America's most esteemed luthiers.

AMERICAN GUITARS

ACOUSTIC

In 1972 and 1973 Acoustic, the well-known amplifier company, marketed an electric guitar and bass, both called Black Widow. The 41-inch guitar featured two humbucking pickups, 24 frets, a rosewood board, and Grovers. Some or all were fitted with a red pad in back; against the ebony-finished maple body, the effect more or less resembled black widow spider markings. Some Black Widows were imported from Japan, and others were built by Semie Moseley of Mosrite (the latter had neck dimensions similar to Mosrites). None was manufactured in Acoustic's Southern California plant.

Acoustic Black Widow bass: rosewood fingerboard, Grover tuners.

ALEMBIC

Committed to high technology, its origins steeped in late-sixties San Francisco psychedelia, the Alembic Company of Northern California is unconventional, to say the least. It pioneered many once esoteric and now common guitar features, including brass hardware, sustain blocks, low-impedance pickups, onboard preamps, and active filtering, as well as aesthetic details such as the use of exotic hardwoods, highly sculpted bodies, and hand oiled finishes.

While various Rickenbacker guitars and reverse Gibson Firebirds had used full or partial length neck/centerpieces, Alembic was the first to emphasize the feature, constructing stunning full-length laminates of contrasting woods. Though a small

Alembics (*left to right*): koa wood bass with a short-scale graphite neck; bubinga wood long-scale bass; walnut bass with an "omega" body cut and a medium-scale neck.

firm, Alembic was revolutionary. Its products were embraced by prominent musicians, and its successes helped open doors for other companies (B.C. Rich, Travis Bean, and Veillette-Citron, for example) offering expensive production guitars as alternatives to the long established brands.

Alembic was founded by Ron Wickersham and his wife, Susan. Both lived in the Novato, California, warehouse where the Grateful Dead practiced in 1969. Susan, Alembic's general manager, remembered, "Owsley Stanley, the prominent figure of the psychedelic era and longtime mentor of the Dead, brought Ron—who is our chief engineer—and me together with [Dead members] Phil Lesh and Mickey Hart. It was actually Ron and Phil's cooperation that developed the first Alembic concepts."

While not an official company founder, the colorful and notorious Owsley was very much a guiding spirit of Alembic, especially in its early days. It was he who had convinced the Wickershams to move to Novato in 1968 in order to act as sound consultants for the Grateful Dead. "Owsley brought us together," said former Alembic president Rick Turner. "It was his idea to assemble it all under one roof—the music, the equipment, the manufacturing, the repairs, everything. One of the main ideas was simply to take recording studio technology and put it into a guitar, even if it cost a lot of money." As Owsley himself put it, "With the technology available to send a man to the moon, it was inconceivable to me that there had been no marked improvements to the electric guitar in decades." He added, "The name *Alembic* is from alchemy. It is a hermetically sealed vessel used for transmutation."

In 1969 Alembic customized a Gibson for Phil Lesh and a hollowbody Guild for Jefferson Airplane bassist Jack Casady. Later Wickersham designed a 20-knob quadrophonic circuit for Lesh's Guild. Rick Turner was hired in May 1970 and was the chief body designer until October 1978. He codesigned pickups with Wickersham and built the first Alembic instrument, Jack Casady's mission-control bass. Still another Owsley acquaintance, Grateful Dead sound engineer Bob Matthews, also joined the company.

In March 1970 Alembic moved to 320 Judah Street in San Francisco; during this period 50 to 60 percent of its business involved the Grateful Dead. In late June of that year Ron Wickersham, Bob Matthews, and Rick Turner incorporated the company. Bob was the first president, followed by Ron, and then Rick.

Alembic was brought to national attention through an article in *Rolling Stone* and soon entered into a distribution agreement with L.D. Heater. It moved to 60 Brady Street in San Francisco. In 1973 Bob Matthews' interests were bought out by fellow employees, and Sam Field joined the company (he later succeeded Rick Turner as president). In November of the same year, the woodworking facilities were set up in Turner's barn in Cotati, while the office and electronics shop were relocated in the Wickershams' barn in nearby Sebastopol. The crew, numbering about a half-dozen, began building instruments on a regular but very limited basis, only about two per month.

A high point in Alembic's history was the design and construction of the Dead's towering P.A. system. With hundreds of components, it was unbelievably big, it was *Ben-Hur*.

The L.D. Heater association ended in 1976, and only weeks later Alembic affiliated with Rothchild, a glamorous but short-lived distribution company whose distinguished lines included Travis Bean, Taylor, and Canada's Larrivee. In June 1977 Alembic consolidated its shops and offices at 8360 Industrial Avenue in Cotati, building about 20 to 25 instruments per month, approximately 85 percent of them electric basses. Also in that year the graphite neck was developed by Rick Turner and Geoff Gould; the latter founded Modulus Graphite, later associated with Alembic.

In October 1978 Turner's interests were bought out by the company, and the following month the Rothchild distributorship terminated. About six weeks later Alembic moved to 45 Foley Street in Santa Rosa.

By early 1982, Alembic had built 2,350 instruments, the great majority of them electric basses. The company makes about 30 of its standard models each month. (From November 1979 to June 1981 Alembic built some guitars for Yamaha.) Employees who became noted builders in their own right include Bruce Becvar, Doug Irwin, Brian Smith (Hyak), Glen Quan (Leo Quan), Ron Armstrong (Stars Guitars), and Rick Turner (Turner Guitars).

1992 Update

Alembic continues its quest to combine the best traits of a production facility and a custom shop. "We make everything we can," reports Mica Wickersham, "including parts as diverse as printed circuit cards, brass bridges, and highly-crafted woodworking." In 1989 Alembic moved to a larger facility in Santa Rosa, California, and by 1990 employed 24 people. Alembic offers about a dozen models, with production at about 80 guitars and basses each month.

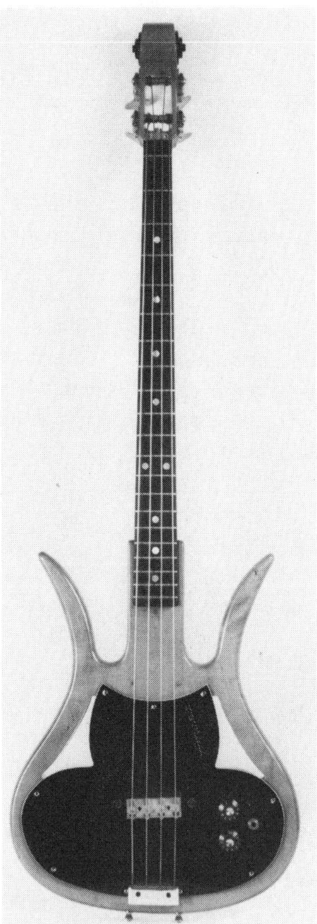

Mid-1960s Ampeg bass. *Gruhn/Baxendale*

ALOHA

The Aloha Publishing and Musical Instrument Company was organized in 1935 by J.M. Raleigh. Its executive offices were located at 7947 South Halsted Street in Chicago, and their low-priced electric guitars were made by various companies and marketed under the brand names Aloha and Raleigh.

AMPEG AND DAN ARMSTRONG AMPEG

Ampeg amps and bass. Note the instrument's scroll peghead and body cutouts.

Everett Hull was a New York jazz bassist who in 1947 perfected a design for a supporting rod (peg) for a bass fiddle. The peg contained a Clevite brand pickup positioned inside the instrument. From this *amp*lified *peg,* Mr. Hull took the name for his firm, and in 1949 or 1950 he founded the Ampeg-Bassamp Company, located on the ninth floor at 214 West 42nd Street.

In 1957 Ampeg introduced a complete line of musical instrument amplifiers, and by that time it had moved to Roosevelt Avenue on Long Island. The company's most famous amp of this early period was the Portaflex, designed by Oliver Jesperson (also known as Jess Oliver). It was an enclosed reflex baffle amp with an internally housed chassis that, like a sewing machine, turned upside down and mounted on top of the speaker cabinet when in use. In 1962 Mr. Hull introduced his company's first instrument, the all-electric Baby Bass, an upright model slightly smaller than a cello. Ampeg electric guitars and standard electric basses were on the drawing boards at the time.

By 1962 Ampeg had moved to 1570 West Blancke Street, Linden, New Jersey, and by 1966 the company had introduced two very unusual solidbody scroll-head basses. These models were assembled in the Ampeg factory after the bodies had been built elsewhere in New Jersey. The company also imported electric guitars from Burns of London.

In early 1968, new owners of Ampeg bought the Grammer guitar plant in Nashville. Company executives consulted Dan Armstrong—the respected designer, retailer, and repairman—concerning possible improvements to the Grammer steel-string. Armstrong suggested that electric guitars were a more promising investment for an amplifier company. Ampeg concurred and contracted Dan to design new products. Work was begun in Ampeg's factory in Linden, and the prototypes were ready in early 1969.

There was one bass and one guitar, each selling for $330. Dan

Ampeg's Portaflex, a classic American bass amp.

explained in *Guitar Player* magazine: "My intention was to make a guitar that sustained extremely well. Plastic was obviously one good material for the body because of its rigidity." The guitar's most obvious physical attribute is its clear body. Although the instruments were officially labeled Dan Armstrong Ampeg models, they generally became known as See Throughs, and Ampeg eventually trademarked the term. Keith Richards' use of one on the Rolling Stones' 1969 American tour gave the guitars a tremendous boost in popularity.

The Dan Armstrong guitar featured interchangeable single-coil pickups that slid in and out of the body. Varying in coil arrangement and magnetic construction, they were codesigned by Armstrong and pickup specialist Bill Lawrence not long after the latter's arrival from Germany. The wiring harness was attached to the Formica pickguard, and the whole package was mounted from the top for easy removal. The bass had a different wiring system with two single-coil pickups, one *on top* of the other and both encased in a bar of potting compound, a rubberlike material.

Armstrong's electrics were among the first to feature a two-octave, 24-fret fingerboard; furthermore, all frets were clear of the body.

Other details of both the guitar and bass included a maple neck, rosewood fingerboard, and chromed brass bridge base. Part of the surface underneath the bridge inserts was sandblasted to increase saddle stability; the earliest Dan Armstrongs did not have this feature. Also, the neck's contour was modified after 60 or 70 instruments had been made. Special-edition models included 8 guitars and 8 basses with all-black butyrate plastic bodies. Ampeg also made about 150 fretless Dan Armstrong basses.

According to Mr. Armstrong, he and an associate designed Ampeg's very successful V-3, V-4, and VT-22 amplifiers. A disagreement over payment for these projects caused a split between Armstrong and Ampeg in 1971, by which time the company's output was about 600 instruments per month.

Dan Armstrong remains very active as a designer. His projects include the Dan Armstrong line of special effects, and the circuitry for Fender's The Strat. Also see Danelectro.

Ampeg/Dan Armstrong; note removable pickup. *Charley's/Crump*

Mid-1960s Ampeg (with Wild Dog Sound) by Burns of London. *Gruhn/Baxendale*

B. C. Rich 12/6 Bich doubleneck with mother-of-pearl cloud inlays. Note body-mounted tuners. The Bich single-neck guitar is a 10-string with four body-mounted tuners.

B.C. RICH

Bernardo Chavez Rico was born October 13, 1941, in Los Angeles. For years he built classical and flamenco guitars at the family's business, Bernardo's Valencian Guitar Shop. To capitalize on the mid-sixties folk-rock boom, Rico concentrated more on steel-strings. Because a distributor advised that "Spanish surnames just didn't make it on country music guitars," he changed his professional name to B.C. Rich. In 1970 he restored Bo Diddley's rectangular Gretsch (see the last photo in this book), which had been run over by Diddley's van. These repairs proved to be something of a turning point, for it sparked an interest in the electric instruments that eventually made the B.C. Rich name world-famous, at least among rock musicians.

Soon the company began producing custom electrics, many of which were copies of Les Pauls and Stratocasters. As a youngster Rico had usually confined his artistic expression to spray-can graffiti, but now he took pen to paper, designing a guitar with sufficient flash to reflect his personality (among his primary interests are fast cars, jet boats, and fine clothes). The result was B.C. Rich's first production solidbody, the Seagull of 1971. Inspired in part by the curves, recurves, and laminations of the archery bows that had fascinated Bernardo Rico in his youth, the Seagull was clearly a rock and roll guitar, with a sharp-pointed body, hot-rod circuitry, and a fast neck. Some of Rich's later guitars were designed by Neal Moser, who joined the company in 1974. They were also named after birds—Mockingbird, Eagle—and they were even more highly stylized than the Seagull. The ad campaign for the Rich Bich model depicted a scantily clad model in a provocative pose. It netted the company some controversy (it was cited by *Ms.* magazine) and considerable publicity; the poster itself, the *Playboy* foldout of guitar literature, had sold some 30,000 copies by 1980.

With their versatile and sensible wiring schemes, radical contouring, and high-dollar appointments, the B.C. Rich electrics are perfect embodiments of a phenomenon that arose in the 1970s, the luxury rock and roll guitar.

1992 Update

In the mid-1980s, B.C. Rich moved from Los Angeles to El Monte, California. It began to import a line labeled NJ (for Nagoya, Japan). Soon after, the NJs were imported from Korea. Production of the U.S.-made B.C. Riches peaked at about 15 guitars a day in 1989.

In 1990, Bernie Rico sold his design licenses to Class Axe. B.C. Rich International will continue to operate, but will no longer build the models that made B.C. Rich a famous name. Instead, it will produce its new Mason Bernard guitars. The Mason Bernards feature custom Strat-styled bodies, 25½-inch scale lengths, 24-fret necks, and ebony fingerboards with side markers only (no markers in front).

Class Axe had already acquired B.C. Rich's import lines (NJ, Rave, and Platinum), and reports it will manufacture the U.S.-made B.C. Rich guitars in its Warren, New Jersey facility.

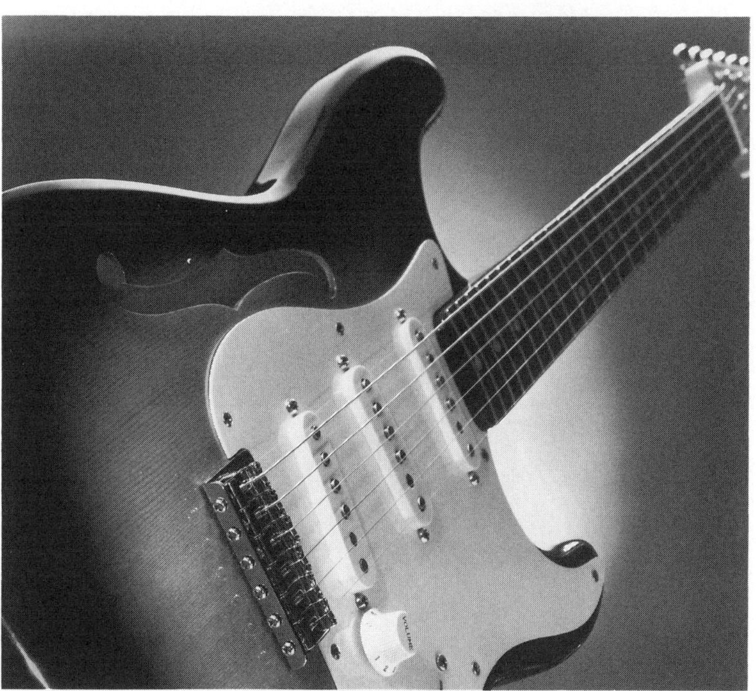

BENEDETTO

Using traditional violin woods such as curly maple, spruce, and ebony, Bob Benedetto has handcrafted exceptional arch-tops for such performers as Bucky Pizzarelli, Joe Diorio, and Ron Eschete. The New York-born luthier began building instruments in 1968 in Lake Hopatcong, New Jersey, relocated to Homosassa Springs, Florida, then Clearwater, Florida, and is next looking forward to living in Stroudsburg, Pennsylvania.

BENEDICT

Roger Benedict's spruce-body Groove Master—named by Jackson Browne, for whom Benedict built two guitars in 1988—combines the familiar feel and comfort of a Strat-type guitar with the light weight and resonance of an acoustic.

The Groove Master line includes semi-hollowbody guitars and fretted and fretless basses. Stock guitars feature a 25½-inch scale, either a bolt-on or through-body maple neck with rosewood fingerboard, and Seymour Duncan pickups—although many Benedicts are built to customer specs.

Benedict began making guitars in 1974 in Elizabethtown, New York, and moved to Minneapolis in 1981. Working with a single apprentice, Benedict builds about two or three Groove Masters each month; their prices start at about $1,650.

BIGSBY

In the late 1940s one of history's most influential guitarists sketched a radical guitar shape on a Pasadena radio station's program sheet. He poked it across the table to his buddy, the late Paul Bigsby. "Can you build me this thing?" said Merle Travis. "*I can build anything!*" said Bigsby with a characteristic loud laugh. The resulting instrument became one of American guitar's most controversial pieces, for Merle Travis claimed that the idea for the Fender Broadcaster—the first large-scale commercial solidbody and thus one of the most important guitars ever developed—was taken from the Bigsby that he designed.

On more than one occasion, Merle stated that Leo Fender came to a gig one night to see the guitar, borrowed it for a week, and returned with his own hastily built instrument. "I designed the Fender guitar, you know," Merle told *Guitar Player* in 1976, "and Paul Bigsby built the first one." Leo Fender disagreed. A quiet controversy between these two gen-

Paul Bigsby with one of his first guitars. ***Forrest White***

The historic Bigsby/Travis guitar, designed by Merle Travis and built by Paul Bigsby. *Country Music Hall of Fame*

tlemen endured for decades, and more than one of Merle's good friends confided that Travis was at least a little bit hurt by all of the success and credit that fell upon Fender.

Both Leo and Merle recounted with impressive conviction and detail the time when Fender first saw Travis' Bigsby, but the stories vary considerably in the particulars and especially in the implication. Fender stated that the Broadcaster was designed well in advance of his first encounter with Merle's solidbody, that he never borrowed it, that it didn't influence his designs, and that his own solidbody prototypes predated the Bigsby/Travis by three years or so. A fair amount of research failed to reconcile the Fender and Travis recollections, and no attempt is made here to lend more credibility to one man than the other.

But it seems unlikely that the 1948 Broadcaster (later Telecaster) was directly influenced by Paul Bigsby's guitar, for the two are dissimilar in almost every way. One could argue that, if anything, the Bigsby/Travis, with its beautiful bird's-eye maple body and remarkably contemporary peghead, was fancier and more ahead of its time than the plain-Jane, plank-bodied, homely pegheaded Broadcaster. Thus it appears that if Fender took anything from Merle Travis it was either the very concept of the solidbody Spanish guitar or the peghead shape, which closely resembles that of the Stratocaster as well as most other Fender solidbodies.

Regarding the solidbody concept, electric Spanish guitars had been marketed in the 1930s by both Vivi-Tone and, to a greater extent, Rickenbacker. Rickenbacker is located in Southern California's Orange County—Leo Fender's back yard. By the mid 1940s more than 15 years had passed since the introduction of Rickenbacker's Frying Pan lap steel; surely several people had considered the next logical step, a solid Spanish guitar. During the early 1940s, even before the Fender company was founded, Leo's only partner had been Doc Kauffman (see Fender), a chief designer of electric guitars for Rickenbacker in

Left to right: Hank Garland with a very unusual bird's-eye maple Bigsby solidbody, Eddy Arnold with a Gibson J-200, and steel guitarist Roy Wiggins. The Bigsby guitar body resembles that of Tiny Moore's Bigsby mandolin. *Doug Green*

the late 1930s. O.W. Appleton built a Spanish solidbody in 1941. Forrest White (see Fender) made one in 1944. Then there is Les Paul (see Gibson). Thus it seems almost impossible that Leo would have been unaware of the idea of a solid Spanish guitar at the time he saw Merle's Bigsby, regardless of whether that event occurred as described by Travis or by Fender. There is no reason to doubt that Fender and Travis, like other prominent guitar figures before and since, could have been working independently on similar ideas.

As to the peghead shapes of the Bigsby and Stratocaster, the similarities can't be ignored: they're striking, undeniable. At the very least, Merle Travis sketched the headstock silhouette that became a world-famous Fender hallmark five or six years before it appeared on any Fender.

Whatever its ultimate influence, the guitar that Paul Bigsby built for the first Travis picker was remarkably modern, especially when compared to, say, Vivi-Tone's board-body guitars or Rickenbacker's noncutaway Spanish solidbodies, which almost resembled baritone ukuleles. Regardless of how one interprets all the facts and stories, the Bigsby/Travis guitar's destiny, like that of Les Paul's "Log," was to be one of those instruments whose historical significance derives not from their evolutionary influence but rather from an association with a famous player and from their exalted but commercially untenable status of being ahead of their time.

Here are Merle Travis' recollections of Paul Bigsby:

> I never knew anyone who called him anything except P.A. He was a pattern maker who also spent a lot of time working on motorcycles. Paul Bigsby was a big, bold fellow, and his hair always seemed to look like he'd just come in from a windstorm. His teeth parted a little bit right in the middle, and he constantly grinned and talked loud. To all the girls he'd say, "Hey you, you're getting prettier all the time."
>
> I spent hours out at his workshop [8114 E. Phlox St.] in Downey, in Southern California. If something went wrong with my motorcycle, I'd just take off and go out there. He'd have pieces all over the floor in no time at all. He'd put it back and it'd be in perfect condition. That's the sort of person he was, a perfectionist. He was a fine man and never got the credit he deserved.
>
> The first thing P.A. built for me was the hand vibrato that became the famous Bigsby. I had an old Gibson L-10 with a crude Vibrola [see Rickenbacker] that was pretty well worn. I had traded somebody out of it, and it worked okay except that it pulled the strings out of tune. They wouldn't return to their proper pitch. Me and Bigsby got to be pretty good friends, and I said, "Do you think you could fix it?" He said, "I can fix *anything.*" I suggested that he try to build one himself, and he said, *"I can build one perfect."* After a certain length of time, P.A. came over with the first Bigsby tailpiece. I put it on, and it worked just fine. I've still got that first vibrato. I was about 28 at the time, and Paul was maybe 10 or 15 years older. This was in about 1946 or 1947.
>
> Well, I had always hated to change the strings on a guitar because you had to reach underneath to turn the keys for the first three. I thought that somebody would notice that people over in Europe had built instruments where they lined up all the keys on one side, so

Paul Bigsby installed the neck on this Martin D-28 in late 1949 or early 1950 for Zeke Clements, who used it on the *Grand Ole Opry*. *Dick Allen*

One of the rarest guitars ever encountered by the author, a Bigsby doubleneck. *George Johnston/ Duwane McCraney*

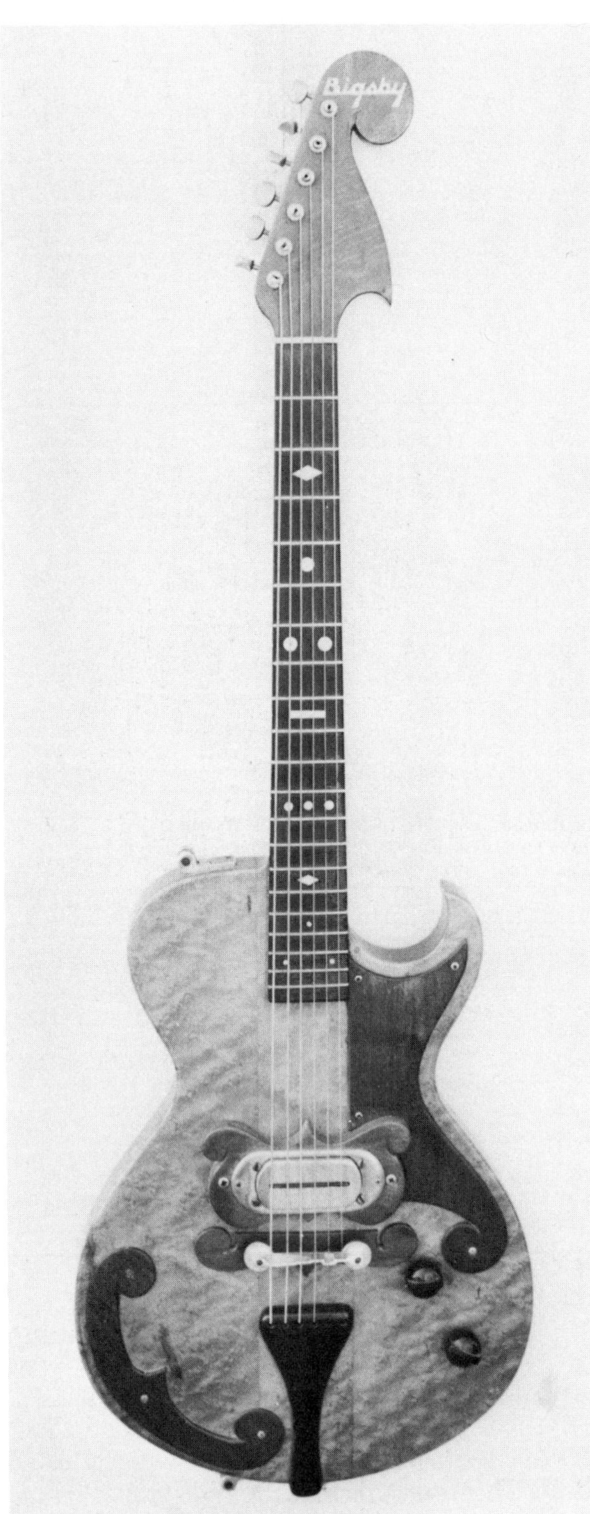

Bigsby solidbody dated 8/18/48. Originally a noncutaway, it was altered by the maker to resemble Merle Travis' guitar. The lower bout body trim is typical of Bigsby's work and also of the early guitars of Semie Moseley, at one time a Bigsby associate. The cast-aluminum saddle is the type used on Bigsby vibratos. ***Dick Allen***

that was where I got the idea for the head.

And then I wanted a guitar that would sustain for a long time, and I thought, man, I'd love to have a solid guitar that was like a steel but with a regular neck on it. So one day I said to Bigsby, "Can you build me this thing?" And I drew him a picture of it. I've always been an amateur cartoonist, see, so I made a detailed drawing on a piece of the program paper from a radio show and drew a little hook on the peghead and put all the keys on top. I told him that I wanted a solid body with a cutaway and to put pickups on it just like a steel. Then I started getting fancy with my pencil and drew a little tailpiece like you have on a violin, and an armrest like you have on a tenor banjo. "*What's them for?*" he hollered. "For decoration," I said, "cosmetics." The more he looked at it the louder he talked—"*I can do it!*"

I don't know exactly how long it was, but P.A. called me up and said, "Well, that funny-looking thing that you wanted, I've got it." I opened up the case and there it was—made out of bird's-eye maple, pretty as you please. I plugged it in and played it, and the neck was just perfection. In fact, it was so good that later I had Gibson build me a Super 400 with a neck just like the Bigsby. I also had P.A. build me a neck to put on my D-28 Martin.

I don't think I paid anything for that solidbody. We were just a couple of motorcycle enthusiasts; one of them played guitar and one of them built things. I had never seen a solidbody guitar before except a steel, but I just thought, well, if it's electric you don't need that hollow body. I don't know how many Spanish guitars Paul Bigsby built, but there weren't very many. Mine is now on display at the Country Music Hall of Fame in Nashville.

Paul once told me: "A fella came out today and wanted one of them crazy things like you got. I said I ain't got time to turn around building them stupid-looking things. If you want one, go to Fullerton. Leo Fender will do it for you." And you see, Leo Fender certainly had a good product, because it more or less revolutionized guitars.

Former Gibson president Theodore McCarty retired from Gibson and bought the Bigsby company in 1965. He and his partner, an old friend and longtime Gibson company officer named John Huis, soon moved the Bigsby operation to Kalamazoo, Michigan, home of Gibson.

Pedal steel pioneer Speedy West recalled of Paul Bigsby: "He built my first pedal steel and I got delivery on February 8, 1948. I remember it as good as yesterday. I'm proud of it. For some reason Paul really trusted me. I'd just come off the farm and got me a job in a dry-cleaning plant and was playing beer joints at night. I says, 'I can pay you $50 down,' and that wasn't very much because the guitar was gonna cost $750 in all. It was a tripleneck with four pedals on it. But I said to him, 'I will never be one minute late with the payments until it's paid for. I'm not a great steel player now, but I'm going to be. I'm gonna be on the top rung one of these days because I've got that desire and I know it's going to happen.' And he sold me that guitar that way.

"He was a perfectionist. He did all of his own work, even his secretarial work. He would not hire any employees. He could have been a giant in manufacturing if he would have had more faith in the ability of other people, but he just didn't think that anyone else could do what Paul Bigsby could do."

BOŽO

During the late 1940s, Božo (christened Božidar) Podunavac was apprenticed to his godfather Milutin Mladenuvic, a master luthier, in his native Yugoslavia. After passing the mandatory government examination, Božo opened a shop in Belgrade and began building 5-string tamburitzas. In 1959 he and his wife, Mirjana, fled the Communists, emigrating to Chicago, where he repaired guitars for various stores. In 1965 he opened his own business. Božo (pronounced *Bo*-zho) built dreadnoughts until 1968, when he developed his unusual Bell Western body shape, with its small, squared upper bouts and extra-large, round lower bouts.

Chicago's winters were too cold for the Podunavacs. In 1972 they moved to Escondido, near San Diego, and three years later they relocated in San Diego proper. In March of 1978 Božo opened a school of lutherie, where he imparts to aspiring guitar makers the skills acquired over a lifetime of experience. All Božo guitars feature especially ornate inlay and detailing as well as extra-large pegheads.

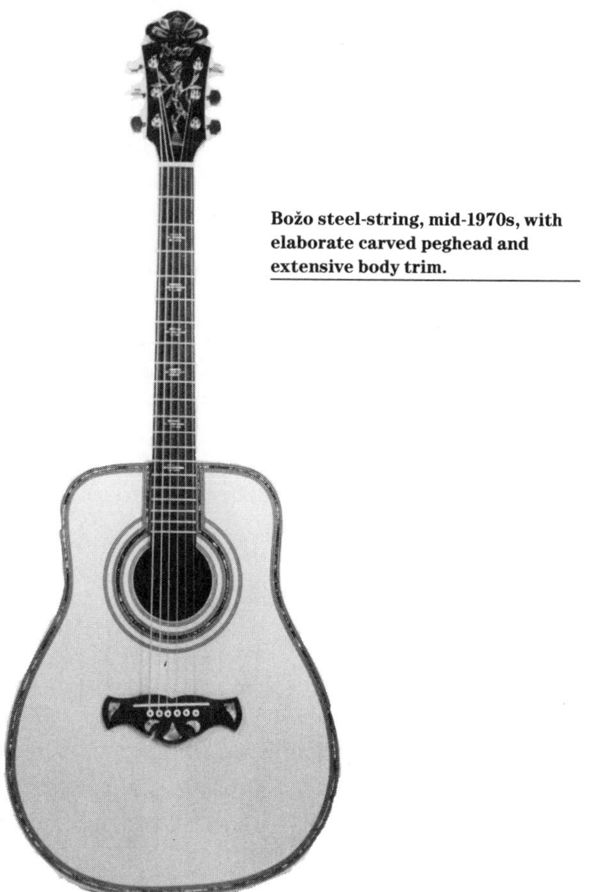

Božo steel-string, mid-1970s, with elaborate carved peghead and extensive body trim.

BORYS

The high quality of Roger Borys guitars, such as this top-of-the-line B420 Special, is suggested by the clientele, which has included jazz artists such as Jimmy Wyble, John Collins, Emily Remler, Larry Coryell, and Mundell Lowe.

Borys, of Burlington, Vermont, began working on guitars in 1974, finishing his first instrument two years later. In 1980, Borys, Jimmy D'Aquisto, and jazz guitarist Barry Galbraith began designing the elegant BG100 Jazz Electric. Borys and Chip Wilson built the instruments, which were later labeled B120. *Guitar Player* reviewer Harvey Citron, himself a builder, called Borys' B120 "comfortable and effortless to play, a professional's instrument."

Other models include the unusual B222 Jazz Solid, of which Citron said, "The amazing thing is that although the size and shape are somewhere between a Les Paul and an L5S, it has a real jazz sound [and is also] capable of performing well in rock and country idioms—very versatile."

Distinctive Borys features include single-piece quartersawn (rather than flatsawn) necks and custom-wound Kent Armstrong pickups, which are clean and clear—ideally suited to the Borys' full sound.

BRUNO

C. Bruno & Son, Inc., of New York was founded in 1834. Although many Bruno guitars were distributed, the company was primarily a wholesaler rather than a manufacturer. Founder Charles Bruno and C.F. Martin entered into a partnership on May 1, 1838, although according to *Martin Guitars* (by Mike Longworth, see Martin), the agreement was likely dissolved by the following year, when Martin moved to Nazareth, Pennsylvania. Instruments bearing both the Martin and Bruno names on the label were made in New York by Martin and, it is assumed, distributed by Bruno. But contrary to a common rumor, Martin made none of the guitars labeled simply *Bruno* or *C. Bruno & Son.*

Mid-1800s Brunos are typical instruments of the period (though superior than average in general construction) with 12-fret necks and small bodies approximating Martin's Sizes 2 and 2½. As of this writing, C. Bruno is still in business, as a distribution arm of the Kaman organization (see Ovation).

BUNKER

In 1966, Dave Bunker patented an unusual guitar that featured micrometer-type, body-mounted tuners, and went on to build some of the most radically designed guitars of the 1970s. Though too unconventional for mass commercial success, Bunker's guitars are prime examples of rugged individualism in instrument design.

The body-mounted tuners were ahead of their time. Bunker also designed small cylindrical pickups for each string. He came up with H-shaped bodies with headless, full-length neck centerpieces, and snap-on sidepieces offered in wood, vinyl, leather-bound denim, or Naugahyde.

While later Bunkers had more traditionally shaped bodies, Bunker remained an innovator. The 1983 doubleneck Bunker-Artisan was billed as a bass/guitar/organ. It featured guitar and bass necks and electronic organ components. The Bunker-Artisan came in a stand-up carrying case that housed a top-mounted microprocessor control panel.

A more recent design is the 1988 Touch Bass/Guitar, available in two models. The TG100 has four pickups for the lower bass neck and six for the guitar neck. Each pickup can be adjusted for distortion and filtering. The TG200 has 20 adjustable pickups. Using upper-neck pushbuttons, the player can select settings controlling pickup, filtering, and distortion. The strings are supported by a rod mounted inside the neck, so that the "floating neck" is impervious to warp. The upper neck is played with the touch technique, while the lower may be either touched or plucked.

Formerly based in the Seattle/Tacoma area, Dave Bunker now lives in Utah. His son, David L. Bunker, produces his own guitar, the Treker, which features the floating neck but uses a conventional body. The younger Bunker builds about 20 to 30 Trekers a month.

Left: C. Bruno & Son, Inc., of New York was founded in 1834. This small-body Bruno dates to the World War I period. ***Spitzer's/Sievert*** ***Right:*** **Bruno Model B, serial no. 16715; note body trim.** ***Music Shop/Madsen***

Top-of-the-line Carvin DC400 Limited: maple-topped koa body, through-body koa neck, maple headstock overlay, ebony fretboard with abalone inlays, active electronics, and Floyd Rose. Among many options: left-handed model (no extra charge—congratulations, Carvin!), Kahler tail-piece, V headstock, mother-of-pearl inlays, and maple fingerboard.

DC135C with optional koa body, two stacked hum-buckers plus M22 bridge pickup, neck-through-body construction, and Floyd Rose.

CARVIN

Lowell Kiesel played Hawaiian steel guitar on Kansas radio shows before moving to Los Angeles, where in 1946 he established the Carvin Company. Lowell had five sons. All of them worked for the firm, and it was from the two eldest, Carson and Gavin, that Kiesel took the name Carvin.

After about three years of production he moved east to Covina, California, working out of his garage and making pickups, lap steels, and small tube amps. One early-fifties customer was Semie Moseley, who used Carvin pickups on the famous doublenecks he made for Joe Maphis and Larry Collins. Soon Carvin branched into guitar parts (including Fenderish necks), kits, and solidbody Spanish models, all of which were sold direct to customers through mail-order; Carvin was and is the only sizable guitar maker that sells most of its merchandise in this manner.

From 1964 to 1978 Hofner necks were used on Carvin products, and in 1978 bolt-on necks were replaced with glued units. In 1968 or 1969 Carvin moved south to Escondido, near San Diego. The major products are P.A.s and amps.

Carvin catalogues from the 1950s were of particular interest, for their photos of unassembled kits were among the very few sources where a player might learn at least a little about electric guitar manufacture.

1992 Update
Carvin employs over 100 workers, producing 2,000 guitars and basses a year in the 40,000-square-foot plant in Escondido, California. The company is noted for affordable prices. The sleek, single-pickup DC125 listed at $470 in 1990, with prices ranging upward to $1,430 for the DC400. Carvin's well-made basses are also bargains: *Guitar Player*'s Tom Mulhern tabbed the $649 LB75 as "one of the best 5-string deals yet."

DAN ARMSTRONG

See Ampeg

1956 Danelectro Model C: aluminum neck rod, solid-core body with hollow "wings." *Anthony Manfredi*

Silvertone electric, one pickup; made by Danelectro and sold in America by Sears, Roebuck. *Dan Torres*

Stan & Dan strike a classic early-1960s pose with their Danelectro doublenecks. *Angela Inst.*

DANELECTRO AND CORAL

A player often holds fond memories of his or her first guitar, and for many that special item was a Danelectro Silvertone. If company founder Nathan I. Daniel had put his own name on his instruments he would have been famous, but he sold most of them to Sears, who marketed them through their catalogues under the Silvertone brand. These Sears electric guitars of the 1950s and 1960s were like the Volkswagen Beetles of the same period—reliable and cheap.

Nathan Daniel was a New York electronics buff who in 1934 started assembling amplifiers at home. In the mid-thirties he was contracted to build the Electar amplifiers for Epiphone, and by 1948 he had founded the Danelectro Corporation, a manufacturer of amplifiers and echo units with its factory and offices in Red Bank, New Jersey.

By 1955 the first Danelectro guitar had been designed and was ready for its 1956 introduction. In 1959 or 1960 Danelectro moved from Red Bank to 207 West Sylvania Avenue in Neptune City, New Jersey, where it remained until its demise in 1968 (some catalogues were advance-dated for 1970).

"Sears, Roebuck put Nat Daniel in the guitar business," recalled George Wooster, once Danelectro's production manager. "They came along and asked him if he knew how to build gui-

Left: **Danelectro Pro 1, $59.95, 23½-inch scale, "baked Melamine" pickguard.** *Soest/Rountree* *Right:* **The Convertible was a roundhole acoustic-electric that could be ordered with or without the pickup. In the latter case, the pickup notches were drilled so that the buyer could install a pickup at a later date; on these models the control holes were filled with decorative inserts.** ***Jan Cuccia/R. Nelson***

Left: **Danelectro with two pickups and dual concentric knobs.** *Soest/Rountree* *Right:* **Short Horn 6-string bass, model 3612.** ***McPeake's/Robt. Foust***

Three-pickup Deluxe model, $145, available in white or walnut. *Gary Jeffers/ Margaret Banker*

tars, and he wasn't one to say no. That's how the ball started to roll."

Every step of assembling the Danelectro Silvertones was completed in the Neptune City factory, including application of the logos. Sometimes Danelectro would, on Sears' order, send an instrument directly to the customer, though it was more common for the guitars to be warehoused at a Sears facility prior to delivery. According to George Wooster, "The only thing Sears ever did was take it out of the box."

Many of Danelectro's most popular guitars during the 1950s and 1960s are generally considered solidbodies; in fact, they are more of a semisolid design, with a Masonite top and back mounted to a pine frame cut from stapled wooden blocks.

After the Masonite plates were installed, a strip of pebbled vinyl fabric was often attached to the sides with a "wood lock" glue that resembled Elmer's white glue.

Players often joke that the company's long, rounded pickups look like lipstick tubes; according to George Wooster, that's exactly what they are. Danelectro bought the lipstick casings from a manufacturer who serviced the cosmetics industry, and then sent them to another contractor for plating before the pickup windings and magnets were installed.

Vincent ("Vinnie") Bell, one of the East Coast's best-known

Left: Unusual Danelectro Short Horn bass with only 15 frets. *Soest/Rountree* *Center:* The guitarlin was intended to be something of a cross between a guitar and a mandolin. Its 31 frets provided an extended range into upper registers. *Karl M. Sandoval* *Right:* Your first electric? The Sears Silvertone with the amp-in-the-case, a better bargain than many. Made by Danelectro.

Long Horn bass, circa 1960, dual concentric knobs, bronze and white sunburst, "lipstick" pickups. *Soest/Rountree*

The Coral electric sitar was one of the more original instruments to appear in the late 1960s. The Sitarmatic bridge's wide surface produces a string buzz that, when amplified, is reasonably effective in approximating a sitar's tone. The 13 drone strings on the left side are tuned in half-steps. Danelectro advised, "For today's 'IN' sound, put the Coral Electric Sitar in your bag." *Jim Brown*

Unlike the Coral model, the Danelectro brand electric sitar had no drone strings. The right-hand bout originally held a thin metal band that supported the instrument on the thigh. Brochures asked, "At $139, shouldn't you be a sitarnick?" *Wagener/Beaty*

Allen Woody

Soest/Rountree

young session players during the 1960s, became the resident pro consultant and product demonstrator for Danelectro and was very close to the company's founder and president. His influence resulted in the Bellzouki 12-string and the Danelectro and Coral electric sitars.

Like much of the industry, Danelectro grew quickly during the mid-sixties guitar boom, increasing its full-time factory roster from fewer than 100 employees to nearly 400. According to John Kahrs, a former personnel director, the highest number of employees was 503, including office personnel. Mr. Wooster estimated that during peak periods the plant produced 150 to 200 guitars a day.

In late 1967 MCA, the entertainment conglomerate, bought Danelectro and soon introduced the Coral line. Mr. Wooster remembered: "About 85 percent of our business was for Sears. We were making many of their Silvertone guitars and amps, but our own name started getting around and we needed a catalogue for our line. That was the Coral series." While the bodies for the hollow Corals were manufactured in Japan, the other Coral parts and all Danelectros were made in the New Jersey plants.

MCA folded Danelectro in 1968. John Kahrs said, "After MCA purchased the company, they started to do business with individual music shops instead of big distributors, and they were going into competition with Gibson and Fender, which wasn't their style."

Veteran retailer-manufacturer-repairman Dan Armstrong [see Ampeg and Dan Armstrong] acquired an interest in Danelectro not long after it had been shut down by MCA. According to him, "MCA had the company only for about a year. Then in 1969 I went to a swap meet in Englishtown, New Jersey, and met a guy who had some Danelectro stuff in a truck. His name was William C. Herring, and he had bought Danelectro's factory from MCA for $20,000 in late 1968 or early 1969. I went with him down to the factory, and it was ghostly—all empty, with three-story ceilings and nobody there, just all kinds of equipment and partially completed guitars.

"Ampeg had had some trouble financing the production of the Dan Armstrong See Throughs, so we contracted to make some Danelectros for them in the interim. Then Ampeg decided that they couldn't pay for them—they were in deeper financial trouble than anyone knew at the time. These guitars had Danelectro single-cutaway bodies with one *humbucking* pickup, nothing written on the peghead, and 'Dan Armstrong Modified Danelectro' on the pickguard. So I started selling them in my store, and they did well. Other dealers wanted them, so we went into regular production—in all we must've made 650 or 700 of them. Bill Herring got sued and lost the Danelectro stock in about August of 1969. My lawyer and I finally located the guitars and parts—they'd been stored in a bunch of chicken coops in New Jersey. They'd been rained on for a few days and were just about scrap by that time, thousands of bodies. I retained the Danelectro name."

Single- and double-pickup versions of the Danelectro Bellzouki, a 12-string guitar developed from the plans of Vincent Bell. Still another version had a protruding horn on the upper right bout.

1967 Danelectro Slimline SL3N with adjustable neck and Gator finish; also available in two-pickup, vibrato, and 12-string versions. Coral's Hornet models were made from the same body, which may have been inspired by Fender's Jazzmaster. For a time these guitars were marketed under the Danelectro Dane Series name. *Third Eye*

Coral Firefly, also available in bass and 12-string versions. *Artie Leider*

Coral Long Horn L2N6, circa 1968. *Artie Leider*

D'ANGELICO

D'Angelico. It's a lyrical word, saturated with guitar magic and resonant with memories and impressions of an old man, a small shop, elegant guitars, and Jazz-age Manhattan. The man behind the legend, John D'Angelico, was a native of New York City, born in 1905, the eldest of four children. His uncle, a Mr.

An early photo of John D'Angelico contouring a neck. *DiSerio*

Acuff

Gruhn/Baxendale

Compare the early Excel (circa 1937) with the later version at right, and note differences in pegheads, fingerboard markers, pickguards, f-holes, and tailpieces.

Ciani, was a successful maker of Italian style flat-tops and mandolins. In 1914 young John was apprenticed to Ciani, and when the old man died, D'Angelico took over supervision of Ciani's crew of about 15 craftsmen and apprentices.

D'Angelico established a small workshop of his own in 1932 at 40 Kenmore Street in New York City, building 16½-inch-wide arch-tops whose bodies, nearly parallel bracing, and headstocks may have been patterned after Gibson's 16-inch L-5. For two years there were no model names, but by 1934 D'Angelico had settled on four basic styles (by 1937 they were more standardized). Styles A and B were generally similar to Gibson's *later* Advanced L-5s and had 17-inch bodies and parallel top braces, while the 17-inch Excel had X bracing, like *early* Advanced L-5s. The top-of-the-line New Yorker was also X braced and, at 18 inches across, was the same general size as Gibson's Super 400.

115

1282 Excel	Leo Celistino	Aug 4 1937
1283 Excel	Silver & Holand	Aug 21 1937
1284 Excel	Tom LaTone Syracuse, N.Y.	Aug 20 1937
1285 New Yorker	Pete Barton	Aug 21 1937
1286 Style B	Barth. Fienberg	Aug 28 1937
1287 Style B	Fordham Music	Sept 1 1937
1288 Excel	Maresco	Sept 22 1937
1289 New Yorker	Willie Mure	Aug 22 1937
1290 Style A	Gravois Music Sh.	Aug 27 1937
1291 Style B	Silver & Holand	Aug 25 1937
1292 Style A	Fordham Music	Aug 28 1937
1293 Excel	Maresco	Sept 28 1937
1294 New Yorker	Silver & Holand	Sept 23 1937
1295 New Yorker	Fordham Music	Sept 5 1937
1296	[illegible]	

A page from D'Angelico's ledger, showing serial numbers, styles, customers, and dates. *DiSerio*

John D'Angelico built 1,164 guitars, all by hand, and many were custom ordered. This individuality led to substantial variations in body size, scale length, body depth, and fretboard dimensions (from classical width to ultra-narrow). Some of his construction principles were borrowed from violin-making, an art which John had studied as his uncle's apprentice. On his guitars D'Angelico used both Grover Imperials and less expensive open-back Grover tuners. At least through the late 1930s the metal-reinforced necks were nonadjustable; these early guitars are readily identified by the absence of a truss rod cover on the peghead. Later models had a truss rod adjustment designed

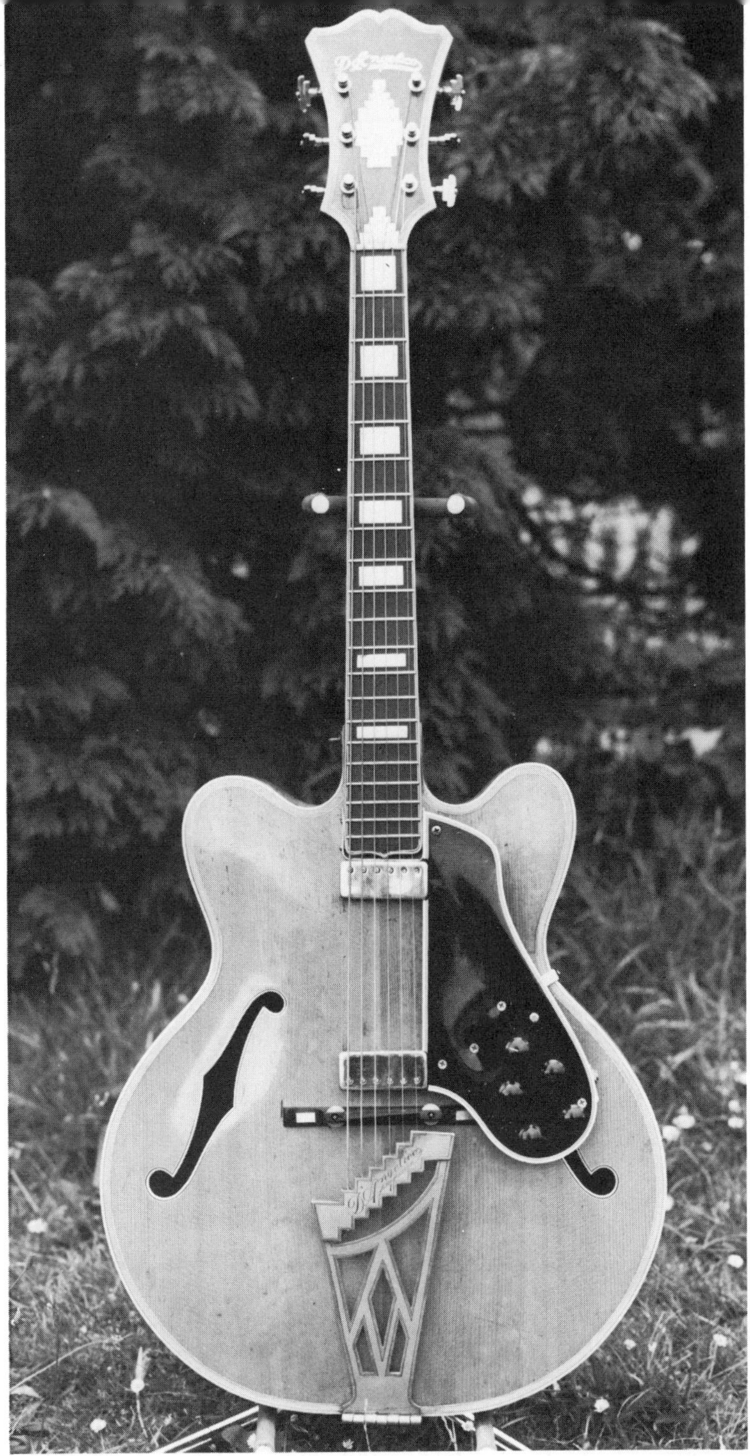

Perhaps the most unusual D'Angelico ever built, this guitar was constructed in 1949 for Lefty Schevak, a New York jazz guitarist. It was originally designed as a left-handed model and later modified to become the only double-cutaway that D'Angelico ever made. It mixes features from the Excel (17-inch body, fingerboard markers) and New Yorker (tailpiece, black-and-white f-hole trim, pearl bridge inlays). The guitar belonged to Pete Townshend. *Ian Vicentini*

by D'Angelico after the expiration of Gibson's patent on a similar mechanism.

Styles A and B were dropped in the late 1940s, and D'Angelico concentrated on the Excels and New Yorkers. Cutaways were introduced on a special-order basis and soon became the favorite body type. During the 1950s most or all work was done on a custom basis. D'Angelico built a few exceptionally good mandolins, and a very few roundhole arch-tops. He also fash-

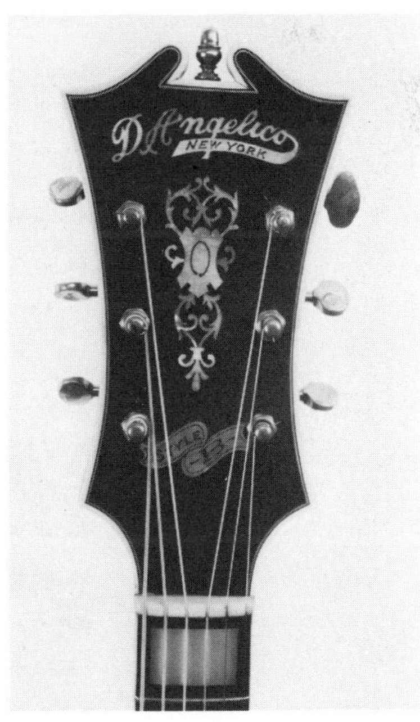

D'Angelico Style B headstock with decorative center pedestal, no truss rod adjustment. For full-length pictures of the Style B see color plates 70 and 71.

ioned necks that were joined to bodies made by other manufacturers, including the United Guitar Company of New Jersey.

John relocated his business in another small shop across the street when his original building was condemned in 1959. That same year he suffered a heart attack, followed by another one two years later. During this period he was also stricken with pneumonia, and he died in 1964 at the age of 59.

The late Jimmy DiSerio is the forgotten man in the D'Angelico story. Although his name rarely appears in historical accounts, he was D'Angelico's right-hand man for many years. Mr. DiSerio's widow recalled: "My husband Jimmy was very close to John D'Angelico. John was Jimmy's godfather, and also our daughter's godfather. My husband went to work for him in 1932 at the age of 12, sweeping up the shop. As he got older he learned the business from John and from John's uncle, Mr. Ciani. He was with him from the beginning.

"John lived with his sister until she got married. They had a place over the shop. It was in the neighborhood where my mother-in-law lived, and we stopped by frequently. John was a very trusting person, very generous. When the building was condemned, John and Jimmy split up. This was in about 1960."

D'Angelico was commissioned by some of jazz guitar's most knowledgeable practitioners, and he sought their counsel regarding the arch-top's expanding role in orchestras and ensembles. Over the years these interactions not only fostered an extraordinary customer loyalty but also helped the old master to keep up to date. D'Angelico's work thus epitomized a quality often touted but rarely achieved—a mixture of Old World craftsmanship and modern design.

Jimmy D'Aquisto with a finished solidbody. ***Tim Olsen/GP***

D'AQUISTO

James L. D'Aquisto was a young jazz guitar player when he became apprenticed to the renowned John D'Angelico in 1952. The elder luthier, a bachelor, took a fatherly interest in Jimmy ("the kid," as he was nicknamed by customers) and the two became very close. After D'Angelico's health failed, D'Aquisto assumed the heavier tasks such as carving tops and backs.

D'Aquisto acquired legal rights to the title "Successor to D'Angelico" and lost them in 1965 in a disputed partnership with the D'Merle String Company, but he did retrieve some of D'Angelico's wood stocks and tools, and he set up shop in Huntington, New York, and later in Farmingdale, New York. Over the next decade he became a distinguished luthier in his own right, building arch-tops that continued the D'Angelico heritage in the woods, general body shapes, and pegheads, while manifesting his own innovation and artistry throughout, especially in the modified body silhouettes, unusual S-shaped soundholes, ebony tailpieces, and complex dovetail neck joints.

DEAN

Dean Zelinsky, a native of Chicago's Highland Park suburb, started manufacturing guitars at a very early age and was well established by the time he was only 22. As a teenager he was interested in collecting and repairing guitars, and to re-float a sinking academic career he opened the Dean Custom Guitars repair shop as an accredited work-studies program.

At 19 he began manufacturing solidbodies. They were based on Gibson Explorers and Flying V's, but had the Dean hallmark, an oversized V-shaped headstock. They caught on, and soon original designs appeared, including the M.L., the Flame, and the E'Lite. By mid 1982, Dean Guitars employed 25 craftsmen, had over 300 dealers, and was completing 50 instruments each week.

Dean ML Standard in opaque black.

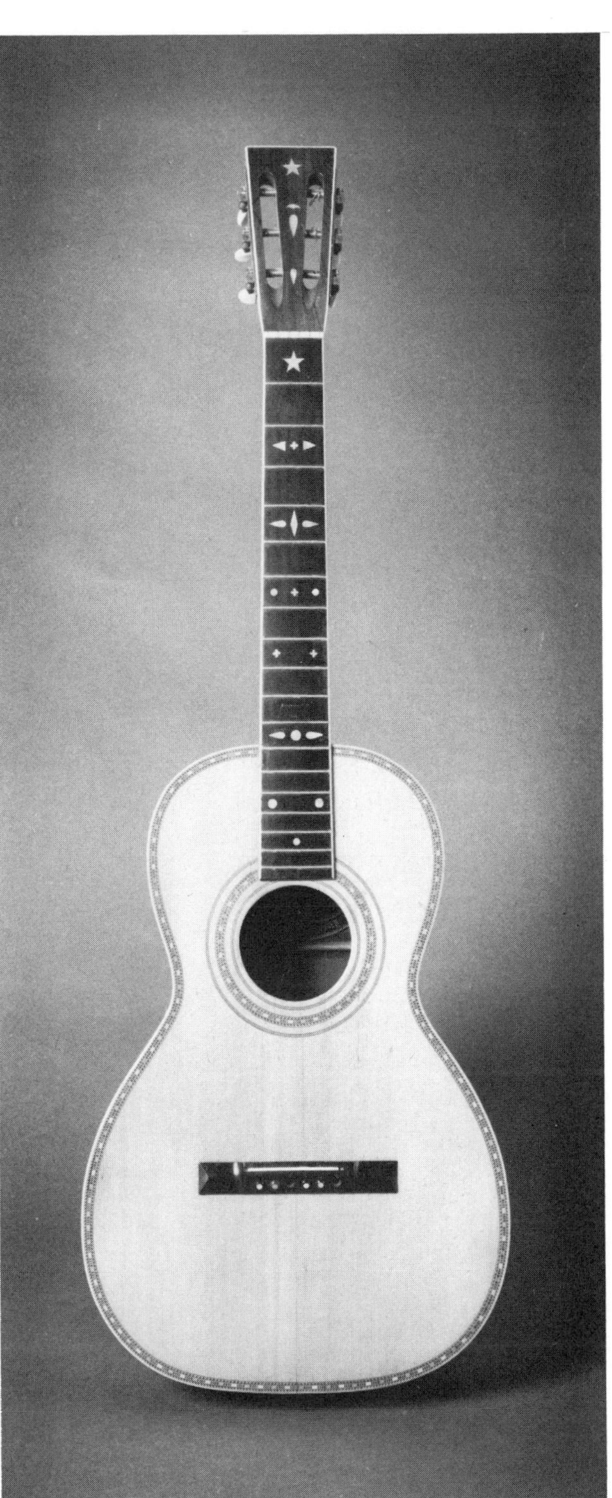

Bay State guitar. Note inlays and intricate body marquetry. ***Harry Wiard/Tom Erlewine***

DITSON, HAYNES, BAY STATE, AND TILTON

The Oliver Ditson Company, Incorporated, had its roots in Colonel Ebenezer Battelle's Book Store (established 1783) and was founded as a separate entity in 1835 by a music publisher, Oliver Ditson (1811–1888). The founder's early partner was Colonel Samuel H. Parker. Ditson acquired Parker's interests in 1842, and Parker left the company in 1856. Ditson was perhaps the pre-eminent figure of the East Coast's turn-of-the-century music merchandising scene, and aside from his publishing, distribution, and retailing businesses he established at least two musical instrument manufacturers: Cincinnati's John Church Company in 1860, and Chicago's Lyon & Healy in 1864; the latter was Ditson's exclusive Chicago agent (see Washburn).

This Bay State gut-string came in a pine "coffin" case with brass hardware. Note the guitar's rope binding. ***Vintage Fret Shop/A. Caswell***

The founder installed family members as heads of his various branch offices, which included Chas. H. Ditson & Company (established 1867) in New York; and Philadelphia's J.E. Ditson & Company, which operated from 1875 to 1910. Ditson shut down its Boston retail store in 1930, at about the time of the Ditson/Martin collaborations that produced Martin's dreadnought style guitar (see Martin).

John C. Haynes, a leading member of the late-nineteenth-century musical instrument community of Boston, came to work for Ditson as an office boy in 1845. He became a partner in 1857, when the company changed its name to Oliver Ditson & Company. When Ditson died in December 1888, Haynes assumed the presidency and held it until 1907.

Oliver Ditson expanded his publishing enterprise to include a manufacturing operation. It was placed under Haynes' supervision and called the John C. Haynes Company (founded 1865). The Haynes division was reunited with the parent company under the Ditson name in about 1900. Haynes guitars were made in a factory in the rear of Boston's Pope Building. This facility was sold to Vega when Haynes discontinued business not long after the turn of the century.

The John C. Haynes Co. sold guitars under several brand names, including Bay State, William B. Tilton, and Haynes Excelsior ("the highest grade of the Bay State make"). The company's West Coast representatives were Kohler & Chase of 26 O'Farrell Street in San Francisco. John Haynes died on May 3, 1907, and was succeeded at the Ditson helm by Charles Healy Ditson, son of the founder.

Tilton was actually a violin maker best known for "Tilton's Improvement," a longitudinal wooden tone bar mounted inside the body. The guitar pictured on page 27 has such a device, and it supports the wooden disk seen through the soundhole. The bracing is a Martin X type, and the guitar may have been commissioned by Tilton and built for him by Martin. Although the patent date on the disk is 1856, the Tilton device was introduced (on violins) to Germany at least as early as 1852, according to a treatise by Jacob Otto, Instrument Maker to the Court of the Grand Duke of Weimar.

Pehr A. Anderberg was a Swedish immigrant who came to America during the Civil War, worked for C.F. Bruno in New York City, and later (circa 1880) moved to Somerville, near Boston, and went to work for Haynes. The Haynes shop on Fremont Street became a training ground for several luthiers, including a Mr. Swenson and C.A. Sundberg, two of the founders of what was to become the Vega Co. It was Anderberg who supervised the actual construction of the Haynes Excelsior, Bay State, and Tilton guitars, and he later took over the management of the guitar operation of Philadelphia's Stewart & Bauer Company.

DOBRO

See National

This Civil War antique, a mid-1850s Wm. B. Tilton, is one of America's most distinctive, elegant, and unusual guitars ever. Details: Small (37-inch overall length) rosewood body bound with ivory and inlaid with particularly colorful abalone, ivory tuning buttons, and ornate silver-plated copper tailpiece engraved with two medallions—one reading "American Institute, New York, Lovett," the other "Awarded To Wm. B. Tilton for the best Guitars & Violins." *J. Webster, Music Folk/Roberta Hudlow*

One of several variations of Epiphone's Recording model acoustic guitar, probably made in the middle or late 1920s. This is the "D" model; the Recording "A" was a flat-top. *Gruhn*

1950 Emperor Cutaway (on the label, *Cutaway* is actually part of the model name). *Wagener/Beaty*

1942 Emperor, sunburst. Also see the natural finish model, page viii. *Wagener/Beaty*

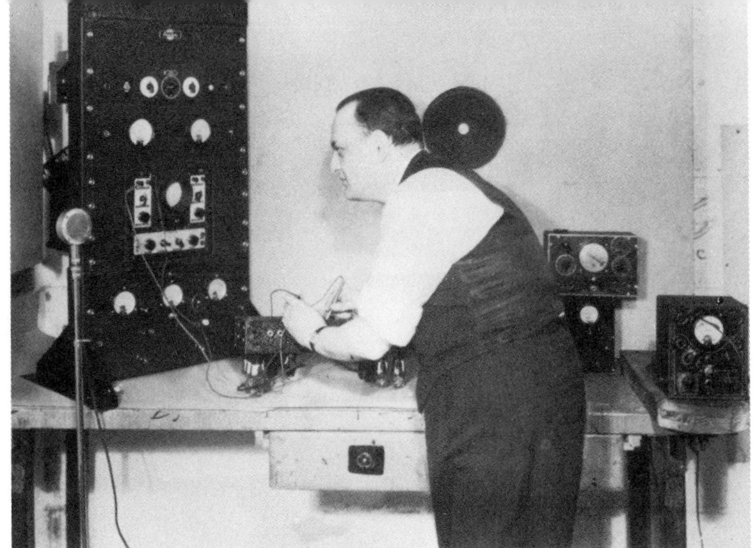

Herb Sunshine with testing gear, circa 1936.

EPIPHONE

The Epiphone Company of New York grew out of the House of Stathopoulo to become one of the most esteemed names in arch-top guitars. During the 1930s no major manufacturer had a better reputation, and Epiphone's endorsers included many of America's best-known studio and radio personalities, such as Dick McDonough, Carl Kress, and George Van Eps.

The House of Stathopoulo was established in 1873 by a Greek violin and lute maker named Anastasios Stathopoulo, and it manufactured a wide variety of stringed instruments. In 1923 it incorporated and began to concentrate on banjos ($50–350) and related products such as banjo-mandolins and banjo-ukes. The factory was located at 68 West 39th Street in New York. The House of Stathopoulo used the trade name "Epiphone" on some of its products, a name taken from luthier/company president Epi Stathopoulo, son of the founder. (Epi's full first name was Epaminondas, after the great general and statesman of the ancient Thebans.) Other early officers included A.G. Malamas, treasurer; and Epi's brother and company secretary, Orpheus ("Orphie") Stathopoulo.

In July 1925 the company bought out the Fairovon banjo manufacturing operation, and in August that year it moved to 35 Wilbur Avenue, Long Island City, New York. In 1928 the House of Stathopoulo changed its name to Epiphone Banjo Corporation.

In June 1931 the firm officially announced its already-established line of Masterbilt guitars, and in October of that year reported that it had made 20,000 banjos, 25,000 mandolins, and 30,000 guitars thus far. The following February, Epiphone opened a showroom in New York City's Strand Theatre building.

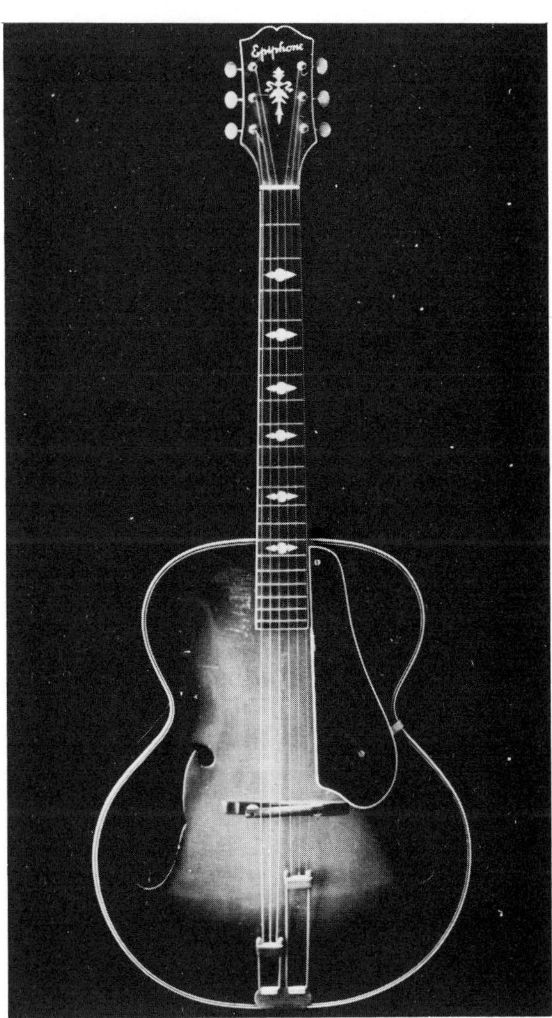

1934 Deluxe Masterbilt. ***Prune***

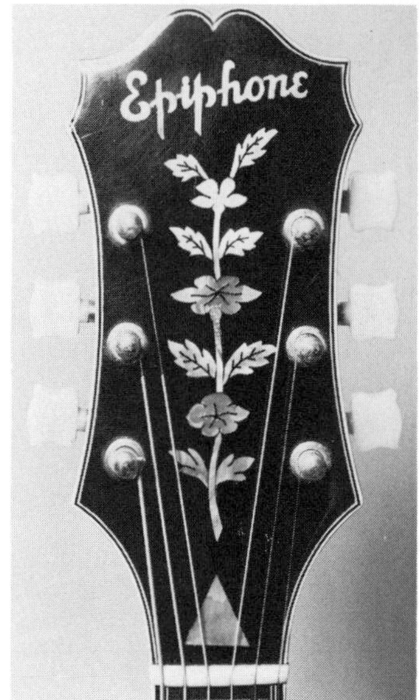

A trio of Emperor headstocks. ***Left:*** **late 1930s.** ***Center and right:*** **circa 1953. Note variations. These are typical examples; slightly different inlays sometimes appeared on models from the same period.** ***Wittrock***

In April 1935 the company moved from Long Island City to 142 West 14th Street, New York City, doubling its floor space. The distributor at this time was Continental Music, a division of C. G. Conn. By November 1935 the earliest Electar electric instruments had appeared. A December 1936 ad promoted the $100 Electar Hawaiian guitar with its amplifier in the case. Epiphone again doubled its floor space in September 1937, and in November of 1938 it formally introduced a line of gut-string guitars ($75–225).

The company officers during this period were Epi, president; Orphie, vice-president; George H. Mann, sales director; and Epi's brother Frixo Nicols (later anglicized to Fritz North) Stathopoulo, an orchestra director who was head of professional relations. Epi died in Florida of pernicious anemia in the early 1940s. Orphie succeeded him as president, and Frixo succeeded Orphie as vice-president. Frixo sold his interest to Orphie in January 1948, and George Mann became vice-president.

Zephyr Emperor Regent, circa 1952. "Zephyr" means "electric"; "Regent" means "cutaway." ***Prune***

Salesman/inventor Herb Sunshine came to work for the Stathopoulos in the mid-thirties and during his six- or seven-year tenure his influence was very important. He designed Epiphone's electric guitar line, invented its individual-polepiece pickup and Frequensator tailpiece, commissioned Nathan Daniel (later founder of Danelectro) to build Epiphone's amplifiers, coined the name *Electar,* and was instrumental in developing the Emperor, the flagship of the arch-top fleet. (Herb also ran the Guild plant for a time after leaving Epiphone.) Here are some of Herb Sunshine's recollections of the early days of Epiphone:

> I'll tell you how that Frequensator tailpiece came about. It seemed like Gibson was coming out with a new tailpiece every few months, so I got to work with a guitar and an oscilloscope. My theory was that a heavy tailpiece muted the sound. The ideal thing was to have a separate fork—an individual length—for each string, but that was too complicated to manufacture and might cause buzzes with all the extra hardware. So I came up with the two-length Frequensator. The name came from "frequency compensator." A discriminating

Early-1930s Epi Zenith with segmented f-holes. By 1935 it had a more conventional body shape, and the end of the fretboard was flat rather than rounded. ***Music Shop/Madsen***

1951 Zenith. The Zenith was a low-end model ($50) just above the bottom-of-the-line Olympic. Mid-1930s: Masterbilt peghead, small body, maple back, segmented (three-section) f-holes. Increased to 14¾-inch walnut body, segmented f-holes. Early 1940s: 16⅜-inch wide walnut body, standard f-holes. ***Wagener/Beaty***

1941 Olympic. ***Wagener/Beaty***

player could reverse the long and short pieces and tell a slight difference in tone.

The Emperor guitar also came about because of Gibson. For a long time their best and largest guitar was the L-5, and our De Luxe, the top of our line, was the same size. Well, they came out with the Super 400 [circa late 1934] and we felt we had to follow suit. I came up with the name Emperor. The Duke of Windsor became the king of England, but he renounced the throne to marry an American commoner. He gave up the crown to marry the woman he loved. It was romantic and everybody ate it up, the biggest story in years. I came up with this idea: the Emperor and the Maid. We photographed a nude model posing with the Emperor guitar in front of her—it was *decent,* you know—and we brought the display to the New Yorker Hotel for a trade show. It was the hit of the show and we stuck with that name.

Epiphone needed some amplifiers, so I looked up Nathan Daniel. In 1920 and 1921 I had worked on Cortlandt Street in Manhattan, which was sort of the center for all the ham radio operators, so I knew about electronics. Nat had a hell of a background in amplifier design. Back in those days most of the country was set up for AC power, but lower Manhattan had DC; so I asked him to build an amplifier that would work on both AC and DC. He made all of the early Epiphone amplifiers, and that was a secret for a long time.

Epiphone finally folded. It was a shame what happened. There were some disagreements. Every single discussion among the family members was the subject of heated debate—that was the Greek in

Dating early Epiphone guitars, general

no truss rod: early and mid-1930s

truss rod adjustment on neck, near body: late 1930s and 1940s

rod adjustment on peghead: post-1951

Epiphone Century, circa 1939, nonadjustable pickup. The only other electric Spanish guitar at the time was the blonde Zephyr ($100), which had a curly maple top, adjustable pickup, and "Mastervoicer" tone knob markings. ***Gruhn/ Baxendale***

Electar amp with angled top panel. ***Jacksonville***

1946 Epiphone Deluxe, "cloud" inlays. ***Wagener/Beaty***

Early-1950s Deluxe Electric, gold plating, maple top. *Spitzer's/Sievert*

1932 Broadway Masterbilt. Note asymmetrical peghead, three-segment soundholes. *Wagener/Beaty*

1951 maple-body Broadway Regent. On this Frequensator tailpiece, the bass-side section is longer than usual; the more conventional type is found on both earlier and later models. *Wagener/Beaty*

Broadway pegheads evolved from: asymmetrical Masterbilt, early 1930s (*left*); asymmetrical with vine inlay, mid-1930s (*center*); center dip with vine, circa 1940; center dip with flower inlay and no truss rod cover, mid-1940s through 1951 (*right*); to flower with rod cover, by 1952.

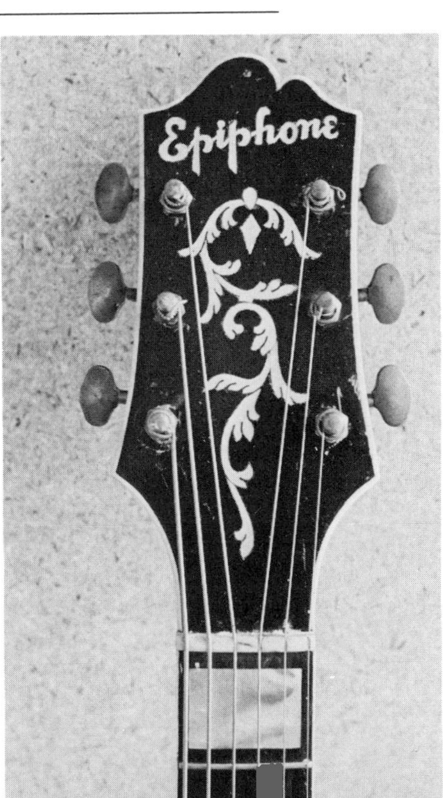

Compare the shape of this early-1930s Broadway headstock to the one on the left in the preceding sequence. The Masterbilt name was included on Epiphone labels for years after it disappeared from the headstocks.

them. They were very vociferous. Epi had avoided the unionization of his plant, but he finally moved from New York to the suburbs of Philadelphia following some union disputes. Several of the best workers were living in the Little Italy section of New York and didn't want to leave. [Sales manager] George Mann knew Al Dronge, who'd made a lot of money in the accordion business during the war, and George and Al went into business together along with the Epiphone artisans who stayed behind in New York. Al and George split up, and Al went on to set up a factory in Hoboken. He called his new company *Guild.*

So Epiphone moved to Philadelphia around 1953. They never really got off the ground again after the war. After Epi died, Orphie acquired all the stock and later sold it to Ted McCarty [see Gibson]. Orphie sold Epiphone for a ridiculously low price. I don't remember the figure, but he could have gotten four times as much. It was a pittance.

Public records of 1952 show a company address for Epiphone at 130 West Third Street in New York City. However, the factory was listed as being in Philadelphia from 1953 to 1955. There were no entries in music industry directories for Epiphone in 1956, and in 1957 it became a wholly owned subsidiary of Gibson.

1935 style Triumph, small body (16⅜ inches). ***Dick Allen***

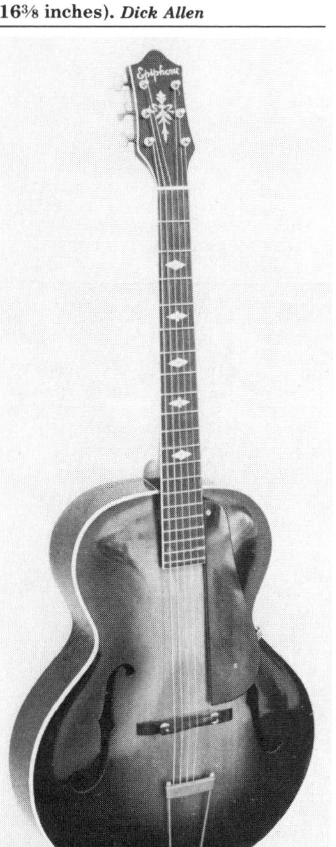

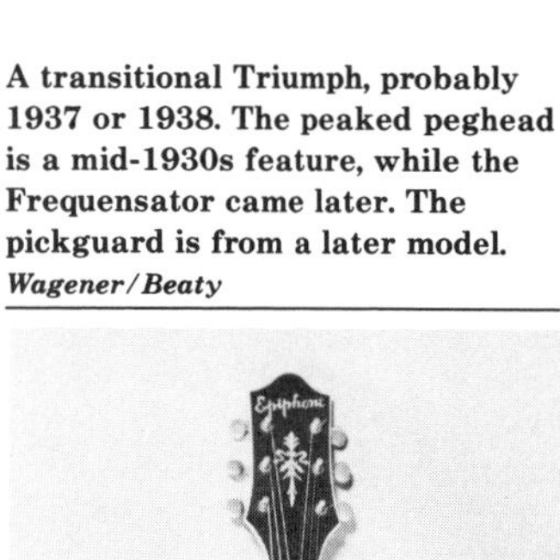

A transitional Triumph, probably 1937 or 1938. The peaked peghead is a mid-1930s feature, while the Frequensator came later. The pickguard is from a later model. ***Wagener/Beaty***

Mid-1940s Epiphone Blackstone. ***Wagener/Beaty***

1951 Epiphone Triumph Regent, DeArmond pickup, Frequensator tailpiece. Note fingerboard inlays. ***Wagener/Beaty***

EPIPHONE GUITARS

An early-thirties catalogue depicts seven Masterbilt models, all with rosewood fingerboards and arched spruce tops. At $275 the De Luxe was the top of the line: flamed curly maple Grand Auditorium body with alternating black/white "rope" body

EPIPHONE SERIAL NUMBERS, 1930–1953

The following numbers are from the records of Petty Music Co., Pittsburgh, an Epiphone distributor. They may not apply to every Epiphone made between 1930 and 1953, but do apply to most. Note that the numbering system changes twice, in 1933 and 1944.

Year	*Series*
1930–1932:	10,000 series
1933:	6,000
1934:	7,200
1935:	8,000 and 9,000
1936:	10,000
1937:	11,000
1938:	12,000
1939–1940:	13,000
1941–1942:	14,000
1943:	18,200
1944:	19,000 and 52,000
1945:	52,000
1946:	54,000
1947:	56,000
1948:	57,000
1949:	58,000
1950:	59,000
1951:	60,000
1952:	64,000
1953:	64,000–66,000

Early-1950s Epiphone Zephyr Electric, also available with blonde finish and/or cutaway body. ***Dan Erlewine/Tom Erlewine***

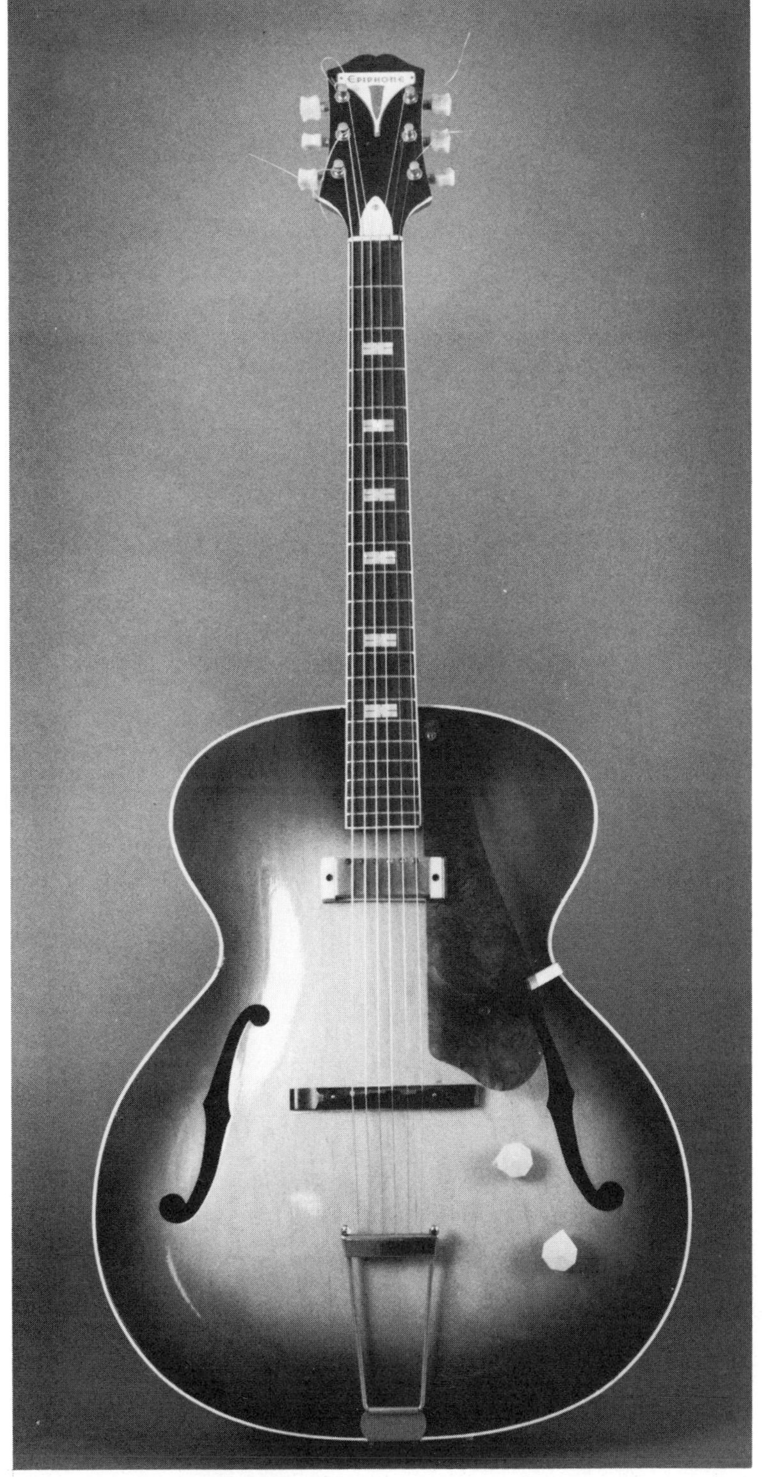

Epiphone Navarre, mahogany body, spruce top. Note the peghead's rounded peak and inlay, as well as the body's unusually full, rounded shape. ***Vintage Fret Shop/A. Caswell***

Early-1950s Zephyr Regent with "New York" style pickup. *Music Shop/Madsen*

Late-1950s Gibson-made Epi Century, New York pickup, Gibson knobs. Gibson used up its stock of original Epi parts before building its own; some Gibson Epis have New York necks and Kalamazoo-made bodies. *Chris Kondrath/Jeff Purcell*

Early Electar amp with wooden cabinet. *Spitzer's/Sievert*

trim. The other models were the Broadway (walnut body, $175), Triumph (walnut, $125), Royal (mahogany, $85), Blackstone (maple, $70), Zenith (maple, $50), and Olympic (mahogany, $30).

Also included were two flat-tops: the Madrid (maple body, f-holes on upper *and* lower bouts—four in all, $90) and the Navarre (mahogany body, $50). There were six tenor guitars: Empire ($250, comparable to the De Luxe), Bretton ($175, like the Broadway), Hollywood (walnut body, $125), Regent (mahogany, $85), Melody (maple, $50), and Beverley (mahogany, flat spruce top, $30).

The formidable Emperor of late 1936 cost $400 and had a heavy tailpiece consisting of a flat plate perforated with decorative holes (later replaced with a Frequensator). Other features included a large 18½-by-21¾-inch curly maple body, oversized pickguard, sunburst finish, ebony fingerboard, particularly elaborate peghead and fingerboard inlays, and gold-plated parts. Here are other details of Epiphone's line:

DE LUXE

Pre 1935: Masterbilt peghead, rope binding, fingerboard inlays vaguely shaped like diamonds and triangles, three-segment soundholes, and a lightweight trapeze tailpiece.
1935: same body, binding, f-holes, and tailpiece, but with vine-inlaid peghead, and inlays generally shaped like diamonds.
1937: a new guitar with enlarged body (17⅜ inches wide), nonrope binding, standard (nonsegmented) soundholes, heavy flat-plate tailpiece, enlarged fan-shaped ("cloud") markers, and an enlarged pickguard extending below the bridge.
Circa 1939: Frequensator tailpiece.

TUDOR

The Tudor ($225) was a rare and short-lived model appearing in the line for only two or three years at most. It ranked between the De Luxe and Broadway and featured a Broadway type vine peghead, diamond and triangle inlays, three-segment soundholes, a trapeze, maple body, and gold-plated parts. Its fingerboard was unusual among other mid-thirties Epiphones—slightly rounded at the treble end. Unlike the De Luxe, the Tudor had no inlay at fret 1.

BROADWAY

Pre 1935: Masterbilt peghead, small walnut body, both standard and three-segment f-holes, diamond-shaped inlays, and a thin trapeze tailpiece.
1935: same body, soundholes, and trapeze, but new vine peghead and large rectangular markers (none at fret 1).
1937: larger 17⅜-inch walnut body, nonsegmented (standard) soundholes, heavy flat-plate tailpiece, enlarged pickguard.
Circa 1939: maple body, Frequensator.

TRIUMPH

Pre 1935: small body, 16⅜ inches wide, asymmetrical Masterbilt peghead, pairs of tiny, inlaid diamonds at each of several frets, trapeze, three-segment soundholes.
1935: same body and soundholes; symmetrical, peaked peghead with a new logo.
1937: wider (17⅜-inch) body, nonsegmented soundholes, enlarged pickguard, and a new, heavy flat-plate tailpiece.
Circa 1939: Frequensator.

SPARTAN

The Spartan appeared in 1935, and at $100 it replaced the $95 Royal. The first Spartan was an arch-top with a round hole, almost certainly a direct attempt to compete with Gibson's $100 roundhole arch-top, the L-4 of 1932–1934. Other details of the premier Spartan were: dot inlays, a peaked peghead, and a 16⅜-inch maple body. By 1937 the Spartan had converted to a walnut f-hole guitar; a distinguishing ornament was the Greek column peghead inlay.

Dale Goens, pictured here with his Electar Rocco model doubleneck, reported in 1980: "This photo was taken 42 years ago when I was playing in western swing bands in Oklahoma City. To the best of my knowledge it was the first doubleneck brought into the state. Noel Boggs came to inspect it, and Leon McAuliffe called to ask how I liked it."

Left: **Early-1950s Epi Devon, $185.** ***Spitzer's/Sievert*** ***Right:*** **Epiphone prototype electric, circa 1944. According to a former company employee, there is only one other like it.** ***Wagener/Beaty***

Gibson-made Epi Crestwood Deluxe, circa 1959, with an interesting mix of standard Gibson parts (tune-o-matic bridge, tailpiece) and New York pickups and knobs. ***Third Eye***

Unusual Epi 6-string bass, early 1960s. *Gruhn/Baxendale*

Early 1960s Epiphone Coronet. *Jim George/Tom Weigand*

Wilshire, circa 1962. Gibson used the same pickups on some Les Pauls, SGs, Firebirds, and others. *Third Eye*

Coronet, circa 1963, note symmetrical body. Within a year or two it had gone to an asymmetrical body (larger left-hand horn), metal pickup cover, and six-on-a-side tuners. The 1967 version had ribbed barrel knobs and a flat-handled vibrato. *Jacksonville*

Broadway electric, circa 1963. Among Gibson-made Epiphones, all of the arch-top bodies were patterned after original Epiphone shapes. *Bill Carson*

Crestwood Deluxe, batwing peghead. *Gruhn*

One-of-a-kind 4-string tenor guitar, factory original, modeled after the Gibson-made Epiphone Wilshire. Note the small, circular plugs that fill the extra polepiece holes. *Gruhn/Baxendale*

Epiphone Riviera, circa 1963, based on Gibson's own ES-335. This type of pickup was not used on any of the standard Gibson guitars of the time, though it later appeared on Les Paul Deluxes. *Jacksonville*

Epiphone Howard Roberts, 1965, made by Gibson. Note oval soundhole, a very unusual feature for the mid-1960s. *Wagener/Beaty*

Gibson-made Epiphone Texan, circa 1967. *Soest/Rountree*

1966 Epiphone E212T Sheraton, made by Gibson. From 1961 to 1970 Gibson made six versions. Production totals for the decade: cherry, 53; cherry/vibrato, 20; natural, 59; natural/vibrato, 49; sunburst, 243; sunburst/vibrato, 197. The cherry versions were available only from 1967 to 1970. With its pearl and abalone trim and gold plating, the Sheraton was perhaps Gibson's most elegant thin-line, though it lacked the ES-355's sophisticated electronics. *Wagener/Beaty*

Epiphone used the Electar brand name on its electric guitars and amplifiers. A 1937 catalogue illustrated a complete line: 6-, 7-, and 8-string jet-black Model M lap steels, the sunburst Model C lap steel with a curly maple top, an electric Spanish (no model name) with a Rickenbacker type horseshoe magnet pickup, the (Tony) Rocco doubleneck Hawaiian, an electric tenor, an electric mandolin, an electric banjo with a curly maple top, and several squarish amps with Keratol covering and "Detacho" rear panels.

The electric banjos, mandolins, and noncutaway guitars came in two styles: Zephyr ($100, blonde, maple top), and Century ($72.25, sunburst). The guitars had metal hand rests that straddled the strings. The Coronet guitars came in two types: the $80 Spanish with a brown finish, oblong pickups, and no hand rest; and the $75 Hawaiian. The Coronet amps had round grilles. The Electar Grande was a beautiful blonde console steel that knocked down and folded up into two pieces of luggage.

The 1954 acoustic arch-top series included the Emperor, Deluxe, Broadway, Triumph, Devon, and Zenith. The electric line included the Emperor, Deluxe, Zephyr, and Century. Like other postwar, pre-Gibson Epi electrics, the 1954 models had "New York" parts: eight-sided knobs and thin bar pickups with cream-colored pickup surrounds.

ERLEWINE

In 1970, luthier/repairman Mark Erlewine began building guitars and basses with his cousin, Dan Erlewine, in Ypsilanti, Michigan. Mark moved to Austin, Texas in 1973, and in 1979 he and ZZ Top's Billy Gibbons developed the Chiquita Travel Guitar shown here. The Chiquita is the best known of the portable mini-electrics.

Soon after, Erlewine and Gibbons began trying to blend the best elements of Stratocasters and Les Pauls. The result was the Erlewine Automatic. (Gibbons sports a double-neck version on *Guitar Player*'s February 1981 cover.) In 1982, Erlewine conceived the Lazer, a radical headless guitar favored by Johnny Winter. As the 1980s drew to a close, Mark reported that he and four employees were producing about five guitars per month.

Earthwood acoustic bass.

ERNIE BALL

Ernie Ball is the founder of Earthwood, the originator of the walnut, guitar-shaped Earthwood acoustic bass, and the dean of modern accessory manufacturers. A Cleveland native born in 1930, he came from a musical family (his grandfather wrote "When Irish Eyes Are Smiling"). The Depression forced the family west to Santa Monica, California, when Ernie was only two. At age nine the youngster took up Hawaiian guitar from his dad and fell in love with the sound of the legendary but obscure steel guitarist Joaquin Murphey.

Ernie's interest in music led to a 20-year career as a professional steel player, teacher, and retailer. He bought a $500 Burbank studio in 1955 and soon had a revolutionary idea—a music store that sold *only* guitars. In 1957 Ernie Ball opened just such a store in Tarzana, near Los Angeles.

During the 1950s the steel guitar was still comparatively young, and Ernie and his fellow steelers had long hassled with mixing up specially gauged string sets to suit the instrument's various necks and tunings. Electric Spanish guitar players were mixing guitar and banjo string sets in order to yield lighter gauges better suited to rock and roll styles. Ernie accommodated these needs with custom-gauge string sets, and he couldn't make them fast enough. A healthy mail-order business encouraged further expansion, and under the wings and glazed eyes of the Ernie Ball cartoon eagle, noble and stoned, there soon developed a nationwide wholesale operation with an ever-increasing line of products—custom personalized picks, steels, and other accessories. Having sold his retail store, Ernie moved south to Newport Beach in 1967. The mail-order and wholesale businesses bloomed, and Ball soon put his three sons to work.

The idea for the radial-braced Earthwood 4-string acoustic bass [also see Guild and Harptone] came from an experiment in which Ernie stuck some frets into an old guitarrón, or Mexican bass. Ernie's friend George Fullerton built the prototype.

In 1972 Earthwood's lacquer-finish steel-string guitars were officially inaugurated, and they included several unusual details (e.g., optional walnut body), some of which reflected the back-to-nature commitment suggested by the company's name: rosewood pickguards, walnut headstock binding, wooden strap buttons and fingerboard markers, no-heel necks with tilt adjustments, large sound chambers, and maple fingerboards.

Earthwood folded in February 1973 and was revived in April 1975. The guitars were discontinued, but the bass operation resumed on a limited-production basis.

The man behind one of American guitar's best-known names, Ernie Ball. ***Guitar Player***

FAVILLA

The Favilla family built instruments for three generations. In 1888 John and his brother Joseph Favilla emigrated from their native Italy to Manhattan, where in 1890 they founded Favilla Brothers, which evolved into Favilla Guitars, Inc. The shop was moved to Brooklyn in 1929 and relocated in Manhattan six years later.

In the late 1940s John's elder son Frank took over the administration of the business; John continued to work in the plant until his death in 1956 at age eighty-five. John's younger son Herk (Hercules) began working at the shop at age fourteen and later performed as a vaudevillian. When Herk's son Tom was born in 1942, Herk began to concentrate more on the family business. On June 26, 1959, he took complete control of the operation and moved the factory from Manhattan to a new 6,000-square-foot facility in Brooklyn.

In 1965 the company relocated to a 20,000-square-foot plant in Farmingdale, Long Island, where the fifteen to twenty workmen produced about 3,000 acoustic guitars a year. Five years later Tom Favilla began importing guitars from Japan; their logos display the company's name in script, while genuine American-made Favillas bear the family crest. Due to escalating production costs and reported undercapitalization, Favilla closed its doors in the summer of 1973.

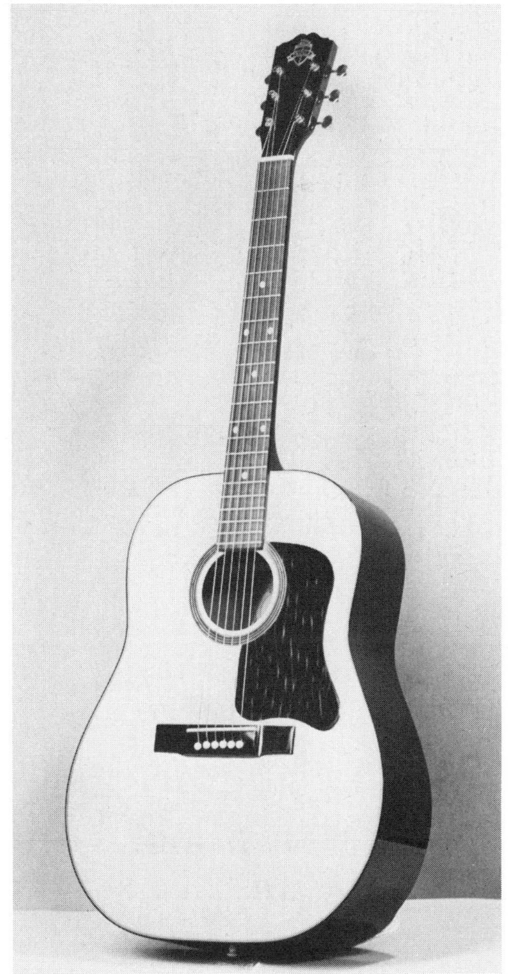

Favilla steel-string, with especially wide waists and rounded body. ***French Art***

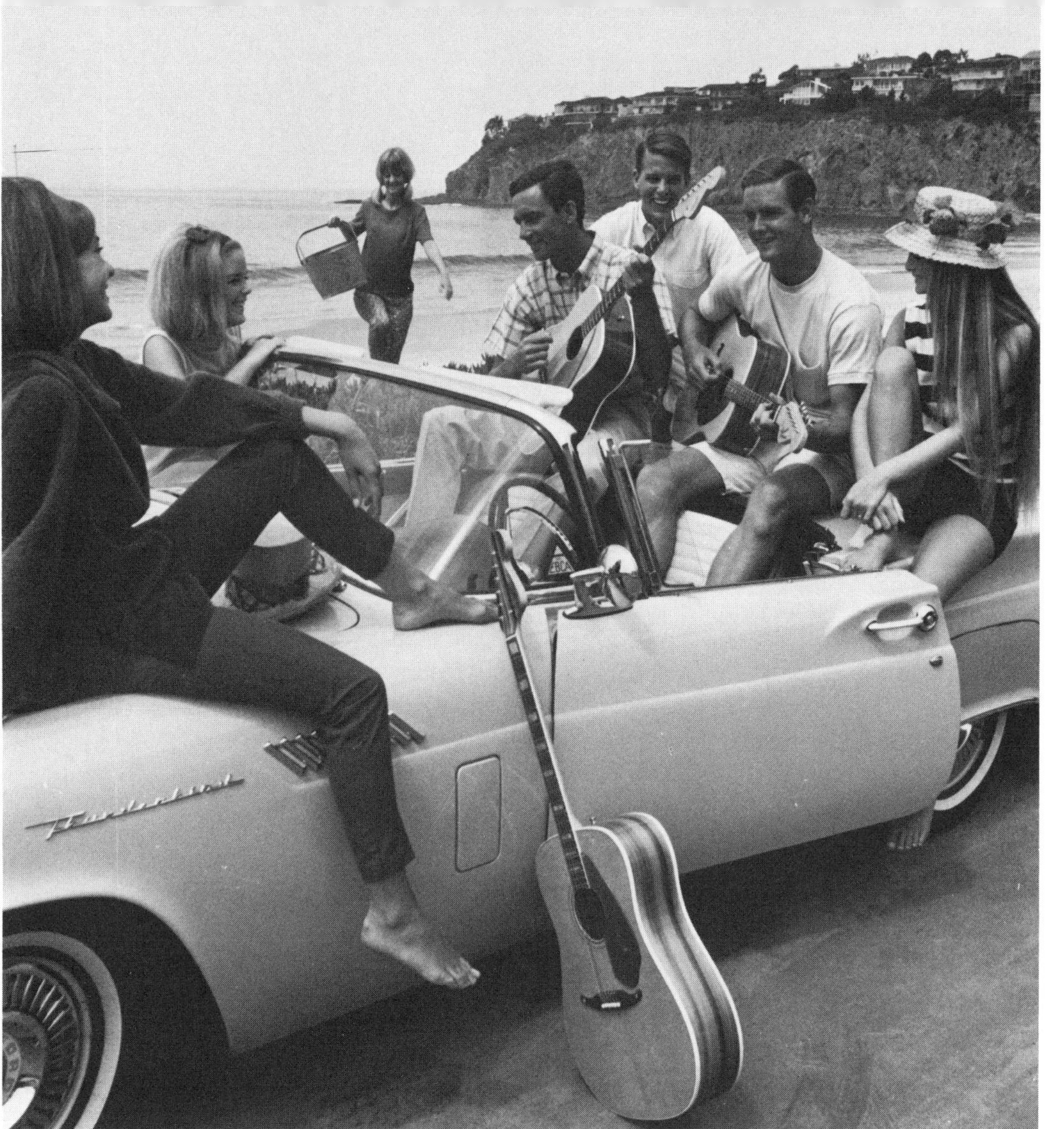

California dreaming: clean-cut kids pose with acoustic guitars and photographer Robert Perine's T-bird for this classic 1967 Fender ad.

FENDER

The following article and interview were written by the author and are reprinted courtesy *Guitar Player* magazine.

There is a good chance that his office at CLF Research would disappoint the lowest federal bureaucrat in Washington. It's a small room, sparsely furnished—no carpet, functional lighting, with a drafting table piled high with blueprints; the monotonic paint is vaguely institutional. A metal bookcase is crammed with miscellaneous speaker parts and catalogues from electronics suppliers. On the modest desk is a Styrofoam coffee cup that, while disposable, is nevertheless being saved; it is labeled with a name carefully printed on masking tape in ballpoint pen: Leo. A side door opens into a large room full of industrial drills and punch presses. There are no clues to the fact that the occupant of the office is a millionaire executive and a leader of his industry, though the absence of frills and the decided air of utility and frugality befit the man who designed it, Clarence Leo Fender.

No one knows for sure who invented the electric Spanish solid-body guitar. In fact, there is no consensus concerning the criteria required to establish such an event. Did it occur when someone strung up a lap steel with six strings tuned to standard pitch? Or when someone else stuck some frets on his electric Hawaiian guitar? In fact, simultaneous development of the electric guitar by independent builders—each with diverse inputs, resources, and influences—

Stratocasters and white Tolex-covered amps, from the 1961–1962 catalogue.

Leo Fender's first guitar, a small Hawaiian model now on display at the Acuff Museum in Nashville's Opryland.

The extremely rare Fender Dual Professional amplifier with angled front panel. *Spitzer's/Sievert*

From the "You won't part with yours either" ad campaign.

appears much more likely than a straight-line evolution traceable to a single, hallowed First One.

This issue of who-came-first, while fascinating to some and historically important, to be sure, sometimes obscures an essential fact: it was Leo Fender who put the solidbody on the map. Was Les Paul a genius? Yes, he was. Were Merle Travis and Lloyd Loar [see Vivi-Tone] visionaries? Undoubtedly they were, and there were others. But Leo possessed something beyond a knack for mechanics, or foresight, or a belief in a dream: He could make it happen; herein lies the peculiar genius of Fender. He first developed a process by which solidbodies could be profitably manufactured on a large scale; therefore, in a very real sense, it is Clarence Leo Fender who is the father of the solidbody guitar.

Given Mr. Fender's low-key personality and the distinctly conservative tenor of the Orange County, California, surroundings where he grew up, his radical guitar designs seem all the more impressive. Their appearance in the early 1950s presented a fundamental alternative to existing electrics. Whereas Gibson, for example, exploited its tradition and long, distinguished history, Fender was as new as this year's Coupe de Ville and purely Californian. Its guitars were neither neo-classical period pieces nor elegant, sunbursted jazzers. There was nothing tuxedo about a Telecaster, nothing Barney Kessel about a sky-blue Strat. Instead, Fender guitars were rock and roll, jet age, outrageous. They were as futuristic as Sputnik, or as tacky as all the sequins in Webb Pierce's wardrobe, depending upon your point of view. Before Fender there were no turquoise musical instruments, no Candy Apple Red scoop-body dragsters with gold-plated hardware and white plastic knobs. Fenders were unique in every way. The vibratos were distinctly un-Bigsby—no hefty external machinery, just a wisp of a plastic-tipped curvy metal rod that disappeared into the guitar's interior. Whereas Gibson guitars

"Here we're at a Christmas party at the factory in the mid-1950s, holding our presents. Forrest is on the left, I'm in the center, and George is on the right."

First-person captions by Mr. Fender.

"Bob Wills and other musicians used to drop by quite often. Here's Freddie Tavares on the far right and Forrest White in the center with some other folks, and Bob Wills' bus. These bands would come by and have all their equipment refurbished."

were spotlighted against velvet curtains in catalogues that oozed company history (and why not?), Fender catalogues were glossy magazines that depicted guitars alongside T-Birds, beatnik paintings, cowboys, and hot-rodders. Gibson flyers featured Tony Mottola wearing a suit and sitting in a studio; Fender ads showed a man with a guitar on his back calmly walking straight into the ocean, or a grinning skydiver leaping into space with a Jazzmaster around his neck, or a man playing electric guitar while surfing—as if it were customary California behavior. Even the cases were different—rectangular, as though conventional luggage just couldn't contain a Fender.

The electric bass is one instrument that, unlike the electric guitar, can be traced to a single prototype. Leo Fender invented it, introduced it in 1951, and in so doing, changed the sound of popular music. The electric bass became known generically as the Fender bass, regardless of who manufactured it. Fender tube amps were

The K&F nameplate, mounted on one of the company's first lap steels. Note the crinkle finish on the body, caused by subjecting the painted instrument to high temperatures. While Doc and Leo were building their first industrial gas oven, the guitars were baked in the Kauffman family's kitchen stove.

Don Randall.

Freddie Tavares.

enormously popular; competitors envied both their design and sales records. They sounded great, and they were hip—you could get a Fender with JBLs more than 20 years ago. Jazzmaster and Jaguar guitars enjoyed a vogue, particularly during the *Beach Blanket Bingo* phase of guitar history, and beginners and folks with limited budgets liked the Musicmasters and Duo-Sonics, though the company staples were always the Tele, the Strat, and the Precision Bass. They are still world favorites. Through the years, Fender's popularity among professionals was a huge promotional asset. Ventures album covers looked like Fender ads; in a sense, they were. The Hendrix/Stratocaster association sold warehouses full of Fenders.

It's difficult to overstate Mr. Fender's impact on his industry. He changed it, revolutionized it—turned it upside down, for that matter. Almost like a superstar or a celebrated trend-setter, he helped to alter the look, the sound, and the personality of American music, and yet it would be hard to imagine a man of plainer appearance or fewer affectations. Freddie Tavares, an assistant to Leo for many years, said, "People didn't have the slightest idea that he was any kind of a wheel. On more than one occasion I would have to point him out to someone who didn't know him. 'See that man over there?' I'd say. 'He owns everything.'"

Although Mr. Fender is not an outgoing individual, his offbeat sense of humor often entertained employees. He neither drinks nor smokes and has few close friends. He is described by more than one associate as something of a recluse. He likes a good car—meaning one that is mechanically sound—but shuns most trappings of the successful executive. Should he invite you to lunch, you'll likely go to Arby's for sandwiches and shakes. He rarely wears a suit, and he's almost never without his little leather holster full of screwdrivers. In his shirt, he keeps a plastic pocket protector stuffed with pens, pencils, and a metal ruler.

When someone does a job for Leo Fender—no matter how good it is—it rarely meets his standards. He splits hairs. Yet his employees like him; some practically worship him. Forrest White's opinion—"I

Fender-made White amp, named after Forrest White. The nameplate promises "Higher Fidelity." ***Dennis Fullerton***

Flat-tops and suits—an out-take from the 1958–1959 catalogue photo session.

"There is my old partner, Doc Kauffman, on the left, and we're holding one of our early K&F guitar and amp sets."

wouldn't trade the years I spent with Leo for anything"—is not uncommon among his associates. He dabbles in photography, likes to play pinochle on a Saturday night, and owns an expensive boat. Still, his only true hobby, perhaps his obsession, is his work. He is a man of few words. He does not play guitar.

Leo Fender has a passion for things mechanical. He routinely annoys representatives who sell him parts and supplies by grilling them with probing inquiries about their own products and then explaining the answers in detail. He is ever curious; he has been known to suddenly slide under a parked car to check out various aspects of its construction. According to Don Randall, president of Fender Sales for years, "Leo likes machinery. He had very expensive and high-powered machinery that probably didn't run more than five days a month, but he liked it—the big presses and everything. Leo designed all the equipment, which was unique, and he was a genius for figuring out the manufacturing process. A very clever man." By his own estimate, Mr. Fender owns between 50 and 75 patents. Clever, indeed.

Don Randall, later president of Randall Instruments, worked for a local radio parts supplier before joining Fender. He established Fender Sales, a separate entity that promoted Leo's instruments nationwide. Essentially, Randall took care of business, including the negotiation of the Fender Company's sale to CBS, while Leo did what he liked to do best—he built guitars. In order to allow him more time to work in R&D (research and development), Leo hired Forrest White in 1954 to be his plant manager. Forrest and Tom Walker—for years a chief Fender salesman—formed the Music Man company in March of 1972. Leo's later company, CLF Research, built the Music Man guitars.

Clayton Orr "Doc" Kauffman was a key person in Leo Fender's

Gene Vincent (*center standing*), rock's consummate greaser and a fine rockabilly bopper, visits the Fender plant along with his band, the Blue Caps.

Fender 4-string electric mandolin.

From Fender's very successful late-1950s ad campaign.

Early Ventures albums were showcases for the Fender sound, and photos like this (who cares if they weren't plugged in?) helped define the rock and roll combo look.

From the 1960 catalogue cover photo session.

introduction to guitar manufacturing. He came to California from a farm in Kansas in 1922 and played various instruments in local bands around Orange County. Like Leo, he is a relentless tinkerer, having fashioned steam engines from five-gallon milk cans when he was a kid and having built farm machinery, sanders, tools, radios, police transmitters, and a motorcycle. He also claims to be the first man to install amplifier components in the top of the cabinet—the way it's done on most amps today—simply to avoid the trouble of having to bend over to make adjustments. "Leo came in one day," recalls Doc, "and he said, 'Hey, you've been building guitars around here—do you want to build some together?' And I said, 'Well, sure; sounds okay to me.'" Kauffman and Fender called their company K&F. The partners expanded their operation and bought a lot on Valencia Street, moved in, set up shop, and got to work. Partly because of the popularity of both country and Hawaiian styles of music, the venture proved successful. They taught themselves how to weld and made many of their own tools.

Doc explained: "I got scared of the business. I had been saving money through the war, and I wanted to get a home and pay for it. My dad was a credit boy all his life—owed money on the farm and everything—so I told myself that I'd never go into debt for anything. Leo was different—he'd go into debt on an investment like a house afire! He didn't care. Besides, he was smart. He's a pursuer, boy—day and night. That's what put the guitar where it is. Anyway, I didn't have much faith in guitars, and I asked Leo to buy out my half of the business. He kept making those little ol' K&Fs for a while after I left him, until all the nameplates were used up. Then he went on his own. You know, he never talked about the future. I never dreamed he'd become wealthy. I respect him, and one day he told me—I'll never forget—I asked him, 'Leo, what in the world would you be doing if you and I had never met?' He said, 'Well, I'd probably have maybe two or three radio stores or TV repair shops.'"

Though he is quick to downplay his role, calling it "inconsequential," Donald D. Randall was in fact responsible to a great degree for the worldwide success of Fender. Before World War II he worked for the Santa Ana Radio & Television Equipment Company and later for the Radio-Television Equipment Company, or Radio-Tel.

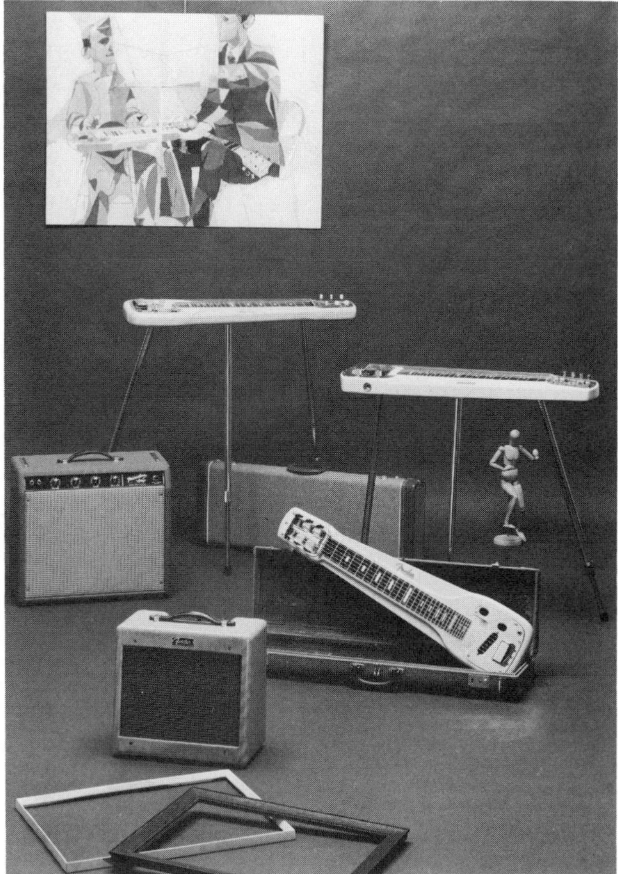

Princeton (*rear*) and Champ amps with steel guitars, 1961.

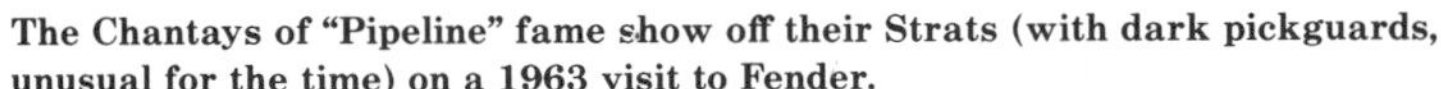

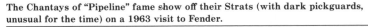

The Chantays of "Pipeline" fame show off their Strats (with dark pickguards, unusual for the time) on a 1963 visit to Fender.

Preparing for a late-1960s beachside promo shot.

1960–1961 style Fender amps.

Some early-1960s Fender amps had volume controls in the center.
Dan Torres/Norm Mayersohn

The latter firm was owned by Francis Hall, later owner of Rickenbacker. As a wholesale parts supplier, Randall provided Fender with radio equipment. During the war, Leo got into the instrument business, and shortly after Don came out of the service, he returned and began to handle the distribution of K&F guitars. Radio-Tel only had one or two salesmen, being confined to Southern California, but as the new Fender Electric Instruments Company grew, Don began devoting more and more of his time to musical instrument distribution and less to radio supply. Charlie Hayes became a salesman in Radio-Tel, and together, Don and Charlie helped the business to grow during the late 1940s and early 1950s. Doc Kauffman describes Randall's importance: "He set up a sales distributorship like nobody had ever seen in the world. Nobody appreciates what part of Fender he was. Nobody knows."

Don found guitar distribution to be much more interesting than supplying electronic parts. "Nobody had ever seen stuff like ours before," he says. "You could go out and promote it and sink your teeth into it. It was an exciting field." In 1953 a new organization called Fender Sales, Inc., was established to handle exclusive distribution of Fender products. There were four equal partners: Leo Fender, Don Randall, Charlie Hayes, and Francis Hall. They built their own facilities and grew at an impressive rate. Randall ran the business, while Fender Electric Instruments continued to function as a separate operation.

According to Mr. Randall, Francis Hall, while a partner in Fender Sales, purchased the Rickenbacker company and began promoting it with vigor. In June of 1955, Charlie Hayes was killed in a car accident, and Leo and Don bought out the interests of Hayes' widow and Hall at the same time, leaving the two of them with 50/50 shares in Fender Sales. "From then on," Don recalls, "Leo and I just continued to promote Fender, working hard, very hard, 14 to 16 hours a day—no vacations or anything for either of us. Leo was a very hard worker and devoted all his time and energy to the product, and I devoted myself to sales, product information, promotion, recruiting salesmen and so on. Leo was content to stay close to the shop, or the lab, as he called it, while I was out in the mainstream. It worked out very well, because he did his job, and I did mine. We helped each other, and it turned out to be a very successful arrangement. I did all the sales work, laid out the catalogues, and, although some people might dispute this, my assistant, Stan Compton, and I also picked out the names of several products."

"For Sale: early '60s Strat, pre-CBS." Such ads are common, and the issue of "pre-CBS," seemingly a part of practically every transaction involving an old Fender, dates back to the period immediately following the sale of Fender in 1965. The acquisition generated numerous stories about a decline in quality—stories that persist to this day. Like many rumors, they had some factual basis. Here was a classic case where a huge conglomerate absorbed a company that, while large, was nevertheless previously identified with the one man whose name appeared on the peghead. Perhaps guitar players felt a sense of loss, or they worried that hotshot corporate execs in coats and ties couldn't possibly turn out a product as personal as a musical instrument.

It is true that after the sale CBS imposed fundamental changes in production techniques as well as management. Based upon detailed accounts of former employees who were there at the time, it is fair to say that some products—including both guitars and amplifiers—suffered a loss in quality, especially during the first year or two following the acquisition.

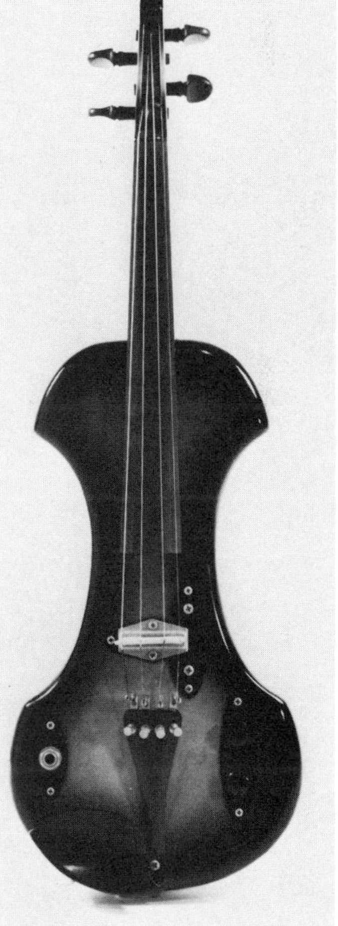

Fender electric violin. *Soest/ Rountree*

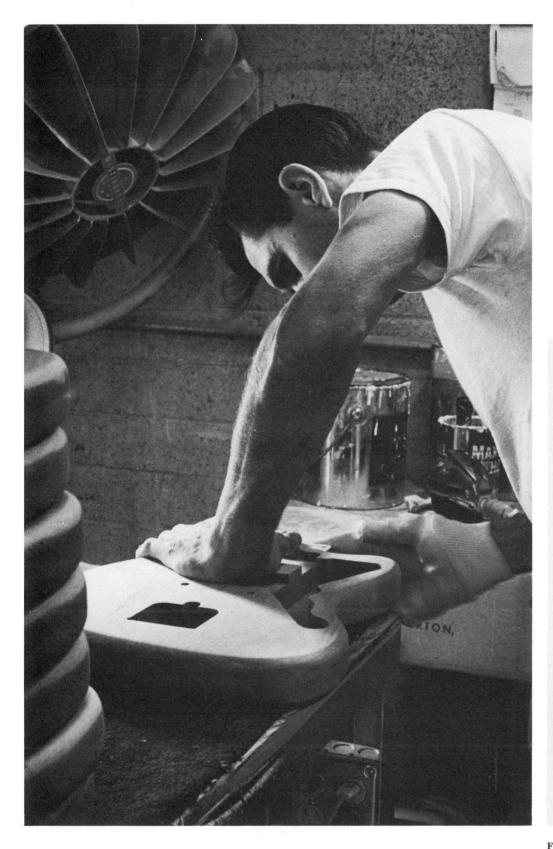

Chuck Lewis preparing an early-1960s Jazzmaster body for finishing.

An aerial view of the Fender plant, with the original nine buildings on the right and the huge CBS addition at left.

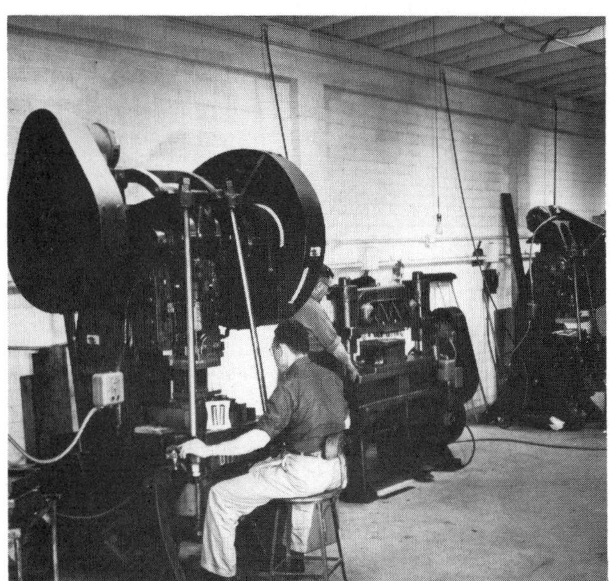

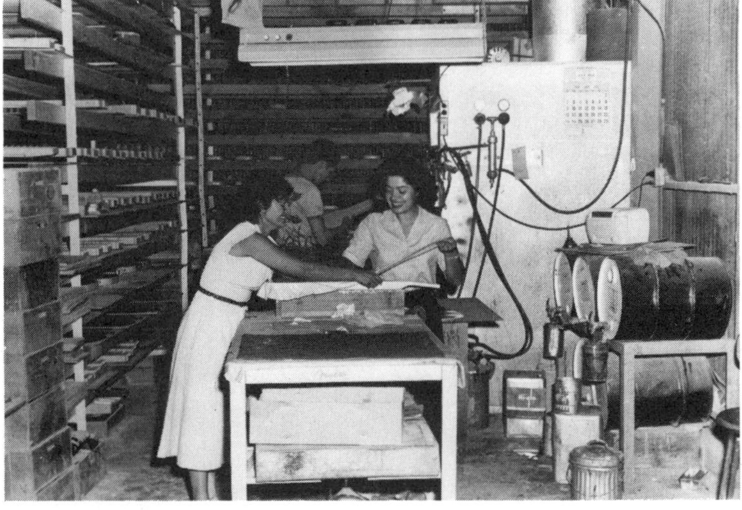

Upper left: **"This is Freddie at the punch press. He's a little out of character here because he didn't really run this kind of equipment. He's just there for the photo. We would punch all sorts of things on equipment like this. Later we bought a punch press that was so big we had to make a hole in the roof to get the thing erected with a crane. We had six or seven more presses of different sizes. The biggest one was around 100 tons. We did our footpedals and transformer covers and all sorts of things on it."** ***Lower left:*** **"Here is a row of people assembling amps. Later we had four of these rows. There was a time when we were putting out 1,000 amps a day. See, we were the largest dollar-volume producer in the world at the time we sold to CBS, and we were also selling something like 80 percent of all the basses of professional quality in the world. On one of our guitars, the Mustang, we were 15 million dollars back ordered. That's a successful little guitar."** ***Above:*** **"This is Geraldine Herrera on the right putting cellulose nitrate skin over a lap steel. There's an electric flare heater at the bottom and just above that is a tank of acetone. This place was a bomb [*laughs*]. It's even dangerous to *look* at a picture of a place like this. They used to stretch this stuff over toilet seats, too, and this was the way it was done—dangerous as hell, oh so dangerous. Over in the drums on the right we had lacquer and lacquer thinner. The whole room was just like a powder keg. One time a fire inspector came, took one look, and left right away. He went about a block away and *phoned* us [*laughs*]. He was pretty upset with the whole thing and wouldn't go near the place."**

First-person captions by Mr. Fender.

"A while after this shot was taken we installed a big canopy over the space between some of the buildings. We would do our unloading in that space."

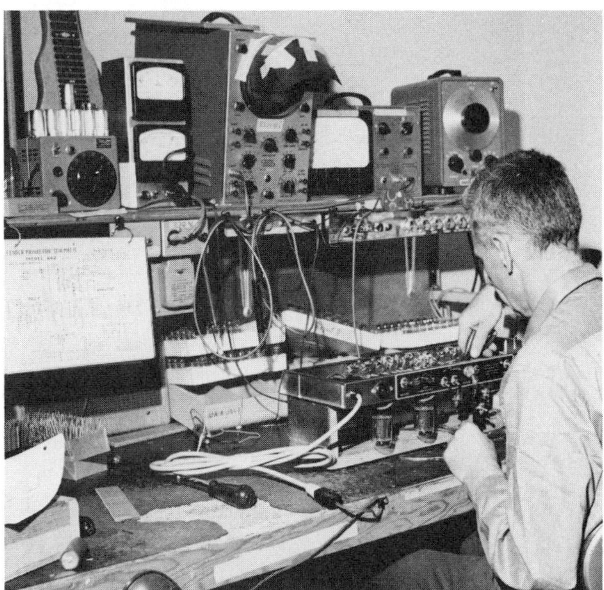

Amp technician Bob Standen at his workbench in 1967 working on a Princeton chassis.

In most cases the best way to determine whether an old Fender is pre-CBS is simply to pop the neck and check the date that appears written inside. The problems arise for guitars made during the transition period. As is the case with any large company, many months may pass during component manufacture, shipping, and sale. Thus, an instrument purchased in mid 1965 or even later may be "pre-CBS" in terms of parts and methods of construction, though actually marketed by CBS. Another complicating factor is that some production techniques did not change at all when CBS took over. Furthermore, there is no neat correlation between any of several product alterations that *did* occur and the transfer of control. Having made these various qualifications, however, the generally applied indicator for a CBS instrument is the appearance of a large *F* on the neckplate. Most dealers rate these as CBS instruments, though there are plenty of Fenders dated 1965 that do not have the *F*. According to collector George Gruhn, the guitars that did change generally begin to "look like CBS" in 1966.

Mr. Randall was Fender's sole negotiator for the sale. He met with an agent from Merrill Lynch, who introduced representatives from CBS. Randall and CBS started negotiations in late August or September of 1964 and completed the deal, to be effective January 5, 1965. Don recalled: "Leo wouldn't even go back to New York and pick up his check [his share of the 13 million dollar selling price], wouldn't go back for the closing. I picked up his share of the booty and deposited it in his bank for him. He was busy working at Fender."

Randall had a five-year contract with CBS to stay on and run the company. He didn't last five years, however, because he and the CBS executives "weren't of the same cut," as he put it. CBS' corporate bureaucracy hit Fender like a blizzard, blanketing various operations in layer after layer of paperwork. Employees found their simple but reasonably efficient procedures under close scrutiny by a horde of systems analysts. There was plenty of confusion, and many employees resented the changes.

Behind the commotion was an attempt by the new owners to standardize operations. According to Mr. Randall, "Any large corporation would likely have the same problems of immediately trying to understand a unique process like guitar manufacture. They thought, well, you know, 'You ought to be able to stick in a plank here and have the neck come out there.' But they caught on."

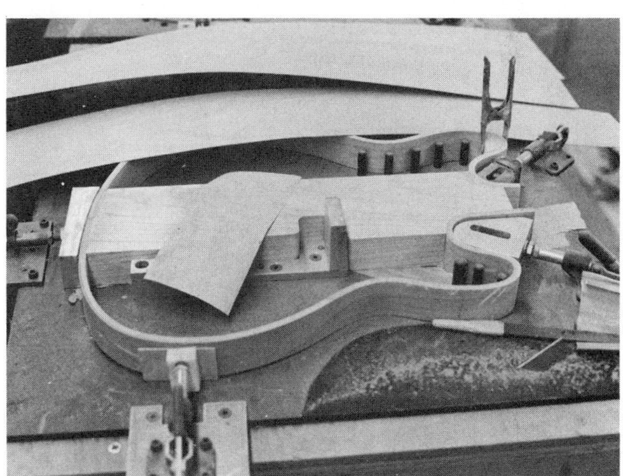

Starcaster body in a shaping jig.

The binding on these Starcaster bodies has been wrapped tightly until the glue dries; the metal forms and heavy rubber bands facilitate the process.

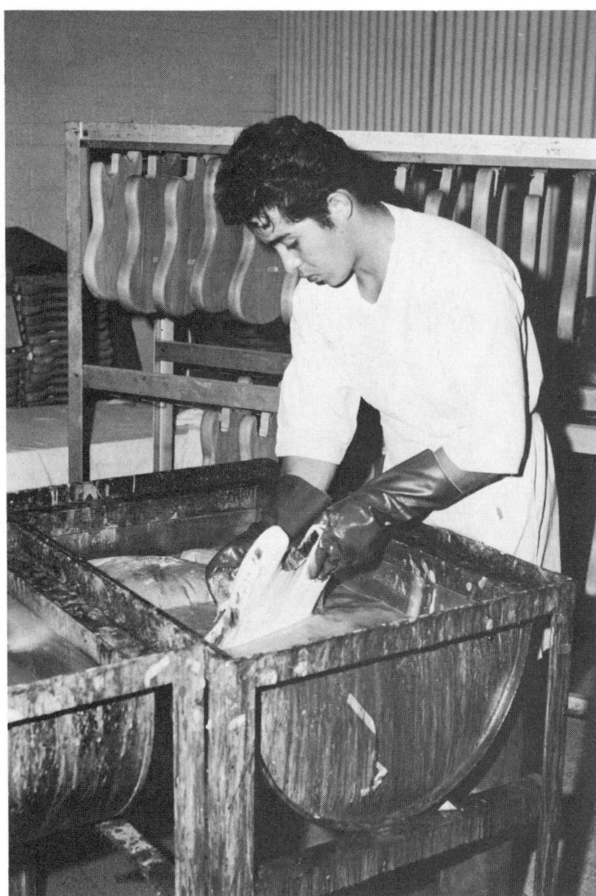

Dipping a solidbody in a vat of Fullerplast stain in preparation for sunbursting.

Randall left in April of 1969 after the differences between himself and the new management became intolerable. "I laid low for a while," he explained, "and then I formed Randall Instruments."

For more than 25 years Freddie Tavares has worked for Fender as a designer and engineer, a mainstay of CBS/Fender's R&D department. Though he helped design guitars, he is quick to set the record straight concerning the extent of his involvement. Once, when asked if the Stratocaster was essentially Leo's design, he replied, "All of the guitars were essentially Leo's design."

Forrest White met Leo Fender in 1948—he recalls every detail of the event—and came to work for him as plant manager on May 20, 1954. At that time Mr. Fender had only about three dozen employees, so as an executive, Forrest was able to witness the company's long growth from a perspective that provided much insight. He became one of a trio of ex-Fendermen who set up the Music Man plant in Anaheim, across town from their old factory. Fortunately, like Julius Bellson of Gibson, Forrest took on the role of unofficial company historian, maintaining a remarkably complete collection of catalogues, price lists, bulletins, clippings, and other information. In direct contrast to Leo's sparse working area, White's ample office at Music Man is full of Fender memorabilia, which he treasures. "Don't you wrinkle that, boy," he says, displaying a quarter-century-old catalogue that looks new.

Forrest was vice-president and general manager of Fender, but CBS changed his function to director of manufacturing. In December of 1967, he quit Fender after angry disputes with CBS over production methods. He and Tom Walker, an important Fender sales-

Sam Mahoney at the spray booth, January 1964.

Art Cordero beveling pickguards in 1959.

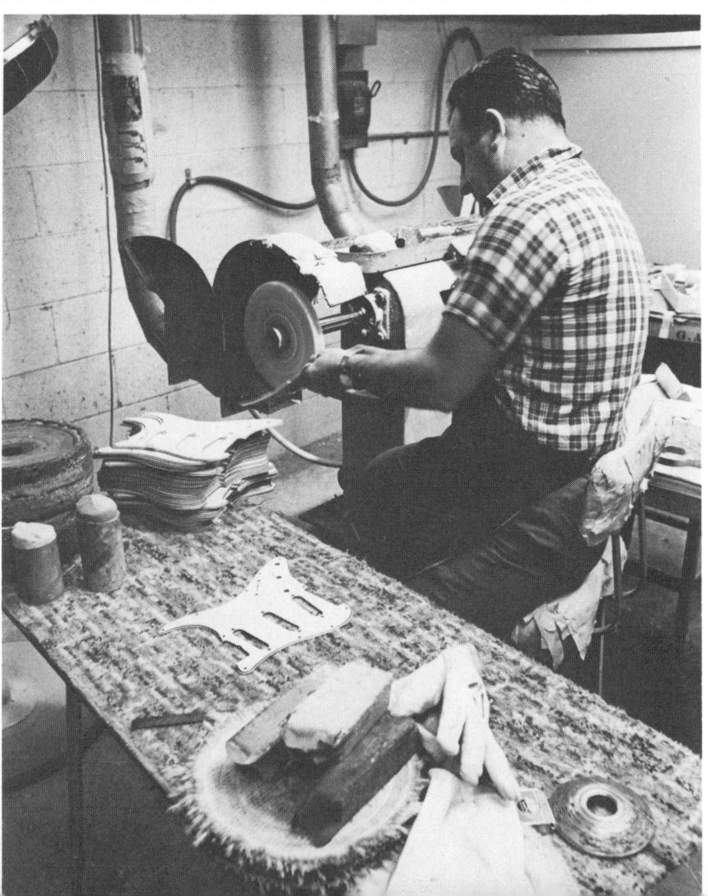

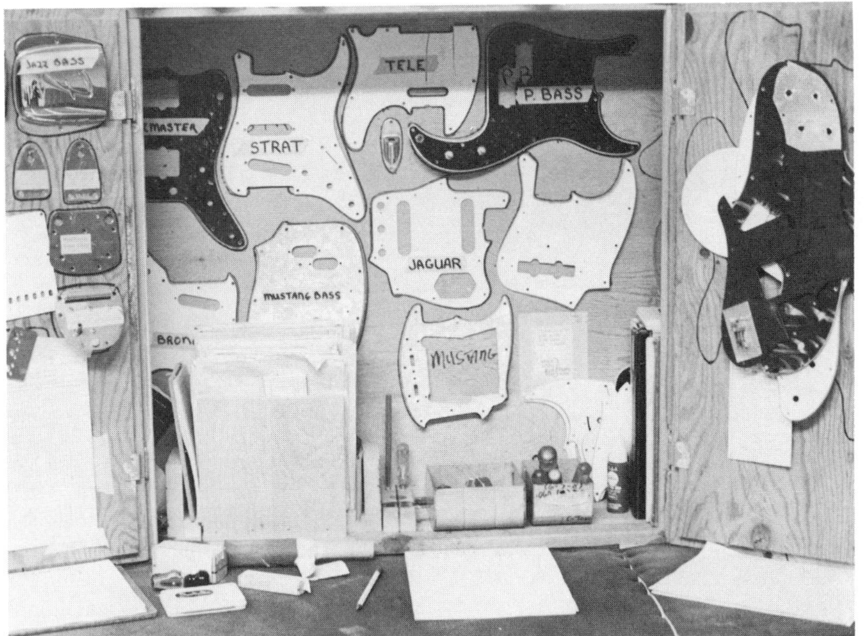

Pickguard templates.

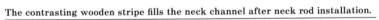

A stack of roughed-out neck blanks.

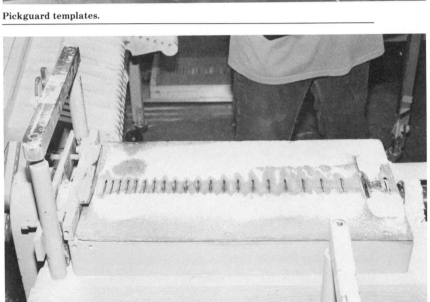

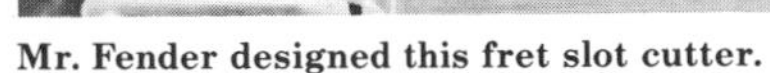
Mr. Fender designed this fret slot cutter.

The contrasting wooden stripe fills the neck channel after neck rod installation.

Inlaying block position markers with white glue.

The end clamp and side clamps are used to hold neck binding in place until the glue dries.

Ted Ledbetter dresses frets on December 1, 1963. Note the stamp at the end of the neck, which reveals the date as well as the neck contour, in this case "B."

These finished necks await installation of tuners and final assembly.

man for many years, got together toward the end of 1971 and formed a corporation on March 3, 1972, which eventually became known as Music Man.

Music Man got under way marketing amplifiers designed by Tom Walker; many of the employees are former Fender workers from the old days. At this writing, Leo works at his own company, CLF Research, where he is assisted by George Fullerton, for 30 years his close friend and right-hand man. CLF has an exclusive agreement with Forrest White and Tom Walker to build guitars and basses for Music Man, and Leo Fender works at it the only way he knows how—full-time. CLF has about 40 employees, which suits Leo Fender just fine. Forrest and Tom run the business; Leo and George build guitars. The arrangement has a familiar ring.

In the summer of 1980, Leo Fender and George Fullerton announced several guitars and a bass to be marketed through their new company, G&L Music Sales, Incorporated. Though a separate firm, G&L shares facilities with CLF Research.

Worker installs strings on a Stratocaster with an automatic key turner.

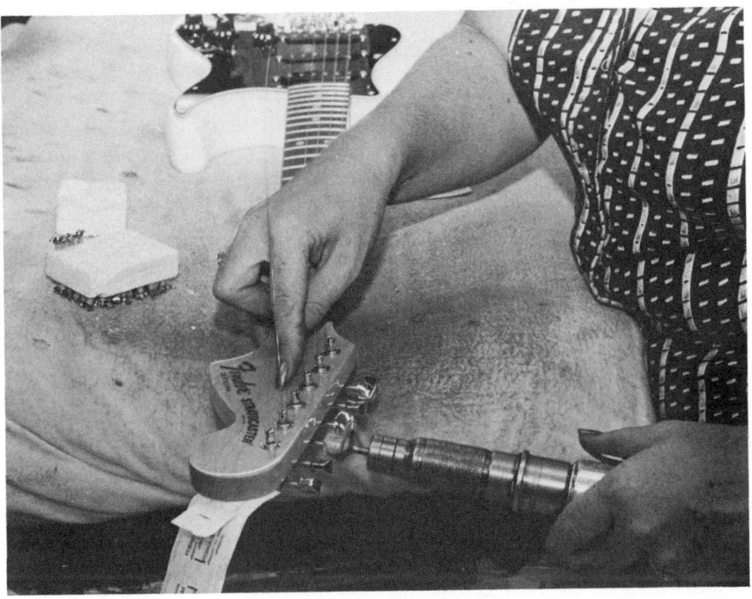

Installing the Micro-tilt device.

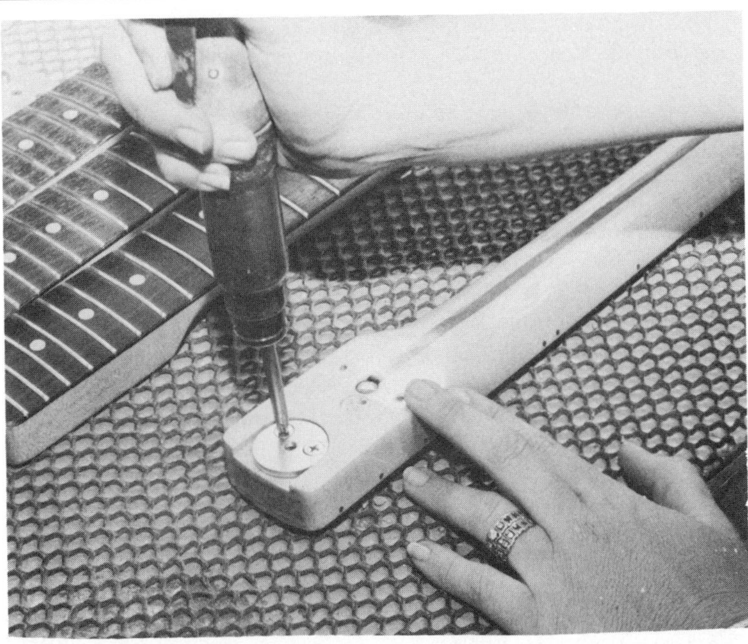

1992 Update

Fender Japan was started in 1981 by CBS—a joint venture involving Fender, distributor/wholesaler Kanda Shokai, and the huge retailer Yamano Music.

Fender Japan distributed made-in-Japan Fenders and Squire products to the Japanese market, and distributed Japanese-produced guitars bound for the U.S. Both Squires and Fenders were built by a couple of Japanese factories, principally Fuji Gen Gakki. Fender's Dan Smith adds: "We never put those pull-off stickers on the guitars. On our decals it always specifies the country of origin; the only exceptions are the Vintage series [which are made in the U.S.], because the originals didn't say it on their decals. On the neckplate on the vintage-type guitars, it begins with a V for U.S.-produced models and a JV for Japan-produced models."

In 1985, CBS sold Fender to an independent group which included several Fender veterans. After trimming the staff and refocusing their efforts, the new group got Fender back on track. As we go to press, the company is strong, with innovative, popular guitars such as the Strat Plus and the American Standard Series.

The new factory is in Corona, California, not far from the original Fullerton facility. About 200 people work there, including the engineering staff. Most guitars and basses whose catalog numbers start with a "1" are built entirely in the California facility. The few exceptions include the Strat H.M. (some parts made in Japan) and new Fenders with code numbers beginning with "14," such as the JP-90 bass (sanding and painting done in Ensenada, Mexico).

In December 1985, Fender bought the Sunn amplifier facility near Portland, Oregon, and most new Fender amps are made there (although the cabinets are made in Mexico). Exceptions include the Fender 15 and Champ 12 amps, made entirely in Mexico, and the Sidekicks, made in Taiwan.

A CONVERSATION WITH LEO FENDER

Clarence Leo Fender's story is told in part in the accompanying article, which describes the history and many successes of his company. But what about the man himself? Here is Mr. Fender's own account of his life and career.

"I always had tools around. I like tools."

WHERE WAS your family from?

☞Mother was born in Covina, a community east of Los Angeles. Dad was born in Illinois. He got through the third grade, and when he was older he went to work for a creamery in Kansas City. He was a farmer all his life. In 1906 he came here to Orange County and got a place west of Anaheim. He sold it, got another place, and that's where he spent the rest of his life.

Were you born in Orange County?

☞Yes, in a barn on our farm near Anaheim. That was 1909. My folks didn't build their first home on that property until the following year. I've lived around Anaheim and Fullerton all my life.

When did you get interested in tools and electronics?

☞Well, as far back as I can remember, I always had tools around. On a farm you have a lot of them. I like tools. Always have. Though my dad was a farmer, I was more interested in electronics and design, so I decided to pursue that sort of a course. I did janitor work in high school, and during my second year of junior college over in Fullerton I had a job with a bookkeeper. I took a Civil Service exam in about 1928, passed it, and later got some work in the motor vehicle department in 1932, 1933. Right after that I worked full-time for the state as an accounting clerk. That lasted about three years. I didn't really like it, but I had a wife to support as well as me—we were married in 1934–and it was a living.

When did you begin to work on guitars?

☞Well, I don't play—never had time to learn [*laughs*]! Too busy making them. I built an acoustic guitar in the 1920s when I was 16. I got into working with pickups in the 1930s. People would come by, and they weren't happy with the pickups that they had, so I'd work on them or repair them, and I started to design my own. I noticed that with those big bar magnets and horseshoe magnets that they didn't always respond evenly, and that led to the development of individual polepieces. I think that perhaps I was the first person to use separate magnets—one for each string.

Were you interested in electric guitars by the time you met Doc Kauffman?

☞I had seen Doc back in the middle 1930s. He used to play in storefronts to draw a little business for the store and also to sign up a few students for himself. But I didn't meet him and talk to him until maybe 1941, right around in there.

When did you and Doc make instruments?

☞Not until the armistice was signed in the fall of 1945—from then until about February of 1946. The new business, K&F, began to take up so much of an investment that Doc began to get worried, and he was afraid that some property he had in Oklahoma might go down the drain if we failed. So he thought that he'd better get out while he had a full skin.

When did George Fullerton come to work for you?

☞Early 1948. Doc and I separated in early 1946, and George came on after I started up Fender Electric Instruments. Doc had released everything to me; he took a small punch press and we called it an even trade.

1957 maple-neck Musicmaster, gold anodized pickguard. ***Charley's/Crump***

Then you decided to make a go of it on your own?

☞ Well, yeah, didn't have much choice—when you jump out in the middle it's just about as far either way [*laughs*]!

Was George your first employee at Fender?

☞ No, we had a crew working there. That was one of the things that worried Doc—this big payroll every week.

Did Fender Electric Instruments grow out of K&F, or did you start from scratch?

☞ We had some of the same employees; it grew out of it. I just continued the thing and expanded it and changed the name.

Les Paul used to live in L.A., in Hollywood. Did you ever have any contact with him?

☞ He came out to the plant one time in about 1950. He wanted to see what we were doing, and he brought Mary Ford out with him, and we went to lunch. Later I gave him an amplifier. Sometime along about then he came into possession of one of our Telecasters. I met him again up in Los Angeles, maybe in the early 1950s, for just a few moments.

Did he ever influence you, or contribute to your work?

☞ No.

There are so many claims and rumors concerning who invented the solidbody guitar. Do you think it could be said that any one person gets the credit?

☞ I don't think anybody knows who invented the first one, but we had the first commercial production; I don't think there's any doubt about that [also see Rickenbacker, Vivi-Tone, and National]. We also had a solidbody standard guitar back in 1943 or 1944 that we rented out while the war was going on, and it was popular. We'd have a waiting list of two weeks on the thing.

Did you design that guitar?

☞ Largely, yes, but I had a business to run, too, and Doc did a lot of the work on it. It was an extreme cutaway—didn't look anything like the Fender guitars.

Was Fender Electric Instruments successful from the very beginning?

☞ Pretty successful, yes. We moved several times—to two steel buildings and one brick building with 3,600 square feet all together. We had about 15 employees by 1947 or so. Then we expanded to 5,400 square feet in about 1949, and then we moved again in 1952 or 1953 into four buildings. We grew pretty fast, because in 1955 we had about 50 employees, but by the end of 1960 we were up to well over a hundred. We built more buildings, and we leased another 6,000 square feet in 1960. Then we had a new warehouse and sales office—a 38,000-square-foot, one-story building with about 11,000 square feet of office space and a recording studio where musicians could come in and record for free on Ampex machines. By the end of 1964 we were occupying 27 buildings. We were bursting at the seams in those days, with about 500 employees in the manufacturing proper, and 600 in all.

Did you design a lot of your own tools and machines?

☞ Yes. We'd have a specific job to do, and we'd design a machine to do it. Perhaps that was a little unusual, because a great many companies are run by people who are principally executives. Often, an executive is not adapted to the machinery end of the business. Maybe I came in through the back door, I don't know [*laughs*].

Your guitars were so radical, so unlike anything that had come before—what was your inspiration for the designs, the shapes?

☞ I had so many years of experience with work on radios and elec-

1960 Duo-Sonic with anodized pickguard, virtually identical to the Musicmaster except for the latter's single pickup. Both introduced in 1956, both restyled in 1964 to resemble the Mustang. ***Spitzer's/Sievert***

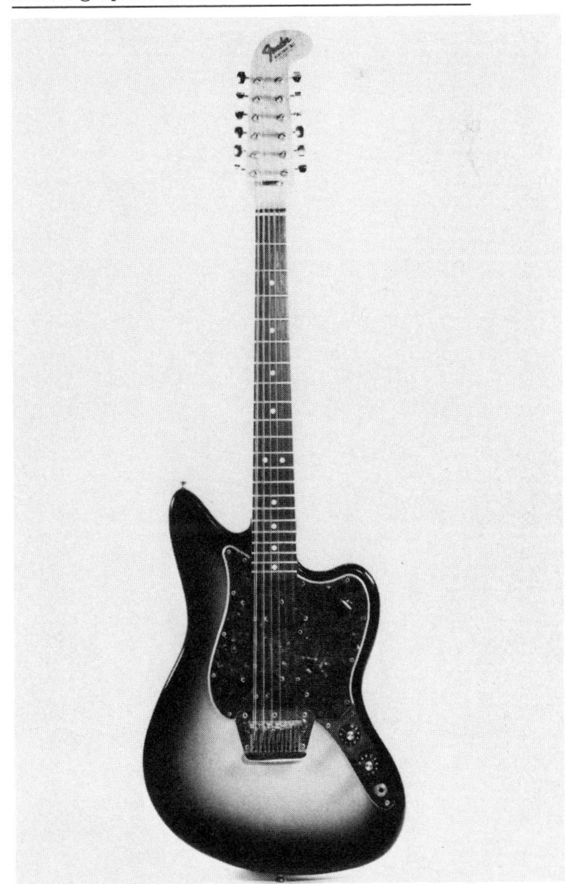

1965 Electric XII. The model was discontinued after the following year. ***Thel Rountree***

1966 Electric XII models and Telecasters.

Marauders (with concealed pickups) and Jaguars, 1965–1966 catalogue.

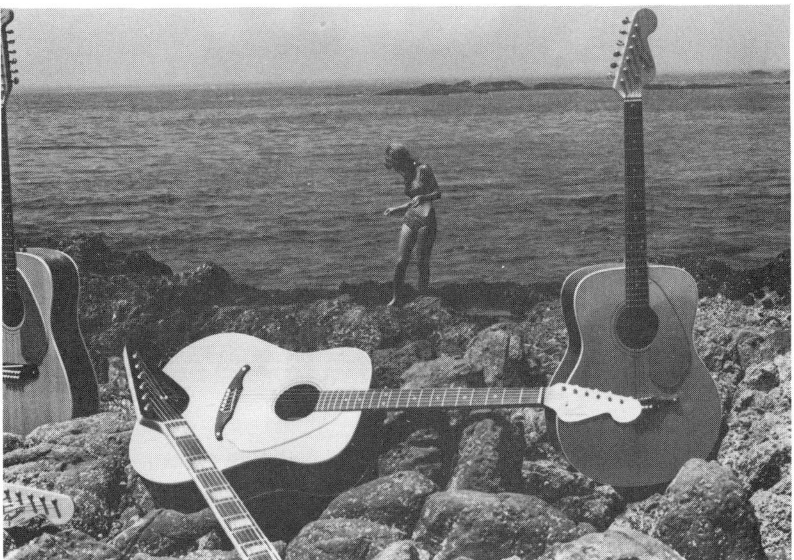

Fender flat-tops at oceanside, late 1960s.

tronic gear, and my main interest was in the utility aspects of an item—that was the main thing. Appearance came next. That gets turned around sometimes.

What were you trying to accomplish with the Broadcaster? What were your criteria?

☞At that time, the steel guitar was extremely popular, and we wanted a standard guitar that had a little bit more of the sound of the steel guitar. I always liked western music, and it was popular. There were problems with the guitars that had gone before. On an acoustic electric guitar you have a string fastened to a diaphragm top, and that top does not have one specific frequency. If you play a note, the top will respond to it and also to a lot of adjoining notes. A solid guitar body doesn't have that, and so you're dealing with just a single note at a time.

How did the neck design come about?

☞On most of the necks at that time—all of the ones that we ran into—the frets weren't properly spaced for noting, and that had gone undetected in the acoustic style guitar, because the diaphragm top gave you a tone that had these adjoining tones, so it wasn't so specific and clean. You could be a little out of tune and not know it. So we developed a method that allowed us to measure fret placement to one ten-thousandth of an inch; we reduced that to the closest thousandth, and then we gave that figure to our tool maker, and he had to then create our system of fret saws in increments of a thousandth of an inch.

Did anyone use the process of bolting on necks before you?

☞Yes, I think they bolted necks onto banjos. I did it because when you build a guitar and neck that are joined in one piece or bonded, then, when you have a flaw in the neck, you have to decide between putting up with it or junking the whole damn thing—body, neck, and all. So I decided that it'd be best for the customer if I built the body and neck separate. It's functional. That's why we did it.

What are the advantages to the tilt-neck adjustment?

☞Well, originally we put shims in there in between the neck and the body at the point where they come together. We'd do this in the last stages of building as a final adjustment to get the string clear-

"Utility—that was the main thing."

Roger Rossmeisl built two three-quarter size Songwriters in about 1967. It was "available in seven fashion colors . . . the ladies will love it." The model was never released. *Bill Carson*

The very rare Musiclander was made in 1966 and 1967. ***Swift Music/Jim Colclasure***

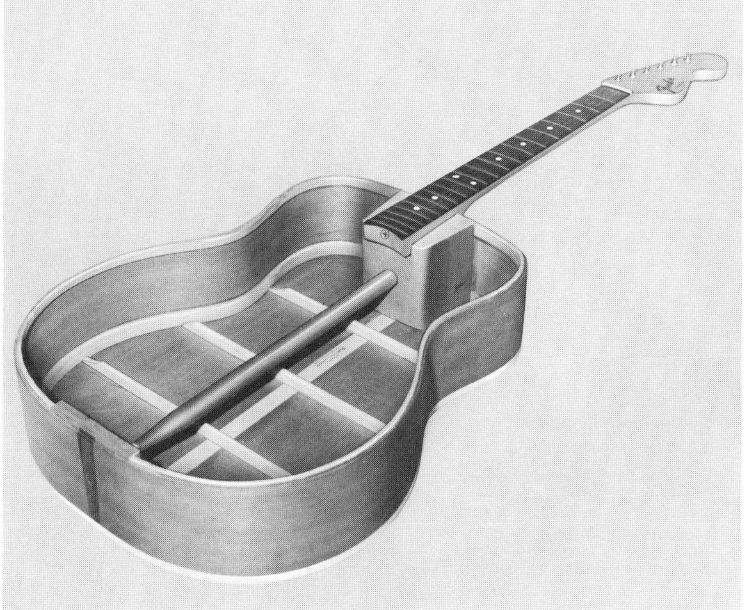

Many Fender steel-strings were equipped with an interior aluminum support rod. Note the unusually massive headblock.

ance just right. With the tilt-neck, you could get a minimum amount of clearance full-length for the easiest kind of playing. We can make adjustments, the dealer can do it, the customer can do it—it was better all around.

Your maple fingerboards were another substantial change in that they looked different and felt unlike previous fingerboards. What was your aim in using maple?

☞ I don't know if I actually remember, but at the time that we came out with our guitars, there was a big trend toward instruments with blonde finishes on the body. Epiphone was very popular, and some of them were just about as blonde as you could make an instrument. People seemed to like that look.

Back in those days, did you realize the potential for what you were doing? Did you set out to revolutionize guitar manufacturing?

☞ I didn't look at it in that way, no. I wanted to build a guitar that would have the sound that I thought that a stringed instrument should have. The guitar has such a range, to expect a diaphragm top to respond to all of those frequencies with equal volume treatment, it's kind of an unreasonable demand. I never had too much feeling for the acoustic guitars: I had always felt that the guitar could do a much better job if it wasn't limited by the properties of that vibrating top. I didn't really think about revolutionizing the industry or anything of that sort. We were spending all of our time thinking about doing a better job for the musician. We weren't trying to harm the acoustic guitar or anything like that. In some cases, a musician likes an acoustic guitar better; well, fine and dandy. In some cases, an acoustic won't do the job. That's where we come in.

"I didn't think about revolutionizing the industry."

Did you originate the headstock with the tuners all on one side?

☞ Well, that was my design, but I shouldn't just say that without telling you a little about it. It was originally a Croatian design, or maybe it's even older. Over there in eastern Europe, in Yugoslavia—where Croatian people come from—they had instruments like this. But I've seen African relics that had it, too, and they were maybe thousands of years old. My main reason was that it put all the strings in a straight line to the tuners—right straight through the nut to the peg. I didn't want to fan out the strings like you have to do with pegs on both sides.

Was the Stratocaster initially as popular as the Telecaster?

☞ No, I don't think it took off quite so fast in the very beginning.

What degree of success did you predict for the Stratocaster?

☞ You never know about those things. We knew it was good, and we were excited about it, but I never thought it would be that popular.

When did you start work on the Strat?

☞ Let's see—it was mostly before Freddie [Tavares] came to work. It'd be around 1951. We had the neck and body designed, and the pickups.

Where did you get the idea for the scooped-out back of the Stratocaster?

☞ An entertainer named Rex Gallion was the one who wanted me to make the relief on the backside of the guitar so that it wouldn't dig him in the rib cage. And he also wanted that little carving away of the corner on top, to make it more comfortable for the right arm.

How did you come up with the multispring vibrato, or hand tremolo?

☞ Paul Bigsby was having a lot of success with his vibrato, the one that was introduced largely by Merle Travis. So the sales force thought that we had to have a vibrato, too. So we came up with one for the Stratocaster. The first one, which we never produced for sale, had some problems, because it didn't sustain a tone too well. We used the multiple springs because it gave us the tension and action we wanted, and also, we had this physical restriction—we had to fit the thing into a certain space inside the body. But I don't want to go into it, really, because I'd give away the trade secret.

Did you design the Fender tremolo yourself?

☞ Yes.

Setting up a photo session for the 1969 catalogue. *Left to right:* Mustang, Mustang Bass, Duo-Sonic II, Mandolin, Musicmaster.

On the Stratocaster, why have a three-way selector switch that is not intended to allow pickup combinations?

☞ Well, there weren't too many convenient styles of switches back then. It wasn't a matter of what we would like so much as it was a matter of what we could get to work with. It was a young industry then—they didn't have these guitar specialty suppliers like they do now. We were limited to the thickness of the body, and this was before all the miniaturization, so we couldn't fit a lot of things in there.

Did you ever consider changing the electrical layout of the Strat in later years?

☞ I would say yes, we did. But it's not so good to alter a model, because then it gets complicated when they need to order replacement parts. It's better just to go to a whole new model and keep it simple. We came up with the Jazzmaster.

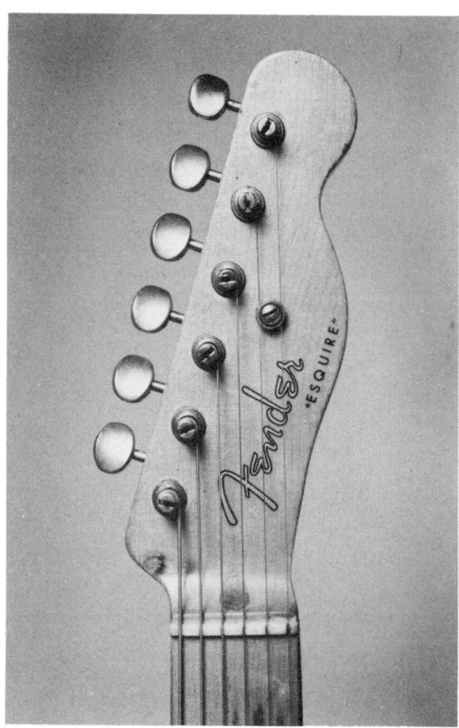

Esquire headstock, 1951.

How did the asymmetrical body and offset waist come about?

☞ That was another thing that just made sense. Normally the player is forced to hold a guitar at an angle to play it, because it's not balanced. So it was part of fitting it to the rib cage. The offset waist, like we had on the Jazzmaster, went right along with the idea of the dressed-away portion in the back. It was just a matter of function.

The Jazzmaster scored with surfers; was it intended to compete in the jazz market with hollowbodies?

☞ It was, yes, though you're right about the surfer thing. We sold a lot of them for quite a while there. The pickup wasn't so deep, and it was wider, thinner, more spaced out. See, the more spaced out the coil is—the wider the spectrum under the string—the warmer the tone. But a broad spectrum of tone places a lot bigger demand on the amp, and the earlier tube amps we had were kind of limited in the amount of power they could handle—I mean the actual wattage—but if you can concentrate your energy into a narrower spot under the string, you can deliver a little more usable power with less apparent distortion.

Is that why you came out with the Jaguar style pickup?

☞ Yes. The Jaguar pickup was narrower, and it put out a little more punch and a cleaner sound.

Where did you get the idea for inventing the electric bass?

☞ There were lots of things. We needed to free the bass player from the big doghouse, the acoustic bass. That thing was usually confined to the back of the band, and the bass player couldn't get up to the mike to sing. And besides, bands were getting a little smaller—combos—and sometimes guitar players would have an advantage if they could have an instrument with frets that would make doubling on bass easier for them. The doghouse was uncomfortable, too, and the player would have to hunch over right next to the peghead to hear whether or not it was in tune—he's got somebody blowing trumpet in his ear, you know. The old bass took up so much room, and it was difficult for the player to haul it all around. Another thing—the electric bass allowed the player to move around and do dance routines. You sure couldn't do that with a doghouse [*laughs*]! The new one lent itself to choreography, which was popular in the 1950s. I don't know whether it is today or not.

"The electric bass allowed the player to do dance routines."

Did the Precision Bass catch on fast?

☞ Yes, it did; it didn't take too long. Probably about 1950 I had the prototype, and we came out with it in 1951, I guess. In a couple of years it was real popular.

What was the concept behind the Jazz Bass?

☞ Well, it's like a car, you know: You come out with the standard model, then you have a deluxe model, a Cadillac version. It had a narrower neck and the offset waist; it was fancier.

How did Jazz Bass pickups differ from those on the Precision?

☞ We had some trouble in speakers with using the Precision, and so the Jazz Bass had the strings running between the poles on the pickup. When the string was pulled one way, it would charge with that pole. Then it would fly to the opposite pole, still carrying the charge, so the initial attack, the punch, was lessened a bit; it wasn't so destructive to the speakers, not so percussionized.

How did you get into acoustic guitars?

☞ That was through a fellow named Roger Rossmeisl [see Rickenbacker and Mosrite]. He first went to work for Gibson, but he wanted to live in California—maybe Michigan was too cold. He went to work for [Francis] Hall at Rickenbacker, and he was living up on the west side of Los Angeles. He wanted to work for me, so he sold his house and made a deal on a home down here and moved all his stuff here—he was determined to work for me, so he made his entire move first. Our sales department was giving us so much urging to build an acoustic.

Was this in 1962?

☞ Right in there at about that time, yes. I told Roger that there were certain things that I wanted in an acoustic, and he brought down the sketches, and it looked like it'd do a pretty good job. Then I told him that I had no area for him to work, and that he'd have to go select a place. He'd have to buy the equipment, too. He did all that and got it going. He was fantastic.

How did those guitars do?

☞ Some of them are still around. Roger had an arrangement with someone who would inject dye into trees and such, to make the wood grain turn colors—blue, red, green. CBS took away a lot of Roger's responsibility, and it discouraged him. They finally fired him, and then they hired him back a couple years after that.

Given your enormous success in the industry, why did you decide to get out of it?

☞ I was sick. On a vacation in 1955 through Yellowstone and across the Rio Grande and all around—somewhere I picked up a strep infection, and I had a bad fever, and it stayed with me for years and years. I got acquainted with a doctor in Fullerton. He cured me in a couple of days with massive injections. I thought I'd be out in the daisy patch in a couple years—I was in bad shape. If I hadn't had that sickness, I probably never would have gotten out.

What sort of changes occurred when CBS took over? I'm sure you know the stigma that attached to some instruments shortly thereafter. Were the guitars lower in quality?

☞ I really don't think so; they weren't trying to cheapen the instrument. Maybe they tried to accelerate production, but it was natural for them to do that, because on one instrument alone, I think it was the Mustang, we were back ordered something like 150,000 units. Well, on a back order of that size—and there were others, too—you can't just sit around. But whether or not the instruments were lower in quality—I really don't have any comment on that. I was over here at CLF at that time, working on guitars.

How did you occupy yourself between your careers with Fender and Music Man?

☞ I retired, but just for two months or so. I got a stack of Zane Grey books and read all those. That was it. After a couple of

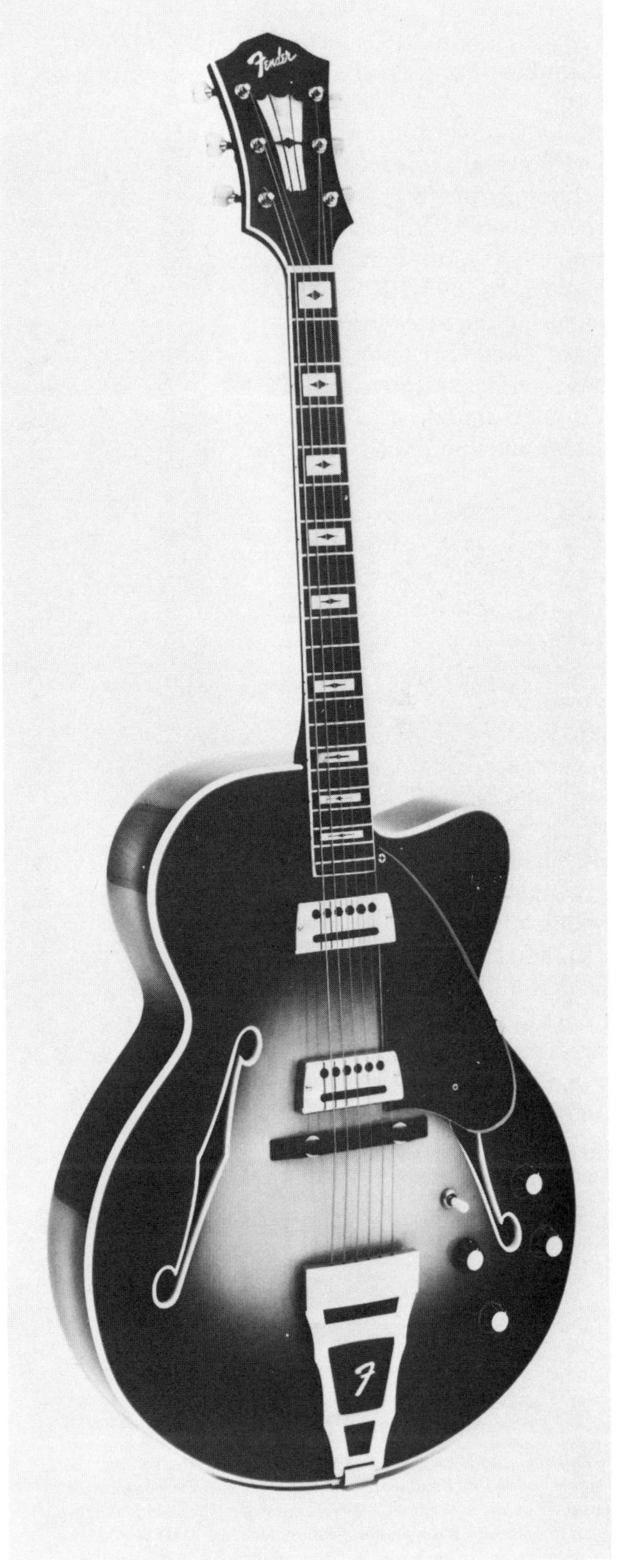

Montego II, 1970. Montego I was the single-pickup version.

KUBICKI

In the 1970s and 1980s former Fender employee Philip Kubicki earned a well-deserved reputation as one of the West Coast's finest custom guitar builders. His company, Philip Kubicki Technology, or PKT, also produced acoustics, wood components, and short-scale electrics. In 1983, PKT began to develop the extraordinary Factor 4 and Ex Factor 4 basses—among the most innovative and distinctive instruments produced anywhere in the world. Kubicki's basses were also a welcome relief from the many "radical" designs of that time, which emphasized odd shapes and flashy graphics over playability and tonal versatility.

In January 1988, in order to concentrate on research and development, PKT entered into a trademark and licensing agreement with Fender, which built, marketed, and distributed Kubicki instruments worldwide. By January 1992, Philip Kubicki and Fender had dissolved their association, and Kubicki was back at work in his Santa Barbara shop.

The Ex Factor 4 shown here has a high-tech, aesthetically pleasing body, whose contours and weight distribution improve the bass' ergonomic qualities. Details: a 3⅓-octave range, both high- and low-impedance circuits, a 32-laminate maple neck, "aircraft bolt" neck mounting (bolts are anchored into threaded metal neck inserts), and a cast aluminum string clasp that allows the choice of either open E (32-inch scale) or the lower D (36-inch) without retuning.

months, I went back to work as a design consultant for CBS. After about two months into 1965, I was back on the job.

What instruments did you work on?

☞ I spent a lot of time helping to develop their piano, the Rhodes. I didn't take out any patents on it; I left it all to Harold Rhodes.

Did you work on any guitars?

☞ I worked on one [Fender Bender] that I thought had a lot of merit. It was a pitch-changing guitar where you'd pull down on the strap, and it had a lever system that would change the pitch on one or more strings.

Were you familiar with the pull-string developed by Gene Parsons and Clarence White?

☞ Yes, I knew about it, and I got to be familiar with them while I was doing this, but mine was a different type. Anyway, CBS didn't think that there was enough sales potential to justify the expense of tooling up. That was a little bit of a difference between their concept and mine. I always felt that even if you had some items that were not too profitable, you should have them anyway in order to provide a full dealer selection. Anyway, I also worked on the Mustang bass for CBS. I don't know if they ever did anything with that.

They've been selling them for about 15 years now.

☞ That's good.

You were selling amps before you began to build guitars; is that right?

☞ For a while there, yes. One successful amplifier was the first Super; you know, Fender's had the Super amplifier in one form or another for, what—32 years now? The first one was unique. It had twin speakers—pretty unusual in those days.

What inspired you to come up with the piggyback design?

☞ As bass amplifiers got more powerful, we thought that it would be better to isolate the speakers from the vibration of the amp chassis—put the speakers in their own enclosure. We initiated it on bass amplifiers, and then we extended the idea to several of the guitar amplifier models.

The "presence" control on Fender amps was a unique and much-discussed feature; what did it do?

☞ That was a real popular thing. Really, it took the place of the bright switch that we used later. You know, most amplifiers don't have such a good response in the higher frequency ranges, and we felt that the guitar player should have the option of giving the treble a little extra boost.

Fender tube amps set standards for the world industry; why the switch to solid-state with CBS? Was that your idea?

☞ No, but I think that it was a good step for them to do, except that the item had problems in it the way they went about it. Transistor amps are good, if you do them right. Tubes are also good.

About this time Fender announced the Marauder guitar, with four pickups concealed beneath the pickguard; it appeared in the 1965–1966 catalog. Why was it never manufactured?

☞ The Marauder was something that was developed over there in R&D after I sold to CBS. I'm not even familiar with what it looks like.

Did you ever regret selling to CBS?

☞ No, I don't think so. A company like we had was sure a job, I'll tell you—it was so big. And then we had so damn many doors to lock up each night; Jesus, George [Fullerton] had a *career* just to lock up at night. By the time we sold we had 27 buildings spread all over. We finally got some security people, but for a long time there we'd have to check all the doors ourselves. We were so darn strung out. I wouldn't want the company back now as a gift. It was just too much, too much trouble.

"I wouldn't want the company back now as a gift."

How long did you stay at CBS after the sale?

☞ Five years, up until 1970 or so. I had built a bunch of industrial buildings, and we named our street Fender Avenue. There's a whole complex of buildings here, with 128 tenants, all of them leasing space for their businesses. There's about 18 acres here.

How much of the design work did you do on the Music Man guitars and basses?

☞ All of it. George Fullerton and me.

Do you think that perhaps you work too hard?

☞ Well, it's what I know. Most every evening I'm up until twelve or one o'clock, sketching at home—guitar bodies, pickups, or whatever's necessary.

Did you ever meet any of the guitar superstars who helped to popularize Fenders—Hendrix, Clapton?

☞ No, but I met Bob Wills.

Any favorite guitarists?

☞ There are several, but one I really like is Roy Clark. I really admire him—not only his playing, but his singing too.

I don't believe he plays a Fender.

☞ Well, we can't all have the best [*laughs*]!

What would you like to do in the future?

☞ Oh, I don't know—just have a small company and build more guitars. I guess—all I've ever really done is work in the guitar business. I like the people in it, and that's a good part to have in your work—it's important—and I like working with musicians and the people who help me.

How did you feel about other companies climbing on the bandwagon with their own solidbodies after your success?

☞ I was too busy, I guess, to pay much attention to it. I didn't give it much thought. But I will say this—*their* first reaction to our solidbody guitars was to make a lot of fun of them. But, you know, I believe that eventually, our dollar volume put us into the number one position in the whole world. But those other companies, they laughed at us at first—thought we were real amusing. [*Pauses, then laughs out loud.*] Maybe they've changed their minds by now.

BROADCASTER AND TELECASTER

Leo Fender is important not only for his durable designs but also for mass-production techniques that revolutionized the manufacture of professional-quality instruments and made possible the $189.50 solidbody. He was the Henry Ford of electric guitars, and the Telecaster was his Model T. Most designs for large-volume instruments result from the convergence of two lines of thought: given the guitar I want, how can I build it most efficiently, and given my tools, what is the best guitar I can make? Mr. Fender's Telecaster represents a classic balance of the two and the purest synthesis of his cardinal principle: function first.

The Tele's immediate predecessor was the Broadcaster, introduced on a significant scale in 1950. It was not a rock and

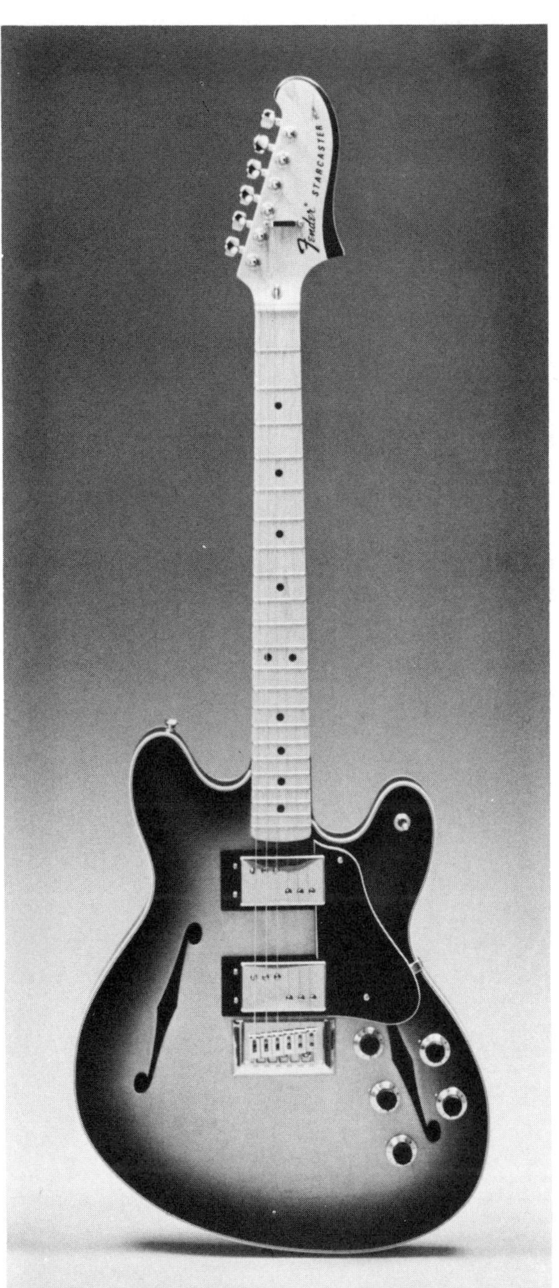

Starcaster, 1976. Fender's semihollow electric departs from the Gibson 335 in several respects. Note offset waists, restyled peghead, and master volume knob.

American guitar's senior solidbody, the Telecaster. This one was built in 1952. *Charley's/ Crump*

roll instrument—rock and roll was seven or eight years away. It was a cowboy guitar. Fender liked steel guitars, and their sounds were crucial influences on him. Conceptually the Broadcaster/Telecaster may be seen in two ways—yes, it was a solid version of a Spanish electric, but it was also a Spanish version of a lap steel, a Hawaiian guitar flipped on its side.

The guitar was plain looking—homely, some would say. With today's technology perhaps it doesn't seem like much, and yet it was everything: a popularly priced electric Spanish guitar, the world's first solidbody of consequence, and ultimately an indispensable tool for thousands of players. Rarely has a single model been so closely associated with certain techniques and styles; indeed, the Telecaster's bright, characteristic twang has fostered a virtual school of esteemed disciples—Roy Buchanan, James Burton, and Albert Lee among them. Its designer's foresight is best demonstrated by the instrument's survival as a world favorite after more than three decades in the intensely competitive guitar marketplace. As dependable as a Zippo lighter, it has seen a hundred prettier challengers banished to the bargain racks.

What passes for "informative" ad copy in the 1980s is drivel compared to the fact-packed literature that heralded the Broadcaster's debut and illustrated its remarkable versatility: ash body, detachable hard rock maple neck, three length-adjustment screws (one for each pair of strings), six height-adjustment screws, three rear pickup elevating screws, two front pickup elevating screws under the pickguard, and an adjustable truss rod. The only nonessential item was a chromed, snap-on bridge cover that, incidentally, is almost never seen on Broadcasters, Strats, or Teles; it's usually removed promptly and either stuck in the case or lost.

Mr. Fender's first occupation was radio repair. It was only fitting that K&F's logo should include a lightning bolt and that Fender's first guitar should be called the Broadcaster. But Gretsch had already registered that name for its drums and banjos, and though Leo was fairly sure that Fender could retain the name if a legal conflict arose, he decided to change it to Telecaster in anticipation of television's popularity. After December 1950 *Telecaster* generally replaced *Broadcaster*; rare exceptions include Broadcasters dated as late as August 1952.

Costing $189.50, the early Telecaster was virtually identical to the Broadcaster, and it was enthusiastically adopted by Southern California cowboy guitarists. Its tone was regulated by a three-position switch that allowed a choice between the lead pickup (rear position), the front, or rhythm, pickup (center position), or the front pickup with a large capacitor (front position). The last setting provided a boomy sound, good for bass lines. However, when moving from one position to another the apparent loudness was changed, sometimes necessitating a compensation with the volume control. Furthermore, the ultra-boomy sound was rendered obsolete by the electric bass; another disadvantage was that the two pickups could not be combined. For these reasons the Telecaster was fitted during the mid 1950s with a conventional three-way pickup selector.

Mid 1954 to mid 1955 saw several changes in the minor details of pre-1960 models. The Broadcasters and pre-1955 Teles have black, single-laminate Bakelite pickguards, barrel-shaped switch knobs (some smooth on top, some rimmed), flush rear pickup polepieces (through mid-1955), a somewhat transparent blonde finish, round string retainers on the peghead, brass bridge pieces, and serial numbers stamped in front on the lead pickup's housing plate. Some of the earliest guitars have three-digit serial numbers.

Though there are overlaps and combinations of old and new features, the post-1955 Telecaster is generally different in all those respects, with a white, single-laminate plastic pickguard (some in 1954), top hat switch, staggered polepiece heights for balanced response, a more opaque finish that reveals less grain, butterfly clip string retainer, steel bridge pieces (a few in 1954), and serial numbers stamped on the neckplate in back.

Examining the more minuscule details of a guitar can sometimes pinpoint its vintage. However, since the vast majority of old Fenders are labeled with the date of manufacture, we'll avoid the ridiculous and limit our exploration of trivia to the merely excessive.

Necks. The first few Broadcasters—no one knows how many—have no contrasting stripe on the back of the neck. The wooden stripe was used to fill the channel after neck rod installation.

Production. No one knows how many Broadcasters were made; Mr. Fender guesses that the number was roughly 400 or 500, and almost certainly less than 1,000.

Decal. During the transition period when the Broadcaster's new name was being decided, the pegheads were labeled simply *Fender.* Thus the chronological order of decals is: *Fender Broadcaster, Fender, Fender Telecaster,* and *Fender Telecaster* plus patent number.

Knobs. Given Fender's consistent use of flat-top knobs in later years, it is generally true that knobs have progressed from dome-top to flat-top. However, there was much inconsistency in the early period, with flat-tops on more than a few Broadcasters, and with at least four knob profiles, a couple of different heights, and varying patterns of cross-hatching on the sides.

Esquire came first: The chronology of Fender's earliest models—first came the double-pickup Broadcaster in 1948, then the double-pickup Telecaster, then the single-pickup Esquire—has been recounted many times, almost always inaccurately. In fact, the 1948 Broadcaster is a myth. Richard Smith (at work on his own Fender history book; it promises to be excellent) has uncovered the real story: Beginning in the spring of 1950, Fender began building both one- and two-pickup models, and both were called Esquires; they had neither truss rods nor string retainers on the headstocks.

Smith wrote in the Aug. '88 *Guitar Player*, "After at least eight months of indecision and manufacturing problems with the non-truss rod Esquires, the Broadcaster became the first full-production version of Fender's two-pickup electric Spanish guitar; all known examples had truss rods. The factory produced the first Broadcaster in fall 1950 . . . . Like the earlier dual-pickup Esquires, the Broadcaster did not have a channel routed from the front pickup to the control plate . . . . After the Broadcaster's introduction, the Esquire was always a single-pickup guitar with a truss rod, with full production beginning in January 1951. Though the Esquire had only a bridge pickup, all known examples had the body rout for a second pickup."

Broadcasters were made for only about six months or even less. In February 1951, Fender dropped the name at the request of Gretsch (who had a Broadkaster drum set) and soon rechristened the instrument the Telecaster. During the interim, probably just a couple of months or more, the guitars featured decals that said simply "Fender," with no model name at all; sometimes dubbed "Nocasters," these are simply '51 Teles with abbreviated decals. Smith also points out that all Broadcasters, "Nocasters," and '51 Telecasters are electronically the same, yet different from Fenders made after 1952. In that year, Mr. Fender changed the Tele's tone control (which in the lead position had previously blended the pickups together) to a conventional capacitor-type control.

Flush rear pickup polepieces (*left*) characterize pre-1955 Telecasters, whereas later models have staggered polepieces (*right*).

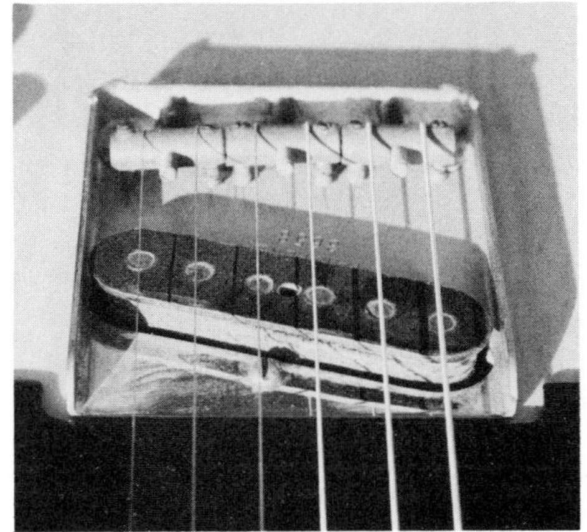

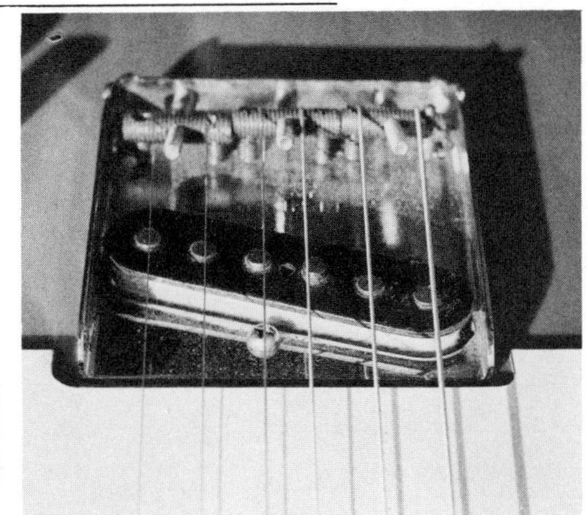

Broadcaster (*top*) and Telecaster. Note the Tele's extra rout. Some Broadcasters have it, most don't.

Date markings. About 80 percent or more of pre-1970s Fender necks are marked with still-legible dates on the lateral surface beneath the pickguard. The early dates are penciled; later ones (circa 1962 and thereafter) are stamped. Other marks are also sometimes found on masking tape or bare wood under pickguards and in neck slots and control wells. Crack open an old Tele and you may be greeted with the name or initials of the person who assembled it—Eddie, Virginia, Maria, and T. G. among others.

In addition to the always-available standard Telecaster, offshoots have included the Thin Line (late 1968), hollow on one side, with a single f-hole (two humbuckings added in February 1972), the Tele Custom (March 1970, with a front humbucking pickup), Rosewood Tele (1969, 1970, 1972), and Tele Deluxe (1973, an all-new guitar with a sculptured body, two humbuckings and new frets, string spacing, and neck). The paisley and floral finishes were offered in 1968 and 1969 only. From 1959 to 1969, the Telecaster and Esquire were offered in an optional "Custom" finish: sunburst with white edge binding. After 1969, "Telecaster Custom" referred to the new guitar with a humbucking pickup.

ESQUIRE

The earliest Esquire known to the author is serial no. 0471, dated January 1951, though company literature said very little

The word *Custom* has been applied to Telecasters and Esquires with at least three different meanings. At left are the Custom Telecaster and Custom Esquire models of 1959 to 1969; they were the only Teles and Esquires with either a sunburst finish or body binding. At right is a different model, a 1971 Telecaster Custom, with humbucking pickup. (Telecasters and Esquires were also available with *Custom* finishes.)

A very early Esquire, dated 1951. *Charley's/Crump*

1969 Telecaster bass and Telecaster guitar with stock Bigsby.

The rosewood Telecaster is quite rare and features a "sandwich" body construction of heavy rosewood pieces with a thin sheet of light-colored wood in between. *Gruhn*

Original 1952 Precision Bass. *Spitzer's/Sievert*

about it until 1953 or 1954. It was simply a Telecaster without the front pickup, and so it entailed modified circuitry, and of course the decal was different. Still, seldom have guitars with different model names been so much alike. Underneath its pickguard the Esquire is even routed for the front pickup that distinguishes it from its near twin. The Esquire's evolution of features was generally like the Telecaster's. It was discontinued in early 1970.

PRECISION BASS, TELECASTER BASS, AND JAZZ BASS

The true significance of particular models is often obscured amid the blah, woof, and quack of promo materials, but the importance of Fender's electric bass was, if anything, understated in early company literature. Furthermore, the electric bass provides a very rare example of when the invention of an instrument—not just a model or a brand, but the species itself—can be traced to a single individual, in this case Clarence Leo Fender. The electric bass looks like an oversized guitar with four strings (its most common name is "bass guitar"), but its function and range are those of the acoustic upright bass. Whether compared to a guitar or to an upright, the electric bass represented a substantial break from all predecessors—a departure arguably greater than that from acoustic to electric guitar, or from hollowbody to solidbody. Fender developed it in 1950 and called it the Precision Bass (substantial production commenced the following year). Popular music has been quite different ever since.

The Precision is distinguished in another way: aside from being the first, it's far and away the most popular. It has dominated its genre more than any model in the history of guitars and related instruments, so much so that for years the term *Fender bass* maintained generic status, like Scotch Tape or Band-Aid.

At a cost of $195.50 its advantages over the acoustic "doghouse" bass were immediately apparent: it was smaller, louder, and more portable; guitarists could quickly adapt to its scale length of 34 inches; and since it was fretted, the bassist could play with "precision."

The original P Bass had the boxy shape of the Telecaster guitar (or of the late-1960s Telecaster bass). Indeed, with its plank body it was the Telecaster guitar's first cousin. The original pickguard was a black Bakelite slab covering both sides of the body's upper half. Other details were: blonde finish only, single-coil rectangular bar pickup, maple neck with no separate fingerboard, and a Tele style peghead.

Soon after the Stratocaster's debut in 1954 (there were a few in late 1953) the Precision Bass gradually began to look less like a Tele and more like a Strat. The square-edged plank changed to a contoured body with a dressed-away face and rear scoop beginning in 1954, though with substantial overlaps between the old and new shapes. The old plank style extends ahead through 1956, and there are reportedly a few 1957s. The blunt peghead changed to a pointed Strat-like profile in mid or

From the 1961–1962 catalogue (*left to right*): a pair of Precisions, a three-switch Bass VI, and an early Jazz Bass with concentric control knobs.

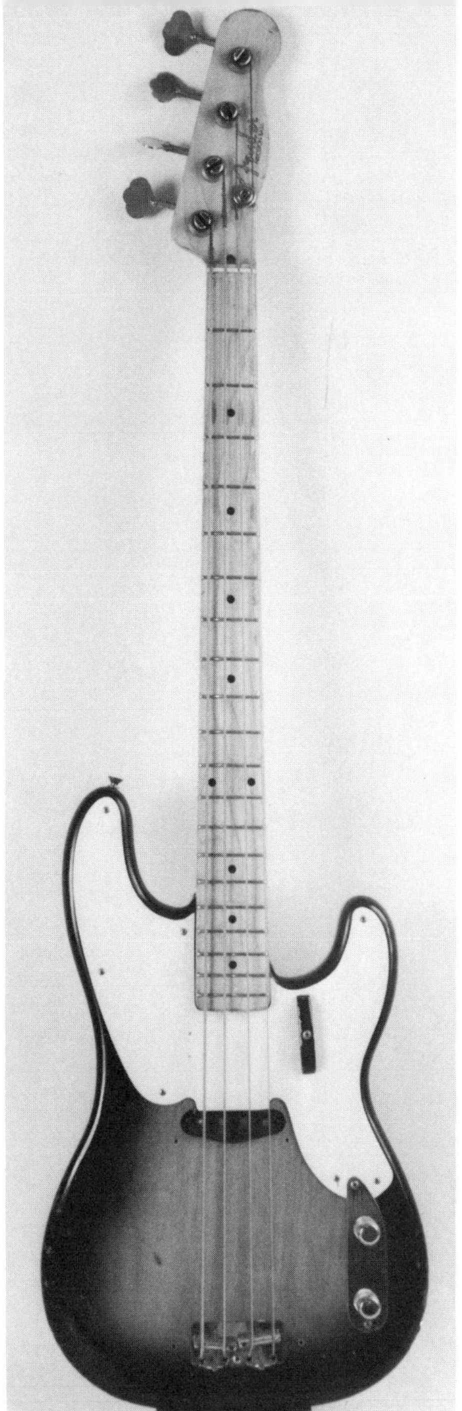

1955 P Bass with bridge cover and pickup cover removed: old peghead, old pickup, old pickguard, and new (contoured) body. *Gruhn/Baxendale*

late 1957; thus there are some 1954–1957 Precisions with the new contoured body and old peghead.

An optional sunburst finish was offered beginning in 1954. In late 1957 a streamlined gold-anodized pickguard was introduced; it was also used on some Musicmasters, Duo-Sonics, and Jazzmasters. In mid 1957 the pickup changed from a single bar to the current split-coil type. Thus by late 1957 the transition was complete to contoured body, modern peghead, gold anodized pickguard, and split pickup; for sheer collector's appeal, the maple-neck model with this combination of features is the world's most esteemed vintage bass.

In 1959 a rosewood fingerboard replaced the maple, and beginning later that year the gold anodized pickguard was replaced by plastic. There are a few 1959 and very few 1960 transition models with rosewood boards and gold pickguards. As with the Strat, the Precision's change from two-color to three-color sunburst was gradual, with the new three-color as early as 1958 and the old two-color as late as 1960, perhaps even early 1961. Maple necks were offered again as an option after the summer of 1969.

The Telecaster bass appeared in 1968, although it missed 1968's catalogue. It had the boxy shape of the earliest Precisions. In February of 1972 a humbucking pickup was added and other changes were made. A variation of the Precision is the fretless model (late 1970), designed for musicians trained on acoustic bass or for those simply looking for that horn-like fretless sound.

The two-pickup Jazz Bass was the next logical step after the popularity of the offset-body Jazzmaster and the more conventionally shaped Precision Bass. Developed in 1960, the Jazz Bass featured a radically tapered fingerboard, narrow nut, and offset body. The earliest production models had concentric, tandem-mounted tone and volume pots and are commonly called *stack knobs*. In early 1962 Fender began to install its three-knob array. (Also see Mr. Fender's interview.)

Post-1957 Precision Bass split pickup.

Precision Bass tailpiece and adjustable saddles. Many of the very early Precisions had hard rubber or Bakelite bridge pieces.

Fender 5-string bass, with a very unusual maple fingerboard, circa 1968. *Soest*

Natural finish Jazz Bass and Telecaster bass.

In 1966, Fender issued a very few hybrid Precisions, and this is one of them, an odd combination of the old plank body and post-1957 features. Courtesy John Entwistle. *Alan Rogan/ Gavin Cochrane*

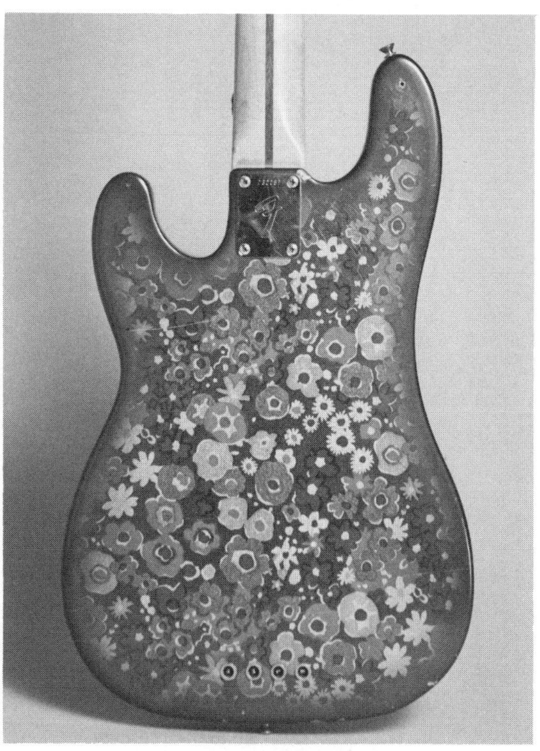

Late-1960s blue-flower print Telecaster bass.

STRATOCASTER

Although a few models had appeared the previous year, the Stratocaster was officially unveiled in 1954. Compared to most guitars of the day it stood out like Dolly Parton in an Amish church, and no one knew quite what to think. People ogled it, giggled at it, and argued over it. Some craved it; most ignored it, at least at first. A good many were indignant, for never had a guitar acted so little like a guitar. To purists, the Telecaster was bizarre enough, but this time that Fender out there in California had gone too far.

The newcomer looked strange with its curvy, contoured shape and body "horns"; later people would call this a double-cutaway. It was the first commercial solidbody with three pickups. Its vibrato bar was a sleek, plastic-tipped tube, and the mechanism itself was mysteriously hidden inside the body. The strings disappeared underneath a snap-on chrome canopy. Now even the lowly output jack was radical—a flush-mounted, teardrop body scoop that looked like it came off a Buick. The Strat's white plastic trim and comparatively huge white pickguard guaranteed its immediate identification from the back corners of a sock-hop ball. It was not a guitar for introverts.

The pre-CBS blonde maple-neck with gold hardware holds a special place in the hearts of Stratocaster lovers. This one is a nontremolo 1957 model. *Charley's/Crump*

The Strat is such a fox, such a rocket ship, that it is easy to forget that the man who designed it poured his talents into making it a workingman's tool. The most important thing to Fender was performance, and through the undeniable Stratocaster sensuousness there emerged an idiosyncratic but sensible instrument, new in every way, recalling Ezra Pound's opinion that genius is the capacity to see ten things where the ordinary man sees one.

The cornerless body fit the guitarist's rib cage and supported the right arm in a natural playing position, and the double cutaway permitted increased fretboard accessibility. Instead of one bridge it had six, and the player could adjust each string individually for length, height, and lateral positioning. The three-pickup circuitry was versatile, and the lead pickup's "crooked" placement increased treble response. The vibrato was a mechanical tour de force, so far ahead of its time that its musical potential wasn't fully explored until more than a decade later in the hands of Jimi Hendrix. Furthermore, the player could adjust its action himself by changing the number of springs. The output jack protected the plug with surrounding wood and allowed the cord to be pulled out (avoiding broken guitars and broken bones) should someone trip over it. There was a lot going on there for $249.50.

Aside from George Fullerton and Freddie Tavares, another person who helped Fender on the Stratocaster was Bill Carson, a Texas country/western entertainer who moved to Southern California in 1951, just about the time Leo began designing the guitar. Mr. Fender, not a musician himself, routinely sought the advice of working performers. Bill Carson, who joined the Fender company in 1957 and eventually became an executive, played the Stratocaster prototype on bandstands around Orange County, generating much interest and giving continuous

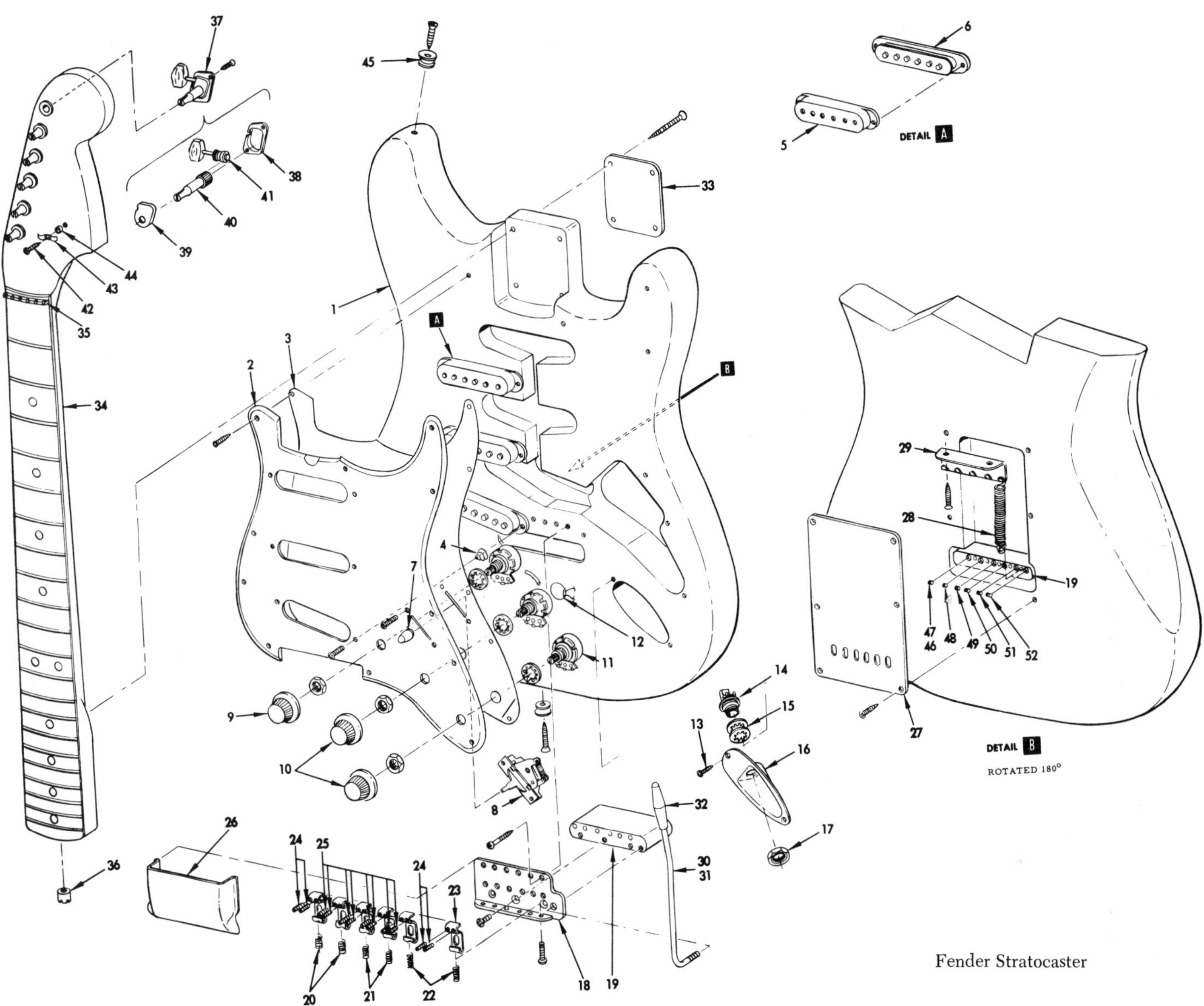

Fender Stratocaster

1 Guitar Body

PICKGUARD ASSEMBLY

2 Pickguard
3 Pickguard Shield
4 Pickup Compression Spring
5 Pickup Cover
6 Pickup Core Assembly
7 Lever Knob
8 Pickup Selector Switch
9 Volume Knob
10 Tone Knob
11 Volume & Tone Potentiometers (Controls: 250K)
12 Ceramic Capacitor

13-17 OUTPUT PLUG ASSEMBLY

BRIDGE ASSEMBLY

18 Bridge Base Plate
19 Tremolo Block*
20 ¼″ Compression Spring
21 5⁄16″ Compression Spring
22 7⁄16″ Compression Spring
23 Bridge Bar
24, 25 Set Screws
26 Bridge Cover
27 Rear Cover Plate
28 Tension Spring
29 Tremolo Tension Spring Holder
30-32 Lever Assembly

*"Tremolo" is used by Fender as a synonym for Vibrato.

NECK AND PEGHEAD ASSEMBLY

33 Neck Plate
34 Neck & Fingerboard, Frets & Position Markers
35 Nut
36 Neck Rod Adjusting Nut

TUNING KEY ASSEMBLY

37 Complete Key Assembly
38 Key Assembly Cover
39 Key Assembly Housing
40 Post and Gear
41 Head and Worm

MISCELLANEOUS

42-44 String Guide Assembly
45 Strap Button
46-52 Strings (Ball Ends)

and valuable advice to Leo about how to improve what local musicians began calling "Carson's guitar."

The Broadcaster/Telecaster had proved the wisdom of Leo Fender's notion that good electric Spanish instruments could be mass-produced out of solid or laminated planks of wood. The Strat was a whole new guitar—still a Fender, only more so. It resulted from the intersection of several ideas: the new headstock, the three pickups, the contoured body, and especially the hand vibrato.

Detail from the most primitive Strat encountered by the author. Note plain metal pickguard and no-skirt metal knobs. Its peghead says only: "Fender, Fullerton, Calif." On some extremely early Strats, the serial number is stamped into the spring coverplate in back.

Vibratos designed by Paul Bigsby and Doc Kauffman had shown definite commercial appeal, but they had tuning problems. Here was a perfect challenge for Fender, who relished his every experiment. (He didn't relish the $5,000 in junked tooling he was forced to sacrifice when the first design, tested by Bill Carson, didn't pan out.) Generally, like other vibrato mechanisms, the Strat's *hand tremolo* lowers the string tension and thus the pitch when depressed, and entails a rocking motion that is a function of string tension and counterbalancing spring pressure.

Fender avoided needle bearings, bushings, roller bearings, and ball bearings in order to minimize the friction that could prevent recovery of true pitch. Instead he took his idea from the design of gram scales, which use a knife-edge surface balancing on a pointed centerpiece. From both sides, Fender countersunk each of the six screw holes (just ahead of the six individual saddles), providing the knife edges against which the entire mechanism would rock. To avoid having the strings move over the bridge and also to avoid a separate rocker bridge, he incorporated the bridge, tailpiece, and vibrato tailblock (or "inertia block") into a single unit.

Stratocaster headstocks, 1957 (*left*) and 1973 (note enlarged peghead and bullet truss rod).

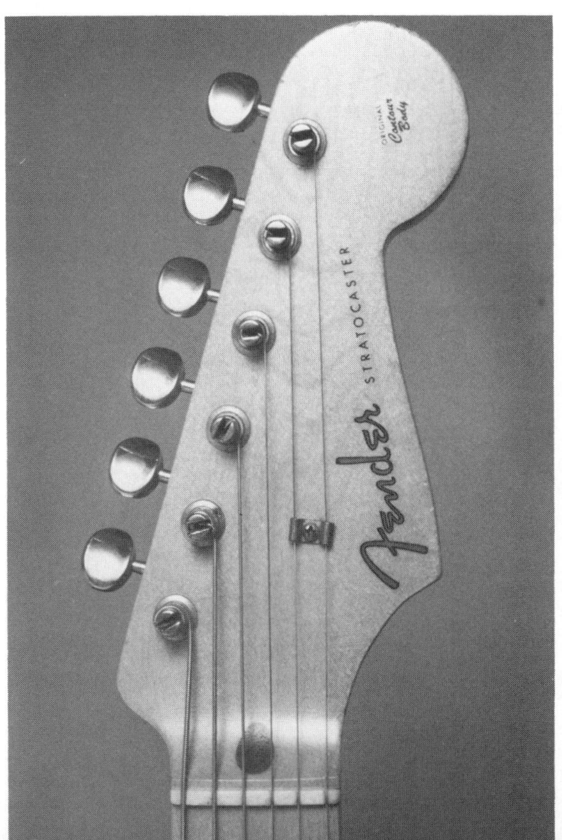

One advantage of the Strat tailpiece is that when the handle is depressed the bridges move not only forward but higher as well. This helps to raise the strings just a little, alleviating to some extent the buzzes that could result from low-tension strings hitting the frets or pickups. Leo Fender believed that most vibrato problems occurred up at the peghead, where strings moving back and forth could hang up on the nut and detune. He minimized this with the straight-line string profile provided by the six-on-a-side tuning key arrangement. Strats without vibratos have always been offered direct from the factory.

The Strat's three-way switch provided the following choices: position 1 (pointed toward the neck) activated only the front pickup and the first tone control (the middle knob of the three); 2 was the middle pickup, controlled by the other tone knob; and 3 was the bridge (rear) pickup, no tone control. The master volume knob was always on. The disadvantage is obvious—you couldn't combine pickups except by balancing the selector somewhat precariously between positions, resulting in an apparent out-of-phase effect.

For years many players ripped up and rewired their Stratocasters to increase their versatility, and accessory manufacturers introduced replacement switches. Fender finally changed the guitar's circuitry, and beginning in 1978 five-way selectors became stock. Positions 1, 3, and 5 duplicate the original choices. The new 2 is a front/middle combination with both tone controls activated, and 4 is a middle/rear combination

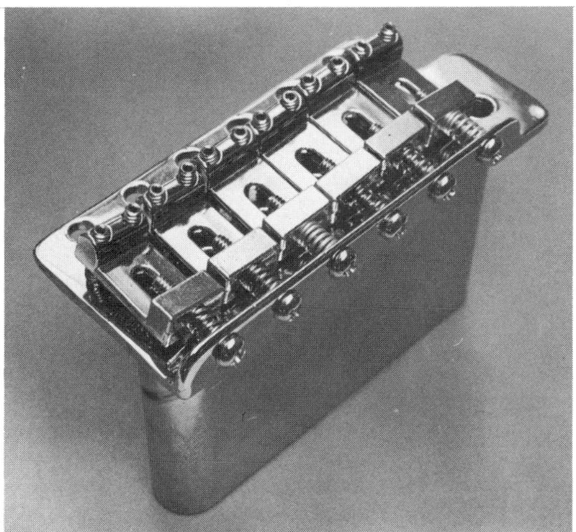

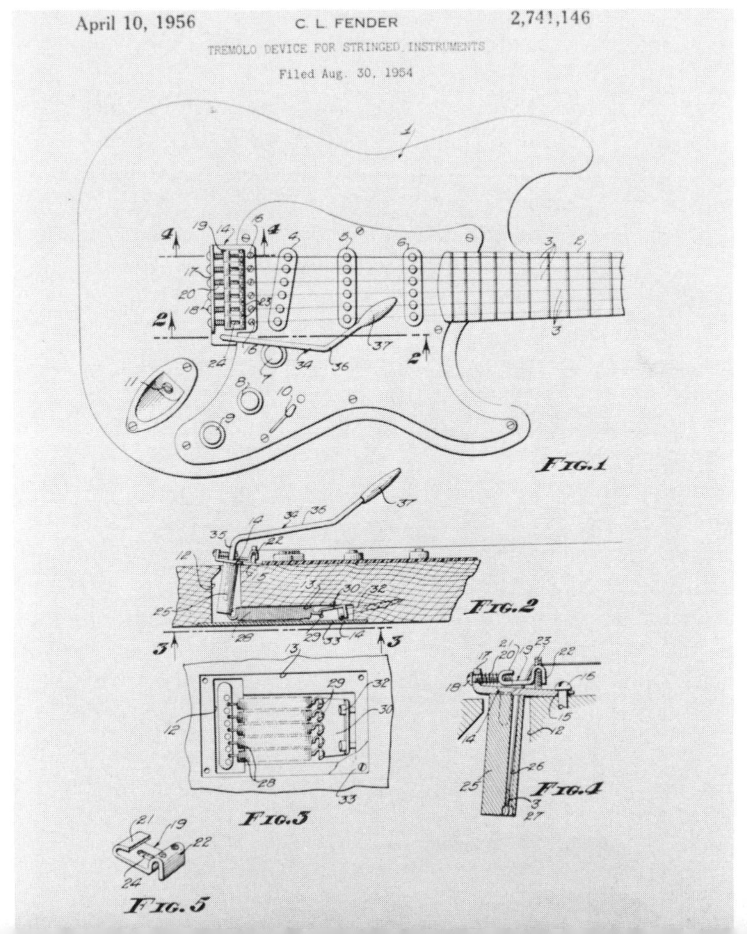

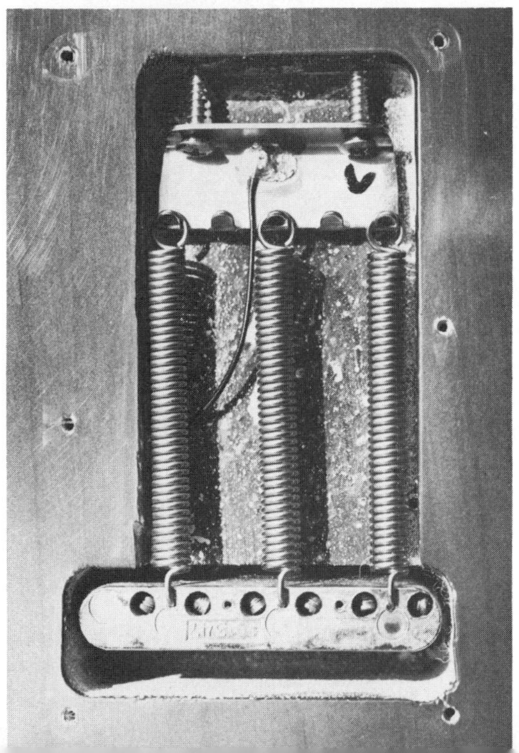

Stratocaster vibrato patent diagram and Strat tailblock (*upper right*). *Lower right:* the removal of the plastic cover plate from the back of the guitar reveals the springs attached to the tailblock's lower surface. Note the two adjustment screws, the ground wire, and the spaces for two additional springs.

with the second tone control. In the new position 2, the tone knob with the lower setting will determine the overall tone of the combination, irrespective of the other control's position. The treble pickup still has no tone control, a curious deficiency for one of the world's most popular guitars.

The master volume knob's location allows the musician to wrap his or her little finger around it while playing, facilitating pedal-steel-type volume swells. As Mr. Fender said, "The Strat is a one-of-a-kind guitar for people who like to play with a tight style—palm ready to mute, little finger near the knob or vibrato bar."

The Strat peghead, so perfect that most other six-on-a-side designs pale by comparison, was Fender's icing on the cake. Leo laughed and recalled: "Well, that Telecaster peghead was sure a minimum profile, wasn't it? You could hardly put a label on it! We didn't think it looked all that good, and we wanted something new, so we came up with the Stratocaster peghead, which is more pointed." (Also see Mr. Fender's interview.)

The Fender company routinely marked each guitar and bass with the date of manufacture. Marks at the neck's treble end are revealed when the neck is substantially loosened or altogether removed. Dates are also often found inside the body routs. Since music dealers frown on customers who walk in with screwdrivers and start disassembling guitars, it helps to be able to fix at least an approximate date based on exterior features.

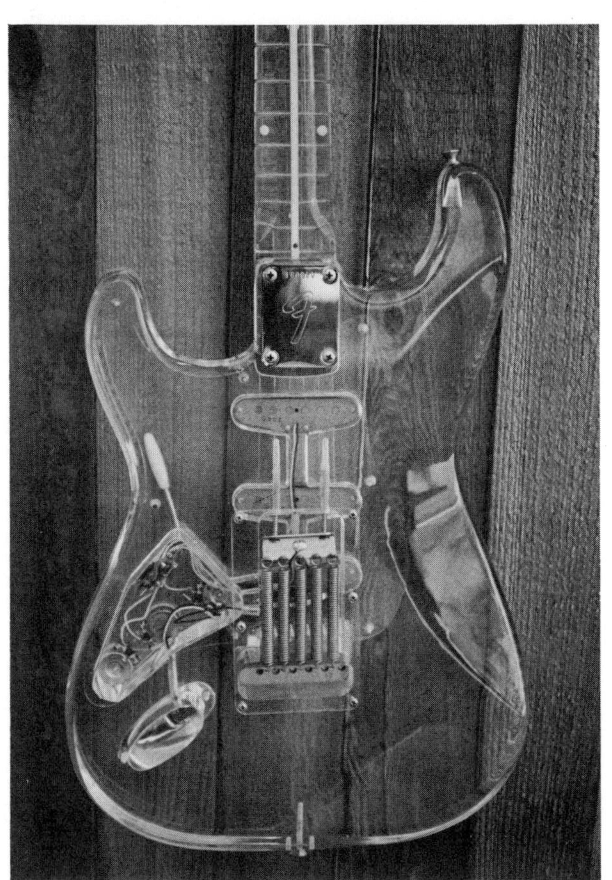

An experimental, one-of-a-kind Strat, made of Lucite (also see color photo 51). ***Bill Carson***

The first Stratocasters were made of alder or ash. Ash was often used for guitars with the somewhat translucent blonde finish, since its attractive grain patterns would show through. There have been scattered sightings of other woods (mahogany was used for at least one custom-colored Strat), but such guitars are rare birds indeed.

A very few of the earliest Strats had gray metal pickguards, but these are so scarce and so early that they may qualify as prototypes. It is safe to say that the first Strats introduced on a significant commercial scale had single-layer white pickguards. They were replaced in the latter part of 1959 with triple-decker white/black/white (w/b/w) plastic laminates, a design that remained intact until the entire Fender line went to the laminated black (b/w/b) pickguard, which made its catalogue debut in 1976. Fender experimented with anodized aluminum pickguards on a few of the earliest Jazzmasters, as well as on Precision Basses made from 1957 to early 1960. A handful of Stratocasters were similarly equipped, but the number is small enough to qualify them as custom items.

Necks have also changed. The standard width at the nut was 1⅝ inches. However, three additional sizes have been offered beginning at least as early as 1961: 1½ (extremely rare), 1¾, and 1⅞ inches (extremely rare).

Over the years from 1958 to 1961, a three-color sunburst (with added red) was introduced, gradually phasing out the old two-color. Probably all 1957s are two-color, and many or most 1958s are three-color. The exceptions include some late two-colors—plenty of 1959s and 1960s, and extremely rare 1961s.

The 1958 and 1959 three-colors have the soft look of the older two-colors, while the three-color sunbursts from 1960 and later have thicker paint with more of a glossy, enameled look, generally permitting a little less grain to show through.

The first Strats had no separate fingerboards; frets were mounted into the maple necks. Rosewood fingerboards appeared in 1959, generally replaced by thinner versions after early 1963. Then in late 1969 or early 1970 separate maple boards appeared as options (a rare guitar is the stock Strat with an early rosewood board and a late two-color sunburst). The rear surface of the early Strat necks was almost V-shaped in cross section. The V necks gave way to the more rounded type during 1957 or 1958. Beginning approximately in late 1971, the Strat switched from a four-bolt neck attachment to the current three-bolt type, which entails the Micro-Tilt adjustment and bullet truss rod.

The major watershed in Stratocaster history is of course the CBS acquisition of Fender, which became official on January 4, 1965. However, it is most unlikely the Stratocasters were built any differently on January 5, and so the definition of a "CBS" Strat may depend on how you look at it. During 1966 the Strat peghead was replaced with an enlarged version. In late 1965 a large "F" logo on the neckplate appeared; this feature is a positive CBS indicator. Also in 1965, shiny pearloid position markers replaced the older "clay" dots; large-head Strats have the newer type.

A typical 1963–1965 pre-CBS Strat has an L serial number, small headstock, and old dots. A typical 1965 has an L number, small head, and pearl dots; 1965 and later: F neckplate, pearl dots, big headstock. However, for the period surrounding the CBS takeover, exceptions and overlaps are not uncommon. Among 1965s, some have F plates, and some have L numbers. Some have old dots, some have pearl. Some have small heads and pearl dots.

There were other minor changes in the evolution of the Stratocaster. For example, when the guitar went to the laminated pickguard, the number of screws around the rim of the pickguard increased from eight to eleven. Over the years the round button string retainers changed to butterfly clips, bone string nuts were replaced with ABS plastic pieces, and the original steel tailblocks were superseded by die-cast zinc units. According to collector Frank Lucido, old maple-neck Strats have extra holes underneath the pickguard where the paint sprayer's gripping device was attached. In about 1959, this method was discontinued, and a handle was clipped to the neck slot for spraying; models built after this change have no interior holes. Decals also changed, as did the profiles of the tuning machines.

These differences in external features are offered only as general guidelines and with a warning: in a huge factory with tens of thousands of ever-changing guitar parts, those parts are going to be assembled in different ways. For example, once a decision is made to enlarge the headstock, the production foreman won't throw out all the old ones. And given the substantial dif-

Stratocaster bodies in transit from the wood shop to the assembly area.

The 62 Jazz Bass, shown here, is one of six recent guitars in Fender's official "Vintage" class that are designated with a specific year: the other five are the 52 Telecaster, 57 and 62 Stratocasters, and 57 and 62 Precision Basses. These fine U.S.-made guitars helped to reinvigorate Fender's reputation in the 1980s.

Other recent U.S.-made Fenders include the American Standard Telecaster, American Standard Stratocaster, Deluxe American Standard Stratocaster, Strat Plus, Deluxe Strat Plus, Eric Clapton and Yngwie Malmsteen Signature Series, HM Series Strat, and Precision Bass Plus.

Note that while Fenders designated with the "Vintage" name are U.S.-made, those officially called "reissues" are imports, including the Custom Tele reissue and Tele Thinline reissue. Other imports include the Precision Bass Lyte, Power Jazz Bass Special, and Stratocaster XII 12-string.

In Fender price lists of the late 1980s and 1990s, model numbers beginning with 10 and 19 indicate American manufacture, while 27 indicates an import.

Bill Carson poses with the silver finish Anniversary Stratocaster model, 1980.

ference in dates that sometimes show up on a single guitar's body and neck, it seems possible that during the CBS transition a small-head Strat could actually have a later body than a large-head model, simply due to the fact that during several periods in the company's history, models were being assembled with both "old" and "new" parts.

At any rate, since exterior features and serial numbers provide general guidelines, and since the great majority of neck dates are still intact (except for quite a few rosewood-board 1959 and 1960 models), we usually need not rely on fine details in order to fix dates.

Over the quarter-century since its introduction, the Strat has undergone many changes, but most have been minor. What is truly remarkable is the extent to which its original design has endured unmodifed. The Stratocaster of the 1980s, so similar to its mid-1950s ancestor, is testimony to the vision of Leo Fender. The company introduced the model's first offshoot in 1980. Called simply The Strat, it has a small peghead with a painted face, brass hardware, and a custom finish. Its new tone selection circuit, designed by Dan Armstrong, features a multimode push-pull knob and new pickup combinations.

JAZZMASTER

Debuting at the top of the line circa late 1957, the Jazzmaster (which is almost never seen in the hands of a jazz player) was still another well-thought-out Fender, an impressively cohesive

1961–1962 catalogue cover shot, featuring a white Jazzmaster, then the top of the line.

This unusual Jazzmaster, one of the first three made, has stock black pickup covers, maple fretboard, and metal pickguard. To avoid worn spots such as the one that appears here, later versions had plastic pickguards. Designed by Leo Fender with the assistance of Freddie Tavares, this Jazzmaster is Mr. Tavares' personal instrument.

1967 Jazzmaster. An unbound neck with dot markers indicates a production date of early 1966 or earlier. A bound neck with dots is a 1966 model, while a bound neck with block markers is late 1966 or later. This also holds true for the Bass VI, Jazz Bass, Jaguar, and Electric XII.

design that marked a significant turn from the Stratocaster. Though its historical significance and long-term commercial success were thoroughly eclipsed by the Telecaster and Strat, it enjoyed a substantial popularity through the surf music era of the early 1960s.

Like all previous Fenders except the Esquire, the Jazzmaster was an all-new guitar and the first model with offset (slanted) waists. This diagonal perspective was extended to the pickguard and body, and overall the Jazzmaster design was a bold shift away from the symmetry of prevailing guitar aesthetics toward the modern art/liquid sculpture styling that remains a Fender hallmark.

Another Jazzmaster innovation was the Trem-Lok button located on the tailpiece. It locked the vibrato assembly and was intended to avoid a detuning should a string break. The bridge was mounted on twin posts, each with an adjustable, pointed allen screw that permitted height adjustments and allowed the bridge to rock when the long vibrato arm was depressed. The Jazzmaster's pickups had single fat coils of wire, and the circuitry was also new, incorporating two independent systems; a selector switch, volume roller knob, and tone roller knob were mounted inconspicuously on the pickguard's bass side.

The earliest Jazzmasters had small pegheads, anodized aluminum pickguards, black pickup covers, and chrome barrel knobs. The next model, late 1959, also with a metal pickguard, had white pickup covers and white plastic knobs. The tortoiseshell pickguard appeared by 1960. Fingerboard markers and trim can sometimes help to fix the date of manufacture of certain 1960s models. Generally, the chronology is this: unbound neck with dull "clay" dots, unbound with "pearl" dots, bound with pearl dots, and bound with block inlays. Pearl dots appeared prior to the CBS takeover, and there are some late 1964 pearl-dot Jazzmasters, Jaguars, and Jazz Basses. The bound fingerboard is a CBS change. (Also see Mr. Fender's interview.)

GEORGE FULLERTON: FENDER'S CUSTOM COLORS

George Fullerton is Leo Fender's oldest associate and one of his best friends. His name appears in several places throughout the Fender chapter. What follows are some of George's own reminiscences about his years with Fender, and some notes on one of the company's most distinctive trademarks—its brightly colored finishes. The company had previously made many colored guitars on special order. The earliest known to the author and probably the first one was a black Strat ordered in November 1955 by the late Howard Reed, one of Gene Vincent's guitarists. But it was George Fullerton who encouraged Fender to put the colors into production.

> I started to work for Leo on February 2, 1948, helping him with the Broadcaster and hand-fretting the first one myself. I first did repairs and eventually worked in different aspects of production. I was later vice-president and supervisor for the entire factory. I stayed on as production manager for five years after CBS bought

the company, until 1970. For a couple of years I transferred into public relations work, and then I left Fender.

One of the things I did at Fender in the early days was to come up with the idea of custom colored finishes. No one, to my knowledge, had ever made colored instruments, but talking to different people it seemed like it might be an interesting way to go. One day I went down to a local paint store on Commonwealth Street in Fullerton—it's not there any more—and I had the man mix it up right there on the spot: put a little of this, now add some of that. We came up with what we later called Fiesta Red. I came back with this paint and had it put on a Jazzmaster. Everyone over at the sales office really got a big laugh out of it, but it turned out to be a very good thing, very popular. In fact, in England that was the only colored finish that they bought for a long time. They'd buy 'em 100 at a time. This must have been 1957 when we got into the custom colors in a substantial way.

By the early 1960s Fender's color chart included Fiesta Red and 13 other Duco and Lucite finishes that, like the blonde, were available on the whole line (excluding the Duo-Sonic and Musicmaster) for an extra five percent retail cost. There were three blues (from dark to light, Lake Placid Blue Metallic, Daphne Blue, and Sonic Blue), three greens (Sherwood Green Metallic, a forest green; the nearly aqua Foam Green; and the light Surf Green), Inca Silver Metallic, Dakota (fire engine) Red, Shell Pink, Black, Burgundy Mist Metallic, Olympic White, and Shoreline Gold Metallic.*

These colors are "compressed" on the color chart and tend to appear somewhat lighter when spread out on a guitar's surface; the Sonic Blue, for example, is a milky, robin's-egg hue, quite light. A paint's color can vary from batch to batch, and guitars of different woods take finishes in different ways. Over the years, varying exposures to sunlight will cause differing degrees of fading. All these factors help account for the varieties of old custom-color Fenders out there.

1958 Jazzmaster, gold anodized pickguard.
Charley's/Crump

JAGUAR

The production Jaguar of 1961 was essentially a souped-up Jazzmaster and seemed to have resulted more from Fender's desire to make a classier guitar than its usual motivations of improved design and functional innovation. Details included individual pickup on/off switches, a tone selector switch, chrome trim, and Strat-like pickups. The flip-up mute, an idea previously used by Gretsch, provided a stacatto, *tick-tick* sound. The Jaguar was dropped after late 1974. Regarding fretboard markers, see the discussion at the end of the Jazzmaster section.

[Note: the Jaguar had a short 24-inch scale and 22 frets, whereas the Jazzmaster had a 25-inch scale and 21 frets.]

BASS VI

Leo Fender thought that the world needed a new instrument, half bass and half guitar, and in about late 1961 he introduced a new, long-scale 6-string. Though Fender's marketers called it

* Fender's custom colors in 1966 were Lake Placid Blue Metallic, Blue Ice Metallic, Sonic Blue, Firemist Gold Metallic, Charcoal Frost, Olympic White, Black, Ocean Turquoise Metallic, Teal Green Metallic, Foam Green, Firemist Silver Metallic, Dakota Red, Candy Apple Red Metallic, and Fiesta Red.

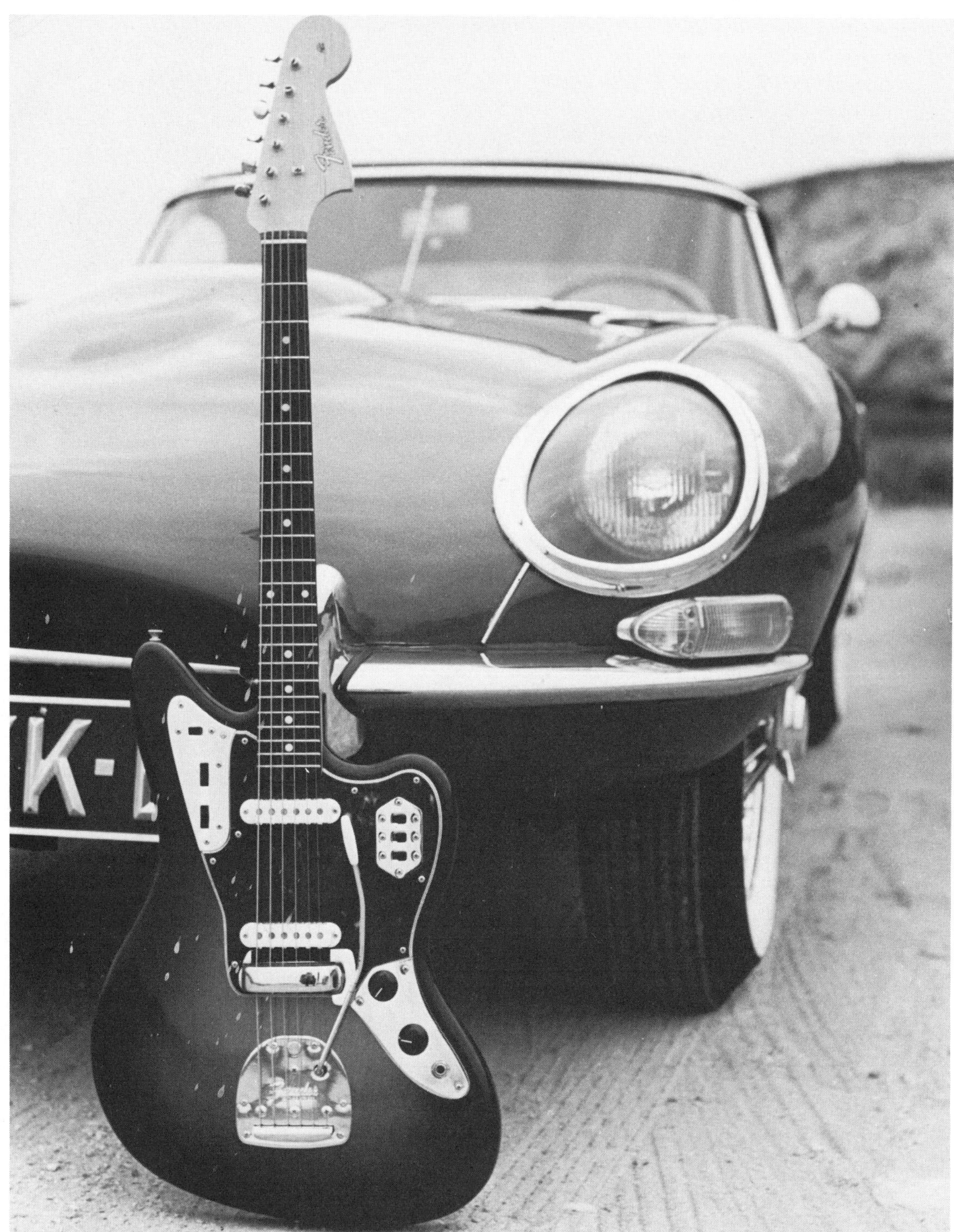

This dot-neck Jaguar was photographed before Fender had decided on the new guitar's name. (There is no model designation on the peghead.)

the Bass VI (see color photo 117), Leo envisioned it as a baritone guitar: "You tune the lower strings just like an electric bass," he explained, "but since the strings are about 4 inches shorter and have a different diameter, the tone is a little thinner—not as deep. It didn't sell too well because it was never promoted to any great degree. Actually, I don't think the sales department was too hep to it." Available in sunburst and various custom DuPont Duco finishes, the 44½-inch guitar featured a 14×1⅝-inch body resembling an elongated Jaguar, with three Stratocaster-like pickups, rosewood fingerboard, master volume and tone knobs, 30-inch scale, 21 frets, a Jaguar/Jazzmaster-type vibrato and rocker bridge, and chromed hardware. A metal plate on the upper right bout housed on/off switches for each pickup.

The late-1963 model showed several alterations: a foam rubber mute mounted on a metal rocker, a fourth slide switch, and Jaguar-like pickups with serrated metal sidepieces. According to Freddie Tavares, who helped design the guitar, the fourth switch was a "strangle switch—that's what we called it. It was a dinky condenser that wouldn't allow the lows to go through; it was like the third switch on a Jaguar."

Manufacture of the Bass VI continued after the CBS acquisition (CBS added neck binding and block markers), but the model was never particularly popular. According to Freddie Tavares, one reason for the Bass VI's lack of success was that the string industry could not at that time produce 30-inch strings

Jaguar bridge. Note adjustable saddles and foam rubber string damper.

The 1963–1964 catalogue's cover featured Fender's latest guitar, the Jaguar.

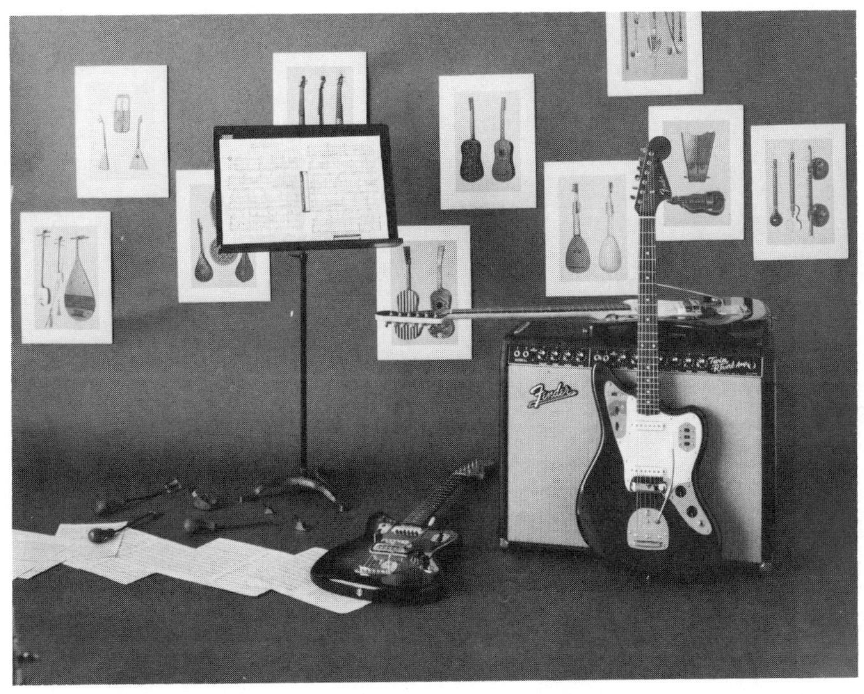

The late-1980s Strat Plus was a remarkable refinement, with its Fender-Lace Sensors instead of conventional pickups, a Fender/Wilkinson roller nut, Sperzel Locking Keys, and a redesigned tremolo. Later versions featured Hipshot's Trem-setter tremolo stabilizer. The Deluxe Strat Plus, Deluxe American Standard, and Clapton models were also equipped with the Lace units, developed by Don Lace.

that sounded as good as 34-inch strings; a desirable balance between length and diameter was never achieved. George Fullerton estimated that only 300 or 400 Bass VIs were made before Fender was sold to CBS in 1965. The Bass VI was discontinued in 1975.

MISCELLANEOUS SOLIDBODIES

Other Fender solidbody electrics have included the Duo-Sonic and Musicmaster (both introduced in 1956, restyled in 1964; Duo-Sonic was discontinued after 1969), Mustang (August 1964), Marauder (1965 only; never produced in large quantities, it was an abortive attempt to build a guitar with four pickups, all concealed beneath the pickguard), Electric 12-string (June 1965–1969*), 5-string bass (June 1965–1970,* with added high C string), Custom (mid 1969–1972, made from the 12-string body), and the Bronco (1969).

Also known as the Swinger, the Musiclander was essentially a sawed-off Musicmaster. One workman who was a member of Fender's production crew recalled: "Fender was sort of hurting for bucks at the time and they had thousands of dollars of left-over parts, so we made the Custom out of 12-string necks and bodies and we made the Musiclanders out of Musicmaster bodies and three-quarter necks." (See photo, page 62.)

FENDER SERIAL NUMBERS: GUITARS AND AMPS

Regarding pre-CBS dates, Fender serial numbers provide few answers but several clues. During the 1950s the numbers were not intended to indicate dates, and any superficial sampling will probably uncover wildly erratic numberings and cause far more confusion than clarification.

But Jim Werner, a diligent collector from Iowa, has documented the serial numbers and dates of more than 800 Fenders. After extensive cross-referencing of his lists and integrating some of Fender's own records for the 1970s, he found some broad guidelines.

In the adjacent tables, it is not only helpful but imperative to check specific models (if listed) as well as the "General" list and L numbers, because some models have their own systems during certain periods while paralleling other models during different periods. *Caution:* There are exceptions to several of the following groupings, and within most of them the numbers do *not* progress chronologically; example: 0260 is a 1953, while 0261 is a 1949. Emphatically, the groupings do *not* fix the dates of all Fenders, but they do suggest the dates of most of them. Check previous sections of this chapter for details of particular features that can help reveal production dates. *(Note: A zero is counted as a digit; for example, 0164 is a four-digit number.)*

Early Fender amps were covered in "tweed," a stitched, light brown cloth covering. Beginning in late 1959, the line began to switch to pebble grained Tolex, and by 1961 the change was almost complete. During 1963 and 1964, the line switched to *black* Tolex.

General (Broadcasters, Telecasters, Esquires, Precisions, and Stratocasters only)

under 0856:	1948 to 1954
0856–7279:	1954 to 1955
7348–22666:	1955 to 1957
28250–37659:	1958 to 1959
38232–53266:	1959 to 1960
55045–76442:	1961 to 1966, most are 1961
76722–90745:	1962 to 1964, most are 1962
91954–98691:	1961 to 1963, most are 1963

See L numbers for post-1962.

MINUS SIGNS

Most five-digit numbers preceded by a minus sign (−) run from late 1956 through 1958.

L NUMBERS

Fender's L serial numbers appear on examples of every model and run all throughout the 1960s, the vast majority from early 1963 through late 1965. Thus most L numbers signify post-1962, up through the CBS transition period. Though there are again a few exceptions, most L numbers indicate production periods for all Fender models as follows:

L00186–L33650:	early 1963 to 1964
L34983–L99809:	1964 to 1965

SIX-DIGIT NUMBERS (ALL MODELS)

first digit 0:	1957 to 1959
100173–124061:	1965 to 1966, most 1965
125115–195270:	1964 to 1969, the great majority 1966
195663–215825:	1966 to 1969, most 1967
217602–240407:	1966 to 1968, most 1968
250025–293692:	1966 to 1972, exceptions through late 1970s
303802–375967:	1968 to 1972, most 1972

According to Fender:

400,000 series:	Apr. 1973 to Sept. 1976
500,000 series:	Sept. 1973 to Sept. 1976
600,000 series:	Aug. 1974 to Aug. 1976
700,000 series:	Sept. 1976 to Dec. 1976

* These guitars were modified in 1966: white neck binding and rectangular fretboard markers were added.

The amplifier's model code number may provide some help in dating the unit. Amps made in the 1950s or 1960s are identified with a number that begins with 5 or 6, respectively. (On early-1960s models, the second character is usually or always the letter *G*.)

Many 1950s and 1960s tube sequence charts are dated by means of a two-letter code affixed with a rubber stamp. The first letter stands for the year (A = 1951, B = 1952, etc.), while the second indicates the month (A = January, B = February, and so on). In general, this system was discontinued after 1967, with a few reported exceptions in the early 1970s.

More confirmation may be found on the chassis' unexposed surface, where the date of manufacture often appears in a five- or six-digit code: the last two digits indicate the year, while the preceding pair of numbers indicates the week.

Finally, the transformer may also date the amp. Transformers made in 1968 and earlier are marked 125A3A, while others made in 1968 and later models are marked 022868. Another transformer number begins with 606 and includes two other figures: the first is the week of manufacture, the second is the year.

FENDER FACTS

Fender Facts was a zippy trade magazine published by Don Randall's progressive sales department. Slick and colorful, the brochure began in late 1962 as a promotional newsletter intended to educate dealers and customers, and to inform them of the latest products from Fullerton. Concerning dates, its accuracy is about that of most catalogues, which is to say approximate at best, but taken overall it adds to a general understanding of Fender product chronology. Here are highlights covering late 1962 to mid 1969.

Issue No. 1, December 1962
The Double Showman (predating the Dual Showman) was available only on custom order with two 15-inch JBLs, $800. The "Go Around" waist belt, designed as a substitute for the guitar strap, was announced. It cost $10.95 and attached to the back of the guitar with hooks and eye screws.

Issue No. 4, August 1963
Fender announced a line of Tarrega classics, proclaiming (with more enthusiasm than accuracy): "As the line of Fender acoustics grows, each will dominate its field for fine tone, craftsmanship, durability, ease of playing, and beauty. These statements are not claims but facts, as will readily be seen wherever these fine instruments are displayed." Steel-strings included the King and Concert, both with spruce tops, Brazilian rosewood bodies, and removable necks.

SEVEN-DIGIT NUMBERS, ON PEGHEAD

76: Aug. 1976 to Apr. 1977
S6: Mar. 1977 to Aug. 1978
S7: Jan. 1977 to Apr. 1978
S8: Dec. 1977 to Dec. 1978
S9: Nov. 1978 to 1981
E0: May 1979 to 1981
E1: May 1979 to 1981

BROADCASTERS

Broadcasters (1948–1952) have four digits or less. The Werner list's lowest verified Broadcaster serial number, 0017, is for a November 1950 guitar, and the highest, 0773, is for an *earlier* model of December 1949. Among Broadcaster numbers there is apparently an utter lack of correlation to production dates.

TELECASTER AND ESQUIRE

under 5221: 1951 to 1954
7045–15304: 1955 to 1956
18160–38881: 1957

For post-1957, see Stratocaster and general list.

PRECISION BASS

37–0347: 1949 to 1952
0852–10146: 1953 to 1955
10299–22459: 1956 to 1957
29039–32029: 1958
32912–45749: 1958 to 1960, most are 1958 to 1959

For post-1959, see Stratocaster and general list.

STRATOCASTER

two or three digits: 1953 to 1954
four digits through 1111: 1953 to 1956, the great majority 1954
7000 and 8000 series: 1955 to 1957
08999–14514: 1954 to 1957, most are 1956
15054–22647: 1957
28250–30747: 1958
30892–43125: 1959
44606–48490: 1959 to 1960
55045–71331: 1960 to 1962, most are 1961
76281–90745: 1961 to 1964, most are 1962
91954–98691: 1961 to 1963, most are 1963

For post-1963, see general list.

1968 Coronados. ***Left to right:*** **model I with tremolo, model II with tremolo, 12-string, Bass I, Bass II.**

Issue No. 5, November 1963
Fender announced two new Regals, the R-2312 acoustic 12-string, and the R-273 three-pickup, double-cutaway, thin hollowbody electric; both were Harmonys with Regal logos on the pegheads. Other news: the Handy-Stand, designed to hold either guitar or bass in playing position, $45; and the Candy-Apple Red Metallic finish.

Issue No. 6, February 1964
The Fender acoustic guitar plant was profiled, and the entire line of Tarrega models received model number changes, confusing dealers and players, not to mention later students of Fender history. Custom neck sizes were announced at 5 percent additional cost for the Jaguar, Jazzmaster, and Stratocaster: narrow (1½-inch), standard (1⅝-inch), wide (1¾-inch), and extra wide (1⅞-inch).

Issue No. 7, August 1964
The new Mustang was announced at $189.50, available in red, white, or blue. The Vibrolux amp was changed to the Vibrolux Reverb, and the Princeton Reverb was added to the line. "Beginning August, all piggyback amps, unless ordered otherwise, will be delivered with *black* vinyl Tolex covering. The new covering will be the same as now used on the single-unit models. It is further anticipated that cases for all instruments except the Musicmaster, Duo-Sonic, and Mustang will be covered in black Tolex." It was also announced that the Champ amplifier "will

DATING FENDER AMPS
Most pre-CBS amps had Jensen or Oxford speakers that were ink-stamped on the back of the frame, with number codes that can help date the amps. According to author/columnist Richard Smith, a three-digit date code followed the company codes 220 (Jensen) or 465 (Oxford). Examples: 220122 is a Jensen (220); the next digit (1) indicates 1951, while the last two indicate the twenty-second week. Speaker 465244 is an Oxford made in the forty-fourth week of 1962.

Does a 2 mean 1952 or 1962? Use overall appearance to fix the decade. General descriptions: tweed covering with wide front panels on the top and bottom: 1952–54; tweed with narrow panels: 1954–59; brown Tolex: 1959–63; blond Tolex: 1961–64; black Tolex: 1963–68.

A tube chart affixed to the amp's interior can also fix the date. The two-character code initiated in 1953 is based on January 1951; 1951 = A, 1952 = B, etc. Similarly, January = A, February = B, etc. The year comes first, thus CH = August 1953 and IJ = October 1959.

shortly be remodeled and will appear in the *front* control cabinet. The first production of the new Vibro-Champ will begin in the latter part of August."

Issue No. 8, November 1964
The new mahogany Palomino augmented the steel-string line. Both the Musicmaster and Duo-Sonic bodies were recontoured to resemble the Mustang; both had large headstocks, were available in red, white, or blue, and could be ordered with either a 22½- or 24-inch scale. No. 8 was the last pre-CBS issue of *Fender Facts.*

Issue No. 9, June 1965
Fender's 12-string solid electric and 5-string electric bass were announced, as was the clear plastic Body Guard instrument protector, which fit over the body's rear surface. The acoustic guitar line was further augmented with two mahogany models at the low end of the price range, the Malibu and Newporter. The Pro Reverb joined the amplifier line.

Issue No. 10, November 1965
For better or worse, CBS/Fender announced its Thin-Line Acoustic-Electric guitars, later to be christened the Coronado series. Two new 12-strings joined the acoustic line: the Villager (a modified Malibu), and the Shenandoah (a 12-string version of the Kingman).

Issue No. 11, March 1966
The Kingman guitars were now available with maple bodies in either natural or sunburst. Leo Fender was pictured receiving

Roger Rossmeisl, with a partially carved top for one of his Fender arch-tops. Note the raised interior ridge, which also characterized some of the guitars Rossmeisl designed for Rickenbacker. While at Rickenbacker, one of his apprentices was Semie Moseley, some of whose Mosrite guitars featured the ridge. The design was extended even further, to the original Acoustic Black Widow, which according to Moseley was patterned after Mosrite guitars.

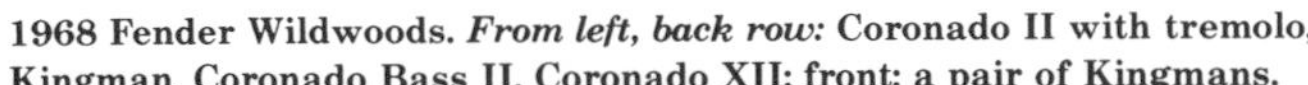

1968 Fender Wildwoods. *From left, back row:* Coronado II with tremolo, Kingman, Coronado Bass II, Coronado XII; front: a pair of Kingmans.

1971 Fender Custom. A seldom-seen guitar (and no wonder), it was made from Mustang parts and sawed-off 12-string bodies. At least one variation was Fender's ridiculously obscure Maverick; specially labeled for a retailer, it was identical to the Custom except for the model designation. Although quite a few Customs left the factory in the early 1970s, many had leftover 12-string necks dated 1965 or 1966.

the Country Music Association's President's Award from Tex Ritter (Mr. Fender shunned the limelight and was rarely if ever pictured in pre-CBS promo literature).

Issue No. 12, September 1966
Marking a low point in Fender's overall quality, this issue announced a solid-state P.A. system, the solid-state Dual Showman, and solid-state versions of a legendary trio—the reverb kit, Bassman amp, and Twin Reverb. As if that weren't enough, the Coronado Thin-Line acoustic-electrics were expanded to include a bass and a 12-string. The Coronado guitars and transistor amps helped contribute to the persistence of the "pre-CBS" dichotomy. There was some good news, too: the Mustang short-scale (30½-inch) bass, designed by Leo Fender, was announced, and it was one of the company's best bargains ever.

The steel-string line converted to the Wildwood series. The beechwood used in the bodies was injected with dyes that expanded throughout the tree along the grain lines. Wildwoods were trendy and short-lived, the Nehru jackets of the guitar world. They weren't Martins, that's for sure, but they were no sillier than many corporate attempts to look hip during the turbulent sixties.

Issue No. 14, July 1967
The Wildwood acoustics were specified to have Kingman bodies, and the Coronados were now available in the optional Wildwood finish; they were accurately described as "truly different." The Coronado I and Coronado II were given new hand tremolos, and the new two-pickup Coronado Bass II joined the line. The Bronco guitar/amp set was announced along with the Bigsby-equipped Telecasters and Esquires.

Issue No. 17, May 1969
The Competition Mustang (with racing stripes) was introduced, and the company announced: "All Mustang guitars and basses now have Fender's exclusive contoured offset waist design and dressed away body." Furthermore, the Bandmaster was now the Bandmaster Reverb. This issue also announced the debut of the ugly-duckling Custom. Among production models the Custom rivals the Musiclander for title of Fender's weirdest guitar ever.

G & L

Dale Hyatt knew Leo Fender for a half-century, making their association one of the longest in the industry. Dale was working for Randall in the late 1970s, when he approached Leo about making a guitar for him. Because Leo was tied up building Music Man guitars through his CLF Research firm, Dale's guitar never materialized. But in 1979, Leo, Dale, and longtime Fender associate George Fullerton got together to form the company that came to be known as G & L—for George and Leo.

Reports Dale Hyatt: "Leo and George owned the factory in the early days, and the three of us owned the sales company. Leo and I bought out George in June 1984. We've used the same facility all along—pretty much the same one where we'd built the first Music Mans—only we've enlarged it. Leo owned the surrounding buildings, so as we needed more space, we just moved in. Leo designed the pickups and things, and the three of us have designed guitars over the years.

"Leo didn't want designs that looked anything like his earlier guitars. The problem was that everyone was doing it. We were the only ones who weren't. Those designs had become standards. The ASAT model [shown here] was our answer to the Telecaster, and now it outsells all other G & L's."

Aside from the obvious cosmetic and structural details, G & L guitars differ from Fender's earlier designs in their unique bridges and pickups.

"Leo's Fender pickups had Alnico magnets and nonadjustable polepieces, while G & L's have ceramic magnets and adjustable polepieces," explains Hyatt. "The way we magnetize the magnet, it lets us have the polepieces all in one field, positive or negative, from where they sit on the magnet all the way to the top of the polepiece. This allows a soft iron polepiece with more output but less wire, so there's less capacitance, which means more highs."

A work force of about 32 produces up to 30 guitars a day at G & L's plant in Fullerton, California.

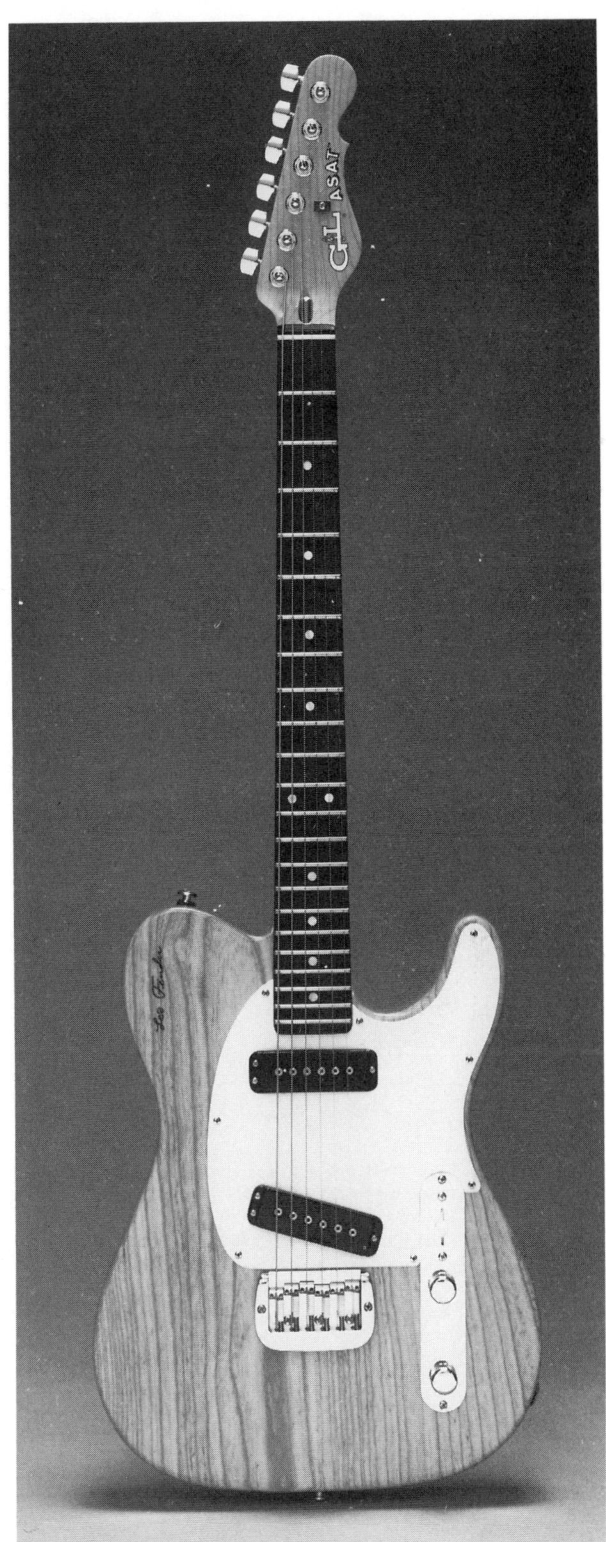

G & L's ASAT model bears Leo Fender's signature on the body.

Silent screen star Priscilla Dean with Gibson Artist model mandolin.

GIBSON

Gibson's position among guitar makers is eminent and unique. Though its quality has varied, and other companies do better at certain things (flat-tops, for one), over the last eight decades Gibson has popularized more influential designs—the modern arch-top, Les Paul, truss rod, 335, tune-o-matic bridge, and many more—and built a greater variety of fine acoustic and electric guitars than any other manufacturer.

COMPANY HISTORY

Orville Gibson

Orville H. Gibson was a skilled guitar builder, and his character reflected a combination of talent, dedication, and eccentricity that epitomized in part the soul of American guitar. Most of his early instruments were elegant and baroque, with sculpted scrolls and points; intricate inlays of ebony, mother-of-pearl, and abalone; and curlicue logos. Their maker's ego bulged with a grand neo-classicism and a marvelous conceit which were reflected in the awesome hyperbole of early company literature. In a fashion common among turn-of-the-century American entrepreneurs flushed with the promise of the Industrial Revolution, Orville H. Gibson assigned a titanic significance to his works, and when his successors proclaimed in an early catalogue that their instruments were "the first serious mandolins and guitars ever manufactured," they weren't kidding.

He was the son of an Englishman, John Gibson. Orville's niece, Barbara L. Seguine, has recounted that John Gibson arrived in America as a small boy with a note pinned to his expensive jacket. The note was addressed to a couple who was on hand to greet him. John received regular financial support from across the Atlantic and settled in or near Malone, New York, where he raised Orville, Orville's brother Osroz, and two sisters.

Orville was born in Chateaugay, New York, in 1856 and moved to Kalamazoo, Michigan. As a young man, he clerked in various business establishments, including a shoe store. His hobbies of whittling, woodworking, and music eventually led to the acquisition of a 10 by 12 foot wood shop. There he began to revolutionize musical instrument construction. Kalamazoo records from 1896 and 1897 list 114 South Burdick as the business location of "O.H. Gibson, Manufacturer, Musical Instruments." The 1899–1902 directories designate a new location, the second floor of 104 East Main, also the young luthier's residence.

The philosophy of Gibson's craft included a belief in the superior vibrating characteristics of unstressed wood. When constructing the sides of a mandolin, for instance, rather than bending flat strips of wood in the previously accepted manner, he would cut them to shape from solid boards. Instead of bending flat sheets into arched tops, he would again carve the arch from a slab. Like the Gibson company's later use of high bridges, elevated fingerrests, and separate tailpieces, this was a violin-making technique he applied to mandolins and guitars (though on each instrument he used an oval soundhole rather than a pair of f-holes). It brought him some ridicule at first, then a good local reputation and some success, and finally a place in history as the father of the arch-top guitar.

Orville's early musical instruments included several highly stylized hybrids—a harp zither, an exquisitely ornamented harp guitar, and the lyre mandolin pictured on early Gibson labels. The headstock decoration on many of these instruments featured a pearl star encircled by a crescent, an inlay attributed to a Turkish pearl cutter in Grand Rapids who was contracted by Gibson.

Orville Gibson.

The Gibson factory at the turn of the century.

Early Years

The Gibson Mandolin-Guitar Manufacturing Company, Limited, was established with the signing of a document at 2:55 PM on October 11, 1902. It was an agreement among five Kalamazoo financiers: John W. Adams (company president until 1944), Samuel H. Van Horn (treasurer), Sylvo Reams (secretary, also production manager for 15 years), Lewis Williams (later secretary and general manager, also developer of Gibson's first pickguard clamp), and Leroy Hornbeck. The newly created "Partnership Association Limited" existed "for the purpose of manufacturing, buying, selling, and dealing in guitars, mandolins, mandolas, violins, lutes, and all other kinds of stringed instruments." Interestingly, it was the instruments of these men and their followers, and not those of Orville Gibson, that made the Gibson name famous.

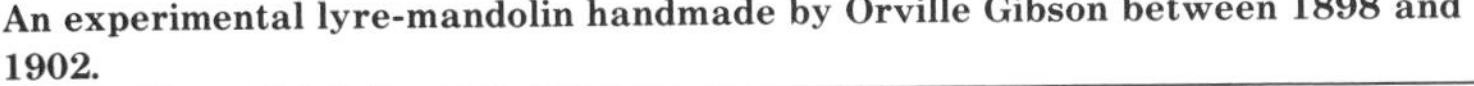

An experimental lyre-mandolin handmade by Orville Gibson between 1898 and 1902.

Curiously, Orville himself was not a partner; rather, he entered into a separate contract under which he assigned his name and sole patent (mandolin, 1898) to the new company in exchange for $2,500. He also agreed to serve as a consultant, training workers in the art of tuning tops and other facets of instrument building.

Shop was set up in an old, cockroach-infested bakery. On May 24, 1904, the Gibson Mandolin-Guitar Manufacturing Company dropped the "Ltd." from its name and incorporated with $12,000 capital stock, but its namesake was not among the 24 charter stockholders, and there are no records indicating that Orville Gibson ever became an officer or shareholder in the company that bears his name.

In 1906, the capital stock was increased to $40,000 and the name further shortened to the Gibson Mandolin-Guitar Company. In November of that year, Gibson expanded its facilities, leasing two brick buildings on the south side of East Exchange Place for $65 a month. The year 1909 saw the granting of patents for the intonation-adjustable bridge and elevated pickguard (with clamp). In the following year, the harp guitar was patented. On April 12, 1915, Orville and the Gibson Company negotiated a new agreement under which Orville was to be paid a monthly royalty for the remainder of his life.

Aside from a smattering of details, little is known of Orville Gibson. An accomplished guitarist, he worked in a local quartet with Thaddeus McHugh (later a Gibson employee, co-author with Lewis Williams of the 1921 patent for the height-adjust-

A trio of stunningly ornamented instruments by Orville Gibson. *From left:* mandolin, fretted zither, and harp guitar.

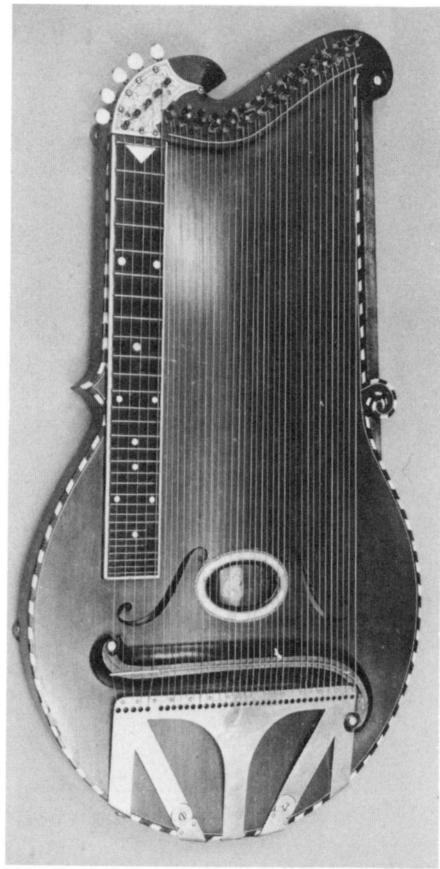

able bridge, and inventor of the truss rod in 1922). Orville Gibson considered all competitors demonstrably inferior. He was left-handed, a characteristic held in high suspicion by superstitious right-handers. He never married. He was treated in 1911 and 1916 at the psychiatric center of St. Lawrence State Hospital (Ogdensburg, New York), where he died of endocarditis on August 21, 1918.

Orville Gibson's financial involvement with the Gibson Company may have been minimal, but his indomitable spirit was as much a part of the firm's rich heritage as his instrument designs. His consuming vision of the glory of Gibson was adopted by public relations personnel. Under the guidance of 20-year Gibson veteran L.A. Williams, the catalogue authors of the proud young company met their destinies with a missionary zeal, erecting and gilding a veritable fortress of company esprit and public image.

Gibson brochures, while biased, were storehouses of knowledge and stimulating advice. How many catalogues today offer exhaustive dissertations on the interaction of the rate, amplitude, and complexity of vibrations? But there was more to Gibson literature than information.

> You acknowledge to being ashamed to own [admit] you are in the wrong, which is acting the part of being no wiser today than you were yesterday. Such is a deceit that beginneth by making falsehood appear like truth and endeth by making truth appear like falsehood, for one misrepresentation must be thatched with another, or it will soon rain through.

PASTE THIS IN YOUR GIBSON CATALOG "K"

REVISED PRICES-CATALOG "K"

Revised September 1, 1919

MANDOLINS

Style	Catalog Page	Net Price
"A"	49	$37.00
With Canvas Case, No. 101		40.00
With "Faultless" Case, No. 360		45.00
With "Faultless" Case, No. 363		49.50
"A-2"	50	47.00
With Canvas Case, No. 101		50.00
With "Faultless" Case, No. 360		55.00
With "Faultless" Case, No. 363		59.50
"A-3"	51	57.00
With Canvas Case, No. 101		60.00
With "Faultless" Case, No. 360		65.00
With "Faultless" Case, No. 363		69.50
"A-4"	52	70.00
With Canvas Case, No. 101		73.00
With "Faultless" Case, No. 360		78.00
With "Faul less" Case, No. 363		82.50
"F-2"	53	108 00
With "Faultless" Case, No. 368		116.00
With "Faultless" Case, No. 371		120.50
"F-4"	54	148.09
With "Faultless" Case, No. 368		156.00
With "Faultless" Case, No. 371		160.50

MANDOLAS

Style	Catalog Page	Net Price

GUITARS

Style	Catalog Page	Net Price
"L-1"	58	$ 54.00
With Canvas Case, No. 135		58.00
With "Faultless" Case, No. 408		67.50
With "Faul less Case, No. 411		74.25
"L-3"	59	70.00
With Canvas Case, No. 135		74.00
With "Faultless" Case, No. 408		83.50
With "Faultless" Case, No. 411		90.25
"L-4"	60	100.00
With "Faultless" Case, No. 416		115.75
With "Faultless" Case, No. 419		122.25
"O"	61	120.00
With "Faultless" Case, No. 242		135.75
With "Faultless" Case, No. 427		142.25

GIBSON BANJO LINE

Style	Net Price
"TB"	$ 95.00
With "Faultless" Case, No. 406	111.40
"GB"	100.00
With "Faultless" Case, No. 441	123.00
"MB"	90.00
With "Faultless" Case, No. 422	102.75
"CB"	95.00
With "Faultless" Case, No. 441	118.00

An early Gibson work crew in a solemn pose with rims for a harp guitar, banjo, and two guitars.

The foregoing isn't a passage from a fundamentalist religious text. Rather, it is a quote from the 1908 Gibson catalogue. It continues with this sombre dictim: "Use the 'Gibson' whether in the Mandolin or Guitar family, and if you have evolutionized from the musical lesser into the greater, you will recognize in the 'Gibson' the realization of the ideals for which you stand." It asks, "Will you then use the old construction which you try to make seem what it actually is not, or will you use the matchless 'Gibson'?"

This wonderfully gooey prose suggests that those who don't play Gibsons are both deceitful villains and deadbeats loitering several rungs too low on the evolutionary ladder. It is buttressed with platitudinous pronouncements, to wit: "The Reckless Indifference of Some Teachers to the 'Gibson' Is Because the 'Gibson' Is So Far Advanced of Some Teachers' Ideals."

The grand result of all this is a quasi-Biblical undertone that threatens nonbelievers with the terrible swift sword—the kind of pressure that advertisers would no doubt use today if they thought they could get away with it. The following passage (p. 61, 1908 Gibson catalogue) is quite possibly the zenith of two centuries of American advertising:

> Awakened souls know that perfect voicing cannot be in an orchestra of a hodgepodge of makes of instruments. The musical inane are not expected to appreciate this statement, but the memory of it and the hosts of evolutionized Mandolin Orchestras universally using the "Gibson" instrumentation pursue with a whip of scorpions and are bringing the days of musical inanity to a speedy end. *Live not longer in a light that is past, when "Gibson" instruments of the classic Violin construction can be purchased at $1.00 down and $1.50 a month.*

Gibson's colossal bass banjo, 1931.

Well, whether because of the fear of Jehovah's wrath, the high quality of Gibson instruments, or the unprecedented effectiveness of its sophisticated marketing, entertainers and amateurs alike pledged their allegiance to Kalamazoo. In association with schools, societies, churches, YMCAs, universities, and clubs, and fueled by widely distributed music periodicals and by regular conventions of instructors, they formed combos and whole orchestras of Gibson-equipped musicians, sometimes calling themselves Gibsonians, Gibsonites, Gibson Girls, and the like. Accolades poured in and were quoted at length in catalogues under the formal portraits of stiff performers with their Gibson mando-basses, mandolins, mandolas, mando-cellos, guitars, tenor guitars, and harp guitars.

In 1915, Gibson's capital stock increased to $100,000. The company thrived during World War I, introducing the low-priced Army and Navy Special mandolins for the armed services. The firm moved into its present location on Parsons Street in 1917.

During 1920 and 1921 the mandolin's popularity was eclipsed by the banjo. Gibson was prepared, having made its first banjos in 1918. The endorsements continued unabated with the catalogues' staid, tuxedoed mandolinists replaced by banjo choirs

One of Gibson's many mandolin ensembles.

Lloyd Loar at left, with ensemble. The huge instrument at center is a Gibson Style J mando-bass ($150 list). Although Fender's Precision is widely assumed to be America's first production guitarlike bass instrument, the mid-1920s Style J was tuned an octave below a guitar's bottom four strings and could be played in either of two positions: standing, like an upright bass, or seated, like a guitar. Gibson promised that it provided "deep, profound pulsations." Note armrest across strings.

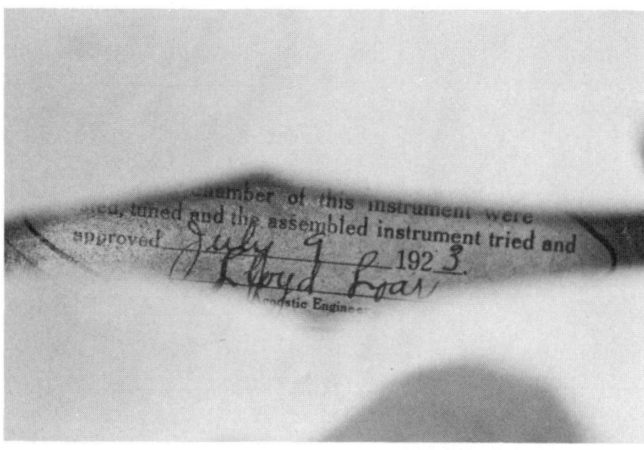

A Lloyd Loar signature label from July 9, 1923. *Bizarre Guitar*

and peppy combos playing mandolin-banjos, tenor banjos, ukulele-banjos, and the like. During the 1920s, Guy Hart was instrumental in designing, building, and securing the patents for various Gibsons. He became secretary and general manager in 1924 and served in that capacity until his retirement in 1948.

Lloyd Loar

Lloyd Loar [see Vivi-Tone] joined the company in 1919 and during his five-year tenure became a Gibson superstar. To this day he stands in a shaft of light in the annals of the history of instruments, the Stradivarius of Kalamazoo. He was an acoustics engineer and mandolinist renowned in both America and Europe, as well as a composer for violin and cello, lecturer on harmony and arranging, recipient of the Chicago Conservatory's Master of Music Award, and consultant to both General Motors and the Virzi Brothers violin company.

At Gibson, Loar's responsibilities were awesome—chief engineer, patent applicant, head of what we would now call R&D (research & development), traveling company rep, trainer of sales agents, director of customer service, purchasing agent, music publisher, and author of articles in periodicals.

Loar is credited with the development of the F-5 mandolin, one of the most esteemed instruments in American manufacturing history. (Loar was not a luthier; he supervised, tested, and approved the instruments.) A strict advocate of quality control, he would stalk the production line, making spot checks. Certain models were blessed with his signature, and this led to Gibson's much touted and genuinely superior *Master Line Master Tone* series, which included among others the magnificent L-5 guitar, H-5 mandola, and K-5 mando-cello. Loar's signature appears only in Style 5 instruments made from late 1922 until late 1924. Though his name is included on no Gibson patents (except as a witness), he is credited with a number of projects in large measure actually the work of others—developing or improving the elevated fretboard, elevated fingerrest, the all-purpose intonation-adjustable bridge, the f-hole design, and the Mastertone banjo's floating head, ball bearing rim, and tone tube.

Late-1920s PG-1. Gibson made two kinds of 4-string guitars, plectrum models like this one (27-inch scale) and tenor models (23-inch tenor banjo scale). *Gruhn*

The 1920s, 1930s, and 1940s

The years between the World Wars saw a sustained public interest in ukuleles and banjos and a budding popularity for the guitar. Many of the nation's first guitar stars were rhythm players who had replaced banjoists in dance bands and orchestras. Soon the guitar became an essential accoutrement for whole posses of singing cowboys, most of whom played—or at least posed with—flat-tops with round holes. The arched-top, f-hole guitar was well suited to work in dance bands because of its "cutting power"—an ability to cut through the considerable volume of gangs of horn players. With the rapid spread of radio entertainment, guitars began to assume a larger role in popular music of all kinds—jazz, country, Hawaiian, ballad, and big band.

Developed by Loar, the L-5 was Gibson's only f-hole guitar from 1923 to 1931, though it led to an inevitable arched-top line. The J-200, designed by Guy Hart in association with Hollywood cowboy star Ray Whitley, was an eminent member of Gibson's flat-top family. However, Gibson flat-tops were generally overshadowed by Martin, and it was Orville Gibson's carved tops, the f-holes, and the other innovations that ensured Gibson's stature as a maker of top-quality acoustic guitars. These same arch-tops were the progenitors of another long line of distinguished Gibsons—the electric arched-tops, sometimes called jazz guitars.

By 1927, Gibson's work force had increased to over 130 employees. Then the Depression struck. The public's crushed buying power mandated that Gibson and other companies either produce decent, low-cost instruments or risk collapse. Gibson responded with its Kalamazoo brand, including the KM-21 mandolin, K-TB tenor banjo, KG-11 guitar, and KG-31 guitar.

Gerald Burgeon worked in at least half a dozen departments at Gibson. Here are his recollections of the company's activities during World War II. Although it was a half-century ago, Gerald still remembers the day he came to work for Gibson:

> It was August 13, 1933. Gibson was making a lot of flat-tops back then and also the Kalamazoo line. The company was busy making instruments right up until we switched to war work in 1942. We had several hundred people working there, making spars and skids for the military gliders. There were a few fellows on the top floor in the back who repaired a few guitars. Some of the instruments that we had in stock were put together for the Army and the Navy, but except for that there was very little instrument production during the war.

In early 1944 the Chicago Musical Instrument Company acquired controlling interest in Gibson, and with CMI's capital investment Gibson was able to expand year after year. Maurice Berlin, then a director of CMI and later the "lin" of Norlin, was a giant of American musical instrument manufacturing. He foresaw the postwar guitar boom and ordered a 15,000-square-foot mill room addition and expansion of the factory's lumber storage area. Employees returned from the service and went back to work making musical instruments. Gibson, already a world leader, was about to double and redouble its production.

EARLY GIBSON GUITARS

The following dates are approximations based on Gibson literature, which is abundant, colorful, and sometimes inconsistent. Catalogues and price lists have been crosschecked with company documents, memos, and interviews, and some "official" mistakes have been corrected or noted. Still, plenty of information rests on brochures that were intended only for promotional purposes, and the announcement of a new guitar may precede or follow the instrument's actual appearance by months (especially in the case of pre-1930 models). Furthermore, "actual appearance" is itself a murky area, since a year can go by while a

Gibson Recording King model M-2. *Bob Coward*

Gibson introduced the low-budget Kalamazoos like this Sport Model flat-top toward the end of the Depression in order to provide low-priced guitars to a public reeling from the nation's economic woes. *Music Shop/Madsen*

new design is produced, test-marketed, formally announced, and distributed.

What follows is a review of Gibson's own documentation (researched, refined, and at least partially corrected), and some dates refer to an instrument's "official" (i.e., approximate) membership in the line. In each case there may be overlaps at the beginning of a chronology (prototypes, test-market guitars) and at the end (since leftover discontinued models were routinely shipped until they ran out).

Carson J. Robison round-hole steel-string, made by Gibson and sold by Ward. *Dan Lambert*

Depression-era Kalamazoo, an inexpensive round-hole Gibson steel-string. Mahogany body, spruce top. *Vintage Fret Shop/A. Caswell*

A Summary of the Gibson Acoustic Line: 1903–1942

The 1903 catalogue listed eight guitars, more than the company would offer during the next two decades. Increasing in list price, they were the Style L, L-1, L-2, L-3, O, O-1, O-2, and O-3, and they ranged from the $44.32 Style L to the $212.17 Grand Concert Style O. These instruments had fixed bridges with pins and arched, graduated tops with round or oval soundholes, thus mixing features now almost exclusively associated with *either* the modern flat-top (round hole, fixed bridge) or arch-top (f-hole, rim-mounted tailpiece).

The 1906 brochure, Catalogue E, listed only three guitars: the L-1, L-3, and Style O. In 1908 (Catalogue F), the L-1 and L-3 were restyled, and the top-of-the-line Style O metamorphosed to the highly stylized single cutaway version, arguably Gibson's strangest guitar ever. These three, which also appeared in Catalogue G, were accompanied by six mandolins, a harp-guitar, two mandolas, and two mando-cellos. Catalogue H added the L-4 Grand Concert model, now the top of the L series and second only to the Style O in price. This four-guitar selection remained intact in Gibson's Catalogue I of 1914–1915, and in Catalogue J as well.

The lineup remained unchanged until 1919 or 1920, when two lower-budget models were added; these were listed in the January 1921 price list as the GY and the L-Jr. The GY was quickly dropped, but the L-Jr. remained for at least a year. It was omitted from the January 1922 and January 1923 price lists, but rejoined the line by May of 1923.

April of 1923 saw the first L-5 and the last Style O. In the January 1924 price list the L-1 and L-3 were dropped, and the L-2, unseen since 1903, reappeared. Thus the 1924 line was, according to the price list, the L-Jr., L-2, L-4, and L-5. (Catalogue N, oddly enough, pictured only the L-2 and L-4.) By December of 1924, the L-3 had also "officially" reappeared (it never actually disappeared), completing a five-guitar line.

By February 1926 the L-Jr. and L-2 were dropped, the L-0 appeared for the first time, and the L-1 reappeared. The L-0, L-1, L-3, L-4, and L-5 comprised the guitar line until early 1928, when it was supplemented with the Nick Lucas Special. For the first time since 1903, Gibson offered as many guitars as mandolins, and by 1928 all six were available in Hawaiian models with high string nuts for lap-style playing. These were identified as the L-0H, L-1H, and so on.

In late 1929, the L-0¾ was added and the L-2 reappeared again—this time as a flat-top—making guitars Gibson's most extensive line. In increasing price, the models for 1930 were the L-0¾ ($35), L-0 (also $35), L-1 ($50), L-2 ($75), L-3 ($100), Nick Lucas Special ($125), L-4 ($150), and L-5 ($275); the L-5 was thus far and away the top of the line.

Beginning in late 1931, Gibson price brochures began listing the guitars first, reflecting the instrument's growing popularity. In 1931 the L-00 was added, the L-0¾ dropped. At this time the price lists began to distinguish arch-tops (the L-3, L-4, L-5, and the new L-10) from the L-00, L-0, L-1, and L-2. Three more guitars were added by late 1932: the L-50 ($50, the bottom of the arch-top group); the L-75 ($75); and the L-12 ($200), which ranked between the L-10 and the L-5. In 1933, the L-C, or Century model, was added between the L-1 and L-2 flat-tops, and the L-0 and L-3 were dropped. This series remained unchanged through 1933.

In mid 1934 the extra large Jumbo flat-top ($60) and the L-7 arch-top augmented the regular line, now consisting of five flat-tops and seven arch-tops. Special instruments included the Nick Lucas and two Roy Smeck acoustic Hawaiian flat-tops: the Radio Grande ($100) and the Stage DeLuxe ($50).

The year 1935 was a landmark for Gibson due to the formal introduction of the extremely expensive Super 400 arch-top. It cost $400, which included a genuine leather-covered case. In that same year the L-2 was dropped, and the L-30 ($30) and L-37 ($37.50) budget arch-tops were added, reflecting Gibson's increasing concentration on arch-tops. Excluding the Lucas and Smeck models, the company now had five categories of 6-string guitars: flat-top (L-00, L-1, L-C); large flat-top (the Jumbo); carved-top L models (30, 37, 50, 75, and 4); the new "Advanced" L series with its larger body width of 17¼ inches and longer scale length of 25½ inches (L-7, 10, 12, and 5); and the Super Guitar category with its solitary member, the Super 400. There were no changes in 1936.

By mid 1937 the Jumbo was replaced by two instruments: the Jumbo 35 ($37.50), and the fancier Advanced Jumbo ($80). The L-1 and L-75 were dropped, and the L-0, not seen since 1932, reappeared. In 1938 the L-75 reappeared and the Super Jumbo was added. In 1938–1939 the L-10 and L-75 were dropped, and the Super Jumbo and Advanced Jumbo were replaced by the Super Jumbo 200 and Super Jumbo 100. The Jumbo 55 was added, the L-C was dropped, and the gut-string GS-85 ($85) and GS-35 ($35) were added. In 1941 the L-37 was dropped, and the L-47 added. There were no changes in 1942. Gibson guitar production effectively ceased from 1942 to 1945. All models mentioned above are discussed in detail below.

Hollow-Body Acoustic and Electric Guitars

STYLE L

The short-lived Style L, which appeared only in the 1903 catalogue, listed for $44.32 and had an orange-finished Norwegian spruce top, a maple body and neck finished in a dark mahogany

Experimental multi-soundhole steel-strings. The model on the left has interior sidewalls (like the multi-hole flat-top on page 137). The model at right is remarkably similar to some Paramount guitars made by Martin.

color, a veneered headpiece, an oval ebony fingerboard with pearl position dots, and a round soundhole decorated with inlaid woods. It could be ordered with either steel or gut strings.

STYLE L-1

The Style L-1 was a charter member of the Gibson line, appearing in 1903's debut catalogue. Until the mid twenties it was near the bottom of the line. Except for a two-year period it was offered until the late 1930s, changing from Orville Gibson's rounded guitar back to the narrower style of the 1910s, and finally to a budget flat-top model.

There was no illustration in the earliest brochure, but the guitar's description was repeated in the 1906 catalogue, and the model picture there featured a slotted headstock in the modern Gibson shape, without brand name or logo. The maple neck had an unbound ebony fingerboard that joined the body at fret 12. There were pearl position dots at frets 5, 7, 9, 12, and 15. The illustration shows 19 frets while the text specifies 21, inaugurating a tradition of occasional contradictions that would carry through Gibson's catalogues right up to the present. Another example: The L-1's body was specified to be maple, but in fact most of the pre 1925 models were made of birch.

Gibson made fundamental changes throughout its line that were reflected in the 1908–1909 Style L-1. The newer body was narrower and less rounded, and its waists were more sharply indented in a fashion that would distinguish the L series for years to come. The slotted peghead was replaced with the solid type decorated with *The Gibson* written at an angle in script. The new fingerboard was bound, and now joined the body at fret 13. (There were 19 frets in both the illustration and the accompanying text, suggesting that the earlier L-1 also had 19 frets.)

The fixed, top-mounted combination bridge/tailpiece of the 1906 model was replaced with a separate, slim wooden bridge and an unusual trapeze tailpiece to which the strings (either gut or wire) were attached with pins—another mixture of current flat-top and arch-top features. The new bridge was an application of violin construction theory, and the tailpiece, or "stringholder," was intended to reduce string breakage by eliminating the bone saddle and decreasing the angle of string breakover at the bridge. Only the Concert size was available for the Style L-1, and it listed for $62.05.

In approximately 1918 Gibson began specifying a neck of Honduras (rather than Mexican) mahogany, and fingerrest clamps of white copper rather than German silver, perhaps reflecting more of a change in marketing strategy than in materials (during World War I, patriotic pickers were unlikely to favor instruments tainted with parts of "German" origin).

The L-1 reintroduced in 1926 was a new guitar from top to bottom, a fairly conventional flat-top. *The Gibson* was written straight across the peghead rather than at an angle. The flat, amber-colored spruce top had a round hole and a glued ebony bridge with a bone saddle; gone was the pin tailpiece. The mahogany body was finished in Sheraton brown. Other details were ivoroid body binding (top and back), mahogany neck, and a 19-fret ebony fretboard again joining at fret 12 rather than 13.

The 1928 model had a stock brown sunburst finish, a fatter, heavier rosewood bridge with white pins, an adjustable truss rod, a fingerboard of rosewood rather than ebony, and multiple black and white binding on the top and back.

The 1929 L-1 had still another new bridge shape; otherwise it was the same as the 1928 model. Due to the Depression, the L-1 had changed again by 1932, becoming a still lower-budget instrument, dropping in retail price from $50 to $35 and increasing to a larger (14¾ inches wide, 19¼ inches long) body. Its shape was now squared off and flat along the bottom, somewhat resembling a Martin with a twelfth-fret neck/body joint.

The neck soon changed to a fourteenth-fret joint, the bridge was reduced in size, and a brown celluloid fingerrest was added. The peghead now said *Gibson* instead of *The Gibson.* Other features: spruce top, mahogany neck, back, and rims, offset bone saddle, and a rosewood fingerboard. By 1937 the inexpensive but remarkably good-sounding L-1 had been dropped from the line.

STYLE L-2

The L-2 of 1903 was essentially a slightly fancier L-1 with added pearl ornamentation on the peghead and three (instead of two) inlaid rings around the soundhole. There were three sizes—Standard ($62.05 list), Concert ($70.91), and Grand Concert ($79.79). The L-2 disappeared until early 1924, when it was reintroduced at a list price of $95. By early 1926 the L-2 had vanished again, this time until about late 1929.

The top of the 1929 L-2 was very slightly arched, though the guitar could still be considered a flat-top. Its design was ahead of the more rounded L-1, Nick Lucas, and L-0 in that it was the first Gibson with the fairly flat bottom rim (a slightly more bell-shaped body) that characterized the next generation of flat-tops. These L-2s have gold sparkle top and soundhole trim.

The company's literature, as always, described the shape much more poetically: "exquisitely designed with graceful outline of figure . . . suggesting the flair and charm of the dusky dark-eyed Belles of Ancient Spain." At any rate, the guitar was dropped in 1935.

STYLE L-3

The 1903 L-3 was simply a fancy L-2 with a bound fingerboard and pearl position markers both on the fingerboard and along the neck. It came in the Standard ($75.35), Concert ($88.65),

L-1 (*left*) and L-3, both circa 1918. *Music Shop/Madsen*

and Grand Concert ($101.95) sizes. The 1906 L-3 retained its distinctive ornamentation, while its extensive structural changes—body shape, neck/body joint, pickguard, bridge, tailpiece—paralleled those of the 1906 L-1. Only the Standard and Concert body sizes were listed.

The 1908 L-3 was almost identical to the L-1 except for its dots (along the side of the neck), three decorative rings, and extra body binding along the back/rim joint. It was available only in the Grand Concert size, for $88.65. Within a couple of years it was further decorated with added peghead inlay. Incidentally, the L-3 was the only Gibson with herringbone soundhole decoration. Bridges gradually changed from (1) noncompensating, non-height-adjustable to (2) compensating, nonadjustable (circa 1915), to (3) compensating, height-adjustable (circa 1921).

By 1924 the L-3 had received an internally mounted truss rod whose cover plate necessitated the omission of the extra peghead inlay. The neck was specified to be British Honduras mahogany rather than Mexican mahogany. The fingerboard was Tamatave ebony, and there was one pickguard clamp instead of two. The finish was a red mahogany sunburst, and the tailpiece's crossbar (where the strings attach) had evolved from the unusual pin type to a more conventional metal rectangle. (Strings wrapped over the top of these tailpieces until the early or mid-thirties.) The guitar's total length was 37⅝ inches. The 1928 catalogue specified the sizes for the Concert (13½ inches wide, 37½ inches long) and Grand Concert (16 inches wide, 38½ inches long) guitars. The L-3 was dropped in 1933.

STYLE L-4

The L-4 Grand Concert guitar made its debut in Catalogue H, dating it to 1911. It would become the Gibson line's senior member, though it changed many times—from a large non-cutaway arch-top with an oval soundhole (through the late 1920s), to an unusual arch-top roundhole (mid 1930s), to an f-hole (late 1930s), and finally to a cutaway (the L-4C).

The debut L-4 was larger than the L-1 or L-3, and it had rounder shoulders and an ample, bulbous body—16 inches across the lower bout. One of its notable features was the 20-fret mahogany neck, whose fingerboard had a graceful point slightly extending over the distinctive oval soundhole. Other details included a spruce top, maple body, *The Gibson* inlaid in pearl script on the ivoroid-bound peghead (with fleur-de-lis), pearl dots and side markers, bound soundhole, three decorative soundhole rings with diamond patterns, black finish, bone nut, one-piece wooden bridge, separate pin tailpiece, body binding on the top and back, and a list price of $124.10.

The 1914 to 1916 model had a standard red mahogany finish, though the ebonized black and golden orange were available on custom order. Like certain L-5 guitars, L-Jr. guitars, K-5 mandocellos, and others, L-4s had "snake head" pegheads, narrower at the top, for a year and a half or two years in the 1923–1925 period. After the late twenties the diamond pattern soundhole inlay was replaced with more conservative trim.

By 1924 the pin tailpiece was replaced with a standard trapeze, and a height-adjustable compensating bridge replaced the one-piece unit. Specifications included an Adirondack spruce top, birch body (which was said to be maple in catalogues), Gaboon ebony fingerboard, and restyled soundhole ornamentation. After about 1925 maple was used for the bodies.

In May 1932 the L-4 changed significantly. The body shape became less exaggerated, more conventional. The oval soundhole was replaced with a round one. The fingerboard's ebony was replaced with rosewood, and the little point up at the end disappeared. The tilted *The Gibson* inscription was repositioned horizontally. In 1933 or 1934 a large, elongated diamond-shaped inlay was added to the unbound peghead, and the *The Gibson* logo became simply *Gibson.*

In mid or late 1935 the L-4 was restyled again, this time changing from the odd combination of arched top and round hole to a beautiful, modern arch-top with f-holes. A new pearl fleur-de-lis graced the bound peghead, and the position dots were replaced with large, L-7 type pearl-inlaid ornaments on frets 1, 3, 5, 7, 9, 12, 15, and 17. (Note: When the L-7 went to the Advanced model and took on the wreath inlays of the L-12, the L-4 took *its* new markers from the old L-7; the 1935 L-4 and pre-Advanced L-7 are virtually indistinguishable.) The trapeze crossbar had the raised horizontal diamond that would be used on various Gibsons for decades to come. The body was increased ¼ inch in both length and width. Other specifications included maple sides and back, spruce top, rosewood fingerboard, sunburst, Grovers, and an adjustable rosewood bridge.

The 1937 L-4 was available with *either* the round soundhole or f-holes. Roundhole models from 1937 can be distinguished from 1935 or earlier roundhole L-4s by the features acquired in 1936—larger 16¼ by 20¼ inch body, trapeze crossbar diamond, and fancy inlays on the peghead and fingerboard.

In 1938 the roundhole option was dropped (f-holes were here to stay), and the L-4 returned to its style of 1936. There were no changes through 1939–1940. The 1940-1941 model had a restyled fleur-de-lis, an optional natural finish, and a modified tailpiece crossbar—shorter, thicker, and without the diamond. There were no changes through 1942.

The years 1937 and 1938 had seen the confusing death throes of the roundhole arch-top design that traced back to Orville Gibson himself. To recap, in early 1935 the L-4 had a round hole, as it had for years. In 1935 it evolved into the more modern f-hole model. Then, in 1937 only, the round hole appeared as an option. In 1938 and thereafter, only f-holes were used.

The L-75's evolution was similarly convoluted during this period. It had entered the line as an f-hole, but the 1936 edition was a roundhole—the only such arch-top remaining in the line. In 1937 it was dropped altogether, but it reappeared in another roundhole version in 1938. That was the last gasp. By 1939 the

L-75 was gone for good, and the entire Gibson line had evolved into the two modern categories: all arch-tops had f-holes, and all roundhole guitars were flat-tops.

Postwar L-4

The noncutaway spruce-top L-4 declined after the early 1950s and was gradually replaced by Florentine (sharp) cutaway versions: the sunburst L-4C and the natural finish L-4CN. Identical in shape to an ES-175, the Florentine L-4 was readily identified by its split-parallelogram fret markers. Appearing at various times both at the bottom and near the top of its class, the noncutaway L-4 joined the line in approximately 1912 and left it in 1956, making it Gibson's longest running model.

STYLE O

The 1903 Style O was very much Orville Gibson's guitar, manifesting several characteristics of his preproduction models, including an oversize paddle-shaped peghead, a wide, oval soundhole, and a large, rounded body. Available in all three sizes, the Style O could be ordered with either gut or steel strings. During the first few years of production, there was no *The Gibson* logo on the peghead.

The Style O stayed at the top of the line for 20 years. By 1906 the paddle peghead was replaced with the slotted type, the oval hole was reduced slightly, and the body's lower half was specified to be 16 inches wide. The fingerboard now had a slight point at the treble end, and the black ebonized finish was standard.

In the 1908–1909 catalogue, the Style O had a most unusual single-cutaway ledge that extended straight out from the body and turned up into a sharp Florentine point. The neck joined at fret 15, facilitating access to upper registers. The upper left-hand bout of the Grand Concert body had a mandolin-type carved scroll with a pearl dot decoration. The fingerboard was asymmetrical at the treble end, and now extended over the soundhole, the last two frets (21 and 22) being less than half the normal length. The glued pin bridge was replaced with the separate bridge and pin tailpiece arrangement.

Until about 1915 most of the Florentine Style O's had a black finish. Most of the later models were finished with Gibson's beautiful shaded mahogany red, while others were golden orange.

By 1918 the original fleur-de-lis was reduced in size and moved down to the center of the peghead. *The Gibson* was added in pearl script, the piece to which the bridge pins attached decreased in size, and a second fingerrest clamp was added. The bridge was slightly enlarged, and the neck was specified to be British Honduras mahogany. A truss rod was added circa late 1922. There were no other changes through 1923, the Style O's last year.

The bizarre and fabulous Style O was a baroque period piece from the century's first decade, and it was one of Gibson's most

Pre-1908 Style O, almost identical to the pre-1920 L-4. Note the pointed fingerboard, oval soundhole, and pin tailpiece.
Gruhn

distinctive guitars ever. The heir to the top of the line was the exquisite L-5.

STYLES O-1, O-2, AND O-3

The Style O-1 appeared only in the 1903 catalogue and differed from the Style O solely in its celluloid-bound headpiece and extra body binding on the back rim.

The O-2, one rung further up the ladder, was essentially an O-1 with an alternating pearl and ebony "rope" pattern inlaid into the body's upper rim, a pearl-inlaid bridge, and pearl-inlaid ivory bridge pins.

The O-1 is not pictured in the 1903 literature, but differences between the illustrated Style O and O-2 are apparent, including (on the O-2) a stylized peghead—pointed at the top center and lower sides, and inlaid with a Turkish star and crescent. The O-2 also had a small, diamond-shaped inlay between the last two frets.

The O-3 used special Sydney pearl in the peghead inlay and also in its full-length fingerboard ornamentation. The rope binding was green and white with fancy wood purfling.

L-0, circa 1928, with pyramid bridge. ***Music Shop/ Madsen***

L-0

The $35 L-0 appeared in late 1925 or early 1926 right at the bottom of the Gibson line. It was a respectable, if inexpensive, concert size guitar of the same dimensions, shape, and weight as the $50 L-1. It had a spruce top and maple body, and the whole guitar, including top, was finished in amber brown. It had a mahogany neck, a 19-fret ebonized fingerboard with pearl dots (joining at fret 12), a one-piece ebony pin bridge with a carved, four-sided pyramid on each end, a bone saddle, and *The Gibson* on the peghead in silver painted script.

The 1928 L-0 received several changes, including an all-mahogany body and a rosewood fingerboard. The nut and saddle were composed of an unusual material—ebony. In 1929 the L-0's pyramid bridge was replaced with a shorter piece, and extra fingerboard dots appeared at frets 3, 12, and 15. The guitar shown in 1929 literature was quite dark, though the text still specified a light amber finish.

Within a year or two the body shape changed, following the lead of 1929's L-2. The L-0's shoulders were now less rounded and the bottom was clearly flatter, whereas the original shape roughly entailed a small circle (upper bouts) over a large circle (lower bouts). The body was now more bell-shaped and slightly less pinched at the waist, much like modern Gibson flat-tops.

The L-0 remained in the line until early 1933, when the price of the L-1 was lowered from $50 to $35, making the L-0 commercially obsolete. The L-00, added in 1931, was now at the bottom of the line. The L-0 reappeared in 1936 or 1937 at a rock-bottom list of $25. It had a fourteenth-fret joint, *Gibson* instead of *The Gibson,* and a bone saddle instead of ebony. It left the line in 1941–1942 at a list price of $29. In 1929 and 1930 the L-0 was offered in a three-quarter size ($35), 12¾ inches wide, and 17¼ inches long.

L-JR.

The short-lived L-Jr. was conceived between 1918 and 1920 and was a budget model arch-top based on the design of the L-1. It had a round hole, a trapeze tailpiece, and a 19-fret fingerboard that joined at fret 13. It was discontinued in the mid-1920s.

L-5

By the early 1920s, the Style O was done for. It was beautiful in an odd sort of way, with its bizarre silhouette and Florentine cutaway, but it was clearly a relic, more akin to Gibson's guitars of the 1910s than anything else in the line. The twenties had begun to roar, and Gibson desired a hot, thoroughly modern arch-top. The Style O was something of a dinosaur. Obviously, it couldn't fill the bill.

Equally obviously, the L-5 could. Gibson called it a masterpiece, and it was, magnificent in every way. It became the company's pride and joy, an industry standard, and a milestone in American guitar evolution. Evidence suggests that it was in production by April 15, 1923 and ready for its official debut later that year. Gibson, never at a loss for words, called it The Master Line Guitar L-5 Professional Special Grand Concert Model. At $275, the L-5 was far and away the top of the line (the second most expensive guitar was the L-4, at $150). The L-5 stayed at this price through the 1920s and 1930s, and it was Gibson's paramount arch-top until the Super 400 joined in late 1934 or 1935.

Designers stake their reputations on their balancing of function and ornamentation, and some would argue that the debut L-5 was Gibson's most aesthetically perfect guitar—luxurious, pristine, elegant. While earlier Gibsons had headstocks generally like those of today—wider at the top than the bottom—the L-5 (like its companion K-5 mando-cello, introduced in late 1923 or early 1924) had a reversed peghead, narrower at the top. *The Gibson* was inlaid diagonally in pearl script, and below that was the stylized neo-classic flowerpot inlay that also decorated other members of the Master Line as well as later electric guitars such as the L-5CES and Byrdland.

Unlike most other guitars of the day, the L-5 was exclusively a steel-string, with its f-holes, elevated fingerrest, elevated fingerboard, and adjustable bridge. It was America's first modern orchestra guitar, well ahead of its time. In fact, it appeared years before the popularity of the big band music for which it was so well suited. When the L-5 was introduced, the L-4 still had the oval soundhole, and the L-3 still had a round soundhole and a high-waisted body reminiscent of its ancestors. Even at the turn of the decade the L-5 was still the only f-hole Gibson, but its gradual acceptance soon left no doubt that f-hole guitars were the arch-tops of the future.

The debut L-5 was simple in appearance, and its decorative appointments were subtle. There was a slight point at the end

1924 L-5, its label signed and dated by Lloyd Loar. Note peghead's shape and inlay. ***Gruhn***

1928 (*left*) and 1931 L-5s. Compare markers. On the 1928 model, note the fingerboard's pointed tip. ***Gruhn/Baxendale***

of the ebony fingerboard, a detail borrowed from the L-4 and the early noncutaway Style O. The peghead, fingerrest, top, and back were triple-bound in white/black/white.

Catalogue N of 1924 makes no mention of the L-5, but a couple of them appear in artist endorsement photos; these 1923 models have no pickguard binding and are thus among the very earliest L-5s and extremely rare. Oddly enough, the top-of-the-line L-5 was bound in plain white celluloid rather than the grained ivoroid used on F-5 mandolins. The fretboards on Loar-era L-5s were bound in white with a thin black border, while later ones had white/black/white binding.

The back of the peghead was black, and its lower point extended into a thin line that ran the length of the three-piece neck. The body was 16¼ inches wide and had a sunburst all over in Cremona brown (a finish introduced by Loar), with

A highly retouched catalogue illustration of a late-1935 or early-1936 L-5.

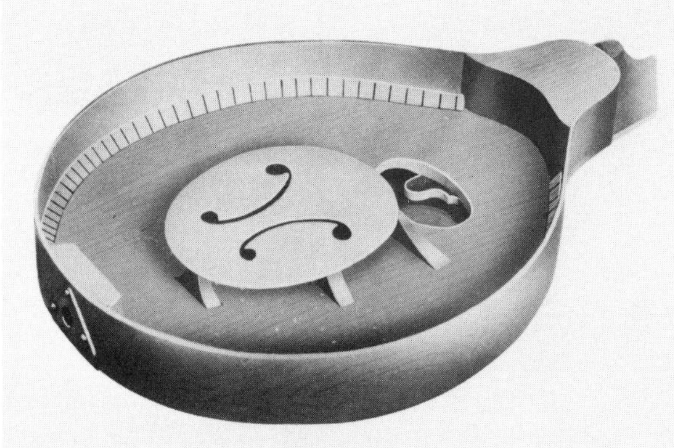

A Virzi Tone Producer mounted in a mandolin.

light patches on the maple neck, spruce top, back, lower bouts, upper bouts, and sides of the peghead. Though specified to be maple, the back was made of birch; maple was used beginning in 1924. The wooden bridge was adjustable, the steel tailpiece simple and unadorned. The L-5 was America's first guitar with *both* a 14-fret neck/body joint and an adjustable truss rod. The scale length was 24¾ inches, and there were pearl position dots at frets 5, 7, 9, 12, and 15 (beginning in the later 1920s, dots began at fret 3).

There were two labels inside the body. The "Gibson Master Model" label was used exclusively on mando-lutes and Style 5 instruments. The other label reads: "The top, back, tonebars and air chamber of this instrument were tested, tuned, and the assembled instrument tried and approved [date], Lloyd Loar, Acoustical Engineer." Loar's signature was written by hand, as was the date, model designation, and serial number. According to George Gruhn, Gibson stopped using the signature label when Loar left in late 1924 but continued using the Master Model label until 1928. The guitar's combination of f-holes, arched top, and internally mounted tone bars was at the time a departure from generally accepted construction principles, and in certain structural respects the L-5's closest relative wasn't a guitar at all, but rather its sister Master Model instrument, the F-5 mandolin.

Some of the early L-5s were fitted with a Virzi Tone Producer, a perforated interior sounding board first used in violins. The device was manufactured by the Virzi Brothers of 503 Fifth Avenue in New York City, a company for which Loar had served as consultant before his tenure at Gibson. (Loar introduced the Tone Producer to Gibson, though it was actually invented by John and Joseph Virzi, owners of the Virzi company. Their factory was in Palermo, Italy.) Small, oval, and made of wood, the Tone Producer was installed inside the body, suspended from the top directly under the bridge. According to Gibson, the Virzi Tone Producer "increases the amplitude of vibration of the sounding board and the air chamber." The device was short-lived; it disappeared after Loar's departure, and even some Loar models don't have it.

The L-5's silver-plated fittings were replaced with gold-plated hardware beginning in 1925. The neck and body were specified to join at the fifteenth fret in the 1928 and 1929 literature, though the illustrated guitars in both cases have fourteenth-fret joints.

The early L-5s had silver-plated tuning keys with mother-of-pearl buttons and gear wheels positioned above the shafts; the first post-Loar models had gold-plated tuners with wheels above the shafts; and later ones had three-on-a-plate, engraved, pearl-buttoned Waverly tuners with wheels below the shafts.

By 1930 individual Grover tuners were standard, the *The Gibson* logo had changed from diagonal to horizontal script, the neck point had given way to a straight edge, the fingerrest was lengthened, the neck was smaller and less triangular, and the position markers had changed to pearloid rectangles at frets 3,

5, 7, 9, 12, and 15 (the squared fretboard and block inlays appeared in late 1929 or early 1930).

George Gruhn reports that just before the unveiling of the Advanced models, there was a brief period when the L-5 was distinguished by pearl blocks beginning at fret 3, a neck point, and a peghead inlay that read *Gibson* rather than *The Gibson.*

The enlarged Advanced L-5 of 1935 was a substantial alteration, with five-ply black/white binding on the peghead, fretboard, top rim, and fingerrest; and three-ply binding on the back rim. There were extra rectangular markers at frets 1 and 17, and the tailpiece was beefier, with an engraved *L-5* in script. The f-holes had been widened, the new Advanced body was 17 by 21 inches, and the scale length was increased to 25 inches. Other details included gold Grovers. In 1937 the L-5 received its gold and silver tailpiece, like the 1980s version but with three engraved diamonds. There were no changes in 1938.

The 1939–1940 model had today's tailpiece (without diamonds), Kluson "Seal-Fast" tuners, and the Vari-Tone control. The Vari-Tone was a string tension adjustment mechanism identified by a small hole in the bottom center of the tailpiece. It was described in a catalogue paragraph that neglected to mention what it did, where it was, or how it worked (anticipating by decades the advertising copy of electronic effects manufacturers). It was, however, specified to be "amazing."

Also in 1939 the single-cutaway body—known as the "Premiere," or "Premier"—and the natural blonde finish became available on both the Super 400 and L-5. The L-5 Premiere, which later became the L-5C ("C" stood for cutaway), listed for $290, $15 over the noncutaway.

The early L-5 was not a commercial bonanza for Gibson, be-

An early-1940s experimental Gibson with a see-through body. *Umanov/Peden*

Compare the early 1940s (*left*) and 1948 L-5. Note differences in tuners, bridges, and tailpieces. The early-1940s model has a rosewood fingerboard because of wartime ebony shortages. *Wagener/Beaty*

L-5CES, circa 1952. In about late 1960 the L-5's cutaway went from rounded to the sharp Florentine, where it stayed at least through 1968, and then back to round again, where it remained all through the 1970s. Compare this L-5 to the two later models shown in color photos 82 and 83. Note tuners, truss rod covers, pickups, cutaways, bridges, knobs, and tailpieces. *Wooden/Goodman*

cause its introduction preceded the demand for orchestra style instruments. But its influence on American guitar making was ultimately profound, and during the early and mid-thirties the L-5 became both a model and a standard of excellence for other eminent guitar makers, including Epiphone, Stromberg, and D'Angelico.

Postwar L-5, L-5CES. The noncutaway L-5 sold in very small numbers through the 1950s and was finally dropped after 1958 (see shipping charts). A total of 450 acoustic *cutaway* L-5s were shipped from 1948 to 1960—253 sunbursts, 197 in natural. After a general decline of Gibson acoustic cutaway arch-tops, the L-5 remained one of only a few such models in 1980.

The L-5CES Electric Spanish joined the line in 1951 and went to a tune-o-matic bridge and humbuckings by 1957. Though made in small quantities it remains in the line as of this writing.

SUPER 400

Gibson's 1935 price lists included several new models that reflected the increasing popularity of arch-tops. The L-30 and L-37 were added at the bottom of the line, the Super 400 at the top. For more than a decade the elegant L-5 had been the company's pre-eminent carved-top, but now it was time to surpass even that masterpiece, and the company went all-out in designing the grand slam: the Super 400, priced at $400 (with case).

The Super 400 was literally and figuratively in a class by itself, the Super category, and along with the Epiphone Emperor and certain D'Angelicos and Strombergs it became a 6-string status symbol. The Super 400 was made of Gibson's choicest figured maple. The peghead was larger than that of any previous Gibson and was ornamented with a new inlay (the split vertical diamond) and an enlarged, squared-off truss rod cover. The fingerboard had diagonally split rectangular markers and was pointed at the treble end, a feature which at the time was found on only one other Gibson guitar, the L-5.

The compensating bridge had a triangle inlay at either end, pointing inward. The heavy tailpiece had a wide crossbar with small engraved diamonds, plus *Super 400* enclosed in a block that was pointed at both ends. The tailpiece's rear section had

L-5 CT, often nicknamed the "George Gobel" model. The body is 2 $\frac{7}{16}$ inches thick, thinner than a stock L-5 but not as shallow as the thin-line models. Originally an acoustic guitar, it was often special ordered with humbuckings. Only 43 were made, from 1959 to 1961. Factory red finish. *Swift Music/Jim Colclasure*

a Y-shaped centerpiece. All metal parts were gold plated, and the tuning keys were engraved, open-back Grovers.

The 1938 catalogue specified gold-plated Grover DeLuxe tuners with terraced, or "stairstep," buttons. In 1939 the tailpiece changed from a sharp-cornered Y to a rounded Y, and the crossbar's *Super 400* engraving was now enclosed in a flat-sided rectangle without points. The new tailpiece featured the Vari-Tone control (see the L-5), and extra binding appeared throughout. A natural finish was now offered in addition to the Cremona brown sunburst, and the short-lived Grover DeLuxes were replaced with "butterfly" Kluson Seal-Fast tuners. The 1939 catalogue showed a back view revealing a black-finished rear peghead with a large diamond ornament. The cutaway Premiere body (see L-5) was first offered in 1938 or 1939 for an

1948 Super 300. *Wagener/Beaty*

The upper bout width on the Super 400 changed from 12½ inches (*left* and *center*) to 13.5 inches (*right*) in 1937 or 1938; and the f-holes were increased in length from 6.25 inches to 7.75 inches. The tailpiece changed from a hinged type to a one-piece design. Note the highly figured maple back and rear peghead inlay. Compare f-holes and tailpieces. The blonde Super 400 on the right has an added pickup.

Walecki

Charley's/Crump

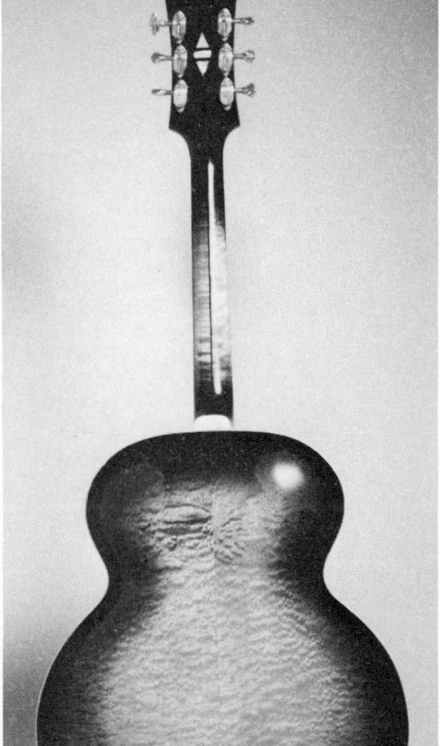

Wagener/Beaty

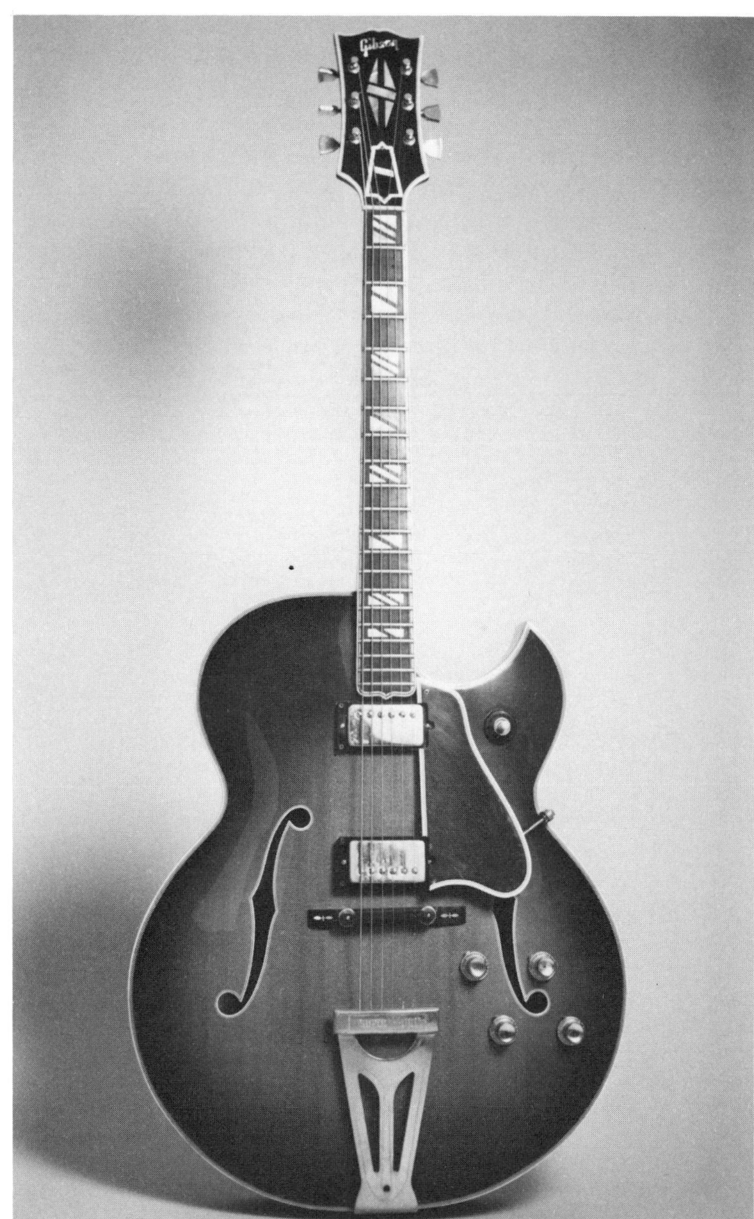

1960 Super 400CES, Florentine cutaway. On both acoustic and electric 400s, the most obvious identifiers are the large peghead, split diamond peghead inlay, squared-bell truss rod cover, split rectangle markers, and tailpiece. The rear of the peghead has a smaller split diamond inlay, and the neck heel is engraved with *Super 400*. *Charley's/Crump.*

extra $25. Such models are often pictured with a decorative ribbon encircling the body at the waist. This grand, new guitar merited comparably grand hyperbole, and Gibson, never one to pull a punch, proclaimed, "It is worth any sacrifice made for its possession."

Postwar Super 400, Super 400CES

After 1949, sales sagged to a trickle and the noncutaway 400 was dropped after only three were sold in 1955. The cutaway acoustic remains in the line as of this writing. The electric ver-

Mid-1960s Super 400C. ***Wagener/Beaty***

sions, CES and CESN, first appeared on the shipping lists in 1951 and 1952, respectively, and sold in small but, considering the price, sufficient numbers all through the 1950s, 1960s, and 1970s, when they remained the top Gibsons in their class (certain custom-order guitars, like the Citation, are more expensive).

The Alnico 5 single-coil pickups changed to humbuckings by late 1957. Like the L-5, the Super 400CES went from rounded cutaway (up through late 1960) to Florentine (early 1961, through 1968 or 1969) and back to rounded, where it remains as of this writing. Production is limited; only 130 were shipped from 1971 to 1978.

Super 400CES, from left: 1954, 1958, and 1979. Compare tailpiece engravings (none on the 1979), pegheads (note the center peak), pickups, bridges, saddles, and knobs; also note the small holes in the earlier tailpieces. The earliest electric 400s had standard Gibson single-coil pickups. They were replaced by the Alnico type (*above left*) around 1953. ***Wagener/Beaty***

JUMBO AND JUMBO 35

In 1934 Gibson brought out the Jumbo, the first in a series of guitars that reflected the growing popularity of vocal duos, trios, and small combos in need of booming accompaniment. The Jumbo had a new shape—boxy, less pinched at the waist—and a new size as well. It was 16 inches wide, equaling the Grand Auditoriums and exceeding the other Gibson flat-tops (except Hawaiian models) by 1¼ inches.

The Jumbo was 20¼ inches long (an extra 1 inch) and 4½ inches deep (an extra ½ inch), with a *Gibson* peghead logo in script. In 1936 the guitar was somewhat less fancy, and it was given a new name—Jumbo 35—to help distinguish it from the expensive new Advanced Jumbo, a rosewood guitar. The Jumbo 35 also had a new finish: red mahogany on the back, rims, and neck; and brown sunburst on top.

In 1939 two small white dots appeared on the bridge in line with the pins; the top was specified to be natural blonde, the body mahogany brown. In 1941 both the sunburst and blonde finishes were available. The Jumbo 35 was not reinstated after World War II.

ADVANCED JUMBO

The Advanced Jumbo followed the Jumbo by a little less than two years. The pair now comprised Gibson's new Jumbo class of enlarged flat-tops. The $80, late-1936 Advanced model was distinguished from the mahogany Jumbo by its rosewood body and three-piece inlays (a diamond bordered by arrowheads) on the peghead and fingerboard. It was discontinued in 1940.

It was an especially fine instrument. As collector George Gruhn said: "The Advanced Jumbo was probably the best flat-top in Gibson's entire history, a wonderful guitar. Whereas the early J-200s had a lot of handwork and varied from guitar to guitar, the Advanced Jumbos were well-made and consistent."

J-200 co-designer and cowboy star Ray Whitley. ***Guitar Player***

SUPER JUMBO, SUPER JUMBO 200, AND J-200

By late 1937 the Jumbo 35 and Advanced Jumbo (and their predecessor, 1934's Jumbo) had revealed the existence of a strong market for the oversized steel-string. It was now time for the coup de grace, the Super 400 of flat-tops. Ray Whitley was a cowboy screen star at the time, and while at Madison Square Garden for a rodeo gig he suggested to Gibson's Guy Hart that the firm build a guitar especially suited to country music, something big and bassy. Later a guest in Kalamazoo, Ray detailed his suggestions to company engineers: enlarge the body—especially the lower bouts—make it deeper, relocate the bridge, and increase the scale length. Gibson went to work that day and soon produced the forerunner of the J-200, a sunburst rosewood jumbo with a 16⅞ by 21 by 4½ inch body, nine-ply binding, a narrow L-5 neck, custom pearl inlay, and a long 26-inch scale.

The late-1937 (or early-1938) Super Jumbo production model had a pickguard nearly twice as long as any previous design; it was Gibson's first decorated pickguard, bearing the flower motif that remains to this day on J-200s. The ebony combination bridge/tailpiece was another Texas-sized feature that made all predecessors look petite by comparison. It had decorative cutouts, plus a row of height-adjustable bearings (one for each string) just ahead of the slightly arching row of bridge pins.

The treble end of the 20-fret fingerboard had the center point that Gibson reserved for its fanciest models. With all of its ya-hoo ornamentation, the Super Jumbo was a cowpoke's Cadillac. Gibson proclaimed it "King of the Flat-Top Guitars."

In 1939 the company added a new model, sort of a budget Super Jumbo. To distinguish the two, the Super Jumbo became the $200 Super Jumbo 200, and the new $100 guitar was christened Super Jumbo 100. The Super Jumbo 200, soon to be called the SJ-200, had a 17 by 21 by 4½ inch body—even larger than the previous year's Super Jumbo. Where the 1938 catalogue specified multi-ply binding on the top rim, the 1939–1940 catalogue listed it for the top, back, fingerboard, and peghead. The 1939–1940 model was also listed as having marquetry inlays on the back. During the late 1930s, Montgomery Ward distributed Gibson-made budget Ray Whitley models with the Recording King brand name.

The first Super Jumbo (SJ) 200. *Country Music Hall of Fame*

Rosewood J-200 with original horseshoe fingerboard inlay. Prewar J-200s are rosewood, while postwar models are maple. Few or none were made during the war. Note the tailpiece's two pearl dots, and split-bar inlays on either side of the pins. *Gruhn*

The 1941 Super Jumbo 200 switched to a rosewood fingerboard, pearloid button keys, and a standard saddle instead of the individual bearings. It was also specified to have "a new construction, bracing, and engineering feature designed to bring out a more powerful, booming tone." This was a cylindrical, internally mounted tone bar, an addition of dubious acoustical merit that didn't last long. Very soon after World War II, the rosewood body was replaced with maple, which remained standard. The names Super Jumbo 200 and J-200 were used interchangeably at least as early as 1950.

There were several versions of the J-200's oversized bridge. Early units were ebony with six individual height-adjustable saddles. In approximately 1940 the design changed to the rosewood "moustache" bridge with a cutout, or open, portion on either end and a straight bone saddle. Tune-o-matics appeared in the early 1960s on new bridges with no cutouts. Adjustable wood saddles were used near the end of the decade, and in 1970 a restyled bridge with sharp corners and no cutouts replaced the rounded, bulbous type.

As a maker of popular western guitars, Gibson had lagged behind Martin for some time, but with the jumbo models they, like Ray Whitley, were back in the saddle again.

JUMBO 55 AND J-55

The $55 Jumbo 55 joined in 1938 or 1939 and was essentially a fancy version of the $37.50 Jumbo 35. It had the same dimensions, mahogany body, and spruce top. However, the 55's fingerboard was "genuine polished coffeewood." The bridge, also coffeewood, was a narrow version of the cutout type found on the 1939–1940 Super Jumbo 200 and Super Jumbo 100, though it had a standard bone saddle and two pearl dots. The sides of the peghead were carved into stairsteps (see Super Jumbo 100), a feature abandoned in 1941 in favor of the standard Gibson shape. Also in 1941 the bridge was replaced with the three-dot rosewood type found on the 1941 Super Jumbo 100, and rosewood was used for the fingerboard. There were no changes in 1942.

The Jumbo 55 was dropped after the war, but the name J-55 was revived in 1972 for an all-new steel-string which at $385 was priced between the J-50 and the Blue Ridge. Its unusual mahogany back had a pronounced arch. Production peaked in 1973–1974, and the model is still in the line as of this writing.

SUPER JUMBO 100

In 1939 a second Super Jumbo guitar was added, the $100 mahogany Super Jumbo 100. Its most distinctive feature was its peghead, which was carved in stairsteps on the sides. The individually adjustable ebony bridge was very similar to the one on the 1940 Super Jumbo 200. In 1941 the short-lived stairstep peghead gave way to another distinctive though more conventional piece, whose lower points were quite wide. The cutout, individually adjustable ebony bridge was replaced by a solid piece of terraced rosewood with a straight saddle and three pearl dots. The butterfly tuning keys were replaced with oval buttons. There were no changes in 1942. Dropped after World War II, it was reintroduced on a limited basis in the early 1970s.

PREWAR HAWAIIAN AND GUT-STRING MODELS

In about 1918 Gibson began informing customers that along with the standard instrument, they could also receive "complete Hawaiian steel guitar equipment" free of charge. This gear was simply an elevated nut that raised the strings, making the instrument suitable for lap-style playing and providing the lucky buyer with two instruments in one.

Gibson advised in 1927 that the L-0, L-1, and Nick Lucas Special were particularly good for Hawaiian style. In the following year, four "Hawaiian Specials" were offered; these were the Lucas, L-0, L-1, and L-2, all equipped with the high nut. In January of 1929 a client could purchase any member of the guitar line in a Hawaiian version; these were indicated by L-0H, L-1H, and so on.

In March 1934 a pair of Roy Smeck Hawaiian guitars (named after the phenomenally popular Wizard of the Strings) joined the Nick Lucas in Gibson's Artist line. One was the $100 Radio Grande, a bell-shaped flat-top that, like the debut J-200 of four years later, was 4½ inches deep. The earliest Radio Grande was distinguished from the $50 mahogany Roy Smeck Stage DeLuxe by its rosewood body, fancy fingerboard inlays, fingerboard binding, and natural-finish top.

In 1936 the $27.50 HG-00 (twelfth-fret joint) was described as a modification of the L-00 (which had a fourteenth-fret joint). In that year there were only three Hawaiian guitars, the HG-00 and the two Smeck models. Also in 1936 the Radio Grande switched to a sunburst, and the following year it was dropped. In 1938 Gibson began referring to the Roy Smeck Stage DeLuxe as simply the Roy Smeck.

Prior to the development of modern strings, guitars were strung with sheep intestines or other similarly unsavory materials. While the very earliest Gibsons could be ordered with either gut or wire strings, the company did not begin offering what we now consider classical guitars until 1937 or 1938.

The 1938 catalogue announced two gut-string models, the $85 rosewood GS-85 and the $35 mahogany GS-35. Both remained in the line through 1942.

NICK LUCAS

Among Gibson's many successful marketing tools were its Artist guitars, instruments ostensibly developed in cooperation with, and named after, various famous guitar players. The first of these was an extra-deep flat-top named after the giant of late-twenties radio guitarists and composer of "Tiptoe Through The Tulips," Nick Lucas, The Crooning Troubador. The Nick Lucas, also known as the Nick Lucas Special, was introduced in early 1928 and was sort of a mini J-200 in shape. Costing $125, it was by far Gibson's nicest flat-top. (In fact, the *only* other true flat-tops were the L-0 and L-1.) It had a spruce top, ma-

Super Jumbo 100, circa 1939. Note individual height-adjustable saddles and carved stairstep peghead. It is sometimes confused with Gibson's SJ (or Southern Jumbo, or Southerner Jumbo), a mahogany flat-top with parallelogram markers. *Wooden/Goodman*

Nick Lucas with his original Gibson Nick Lucas model. *Nick Lucas/Guitar Player*

hogany body and neck, brown mahogany sunburst finish, rosewood fingerboard, a large rosewood bridge with a carved pyramid at either end, bone saddle, white pins, and white/black ivoroid binding on the top, back, and neck. The neck joined at fret 12, and the fingerboard featured fancy position markers.

In 1933 the neck joined at fret 13. The body was specified to be 14¾ inches wide and 19¼ inches long, was rosewood rather than mahogany, and had an odd combination of flat top with a raised fingerboard, a trapeze tailpiece, and an unglued bridge—features usually found on arch-tops. The fingerboard inlays were enlarged, resembling those of the new L-7, and the guitar had by this time received a brown celluloid fingerrest. The following year, the price dropped to $90 and the wood was changed again, this time to maple. The maple Lucas models have 14-fret necks. The bridge was reduced to a simple rectangle without pyramids, and the extra-deep body was specified to be 4½ inches deep.

The Nick Lucas was manufactured until 1938. Some of the last models, which did not appear in catalogues, went back to mahogany bodies. The maple-body Lucas guitars are not only superior to the other versions, but they're also certainly among Gibson's very best flat-tops ever.

L-00

The black flat-top L-00 was introduced in mid 1931. At $25 it was Gibson's lowest priced guitar, very similar to the $35 L-0. In 1933–1934 the neck changed from a twelfth- to a fourteenth-fret joint. The top was now shaded brown, the back and sides a dark mahogany red. A brown celluloid fingerrest was added, and the *The Gibson* peghead logo that had characterized the earliest L-00s was changed to *Gibson*. The body was specified

1935 Gibsons, Grossman catalogue.

GROSSMAN MUSIC CO.
KLEARTONE
CLEVELAND, OHIO
Gibson
WORLD'S FINEST GUITARS
Here is one of the biggest reasons for the famous Gibson tone and volume—a piece of carefully selected and seasoned wood is carved and graduated into a top or back. No heating, soaking, or pressing—that is why Gibson instruments improve with age.
Style
L-75
$75.00
Style
L-10
$150.00
Style
L-4
$100.00

L-75, L-10, and L-4 in Grossman's 1935 brochure. Note the L-75's round hole and arched top; the L-10's peghead, markers, and body trim; and the L-4's peghead and markers. ***Gruhn***

to be 14¾ inches wide and 19¼ inches long, like the L-C and L-1. Except for slight price increases the L-00 stayed the same through 1940, and the following year the natural finish became optional. The guitar was discontinued during the war.

L-10

In 1930 there was a large price spread between the senior roundhole arch-top—the $100 L-4—and the new $275 L-5 f-hole arch-top. If you wanted an f-hole guitar and couldn't scrape up 275 bucks, you were out of luck. This was clearly an intolerable situation, and in mid 1931 Gibson introduced the black, $175 L-10 to fill the gap.

The L-10 was spiffed up considerably in 1934 with a bound peghead heavily inlaid with pearl, and a bound fingerrest. The most distinctive new features were the fingerboard inlays, enclosed in rectangular pearl borders. (The similarly ornamented early-thirties L-12 can be distinguished by its red mahogany sunburst and gold tuners.) By 1934, the *The Gibson* peghead logo that had distinguished the earlier L-10s had changed to *Gibson.*

By mid 1935 the L-10's ornamentation had again changed substantially, now featuring black and white checker binding on the top rim. The fingerboard markers were also different: split diamonds replaced the rectangle-enclosed inlays, and markers were added to frets 1 and 17. The body was increased from 16 by 20 inches to 17 by 21 inches. The peghead inlay was less ornate, and the standard finish was now red mahogany sunburst. The trapeze tailpiece's flat rectangular crossbar was replaced with a fancier version—pointed at the ends and featuring a raised diamond pattern. In 1937 the trapeze's thin tubular rods were replaced by a heavy flat plate perforated with

On this especially beautiful 1934 L-10, note the fingerboard markers. *Gruhn*

various designs. (Compare these differences to those between the 1936 and 1937 L-12s.) There were no changes in 1938.

The L-10 was a groundbreaker of sorts, the first newcomer to the $100-and-up category since late 1924, and it opened the door for several new arch-tops. Within three years after the L-10's appearance, the arch-top line had nearly doubled, supplemented by the L-50, L-75, L-7, and L-12. But by 1938 the growing popularity of guitars on either side of the L-10 (the $125 L-7 and the $175 L-12) rendered it commercially obsolete, and it was dropped by 1939.

L-12

The year 1932 was a big one for Gibson. The L-10 had been the first expensive newcomer in years, and it nearly evened up the composition of the line: five flat-tops (Nick Lucas, L-00, L-0, L-1, L-2) and four carved-tops (L-3, L-4, L-10, L-5). Late 1932 tipped the scales. Three more arch-tops were added: the L-12, L-50, and L-75.

The L-12 was like the L-10 (which it eventually helped replace) in that it was a high-quality instrument for serious buyers not quite ready to take the L-5's $275 plunge. The L-12 listed at $200, between the $150 L-10 and $275 L-5. It dropped to $175 in 1934.

The L-12 was similar to the L-10—too similar for both of them to remain in the line. The L-12 even had the L-10's rectangle-enclosed inlays and peghead ornamentation. It was distinguished from the L-10 by gold-plated (rather than nickel-plated) tuners with genuine mother-of-pearl buttons, and a red mahogany sunburst instead of an ebony finish, but that was it, that and the price tag.

Near right: L-10, circa 1938. Note checkered top binding, split diamond markers, and perforated tailpiece. *Far right:* Advanced L-12, circa 1938. With its increased body size and scale length of 25 inches, the Advanced Series represented a completely new design. The initial Advanced L-12 premiered the classic split-parallelogram markers later used on the ES-350, ES-175, ES-345, and others. *Wagener/Beaty*

During 1935 the L-12, like the L-10, changed substantially. The new one had an Advanced, 17 by 21 inch body, brown sunburst, twin-parallelogram fingerboard inlays, extra markers at frets 1 and 17, and a slightly fancier trapeze with a raised, twin-parallelogram motif. A crisp, no-nonsense peghead inlay (see photo, page 126) replaced the earlier, more ornate decoration. The old white binding was replaced with white/black/white on the peghead, fingerrest, and top edge.

In 1937 the trapeze's slim rods were replaced by a single flat plate with holes in various designs. The price went up to $187.50. A new peghead ornament was designed by 1942, similar to the inlay used years later on the ES-335, ES-175, and several others. Also in 1942 the fingerrest binding returned to a single white layer.

The postwar L-12 and L-12C (essentially gold-plated L-7s) sold poorly, especially after 1948. Counting both models, only 87 were shipped between 1949 and 1955. The L-12C was dropped after 1950, the L-12 after 1955.

L-7

The success of the L-10 and L-12 proved that there was a market for the upper/middle-class arch-top, and Gibson specialized further with 1934's addition of the $125 L-7, priced between the $100 L-4 and the $150 L-10. Since the L-4 was at that time a roundhole guitar, the L-7 became Gibson's lowest priced Grand Auditorium f-hole, with the same dimensions and general construction as the L-5, L-12, and L-10 (the L-75 and L-50 still had 19¼-inch long bodies).

The brown sunburst L-7 was an esteemed addition to the line, essentially a slightly less fancy version of the ebony-finished L-10. Like the L-10, the L-7 had a maple body with a spruce top, mahogany neck, and rosewood fingerboard. The L-7's peghead sported a generous fleur-de-lis, and each fingerboard marker had its own design, though there were no rectangular borders such as those that set apart the L-10 and L-12. (The pattern had been used on certain Lucas models and TB-2 tenor banjos.) Like those two companions, the L-7 remained unchanged through 1935, the year in which Gibson officially began to set apart its four-member class of Advanced Carved-Tops (L-7, L-10, L-12, L-5).

In late 1935 things got confusing. The L-12 and L-10 dropped their fingerboard rectangles, and the L-7 added them (at frets 1, 3, 5, 7, 9, 12, 15, and 17). Like the L-10, the L-7 changed to a pointed diamond-pattern trapeze bar and a larger 17 by 21 inch body. The L-7's new peghead inlay also resembled those of the 1934–1935 L-10 and L-12.

In 1937 the cylindrical rods of the L-7's tailpiece were replaced by flat planks, and the pointed crossbar was replaced by a rounded version. In 1939 a natural finish became available. The 1939 model remained superficially unchanged at least through 1940, but by 1942 the rectangular markers were replaced with split parallelograms (like the L-12's), the peghead inlay was reduced, and the tailpiece crossbar was now pointed again.

1948 L-12 Premiere (cutaway), also called L-12P. *Wagener/Beaty*

1935 L-7 with 16-inch (pre-Advanced) body. Note fleur-de-lis peghead inlay. *Wagener/Beaty*

1954 L-7C. From 1961 to 1972, the model's last year, 702 L-7Cs were made, all sunbursts. *Wagener/Beaty*

1948 L-7. Note the parallelogram motif in inlays and on raised tailpiece markers. *Wagener/Beaty*

L-50

The $50 L-50 was a new idea in Gibson guitars for 1932: a budget carved-top. It was an odd model in that it had an arched top with a round hole and a stubby trapeze tailpiece, and the short (17½-inch) body was flat bottomed and bell-like. In 1935 it became an f-hole, and its 17½-inch body increased in length to 19¼ inches, making it less squatty and necessitating a longer trapeze. The inlaid pickguard was replaced with an elevated fingerrest. (There are some long-body roundhole models.)

In 1936 the L-50's body changed from the slope-shouldered western shape to the larger Grand Auditorium body, 20¼ inches long, 16¼ inches wide, more rounded, and less bell-like. The tailpiece now had a raised diamond, the standard finish was brown sunburst, and Grovers were specified. (The L-75 at this time made an odd change from an L-50 type f-hole to a Grand Auditorium sized roundhole. The L-4, however, moved in the opposite direction, changing from the 16 by 20 inch Grand Auditorium roundhole to the Grand Auditorium in an f-hole guitar.) In 1938 the ebony adjustable bridge was replaced with one of rosewood.

Postwar L-50

The 1952 catalogue's L-50 had the old peghead and script logo (the catalogue photo was at least a couple of years out of date), long pickguard flush with the upper rim, and trapezoidal markers unlike its dot-neck predecessors. In the mid-fifties and thereafter it had a slightly shorter pickguard and the current logo and peghead.

Late 1935–1939 style L-7, Advanced body, accessory pickup; with EH-150 amp.

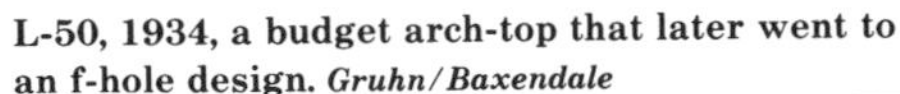

L-50, 1934, a budget arch-top that later went to an f-hole design. *Gruhn/Baxendale*

Wartime L-50, 16-inch body, script logo. The wooden tailpiece crossbar reflected wartime restrictions on metal. *Wagener/Beaty*

1959 L-50. *Wagener/Beaty*

The postwar L-50 sold very well until 1954 or so, but then its sales dropped substantially. Gibson discontinued most of its *noncutaway* acoustic arch-top Spanish guitars over a three-year period: the L-12 and Super 400 in 1955, the L-4 and L-7 in 1956, and the S-300 and L-5 in 1958. Once the pride of the Gibson line, the noncutaway arch-top class was represented for the next ten years only by the budget-priced L-50 and its companion L-48. They appeared in the October 1966 price lists. A year later they were officially discontinued, though remaining stocks were shipped through 1970.

L-75

The L-75 joined the line in 1932, along with a pair of other newcomers: the L-50 and L-12. The f-hole L-75 was half of a two-guitar experiment with white pearloid fingerboards and peghead veneers (the other guitar was the roundhole L-C, or Century). It was an ornamentation that had met with some success on various banjos, but on a guitar it was a radical decoration, making the instrument immediately recognizable from anywhere in a concert hall. The fingerboard markers were mother of pearl designs inlaid in rosewood rectangles. The early L-75 had the squat shape (17½ inches long) and stubby tailpiece of the 1933–1934 L-50, and cost $75. The white fingerboard and peghead did not last long, until 1934 at the latest. The late-1934 L-75 was a new guitar, longer (19¼ inches) and less squat, with a standard trapeze and a conventional rosewood fingerboard with pearl dots. With the white fingerboard

Gibson L-48, a budget arch-top. *Music Shop/Madsen*

ELECTRIC INSTRUMENTS
HAWAIIAN and SPANISH GUITARS
MANDOLINS — BANJOS

EH-150 lap steel and amp. Early Gibson amps were manufactured by Lyon & Healy. *Gruhn*

gone and with the mid-1930s L-50 metamorphosing into an f-hole, it became apparent that the L-50 and L-75 were too similar. The L-75 de-evolved to a roundhole arch-top in mid or late 1935, disappeared in 1937, was resurrected the following year as another roundhole arch-top, and was dropped by 1939. For details, see the end of the discussion of the prewar L-4, page 108.

L-C

In 1932 the concentrated effort to enlarge the consumer's available options entailed the addition of the arch-top L-75, with a white pearloid fingerboard and peghead. The L-C, or Century model, was introduced the following year as a similarly ornamented flat-top companion. It was slightly more successful in that it retained the white decoration during its entire five- or six-year tenure.

The $50 L-C was shaped like an L-1 but made of curly maple rather than mahogany, with a sunburst on the top, back, and rims rather than on the top only. It had extra body binding. Rather than a standard dot neck it had a white pearloid fingerboard with rectangular rosewood markers inlaid with pearl. The earliest L-Cs, made for a year or so, had 12-fret fingerboards and no truss rod adjustments; the 14-fret versions do have rod adjustments.

L-30

In late 1935 Gibson expanded its arch-top line even further, ostensibly adding two guitars lower in price than the L-50 and L-75, which were only three years old themselves. But rather than being truly new models, the L-30 and L-37 were more the descendants of the mid-thirties L-50 and L-75, respectively, which had evolved to the enlarged Grand Auditorium body.

The black L-30 had the same 14¾ by 19¼ inch body as the earlier, red mahogany-colored L-50, as well as the same neck, f-holes, fingerboard dots, and tailpiece. The L-30 was bound only on the top, however, and cost $30 rather than $50. In 1936 a brown mahogany sunburst became standard, and binding was added to the back rim. Two years later the ebony bridge was replaced with a rosewood unit. There were no changes in the L-30 through 1942.

EH-185, circa 1941. *Lira*

L-37, L-47, AND L-48

In some respects the late-1935 L-37 was to the L-30 what the 1934–1935 L-75 had been to the L-50—same body shape, different finish; all four instruments were originally small-bodied arch-tops. At first the $37.50 L-37 differed from the black $30 L-30 only in its red mahogany sunburst and added back rim binding. In 1937 the L-37's price increased to $40, and brown sunburst became standard. In 1938 a rosewood bridge replaced the ebony piece, paralleling the evolution of the L-30. In the following year the L-37 was billed as a smaller version of the L-50, which in 1936 had evolved to a Grand Auditorium guitar.

In 1941 the L-37 disappeared and the slot between the L-30

and L-50 was filled by the new L-47 arch-top f-hole guitar. It was the same size as the L-30 and L-37, but it was distinguished by its dark shell binding on the top and back rims. The L-47 was available in either natural or sunburst, and effective May 20, 1941, it listed at $50 ($5 extra for the natural finish); the price went up $2.50 in 1942. It was discontinued after World War II, effectively replaced by the L-48.

The noncutaway dot-neck L-48, "within reach of every student," was a companion to the L-50 and Gibson's lowest-priced arch-top guitar. Through the early 1950s it had a spruce top and mahogany back. By the mid-fifties the back was maple and the top was specified as laminated, a most unusual feature for a Gibson arch-top, and part of the reason the guitar could be sold for so little, only $97.50 in 1954. In the late 1950s the L-48 was specified to have a very unusual combination of laminated mahogany top, mahogany rims, and laminated maple back. This construction was maintained through 1966. Shortly after that the L-48 was dropped. (See L-50 for additional details.)

Charlie Christian; note "Charlie Christian" pickup. The guitar is a rare ES-250, with a Super 400 tailpiece. ***Duncan P. Scheidt***

PREWAR ELECTRIC GUITARS

Guitar companies, even distinguished ones, act like kids sometimes. If one expresses an idea, another is likely to squawk, "Oh yeah? Well, I *thought* of it first!" If all the people who claimed to have invented the electric guitar were placed end to end, the line would stretch from Orange County to Kalamazoo. Though Gibson later claimed the electric guitar among its many firsts, there were no electric models in the line until four or five years after Dobro (later National Dobro) and Rickenbacker had introduced electrics on a commercial scale. Lloyd Loar had invented an upright electric bass way back in the 1920s, so Gibson engineers were certainly aware of electric instruments, and there were some very early prototypes, but the catalogues through 1935 made no mention of commercial electric models.

A flier dated January 17, 1936, announced the Gibson Electric Hawaiian guitar (there was no other model name or number). This 6-string lap steel had a 13½-inch long maple body bound on the top edge, 29 fret markers, one cobalt-magnet straight bar pickup, tone and volume knobs (one on either side of the pickup), a sunburst finish, maple neck, and a bound rosewood fingerboard.

The matching EH-150 four-stage, six-tube amp was a boxy, 15-watt unit with bump protectors on its squared corners. It was covered with "aeroplane" cloth and housed a 10-inch High Fidelity Ultrasonic Reproducer, also known as a speaker. The amp's removable rear panel was fastened with luggage clasps. The guitar/amp outfit cost $150 ($5 extra with the 7-string guitar). The lap steel was quickly dubbed the EH (Electric Hawaiian)-150. A lesser Hawaiian guitar/amp set, the $100 EH-100, followed immediately. The lap steel was black, had only a volume control, and was available in 6-string ($44) and 7-string ($49) models.

The 1936 catalogue's big news was the arch-top ES (Electric Spanish)-150, Gibson's first electric Spanish guitar. In a way,

The Gibson ES-150 was the first production electric Spanish model to be offered by a long established industry leader and is thus one of the most important American guitars ever made, introduced in 1936. It featured a "Charlie Christian" bar pickup designed by Walt Fuller, a spruce top with X bracing, a maple body, and a one-piece mahogany neck (quite triangular in cross section). Note the pickup's three adjustment screws. In 1940 a more conventional rectangular pickup replaced the original unit. In about late 1945 the 16¼-inch wide L-50 type body was replaced with the Advanced 17-inch type, and the fingerboard changed from 19 to 20 frets. Trapezoid markers replaced the dots in about 1951. ***Robt. Dalley***

its impact was like that of Gibson's first solidbody of 16 years later, the Les Paul, in that Gibson was so big, so esteemed, and so traditional that it helped legitimize any field it entered. At 16¼ by 20¼ inches, the ES-150's maple body was a Grand Auditorium of the pre 1935 size. The single pickup—later nicknamed the Charlie Christian—was single-bound with ivoroid, pointed at both ends, and featured a chromed bar polepiece and an internal height adjustment mechanism with three screws (in a triangular configuration) that protruded through the spruce top. Oddly enough, the early 150s had *flat* backs.

In 1938, the maple, $150 ES-250 electric Spanish guitar was added. This model had the 17-inch wide Advanced body (like the L-5 and others), the rare, carved stairstep peghead like the Super Jumbo 100 of that year, block inlays, Charlie Christian pickup, a compensating saddle, and fancy white/black/white binding. Costing twice as much as the ES-150, the ES-250 demonstrated Gibson's increasing commitment to expanding the electric series.

Switchmaster, late 1955. *Wes Johnson/Allen Johnson*

In 1940 the EH-125 lap steel (with mahogany top) was introduced, along with the 6-pedal Electraharp, the first pedal steel, designed by machinist John Moore. It was accompanied by the new ES-300, Gibson's first electric guitar with individually adjustable polepieces. It had a slanted, oblong pickup like the EH-150 lap guitar and was otherwise very similar to the 1942 L-7 in its dimensions, tailpiece, twin parallelogram markers, and peghead inlay. It sold for $300 with amp.

That same year, the ES-250 was discontinued. The 150 had dropped the Christian pickup in favor of a rectangular, individually adjustable unit mounted near the bridge. The ES-125 replaced the apparently identical ES-100. The 100 appeared in 1938 (L-30 type body; in 1940 its straight bar pickup, mounted near the neck, was replaced with a 6-polepiece unit mounted near the bridge).

The 1942 electrics were the ES-300 (1940; huge diagonally mounted pickup replaced in 1941 by a smaller unit), ES-150 guitar, ES-125 guitar ($73.50), ETG-150 tenor guitar ($105), two mandolins, a banjo, the Electraharp ($477), three lap steels (EH-185, 6-string or 7-string; EH-150, 6-string or 7-string; and EH-125, 6-string only), and three amps (EH-185, EH-150, and EH-125).

SELECTED POSTWAR ELECTRICS

The August 1, 1949 catalogue specified ten arch-top electric Spanish (ES) models, excluding finish options: the ES-5, ES-350, ES-300, ES-175, ES-150, L-7E, L-7ED, L-7CE, L-7CED, and ES-125.

ES-5, SWITCHMASTER

The 1949 ES-5 was called the "supreme electronic version of the famed L-5," even though it was a significantly different guitar. Its features included a maple top (the L-5's was spruce), rosewood saddle, three black plastic-covered Alnico 5 pickups designed by Walt Fuller, a volume control for each pickup, and

ES-350, circa 1952. Both the ES-350 and ES-300 went from one to two pickups in 1948. In about 1952 the 350's upper-bout knob was replaced by the toggle switch shown here. *Dan Torres/Norm Mayersohn*

Only three Byrdlands were shipped in its first year, 1955, but Gibson's fanciest thin-line soon outsold the electric Super 400s and L-5s. The Byrdland's peghead inlay, truss rod cover, markers, and fingerboard (pointed at the treble end) are all patterned after the L-5; see page 115.

a master tone knob on the cutaway bout. A tune-o-matic was added in 1954, perhaps 1955. In late 1955 it was renamed the ES-5 Switchmaster and given separate tone and volume controls for each pickup. A four-way toggle replaced the upper-bout knob and provided a choice of any pickup or all three. A fancier tailpiece was adopted within a year, and humbuckings were stock by mid 1957. The 1960 catalogue was the last to include the Switchmaster. Like earlier versions, that guitar had a rounded cutaway. One of the last Switchmasters made was a very rare model with a Florentine (sharp) cutaway, a feature that distinguished similar Gibsons (L-5CES, Super 400) beginning in late 1960. The Switchmaster did not appear in the 1962 catalogues.

ES-350, ES-350T, ES-350TD AND BYRDLAND

The 1948–1952 ES-350 had a single-cutaway 17-by-21-inch maple body, maple neck, rosewood saddle, two black Alnico 5 pickups, gold-plating, two volume knobs, master tone knob on the upper bout, and a thick body. The 1954–1956 version had a toggle switch, four knobs, and a tune-o-matic.

A new guitar, the ES-350T (later called ES-350TD) made its debut in 1955 with a 2¼-inch *thin* all-maple body, short 23½-inch scale, and a smaller-than-standard neck. Only one ES-350TD and one ES-350TDN (natural finish) were shipped in 1955; the remaining stock of thick-body ES-350s was shipped through 1956.

The ES-350T was a two-pickup thin-line, a less fancy version

Byrdland co-designer Billy Byrd. *Julius Bellson*

ES-300, circa 1950. The original model, introduced in 1940, had a spruce top, blonde finish, and a diagonally mounted pickup. It was the first Gibson to feature the classic crown peghead inlay shown here. The early postwar ES-300 had a laminated maple top and a single, conventionally positioned pickup; that model was replaced in 1948 by the two-pickup version shown here. *Jacksonville*

of 1955's new Byrdland (the only other short-scale Gibson electric aside from three-quarter models). While the 350T had a laminated maple top and back, single binding, rosewood fingerboard, and crown peghead decoration, the Byrdland had a carved spruce top, carved maple back, multiple binding, ebony fingerboard, and flowerpot peghead decoration. While the 350T's original single-coil pickups had standard screw-type polepieces, early Byrdland pickups had rectangular polepieces. Both went to Patent-Applied-For humbuckings from 1957 to 1962.

Both models started with rounded cutaways. The Byrdland switched to the sharp Florentine design in about late 1960, and returned to the rounded type late in the decade, circa 1968. The last short-scale 350Ts (1961–1963) had sharp Florentine cutaways. With the success of the *double*-cutaway thin-lines (335, etc.), it became apparent to Gibson that it didn't need both single-cutaway thin guitars. The Byrdland stayed and the 350T vanished, only to reappear in 1977 with a rounded cutaway and a full 25½-inch scale.

ES-300

The postwar ES-300 was a noncutaway version of the 1949 ES-350 described above, and it featured an "f-hole" tailpiece identical to the type used on one of National's 1950s Del-Mar models (it is not unusual for different manufacturers to deal with the same suppliers of parts). The 300 sold fairly well but was dropped after 1953, though records show that one was shipped in 1956. (The slant-pickup prewar ES-300 is discussed in the prewar electrics section.)

ES-175

This guitar was one of Gibson's all-time classic balances of quality and price. Featuring a press-formed maple top, the ES-175 made its debut in 1949 and became the longest-lived of the postwar Gibson electrics. The original model had one black pickup, two-speed knobs, a Florentine cutaway body, and a rosewood saddle. The two-pickup ES-175D was added in 1953. By 1957 there were humbuckings on both the 175 and 175D. The latter received a fancy new tailpiece, T-shaped in the center with zigzag tubular rods on either side; this unit was pictured at least through 1966, though by the early seventies the tailpiece had returned to its simpler, mid-fifties styling.

The one-pickup 175 remained through 1968, although by mid 1971 it had been dropped. A tune-o-matic bridge was added to the 175D in 1976 or 1977. In 1976 the thin-line 175T made its debut, and in 1978 the 175CC appeared with a Charlie Christian pickup.

ES-150, ES-150DC

In 1949 the ES-150 was a noncutaway guitar with one black pickup, script logo, maple top, and dot neck. By the year 1952 it had trapezoidal fingerboard markers. The model was dropped after only six were shipped in 1956 (also see the section on prewar Gibson electrics). In 1969 the name was revived for the hollow, all-maple ES-150DC, an utterly different instrument. Except for its master volume knob and thick body, it looked like a 335.

L-7 ELECTRICS

Excluding finish options, the postwar L-7 electrics came in four versions, all with integrated pickguard-mounted pickups patented by Ted McCarty: the one-pickup, noncutaway L-7E; the two-pickup, noncutaway L-7ED; the one-pickup cutaway L-7CE; and the two-pickup cutaway L-7CED. All were discontinued after poor sales in 1954. (Also see the prewar acoustic L-7.)

ES-125, ES-135

Dating back at least to 1948, the postwar noncutaway ES-125 was substantially different from its early-forties predecessor (see *Prewar Electrics*). It became Gibson's most popular electric in the 1950s, with over 26,000 sold during the decade. It featured a noncutaway arched body, a single black pickup mounted near the unbound neck, and a trapeze with a raised diamond. Variations on the basic single-pickup thick-body ES-125 include the 125T (1956, thin body, only 1¾ inches deep), 125TD (1957, thin, two pickups), 125T¾ (1957, only 12¾ inches wide), 125TC (1960, thin cutaway), 125TCD (1960, a TC with two pickups), 125CD (mid-sixties, thick cutaway, two pickups), and 125C (by 1968, like the CD but with one pickup). The 1970 TDC was the last remnant of the line; all were gone by the following year.

The 1954–1958 ES-135 was a fancy ES-125: bound neck, multilayer pickguard, trapezoid markers.

LABELS AND KNOBS

In the mid-fifties, hollow Gibsons went from white labels to orange oval labels. These were used through early 1970 and were replaced with white Gibson/Norlin labels. Postwar electrics used flat-sided (no-skirt) barrel knobs until 1955, then unlabeled, clear-top, skirted knobs. Beginning circa 1960, *tone* and *volume* appeared on the knobs.

THE TED McCARTY ERA

In 1950, the legacy of Gibson, Reams, Williams, Loar, Hart, and Berlin was passed into the able hands of new company president Ted McCarty. Several of the products for which he was substantially responsible—the 335, the stop tailpiece, and others—are pictured with captions in the following article, which was written by the author in 1978 and appears here courtesy *Guitar Player* magazine.

Theodore McCarty is an unsung giant of modern guitar manufacturing, and his story is one of talent obscured by modesty. Because he never chose to apply his name to any of his cre-

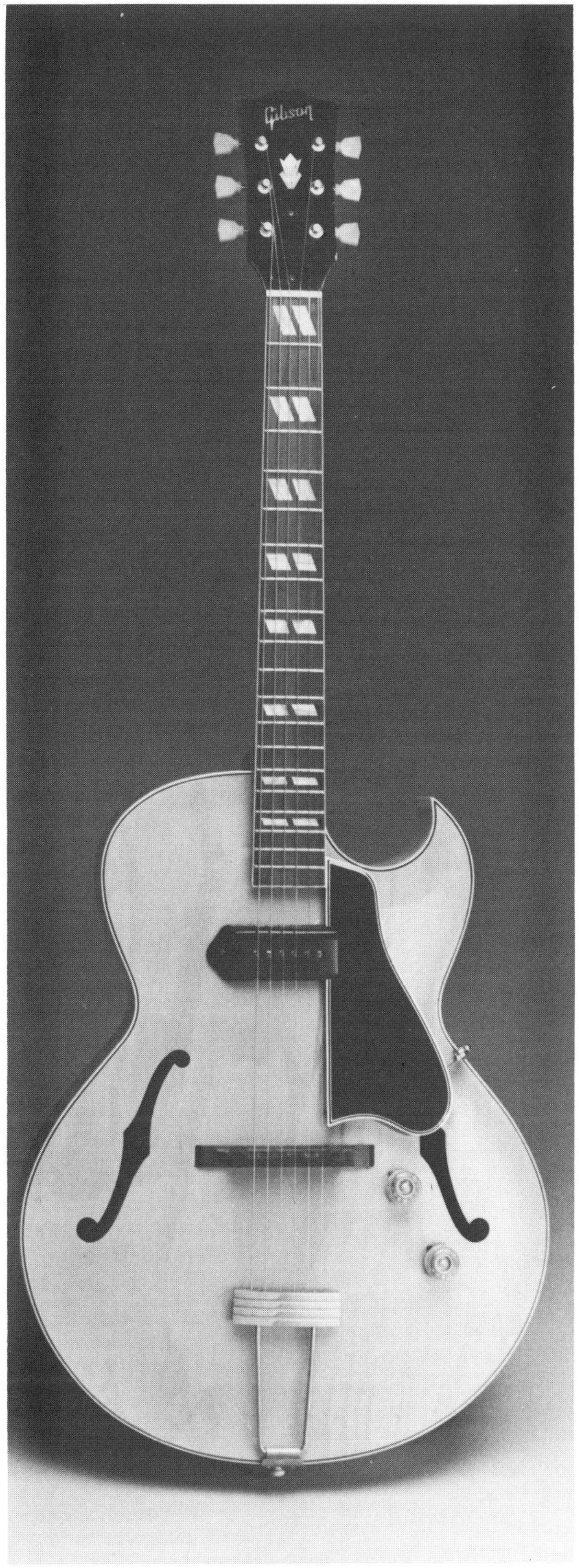

1956 ES-175, tailpiece unoriginal. *Wallace/Perla*

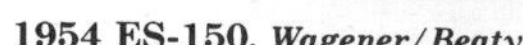

1954 ES-150. *Wagener/Beaty*

Mid-1960s ES-125CD. *Spitzer's/Sievert*

ES-125T ¾. *Spitzer's/Sievert*

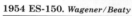

Left: ES-140T ¾, late-1950s/early-1960s style. *Rick Nielsen/Bob Alford* *Right:* A particularly unusual ES-140T ¾ Custom, distinguished by its headstock inlay, fancy neck binding, extra body binding, and position markers. Note the point at the end of the fingerboard and the short tailpiece. The standard dot-neck ES-140 of 1950 was generally a scaled-down ES-175. *Gruhn*

An early-1950s photo with Julius Bellson (*left*) and company president Ted McCarty, who headed the staff that designed the 335, Flying V, and Explorer. *Julius Bellson*

ations, his profound influence remained unheralded for decades.

McCarty came to the red-brick Gibson plant in 1948. At the time, controlling interest in the company was owned by CMI. Only two years later, CMI founder Maurice Berlin chose Ted to succeed retiring president Guy Hart. It was a good move. McCarty was Gibson's top executive for the next 16 years, from 1950 to 1966, a golden age even in that company's long and proud history. A statistical summary of McCarty's presidency is impressive, perhaps awesome: during his career there, the company's labor force increased by nearly 10 times, its profits by 15 times, its sales by 1,250 percent, and its stature by an immeasurable amount.

The upper soundholes were enlarged on this multihole Gibson flat-top, probably in a fruitless attempt to improve the sound. At any rate, the operation revealed the interior rims, or secondary sidewalls. *Allen Johnson/Tom Erlewine*

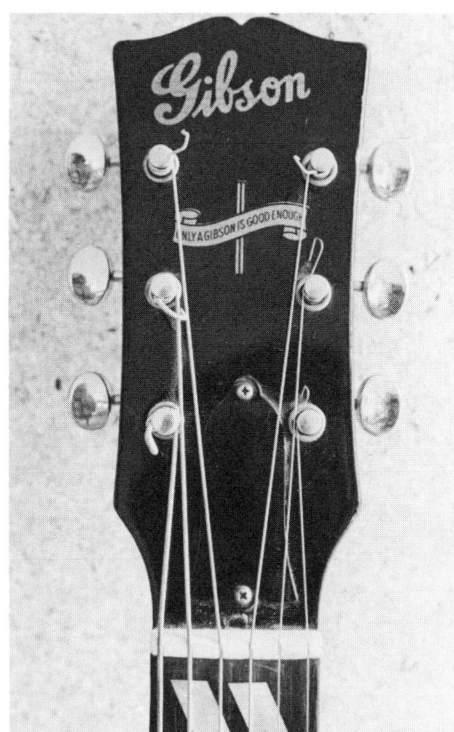

An "Only A Gibson Is Good Enough" headstock from a 1940s SJ. The slogan was first applied to instruments during World War II but was quickly dropped when Epiphone began to use "Epiphone . . . when 'good enough' isn't good enough."

A trio of distinguished Gibson vets, from left: Wilbur Marker, Walt Fuller, and Julius Bellson. Note the two L-5s at left, a cutaway electric with single-coil pickups, and an acoustic version in natural finish. *Julius Bellson*

Wartime J-45 (*left*) with an "Only A Gibson Is Good Enough" peghead. At right is a miniature steel-string built by Gibson for an ad campaign, circa 1939. *Bob Ingram/Michelle LeCalle*

1950s J-45, 16-inch-wide jumbo mahogany body. From 1948 to 1960 its annual sales averaged over 1,200. An adjustable-bridge version appeared in 1956 and sold well. *Gruhn/Baxendale*

The ES-225T, Gibson's first thin-line, shipped from 1955 to 1959. A double-pickup version appeared from 1956 to 1959. Note Les Paul tailpiece.

This bizarre Gibson wide-neck steel-string has a Dobro resonator, seven strings (note peghead), and four upper-bout soundholes. It was made in about 1950, when CMI owned both Gibson and Valco, makers of Dobro. Gibson has no record of this guitar, but it's clearly original. *Gruhn*

Early-1950s LG-1, with sunburst finish and straight bracing. The very similar LG-2 had a sunburst and X bracing, while the LG-3 was natural finished with X braces and triple binding, similar in ornamentation to a J-50. About 2,300 LG-1s were sold each year from 1948 to 1956; the model was listed through 1960. The LG-2's average annual sales from 1948 to 1960 were 750, while the LG-3's average figure for the same period was 385. The hugely successful LG-0 averaged annual sales of 2,483 from 1958 to 1960. *Gruhn/Baxendale*

Early- and mid-1950s type J-50, mahogany body and neck. By the late 1950s it had an enlarged pickguard, pointed at the side. *Music Shop/Madsen*

Late-1960s J-50, essentially a J-45 with a natural finish, adjustable saddle and pickguard logo. Over 700 a year were sold from 1948 to 1960, though the figures dropped off after 1957. The adjustable-bridge version appeared in 1956. *Soest/Rountree*

Stranger than fiction—a stock Gibson flat-top with four f-holes. The holes are merely the visible oddities. Inside the body is a second set of rims, almost a guitar within a guitar. *Fred's Music/F. Bernardo*

THE BIRTH OF THE LES PAUL GUITAR

In his first year as Gibson's president, McCarty, with the help of an able staff, helped coordinate the design of what was to become the original Les Paul guitar (see next section). Les himself had come to Mr. Berlin years before with the idea of a solidbody electric, but Les was too far ahead of his time; Gibson wasn't ready. By the time McCarty took over the company, Leo Fender was on his way to revolutionizing the industry. Gibson decided to move, as McCarty recounted:

> Fender had come out with the solidbody, or the plank guitar, as we called it, and the rest of the industry was watching—Gretsch, Kay, and the others. We didn't like the idea in a way, because it didn't take a great deal of skill to build a plank guitar. But it started to catch on, particularly with the country and western players, and it had a certain tone you couldn't get with the electric-acoustics which all the rest of us were making at the time. We finally came to the conclusion that we had better get on the bandwagon.
>
> We made solid maple bodies, but they were too heavy and sustained too long—couldn't keep them quiet. So the original Les Paul—we didn't call it that until later—had a mahogany back with a carved maple top laminated to it. That gave us the balance.
>
> The reason we carved the top was that Fender didn't have any carving equipment in their plant, so I decided, let's do something that will be different than what they have. So we built this guitar, but then we didn't know what to do with it.
>
> Well, I had heard Les Paul on the radio when he was known as Rhubarb Red. He'd been an Epiphone player for years, and we had

Courtesy Southern Music/Richmond, Inc.

met him at various clinics and tried to sell him on the idea of playing an L-5, but to no avail. But now we had this new guitar, a solidbody, and we thought that here was something that might interest Les. We had it all designed and completed, the gold-top model, although we had our standard tailpiece on it. *[Note: The Les Paul guitar is patented in U.S. Patent No. 2,714,326, filed January 21, 1953, and granted to T.M. McCarty for a "stringed musical instrument of the guitar type and combined bridge and tailpiece therefor." Most of the patent document is devoted to the bridge: the guitar appears to have been included primarily to illustrate the workings of the bridge. The model depicted is essentially the 1954 gold-top with the stud tailpiece.]*

Well, I made an appointment to see Les in New York to show him the instrument and to discuss it with him. I flew in and met Phil Braunstein, Les' financial adviser. The two of us had breakfast the next morning, and he informed me that we were going to a place in Pennsylvania called the Delaware Water Gap, up on top of a mountain. Les and Mary Ford were recording there. They were staying at a hunting lodge. Phil and I drove in Phil's car from New York to Delaware Water Gap—all day long, pouring down rain like you wouldn't believe. We had dinner at a little hash house at the bottom of the mountain, then called ahead. Les said, "You'll never find us." So he sent his brother-in-law down so that we could follow him up. Mary's sister Carol was there, along with Carol's husband Wally Kamin, who was also Les' bass player. You see, Les used to do most of his recording at night—sleep all day, work all night. Delaware Water Gap was secluded, away from the noise of the plane traffic. So we arrived and went through the usual social amenities, and I showed the guitar to Les. Les played it, and his eyes lighted up.

We had designed it over at Gibson. Les had never seen it. Anyway, he said, "They're getting too close to us, Mary; I think we should join them." She agreed. Of course, Les had been working on the design of solid guitars for years; he had sort of championed the idea. Well, Les, Phil Braunstein, and I sat down. Phil was a CPA; none of us were lawyers. I have a theory—the simpler a contract is, the better. The more qualifications you have, the more likely you are to create a loophole.

Les had developed a new trapeze-type tailpiece with a cylindrical bar. The strings wrapped around it, which gave it a little different tone than we'd obtained with the standard Gibson trapeze tailpiece. *[Note: The whole point of the Les Paul tailpiece was to permit the muted technique integral to Les' popular sound. This necessitated wrapping the strings over the crossbar (as on the ES-295) where the palm could rest on them. However, Gibson wished to wrap them under the bar so as to lower the strings relative to the fretboard and thereby avoid production problems when joining the neck to the body. The guitars were reportedly produced with both types of tailpiece, but over-the-bar versions are seldom if ever seen. At any rate, the disagreement between Les and Gibson was "solved" with the introduction of the stop tailpiece in 1954.]* We agreed to call the guitar the Les Paul, and Les would receive a royalty on every one we produced. He agreed to give us exclusive use of his tailpiece and not to appear in public playing any guitar other than a Gibson.

I am sure it was 1950 when we signed this agreement. We worked all night long on that contract and when we were finished it was only a page and a half long on standard stationery-size paper. We wrote and rewrote until everyone was satisfied. We signed it. Mary made us some bacon and eggs, and Phil and I drove back to New

Les Paul and Mary Ford in their home studio, early 1950s. Like most of Les's guitars, the very early Les Paul guitar he's holding is modified to the hilt. Note the vibrato tailpiece, knobs, top-mounted output jack, and replacement pickups.
Courtesy Thomas W. Doyle

1969 Everly Bros. Compare its pickguards to the black mid-1960s model. ***Frank Lucido***

A black mid-1960s Everly Bros. with a replacement bridge. ***Jay Levin***

York. I called Mr. Berlin and told him that we had a contract, and that launched Gibson solidbody guitars.

Fred Gretsch, a good personal friend of mine, called me after he heard about it and said, "I am sorry to see that Gibson has decided to go into solidbody guitars," but I told him that the solidbody was here to stay, and that Gibson was going to get on the bandwagon. The guitar that I took up to Les that night was, except for the tailpiece, pretty much or exactly like the first Les Paul introduced in 1952. After that we submitted things to Les for his advice. We never wanted to do anything that wasn't in keeping with his wishes. He was a consultant to Gibson, a valuable one. He also worked with us when we were improving pickups.*

THE STOP TAILPIECE

The initial success of the Les Paul Model (gold top, single-coil pickups with cream-colored plastic covers, trapeze tailpiece) warranted further development and expansion of the line. The first change was a substitution of the stud, or stop, tailpiece for the original trapeze. The new device was designed by Ted McCarty. As he explained: "Basically, Les Paul triggered the idea with his trapeze bar tailpiece. I got to looking at the bar type and decided that it had a couple of problems. I figured that if we fastened it on studs it would sustain just as well, maybe better, and we could raise and lower the studs; then, with two setscrews, you could intonate it a little. Furthermore, it was versatile. You could use it as a tailpiece if you had another bridge, or you could wrap the strings around it and use it as a combination bridge/tailpiece. Later, on the bridge/tailpiece, we added the raised bridge to improve intonation."

THE TUNE-O-MATIC BRIDGE

Ted's work on the stop tailpiece led to the tune-o-matic bridge (U.S. Patent No. 2,740,313; filed July 5, 1952), an invention that acquired the rare distinction of having its name adopted as a generic term. The design was exclusively McCarty's; had the sales department decided to call it the McCarty bridge, Ted's name would be as well-known as that of Dan Armstrong, Adolph Rickenbacker, or Fred Gretsch.

The early tune-o-matics had a bug that needed to be worked out. The individual saddles were held in place by string tension, and when a string broke, the corresponding saddle sometimes fell out. Ted remedied the problem by devising the restraining wire that Gibson used for years on its tune-o-matics.

LES PAUL CUSTOM

While McCarty worked on the stop tailpiece, an improvement on the original gold-top Les Paul, he was engaged in a broader, concurrent project, a completely new and fancier model. It was introduced in 1954 as the Les Paul Custom and acquired the nicknames Black Beauty and Fretless Wonder. "The Custom was a cooperative effort," Ted said. "We had the basic gold-top and wanted a deluxe model with gold parts, an ebony fretboard, etc. Since it was going to be black, we made the whole thing out of mahogany at first, without the laminated top. You don't

* For details on the Les Paul guitar, see page 154.

have to be quite as careful about the appearance of the wood if you are going to cover it over anyway with black paint. The Custom had fairly flat frets when it first came out. Someone around the shop—it could have been [pickup designer] Seth Lover—made a joke one time and said 'You mean that fretless wonder?' And that nickname stuck. Then, the Les Paul Junior was the economy model." [More details later in this section.]

THE KORINA TRIO

Commenting on the Flying V, Explorer, and Moderne, Ted McCarty explained:

> I designed those three guitars with the help of a local artist. There must have been a hundred sketches around the shop, all sorts of weird shapes. The dealers thought we were too stodgy, too traditional, so we decided to just knock them off their feet.
>
> We were working on this one guitar—since it was a solidbody, you could do just about anything with the shape—and it was sort of triangular. It was too heavy and we had to remove some weight from somewhere and we discovered that we didn't need the back end at all, so we just cut out some material in the middle. We wanted it to look like an arrow. Someone in the shop made a wisecrack and said, "The thing looks like a flying V," and we thought about the name and eventually used it. That's how we came up with the Moderne and Explorer, too, just experimenting with shapes. We must have made dozens of variations.
>
> So here we were, ready to go to town with our new guitars, but then *they didn't go over!* Dealers would buy new Flying V's, but then they'd hang them in the windows just to attract attention. Some of them never tried to *sell* the thing; they were just too radical. I wish I had kept one each of those original models. I hear they are really very highly prized these days.

MODERNE

Most or all of the key executives, designers and other personnel who worked at Gibson at the time were asked about the number of Modernes actually constructed. Unfortunately, their memories vary considerably. Two sources were certain that the number was between 40 and 50, and none suggested a higher figure. We do know that some were destroyed in the Gibson "morgue" subsequent to the industry's unanimously negative reaction to the guitar and the company's decision not to add it to the line. The 22 survivors listed in the shipping totals appeared on routine invoices and do not include Modernes sold at cut rate to Gibson employees or those which were kept at the plant for experimental purposes. Some evidence suggests that at least two or three dozen left the factory one way or another, a surprisingly large number considering the fact that they are presently so scarce as to appear to be nearly extinct. Where are those Modernes? Ted McCarty, who supervised its design, guesses that only a handful were made, perhaps half a dozen.

ES-335

Aside from the Les Pauls, perhaps the most enduring guitar design that came from McCarty's engineering staff was the ES-

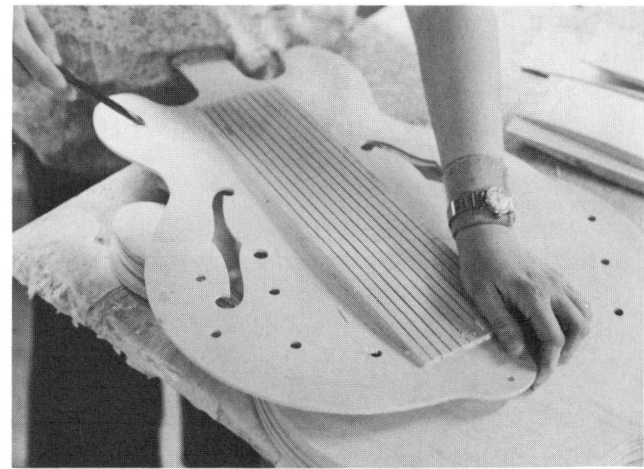

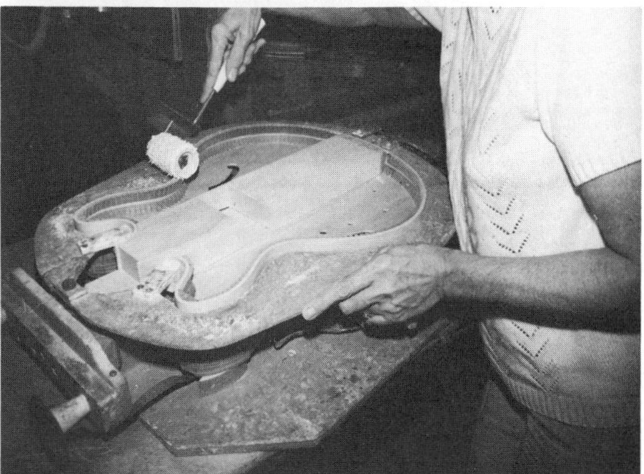

Strips are installed on the underside of the 335's arched top to provide a flat gluing surface for the interior block. After the block is in place, glue is applied to the rims and the back is attached.

A TOUR THROUGH THE GIBSON FACTORY

The old Gibson plant, Kalamazoo, Michigan.

Making the initial cut on a solid slab of wood.

335 semisolid electric, a popular guitar ever since its introduction in 1958. "It was my idea to put the solid maple bar down the middle," Ted said, "but the design for the series—the 335, 345, and 355—was a cooperative effort, as most of them were. In order to glue that center chunk of maple, we put spruce pieces on the inside of the arched top and back to flatten out the arch for the solid maple bar. I had never seen a semisolid guitar before we built ours. *[Note: see Gretsch's Country Gentleman.]* We were after the sustain of the solidbody, but with a little less weight. Those guitars were very successful right from the start."

GIBSON AND EPIPHONE

Epiphone president Epi Stathopoulo died in the early 1940s, and his brother Orphie took control of Epiphone. Ted McCarty, then a buyer for Wurlitzer, got together soon after the war with Maurice Berlin of CMI and established Gibson's line in the Wurlitzer stores. Sometime in the early 1950s, by Mr. McCarty's recollection, Epiphone suffered a long and debilitating strike and was eventually bought out by Continental Music, the wholesaling arm of the C.G. Conn Company. Continental began trucking the Manhattan-made guitar parts to Philadelphia for assembly, and the ensuing complications caused a decline in the instruments' quality. Orphie regained control of the company but resumed only the bass-manufacturing portion of the business.

Gibson had converted to making materials in support of the war effort during the 1940s. Somehow during that time, Gibson's own acoustic bass-building equipment was lost or destroyed. When Mr. McCarty arrived in Kalamazoo in 1948, the bass tooling was missing, and no one knew what had happened to it. CMI's Maurice Berlin wanted Gibson to re-enter the bass business, and at one time or another, McCarty had mentioned to Orphie Stathopoulo that should he ever decide to sell Epiphone's bass-building gear, Gibson might be interested. The stage was set. "In 1957," Mr. McCarty recounted, "I was out buying lumber in Tacoma, Washington, and I got a call from Orphie. His health wasn't too good, and another brother, Frixo, had had a motorcycle accident. Orphie decided to sell out. I talked to Mr. Berlin, and since Epiphones were good basses, we decided to investigate this thing further."

A deal was proposed and accepted (see Herb Sunshine's account in the Epiphone section); it covered the machinery and the Epiphone name but not the company as such. "In other words," McCarty explained, "Epiphone, Inc. existed on paper, and we had Orphie fold that up because we didn't know what liabilities it had acquired."

Gibson bought the bass-manufacturing inventory—the equipment and the work in progress—and McCarty dispatched men to New York and Philadelphia to pick up the newly acquired fixtures. Then, he explained, "We hauled it all up to Kalamazoo, rented space in another building away from our Gibson plant, and set up to make the basses. As we unpacked and got all this stuff together, we discovered that we had acquired not just the equipment for building basses but all the jigs, fixtures, and work in progress for the *guitars* as well. So when I discovered this, I hotfooted it over to Chicago and sat down with Mr. Berlin, and we decided that we could now produce the Epiphone guitar if we wished, exactly like it used to be built before Continental started making parts in one place and assembling them in another."

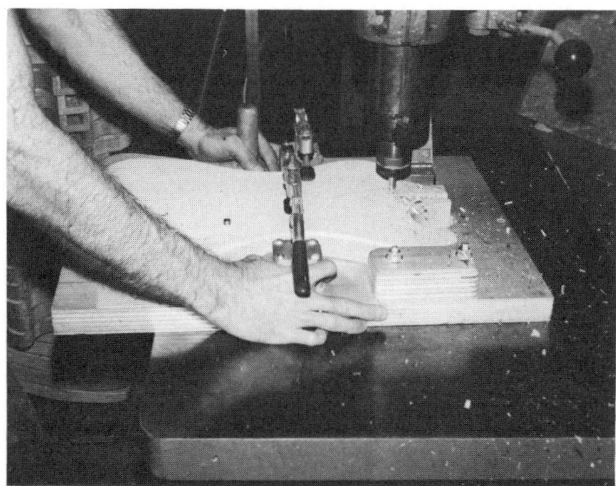

Routing the neck slot on an RD body; note the alignment peg protruding through the toggle switch hole.

Bending a guitar's sides on a heat press.

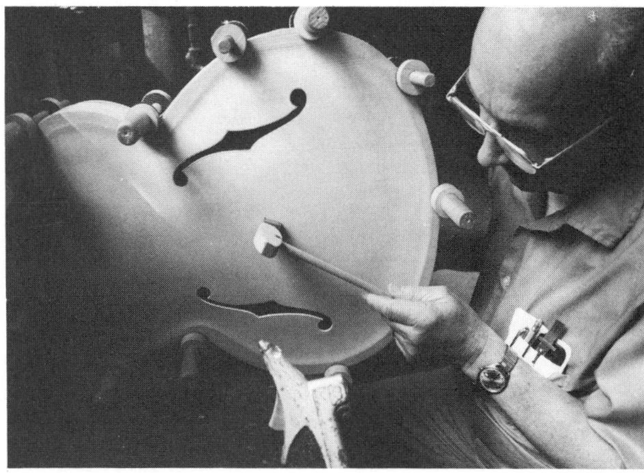

A technician taps a Johnny Smith top with a piano mallet, listens, and makes fine adjustments with sandpaper to the contour of the braces.

Gauging the thickness of an arched top.

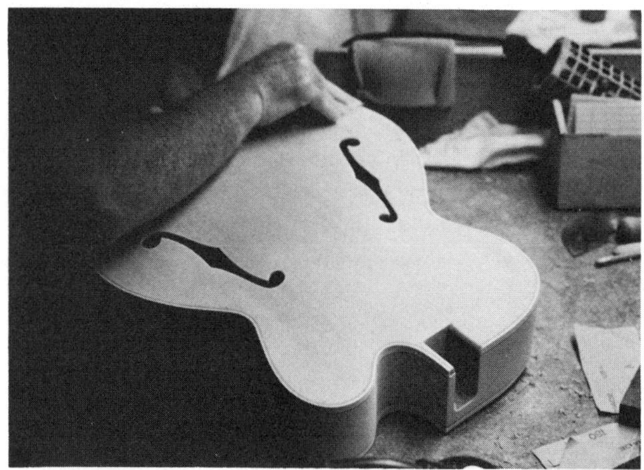

Hand sanding.

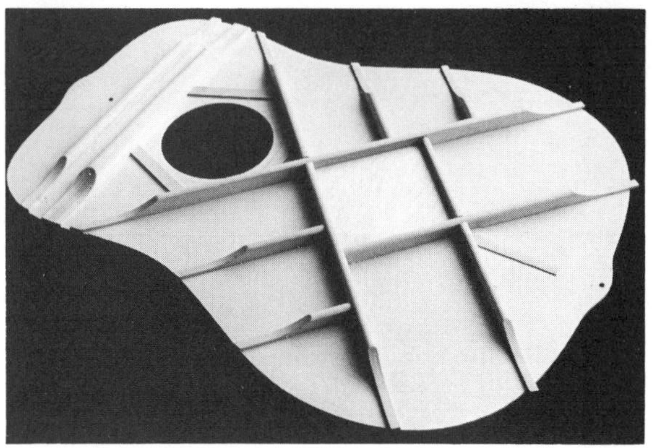

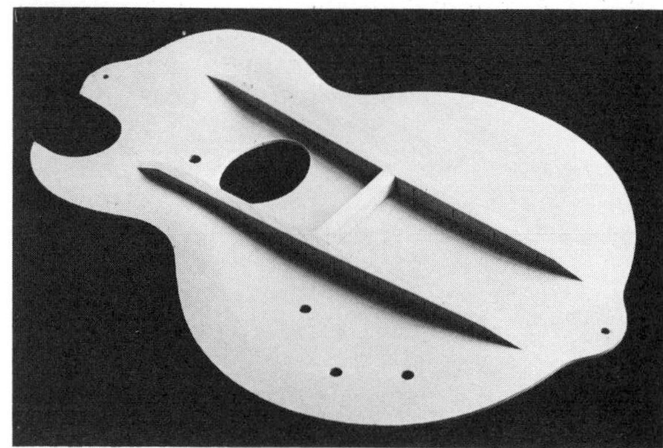

Most Gibson flat-tops have solid spruce soundboards and symmetrically arranged spruce braces. The Howard Roberts (*right*) has a pressed maple, spruce-braced top. ***Photos courtesy Richard Schneider***

Gibson's restrictive franchise program was intended to avoid the hassles of having competing outlets in the same neighborhood, and it necessitated the frequent rejection of dealership applications from reputable retailers, including many who sold

Contouring a neck on an electric shaper.

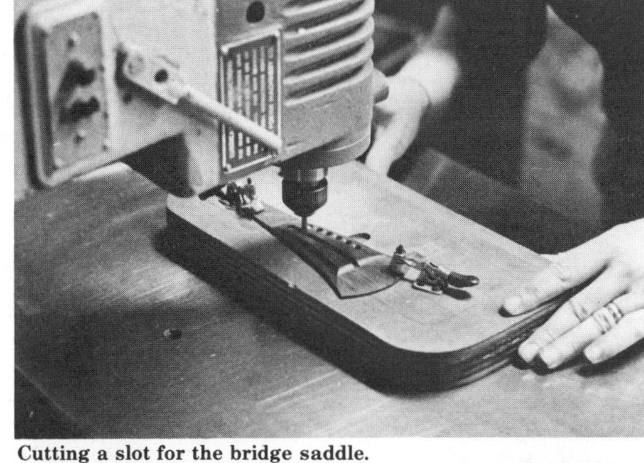

Cutting a slot for the bridge saddle.

Drilling a hole for the truss rod adjustment mechanism.

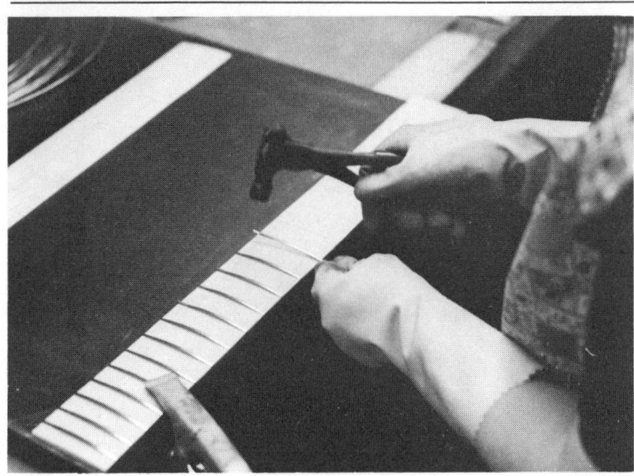

Fret installation; note combination hammer/fret nippers tool.

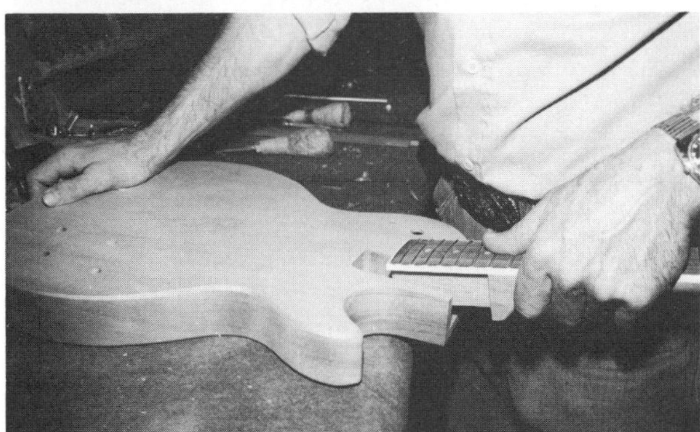

After applying glue from a squeeze bottle, the craftsman inserts the neck into its slot.

other CMI products. The acquisition of Epiphone afforded an ideal solution: if hot-under-the-collar dealers wanted top quality instruments but were located near Gibson outlets, the company could offer them Epiphones and guarantee an exclusive distributorship. McCarty said, "We began building them in 1957, as soon as we discovered we had acquired this equipment. After we got it established, we closed up the original Epiphone plant and moved Epiphone right into the Gibson factory. This was in about 1960. We used the old Epiphone model names and also introduced our own guitars, because the dealers wanted items to compete with Gibsons like the ES-335. Pretty soon Gibson and Epiphone were competing." From 1961 through 1970 Gibson built 86,977 Epiphones, nearly three-quarters of them from 1964 to 1967. The Epiphone name was later applied to guitars imported by Norlin, CMI's successor.

Gibson's humbucking pickup, a milestone in electric guitar evolution.

HUMBUCKING PICKUPS

Gibson's humbucking pickup was designed by Seth Lover, who later went to work for Fender and designed their humbucking as well. Except for a very few of the earliest units, the Gibson pickups were labeled with *Patent applied for* stickers from the time of their first appearance in mid 1957 through 1962. (The patent was granted July 28, 1959.) Later "patent number" units have slightly smaller magnets and other modifications. Although the tone of the patent-applied-for can sometimes be distinguished from its successor by a discriminating listener, there are inconsistencies among both types that make generalizations difficult. The patent-applied-for's popularity, which is unsurpassed, is due to a blend of performance and snob appeal.

FIREBIRDS

A particularly colorful chapter in the McCarty story is the development of the Firebird guitars. With its Les Paul line, Gibson was clearly a leader in the solidbody electric field. However, various personal and legal entanglements accounted for a decision not to renew Les Paul's consultation/royalty agreement. The popularity of Fenders, plus the commercial failure of the Flying V's and Explorers and the discontinuation of the Les Pauls, all added up to imply a gap in Gibson's line. There were no bizarre solidbodies to signify that Gibson shared America's early-sixties space-age consciousness. The SGs were popular and modern, to be sure, but there was nothing in the catalogue with enough pure flash content to compete with a gold-plated Lake Placid Blue Stratocaster. The Firebirds filled the flash gap.

CMI's sales department ensured that the body's outline avoided the angles and corners that had made the V's and Explorers too twisted for dealers to handle. Nevertheless, the various Firebirds appeared at first glance to be so radical as to be almost frivolous; alongside conventionally shaped Gibsons, they stood out like rockets. Despite the craziness, the Firebirds of 1963–1965 were well-engineered and solidly built.

Mr. McCarty remembered: "I hired Ray Dietrich, a car designer, and told him that we needed something new and refreshing. One of his greatest things was his sense of clean design. He never went in for anything curlicue or too fancy. The sketches were simple, with a classic beauty. He came up with the shape and the logo. That's how the Firebird was born. Over at CMI, the sales people actually chose the designs that would be put into production. We'd come up with the sketches and prototypes and then present them to CMI and they, having a closer relationship with the dealers, guided us on which ones to manufacture." *[Note: Firebird details on pages 175–181.]*

Barney Kessel Regular: mahogany neck, chrome parts, understated peghead inlay, and split-parallelogram markers. The Bigsby tailpiece was an option available from the factory. *Gruhn/ Baxendale*

Left: An early-1960s photo of Barney Kessel with a Barney Kessel Custom: maple neck, gold plating, bow tie markers, and jazzy peghead inlay. *Julius Bellson* *Right:* Trini Lopez with a Trini Lopez Custom: thick body, unique headstock, diamond holes, and diamond pickguard. Compare it to the thin Trini Lopez in the color section (93). *Julius Bellson*

Left: The Johnny Smith appeared circa late 1961 and was soon joined by a two-pickup version. It was based on Johnny's custom D'Angelico (a scaled-down, 17-inch New Yorker), although the Gibson's upper neck was flush with the top and also attached to the soundboard's interior crossbracing for improved high-register sustain. The pickup was new in both design (a smaller humbucking) and point of attachment (at the fingerboard's end, so as to leave the top undisturbed). Though the 1962 catalogue illustration depicted a 22-fret prototype, the text specified 20 frets. The discrepancy arose from Johnny's modification of Gibson's original design; production models have 20 frets, as per Smith's request. *Gruhn* *Right:* Johnny Smith in an early-1960s promo shot with his Johnny Smith guitar.

Ted McCarty and John Huis bought Bigsby Accessories, Incorporated, in 1965 and tendered their resignations to Gibson in November of that year. Ted agreed to stay on until June 30, 1966. When he left Gibson and took over Bigsby, he knew the move would fundamentally change his life. In reflecting on the choice he commented: "I never regretted my decision. I had nothing to prove, and I didn't have to set the world on fire or build a dynasty or anything. As far as I'm concerned, Gibson is the greatest name in the industry, not just in this country but in the world. When you pick up, say, a 1958 ES-335 or an old Les Paul, one thing you can see right away—the people who built this guitar cared about it. They cared a lot."

Left: The gifted Tal Farlow, one of jazz guitar's most brilliant exponents. See Gibson's Tal Farlow model, color photo 45. _Lower left:_ The CF-100E was an electrified version of the CF-100 shown in color photo 57. It was introduced in 1951, and about 140 were sold each year through 1959, when it was discontinued. _Jacksonville_ _Center:_ 1962 mahogany-body TG-0, essentially a 4-string LG-0. Gibson tenor guitars date to circa 1927 and remained in the line through the late 1960s _Wagener/Beaty_ _Right:_ Prototype or custom-order Hummingbird, with an L-5 type neck. The first Hummingbirds were maple, but shortly after the maple Dove came out, the Hummingbird went to a mahogany body. _Vintage Fret Shop/A. Caswell_

President McCarty (with shovel), Gibson execs, and local officials at a ground-breaking for a new facility, July 23, 1964. ***Julius Bellson/Kalamazoo Gazette***

The Gibson factory, including the huge 1960 addition (*upper left*), the 1945 addition (*center*), the 1950 addition (*right foreground*), and the three-story 1917 plant (*right rear*). ***Julius Bellson***

ES-335

The early 335 had rounded cutaway bouts, dot markers, a one-piece mahogany neck, PAF humbuckings, a stud ("stop") tailpiece, a long pickguard extending below the bridge, an orange oval label, and cleartop knobs. Immediately successful, it was a highlight of Ted McCarty's tenure at Gibson and progenitor of the semisolid class of electrics that includes Fender's Starcaster and others.

The 335's dots were replaced by blocks in 1962, roughly concurrently with the PAFs' replacement by patent-number pickups. (There are block-necks with PAFs, and 1962 models with dots.) Some stock guitars from this period have one PAF and one patent-number pickup. In late 1964 or early 1965 the stud tailpiece, which was bolted right to the interior block and emphasized the solidbody type sustain of this half-solid, half-hollow guitar, was replaced with a trapeze, which is much more closely associated with the action and sound of jazz guitars and other hollow models. There were three changes circa 1970: discontinuation of the orange label, the addition of a stamped *MADE IN U.S.A.* on the back of the peghead, and a reshaping of the rear of the previously flat neck/peghead joint to include a protruding volute. There are some 335s with *MADE IN U.S.A.* stamps, volutes, and orange labels, another overlap of features.

A *very* few early 335s have no fingerboard binding; otherwise, this guitar represents the premier 335 of 1958, well known as the "dot-neck." ***Erlewine***

ES-330 TDN, introduced in 1959. Often assumed to be very similar to a 335, it actually differs in several respects: hollow body, single-coil pickups, sixteenth-fret neck joint. Starting in 1962 the pickups had metal covers, and blocks replaced the dots. Also available in a single-pickup model, ES-330T, built from 1959 to about 1963. ***Charley's/ Crump***

Soest/Rountree

Glen Quan

Aside from the sunburst there were two other finishes originally offered on the 335, blonde *(near left)* and cherry *(far left)*. Most Gibsons, like this cherry dot-neck, could be ordered with a factory Bigsby; if the holes for the standard tailpiece had already been drilled, they would be plugged with decorative inserts (shown here) or covered with a plastic "Custom Made" tag. See color photos 85-87.

Bottom left: A very unusual dot-neck 335 (circa 1960) with an original sideways vibrato. The tailpiece is unique, distinguished from the gold-plated ones used on 355s of that period by its nickel plating, and from the SG/Les Paul type by its rim (end pin). Thus it appears to be factory-fitted to the guitar. The original finish extends over the stop tailpiece bushings, and the owner apparently requested both tailpieces. *Guitar Trader/Photog. Unlimited* *Bottom right:* ES-335, 1962-1964 style. *Charley's/Crump*

In the 1960 catalogue, the ES-355, shown here, was the only model with the sideways vibrato tailpiece used on later SG-style Les Pauls. The 355 was also pictured with the round Vari-Tone selector (depicted here) until about 1962, when the pointer knob became standard. The 355 was available with or without stereo and Vari-Tone until 1970, after which is was available only with the stereo and Vari-Tone (ES-355TD-SV).

In 1963 the 355's sideways tailpiece was replaced with the type shown here on this early-1970s model. The newer unit was also used on certain mid-1960s Firebirds and SGs. *(Note: Regarding the 355's less fancy sister instrument, the ES-345, see color photos 40 and 74.)*

GIBSON SOLIDBODIES

Les Paul

Les Paul was a visionary, an advocate of solidbody construction who told 'em so way back in the 1940s, before Fender. Born Lester William Polfus in 1915, he became known to country music buffs as Rhubarb Red, a cheerful kid with a guitar. Pop and jazz fans knew him as Les Paul, the architect of a futuristic sound that combined his Django Reinhardt-flavored jazz artistry with his knack for electronics. The first to use the now-indispensible technique of multiple recording, he is credited with developing 8-track equipment. With hot-rodded guitars, muted picking, layered arrangements, speeded-up recording, echo, phasing, and overdubbing—all of which he pioneered—he revo-

1974 ES-325, essentially a budget 335, the only mid-1970s thin-line Gibson with dots. Details: maple body, one f-hole (a most unusual feature for Gibson), small humbuckings, no peghead inlay, bargain-basement pickguard. Mounting the controls from the top, a process resulting in the top-mounted cover plate, did not require the drilling of individual holes for the knobs and switch and thus helped lower production costs. Note that on Gibson's later thin-lines the body horns (cutaway bouts) are more pointed than those on the early dot-necks.

lutionized the sound of the electric guitar. In terms of expanding and popularizing the instrument's range of effects, he had no equal until Jimi Hendrix.

Ted McCarty's recollections of the birth of the Les Paul guitar appear earlier in this chapter. Here is Les Paul's account in his own words:

> I started designing solidbodies back in the 1930s. I went to see the Larson brothers [see Maurer] in 1937. Their shop was still in a barn then, in Chicago, if you can believe it. They were funny fellows. They supposedly hadn't spoken to each other in twenty years. One time one of them said to me, "Listen, I hear you're a pretty good guitar player, but you'll never be as good as that Rhubarb Red." I never did tell him that I *was* Rhubarb Red. Well, the Larsons built a guitar for me with a half-inch maple top, no f-holes, and two pickups.
>
> I was interested in proving that a vibration-free top was the way to go. I even built a guitar out of a railroad rail to prove it. What I wanted was to amplify pure string vibration, without the resonance of the wood getting involved in the sound. After I moved to New York, I went over to the guys at Epiphone and I said to Epi [Stathopoulo], "Is there any chance I could do some experimenting, maybe on a Sunday, and use your machinery?" Epi said, "Be our guest." They were interested in what I was going to build. I built the "Log" out of a 4-by-4-inch board and stuck on some wings, you know, two halves from a regular guitar body for looks. These guys took a look and said, "Gee, this guy's strange!"
>
> A while later I took it over to Gibson—I was a dyed-in-the-wool Gibson man, still am—and I showed it to Mr. Berlin, and he called it the broomstick with a pickup on it. He said, "Forget it." Later on, in late 1949 or so, he said, "Go find that kid with the broomstick and sign him up."

When Les Paul's arm was crushed in an accident, he had it permanently set to permit him to continue playing guitar. ***Guitar Player***

The "Log," Les Paul's early solidbody.

Les made many records with this gear, an Epiphone with a 3/8-inch steel bar running through it, an Ampex recorder, and a Gibson EH-150 amp.
Sievert/GP

I had two models in mind right from the very beginning, [what came to be known as] the standard gold-top, and the black Custom. I specified both colors right at the beginning. I picked gold because no one else had one, and because it's always associated with quality, richness. And I picked black because it's classy, like a tuxedo, and also because a player's hands—if the guy were white—would show up onstage against the black finish. That may sound crazy, but that was my reason. Over the years I had the say-so on all the details—the wood, binding, frets, size of the peghead, number of turns on the coils, etc.

Gibson kind of mixed up a couple of things. First of all, it was the Custom, not the regular gold-top, that was supposed to have the maple top. Maple's the better wood, right? But Gibson sent me one, and when we took it apart to replace the pickups we saw that it had a plain mahogany body, with no maple cap. I called them right away, but the factory was already tooled up to do it that way, so we just said, let's let it drop, forget it. They later started making the Customs with maple tops.

The tailpiece—they got that wrong too. I wanted the strings to go *over* the bar, so you could get that muting sound that I was well known for. That was the whole idea. But they put the strings under the bar at first, so I called them right away and asked them to fix it.

You've seen that ES-295, sort of like a 175 but with an all-gold finish? That was my idea too. The first one was made for a terminally ill patient in a ward in Milwaukee. I do a lot of benefits, and this one patient says, "Les, I'm not going to make it." I said, "Sure you will," and we struck up a conversation. I had a gold-top guitar with me, and he liked that color, but he was an acoustic player, so I called up Ted McCarty at Gibson and asked him to rush a gold hollowbody guitar to this guy in the hospital. They got right on it and whipped it together, but the guy never saw it. It got there too late. I kept it here at home until a friend borrowed it, and it got burned up in a fire.

Now, here's what happened with the SG. The first one I saw was in a music store, and it said *Les Paul* on it. I didn't like the shape—a guy could kill himself on those sharp horns. It was too thin, and they had moved the front pickup away from the fingerboard so they could fit my name in there. The neck was too skinny and I didn't like the way it joined the body; there wasn't enough wood, at least in my opinion. So I called Gibson and told them to take my name off the thing. It wasn't my design.

The following year my contract with Gibson was up. They asked me to renew, but I was going through a divorce, and it just wasn't the time to renew. This was in 1962. In 1967 the legal stuff was all cleared up, so I came back to Mr. Berlin and told him I thought it was time to make the guitar again. Believe it or not, he told me that they were thinking of phasing out the solidbodies altogether. I told him that all the rock players were flying around like crazy trying to find the old, single-cutaway Les Pauls—they were the hottest thing for rock. I talked him into it. We made the deal that night. Gibson came out with the original style Les Pauls again, and they've been making them ever since.

You know something? In my first agreement with them, they originally weren't even going to put the Gibson name on the guitars, because the solidbody was just such a crazy idea. Of course, they finally decided to put *Gibson* on there, but the original plan was just to say *Les Paul,* that's all.

Les Paul's tools of the trade, from left: 1930 L-5, 1952 Les Paul, L-3 (circa 1930), and an aluminum guitar built by Les himself (note very unusual tuning key placement). The photo is of Rhubarb Red. ***Sievert/GP***

Les Pauls, SGs, and Melody Makers

Group I

THE LES PAUL GUITAR

Introduced in mid-1952 (see the Ted McCarty article earlier in this chapter), the first Les Paul had a *single* cutaway, mahogany back and neck, a 24¾-inch scale, two nonhumbucking pick-

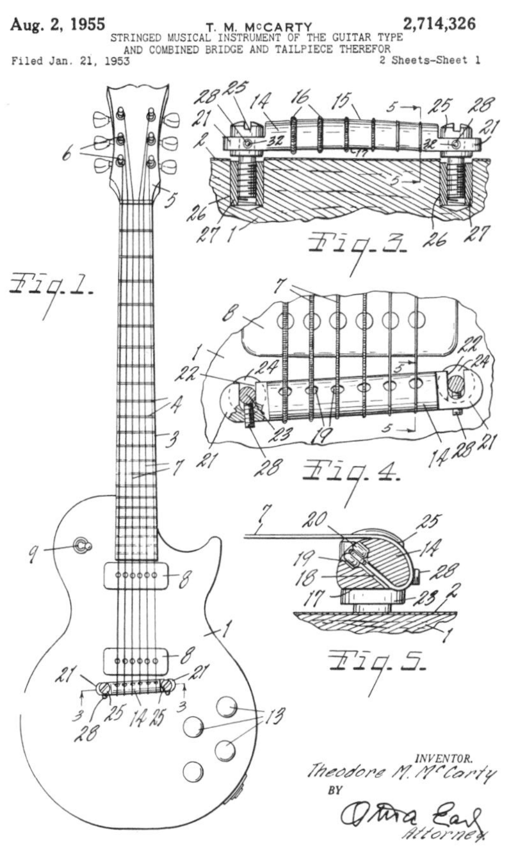

Left: **The patent for the original Les Paul gold-top was assigned to Ted McCarty.**

Right: **1952 Les Paul Model, gold-top. Note trapeze tailpiece.** ***Gruhn***

1959 Les Paul Standard. Note especially fine flamed maple top. *Guitar Trader/Photog. Unlimited*

ups with cream-colored plastic covers, a gold top with ivory-colored trim, 22 frets, and a trapeze bar combination tailpiece/bridge. Some bodies were painted gold on the sides and back as well as the top; this type ran concurrently with the standard gold-top at least as late as 1956. Most 1952s lacked the plastic trim ring around the pickup selector; a very few had unbound fingerboards. On some, the P-90 pickups were mounted with a screw in each of two corners rather than two screws in line with the polepieces.

In late 1953 the stud (or "stop") tailpiece replaced the trapeze, and in 1955 the tune-o-matic bridge was added. Two years later, patent-applied-for humbuckings were substituted—despite 1957 catalogue photos depicting older models with cream covers. In 1958 the cherry sunburst flame maple top replaced the gold top.

LES PAUL STANDARD

Gibson first used the name *Standard* for a Les Paul in 1958, applying it to the 1958–1960 type cherry sunburst ($265). However, dealers and collectors often use the term in referring to older gold-tops as well—technically Les Pauls or Les Paul Models—in order to distinguish them from Customs, Jrs., TVs, and other Les Paul variations.

In 1961 the *double*-cutaway SG style replaced the original, and the body now joined the neck at fret 22. Gibson's vibrato had a swing-away arm, pulled sideways *across* the face of the guitar. This model had a solid cherry finish and cost $290. In 1974 the single-cutaway Les Paul Standard was reintroduced; it

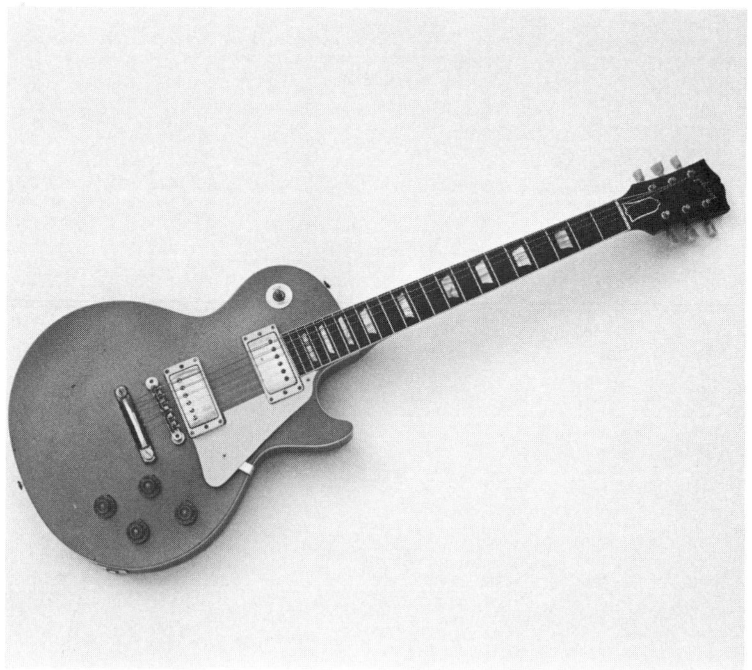

1957 gold-top Les Paul; note humbuckings and tune-o-matic. *Mayersohn*

was the same as the 1974 Deluxe, but with full-sized humbuckings.

SG STANDARD

The cherry-finish 1962 SG (for *Solid Guitar*) Standard replaced the 1962 Les Paul Standard. The new Gibson Vibrola had a large metal base plate, and its arm had a curved white plastic tip. The pickguard was enlarged in approximately 1966, extending over to the left side as well as the right; there were no longer separate plastic pickup frames. The model was replaced after 1970 by the SG Deluxe, and it was reintroduced in late 1972 with a new, enlarged tune-o-matic in a rectangular housing, a 1964–1966 type pickguard (wing-shaped, flush mounted, on the right-hand side only), and 1954 style barrel knobs.

A 1958–1960 style Les Paul Standard with exquisite tiger striping. ***Kosta Kovachev***

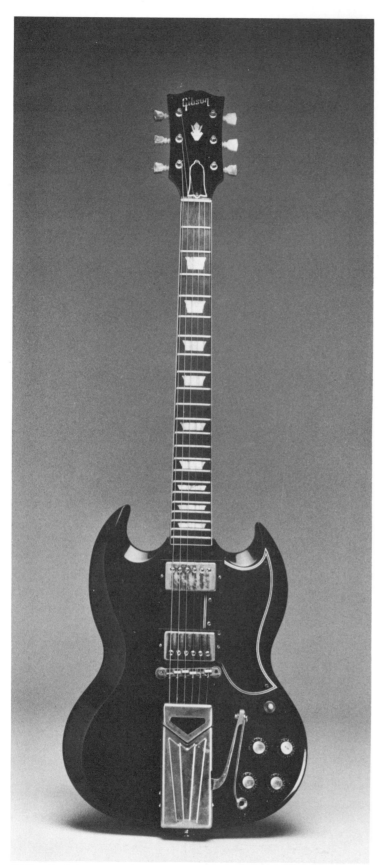

SG Standard, circa 1962. The sideways vibrato was also used on its immediate predecessor, the SG/Les Paul Standard. *Wallace/Perla*

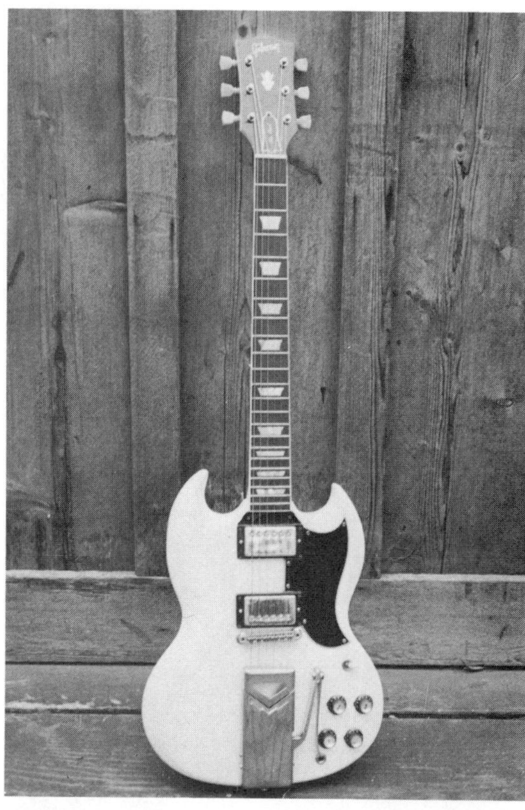

SG/Les Paul Standard in an extremely rare white finish. ***Ax-In-Hand***

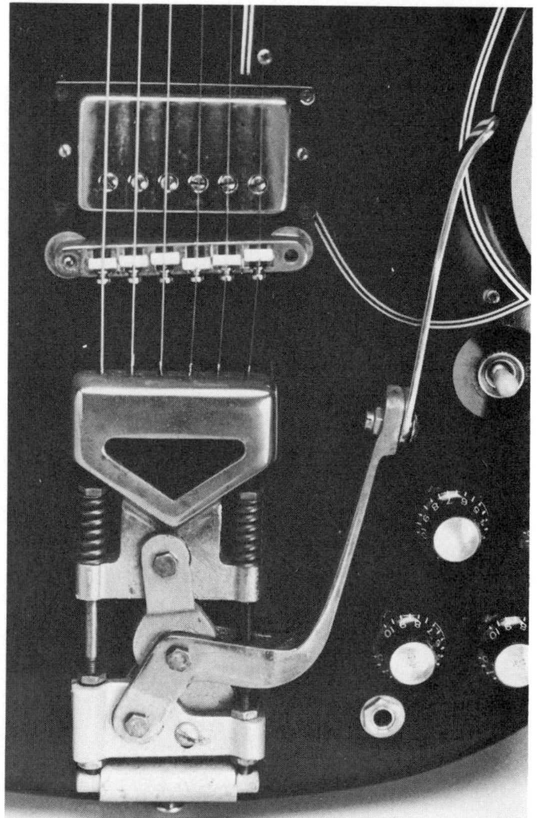

SG, detail; side-to-side vibrato, cover removed.

This 1962 SG/Les Paul has a rare tailblock of ebony with pearl inlay. *Charley's/Crump*

1968 SG Standard. Note enlarged pickguard and vibrato base plate. *Jacksonville*

Left: Five-screw pickguard of thin-neck SG serial no. 1 0127. *Right:* Slightly smaller (note toggle switch area) six-screw guard on a 1965 SG Standard.

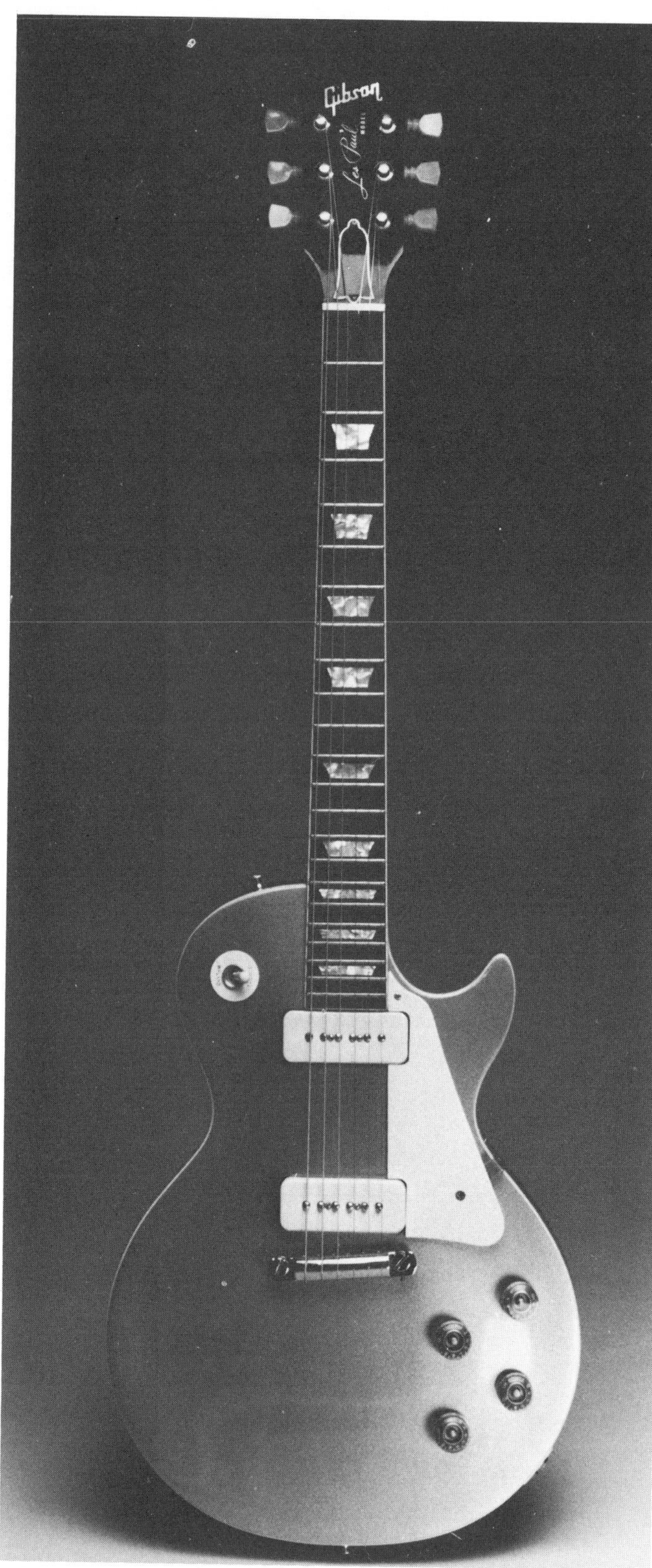

Early-1970s reissue gold-top with P-90 ("soapbar") pickups. The first reissues (of 1968) had tune-o-matics. *Wallace/Perla*

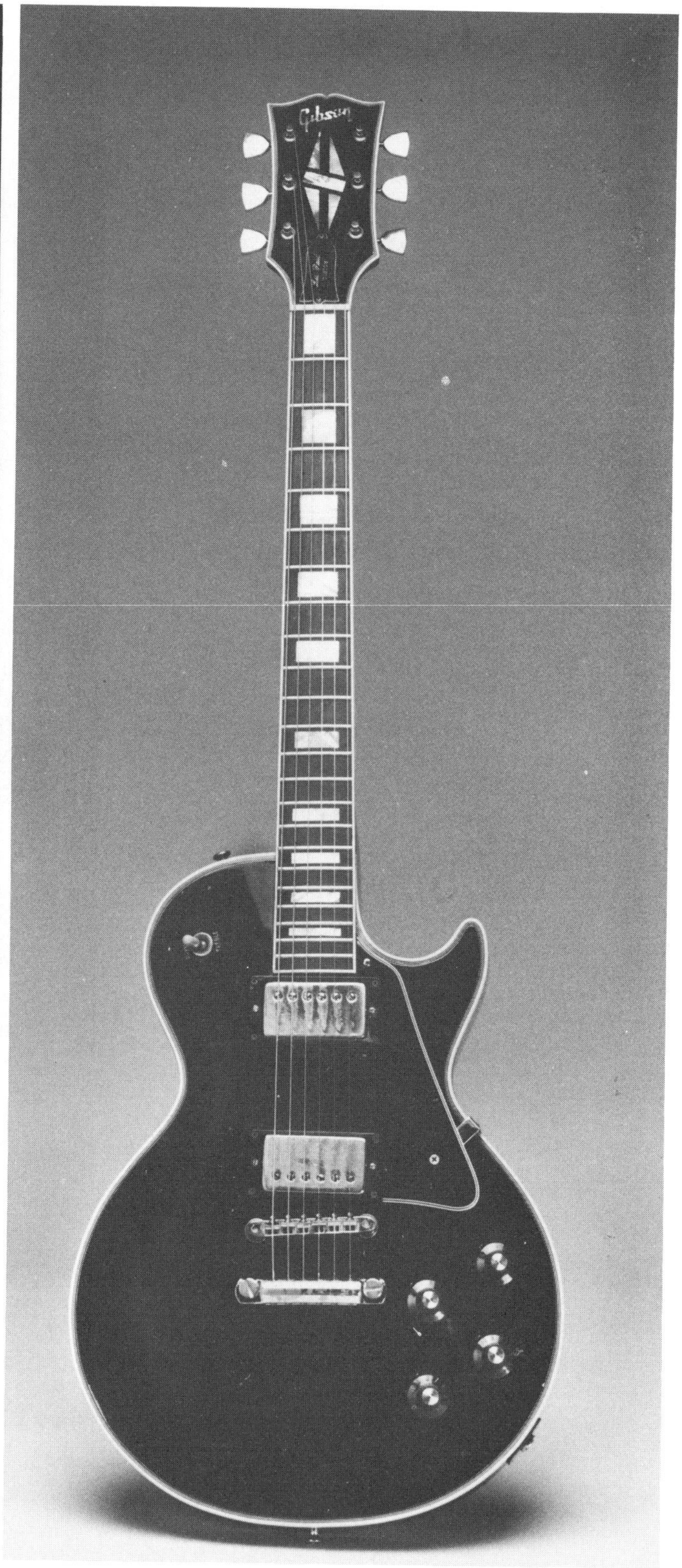

1968 reissue Les Paul Custom. *Wallace/Perla*

LES PAUL REISSUES

There were no single-cutaway Les Pauls available after 1961 until 1968, the year when Gibson reissued the 1955 style gold-top (*with* tune-o-matic). The reissue is easily distinguishable from the original by the binding inside the cutaway; it is exceptionally wide on the newer guitar, covering the edge line between the mahogany and maple pieces.

According to the manufacturer, a very few leftover gold-tops may have been shipped in 1958, still with the cream pickups and either the old 1954 type bridge or the newer tune-o-matic.* Perhaps this is why Gibson called its early 1970s gold-top reissue the "58 style," even though it was really the 1954 type (*without* tune-o-matic). The reissue may be distinguished by the following features, none of which appears on the 1954 Les Paul: *Gibson* on the pickups in raised letters, a raised ridge on the tailpiece (on some models), and the words *MADE IN USA* stamped on the back of the headstock. The original had serial numbers stamped in ink, while on the reissue they are actually impressed into the wood. The 1954 reissue is easily fitted with older parts, so beware of forgeries.

In 1968 Gibson also announced a Les Paul Custom that was claimed to be "an exact duplicate of the original." It was nothing of the sort. (The imprecise description was unfortunately typical of Gibson reissue literature during the 1970s.) The 1968 Custom's *two* humbuckings* distinguished it from the 1954–1957 Customs, which had nonhumbucking pickups, and also from the 1957–1961 models, which had *three* humbuckings. Complying with public requests, Gibson built the new Custom with a carved maple top that produced a sharper tone than the one-piece mahogany body of the original.

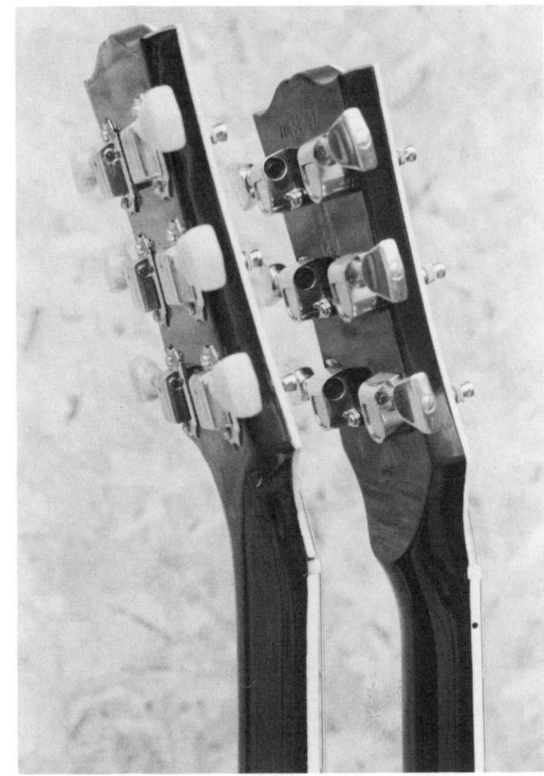

The peghead on the right has the volute that Gibson began using on many models circa early 1970. At about the same time, Gibson began stamping *MADE IN U.S.A.* on the rear surface between the two rows of tuners.

LES PAUL DELUXE

The 1968 reissue of the 1955 type gold-top was made for less than a year. Gibson then decided to install small humbuckings that would fit the holes originally cut for the old cream pickups; this guitar was called Les Paul Deluxe. It featured a three-piece neck, whereas the 1968 reissue had a one-piece neck and a narrower peghead. Transition models have cream pickups, one-piece necks, and wide headstocks.

Late-1970s Les Paul Deluxe.

*Though they were originally Gibson terms, *tune-o-matic* and *humbucking* are spelled here with lower-case letters because of their generic status.

1954 Les Paul Custom. Note front Alnico pickup with rectangular polepieces. *Gruhn*

Left-handed Les Paul Custom. *Guitar Player*

1954–1955 style Les Paul Custom reissue. The vast majority were shipped in 1973.

1958 Les Paul Custom. *Charley's/Crump*

1961 Les Paul Custom ("SG/Les Paul" Custom). Note pearl-inlaid ebony tailpiece. *Wes Johnson/Allen Johnson*

Group II

LES PAUL CUSTOM

The Custom made its debut in 1954 (see the McCarty article earlier in this section), and its low, flat frets and ebony finish gave rise to the *Fretless Wonder* and *Black Beauty* nicknames. Its features included two pickups (the front had bar polepieces) with black plastic covers, a mahogany neck, a bound ebony fingerboard, a one-piece solid Honduras mahogany body (unlike the gold-top, which has a maple cap), gold-plated parts, and a tune-o-matic. The 1954 style Custom (mislabeled *Les Paul Deluxe* in a 1954 price list) was reissued in late 1972 in a limited series.

In November 1957 the guitar was fitted with three humbuckings; it cost $375 without the Bigsby. Its toggle switch allowed a choice of the front pickup alone, center plus rear, or rear alone. The model remained unchanged through 1961. A *very* few were made with two pickups.

In 1961 the Custom was completely restyled, now featuring the SG type double cutaway, an all-white finish, the Gibson vibrato (see late-1961 Les Paul Standard), and again, three humbuckings.

A commemorative Les Paul Custom was unveiled in 1974. It bore the words *Twentieth Anniversary* inlaid in a special fretboard marker.

SG CUSTOM

This model replaced the 1962 SG style Les Paul Custom. It was virtually the same guitar except for its restyled Deluxe Vibrola (see early-1960s SG Standard). In about 1966 the white pickguard was enlarged to cover most of the body's upper half. A walnut finish became available in the late 1960s. By 1972 the guitar was given a new, triangular pickguard, and the controls were housed in a semicircular plate. A Bigsby replaced the Vibrola. In 1973 the smaller, wing-shaped pickguard—roughly the 1966 style—returned. The model also featured a new tune-o-matic in an enlarged rectangular housing, and cylindrical speed knobs.

Group III

LES PAUL JR. AND SG JR.

Originating in 1954, the Les Paul Jr. (sometimes spelled *Junior* in Gibson literature) had a flat, single-cutaway body, one pickup, a mahogany neck, a Brazilian rosewood fingerboard, 22 frets, a combination bridge/tailpiece, and a sunburst top. In mid-1958 it changed to a cherry red double-cutaway with rounded edges, unlike the fairly sharp single cutaway of the 1954 Jr. It cost $120, and a few were made in three-quarter size.

In 1961 it went to the SG type body but retained the Les Paul name. A little over a year later the name changed to SG Jr., and three years after that, a Gibson Vibrola was added. The pickup of the 1964–1966 SG Jr. was separated from the pickguard. In about 1967, the pickguard was enlarged, engulfing the

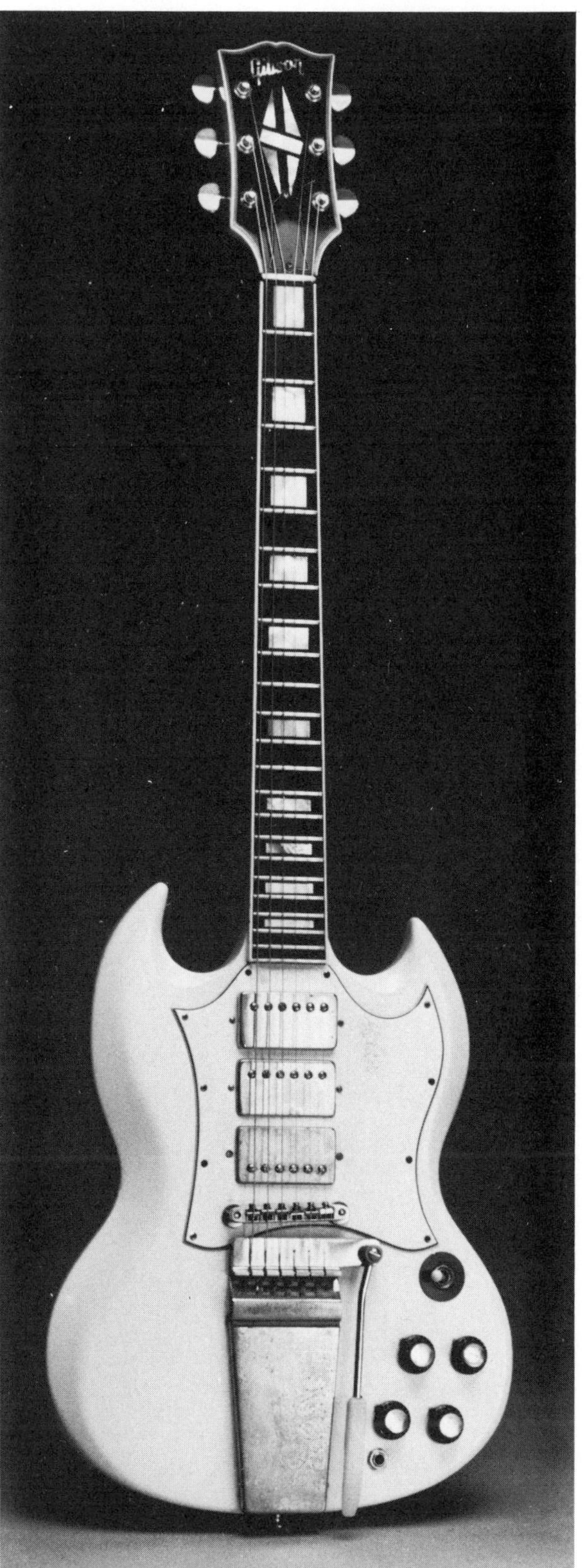

1968 SG Custom. *Wallace/Perla*

1955 Les Paul Jr. Note gold, clear-top, skirted knobs. *Charley's/Crump*

1958 Les Paul Jr. *Charley's/Crump*

1961 Les Paul Jr. *Jacksonville*

SG Jr., 1966 type with Gibson Vibrola. *Ax-In-Hand*

1957 Les Paul TV, P-90 pickup, black skirted knobs. *Charley's/Crump*

1960 Les Paul TV. *Jay Levin*

1955 Les Paul Special, replacement tuners. *Charley's/Crump*

pickup and covering most of both sides of the upper body. The model was discontinued after 1970.

LES PAUL TV AND SG TV

Debuting in 1957, the Les Paul TV had a "limed mahogany" finish and was otherwise identical to the 1954 Les Paul Jr. Like the Jr., it went to a double cutaway in December 1958. The name was changed to SG TV in 1960, but it retained the 1958 shape (compare this to the Jr. above, whose change in body shape *preceded* the name change). In 1961 the sharp-cornered SG shape was adopted, and the guitar was given a white finish. It was discontinued after 1964.

LES PAUL SPECIAL

Introduced in September 1955, the limed mahogany Special was like the Les Paul TV but with *two* nonhumbucking pickups, a laminated pickguard, a pearl "Gibson" headstock logo, and a bound fingerboard. The pickup covers were similar in size to those of the early gold-tops, while those on Juniors and TVs were of the larger, "dog ear" type. In about March 1959 the Special changed to a rounded double-cutaway. Options included a three-quarter size body and a cherry red finish.

SG SPECIAL

The SG Special of 1960 was the same guitar as the 1959 Les Paul Special. In 1961 it was given the SG body, available in cherry or white. In 1966 a Vibrola was added, and in that same year or the year after, the pickguard was enlarged. The model was discontinued in 1971, replaced by the SG Pro. It was reintroduced in late 1972 with the new type tune-o-matic in an enlarged rectangular housing, and it had new, plastic-covered humbuckings. The 1966 type wing-shaped pickguard returned.

Something of a dwarf among solidbodies, the Les Paul Special three-quarter-size guitar, circa 1959. *Gruhn*

1960 SG Special. Except for the name, it's the same as the 1959 Les Paul Special. The earliest Les Paul Specials with this body shape had their toggle switches in a different location—halfway between the tailpiece and the rear strap button and between the front pickup's two knobs. *Charley's/Crump*

SG DELUXE

In late 1971 the SG Standard was replaced by the SG Deluxe, with two humbuckings, an elevated triangular pickguard, a Bigsby, and a semicircular control housing plate. The SG Deluxe was discontinued after 1972, when the Standard was reintroduced.

SG PRO

In late 1971 the SG Special was replaced by the SG Pro, with a Bigsby, two nonhumbucking pickups, and the same pickguard and control plate as the SG Deluxe. It was discontinued after 1972 when the Special was reintroduced.

1965 SG Special. *Ed Seelig*

Extremely rare 4-string Gibson solidbodies. At left is a tenor guitar with a Gibson tenor banjo neck, only 19 frets, and a short 22¾-inch scale. Its other features are like those of a Les Paul Special, circa 1957. At right is an SG-style plectrum model, circa 1962, with 22 frets and a 26¼-inch scale. Note the pickups on each guitar; they have four polepieces instead of six, and the extra holes in the black plastic covers are filled with circular pieces resembling fingerboard position markers. These are the rarest of the postwar Gibsons pictured in *American Guitars.*
Gruhn

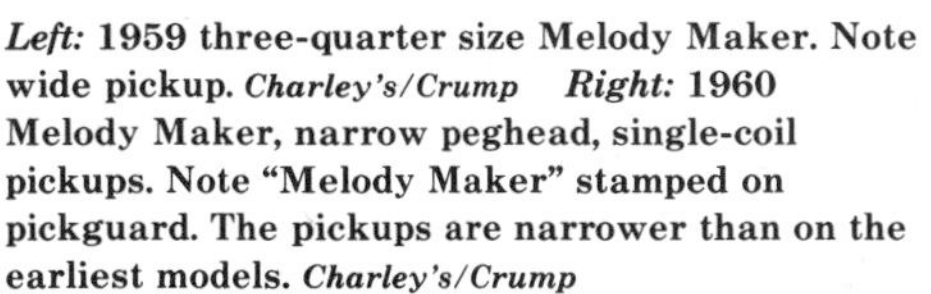

Left: 1959 three-quarter size Melody Maker. Note wide pickup. *Charley's/Crump* *Right:* 1960 Melody Maker, narrow peghead, single-coil pickups. Note "Melody Maker" stamped on pickguard. The pickups are narrower than on the earliest models. *Charley's/Crump*

Gruhn

Melody Makers: 1962–1963 (*left*) and circa 1965. The later version has additional sculpturing, sharper "horns." *Jacksonville*

1968 Melody Maker III: three pickups, Vibrola, available in Sparkling Burgundy or Pelham Blue finish. *Honest Ron's*

Group IV

MELODY MAKER

This guitar, new in 1959, had a single cutaway, a flat body, a small peghead, the same scale and number of frets as the 1952 Les Paul, and a sunburst finish. It was available with one or two pickups of an unusual design for Gibson—single-coil, long and narrow, and rounded at the ends. It went to a double cutaway in 1961. The body changed slightly in about 1964 (photo, previous page), and a red finish replaced the sunburst.

In 1966 the SG-type contoured body replaced its flat predecessor, and a blue finish joined the line. An enlarged white pickguard and a Vibrola were also added. Then in 1970 the red and blue finishes were replaced by walnut, and the unusual slide-type pickup selector was replaced with a conventional toggle. The peghead was enlarged to the standard size.

SG 100, 200, AND 250

In 1971, these guitars replaced the Melody Maker line. They had narrow, single-coil pickups, triangular pickguards, and rectangular tailpiece covers. The controls were housed in a metal plate shaped like a tongue depressor. The two-pickup models had slide switches.

SG I, II, AND III

In late 1972 or early 1973 this trio replaced the short-lived 100, 200, and 250. The new models had triangular pickguards, semicircular control housing plates, and new humbuckers with rectangular *plastic* covers.

1973 SGs, from left: SG-II, SG Special (note rectangular black plastic pickup covers), and SG Standard.

1973 Les Paul Signature bass and guitar (made with a 335 body).

Group V

LES PAUL PERSONAL

This 1969 guitar had low-impedance pickups, *gold* plating, and the old type of tune-o-matic. Its cutaway was more rounded than that of other single-cutaway Les Pauls.

LES PAUL PROFESSIONAL

This 1969 low-impedance model had *nickel* plating and the old tune-o-matic.

LES PAUL RECORDING

This 1971 model replaced the Personal and Professional. It had low-impedance pickups, and a large plastic plate that housed all the controls.

LES PAUL SIGNATURE

The gold-top 1973 Signature used a sawed-off ES-335 body and was the first semiacoustic Les Paul. It had low-impedance pickups.

Les Paul Recording. The original model had a standard, smaller tune-o-matic.

1978 Les Paul 55/78. Announced as a reissue of the 1955 Les Paul, it is in fact a combination of features never before found together on any single Gibson. Basically, it's a 1955–1958 style Special with speed knobs and a tune-o-matic.

The Flying V, Explorer, and Moderne

Prior to Fender, manufacturers fostered an image of the guitar scene that was a blend of upbeat class, hallowed tradition, and innovation. But Fender came out of nowhere, with no tradition, and helped establish a new guitar subspecies. Competitors wondered, as the movie character Butch Cassidy once hollered to the Sundance Kid, "Who *are* those guys?"

It was 1957, the year of "Jailhouse Rock" and Sputnik. Ford and Chevy tailfins went from round to sharp. It had become acceptable for a guitar company to be not only innovative but radical. Gibson, despite its many breakthroughs, had a reputation for being about as radical as *Art Linkletter's House Party.* But Ted McCarty had just the thing: the Flying V, essentially a neck with two tailfins, and the Explorer, a solidbody shaped like a lightning bolt. Both were formally introduced in 1958, along with their companion, the mysterious Moderne. For details of their development, see the McCarty interview earlier in this section.

FLYING V

The following features distinguish an original Flying V from subsequent versions: knobs in a straight line, squared "shoul-

Left: 1970 Les Paul Jumbo, a very odd flat-top with a low-impedance pickup and top-mounted controls. *James Hilligoss* *Right:* 1976 Les Paul Artisan. The 1979 model had a TP-6 tailpiece. Because of the similarity of their names this model is sometimes confused with the Les Paul Artist, which has active electronics, a TP-6, three microswitches, and block markers.

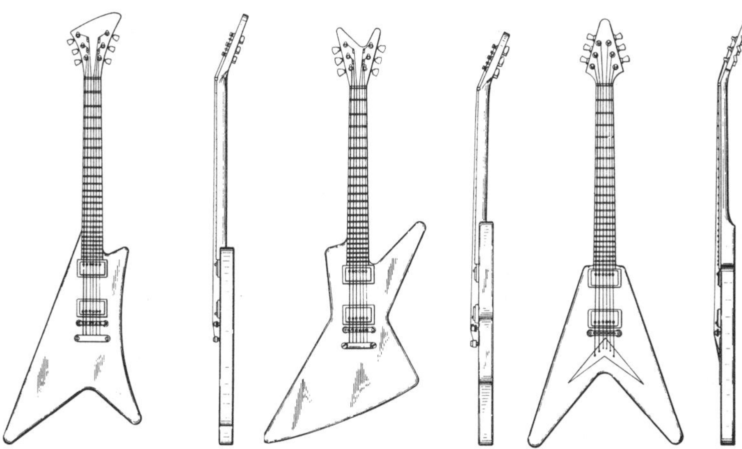

Three of Theodore M. McCarty's design patents for Gibson. From left: the Moderne, the Explorer, and the Flying V. The joint patent application was submitted on June 27, 1957.

ders" (neck/body joint), korina body (*korina* is a trade name for selected pieces of African limba wood), gold-plated hardware, patent-applied-for humbuckings, all frets clear of the body, smaller pickguard with pickup mounting rings, and a raised plastic *Gibson* logo glued on the peghead. Additionally, on the originals the strings passed through a wedge-shaped metal plate and through the body, while later V's had stud tailpieces or vibratos. Finally, the original had an oval groove fitted with a black strip of ridged rubber on the right wing to keep the guitar from sliding off the player's lap.*

The early Flying V's were not taken very seriously (see Ted McCarty's comments earlier in the Gibson section), and they sold poorly when introduced. Some original bodies made in 1958 and stamped with 1958 serial numbers were stored at the factory until 1962–63. Those leaving in 1962–63 are often considered originals, although they had patent-number pickups and nickel-plated parts.

Incidentally, the photo of the Flying V on the back of the March 1959 catalogue was substantially retouched by an artist, and several of the illustrated features never appeared on a production V, including the dark finish, lack of a toggle switch, and the body binding. A very few V's were made with stock black pickguards.

Flying V reissues are easily distinguishable (from the original V's) by all of their following features: an extra large truss rod cover, sloped shoulders at the neck/body joint, a relocated strap button, the treble end of the fretboard rests on the top (rather than all frets clear), an enlarged pickguard without pickup rings, a triangular (rather than straight-line) knob configuration, a relocated switch and jack, a stud tailpiece (rather than strings passing through V-shaped plates), a rear peghead vo-

1958 Flying V. ***Dave Di Martino***

* Some of the very earliest V's lack this feature.

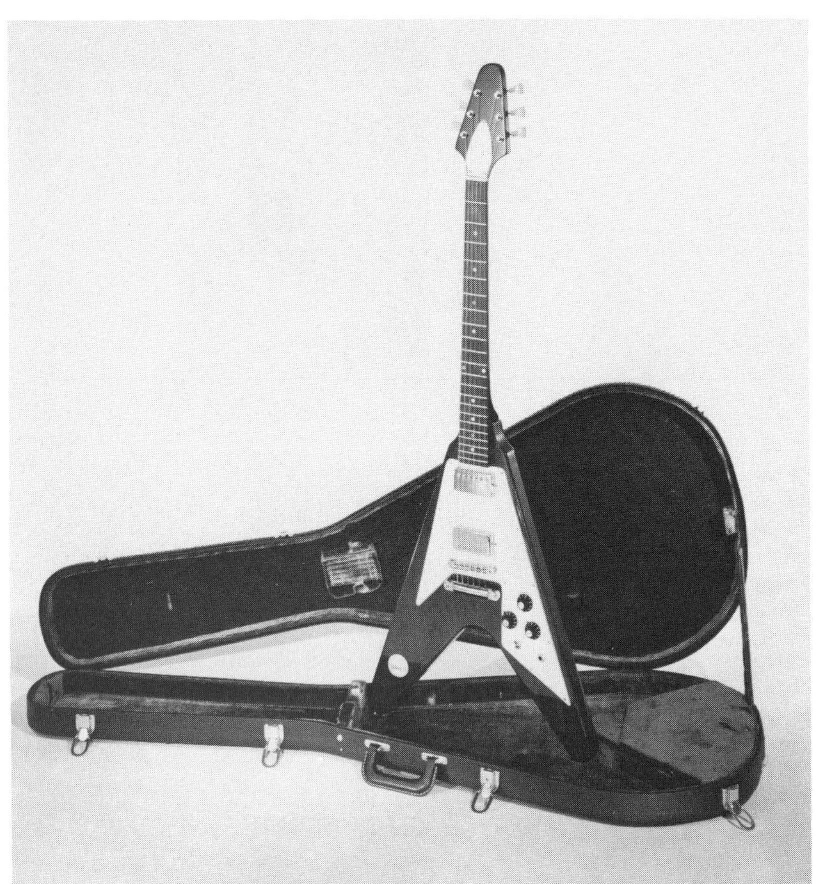

A pair of Flying V reissues (at left is an early-1970s "Medallion" series model).

1979 Flying V-II, Boomerang pickups, brass bridge studs, five-piece maple/walnut body, brass nut.

lute, and a *MADE IN U.S.A.* stamp on the back of the peghead; the volute and stamp are only on 1970 and later models.

Flying V reissues were shipped in 1967, 1969–1971, and 1975–1978, with a smattering of additional shipments in 1966, 1973, and 1974.

EXPLORER

The Explorer was very similar to the Flying V except for its body shape. Like the V, it was ahead of its time and fizzled on the launching pad. During the late 1970s prices for original V's and Explorers sometimes exceeded $4,000, and the body shapes were copied by many replacement parts and kit companies and young manufacturers as well as various Japanese firms—most notably Ibanez, whose V copy was much truer to the original than Gibson's own reissue. Gibson's Explorer reissues appeared in 1975 (only two were shipped that year, but 2,006 were shipped in 1976). While early Flying V's had through-the-body string anchoring and raised plastic *Gibson* peghead logos, the Explorers had stop tailpieces and pearl *Gibson* logos. Some 1958 Explorers left the factory in 1962–63; see Flying V.

The original Explorer prototype, or "Futura," is depicted in a diagram registered with the U.S. Patent Office and represents Gibson's earliest Explorer-like design. According to shipping records, it left the Kalamazoo plant along with ten other handmade experimental guitars in 1955. Refinements of the body and headstock were made both for aesthetic reasons and to conform the design to limitations of the factory's regular production tooling. The restyled version was christened Explorer and introduced in 1958.

Gibson engineers often adopted nicknames or "working titles" for experimental guitars prior to the selection of an official designation by Gibson's parent company, then CMI of Chicago. When this guitar was first displayed at a music industry trade show, it was called the Futura (remembered by some old timers as Futurama or Futuristic). However, that name was never used in catalogs, price lists, *Gibson Gazettes,* or other documents. The Futura is an Explorer prototype with an unofficial nickname and is not a separate model. It is probably one of a kind, though a very few of the earliest Explorers share a similar split headstock.

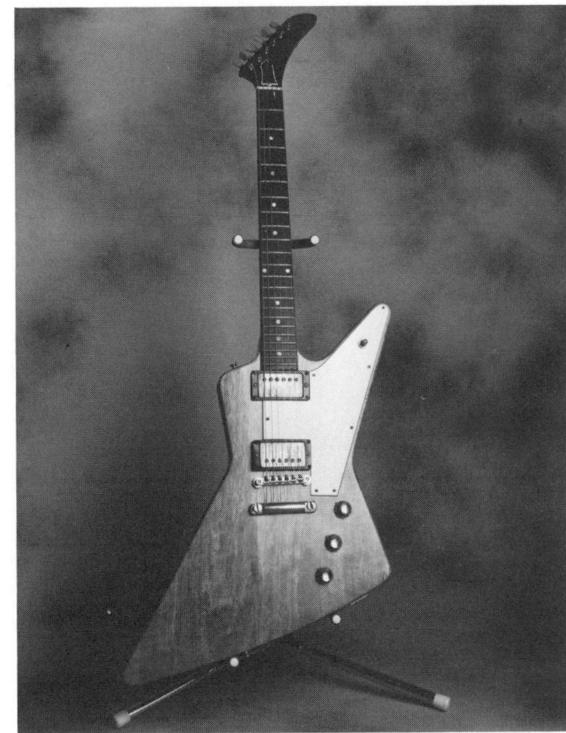

John Entwistle's 1958 Explorer. A very few Explorer basses were also made, circa 1959. ***Alan Rogan/Gavin Cochrane***

Firebirds

Novices sometimes confuse reverse and nonreverse Firebirds, which to a collector is like confusing Errol Flynn and Elmer Fudd. Introduced in mid 1963 and discontinued after May 1965, the reverse-body Firebirds are the "good" ones, the collector's items. Their design, however radical, was nevertheless something of a compromise. In 1958 president Ted McCarty and his drafting-table comrades had unveiled a trio of crazy-shape solidbodies intended to show the world that Gibson was a forward-looking outfit. The Explorer and Flying V took off, fizzled, and died a fiery death (they were later resurrected). Their doomed companion, the Moderne, never made it off the ground. (For details of the development of all these models, see the Ted McCarty article earlier in this section.)

Four years after the expiration of this triumvirate of distinguished duds, McCarty and crew enlisted Ray Dietrich, a Detroit auto designer. They took a full-length neck/centerpiece (cut on an automatic shaper), stuck on some body "wings" that gave it a rounded-off, toned-down Explorer look, added a very distinctive headstock, and, at Dietrich's suggestion, christened the series *Firebird.* Mr. McCarty explained, "Any time you glue two pieces of wood together, there's going to be a little change in how solid the instrument is, and that's why we came up with this full-length idea instead of gluing the neck into a slot in the body. The things that we did—even if they looked crazy—were done for reasons, not just to be doing something."

Commercially, the debut of the Firebirds was more successful than that of the V and Explorer (it couldn't have been much *less* successful); still, the new models hardly set the world on fire. There were four guitars, all with mahogany bodies, the characteristic Firebird humbucking pickups (rectangular nickel silver covers, concealed polepieces, large mounting rings), white/black/white triple-ply pickguards with beveled edges, full-length neck/centerpieces, 22-fret fingerboards, and unique

The Futura, or Explorer prototype. ***Kurt Linhof***

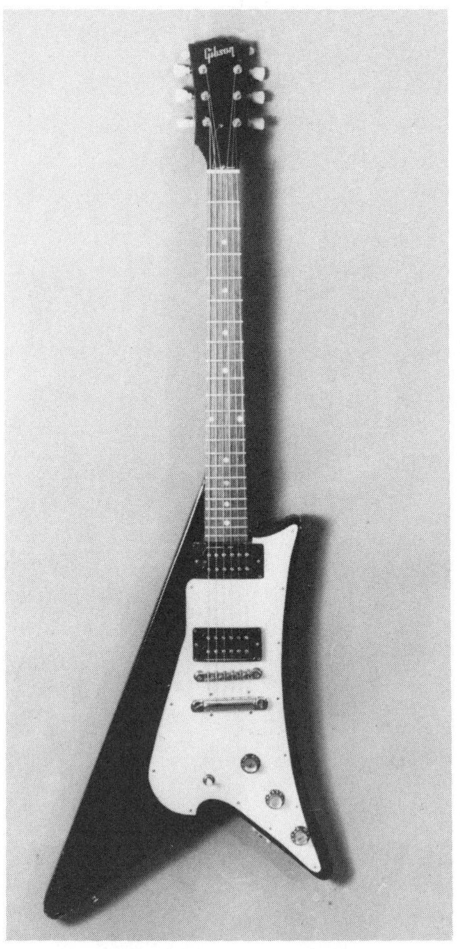

Among electric guitars, the Moderne is perhaps the ultimate collector's item, a veritable Holy Grail. According to George Gruhn, the one illustrated here is unfortunately fake. It has a colorful history of fraud, threatened lawsuits, and intercontinental travel and is now owned by a Japanese industrialist. For details, see the Moderne discussion in the Ted McCarty section, page 143. ***Guitar Player***

Reverse Firebird I. ***Prune***

Reverse Firebird III. ***Apirak Sillapachai***

headstocks with perpendicularly mounted, banjo style tuners. The treble E string's tuning machine was located nearest the string nut, and there was a sculptured ledge around the peghead. Sunburst was standard, and various optional Custom Duco colors were available for an extra $15.

In order to distinguish it from its very different successors, the original style was unofficially dubbed *reverse*, referring to the fact that, like almost no other guitar except the Explorer, the body is "backward": the "horn" on the treble side is higher and more pronounced than the other one.

The initial Firebird headstock is a rare example of one company taking another's design, rearranging it a bit, and coming up with something truly new, something "derived" rather than stolen (granted, it's a fine line, subjectively drawn). Like the original Mosrite body, the early Firebird peghead's shape was essentially a turned-around Fender. "We were very, very aware of Fender," McCarty explained in referring to the Firebird's banjo tuners, "and we never wanted our guitar to look like a Fender copy. If we had used the other kind of machine head it would have looked too much like a Fender. One thing that Gibson would never do, at least while I was there, was copy anybody else. The unusual shape of the headstock precluded our using standard tuners. We also felt that the banjo pegs were simply easier to tune, easier to reach."

Reverse Firebird V. See color photo 125. *Guitar Trader/Photog. Unlimited*

Reverse Firebird VII. See color photo 124, the nonreverse model.

A pair of Firebird headstocks with banjo pegs and sculpted ledges (*left,* 1963; *right,* 1965). Note that both the shapes and the arrangements of the pegs are reversed.

Reverse Thunderbird IV, two pickups. *Jacksonville*

With its single, unobtrusive pickup, minimal hardware, and sleek body ridges down the center, the reverse Firebird I was a classic statement of early 1960s guitar modernism, a spaceship form with a clean functionalism uncluttered by extraneous bolt-on accessories. There was no vibrato. It had a combination bridge/tailpiece with a high-relief ridge designed to ensure accurate intonation, nickel-plated machines, and an unbound rosewood fingerboard with dot markers. It listed for $189.50 (those were the days).

The $249.50 Firebird III had two pickups, a bound rosewood board with dots, and a three-way pickup selector on the treble-side body horn. The remarkably simple but effective Gibson Vibrola was mounted behind the bridge, affixed directly to the top. It operated without springs; the handle simply bent a metal strip that ideally returned to its original position when the handle was released. The slightly curved lever had three mounting holes for an adjustable action. The bridge was originally designed for use on other models, including the Firebird I, as a combination bridge/tailpiece.

The 1963 $325 Firebird V, a prime collector's guitar, had the same pickups and three-way selector as the III. The bound rosewood fretboard was inlaid with trapezoidal markers at frets 3, 5, 7, 9, 12, 15, 17, 19, and 21—the same fret positions marked by dots on the I and III; the V was the only Firebird with trapezoids. Its bridge was a tune-o-matic, and its Deluxe Vibrola was a fancy version of the one found on the III: it had a long, nickel-plated panel (like SG Standards of the period) engraved with *Gibson* and a leaf and lyre decoration. The lever was tubular instead of flat, and capped with a spiffy white plastic tip.

1.
The pearl and rosewood inlays on this mid-1930s Gibson L-C, or Century, are slightly more elaborate than usual. The idea for the pearloid fingerboard was borrowed from Gibson banjos.

2.
This guitar was probably made by Regal and has alternating colored wood top trim, a hand-painted top, and a white plastic fingerboard. Its peghead is like that of the slot-head W&S shown in the Weymann chapter.

3.
Gibson/Epiphone Al Caiola Custom. Note tone switches, bridge inlays, and the lack of f-holes. The body is that of an ES-335. Only 174 were made, all from 1966 to 1970. See the Al Caiola Standard, color photo 46.

4.
This Prairie State is a flat-top with f-holes, an L-5 size body, and abalone trim. Compare this Maurer-made guitar with photo no. 7.

5.
Gibson ES-295 ($295 list), all-gold body, flower pickguard, Les Paul tailpiece. Essentially a fancy ES-175, it changed in 1955 from 19 to 20 frets. Gibson built 1,770 in all, from 1952 to 1958.

6.
1952 Gibson J-185, designed as a compact J-200. Only 643 sunburst (1951–1958) and 270 natural (1951–1959) models were shipped. The bridge's twin inlaid crosses are unique. In 1952 the neck was specified to be maple; mahogany was soon substituted.

7.
Maurer roundhole flat-top with pearl trim. Compare it with the f-hole Prairie State, no. 4.

8.
An exceptionally fine maple-neck Fender Strat, factory green finish.

9.
Stock green Strat, rear view.

10.
1948 Fender Broadcaster, serial no. 0022.

11.
Broadcaster headstock.

12.
1952 Fender Telecaster. Compare it with no. 10.

13.
1958 Fender Stratocaster, maple neck, Dakota Red finish, small headstock.

14.
1954 two-color Strat, serial no. 0642.

15.
1958 three-color Strat.

16.
Gibson's top of the line is the Citation arch-top, and this is the first one made.

17.
The Citation's extremely tight-grained maple back.

18.
Tal Farlow's own Tal Farlow guitar with added pickup, modified bridge base, and improvised string mute.

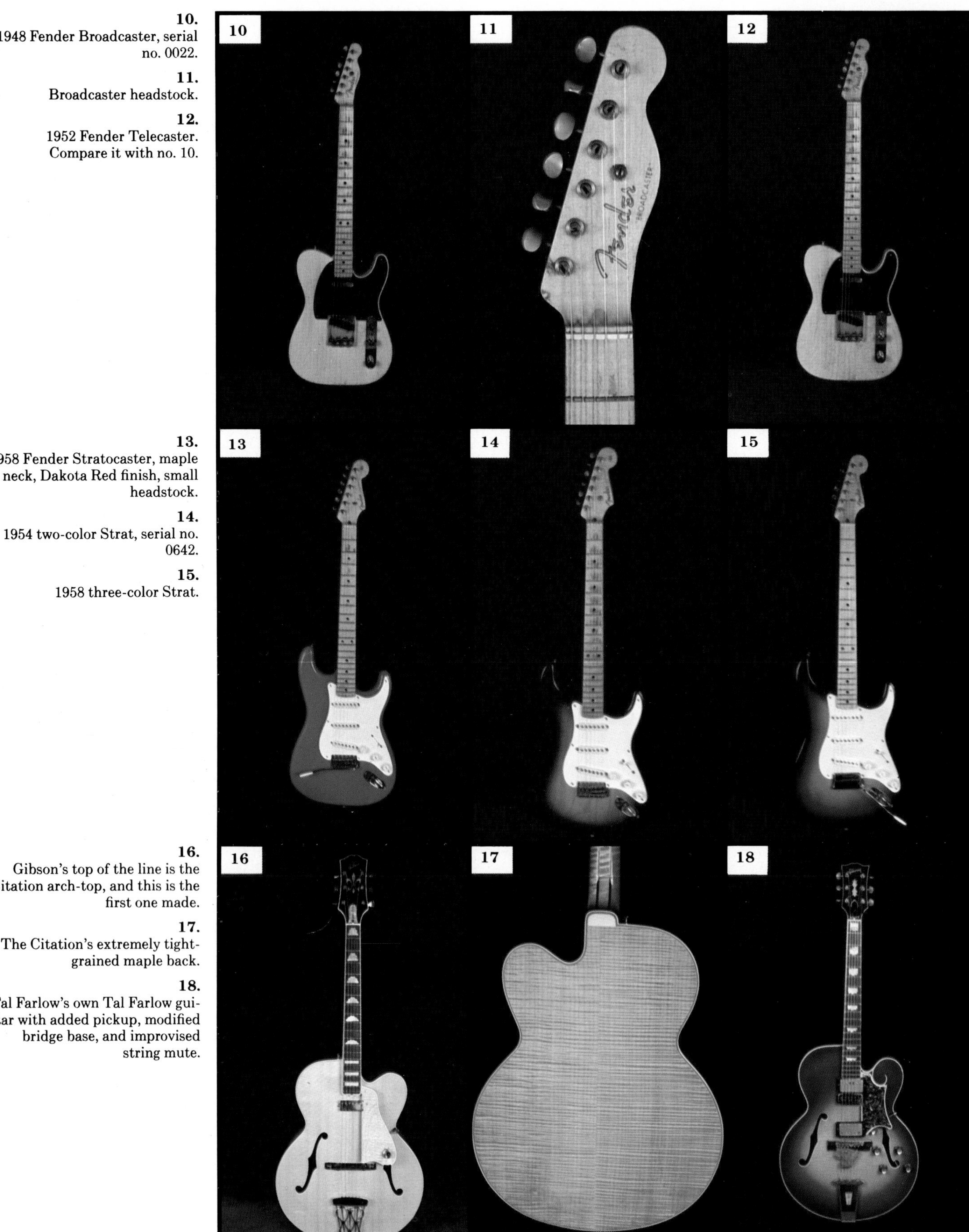

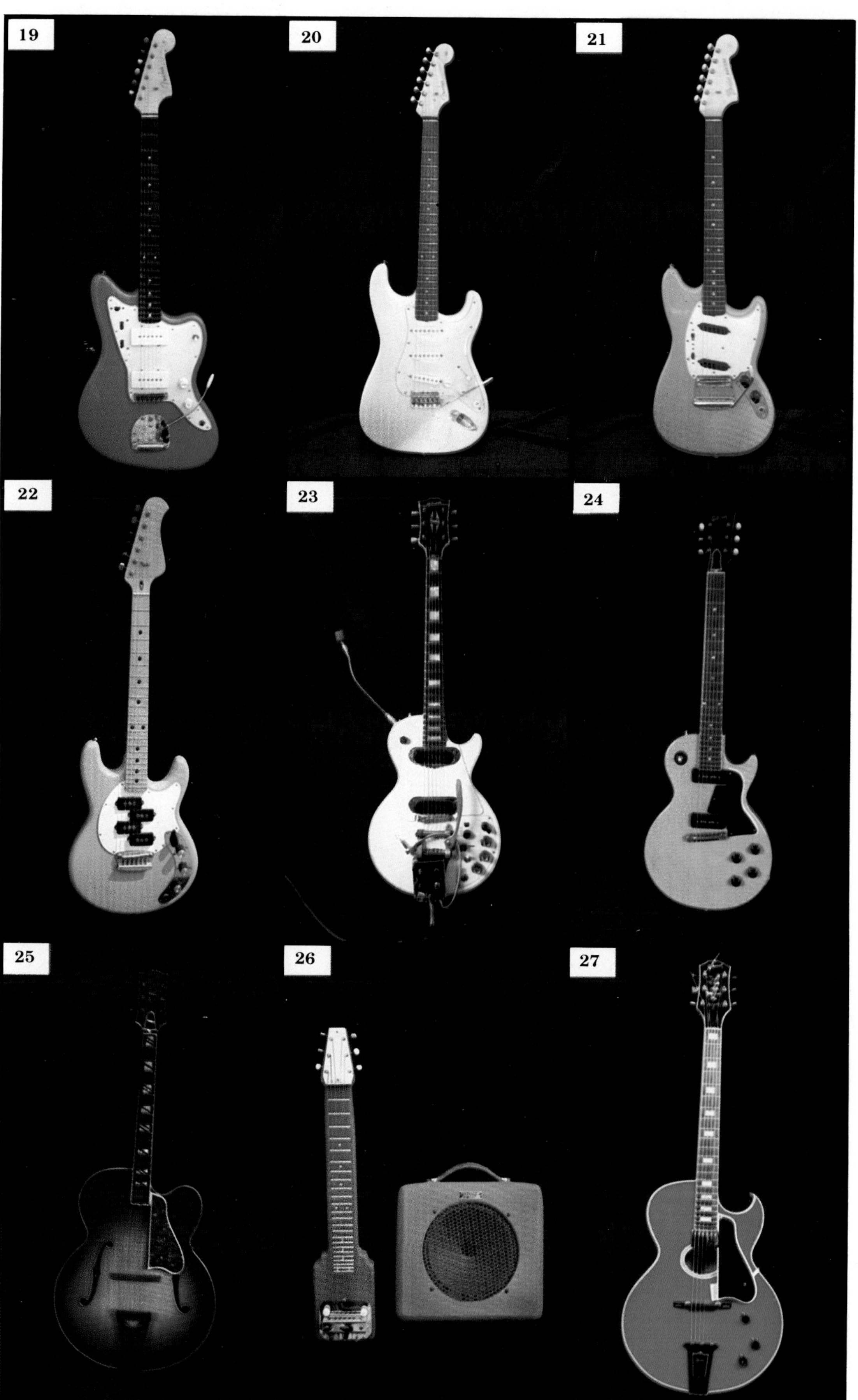

19.
The first official custom-colored Fender, a Fiesta Red Jazzmaster. See George Fullerton's account in the Fender chapter.

20.
White pre-CBS Stratocaster with gold hardware, rosewood fingerboard. Note laminated pickguard, and compare it with the older, single-layer type in color photos 13, 14, and 15; note the difference in the number of pickguard screws.

21.
Fender Mustang, factory blue finish.

22.
The prototype for Music Man's first electric 6-string, built by Leo Fender and his staff.

23.
Les Paul's own Les Paul with built-in microphone and the "Les Paulverizer," a tape recorder remote control and special effects device.

24.
1956 Gibson Les Paul Special; compare it with no. 92.

25.
1957 sunburst Gibson Super 400C.

26.
Mr. Fender's personal K&F lap steel and amp set.

27.
Howard Roberts' own Howard Roberts Custom. (The matchbook serves to elevate the pickguard.)

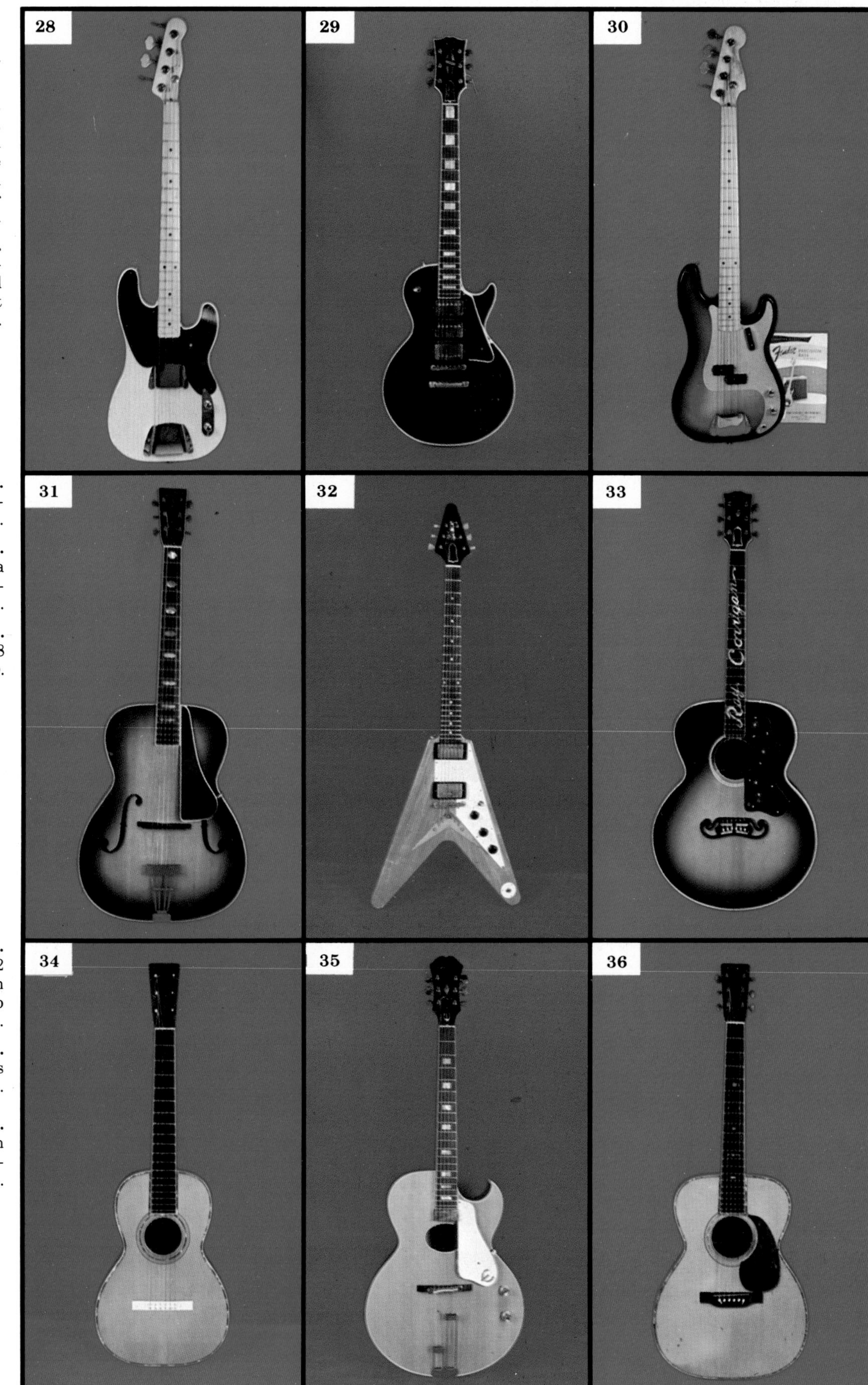

28.
1952 Fender Precision Bass, slab body, small peghead. Compare it with no. 30.

29.
1961 Gibson Les Paul Custom, one of the last of the original three-pickup models. Note the Super 400–type split diamond peghead inlay. Also see color photo 101.

30.
1958 Precision Bass with contoured body, large peghead, gold anodized pickguard, and split pickup.

31.
1939 Martin F-9 arch-top, hexagonal markers.

32.
1958 Gibson Flying V, korina body. Compare it with the reissue Vs in the Gibson chapter.

33.
"Crash" Corrigan's 1938 rosewood Gibson J-200.

34.
Turn-of-the-century Martin 0-42 with ivory bridge, ivory friction pegs, and pearl trim around top and soundhole.

35.
1967 Epiphone Howard Roberts (standard model).

36.
Martin 000–42. Note pearl trim and inlays (bridge dots unoriginal).

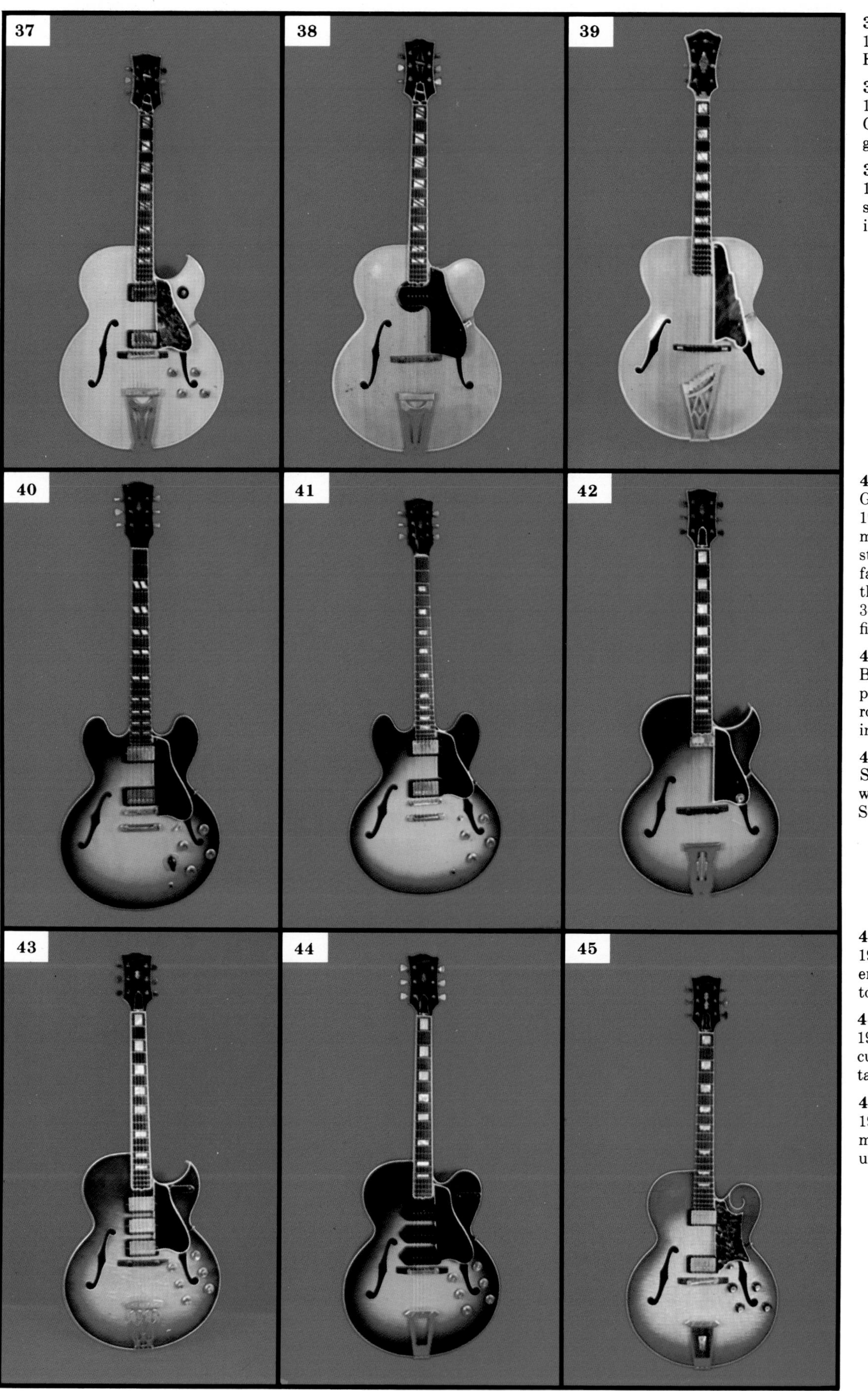

37.
1961 Gibson Super 400CESN, Florentine cutaway.

38.
1954 Gibson Super 400CN with Gibson pickup/pick-guard assembly.

39.
1938 D'Angelico New Yorker, stairstep tailpiece. Note peghead inlay.

40.
Gibson ES-345TD, introduced in 1959; note long pickguard. The model might be considered a stereo 335 with gold plating and fancier trim, though less fancy than the ES-355. (A very few 345s have markers starting at the first fret.)

41.
Block-neck Gibson ES-335. Compare its cutaways with the more rounded type of the earlier guitar in no. 40.

42.
Special-order Gibson L-5C with factory-installed Johnny Smith pickup.

43.
1961 Gibson Switchmaster, Florentine cutaway. Highly figured top, fancy tailpiece.

44.
1955 Switchmaster. Compare its cutaway, pickups, knobs, and tailpiece with no. 43.

45.
1962 Gibson Tal Farlow. Note markers, body scroll, highly figured top, and inlaid tailpiece.

46.
The Gibson-made Epiphone Al Caiola Standard has ES-330 type pickups and no f-holes. Compare it with the Custom model, color photo 3.

47.
Epiphone Zenith acoustic.

48.
1965 Gibson/Epiphone Professional, made with an ES-335 body and featuring built-in "reverb-tremolo Tonexpressor."

49.
1959 National Belaire, with a Gibson ES-175 body and Gibson type tailpiece.

50.
Late-1960s blue flower print Telecaster, a companion to the paisley model shown in color photo no. 63.

51.
The one-of-a-kind see-through Stratocaster, an experimental guitar made of Lucite. See detail on page 80.

52.
1957 Gibson Les Paul Standard, with gold top and humbuckings.

53.
1959 Gibson EB-0 bass. Note friction-type tuners.

54.
Noncutaway 1953 Gibson Super 400 with factory pickup/pickguard assembly.

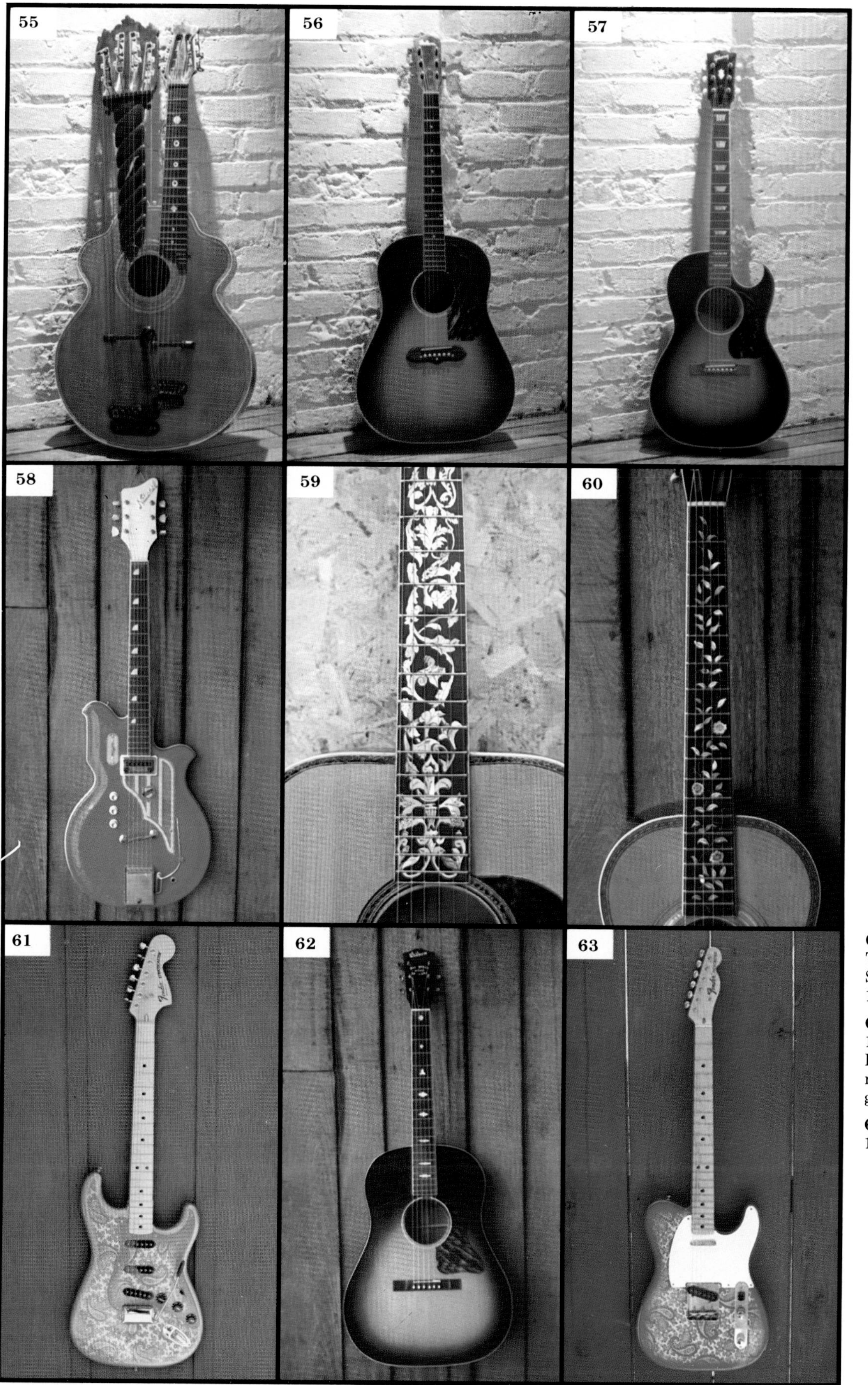

55.
This awesome creature, a harp guitar, was built by Joseph Bowman of Chicago in about 1909. It features seven tunable sympathetic strings *inside* the body, exceptionally fine tuners of Bowman's design, a palm rest, a swirling carved harp neck, and pearl inlays.

56.
1941–1942 Gibson J-55. Note the carved three-dot bridge.

57.
Gibson's CF-100 cutaway mahogany acoustic was shipped from 1950 to 1959. Compare it with the CF-100E in the Gibson chapter.

58.
1964 National Newport 82 with synthetic "Glas" body. The body shape resembles a map of the United States.

59.
Fingerboard detail from a steel-string labeled The Winters, serial no. 0007.

60.
Early Washburn fingerboard inlay detail.

61.
The one and only stock paisley Stratocaster, made in the late 1970s.

62.
1936 Gibson Roy Smeck Stage De Luxe. Its dreadnought body is most unusual for a Hawaiian guitar.

63.
1969 paisley Telecaster.

64.
Early-1960s Gibson Byrdland. Note three-loop tailpiece and L-5 type ornamentation (flower pot inlay, block markers, pointed fingerboard). It was named after two guitarists with whom it was closely associated, Billy Byrd and Hank Garland.

65.
Gibson L-5, circa 1939. Note original tuners. Noncutaway L-5s were sold through the late 1950s.

66.
Gibson ES-175D, zigzag tailpiece. The original version of mid-1949 ($175 in sunburst, hence the model number) was Gibson's first guitar with a modern Florentine cutaway. It changed from 19 to 20 frets in 1955.

67.
Rickenbacker 4001 bass.

68.
Gibson ES-335 12-string, introduced in 1965 to capitalize on the folk-rock boom.

69.
Mosrite Joe Maphis solidbody doubleneck.

64

65

66

67

68

69

70.
D'Angelico Style B (bridge unoriginal). Note peghead.

71.
D'Angelico Style B, back.

72.
Stromberg Master 400, mid-1940s. Note extremely wide (19-inch) lower bouts.

70

71

72

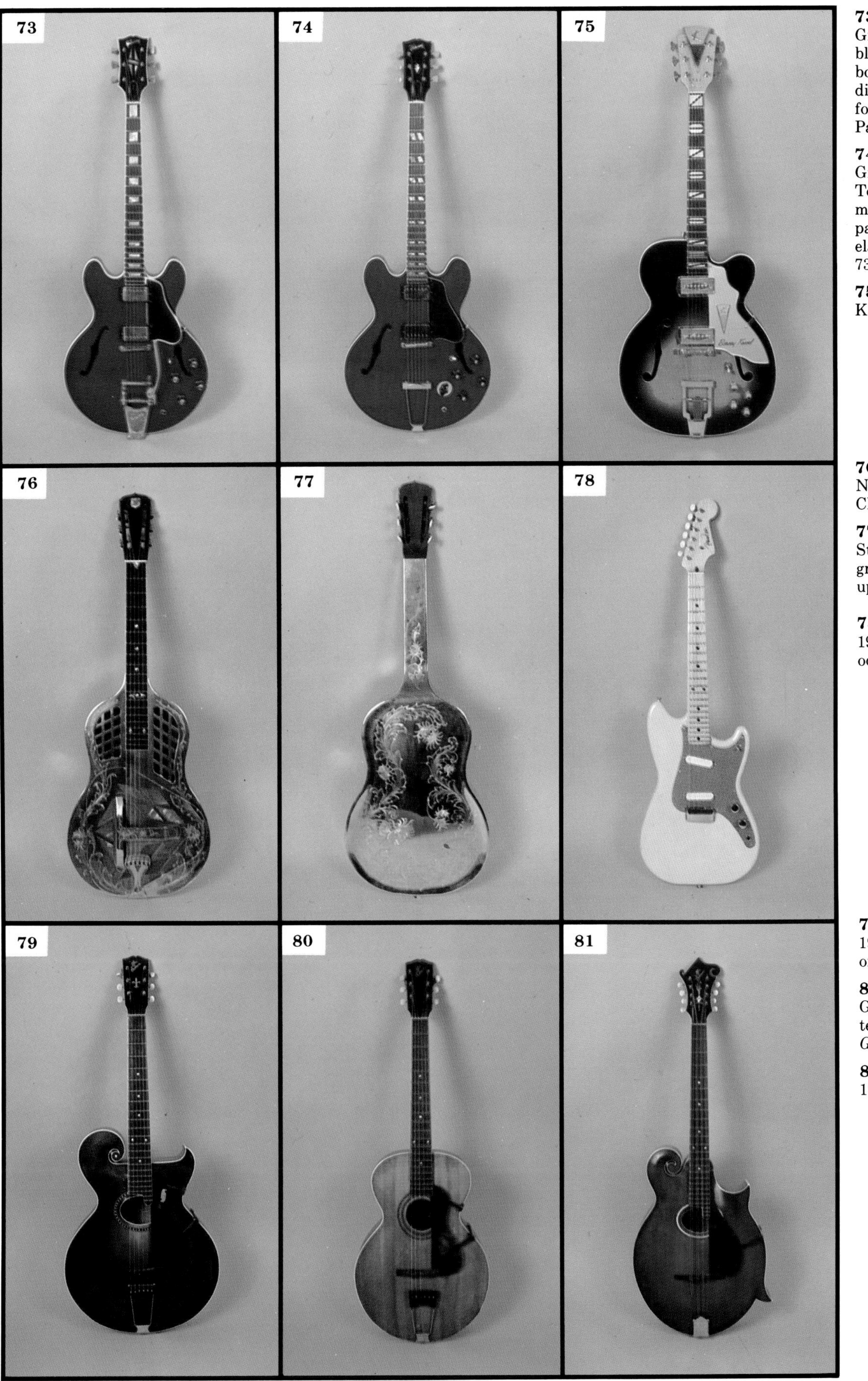

73.
Gibson ES-355 nonstereo, stock block markers and ebony fingerboard. The 355 features the split diamond peghead inlay also found on the Super 400 and Les Paul Custom.

74.
Gibson ES-345TDC. Note Vari-Tone switch, split-parallelogram markers, rosewood board. Compare its binding with the more elaborate ES-355 in color photo 73. Also see no. 40.

75.
Kay Barney Kessel Jazz Special.

76.
National Style 4 Tri-Plate, or Chrysanthemum; Hawaiian neck.

77.
Style 4, rear view. Note heavy engraving and the body's extension up the length of the neck.

78.
1957 Fender Duo-Sonic, gold anodized pickguard.

79.
1919 Gibson Style O (pickguard ornament unoriginal).

80.
Gibson L-1, 1911. Note thirteenth-fret neck/body joint, *The Gibson* peghead inlay.

81.
1915 Gibson K-4 mandocello.

82.
1964 L-5CES with humbuckings, soft cutaway.

83.
Soft cutaway L-5's highly figured maple back.

84.
1961 L-5CES, Florentine cutaway.

82

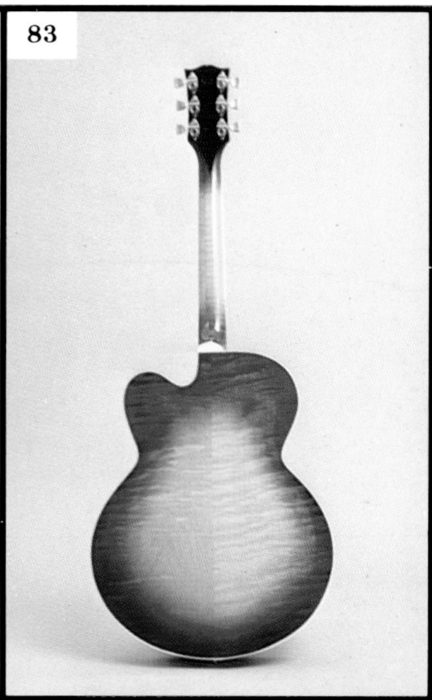

83

84

85.
1958 blonde Gibson dot-neck ES-335, long pickguard. The symmetrical double-cutaway was a completely original design. The earliest sunburst 335s had unbound fingerboards, and some of these lacked the crown peghead inlay.

86.
1960 sunburst Gibson dot-neck ES-335, long pickguard.

87.
1959 cherry red Gibson dot-neck ES-335, short pickguard.

85

86

87

88.
Early-1970s reissue Gibson gold-top Les Paul, without tune-o-matic.

89.
1960 two-color sunburst Fender Jazz Bass with concentric knobs.

90.
1978 Gibson 25/50 Les Paul Anniversary model.

88

89

90

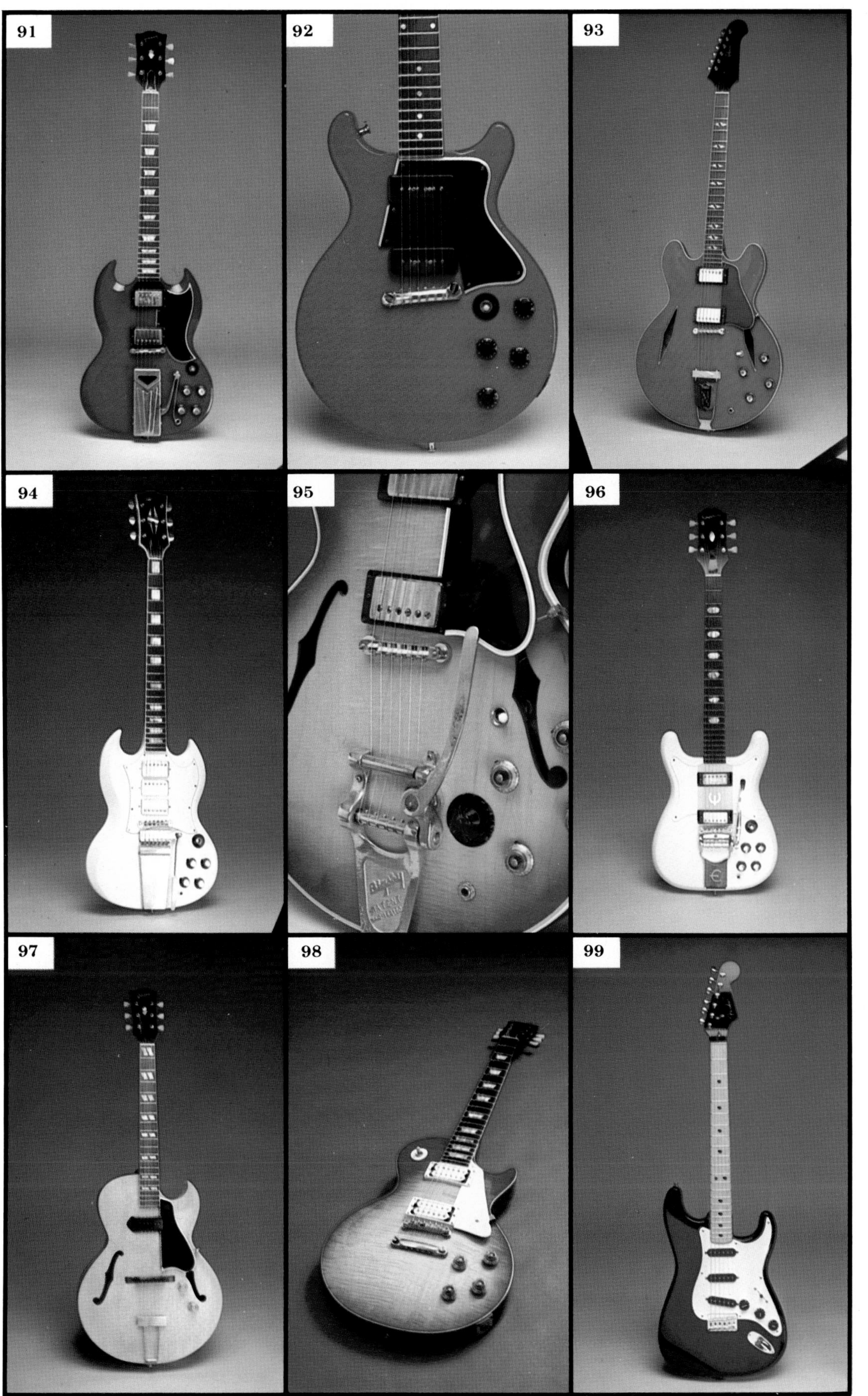

91.
1961 Les Paul (or "SG/Les Paul") with sideways vibrato.

92.
1959 Gibson Les Paul Special, P-90 pickups, double-cutaway.

93.
1965 Gibson Trini Lopez, thin body. Note headstock and soundholes.

94.
1968 Gibson SG Custom.

95.
Gibson ES-355, stock Bigsby, very unusual sunburst finish. Note Vari-Tone switch and clear, skirted knobs. The first 355s were monophonic. The Stereo/Vari-Tone circuit designed by Walt Fuller appeared in 1959 and is featured on the great majority of 355s.

96.
Very early Gibson-made Epiphone Crestwood.

97.
Early 1950s Gibson ES-175N, replacement tailpiece.

98.
An immaculate 1959 Gibson Les Paul Standard with highly figured maple top, double white coil PAFs.

99.
Stock black Fender Stratocaster, maple neck, nonvibrato tailpiece, bullet truss rod.

100.
1950s Gibson L-4C.

101.
1968 Gibson Les Paul Custom reissue. Compare it with no. 29, a three-pickup original.

102.
Gibson ES-125CD. The early postwar noncutaway ES-125 had a single pickup with a very unusual feature: nonadjustable polepieces. Shown here is a later model.

103.
The diminutive Gibson ES-125T ¾.

104.
Mid-1950s Epiphone De Luxe electric. Note triangle fingerboard marker inlays, "New York" pickups, peghead inlay, and faceted knobs.

105.
Gibson/Epiphone Granada, also available with cutaway, mid-1960s

106.
Del Oro bargain-basement special with jazzy body trim.

107.
Gibson EB-2 bass. The pushbutton tone modifier was added in 1959, the string mute about 1960.

108.
A virtually unplayed George Maul of New York City, 1864.

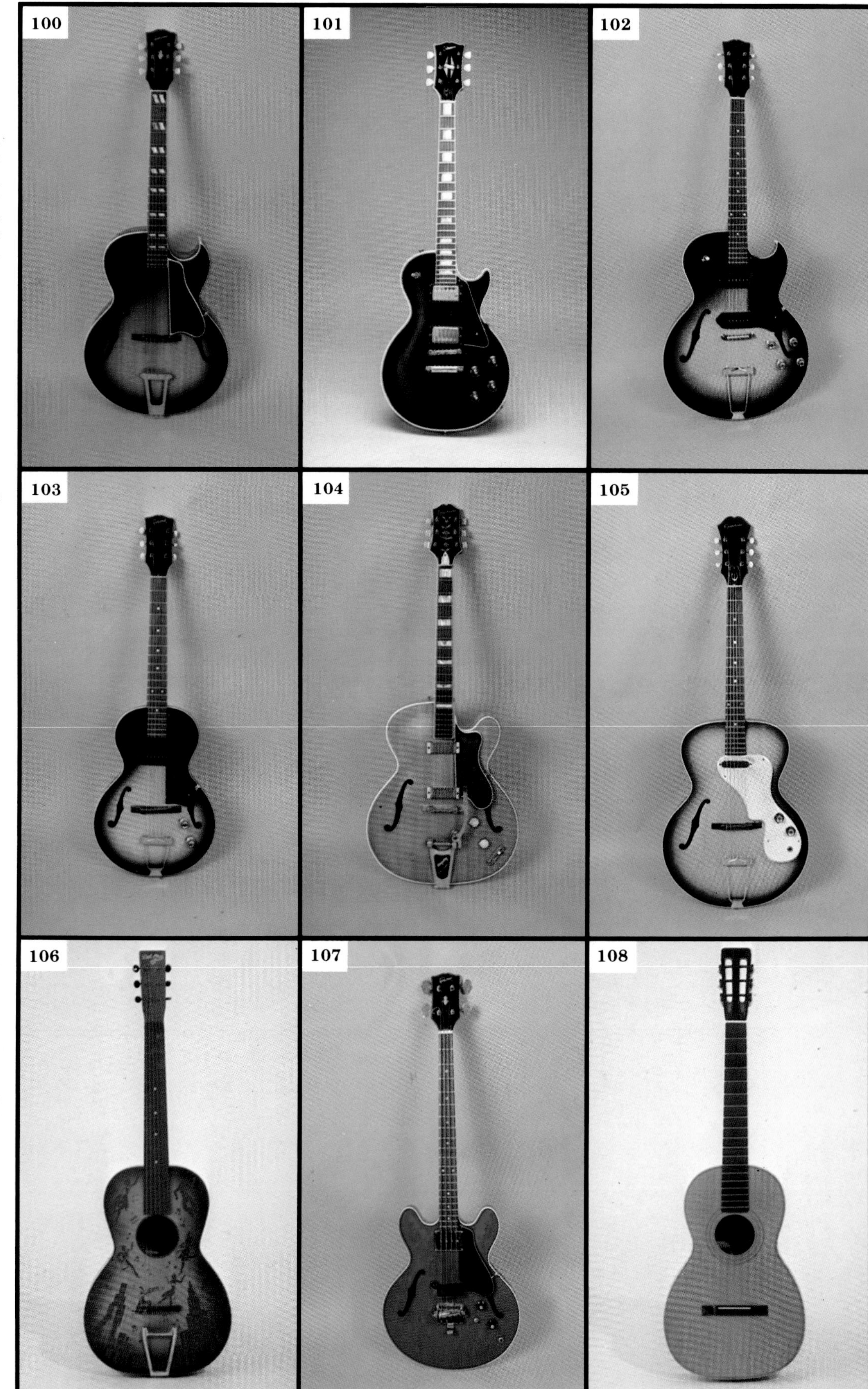

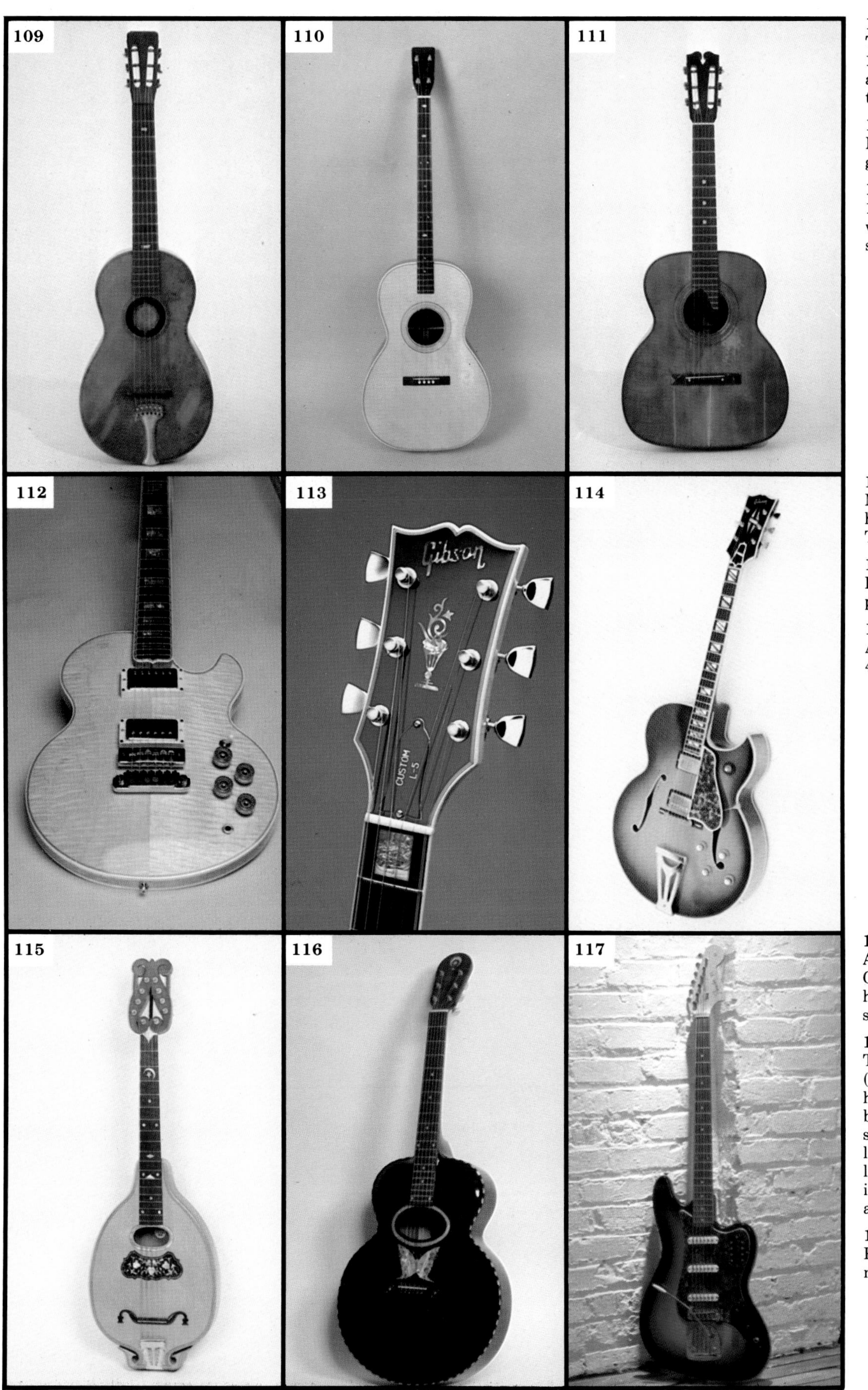

109.
Tilton's Improvement, circa 1905. Note soundhole medallion and extremely unusual diagonal top grain.

110.
Martin 0-28T herringbone tenor guitar.

111.
1907 J. G. Schroeder steel-string with wide body, wide neck, and slot head.

112.
Natural finish Gibson L-5S with highly figured maple top and TP-6 tailpiece.

113.
L-5S headstock with mother-of-pearl fingerboard inlay.

114.
A factory-customized 1964 Super 400CES with two extra frets.

115.
A five-course guitar by Orville Gibson, circa 1894. Note peghead, inlays, and lower body sculpting.

116.
This oval-hole De Luxe O Style (circa 1898) by Orville Gibson has an unusually large, rounded body, pearl and ebony binding, a star-and-crescent headstock inlay, a hollowed-out neck, black lacquered finish, and a butterfly inlay of abalone, tortoiseshell, and mother-of-pearl.

117.
Post-1963 Fender Bass VI with mute and fourth tone switch.

118.
1966 Fender Electric XII, four pickups, Lake Placid Blue Metallic.

119.
1966 Shoreline Gold Metallic three-knob Jazz Bass with bound fingerboard and block markers. Compare its knobs, binding, and markers with photo no. 89.

120.
1965 blue dot-neck Fender Jazz Bass; pickup cover and bridge cover removed. Note matching peghead.

118

119

120

121.
1965 green Fender Jaguar with bound neck, dot markers.

122.
1961 Gibson 12/6 doubleneck. Compare it with the doublenecks in the Gibson chapter.

123.
1958 Fiesta Red left-handed Strat.

121

122

123

124.
Nonreverse Gibson Firebird VII in Pelham Blue, circa 1967.

125.
Sunburst reverse Firebird V. Note sculpted peghead, banjo-type tuners, and trapezoidal markers.

126.
A classic 1952 Les Paul with a body that's gold on the sides and back as well as the top. The absence of a serial number identifies it as one of the earliest of the 1952 models. Among gold-tops the all-gold Les Paul is uncommon but not extremely rare.

124

125

126

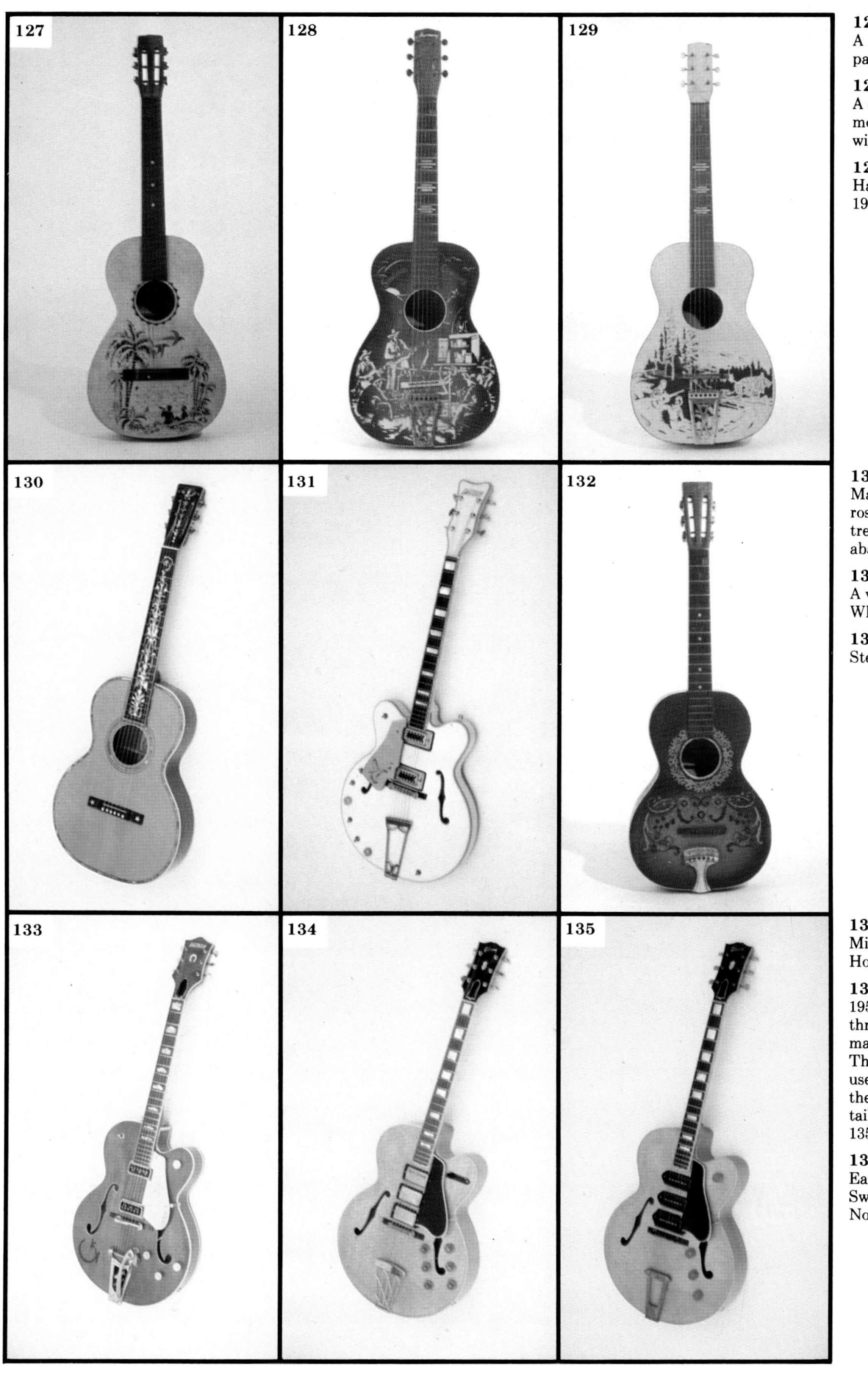

127.
A low-budget Stella flat-top with painted Hawaiian motif.

128.
A classic in its own way, the Harmony *Singing Cowboys* guitar, with a stenciled paint job.

129.
Harmony flat-top, probably early 1950s, with campground motif.

130.
Maurer, circa 1910, Brazilian rosewood back and sides. Note tree-of-life inlay and elaborate abalone body binding.

131.
A very rare left-handed Gretsch White Falcon Stereo, circa 1975.

132.
Stella, with decals.

133.
Mid-1950s Gretsch Chet Atkins Hollow Body with *G* brand.

134.
1959 Gibson Switchmaster with three PAF humbuckings, tune-o-matic, and clear skirted knobs. This tailpiece design was later used on the Citation. Compare the pickups, switch, knobs, and tailpiece with photos 43, 44, and 135.

135.
Early-1950s Gibson ES-5, the Switchmaster's predecessor. Note barrel knobs.

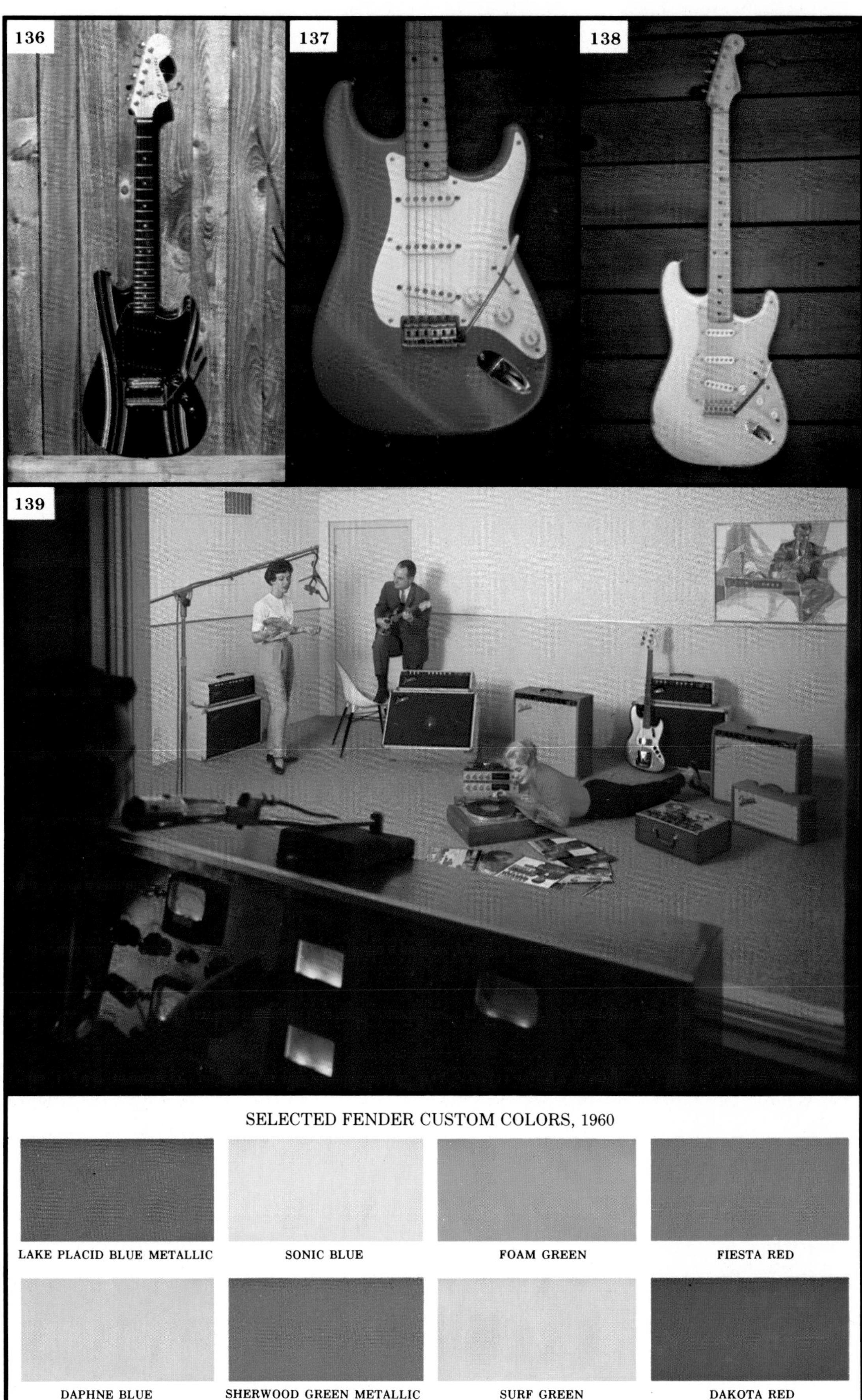

136.
1970s Fender Mustang with an experimental multilaminate body of colored woods—not an important guitar, but an interesting one.

137.
This 1957 gold-plated Lake Placid Blue Strat once belonged to Homer Haynes of Homer & Jethro.

138.
Though not the first one made, this Strat bears the serial number 0001. Note gold hardware and unusual gold anodized pickguard. The guitar belongs to David Gilmour of Pink Floyd.

139.
This highly unlikely but entertaining scene from a 1961–1962 Fender ad features a Jaguar guitar, a blue three-knob Jazz Bass, blonde amplifier cabinets from 1960 and 1961, and 1962-style brown cabinets.

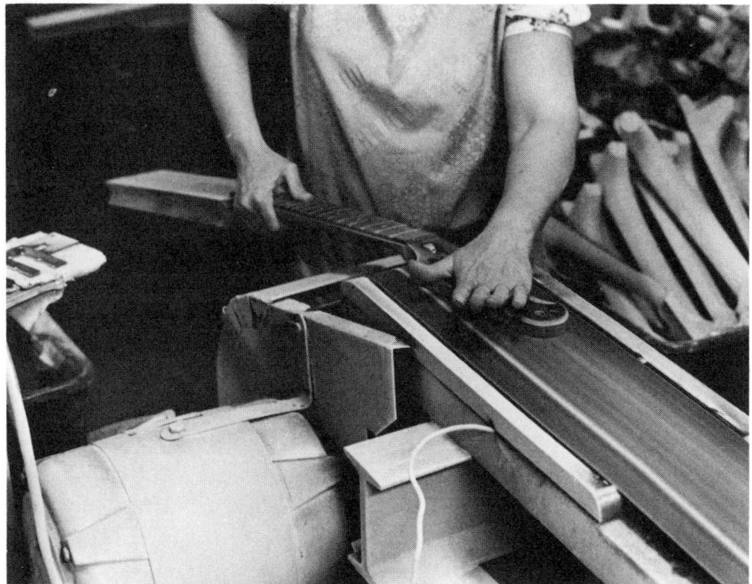

Sanding a Firebird headstock. Note full-length neck/centerpiece.

Nonreverse Firebird I. *Jacksonville*

Nonreverse Firebird III. *Gruhn*

The $445 reverse Firebird VII had three pickups, a tune-o-matic, the Deluxe Vibrola, and banjo pegs, all gold plated. The VII is immediately distinguishable from other reverse Firebirds, since it was the only stock model with any of the following features: rectangular position markers (including an extra one at the first fret), ebony fretboard, gold plating, and three pickups.

The official production totals for *reverse* Firebirds (1963–1965) are: I, 1,377; III, 2,546; V, 925; and VII, 303. Thus, these models had limited but respectable success.

The nonreverse Firebirds (discontinued in 1969, shipped through 1970) were fundamentally dissimilar to their superior predecessors. In fact, Gibson has even applied different model designations to guitars that are more similar than reverse and nonreverse Firebirds (for example, late Les Pauls and early SGs). The nonreverse Firebirds look like flipped-over reverse Firebirds (which look sort of like flipped-over Fenders), but differ in methods of manufacture, pickup array, other features, and in their market value as collector's items.

Each member of the reverse series was unique: the Firebird I was the only model with one pickup, the III was the only one with its type of vibrato, the V had unique trapezoidal markers, and the VII was the only one with three pickups, or an ebony fingerboard, or rectangular position markers, or a marker of any kind at the first fret. While the reverse series comprised individual models that shared certain construction details, the nonreverse Firebirds had a single basic design and, aside from pickups and vibratos, differed mainly in superficial respects. Gone were distinctions between fingerboards and position markers; all stock nonreverse Firebirds had rosewood boards with dot markers. The bodies were much more conventional: separate necks were simply glued on, rather than incorporating the full-length centerpiece found on all reverse models. (Gibson found it increasingly hard to obtain wood in sufficient sizes for the full-length pieces.) Gone were the distinctive if not excep-

Nonreverse Firebird V. *Gruhn*

tionally accurate banjo pegs, replaced by stock tuners. Whereas some reverse fingerboards were bound and some were unbound, all nonreverse boards were unbound.

The nonreverse Firebird I had two single-coil pickups with black plastic covers, while the reverse I had one humbucker with a metal cover. The nonreverse I had a vibrato with a plastic-tipped tubular lever and a raised-ridge bridge.

The nonreverse III had three pickups of the design found on the nonreverse I, and except for its circuitry it was the same basic guitar as the nonreverse I (the color of the knobs differs with various models and finishes).

The V was a classier guitar with two small metal-covered humbuckers such as the type found on reverse models, a chrome-plated Deluxe Vibrola with the long metal panel, and a tune-o-matic bridge. The VII is essentially a V with three humbuckings and gold plating.

Gibson's leadership changed at about the time of the shift in Firebird design, and the nonreverse models were an attempt to standardize production; hence the similarity of fingerboards, position markers, and so on. According to George Gruhn all nonreverse Firebirds even had identical bodies with three pickup routs underneath the pickguards. With the standardization

Nonreverse Firebird VII, custom color. *Guitar Trader/Photog. Unlimited*

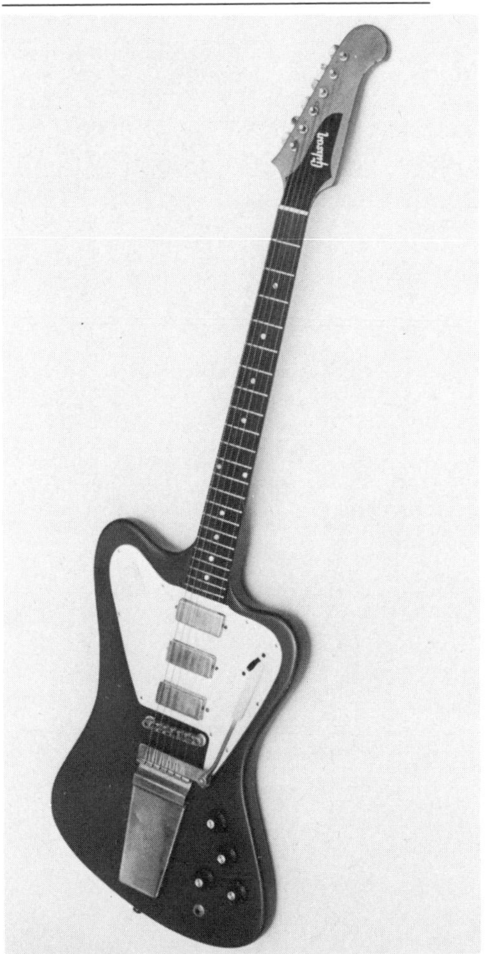

This mid-1960s transition guitar is a platypus of Firebird features: reverse III type body, bridge, pickguard, knobs, pickups, and fingerboard; a *non*reverse I and III type vibrato; and a peghead with a nonreverse shape and nonreverse tuner array (bass E nearest the nut) but reverse style sculpted rim and banjo tuners. ***Jay Levin***

Here is model unlike any normal production Gibson: reverse body with the unbound fingerboard of a Firebird I, the flat-handled vibrato found only on the reverse III, and an array of knobs found on the reverse III, V, and VII. Its pickups are stock only on the *non*reverse Firebird I. Note its peghead—reverse shape, but flat, without the sculpted rim. The tuners are conventional machines—a nonreverse detail—but the treble E string is closest to the nut, as on stock reverse models. Futhermore, the keys are on the right side, whereas stock nonreverse Firebirds have keys on the left (reverse models have banjo tuners). You won't find this guitar in a catalogue—it's far too rare and weird—but it does appear to be stock. *Norm's*

of bodies, vibrato levers, markers, fingerboards, number of knobs, pickup cavities, necks, switches, and position of the output jacks—all features in which various reverse Firebirds differed—the second-generation models were much less costly to produce.

All nonreverse Firebirds had 13¾ by 19¾ by 1½ inch bodies with black sliding pickup selectors rather than the usual toggle switches, 22 frets, and four knobs. All were available in sunburst or any of several custom colors, including medium blue, aqua, misty light green, and red. Each had a red Firebird logo in the upper left-hand corner of the large white pickguard, and all had pickups protruding through the pickguard, without mounting rings.

Aside from the broad categories of original reverse and later nonreverse guitars, there were also a few transition hybrids that mix features of both (see photos). Firebird reissues began with the Firebird V of 1972 and 1973. In 1976, Gibson commenced substantial production of a new reissue, the reverse 1976 Firebird. Available in several finishes and combining features of various original models, the Firebird '76 sold well through 1977 and declined in 1978.

Miscellaneous Postwar Electrics

ELECTRIC BASSES

Soon after Fender's Precision Bass began making waves in 1951, Gibson issued a violin-body model called simply the Gibson Electric Bass. It was first shipped in 1953 and only 546 were sold through 1958, after which it was dropped. Its details included: arched 19 by 11¼ by 2 inch solid mahogany body, 30½-inch scale, 20 frets, a huge Alnico-magnet pickup with a *brown* Royalite cover, bone nut, and a $225 price tag. A telescopic end pin provided a stand for upright playing. The name was changed to EB-1 in 1958 to distinguish it from the new EB-2. The EB-1 reappeared circa late 1969. While the original had an exposed bridge, barrel knobs, and perpendicular tuners, the reissue had a bridge cover, black knobs, a chrome-plated pickup cover, and standard tuners. The reissue was dropped after 1971.

Gibson's Electric Bass became the EB-1 in 1958. Note violin body, perpendicular tuners. *Ax-In-Hand*

Late-1960s EB-2C, a companion to the ES-335 guitar, which it resembles. *Spitzer's/Sievert*

EB-0F with built-in fuzztone. *William Walz/ Patrick Gallagher*

EB-0F, detail.

Gibson's next bass, the EB-2 (or EB-2N, Natural finish), was introduced in 1958 (during 1959 or 1960 a baritone pushbutton was added). It had a double cutaway, a semiacoustic maple body, and one pickup. It was dropped circa late 1961 but reappeared by early 1965 in cherry (EB-2C) or sunburst. The double-pickup EB-2D and EB-2DC appeared circa late 1965. In 1967 or early 1968, walnut and burgundy finishes became available. The EB-2D was dropped after 1972.

Gibson's third bass, the cherry red EB-0, followed in 1959 and within a year was the company's most popular 4-string. It had a slab body modeled after the 1960 double-cut Les Paul Jr., perpendicular tuners, and a 30½-inch scale. It changed to the SG shape circa 1961 and remained in the line through 1972. A long-scale version, the EB-0L, appeared in late 1969 or early the following year and was dropped after 1972. The EB-0F, an EB-0 with a built-in, pickguard-mounted fuzztone, was announced as a new model for 1962 (it likely made its debut the preceding year). It was dropped after 1964.

In 1960 the sunburst EB-6 6-string bass appeared. It was modeled after the 335 and EB-2 and had six strings tuned like a guitar but one octave lower. A year or two later the EB-6 also became known as the Baritone Guitar, and the body went to the solid, SG (or EB-3) type in cherry red; unlike its semiacoustic predecessor, it had no pushbutton tone modifier. Only 133 EB-6's were shipped from 1960 through 1965. None left the factory in 1966, and only two in 1967, the model's last year.

EB-6 6-string bass, circa 1963. *William Walz/Patrick Gallagher*

1970 EB-3L. This type of pickguard was also used on the EB-3 and EB-0; compare it to the 1972 type, which is still in use on the EB-3.

1972 EB-3 (*left*) and EB-3L.

1960 EB-6 6-string bass, or baritone guitar. The pushbutton tone modifier did not appear on the later SG type EB-6. *Jay Levin*

The $310 cherry red EB-3 joined the bass line right at the top (circa 1961) with an SG-type body, string damper, two humbuckings, and a four-position tone switch. It stayed in the line through mid 1979. The long-scale version appeared in 1969 or 1970, and was discontinued after 1972. The late-sixties Melody Maker bass was a double-cut solidbody with one pickup and a mute.

DOUBLENECKS

Gibson's first custom-order doublenecks appeared in 1958. There were two models, each with an arched spruce top, double Florentine cutaways, maple sides and back, one-piece mahogany necks, and bound rosewood boards; both were available in sunburst, white, or black. The four-pickup Double 12 ($475) had a 12-string neck on the upper side and a 6-string on the lower, while the three-pickup Double Mandolin ($435) combined a 6-string with a "mandolin"—actually a short 6-string guitar neck tuned an octave higher than usual.

In 1962 Gibson first offered the SG style Double Bass (catalogued both as the EBSF-1250 and EBS-1265), which consisted of an EB-3 joined to an SG Standard, plus onboard fuzztone (the fuzz was dropped by 1965 though it appeared in later price

Top:* 6/12 doubleneck, 1958, arched top. It was Gibson's first electric 12-string. *Jim Brown* *Left:* Carlos Santana's Gibson Double Twelve (circa 1966). *Center:* Doubleneck, circa 1959. The shorter neck is actually for a 24-fret "octave" guitar—tuned like a standard 6-string, only an octave higher. Arched top, maple body, one-piece mahogany necks, pearl inlays, three PAF pickups. *Apirak Sillapachai* *Right:* Gibson doubleneck, circa 1962, with stock built-in fuzztone. *William Walz/Patrick Gallagher

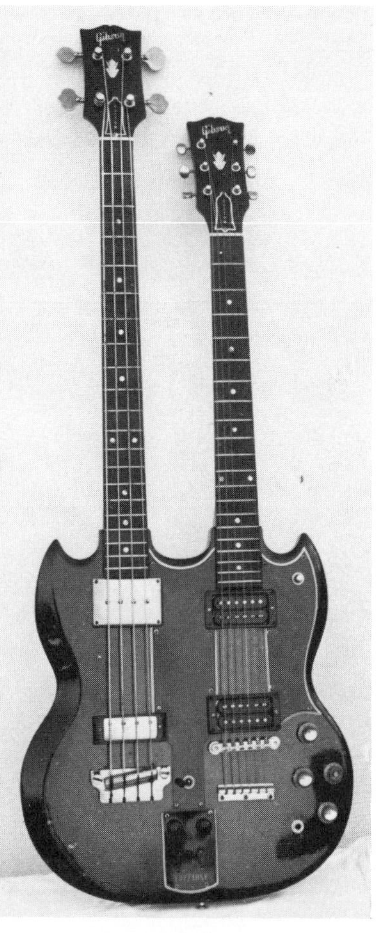

The 1962 catalogue still pictured the $1\frac{7}{8}$-inch-thick arch-top doublenecks, while the 1963 brochure (published 1962) was the first with the $1\frac{9}{16}$-inch-thick SG style doublenecks like this Double Bass, which combines an SG Standard with an EB-3. Earliest models came with a stock built-in fuzztone. The bass tuners suggest that this one was made circa 1970. *Wooden/Goodman*

Unique, customer-ordered Gibson 330 with Les Paul Signature pickups and extensive rewiring. ***Allen Johnson***

John McLaughlin's drone-string Gibson, built by Abe Wechter. ***Mike Aldworth***

lists). The Double Mandolin and Double 12 were catalogued in 1962 but not pictured, perhaps because Gibson was using up the last of the old arch-top bodies and producing the earliest SG type doublenecks.

No doublenecks were offered during the early 1970s, although by 1977 the EDS-1275 (6 and 12) had reappeared, now with 1970s-style control knobs and metal tuning keys (the mid-sixties tuners had the larger plastic buttons).

CUSTOM-ORDER GIBSONS

Taken to its logical extreme, the rare-guitar syndrome would place infinite value on a guitar that never existed. Perhaps the closest thing to such a phantom is the factory-original one-of-a-kind, of which there are two types: the one-off designed by company personnel (perhaps an experimental model, prototype, or promotional item), and the customer-designed, special-order instrument.

The proud owner of the latter type may or may not have an especially valuable piece on his hands; guitar buffs are frequently concerned about how their instruments stack up against others, and when it comes to the ultimate comparator, there's nothing like nothing at all. Still, the guitar may have little market worth above its utilitarian considerations. Sure it's rare, but does anybody want it? If a once-desirable guitar can lose its collector's value because of postproduction alterations by owners, how much difference does it make if the owner's modifications occur on the assembly line?

The unique, customer-designed guitar is thus something of a strange beast—original yet not stock, buyer-designed rather than seller-designed—and the nebulousness of its split personality casts added subjectivity to market value, already a quasi-objective assessment at best. At any rate, Gibson has for many years accommodated those buyers with enough money to indulge their fantasies of the perfect guitar.

SERIAL NUMBERS

With the exception of Martin, most of the major American makers seldom intended to pinpoint manufacturing dates with serial numbers. Without relevant correlation, serial numbers are usually no more than pieces of the identification puzzle.

Over the years Gibson has produced a whole swamp of confusing numbers. Some were assigned according to date; some were not. Certain sequences progress chronologically, while some backtrack and others leap ahead. A few refer to the number of units made within a specific series, while others were chosen literally at random. Some appeared only once, and others were definitely duplicated, sometimes several times.

A significant break in the early serial numbers occurred in late 1924. Up until that time the numbering was coherent and sensible. Many of the flat-tops built after 1926—especially less expensive models—had no numbers at all. Here are serial numbers from 1911 to 1924.

SERIAL NUMBERS, GENERAL SUMMARY, 1911–1924

1911	8750–10850	1918	39500–47900
1912	10850–13350	1919	47900–53800
1913	13350–16100	1920	53800–62200
1914	16100–20150	1921	62200–69300
1915	20150–25150	1922	69300–71400
1916	25150–32000	1923	71400–74900
1917	32000–39500	1924	74900–80300

The following table includes selected serial numbers published by Roger H. Siminoff in *Pickin'* magazine. Single numbers represent the only available listing for the year, while pairs indicate the lowest and highest of available serial numbers for the specified year.

SELECTED SERIAL NUMBERS, 1927–1939

1927	83795, 85369	1933	90740
1928	85473, 87222	1934	92035
1929	87301, 89725	1935	92684
1930	90146	1937	95366
1931	90302	1939	95533
1932	90541, 90693		

Some guitars, banjos, and lap steels made in the late thirties are stamped with two or three *letters* followed by a number.

Gibson's production was severely curtailed during World War II. Here are some very rough guidelines for dating wartime Gibsons.

SELECTED SERIAL NUMBERS, 1941–1946

1941	96244, 97386	1944	97930, 98216
1942	95137, 97618	1945	98343, 98567
1943	96893, 97718	1946	98660, 99346

Gibson instruments are usually made in racks, or batches, each typically containing 40 units. Many postwar flat-tops have numbers (stamped on the wooden headblocks) that refer to these batches. For example, 8000-21 designates the twenty-first guitar in that particular lot of 40, while 8000 identifies the order number. If the second figure exceeds 40 (for example, 8000-60), it suggests that an extra batch of that series was made. If there is no second number at all to distinguish members of a given series, then duplicate order numbers can be expected to be found on other instruments. Such numbers may appear in addition to a serial number on the label.

A summary of the headblock numbers published by *Pickin'* appears on page 188. If one figure is given, it is the only available headblock number for that year; two entries represent the lowest and highest of available numbers for the specified year. There are overlaps, and further confusion arises from the way

The Bossa Nova appeared circa 1969 and promptly disappeared. It was a cutaway rosewood classic guitar with a bridge-mounted pickup. Only seven appear on the 1970s shipping lists: six in 1971 and one in 1973.

1970 Crest, utterly unique among Gibsons. In general construction it's somewhat similar to an ES-330, though it is considerably fancier and has a rosewood body, a *flat* back (note decorative marquetry), and an arch-top type bridge. Unlike other expensive Gibson thin-lines (e.g., ES-355), it is fully hollow. The pickups are positioned over the top, rather than sunk into it. ***Gruhn***

in which some numbers skip around. Notice the big leap in the 1917 entry. Finally, some of the numbers within that gap—for example, 9600–9800—show up more than a decade later.

SELECTED FACTORY ORDER NUMBERS, 1908–1923

1908	259	1916	2667, 3508
1909	309	1917	3246, 11010
1910	545, 927	1918	9839, 11159
1911	1260, 1295	1919	11146, 11212
1912	1408, 1593	1920	11329, 11367
1913	1811, 1902	1921	11375, 11527
1914	1936, 2152	1922	11565, 11729
1915	2209, 3207	1923	11973

Beginning in 1947 Julius Bellson originated the A series, which Gibson used for years. Beginning with A-250, the A series continued at least as late as 1960. Unfortunately, other systems were also used during this period. The following table includes the highest and lowest A numbers that appear on a *partial* list from Gibson. They were applied to several models including the L-4, L-5, L-7, L-12, J-185, J-200, Super 400, ES-5, ES-175, ES-335, ES-345, ES-355, and Byrdland. The A numbers were not used on solidbodies.

SELECTED "A" SERIES NUMBERS, 1947–1958

1947	A252, A1216
1948	A1717, A2615
1949	A2020, A4276
1950	A4801, A5857
1951	A7893, A9216
1952	A9787, A12287
1953	A13820, A15750
1954	A16272, A18617
1955	A20347, A21778*
1956	A22943, A24583
1957	A24874, A26729
1958	A26155, A27671

*A10133 also appears in 1955

Beginning in 1952 factory order numbers on certain guitars were prefixed with a letter that progressed backward through the alphabet, one letter each year for several years. Instruments made in 1952 were designated with a Z, 1953s with a Y, 1954s with an X, and so on. This system runs concurrently with the A serial numbers, and despite a few overlaps it is usually dependable for dating certain models up until 1963, when the system was discontinued with the letter O. Arch-top acoustics and electrics have the factory order number stamped directly into the inside surface of the back, where it can be seen through the f-hole. Again, A series numbers and factory order numbers often appear concurrently. To confuse matters even more, plenty of Gibsons, especially those made during the 1940s, have no identification numbers at all.

A welcome change occurred between late 1953 and 1961, when Gibson applied a system to solidbodies that not only progressed sequentially but actually identified the instrument's year of manufacture with the number's first digit. For example, 6 8219 is a 1956. Les Pauls made in 1952 generally have no serial numbers. Many 1953s have serial numbers, and some do not. From 1954 up until early 1961 the numbers are almost consistent and complete. In most of 1961, however, the numbering system does not apply. Only a small number of 1961 models are labeled with the digit 1.

The numbers applied during the 1950s are in black or yellow ink, depending on the color of the instrument. A number impressed into the wood rather than stamped in ink identifies the guitar as a 1961 model or later. If toward the end of the year the numbers beginning with a particular numerical prefix ran out, Gibson simply went back and filled in the space between the prefix and the remaining four digits with an extra digit, resulting in a total of six. There are many six-digit Les Pauls, for example. Thus during the 1950s Gibson was employing at least three serial number schemes: the reverse alphabetical system, the solidbody year identifications, and the A series.

The previously described systems, despite their many flaws, are paragons of consistency compared to those applied after

The luxurious L-5S was unveiled in late 1971 as Gibson's top-of-the-line solidbody. Its original low-impedance pickups were replaced with humbuckings in 1973, and the original L-5 tailpiece was replaced circa mid-1978 with the TP-6 shown here. Choicest curly maple body, multi-ply bindings, gold plating, abalone inlays. See color photos 112 and 113. *Wallace/Perla*

The Howard Roberts Custom (shown here) with chrome plating joined the line circa 1973, and the gold-plated Howard Roberts Artist joined about two years later. The peghead inlay traces back to various Epiphones of the 1930s, 1940s, and 1950s.

1960. Company ledgers were stamped automatically by a machine before the guitars were produced. Numbers were stamped on the guitars, and then the model names were entered in a ledger next to the corresponding number. Boggling mixups in the sequencing occurred during the mid 1960s, resulting in repeated duplications.

Beginning in the late 1970s Gibson inaugurated a serial numbering system which identifies the actual day of manufacture. In the eight-digit number, digits one and five, when combined, reveal the year. The second, third, and fourth digits together represent the day according to the Julian calendar, in which each day of the year is given its own number in sequence (Julian dates are often listed in small print on desk-model calendars). Finally, the last three digits identify the location of manufacture: Kalamazoo Gibsons run from 000 to 499, while guitars built in the Nashville plant (established in 1975) run from 500 and up.

GIBSON SHIPPING TOTALS

Selected Shipping Totals, 1948–1960

Fortunately, the shipping totals of Gibson's postwar guitars are documented. Reproduced here courtesy of company historian Julius Bellson, they help to profile Gibson's evolving guitar line. Abbreviations: E (Electric), ES (Electric Spanish), N (Natural finish), T (Thin body), D (Double pickup), and adj. (adjustable bridge); on thin guitars *C* signifies *Cherry finish*, otherwise *Cutaway*. If more than one type is specified, the figures represent the totals, not the number of each type. Note the following trends.

Arch-top acoustics. During the 1950s we see the decline of the L-50 and L-48, and the cutaway versions of the L-4 and Super 400 outlasting the standard versions. All the L-7s except the L-7C were gone by 1956. Except for a trickle of S-300s the only late-1950s acoustic arch-tops with noncutaway bodies were the L-50 and L-48. By 1959 only cutaway versions of the L-4, L-7, Super 400, and L-5 remained.

Flat-Tops. Note the J-200's consistent success, the rise and fall of the J-185, the official introduction of the Hummingbird in 1960, and the mid 1950s peaks for the J-45 and J-50.

Arch-top electrics. There were over half a dozen electric arch-tops during 1948 and 1949. Note the mid 1950s expirations of the original 150 and the 300, the expansion of the 175 into double-pickup versions, the mid 1950s shift of the 350 to double-pickup models, the early 1950s decline of the electric L-7s, the ES-5's evolution into the short-lived Switchmaster, the 1955 unveiling of the Byrdland, and the end-of-the-decade introduction of the thin-body 330s. Among the 1960 lineup, note the rarity of the electric Super 400s and the L-5CT "George Gobel" model, and the popularity of double-pickup 175s, and especially the 330s.

SELECTED SHIPPING TOTALS, 1948–1960

Model	*1948*	*1949*	*1950*	*1951*	*1952*	*1953*	*1954*	*1955*	*1956*	*1957*	*1958*	*1959*	*1960*
L-4C & L-4CN		140	199	250	129	165	100	96	96	99	90	89	82
L-4 & L-4N	153	187	134	238	123	125	48	21	2				
L-50	1313	937	1028	1091	712	856	515	277	350	330	177	189	145
L-48	599	1092	1420	1586	890	1099	757	576	692	735	416	514	342
L-7 & L-7N	391	224	201	170	73	91	31	35	1				
L-7C & L-7CN	39	130	143	152	98	235	95	93	87	70	48	89	81
L-7E & L-7EN	34	58	24	24	18		2						
L-7ED		13	6	7	2								
L-7CE & L-7CEN	92	116	81	89	74		14						
L-7CED & L-7CEDN		37	45	44	48		6						
L-12 & L-12C	118	31	12	18	13	11	1	1					
Switchmaster								7	59	56	55	70	46
Switchmaster N									39	30	34	33	20
ES-5		66	111	88	126	72	65	45	4			70	46
ES-5N		22	52	77	93	53	23	11				33	20
Super 400CES				2	7	16	17	5	20	24	15	22	24
Super 400CNES					11	11	6	16	19	15	15	8	7
Super 400C & CN			21	22	17	5	24	12	14	25	20	16	19
Super 400 & 400N	91	44	25	18	30	11	12	3					
S-300	28	20	30	33	22	26	16	11	9	6	3		
Byrdland								1	31	78	38	46	71
Byrdland N								2	25	52	23	34	39
L-5CES				31	29	25	30	19	23	22	21	26	45
L-5CNES				8	17	18	20	31	32	15	27	12	17
L-5C & L-5CN	44	45	41	26	32	23	39	36	20	32	18	55	39
L-5CT (Gobel)												23	9
L-5 & L-5N	87	46	21	40	27	16	15	13	7	11	5		
SJ	439	462	617	674	768	1008	697	532	586	607	265	384	279
SJN							15	498					488
Country West.									813	719	371	679	
J-50	683	358	428	794	825	1212	1081	942	1058	976	339	343	143
J-50 adj.									93	478	581	787	708
J-45	1309	1213	1383	1520	1383	1800	1481	1432	1382	1211	478	627	241
J-45 adj.									384	931	794	1102	1255
J-200	146	88	64	131	112	152	158	90	102	126	80	97	110
J-200N	20	23	37	73	89	49	92	41	59	93	51	75	57
Hummingbird													156
J-185				66	137	119	97	59	65	71	34		
J-185N				11	24	32	31	17	59	33	35	28	
ES-350	87	76	54	70	122	87	58	44	45				
ES-350N	55	89	46	57	67	50	31	14	4				
ES-350TD								1	156	150	104	90	71
ES-350TDN								1	62	74	43	57	15
ES-300 & 300N	273	124	157	161	106	4			1				
ES-175		129	503	559	818	829	599	485	560	353	211	301	226
ES-175N		13	30	105	192	181	141	115	146	92	66		5
ES-175D & DN						268	404	451	567	446	399	453	456
ES-150	555	365	527	543	486	474	298	193	6				
ES-330TC													37
ES-330TD												270	1198
ES-330TDN												79	215
ES-330T												349	772
ES-330TN												82	88
ES-330TDC													98

SELECTED SHIPPING TOTALS, 1952–1960

Model	*1952*	*1953*	*1954*	*1955*	*1956*	*1957*	*1958*	*1959*	*1960*
Les Paul (Gold top & sunburst)	1716	2245	1504	862	920	598	434	643	635
Les Paul Custom			94	355	489	283	256	246	189
Les Paul Special				373	1345	1452	958	1821	1387
Les Paul Special ¾								12	39
Les Paul Jr.			823	2839	3129	2959	2408	4364	2513
Les Paul Jr. ¾					18	222	181	199	96
Les Paul TV			5	230	511	552	429	543	419
ES-335TD (Sunburst)							267	521	405
ES-335TDN							50	71	88
ES-335TDC									21
ES-345TD								446	251
ES-345TDN								32	18
ES-345TDC									252
ES-355TD							10	177	128
ES-355TD-SV (Stereo & Vari-Tone)								123	189
Flying V							81	17	
Moderne							19	3	
Melody Maker								1397	2430
Melody Maker ¾								1676	424
Melody Maker-D									1196

These production figures are complete for the guitars listed, 1952–1960; if a column is blank, none of that model was made that year. The official charts are incomplete in some places and ambiguous in others regarding the number of Explorers made in the late 50s. The lists were compiled by the secretary to the president of Gibson and are based on the number of instruments actually shipped.

The Mark Series featured an unusually shaped bridge with interchangeable saddles.

The alder S-1 joined in late 1974. Bill Lawrence, who designed the circuitry, describes it as a one-pickup guitar with three coils rather than a three-pickup guitar. The Marauder, which joined circa 1974, featured the same body, neck, and headstock, plus one humbucking and one single-coil pickup.

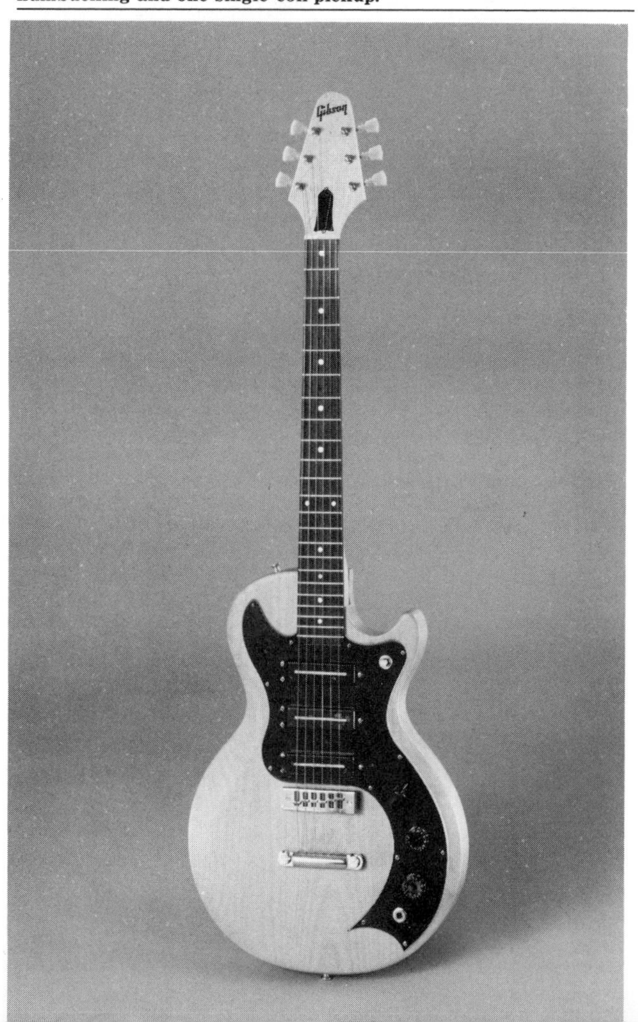

Selected Shipping Totals, 1961–1970

The following table indicates that the Super 400CES, Barney Kessel, J-200, Byrdland, and L-5CES all reached peak production for the decade in 1968–1969. Note the introductions of the Everly Bros. and Tal Farlow in 1962, Firebirds and Johnny Smith D in 1963, Trini Lopez in 1964, ES-335-12 in 1965, and the Crest, Citation, ES-340, and second-generation ES-150 in 1969. Note the rarity of the Everly Bros. (especially in natural) and ES-5, the abundance of late-1960s 335s, the reintroductions of the Les Paul Custom, Les Paul Standard, and Flying V, and the decline of the ES-5, ES-350, and SG-TV. Note the rise and fall of the different colors for the 335 and 345. Unless finishes are distinguished, the figures represent the totals for the various colors. Additional abbreviations: LP (Les Paul), ch. (cherry finish), and wh. (white finish, or lime green).

Gibson L6-S; laminated maple neck, extra-powerful ceramic magnet pickups designed for Gibson by Bill Lawrence.

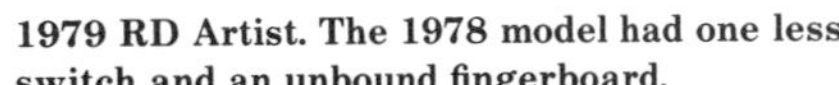

1979 RD Artist. The 1978 model had one less switch and an unbound fingerboard.

SELECTED SHIPPING TOTALS, 1961–1970

Model	*1961*	*1962*	*1963*	*1964*	*1965*	*1966*	*1967*	*1968*	*1969*	*1970*
S-400CES	30	24	29	29	31	25	28	52	120	31
S-400CESN	15	16	14	13	1	4	22	11	45	15
ES-5	41									
ES-5N	11									
ES-350 TD	61	59	35							
ES-350 TDN	21	18	23							
J Smith & JSN	28	91	68	33	23	23	48	81	77	43
JSD & JSDN			34	36	27	23	50	84	100	30
Kessel Cust.	19	43	43	59	42	57	125	263	51	20
Kessel Reg.	43	153	154	141	163	149	31	98	103	34
Trini L. Cust.				2	45	40	92	84	21	23
Trini L. Reg.				3	321	485	783	242	107	25
Byrdland	77	59	102	93	66	45	92	194	160	36
Byrdland N	20	17	32	15	11	3	7	24	60	21
ES-150									465	372
L-5CES	22	30	51	42	34	23	102	189	170	71
L-5CNES	13	11	21	10	10	1	5	11	55	24
L-5C & CN	24	33	45	32	16	34	10	39	89	10
Citation									3	
Crest									56	71
Tal Farlow		2	39	41	77	39	17			
L-7C	79	66	140	119	49	31	34	95	58	12
LP Cust.								433	2353	2612
LP Std.								1224	2751	3559
LP Jr. ¾	71									
SG Cust.	513	298	264	130	236	125	43	264	451	317
SG Std.	1662	1449	1445	1375	1731	1046	1154	1340	3354	5048
SG Spec. red	1186	959	1017	1704	2099	1841	1517	1269	2378	2862
SP Spec. wh.		377	374	318	519	29	147	192		
SG Spec ¾	47									
SG TV	256	457	379	528	716	548	123	54		
SG Jr.	2151	2395	2318	3364	3570	1928	1021	561	751	938
LP Personal									2	
LP Prof.									2	811
Flying V						2	44		15	47
Flying V ch.							67			
Firebird I			80	497	800	1164	200	192	34	1
Firebird III			272	1254	1020	935	463	10	27	12
Firebird V			62	510	353	342	83	50	17	2
Firebird VII			20	173	110	46	9	19	5	6
Firebird-12						248	24			
Thunderbird II			2	501	215	361		67	7	23
Thunderbird IV				235	87	131	120	31	6	22
EDS-1275	7	6	6	10	5	4	33			1
EMS-1235	9	3	4		3	5	2			1
EBSF-1250		1	3	6	6	3	3			3
EB-0	535	815	681	1133	2006	1660	1676	1350	3018	2653
EB-0F		35	74	64	92					
EB-2	39			340	368	884	2746	1903	785	870
EB-3	132	273	214	277	339	467	631	565	1716	1589
EB-6	33	20	10	24	12		2			

SELECTED SHIPPING TOTALS, 1961–1970

Model	*1961*	*1962*	*1963*	*1964*	*1965*	*1966*	*1967*	*1968*	*1969*	*1970*
J-200	73	85	163	209	154	193	226	317	174	126
J-200N	52	54	96	78	50	21	59	87	118	129
Hmgbird	595	503	1461	1283	1522	891	1738	2213	1595	1335
Everly Bros.		2	102	69	41	22	8	48	51	60
Everly Bros. N			46							
ES-355TD	117	72	66	54	130	132	207	144	67	34
ES-355TDSV	174	148	97	198	127	137	198	174	147	101
ES-345TD	174	102	117	218	272	278	501	560	201	230
ES-345TDC	223	204	161	193	216	186	643	378	213	140
ES-340									501	287
ES-335TDC	420	610	807	892	1038	1056	3122	1466	1142	794
ES-335TD	466	266	349	349	712	1468	2596	2294	1055	1246
ES-335TD-12					48	360	451	216	31	34
ES-335TDC-12					7	152	597	124	30	12
ES-330TDC	645	734	652	693	1067	1151	2563	643	515	124
ES-330TD	542	496	521	1231	1318	2000	2335	1223	518	279
ES-330T	267	224	151							
ES-330TC	214	179	152							
ES-175	160	133	156	149	182	163	194	127	84	44
ES-175D & DN	487	441	557	483	562	437	866	994	669	352

Selected Shipping Totals, 1971–1978

Among other things, the following chart reveals the introduction of the L-5S, L-6S, and Les Paul Signature in 1973; Les Paul Triumph in 1975; and the 25th Anniversary Les Paul in 1978. Note the reintroduction of the Explorer, Firebirds, and Thunderbirds, the rarity of the Citation and Crest, the peak production of Les Paul Deluxes and SG Specials in 1973–1975, the Les Paul reissues, and the decline of the low-impedance Les Pauls and Everly Bros. Note that Flying V reissues were sold throughout the decade, although major production commenced in 1975. In several cases, various finishes for guitars of a single model are grouped under one heading. Finish abbreviations include: wal. (walnut), wr. (wine red), csb. (cherry sunburst), tsb. (tobacco sunburst), rosew. (rosewood top), eb. (ebony), wh. (white), and nm (natural mahogany). Additional abbreviations include: Tri. (Triumph) and LPC (Les Paul Custom).

From 1971 to 1978 Gibson built 424,228 instruments in all, with a yearly average of 53,000, a high in 1974 of 73,300, and a low in 1977 of 39,661.

Howard Roberts, 1979, with prototype for the Howard Roberts Fusion: single-cut, semihollow, 24 frets. ***Sievert/GP***

SELECTED SHIPPING TOTALS, 1971–1978

Model	*1971*	*1972*	*1973*	*1974*	*1975*	*1976*	*1977*	*1978*
LP Anniv.								1106
LP Recording	236	1314	1759	915	204	332	362	180
LP Spec.						162	1622	803
LP Personal	95	49	2					
LP Professional	116		2				11	1399
LP Jumbo	43	3	3					
The LP N						24	5	5392
The LP rosew.						9	5	4
LP Artisan						2	1469	641
SG Dlx.	3118	4434	15	1		47		
SG Std.		1009	3009	2295	2042	2823	2618	2503
SG Cust.	395	400	775	939	149	376	279	217
SG Pro	690	2280	24	1				
SG Special	1517	749	3534	2183	593	549	232	2
LP Sig.			3	1046	118	150	123	20
LPC eb.	2390	2654	4807	3900	2006	1694	642	4282
LPC csb.	94	605	2152	2808		621	255	1093
LPC cherry	668	569	68	185	938			
LPC tsb.		106	164	572	335	288	48	1244
LPC left	31	38	32	98	144	75	121	298
LPC wh.					2745	159	47	441
LPC rosew.					36	17		
LPCN					194	108	11	1011
LPC wr.						1271	562	1750
LPC nm.							942	5
LP Tri.					206	169	101	80
LP Dlx.	4466	5194	10,482	7367	2553	168	413	4450
LP Std.					1	24	586	5947
LP Std. "58" reiss.	25	1046	4	1	1			
LPC "54" reiss.		60	1090		3		1	
LP "55" reiss.				1925		2	331	293
L-5S			197	555	211	74	301	358
L-6S & L-6S Deluxe			181	5044	3354	3480	2095	1463
Citation	4							
Trini Lopez & TLD	33							
L-5CES & L-5CESN	127	193	162	231	175	245	247	155
Byrdland	92	128	119	91	206	208	98	111
Crest	38	7						
ES-355	46	232	333	191	148	298	267	243
ES-345	348	397	739	596	128	913	387	382
ES-340	319	198	210	9				40
ES-335	2295	2769	4364	3187	764	1502	1307	1971
J-200	223	161	328	571	109	279	212	146
Everly Bros.	39							
Flying V	350		2	1	1872	423	110	313
Firebird		351	15			1277	1254	199
Thunderbird						543	1270	21
Explorer					2	2006	1087	274

1992 Update

Current Gibson chairman Henry Juszkiewicz and president Dave Berryman purchased the Gibson company from Norlin Industries in 1985 (sale effective in 1986). The company has since acquired Steinberger, Tobias, and the Flatiron banjo and mandolin company. It also distributes Ramirez' world-famous classicals.

Gibson opened a new 25,000-square-foot factory in Bozeman, Montana in June 1989, and has added promotion offices and showrooms for dealers and professional players in Nashville, New York, Los Angeles, and London. As we go to press, the firm has just over 500 employees worldwide and is producing 68 models of guitars, basses, mandolins, and banjos. Although a few recent Epiphones were produced in Nashville, Gibson generally uses that label for the guitars it imports from overseas (primarily Korea). All Gibsons are made in the U.S.—the flat-top acoustics in Bozeman, and the arch-tops (both electric and acoustic) and solidbodies in Nashville. Shown here is the 1989 L-5. Note the redesigned tailpiece.

In August 1975, Gibson opened its new Nashville factory, where about 230 workers build the following solidbodies: various Les Pauls (Artist, Artisan, Custom, Deluxe, Pro, Standard, Heritage Elite, Heritage Standard, The Paul Standard, The Paul Deluxe), L-6S and L-6S Deluxe, Marauder, all Sonex models, *The SG Standard* and *The SG Deluxe* (these two have confusing names and are different from the *SG Standard* and *SG Deluxe*), and the solid 335s. Nashville Gibsons are identified by serial numbers whose last three digits run from 500 and up.

GRAMMER

Nashville's Grammer Guitar, Inc., succeeded the R.G.&G. Musical Instrument Company, and after an investment of $18,000 by country singer Billy Grammer, it ultimately produced over a dozen steel-string models, three small-body guitars with 22-inch scales, and a pair of tenors.

The first Grammer guitar, circa 1965. Note the marquetry along the fingerboard. *Country Music Hall of Fame*

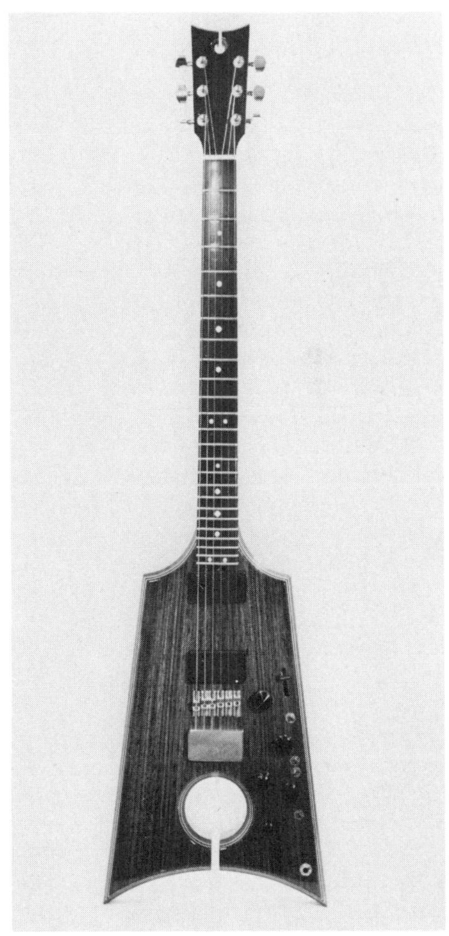

GRD rosewood Wedge PF, with dual parametric filters.

GRD

Strafford, Vermont's School of Guitar Research and Design Center (GRD) was founded in 1972 by designer/luthier/educator Charles Fox. GRD offers some of the most provocative designs to have appeared in the 1970s, including shallow-body cutaway steel-strings and two-channel electrics with either parametric filters or graphic equalizers.

The classic Gretsch electric, a model 6120 Chet Atkins Hollow Body (circa 1957), forerunner of the Nashville. Note peghead inlay, markers, DeArmond pickups, *G* brand, and signpost pickguard logo. See color photo 133. ***Guitar Trader/Photog. Unlimited***

GRETSCH

Gretsch's forte was its orchestra-model arch-tops, some of which were traditional, some classy in a Mae West kind of way—loaded with knobs and options such as tubular vibrato bars, Project-O-Sonic stereo, adjustable felt string mutes, and circular snap-on back pads that lent sort of a Victorian sofa effect.

But all the flash represents only a chapter in the long history of one of America's oldest music companies, one that, like Harmony and Martin, was founded by a German immigrant. Friedrich Gretsch was born in 1856 and came to America at age 16. His father, a Mannheim grocer and former employee of banjo and drum manufacturer Albert Houdlett & Son, brought the family to the New World with the same dreams of prosperity that had lured countryman Christian Martin four decades earlier.

In 1883 Friedrich Gretsch set up a modest shop on Middleton Street in Brooklyn for the manufacture of banjos, tambourines, and drums. The business succeeded and grew for a little over a decade, when in April 1895, the 39-year-old company founder died suddenly during a trip to his native Germany.

Friedrich's eldest son, Fred Gretsch, Sr., found himself head of a prosperous enterprise. Though he was 15 and still in knickers, he had business savvy and served the company well. His energy and enthusiasm inspired his subordinates: he hit the road as a salesman, worked long hours at his desk, tanned drumskins up on the roof—everything. Within five years he retooled and expanded the shop to accommodate mandolin making and began importing other instruments and accessories.

By the turn of the century the Gretsch company was thriv-

Brand names often change hands many times, resulting in identical names but dissimilar guitars made by different manufacturers. The Bacon name goes back to the 1920s and over the years was associated with the A.C. Fairbanks, Vega, Bacon, Bacon & Day, and B&D brands before Gretsch acquired it circa 1940. This mid-1950s Gretsch-made Bacon Belmont guitar (*near right*) has no structural relationship to previous Bacons. Compare its thoroughly Gretsch peghead, f-holes, and DeArmond pickups with the mid-1950s Gretsch Model 6120. *Wagener/Beaty* *Far right:* Pre-Synchromatic arch-top, Model 100, \$100, probably late 1930s. Note pearl-inlaid peghead, engraved tailpiece. Curly maple body and neck, gold plating. Model One Hundred Fifty had block markers, while the Two Hundred Fifty (the top of the line) had a musical note peghead motif. Other models of the period: Models Fifty and Sixty Five arch-tops, Model Two Forty tenor, and Model Forty flat-top Hawaiian. *Music Shop/Madsen* *Below:* A trio of 1940s Gretsch arch-tops.

Presenting the NEW GRETSCH-AMERICAN

ORCHESTRA GUITARS

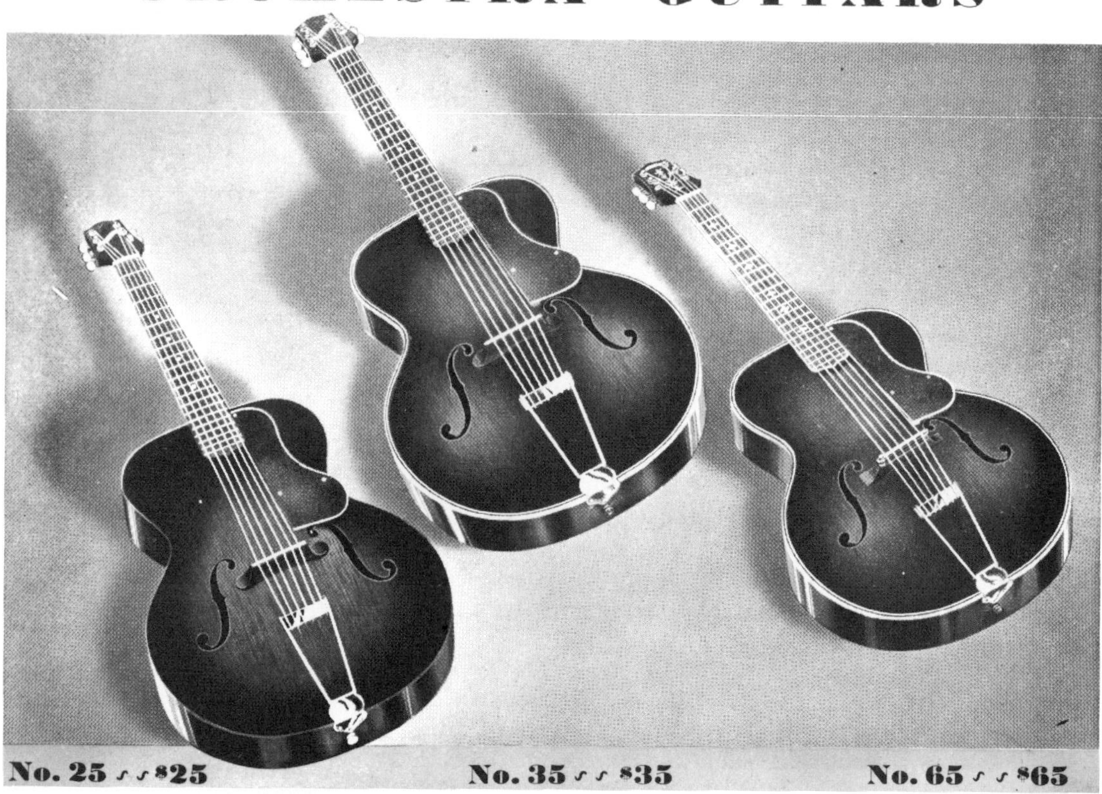

ing, and by 1916 it had enlarged considerably, its warehouse and factory occupying a ten-story building at 60 Broadway. Fred Gretsch, Sr., was now one of America's leading importers and manufacturers.

William Walter ("Bill") Gretsch, son of Fred Gretsch, Sr., was secretary and treasurer during the mid-twenties, a time when the Fred Gretsch Manufacturing Co. expanded its national and international facilities to include offices in Paris and Markneukirchen, Germany, and showrooms in New York and Chicago. In June 1925 Fred Gretsch, Sr., went to Europe to further increase his international connections. During this period the firm published the Confidential Trade Price List, a book well known among industry insiders.

In the summer of 1926 the company acquired all rights to the K. Zildjian cymbal company. In August of the following year Gretsch's tenor guitars were formally debuted. During the Christmas season of 1929 the factory's production capacity was reported to be over 100,000 instruments, and a new midwestern branch was soon opened at 226 South Wabash Avenue, Chicago.

During the Depression, guitars accounted for only a small portion of Gretsch's total production (the bread-and-butter products were drum heads, banjos, harmonicas, Rex Royal accordions, cymbals, strings, and pitchpipes), but soon the guitar line expanded. In late 1933 the firm announced its Gretsch-American Orchestra guitars ($25–100), and in February 1935 the company moved its Chicago facility into expanded quarters at 529 South Wabash Avenue; this operation was again enlarged a few years later, the address changing to 218 South Wabash.

In March 1940 the company announced its acquisition of the B & D trade name from the Bacon Banjo Co. as part of a general plan to increase its output of stringed instruments. However, the nation plunged into World War II, and the restrictions on metals and other raw materials had a profound effect on the industry.

Fred Gretsch, Sr., retired in 1942 and spent the next decade as a most successful banker; he was president of Lincoln Savings and a director of Manufacturers' Trust Co. He died in 1952.

Soon after the war started Gretsch unveiled its Defender drum set, "made with less than 10 percent critical materials." A 1945 notice to dealers said: "We want to thank you for the fine spirit that all of you loyal and patriotic dealers have shown in agreeing that out of our limited wartime supplies of musical equipment Gretsch must first serve the needs of our men and women of the armed forces." William Walter Gretsch became president after his father's retirement in 1942, and he remained in that capacity until his death in 1948 at the age of 44.

Another son, Fred Gretsch, Jr., assumed the presidency when William died, and it was he who captained the company during its guitar heyday. His experience with the firm began at age ten, when he had a weekend job packaging phonograph needles. He graduated from Cornell, and in 1931 he was elected company treasurer.

Gretsch Synchromatic, 1940s style, cat's-eye soundholes.
Wagener/Beaty

In 1980 Fred Gretsch, Jr., recalled some of the details of his half-century tenure at Gretsch:

> I came in on a full-time basis in May of 1926. I was sort of a general office worker, and I moved up the line. My brother William was running our Chicago office while I was running the factory and the New York office. When I went into the service in 1941, he came East and ran the company. *[Note: the Chicago office was quite independent, maintaining its own payroll and accounts receivable departments.]*
>
> During the war we continued making instruments, but only with government-approved materials—no more than a certain amount of metal in each instrument. Probably 90 percent of our business was done with the armed services themselves or with related groups who were providing instruments to soldiers. We went back to our full-time production in about 1946.
>
> The Gretsch & Brenner Company was started by my uncle, Walter Gretsch. He had been associated with my father but decided to go into business for himself, so he started Gretsch & Brenner, which was purely an import organization. They weren't manufacturers.
>
> Jimmy Webster lived on Long Island. He was the chief designer of Gretsch electric guitars. For example, he was responsible for most of the ideas in the White Falcon. The people in production may have

1992 Update

Gretsch is once again owned by the Gretsch family. The new owner is Fred Gretsch IV, son of William Walter "Bill" Gretsch.

Mr. Gretsch recounts that the Baldwin Piano & Organ Co. owned Gretsch from 1967 to 1984. The firm was reacquired by the Gretsch family in 1985. No guitars were made until 1989, although production soon grew to about 200 instruments per month. The company has 40 employees as we go to press, and offers 14 models of hollowbody, semi-solidbody, and flat-top acoustics.

Fred Gretsch Enterprises has its offices in Savannah, Georgia, and a factory across the Savannah River in Ridgeland, South Carolina. Various parts are made there, including pickups, pickup mounting surrounds, body parts, and some of the hardware. These items are sent to Japan, where guitars are assembled from American and Japanese parts.

Mr. Gretsch avows: "The same tools are being used to make much of the product, although today we use superior glues, finishes, and machinery techniques that were not available earlier. This provides the classic Gretsch sound and look in a better-playing version that will last longer."

In 1989 Mr. Gretsch explained that Gretsch will remain a family enterprise: "My son, Fred V, will join the business next year in the same capacity that all family members have joined—learning the business from the ground up."

A pair of early Synchromatics: note the Synchromatic tailpiece on the blonde model, the stairstepped bridge on the other. ***Music Shop/Madsen***

had to refine some of his designs, but most of the ideas were his. He was very involved in the Project-O-Sonic project. The Sho-Bro was designed in collaboration with Shot Jackson, the Dobro player and pedal steel player who cofounded the Sho-Bud steel guitar company. The Sho-Bro was more Dobro than Gretsch.

I sold Gretsch to the D.H. Baldwin Company in 1967. I was president of Gretsch at the time, and I became a director of Baldwin. We continued manufacturing the guitars in our shop at 60 Broadway for three years or so, and we used the same people on the production line. We made the guitars, drums, and pickups right there in the same factory. It was during 1966 and 1967 that we had the largest number of guitar people working there in Brooklyn, about 150.

Mid-1940s Gretsch model Two Hundred Fifty. At least some versions had bound f-holes, and the original pickguard was decorated with the musical note design appearing on the peghead (see the "Oh Man, What A Guitar!" ad opposite title page of this book). The tailpiece was used on National's late-1950s Del Mar and on Gibson's late-1940s ES-300. ***Dick Allen***

As Mr. Gretsch noted above, his firm was purchased in 1967 by the Baldwin Piano & Organ Company of Cincinnati, which reorganized it as a subsidiary. In September 1965 Baldwin had acquired the manufacturing facilities of England's well-known guitar maker James Ormston Burns (see *The Burns Book,* Paul Day, P.P. Publ.) for £250,000. Baldwin assembled the imported Burns parts in Booneville, Arkansas, where it also maintained a banjo factory. To consolidate its businesses (and to escape Brooklyn's increasingly severe labor problems—even the sabotage of instruments) Baldwin moved Gretsch's New York plant to its Arkansas banjo facility in 1970. Former New York plant manager Bill Hagner, a Gretsch veteran since November 1941, found the new crew to be skilled and cooperative, and soon he had re-established substantial guitar production. He recalled in 1980, "We took the people in off the farms and from the small towns and taught them craftsmanship, and they were very good. When you get into a part of the country like that they have a lot of pride in their work."

In early 1972 the New York office was shut down and its administration was shifted to the Chicago outlet, which itself was relocated in Baldwin's home base of Cincinnati within a year or two. In January 1973 the Booneville plant suffered a serious fire. After assessing the damage and estimating the retooling costs, Baldwin was ready to permanently discontinue its guitar operation. According to one former executive, some of the equipment was put up for sale at auction. It was high noon for Gretsch. The employees rallied and put together a long-term loan arrangement. Bill Hagner formed Hagner Musical Instruments and agreed with Baldwin in April 1973 that Hagner would take over the factory himself and sell Gretsch guitars to Baldwin under a contract; Baldwin retained its rights in the Gretsch brand name. On December 15 of that same year the factory was struck by a second fire, this one disastrous. Despite the devastation of equipment, lumber supplies, and stock, the operation recovered quickly. Baldwin regained control in December 1978, and merged Gretsch with Kustom in November 1979. Gretsch ceased guitar making in mid-1981. By early 1982 the company was again gearing up for production, with several hollowbody electric prototypes under consideration, some made at the Arkansas plant, some in West Germany, and some at Baldwin's facility in Juarez, Mexico.

Gretsch New Yorker acoustic arch-top. *Charley's/Crump*

GRETSCH GUITARS

During the late 1930s and 1940s, the Model 400 Synchromatic was Gretsch's contender in the Super 400/Emperor all-out luxury guitar sweepstakes. It had streamlined cat's-eye f-holes, a stairstepped tailpiece with individual anchor barrels for each string, a "synchronized" bridge (graduated to provide a progressively broader contact between string and top going from treble to bass), enclosed Grover tuners, an 18-inch body (similar to the hugest Gibsons and Epiphones), a five-piece maple neck, and gold plating. In cross section its neck was asymmetrically shaped to make it more comfortable.

There were five other maple Synchromatics, their names corresponding to their prices. Models Three Hundred (gold plating, ebony fingerboard), Two Hundred (gold plating, rosewood board), and One Hundred Sixty (chrome plating) all had 17-inch maple bodies and cat's-eye soundholes. Models One Hundred (bound headstock, three-piece maple and rosewood neck), and Seventy-Five (unbound headstock, three-piece maple neck) both had 16-inch maple bodies and conventional f-holes.

Gretsch Synchromatic arch-tops and flat-tops from the 1949 catalogue.

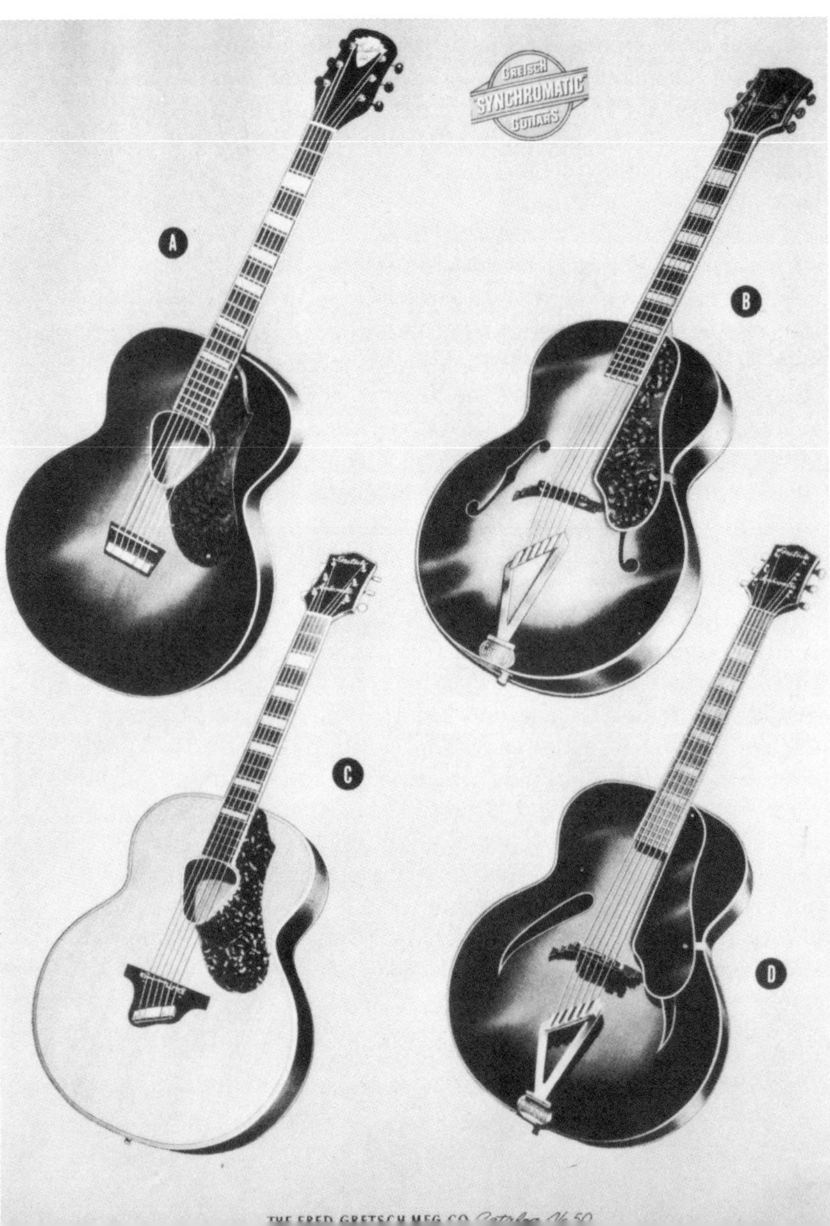

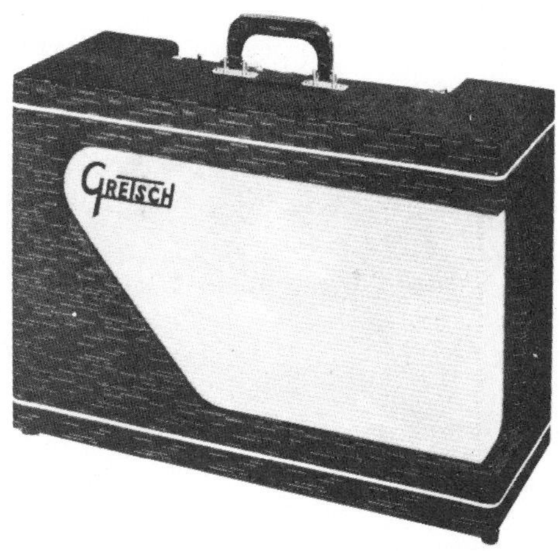

Gretsch Dual-Twin amp with three speakers, also available in western motif with hand-tooled leather belting around the top and bottom.

Other early Gretsch guitars included three arch-tops (models Fifty, Thirty-Five, and Thirty), Model Forty Hawaiian, two student grade flat-tops, the solid mahogany Electromatic electric Hawaiian lap steel ("its pick-up is sufficient to sustain a single stroke of the pick through sixteen measures!"), and the Electromatic arch-top electric Spanish guitar.

Some of the more interesting items in Gretsch's 1949 catalogue were the 16-inch maple New Yorker arch-top ($65) and several Electromatic models (console Hawaiian, single-neck Hawaiian, student Hawaiian, and Spanish). Forties Gretsch flat-tops included the triangular-hole, 16-inch Synchromatic Sierra (with *75* on the peghead); and the 17-inch Jumbo Synchromatic, forerunner of the Rancher.

It was during the 1950s and 1960s that the best known Gretsch guitars were conceived. Their popularity was especially dependent upon a series of official and unofficial endorsers, chief among whom was Chet Atkins. Some "artist" models have little input from their namesake guitarists, but Chet Atkins did in fact contribute significantly to the series that bears his name. Bill Hagner explained, "Chet was definitely very involved. He always had the last approval, and usually we would submit a *lot* of samples before we'd get it just the way he wanted it." Among official recommendations the Atkins seal of approval was all any manufacturer could hope for in the mid 1950s. First, he was incandescent with talent. Second, he was an eminently trustworthy gentleman: if Chet says it's good, it's good. Next, he sold records by the truckload and appeared on TV, and to top it off he was a guitar designer associated with electronic experimentation, often pictured in his home studio with dials and scopes and lights. Chet Atkins was a perfect blend of folksy charm, electronic wizardry, and guitar genius, and as far as modern electric models are concerned, his say-so put Gretsch on the map.

The previously mentioned Jimmy Webster was a traveling musician, teacher, conductor of Gretsch's Guitar-Rama hotel

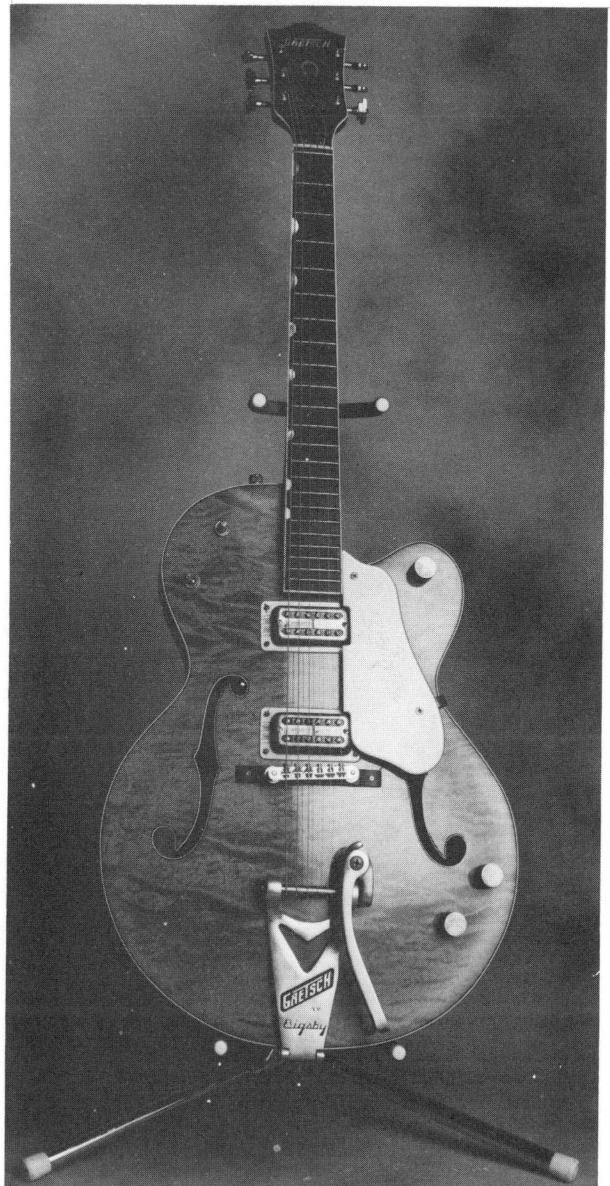

Chet Atkins Hollow Body, circa 1958. Note peghead, f-holes, neo-classic markers, and figured top (bridge unoriginal). Courtesy John Entwistle. ***Alan Rogan/Gavin Cochrane***

Mid-1950s Duo-Jet, with Melita bridge and DeArmonds. *Frank Lucido*

Astro-Jet, 1965, with Super Filter 'Tron pickups: note four-on-a-side peghead array. *Spitzer's/Sievert*

exhibitions, and the company's chief innovator during the 1950s and early 1960s. He was responsible for the White Falcon, White Penguin, and Bikini guitars, as well as the neo-classic markers, padded back, mufflers (string dampers), Project-O-Sonic stereo, and other distinctively Gretschian features. According to Bill Hagner, "Year after year, model after model, Jimmy came up with new ideas."

One such Webster brainstorm was the late-1960s/early-1970s Floating Sound unit, designed to enhance sustain. The strings wrapped over and under a metal "buckle" that "floated" on the string tension and acted as one end of the scale length. This piece connected to a tuning fork which protruded through the top and was suspended inside the guitar body.

It was through Chet Atkins that Gretsch met Ray Butts of Cairo, Illinois, who was contracted in the mid 1950s to design pickups. The result was the Filter 'Tron, originally a unit with individual coils for each polepiece and later a somewhat more conventional humbucker. The Hi-Lo 'Tron, designed by full-time Gretsch personnel, was a considerably less expensive pick-up used on some of the lower priced electrics. (During the 1940s and early 1950s Gretsch pickups were manufactured by Harry DeArmond of Toledo, Ohio. Gretsch gave the DeArmond company invaluable exposure, but terminated the relationship when DeArmond made a production deal with Chuck Rubovits of Harmony.)

Thanks in large measure to Chet Atkins' endorsement, Gretsch electrics became especially popular in the South and West. Several were decked out in country/western trim. For the Beatles' apocalyptic *Ed Sullivan* performance on February 9, 1964, George Harrison showed up with a Gretsch, and the company had again scored a golden if unofficial endorsement that helped broaden its base from jazz and country/western to rock and roll and pop music in general. Sales boomed, and Gretsch sometimes found itself a year behind in fulfilling orders. Bill Hagner claimed, "All hell broke loose when George Harrison came on TV. He was often seen with a Country Gentleman, which took off like wildfire. At our peak we were making 100 electrics a day, six days a week."

CHET ATKINS HOLLOW BODY AND NASHVILLE

In 1955 there were two $385 Chet Atkins models—one hollow, one ostensibly solid. The Chet Atkins Hollow Body, or Model 6120, was a single-cutaway with twin DeArmond (also called *Gretsch Dynasonic*) pickups, a standard Bigsby vibrato, gold plating, an "amber red" finish, a longhorn logo on the peghead, and block markers engraved with western scenes. The pick-guard sported a jagged signpost with Chet Atkins' signature. Perhaps the model's most memorable ornament was its large *G* cattle brand, actually burned into the top with a branding iron.

By 1959 a horseshoe peghead logo replaced the longhorn, neo-classic (half-moon) markers replaced the blocks, Filter 'Trons replaced the DeArmonds, and the *G* brand was gone. The finish, still described as amber red, was orange. (Inciden-

A gleaming black top and gold hardware lent a badass elegance to the 1963 Duo Jet; also available "with spotlight sparkle finish top" in silver, gold, champagne, burgundy, and tangerine.

1963 Corvette, single or double pickups.

tally, the single-cutaway Chet Atkins model is a fine rock and roll guitar. Eddie Cochran played one, and Pete Townshend used one on the Who's classic killer, *Who's Next.*)

By 1963 it was an all-new guitar with a thin double-cutaway body, a padded back, simulated f-holes, a mute, a Gretsch Bigsby (with a V-shaped cutout), and a straight-line metal saddle. The rounded pickguard had a *Chet Atkins* signature. The 1965 literature revealed no changes. By 1968 the guitar was called Nashville and had a straight-line saddle, a rounded pickguard, a mute, and a rectangular metal nameplate on the peghead. The 1972 model had a squared pickguard, a tune-o-matic, Filter 'Trons, no mute, and no peghead plate. The features for 1975 included a crooked-arm vibrato and new pickup housings.

SOLIDBODIES

C. W. "Duke" Kramer came to work for Bill Gretsch in Chicago as a horn polisher in October 1935. He later became a sales executive and one of Gretsch's best-known industry figures. He explained in 1980 that "Gretsch's strength was always with jazz and country musicians and with the hollowbody electric guitar. We never wanted to get into solidbodies too much—that was Fender's strong suit. They had theirs and we had ours. We did build some solidbodies, but like Fender's hollow electrics they were never too successful."

CHET ATKINS SOLID BODY

The Chet Atkins Solid Body of 1955, also known as Model 6121, might be termed a pseudo-solidbody in that, according to Chet Atkins, it was in fact hollow or at least semihollow (see Mr. Atkins' comments later in this chapter). The 6121 shared

1963 Rancher. Compare features: the 1955–1959 version had block markers and a *G* brand on the lower bass side; the 1965 and the 1968 had neo-classics and no brands; and the 1975 had a standard pin bridge and a *G* brand on the *treble* side. The Rancher was a westernized version of the triangular-hole 17-inch Jumbo Synchromatic Flat-Top.

the following details with its larger sister instrument, the hollow 6120: a single cutaway, the longhorn logo on the peghead, block markers inlaid with western scenes, DeArmond pickups, a Bigsby, gold plating, one switch, and four knobs. In addition, it sported hand-tooled, studded leather side trim. The 1959 Model 6121 had neo-classic markers, a horseshoe peghead logo, Filter 'Trons, two switches, and three knobs. The 6121 was discontinued by the early 1960s.

OTHER EARLY GRETSCH SOLIDBODIES

Aside from the Chet Atkins Solid Body, there were four solidbodies in 1955 that vaguely resembled Les Pauls: the black Duo-Jet; the Jet Fire Bird with an Oriental Red top; the Silver Jet with a Silver Sparkle top; and Round-Up, with a *G* brand, tooled leather body binding, belt-buckle tailpiece, block markers with western designs, and longhorn logos on the pickguard and peghead. All had three knobs on the lower right bout, DeArmond pickups, block markers, and a Melita bridge. Designed by John Melita of Philadelphia, the bridge had individual length adjustments for each string, one of the very first with that feature. Melita sent the parts to Gretsch, who assembled and plated the bridges.

By 1959 the Round-Up was dropped (later reintroduced) and the other three models, still single-cutaways, had these changes: two knobs on the lower bout, Filter 'Trons, neo-classic markers, and roller bridges.

The 1963 solidbodies were all *double*-cutaways with non-Bigsby vibratos: Jet Fire Bird, Duo-Jet, and Corvette. The 1968 versions all had Bigsbys and new Super-'Tron pickups. There was only one solidbody in 1972, the black, single-cutaway Roc Jet. Unlike the single-cuts of the 1950s, it had five knobs and a tune-o-matic. In 1975 it was shown in black, red, and walnut. There was a country version, the orange Country Roc; unlike the mid-1950s Round-Up, it had five knobs and a tune-o-matic, among other differences. The Broadkaster solidbody guitar and bass were also shown in 1975.

Manufacturers have sometimes tried to attract women with ad copy like, "The gals will especially like the slim body and three-quarter neck." Gretsch's 1963 Princess, built with a Corvette body, was an all-out attempt. It was marketed like an evening gown: "a guitar that is unmistakably hers. When she's out in front of others she'll see the admiration in their eyes. Her guitar is especially finished in a variety of pastel colors. Feminine in size, light in weight. Everything designed and scaled for her ease of playing. The white back is comfortably padded. 24K gold-plated metal parts. Shoulder strap is of white leather. Matching amp with jeweled pilot light."

Pete Townshend's mid-1950s White Falcon, with DeArmond pickups, Melita bridge, and *G* tailpiece.
Alan Rogan

MISCELLANEOUS MID-1950s GRETSCHES

The single-pickup hollow electrics for 1955 were the 17-inch-wide gold-plated Convertible (Lotus Ivory top, Copper Mist

John Entwistle's nonstereo White Falcon, circa 1959. *Alan Rogan/Gavin Cochrane*

The extremely rare gold-plated White Penguin Model 6134 was inspired by Jimmy Webster's idea of a solidbody White Falcon. Informed guesses as to the maximum number produced range from 20 to 100. It listed for $490 in January 1959, though rarely if ever appeared in catalogues. This one belongs to John Entwistle, bassist for The Who, and dates to about 1955. Note peghead logo, DeArmond pickups, and metal armrest. *Alan Rogan/Gavin Cochrane*

This White Falcon is an interesting transition model, circa 1958. It combines several mid-1950s features (Melita bridge, DeArmond pickups) with the newer neo-classic fingerboard markers. *Artie Leider*

1975 single-cut nonstereo White Falcon: block markers, crooked-arm vibrato.

body, knobs mounted on a Lucite pickguard), the 16-inch chrome-plated dot-neck Corvette, and the 16-inch thin-body Streamliner. (The single-pickup Sal Salvador and Clipper models were added by 1958.)

Gretsch's 1955 cutaway arch-top *acoustics* included the Fleetwood (ebony fingerboard, Synchromatic neck), and the Constellation (rosewood board). The other acoustic arch-tops were the 18-inch Eldorado (cutaway or noncutaway, with a terraced bridge reminiscent of the 1940s Synchromatics), 16-inch noncutaway Corsair (block markers), and 16-inch noncutaway dot-neck New Yorker. In 1955 Gretsch also had two 17-inch jumbo maple flat-tops, both with triangular soundholes—the Town and Country; and the gold-plated Rancher, with a *G* brand on the body.

GRETSCH BASSES OF THE 1960s

The company offered no electric basses until 1964 or 1965, when it came out with the double-cutaway PX6070, or simply Gretsch Electric Bass. It was a high-dollar item, with several Gretsch goodies—gold plating, padded back, string mute. Its most unusual characteristic was its retractable "cello pin," inserted near the tailpiece for stand-up operation. The 1968 literature described four hollow basses, all single-cutaways. The two short-scale models had vaguely Fenderish headstocks.

WHITE FALCON

The White Falcon was initially a promotional item, an experimental guitar built as a showpiece for a music industry trade show in Chicago. Bill Hagner remembered, "We lacquered it white, trimmed it all in gold, called it 'The Guitar of the Future,' and put it way on top of our display. It caused so much commotion that we worked it into the production line by the mid 1950s."

The 1955 single-cutaway, nonstereo White Falcon had a 17-inch-wide body, one switch, four knobs, Melita bridge, 24 carat gold plating, block markers, DeArmond pickups, a *vertical* "Gretsch" peghead logo (parallel to the neck), and an ornamental plate located on the peghead just above the nut. Its tailpiece had a V-shaped crossbar plus a metal *G* suspended between two rods. The glittering body trim—crushed, gold-colored glass between layers of clear plastic—was the same material as that used on the outer shells of Gretsch's Sparkle Gold Pearl drums.

In 1959 there were stereo and nonstereo versions, each with a single-cutaway, roller bridge, neo-classic markers, Filter 'Trons, *horizontal* "Gretsch" peghead logo, and a 1955-type tailpiece. The 1963 model was a double-cutaway with neo-classic markers, a 1955-style *G* tailpiece (i.e. no vibrato), and a roller bridge.

The 1965 White Falcon had *mini* knobs on the two muffler adjustments and (on the stereo) six switches, *four* of them on the upper left bout. It was the first White Falcon with a stock Gretsch vibrato, and except for its plastic tip the handle was a *straight* tube. The '68 model had the Floating Sound, plus large new rounded tuner buttons in place of the stairstep type of

Built for comfort—a late-1960s White Falcon Stereo with padded back, crushed-gold trim, 24-karat gold plating, built-in muffler, ruby-jeweled knobs; note Floating Sound (between muffler and bridge) and straight-tube vibrato arm.

1965 and earlier. The stereo version had six switches, *none* on the upper left bout. The vibrato was redesigned, this time with a hefty knurled adjustment nut at midlength on the arm.

In 1972 there were again two White Falcons, each with a squared-bottom pickguard, neoclassic markers, and Floating Sound; the vibrato arm was now a *crooked* tube. The standard mono guitar had larger f-holes, plus two switches on the upper left bout, while the stereo had no switches in that location. In 1975 there were three White Falcons, none with Floating Sound and all with small f-holes, tune-o-matics rather than roller bridges, block markers rather than neoclassic markers, and crooked-arm vibratos. Like the debut White Falcon of the 1950s, Model 7593 was a single-cutaway (it was different from the original in virtually all other respects). The double-cutaway nonstereo Model 7594 had three switches, while the 7595 Stereo had six. There were no apparent changes in 1978. The two-piece string mute ("double muffler") had two *full-sized* knobs.

COUNTRY CLUB

The 1955 catalogue depicted the 17-inch single-cutaway Country Club with two DeArmond pickups, block markers, Melita bridge, stairstep Grover Imperial tuners, and one switch. The 1959 model had Filter 'Trons, neoclassic markers, a roller

Mid-1950s Country Club, unusual two-tone gray finish. ***Don Hager/Beaty***

("space control") bridge, and two switches. The distinguishing feature of the 1963 model was its mute; the guitar was also available in stereo.

The 1965 Country Club had the same roller bridge, Filter 'Trons, and stairstep tuners, but no mute. The 1968 version (mono only) had the same roller bridge but also sported new large rounded tuning key buttons instead of the stairsteps. By 1972, the roller had been replaced by a tune-o-matic; other features included smaller f-holes, a squared pickguard, neoclassic markers, and a *G* tailpiece. The 1975 model had one switch, five knobs, and *block* markers; the tailpiece now said *Country Club.* There were no changes in 1978.

1969 custom-ordered single-cutaway Country Gentleman with simulated f-holes.
Don Hager/Beaty

COUNTRY GENTLEMAN

There were four guitars in 1959's Chet Atkins line: the Country Gentleman, the Chet Atkins Hollow Body (6120), the Tennessean, and the Chet Atkins Solid Body. All had neoclassic markers, Filter 'Tron pickups, and Bigsby vibratos. The 1959 Country Gentleman had a thin, 17-inch closed body, stairstep Grover Imperial tuners, an ebony fingerboard, gold plating, and a single cutaway. According to Gretsch executive Duke Kramer, the new design was intended to accommodate Chet Atkins' wish to maximize the guitar's purely electrical properties. This was accomplished with heavy interior bracing almost substantial enough for the model to qualify as a semisolid (see Chet Atkins' comments later in this chapter). Standard soundholes were replaced on the earliest models by inlaid plastic inserts and later by simulated, silkscreened f-holes in order to further de-emphasize body resonances. Due to the instrument's excessive weight, the interior block was later reduced in size, though the top still connected to the back, this time through interior soundposts.

By 1963 the Country Gentleman was a double-cutaway with stairstep Grovers, padded back, simulated f-holes, and a double mute (entailing an extra knob to the left of the Bigsby); the pickguard said *Gretsch.* Those features appeared again in the 1965 literature, but the 12-pole Filter 'Tron in the rhythm position was replaced with a twin-bar Super-'Tron II pickup with concealed polepieces. The body was specified to be hollow.

By 1968 there was a single mute (without the extra knob), rounded tuners, and a rounded pickguard that said *Chet Atkins Country Gentleman/Gretsch.* By 1972 the model had real f-holes, a squared pickguard saying only *Chet Atkins Country Gentleman,* and no mute. The Bigsby was still the standard type. The 1975 model, however, had a crooked-arm Bigsby, and also a 24½-inch scale. By 1978 the scale was 25½ inches.

TENNESSEAN

The late-1950s cherry red Tennessean was a single-cutaway hollowbody with one Filter 'Tron, neo-classic markers, real f-holes, a Chet Atkins "signpost" signature on the pickguard, and a standard Bigsby. By 1963 it had two Hi-Lo 'Tron pickups, simulated f-holes, no signpost, a Gretsch Bigsby with a *V* cutout, a straight-bar saddle, and a rounded pickguard. Those characteristics were again depicted in the 1965 catalogue. The 1967 model was almost identical, though it had a rectangular metal nameplate on the peghead. In 1972 it had a tune-o-matic, a squared pickguard, and no nameplate on the peghead.

ANNIVERSARY

The two-tone Smoke Green single-pickup Anniversary (or Single Anniversary) was added to the line in the late 1950s. By 1963 it was joined by the two-pickup Double Anniversary. Both had metal nameplates on the peghead, Filter 'Trons, and roller bridges. By 1963 both had Hi-Lo 'Trons; there were few or no changes through 1968.

By 1972 the Single Anniversary had been dropped and the Double had smaller f-holes, no nameplate, a squared pickguard saying *Gretsch,* a tune-o-matic, neo-classic markers, and a *G* tailpiece. The 1975 model had a squared pickguard saying *Anniversary,* a tune-o-matic, block markers, and a new tailpiece without the *G.* A few Anniversarys were made in sunburst.

PROJECT-O-SONIC

The 1959 catalogue detailed Gretsch's Project-O-Sonic electric, sort of the '59 Coupe deVille of the guitar world. Its circuit involved split pickups, a jack box, and separate amps for treble and bass. The system was available on the White Falcon and also on the three Country Club models (sunburst, natural, and Cadillac Green), which were renamed the Project-O-Sonic Series.

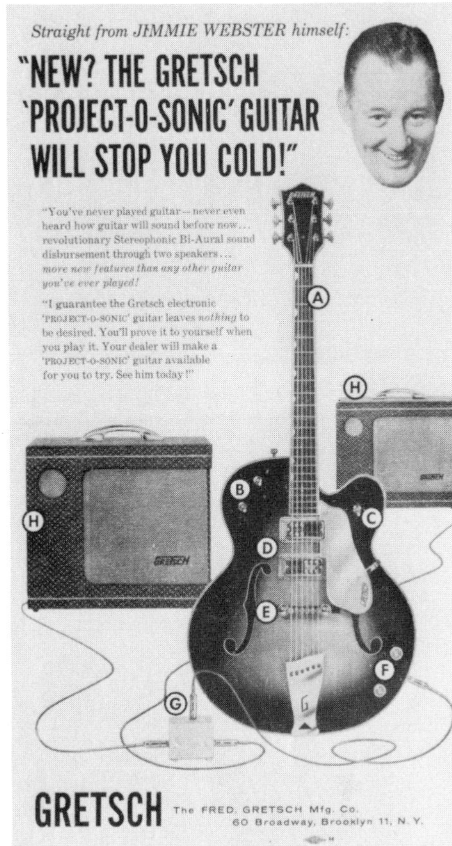

The Project-O-Sonic guitar entailed a stereo output and separate amps for bass and treble.

CHET ATKINS TALKS ABOUT GRETSCH

The first Gretsch Chet Atkins model was the 6120. Fred Gretsch and some engineers and I sat around all day and designed the thing. It was a hollow guitar. I kept trying to talk them into making one with more solidity from the neck down through the body, although they never did get it exactly like I wanted it. Still, they built a lot of good guitars and were very good to me.

I never did like the big old Gretsch f-holes—I thought they were a little too big and gaudy. I copied the holes on a D'Angelico and asked Gretsch to copy them and they did, and eventually they changed over to using them on all their guitars. Later on I suggested, "Well, why don't we fill up the f-holes—cover them over. Maybe that will make it sustain more."

Jimmy Webster was a chief designer for Gretsch and he had the idea of putting the thumbnail [neo-classic] markers on the fretboard. I specified the zero fret on there, because I'd seen one on a Maccaferri guitar that Django was playing, and it looked like a real good idea. I had had a lot of trouble with the string nuts and it seemed like I had to adjust the height of each one, so I thought the zero fret would help.

The Bikini doubleneck was a folding guitar with its necks mounted on slides for quick disassembly.

1968 Model 6119 Tennessean: straight-line saddle, Hi-Lo 'Tron pickups, rounded pickguard.
Spitzer's/Sievert

Sho Bro Hawaiian, made by Gretsch with Dobro parts, also available in a 7-string model. Gretsch also made a Sho Bro cutaway Spanish model.
James Hilligoss

I had used a mechanical tremolo since before the war. I wanted to have a crooked arm on mine so I could play pizzicato notes, muted against the bridge with my palm. Before he died, Mr. Bigsby [see Paul Bigsby] made me several attachments where I could take a round bar of quarter-inch cold-rolled steel and just bend it the way I wanted it. Now, mine didn't swivel, and Gretsch told me that for the average guy, my kind of tremolo would get in the way. On the later models they put a swivel on there, but I could never use it. Mine's in place and always will be, because that's the way I learned from the beginning. The cattle brand—that was someone else's idea. I didn't especially like that, but I was so happy to have a deal that I didn't complain about anything. I had them put on a metal bridge and a metal nut right from the beginning, and that was a part of trying to get a more solid guitar—an acoustic-looking guitar with more solidity.

The models that I was really involved with were the 6120, the Country Gentleman, the Super Chet, and Super Axe. The bracing inside the original Country Gentleman was solid, although not a solid block of wood down the middle. It was a pretty good guitar. George Harrison played one for years and helped sell thousands. Without asking me or consulting me, Gretsch decided to put some sponge rubber mutes on there, and they had to take the bracing that connected the top to the back and cut it in two. I always thought that that hurt the sustain of it. I always wanted the Country Gentleman to have a solid block down the middle that ran all the way through the body, but I never could talk them into it.

Ray Butts made a very early humbucking pickup. I was having a hell of a problem with those old DeArmonds humming. Ray was up in Cairo, Illinois, and he built that Echosonic amp, and I bought about the first or second one. Scotty Moore bought one and then a lot of people around Nashville got one. I kept telling Ray how unhappy I was with the DeArmond pickups, and I had to twist my body around to get the guitar in a certain position relative to the amp to get rid of this humming. One day he came down to Nashville and had this rough-looking pickup on an old guitar. He said how would you like a pickup that doesn't hum, and he tried it out for me. I said it's wonderful. Let's call Gretsch and put it out. It was a great invention as far as I was concerned.

Most of those gadget type features were Jimmy Webster's ideas. He always told me that the people out there in radioland liked to buy gadgets and you've got to give them more and more. Some of his ideas were good and some weren't. Personally, I like having a good quality guitar with no gimmicks, but he thought differently and he must have been right because they sold a lot of guitars. You know something—that Floating Sound with the tuning fork actually worked, at least on the treble strings, but it took the bottom out of the bass strings.

The Chet Atkins Solid Body was Gretsch's design. And it wasn't fully solid inside. It had a top and a back that were separate pieces. For the Super Chet, I just wanted to build the most beautiful guitar around. You know the extra binding along the side in the center? That's on a guitar that I have that's about 200 years old. The shape, which is really beautiful, was designed by Clyde Edwards up at Baldwin. Again, it did not have the solidity from the nut to the end of the guitar so it didn't turn out quite as I had hoped, but it was still very good. The Super Axe was our attempt to build a solid guitar that was a pretty good size—it still has some romance to it—

George Van Eps, the nearly incomparable chord-melody specialist, with his custom Gretsch 7-string. The company marketed a Van Eps 7-string in the early 1970s with a roller bridge, Floating Sound, and *G* tailpiece. Note peghead and extra polepieces. *Guitar Player*

With its lavish abalone inlay, the early-1970s Super Chet was one of Gretsch's fanciest guitars. Its controls were pickguard-mounted to avoid holes in the top; circa 1976 it went from a 24½-inch scale to 25½ inches. The Deluxe Chet was made from the same body and had standard markers, top-mounted controls, and a Bigsby.

and wasn't just another Les Paul copy. We put some effects in there and it's quite solid, a good guitar for contemporary playing.

In the middle of 1979 Gretsch and I gradually started to drift apart. We had some differences of opinion about design, but they've been very nice to me and I still love them. I still play my single-cutaway Country Gentleman.

1966 Gretsch Monkees model. Note "Monkees" logo on pickguard and peghead. *Anthony Manfredi*

GROSSMAN

Prior to World War II, the great majority of guitars were sold through mail-order distributors, such as Grossman, Tonk Bros., CMI (Chicago Musical), and Progressive, many of whom affixed their own names.

This page from Grossman's 1939 catalogue displays Grossman's Kleartone models. (The six-guitar Champion assortment cost a total of $45.)

GROSSMAN MUSIC CO . . CLEVELAND OHIO

GUITARS

No. 815

$8.50

No. 837
Super
Auditorium

$15.00

No. 823
Auditorium

$9.50

No. 815—"Stella" Guitar. Imitation Amplifying Model. Grand Concert Size of birchwood construction with F-Shaped soundholes and large nickel-plated Cover-plate. Finished in rich shaded, curly-maple grained-effect; white striped top edge, trapeze tailpiece, fingerboard neatly decorated with diamond designs. Distinctive model with striking sales appeal ... $8.50

No. 815-B—"Stella." Constructed same as above, but with all metal parts in beautifully polished bronze ... $9.50

"KLEARTONE" PANEL MODEL

No. 837—Super Auditorium Size with Violin arched top and back. Has neatly bound front and back white edges; adjustable bridge; F-shaped soundholes. Artistically designed panel with beautiful graining on back and sides. Polished finish throughout. Carefully shaped neck with accurately fretted fingerboard. A beautiful model with big, powerful tone, especially suitable for modern orchestra use ... $15.00

Cartons of 6
Each $13.50

No. 400—Case, "Economo," side-opening. Fleece lined, strong handle ... 4.30

"WINDSOR" GUITAR

No. 823—Auditorium Size. Will outsell and outperform any Guitar in its price class. Beautifully grained polished finish; diamond shaped panel in contrasting shade; both edges and headpiece white striped. Artistic. Lyre-shaped soundhole. Sells on Sight. ... $9.50

No. 750
"CHAMPION"
GUITAR
Assortment
(6 Guitars)
$45.00

No. 750
"CHAMPION"
GUITAR
Assortment
(6 Guitars)
$45.00

"CHAMPION" GUITAR ASSORTMENT

GUILD

Guild is a proud company whose finer steel-strings and arch-tops rank with the industry's best, and whose middle-level models pack exceptionally high value. As guitar manufacturing firms go, Guild is a young company, but even so, a few myths about its origins have already sprung up. One holds that it was founded by displaced Epiphone employees after the original Epiphone Company folded, and most of the stories share a similar theme that confederated craftsmen, in recognition of their cooperative venture, chose the name *Guild.*

The truth is that Guild was not founded by any ad hoc guitar-making collective, but rather by one man: Alfred Dronge, a one-time music store owner, music teacher, and professional guitarist. Dronge did in fact capitalize on the demise of Epiphone, a New York company that he, as an avid player, had frequently visited. Reliable sources vary as to whether he acquired any of the fixtures and equipment from Epiphone's Manhattan factory, but there is no question that he did retain several former Epiphone employees when he founded his small company in 1952.

Guild originally had headquarters in a modest New York City loft, space enough for the five-man staff Al Dronge had assembled. (Company historians are fond of emphasizing that the combined guitar-making experience of Dronge's personnel exceeded 200 years.) The founder and his employees devoted their first efforts to making large-bodied acoustic and electric arch-tops that manifested definite Epiphone bloodlines. Many early clients were professional guitarists, Dronge's friends in the New York studios. The company's output was small enough to allow Dronge to inspect personally every instrument as it

1968 Guild A600 B acoustic electric purchased from Guild founder Al Dronge: maple body, checker trim, gold plating.
Peter Budd

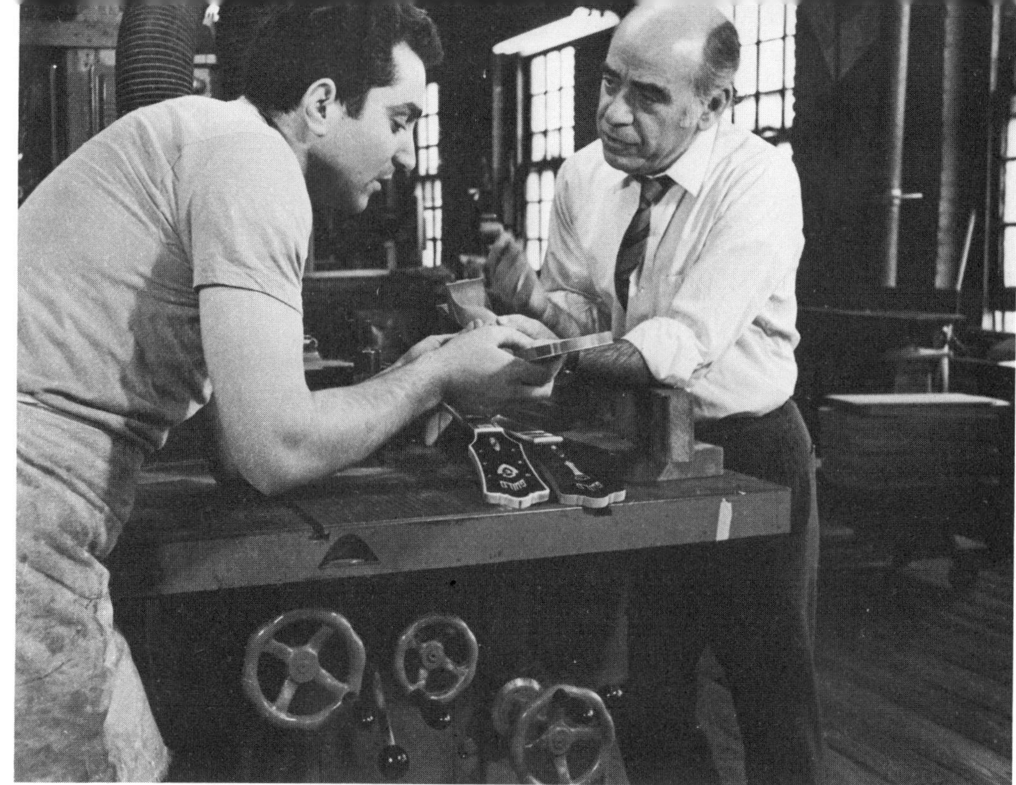

The late Alfred Dronge (*right*), founder of Guild Guitars, with a craftsman in the Guild woodworking shop, April 1969.

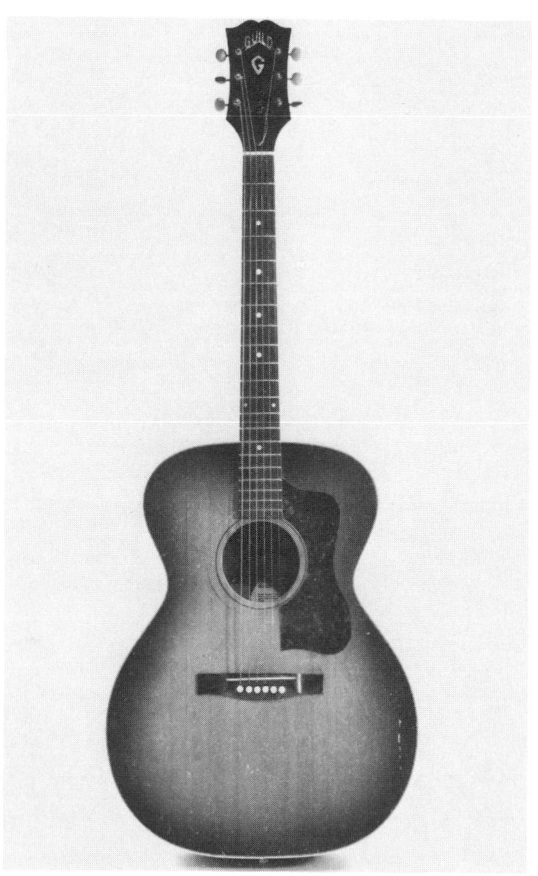

1960 Guild F-20. Note Gibson-like peghead. ***Soest/Rountree***

came off the line, and he let his acquaintances uptown know whenever a particularly good guitar was available.

Al was fortunate in obtaining rising jazz guitarist Johnny Smith as one of Guild's first endorsing artists, and Smith's picture graced one of the company's earliest catalogues. Smith was shown playing a Stuart 500, tops among the seven mid-1950s electrics. The 17-inch guitar had a single, Venetian (rounded) cutaway, volume and tone controls for each of its two pickups, gold-plated hardware, and Guild's graceful "harp" tailpiece. The top was spruce, the back and sides were flamed curly maple, and the five-piece maple neck had a rosewood fretboard featuring pearl block inlays with inverted abalone triangles, the same motif that had been used on Epiphone's top-of-the-line Emperor; the pattern was adopted as the heritage of top-of-the-line Guilds.

The Stuart 500's body, neck, and peghead were bound in ivoroid, and the peghead was inlaid with both the company logo and an insignia that was to become the hallmark of Guild's finest guitars, the *G* shield emblem.

A step down was the Stratford 350—the hot rod of Guild's debut models and the clearest link to Epiphone. In most respects, it was a smaller version of Epiphone's 18½-inch-wide Emperor Electric. The Stratford 350 had most of the features of the Stuart 500, except that it had single volume and tone controls and *three* pickups. In lieu of a pickup selector switch, it boasted a battery of six pushbuttons below the treble f-hole—as had the Emperor Electric. This "automatic Multi-switch changer" was said to provide "the versatility of an electric organ at the fingertips of the player." Though perhaps a little clunky looking, the arrangement was significantly more versatile than those offered on later and far more popular three-pickup guitars such as the Stratocaster and certain Les Paul Customs.

The rest of Guild's arch-top electric line included the Manhattan 175 (Epiphone, incidentally, had long offered a "Broadway" model), the Aristocrat M-75, the Capri CE-100, the Savoy 150, and the Granada 50. The Manhattan 175 was essentially an economy version of the Stuart 500, offering a three-piece mahogany neck, single tone and volume controls, chrome plating, and simpler appointments. For more frugal buyers, the Savoy 150 was simpler still, with a single pickup, nickel plating, and a plain trapeze tailpiece.

Standing apart from the other midpriced models was the unusual Aristocrat M-75, which had both gold plating and a harp tailpiece, and lacked f-holes. It was billed as a "light-weight, semisolid midget model," with a mahogany body 2 inches deep and 13½ inches wide, and a single Venetian cutaway. The Aristocrat was the only model aside from the Stuart to offer tone and volume controls for each of its pickups. Guild's Capri CE-100 was more or less the Savoy 150 with a pointed, Florentine cutaway in place of a Venetian cutaway. It was also distinguished by utilitarian volume and tone knobs that looked as though they had been borrowed from a toy oven. More significant, the Capri's Florentine cutaway made it the forerunner of the successful thin-line electric Starfire series that Guild was to introduce early in the following decade.

At the bottom of the line, the student-grade Granada 50 was a plain arch-top with a single pickup. Unlike the other models, it had an unbound neck and dot inlays. Available only in sunburst, it listed at $137.50. Because of Guild's small size, however, the company was almost a custom shop, and an early artist endorsement photograph (of one Betty Reilly, "the Irish Señorita") shows a *blonde* Granada with a *G* shield on the peghead and a block-inlaid fretboard.

Guild's acoustic models of the period included three arch-tops and four flat-tops. Though Al Dronge was a classical guitarist, the company did not begin offering classic models until after its 1956 move out of New York. The arch-tops were simply acoustic versions of electric models: the Stuart Acoustic A-500, the Stratford Acoustic A-350, and the Granada Acoustic A-50.

A very distinguished steel-string: Guild's F-50.

The premium model of the flat-top line was the jumbo Navarre F-50, larger and more expensive than the flat-tops Epiphone had offered. (Epiphone had previously offered a Navarre model acoustic Hawaiian guitar.) The F-50's peghead bore the *G* shield. Though in later years Guild adopted a pickguard shape that generally followed the contours of the body, the pickguards of the first F-50s, like those of the other Guild flat-tops of the day, curved downward from the nineteenth fret.

The Valencia F-40 was a smaller version of the F-50, with a simpler bridge shape and less purfling (trim) around the soundhole. The Aragon F-30 steel-string was smaller still, and though of similar construction, it had only modest dot fretboard inlays

Early-1970s Guild Artist Award amplified carved-top. The Epiphone legacy is revealed in the pearl fingerboard markers with abalone wedges. See the cutaway Emperor on page 28, for example.

and a simple logo on the peghead. Guild's cheapest guitar of all was an economy version of the F-30, the $85 Troubadour F-20.

By 1956, Guild's operations had become too extensive for its New York loft. Dronge moved the company to a larger facility in Hoboken, New Jersey. In the meantime, he had made two additions to the acoustic arch-top line. Guild had come out with the Capri CA-100, an acoustic version of the CE-100; and more significant, it had brought out its Johnny Smith model. For all intents and purposes, the Johnny Smith was an electric guitar, but for years Guild persisted in listing it among the acoustic models. The company made the distinction because no electric hardware was mounted on the body itself. Similar to the Stuart A-500, the Johnny Smith had a spruce top, flamed maple back and sides, gold plating, an engraved harp tailpiece, and an ebony fretboard with pearl blocks. A small, single pickup floated clear of the top below the end of the fingerboard; it was attached to the pickguard, which also housed the single volume knob.

Smith later transferred his allegiance to Gibson, which brought out a somewhat similar Johnny Smith model of its own. Bereft of its endorser, Guild changed the designation of its guitar to "Artist Award," adding to the peghead an elaborate pearl-and-abalone inlay that depicted a trophy cup on a plaque. Subsequent company literature took pains to characterize the suspended pickup and the pickguard control knob assembly as "Guild-developed" (though the concept dates at least to DeArmond's much earlier units).

Guild grew steadily in its Hoboken factory, branching out with engineering and research departments in addition to its production staff. In 1961, five years after leaving New York, the firm incorporated and became a stockholder-owned enterprise. By 1964, the year the Beatles arrived in America, Guild was offering a line of 26 arch-top and thin-line electrics, three solidbodies, eight flat-tops (including a 12-string model), six classics, five acoustic arch-tops, five amps (including a stereo model), and a baritone ukulele.

The better electrics were now equipped with humbuckings (generally patterned after Gibson's very successful units), and the harp tailpiece had become standard on all arch-tops. A "stairstep" pickguard, which in the next few years would become as much of a fixture on the arch-tops as the harp tailpiece, had appeared circa 1963 on the Artist Award and on the new models endorsed by George Barnes.

The more intriguing of the 1963 Barnes-endorsed models was the mahogany-body Guitar In F. Featuring a Venetian cutaway, it was merely 13½ inches wide with a short, 22¾-inch scale and an unengraved harp tailpiece. There were no f-holes in the carved spruce top; rather, there were only rectangular cutouts for the pickups, which protruded from an internally suspended longitudinal support bar. As with the Artist Award, the idea was to avoid having any electrical hardware touch the top. The knobs were installed on the pickguard, and the pickup selector switch, mounted on the cutaway, was the only exception. The

The "Guitar in F" was tuned higher than standard, A E C G D A, and intended to fulfill an alto sax's role in an ensemble. No soundholes, pickups affixed to internal strut. *Right:* Acousti-Lectric, no soundholes.

result was an odd but undeniably sleek exterior that made the Barnes guitars Guild's most distinctive electrics ever. The company claimed that the "innovations completely eliminate undesirable harmonics or feedback."

The Guitar In F was labeled with a script *F* peghead inlay. It was intended to be tuned a fourth higher than a standard guitar: A D G C E A, low to high. Guild explained that Barnes used the instrument "in ensemble as he would an alto saxophone—usually two or more to the section." The George Barnes Acousti-Lectric was a full-sized, standard-tuned version of the Guitar In F, with curly maple back, sides, and neck, a spruce top, a *G* shield, and an engraved harp tailpiece.

Duane Eddy, King of Twang, was arguably America's first rock and roll guitar star, certainly the first to take center stage strictly as an instrumentalist. He became another Guild endorser. Concurrent with the introduction of the Barnes models, the company brought out two guitars carrying Eddy's signature on their pickguards. The Duane Eddy DE-500 Deluxe was essentially a full-size Venetian-cutaway electric with a 2-inch-deep curly maple body, spruce top, two humbuckings, gold plating, a Bigsby, a maple neck, an ebony fretboard, pearl blocks, a *G* shield, and Eddy's name on the truss rod cover. The Duane Eddy DE-400 Standard was the same guitar with maple sides and back, mahogany neck, rosewood fretboard, and both chrome and nickel plating. In place of the *G* on the peghead, it sported Guild's Chesterfield inlay—an outlined crown atop a stylized, three-footed pillar.

Duane Eddy.

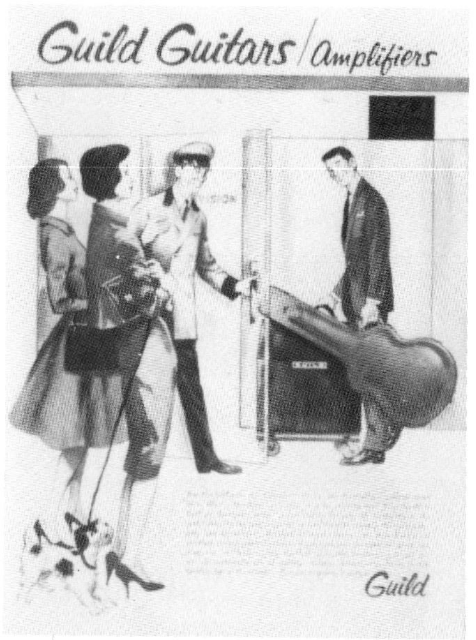

The look-sharp look—Guild's 1964 catalogue.

Elsewhere in the electric line, the Capri CE-100 had come out in a two-pickup version as the CE-100D and had been joined by the Slim Jim T-100 and Slim Jim T-100D—Capris with 2-inch-deep bodies. All bore Chesterfield inlays. The Aristocrat M-75 had vanished, but it left a legacy of a shoulder-mounted pickup selector switch on the twin-pickup Capris and Slim Jims. The Stratford 350 was still surviving, but its end was near, despite the catalogue copywriter's enthusiastic 1964 description of the three-pickup pushbutton behemoth as "a marvel of electronics, a masterpiece of the guitar maker's art, an instrument for the swinging soloist and technician."

Though some of the older models were in their declining years, Guild was to revitalize its electric line with the new Starfire (SF) series. The first Starfires were basically Slim Jims with humbucking pickups, dot-inlaid fretboards, and eye-catching cherry-red finishes. (Special-order finish options included emerald green, honey amber, and ebony grain.) The SF-III had twin pickups and a Bigsby, the SF-II was the same guitar without the vibrato, and the SF-I was a single-pickup version.

Rounding out the cutaway hollowbody electric models were two small-body, single-pickup guitars built along the lines of the Guitar In F, though with shallower (2-inch) bodies: the Freshman M-65 and the short-scale (22¾-inch) Freshman M-65¾. The noncutaway single-pickup Granada had been superseded by the thinner (2⅞ inches deep) Cordoba X-50, which was available in a still thinner (2 inches deep) version known as the Cordoba T-50 "Slim." All Freshman and Cordoba models had unbound, dot-inlaid fretboards, and script Guild peghead logos in place of the usual peaked block-letter type.

Guild's new solidbodies, like the George Barnes and Duane Eddy hollowbodies, had come out in 1963. The top model was the Thunderbird S-200, which had two humbucking pickups and a vibrato tailpiece of Guild's own design, with springs inside the body and a tubular arm. The shape of the double-cutaway body was somewhere between that of a Fender Jazzmaster and a Hershey bar left too long in the sun. Guild sought to further distinguish it by giving the top of the peghead an asymmetrical, quasi-Florentine profile. The S-200 had a thunderbird peghead inlay, block fretboard inlays, and—"at no extra cost"—the Guild Built-In Guitar Stand, a hinged leg recessed into the back of the instrument. When folded out, it formed a tripod with the "feet" of the sculptured body, and the guitar could stand by itself.

Sharing the peghead shape, vibrato tailpiece, and built-in stand of the Thunderbird S-200 was the Polara S-100. The body had a slightly more conventional shape, closer to that of a Gibson SG, but the bottom was carved out to create the feet of the built-in stand. A single-pickup version was offered as the Jet Star S-50. A general note: during the mid 1960s, Guild pegheads changed from a Gibson-like design to the center-peak type.

By 1964 Guild had filled out its flat-top series with a new jumbo, the Bluegrass F-47, and two new dreadnoughts: the

Bluegrass Special D-50 and Bluegrass Jubilee D-40. The F-47 had a spruce top, mahogany back and sides, and a rosewood fretboard with pearloid block inlays. The rosewood D-50 had an ebony fretboard and chromed Grover Rotomatics. The D-40 had mahogany back and sides, a rosewood fretboard, and nickel-plated Guild tuning machines.

Another noteworthy addition was the highly regarded F-212, basically a 12-string version of the F-47. The F-40, meanwhile, had been discontinued, and the company had added a new, small-body budget flat-top in the Economy M-20.

Charlie Byrd had joined the ranks of Guild endorsers, lending his name to the company's six classical models. The rosewood Classic Mark VI was the most distinguished of the series, featuring an ebony fingerboard and bridge, wood binding, gold-etched tuning machines, and natural bone "rollers" (tuning key shafts). It was first available "on special order only," but by 1966 it had become a regular production item. The *crème de la crème* Guild classic was the limited-edition Mark VII, with still finer selections of the same materials; it waltzed through Guild catalogues for several years, finally leaving for good in the mid 1970s.

In 1966 Guild was purchased by Avnet, Inc., a corporation with interests in consumer electronics, automotive products, and other industrial fields. The acquisition did little to change the day-to-day operations at Guild, which continued to function as a virtually autonomous entity.

By 1967 the Starfire series had come into its own. The single-pickup SF-I had been dropped, displaced by more advanced models, and although the introduction of the SF-III was hardly a dim memory, it was already being labeled "a favorite for many years." The spotlight had been usurped by the SF-IV, SF-V, SF-VI, and SF-XII. The SF-IV was similar in appearance to Gibson's phenomenally popular ES-335, introduced in 1958. It had two humbucking pickups on a thin double-cutaway body. The SF-IV's pickup selector was mounted on the treble cutaway (the Gibsons had their switches positioned near the treble f-hole). The SF-IV also had a Chesterfield peghead inlay, dot markers, and a harp tailpiece. The SF-XII was simply a 12-string version of the SF-IV.

The SF-V was distinguished from the SF-IV by its Bigsby style vibrato tailpiece, a master volume control, fancier tuning keys, and block inlays. The SF-VI was a luxury SF-V, with gold plating, a *G* shield peghead inlay, and pearl blocks with abalone wedges on its ebony fretboard.

In April 1967 the still-growing company started work on a new factory in Westerly, Rhode Island, with the intent of moving all its flat-top and classical production there. Manufacturing efforts continued to be shifted from the Hoboken plant through 1968 and 1969, and the company found the Rhode Island economic climate and labor pool so agreeable that it decided to consolidate all its production facilities in Westerly. The move was completed by the fall of 1971, but some instruments made after that time still carried *Hoboken* labels because the

Starfire III, circa 1967. *Spitzer's/Sievert*

1969 Starfire IV.

Starfire V.

Starfire VI.

company didn't print new labels until its supply of old ones had been exhausted. Westerly remains the site of the Guild manufacturing plant. The company's administrative offices, however, are in Elizabeth, New Jersey, near New York City.

By 1969 Guild was able to claim Tommy Smothers, Richie Havens, George Benson, and (the subject of a much-used publicity photo) Eric Clapton among its endorsing artists. Duane Eddy's star had fallen, and his name no longer appeared on the pickguards of the DE-500 and DE-400, though the models survived. By this time, the stairstep pickguard was used on all Guild arch-tops.

The old small-bodied Aristocrat electric resurfaced, billed as the M-75 Semi-Solid 3/4 Size Body Guitar, with humbucking pickups, a Chesterfield inlay, and a body ⅛ inch deeper than that of the first model. Its companion was the new M-85-II bass, built along the same lines but having a 2⅞-inch-deep body and a 30¾-inch scale, and featuring a master volume control on its cutaway. A single-pickup version, the M-85 bass, was also sold. At this point the flat-top division added a new dreadnought, the D-35, a slightly more modest edition of the D-40; it also introduced a built-in pickup option on the F-212.

The year 1972 was a watershed for Guild. Alfred Dronge was killed in May when his private plane crashed during a storm. After several months the presidency was assumed by Leon Tell. By 1975 the Guild line had undergone some significant changes, most notably in the solidbody electric division, where the S-100 had shucked the name *Polara* and metamorphosed into something similar to Gibson's long popular SG. The S-100 DeLuxe featured a contoured double-cutaway mahogany body with dual humbucking pickups, a phase switch, a Bigsby vibrato, Grover Rotomatic tuners, a Chesterfield inlay, and pearloid block markers. The S-100 Standard had a chrome-plated, angled brass tailpiece instead of a Bigsby, and was also offered with a natural wood finish, clear pickguard, and relief carvings of acorns and oak leaves on the top.

The old semisolid Aristocrat had become the carved-body M-75CS. Gone was the harp tailpiece, replaced by the same angled brass tailpiece that graced the updated S-100. New features included a polarity reversal switch, a master volume, an ebony fretboard with pearl blocks, and Schaller machines. The M-75CS had lost its aristocratic gold plating, but well-heeled purchasers could get a special version with gold plating in the M-75GS.

The Starfire series had dropped the SF-III, SF-V, and SF-XII and substituted Arabic numbers for the old Roman numeral designations. The Starfire 6 remained the top model, the only member of the series still offered with a Bigsby. The SF-4 inherited the SF-V's master volume control, while the Starfire 2 carried on the single Florentine cutaway look that had ushered in the series more than a decade before.

Attrition had also hit the full-sized arch-top electric line, reducing it to four models. The Artist Award was now listed among the electrics simply because Guild had ended production of its beautiful arch-top acoustics in mid 1973. The Stuart 500 survived as the X-500, now with the additions of a master volume control, Grover Rotomatics, and an ebony board in place of the original rosewood piece. The X-175, formerly the Manhattan 175, had also acquired a master volume control in the interim. The knob was located on the cutaway, exiling the selector switch to the upper bout. Stereo versions of all double-pickup guitars and basses were now available on special order, and Guild also offered left-handed editions of all its electric models. The flat-top line added a new premium dreadnought, the D-55. Another addition to the flat-top line was the arched-back G-37 dreadnought, which originated as a special-order model for a New York dealer and was incorporated into the general line in 1973. That year also saw the official resurrection of the F-40, now carrying a Chesterfield inlay and Grovers. Joining it in the jumbo ranks was the new F-48, ¼ inch shorter and ⅛ inch shallower than the F-50, with mahogany sides and back, a rosewood fretboard, chrome-plated Grovers, and a Chesterfield inlay. By the end of 1975 both the F-47 and F-48 had been discontinued, as Guild put more effort into enlarging its distinguished dreadnought series.

The D-44 Bluegrass Jubilee, a D-50 with a back and sides of pearwood, appeared in 1970. It became the D-44M, with maple substituted for increasingly scarce pearwood as the decade went on. (It finally dropped out of production in 1979.) In 1974, Guild introduced the big-bodied G-41, as well as the G-75, a three-quarter edition of the D-50.

Dreadnought 12-strings became available in 1974 with the introduction of the G-312 and the G-212, 12-string versions of the D-50 and D-40, respectively. (During the mid 1970s, the jumbos received invaluable exposure in the hands of John Denver.) The Guild 12-strings had become more luxurious by this time with the introduction of the F-512 and the F-412. The former, with a spruce top and rosewood body, superseded the dropped F-312; it featured a larger body and a bound ebony fretboard with pearl blocks. The F-412 was the same guitar with an arched maple back and curly maple sides.

The B-50 flat-top acoustic bass was introduced in 1975. A full 6¾ inches deep, it had a 31-inch scale, an unbound dot-inlaid rosewood fingerboard, a split saddle, and optional Barcus-Berry Hot-Dot transducers.

The full-sized arch-top electrics were essentially unchanged at the end of the decade. The Starfire 6, however, was first shorn of its Bigsby and then discontinued altogether by early 1979. The Starfire 2, the last vestige of the original Florentine-cutaway models, also expired. Only the Starfire 4 endured as the 1980s dawned.

In 1977 Guild completely redesigned its solidbody guitars and basses. The first fruit of that effort was the B-301 bass, a single-pickup instrument with a new, bell-bottom body. The treble cutaway was short and blunt, reminiscent of the defunct M-80CS, while the cutaway on the bass side was more protuberant, resembling that of a Stratocaster. By 1979, the new

S-100 solidbody.

Mid- and late-1960s style Thunderbird. The built-in stand didn't catch on. ***Ax-In-Hand***

Guild X-500.

shape had supplanted all previous Guild solidbodies. The leading guitar was the S-300, with a 24-fret dot-inlaid ebony fretboard. It was offered with a maple neck and an ash body as the S-300A; as the S-300D or S-300AD, it came with DiMarzio pickups.

Guild brought out its first triple-pickup electric since the old Stratford when it introduced the S-70D, similar to the S-100 but with a rosewood board and a pickguard extending onto the bass side of the top. Its three DiMarzio SDS-1 units were in a Stratocaster configuration (angled bridge pickup). The lowest priced of the new Guild solidbodies were the S-60D, essentially a two-pickup version of the S-70D, and the S-60, with a single humbucker. Both lacked the more expensive models' Chesterfield peghead inlay.

Guild ended its twenty-seventh year vastly changed from the small loft/workshop enterprise that Alfred Dronge had started in 1952, but one important similarity remained: it was still striving to grow. During 1980 and 1981, Guild introduced the limited-edition luxury flat-top D-70, the flat-top D-46 (with a body of ash, a most unusual wood for an acoustic guitar), and prototypes for new solidbody guitars with active onboard electronics.

1990 Update
In August 1986 Avnet sold the company to Guild Musical Corp., a group of investors. In November 1988, that group defaulted on bank obligations and filed for Chapter 11, a court-supervised financial restructuring. The Faas Corp. of New Berlin, Wisconsin, owners of Randall, bought Guild on January 25, 1989, for 2.1 million dollars. Owner Chuck Faas made no fundamental changes in either the work force or the 50,000 square foot factory (located in Westerly, Rhode Island, since 1967). Guild discontinued solidbody production in order to concentrate on about 30 acoustic and acoustic-electric models, including the Nightbird, familiar guitars such as the D-55, and the JF-55, a reincarnation of the F-50R. There are 55 employees, and production is running about 450 instruments per month.

SELECTED GUILD SERIAL NUMBERS, 1960–1979

Year	*From: Number*	*To: Number*
1960	12035	14713
1961	14714	18419
1962	18420	22722
1963	22723	28943
1964	28944	38636
1965	38637	46606*
1966	46607	46608*
1967	46609	46637*
1968	46638	46656*
1969	46657	46695*
1970	46696	50978
1971	50979	61463
1972	61464	75602
1973	75603	95496
1974	95497	112803
1975	112804	130304
1976	130305	149625
1977	149626	169867
1978	169868	195067
1979	195068	211877

* See following charts.

SELECTED SERIAL NUMBERS, 1965–1969

Artist Award
1965 AA 101
1966 AA 102–113
1967 AA 114–139
1968 AA 140–157
1969 AA 158–167

Starfire 6
1965 DB 101
1966 DB 102–174
1967 DB 175–274
1968 DB 275–329
1969 DB 330–339

DE-500
1965 EI 101–107
1966 EI 108–116
1967 EI 117–136
1969 EI 137–141

CE-100
1965 EF 101–211
1966 EF 212–396
1967 EF 397–649
1968 EF 650–719
1969 EF 720–760

Starfire 12
1966 DC 101–586
1967 DC 587–896
1968 DC 897
1969 DC 899–910

D-50
1965 AL 101–192
1966 AL 193–301
1967 AL 302–513
1968 AL 514–584
1969 AL 585–698

Starfire 2 and 3
1965 EK 101–387
1966 EK 388–2098
1967 EK 2099–2819
1968 EK 2820–3028
1969 EK 3029–3098

S-200
1965 SC 101
1966 SC 102–153
1967 SC 154–166
1968 SC 167–191

X-175
1965 EG 101–107
1966 EG 108–160
1967 EG 161–239
1968 EG 240–322
1969 EG 323–346

Starfire 4
1965 EL 101–276
1966 EL 277–1167
1967 EL 1168–1840
1968 EL 1841–2223
1969 EL 2224–2272

F-50
1965 AD 101–119
1966 AD 120–190
1967 AD 191–291
1968 AD 292–355
1969 AD 356–418

X-500
1965 DA 101–106
1966 DA 107–138
1967 DA 139–180
1968 DA 181–235
1969 DA 236–244

Starfire 5
1965 EN 101–194
1966 EN 195–927
1967 EN 928–1807
1968 EN 1808–2141
1969 EN 2142–2278

DE-400
1965 EH 101–126
1966 EH 127–233
1967 EH 234–276
1968 EH 277–301

Guild B-50 acoustic bass.

Michael Gurian.

GURIAN

Michael Gurian was both a major American wood supplier and a builder of some of the most distinctive steel-strings to appear in a long time. Born in 1943, a Brooklynite of Armenian descent, he took lessons on various instruments and developed a fondness for wood. He later studied sculpture at Long Island University, took up classical guitar, and taught music in Roslyn, New York.

With his studio apartment for a workshop, Michael built his first guitar—a copy of a classical made by Victor Manuel Piniero, a student of Velasquez. In 1965 he moved to a three-room shop in Greenwich Village, and with two assistants began building classical instruments. Traditional steel-strings were added four years later, and Gurian introduced his own distinctive body shapes soon after that. The company moved to Bedford Street and then Grand Street, his crew of builders growing to 15. In 1971 he relocated in Hinsdale, New Hampshire, because of that state's favorable business climate. Vintage retailer Matt Umanov encouraged him to build a cutaway, and he did. It became a regular member of the line.

A terrible 1979 fire resulting from a boiler explosion destroyed not only all of Gurian's guitars but also his tooling and machinery as well. After the half-million-dollar loss he rebuilt and grew, recovering with remarkable perseverance from a defeat that would have sent a lesser person back to guitar teaching for good. By late 1979 Gurian was employing over two dozen people and servicing nearly 200 dealers worldwide. In early 1980, with 90 percent of his prefire craftsmen still with him, he was looking forward to manufacturing guitars once again.

Gurian's background as an expert with old-fashioned techniques manifests itself in his instruments, whose unusually rounded bodies are most appealing. They combine classical appointments and modern interior construction; the tone is bright and strong.

Because of the unfavorable economic climate, Michael Gurian was forced to close his business in the winter of 1981–82.

HAMER

Located in Palatine, Illinois, Hamer was named after cofounder Paul Hamer; the other principal designer/administrator is Jol Dantzig. In a sense they represent a new generation of guitar builders, in that while most of their designs are firmly rooted in the traditions of a major manufacturer (in this case Gibson), they believed that they could improve upon those revered Les Pauls and Explorers. The Hamer Sunburst, for example, is patterned in general outline after Gibson's earliest double-cutaway Les Paul Specials and Juniors, though it bears a much fancier complement of parts, woods, and finish (the model's name is of course the common nickname for Gibson's 1958–1960 Les Paul Standard, perhaps the world's most esteemed solidbody ever). Aside from its regular line, Hamer has also built notable special-order instruments, including a 12-string quadraphonic bass, and Rick Nielsen's many custom guitars (checkerboard-finish V's and Explorers, etc.).

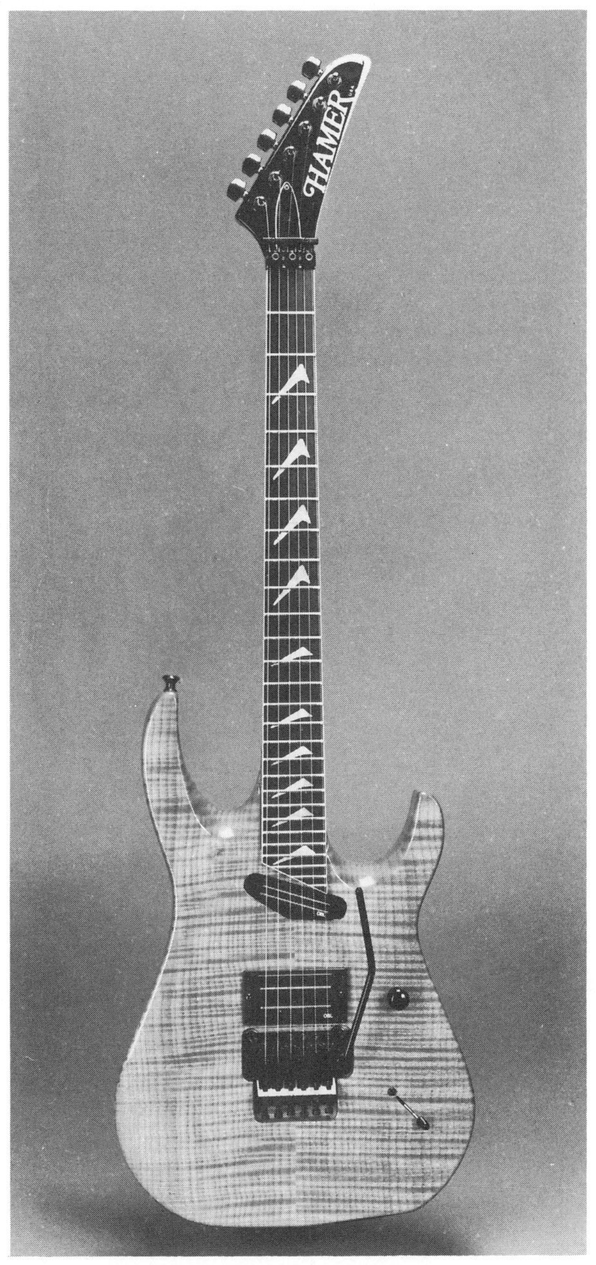

The elegant 1989 Californian Custom is a typical Hamer instrument, blending choice woods, knockout looks, no-nonsense electronics, sonic versatility, comfortable neck, and precision craftsmanship.

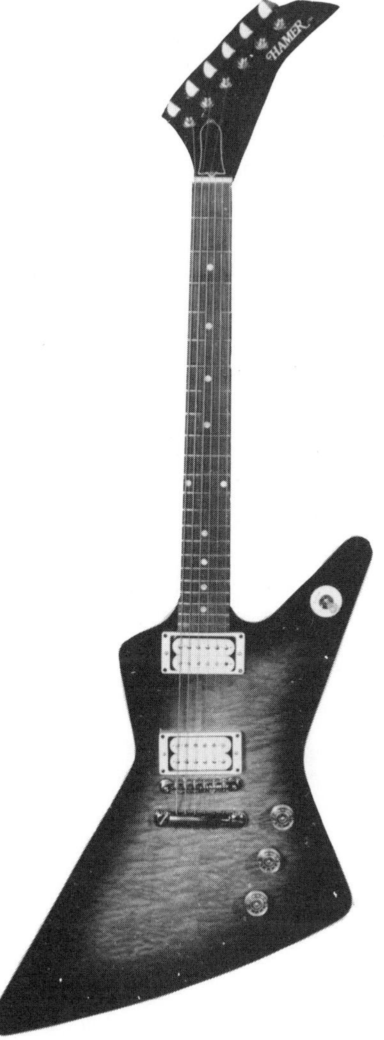

The inspiration for this Hamer was clearly the original Gibson Explorer, but the Hamer's two-piece curly maple top is much more dazzling than the Explorer's limed korina body. Aside from flashy looks, the zigzag shape is practical, balancing the right arm in a comfortable playing position.
Goodman

1992 Update
In 1980, Hamer relocated from Palatine, Illinois, to a larger, 12,500-square-foot facility in nearby Arlington Heights, on the northwest side of Chicago. Every Hamer is built entirely within this building. Head of sales Paul Hamer left the company in 1987, and in 1988 Hamer was acquired by Kaman Music Corp., makers of Ovation. All staffers were retained, including managing director Frank Untermyer and co-founder Jol Dantzig, the director of design. No changes in manufacturing were instituted.

In 1990, 25 workers produced approximately 50 instruments per week. Although there are eight guitar and four bass models in the line, many custom features and options are offered.

Harmony "Singing Cowboys," stenciled paint. *Umanov/Peden*

HARMONY

Harmony was at one time the production king of American instruments, and during its heyday it accounted for over half the guitars built in this country each year. The proud old giant had a modest beginning in the last decade of the nineteenth century. A Hamburg mechanic named Wilhelm J.F. Schultz emigrated to America to work for the Knapp Drum Company of Chicago. When Knapp was bought out by Lyon & Healy, he was promoted to foreman of the drum division.

In 1892 Schultz struck out on his own, buying a two-room loft on the top floor of the Edison Building at Washington and Market Streets, later the site of Chicago's Civic Opera House. He and four employees began production on a modest scale—the first transaction was the sale of two guitars in 1892 to the Chicago Music Company. Schultz's business grew fast and boasted 40 employees by 1894. There were several factory locations in Chicago before 1904, when Schultz and crew settled into their own three-story, 30,000 square foot plant at 1738–1754 North Lawndale Avenue. A new wing was added in 1906, and by 1915 Harmony had a quarter of a million dollars in annual sales and 125 employees.

When the ukulele became popular following its introduction at the Hawaiian exhibit of the 1915 San Francisco Fair, Harmony became the first (and for a time the only) large-scale ukulele manufacturer. In 1916 Sears, Roebuck acquired Harmony in order to gain its substantial ukulele production. When World War I severed the industry's German wood sources, Harmony became America's only large-scale violin manufacturer. It also made mandolins, banjo ukes, tenor banjos, and other instruments and by 1923 its annual production capacity was 250,000 instruments.

Max Adler was a Sears executive and later the donator of Chicago's Adler Planetarium. He appointed his nephew, Jay Kraus (sometimes spelled *Krause*), to be Harmony's vice-presi-

HARMONY FEATURES...
A "Reasonable" Blonde
THE GLEAMING WHITE, NATURAL FINISH
PATRICIAN
Nu-Tone
SENSATIONS of the season—4 brilliant new additions to the Patrician line of guitars. . . . Traditional in their fineness of tone quality and superb character of workmanship—yet most "reasonable" at their featured prices of $25.00 to $75.00.
Here is a blonde worth getting excited about! Outstanding in appearance, it individualizes the guitar player—whether professional or amateur. In the grand auditorium size, its back and sides are of curly maple, its top of selected spruce. Its features include heavy tortoise shell celluloid binding, heavy plastic shell guardplate, and ovalled rosewood fingerboard.
Ask your jobber—leading wholesalers have "Patrician Nu-Tone" available. Write us for details.
THE MODEL ILLUSTRATED IS NO. 1450, LIST PRICE $25.00. MANDOLIN TO MATCH NO. 417, $25.00
THE HARMONY CO.
1748 NORTH LAWNDALE AVENUE
CHICAGO
The World's Largest Manufacturers of Stringed Musical Instruments

A 1940s ad for Harmony's Patrician arch-top. *Chuck Rubovits*

dent in 1925. Kraus was well liked and highly respected, with outstanding skills as a businessman and company leader. He succeeded founder Wilhelm Schultz as Harmony's president in January 1926, and along with Fred Gretsch, Jr., Hank Kuhrmeyer of Kay, and others he ultimately became one of the great captains of the Chicago guitar manufacturing community of the 1930s, 1940s, and 1950s. Jay Kraus was one of the six men who met in 1947 to found the American Music Conference (AMC), and he served as president of both that organization and NAMMM, forerunner of NAMM, or National Association of Music Merchants.

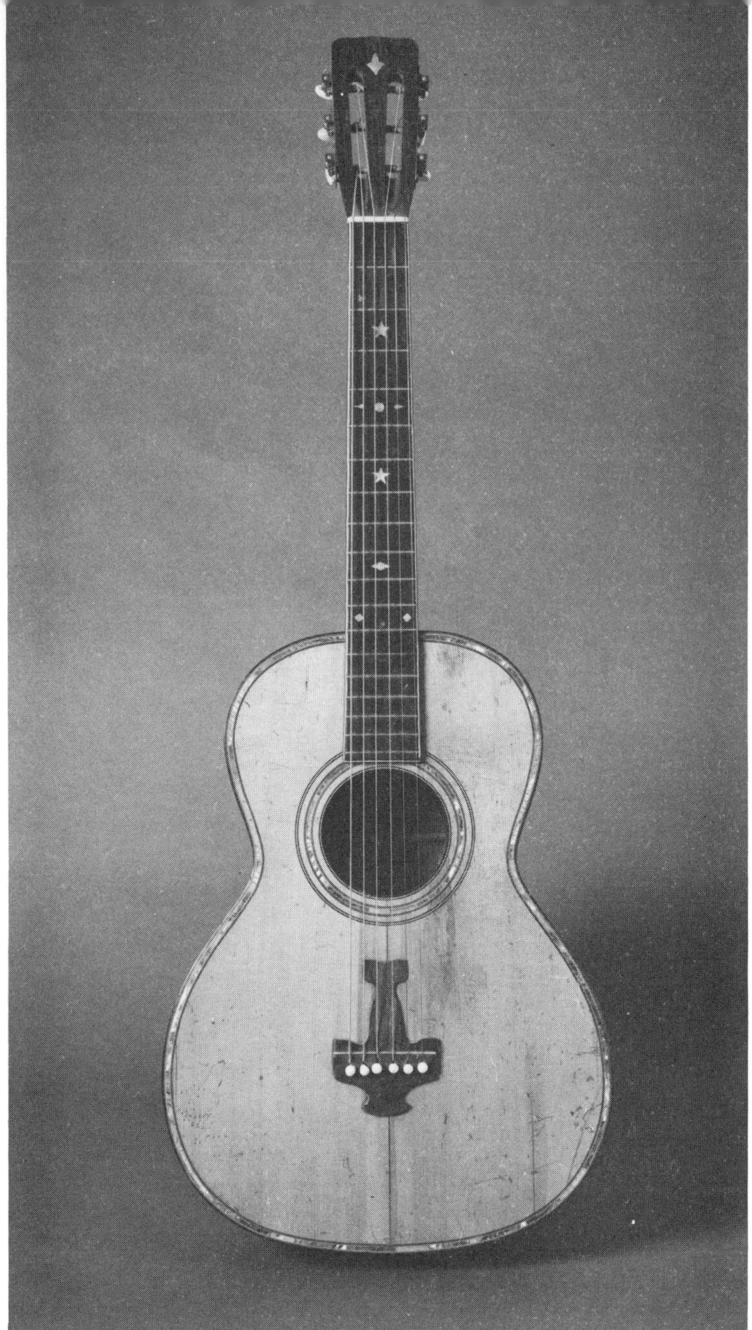

Unlabeled flat-top (early 1930s) with fancy body trim, made by Harmony for a wholesaler. The airplane tailpiece, probably inspired by Lindbergh's 1927 Atlantic crossing, appeared on several models. *Carl & Brenda Vanover/T. Erlewine*

In February 1928 Harmony introduced its Roy Smeck Vita series—standard, tenor, and plectrum guitars, all distinguished by their soundholes, which were shaped like seals (the kind that bark and swim). In January 1930 the Roy Smeck Grand Concert and Hawaiian models were unveiled. By the following year, Harmony claimed an awesome annual production capacity of 500,000 instruments. In March 1931 the Vagabond guitar line was first produced, and in the following September the Cremona professional guitar appeared; it became one of Harmony's most respected arch-tops.

In July 1938 Harmony returned to violin production after a 19-year hiatus, and in September of that year the Patrician guitars made their debut. In May 1939 Harmony bought several brand names from the bankrupt Oscar Schmidt Company (which was succeeded by Fretted Instrument Manufacturers), including La Scala, Stella, and Sovereign; the latter two were used on many of Harmony's most popular guitars. During this period Harmony substantially increased its trade names to include Valencia, Monterey, Harmony Deluxe, Johnny Marvin, Vogue, and many more.

Jay Kraus resigned in February 1940, and two months later John T. Higgins was elected company president. Then Kraus bought the firm for himself in December of the same year by acquiring controlling stock, and in January 1941 he moved Harmony into new quarters at 3633 South Racine Avenue.

The 1941 Harmony catalogue illustrated acoustic guitars ranging from $7.50 to $75, and during that period the company was reportedly manufacturing about 130,000 of the 250,000 American guitars produced each year. There were no field forces or branch offices, and no territorial restrictions on Harmony's wholesalers. Competition was fierce.

Except for the year 1949, total music industry retail sales

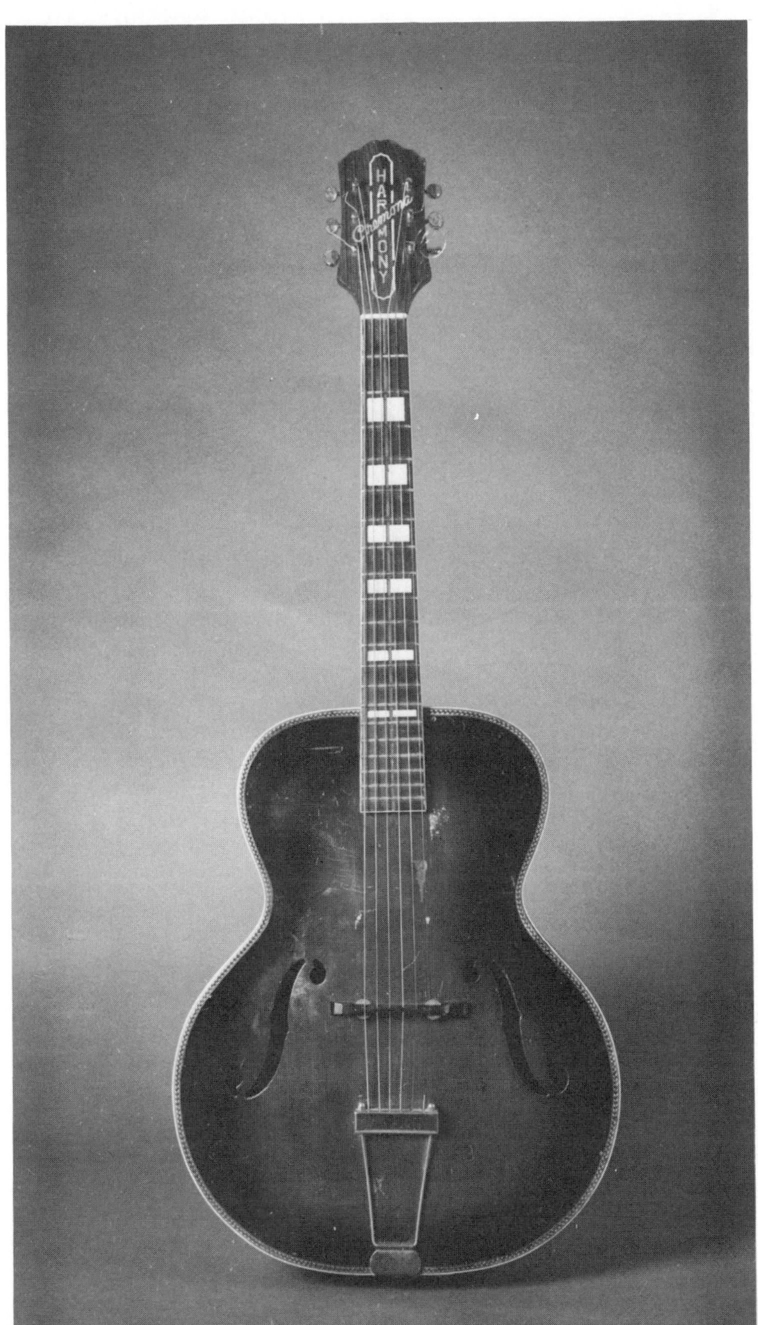

Harmony Cremona, circa 1941. *Mark Sneden/Tom Erlewine*

grew steadily from 1941 to 1960: 90 million dollars in 1941, 235 million in 1950, 380 million in 1955, and 590 million in 1960. The mid 1950s saw a staggering boom in the growth of fretted instruments, accounting for a volume of 8½ million dollars in 1955, 12½ million in 1956, and almost 16 million in 1957. Harmony was a primary benefactor of this growth.

By 1961 Harmony had outgrown the Racine Avenue facility and acquired a new 80,000 square foot woodworking plant on Kolin Avenue. Another boom in sales followed, and even in its enlarged factory the company was bursting at the seams trying to keep up with demands for guitars, guitars, guitars. Dollar-volume business reportedly tripled in two years, and in July 1964 a second plant was opened on 44th Street. Plant No. 1 was the site of all manufacturing operations except final assembly, inspection, packing, and shipping. These were shifted to the new 40,000 square foot facility about a mile away. A third building (12,000 square feet) served as a warehouse. The complex system worked, thanks to some very busy truckdrivers and also to the exceptional organizational skills of Jay Kraus, manufacturing director Jerome King, Plant No. 1 superintendent Frank Elias, Plant No. 2 administrator Harold Klopping, and Plant No. 2 superintendent Robert Andrlik.

While Harmony did not sell directly to dealers, it sent coupons, inquiries from the media, and other sales leads to those who used the company's own merchandising aids.

The June 24, 1969, issue of *down beat*'s *NAMM Daily* contained a bulletin that, as we will see, was heavy with prophetic significance for Harmony and other American guitar makers: "It is no secret that imports, particularly in the guitar field, have become a force to be reckoned with in the music market. Electric guitar imports peaked in 1966 when the entire industry was in short supply. In that year a total of 537,000 units entered the U.S., with a declared value of $6,828,000 (perhaps one-third of actual retail value). Today there are more guitars (electric plus acoustic) coming into the country than are produced by U.S. manufacturers. Harmony is relying on its experience, its distribution system, and its time-proven marketing methods to stay ahead. . . ."

Charles A. "Chuck" Rubovits joined Harmony in 1935 when the company had about 200 employees. He eventually became its president, as well as president of NAMM. He was Jay Kraus' right-hand man and personally supervised the sale of over five million guitars. Here are his recollections covering the last three decades of Harmony's history:

> When I joined we were making primarily commercial grade flat-tops with a modest line of arch-tops. We sold a lot of guitars to the wholesalers for $2.50 apiece, and they were selling them for $7.50 or so. We were into electrics by 1938 with some Hawaiian models that had a pickup we bought from Rickenbacker. That was the early days of electrics, I'll tell you. That was long before Fender ever had a dream.
>
> We made thousands and thousands of guitars with the Stella name on them. The Kay Company was making most of the Airline

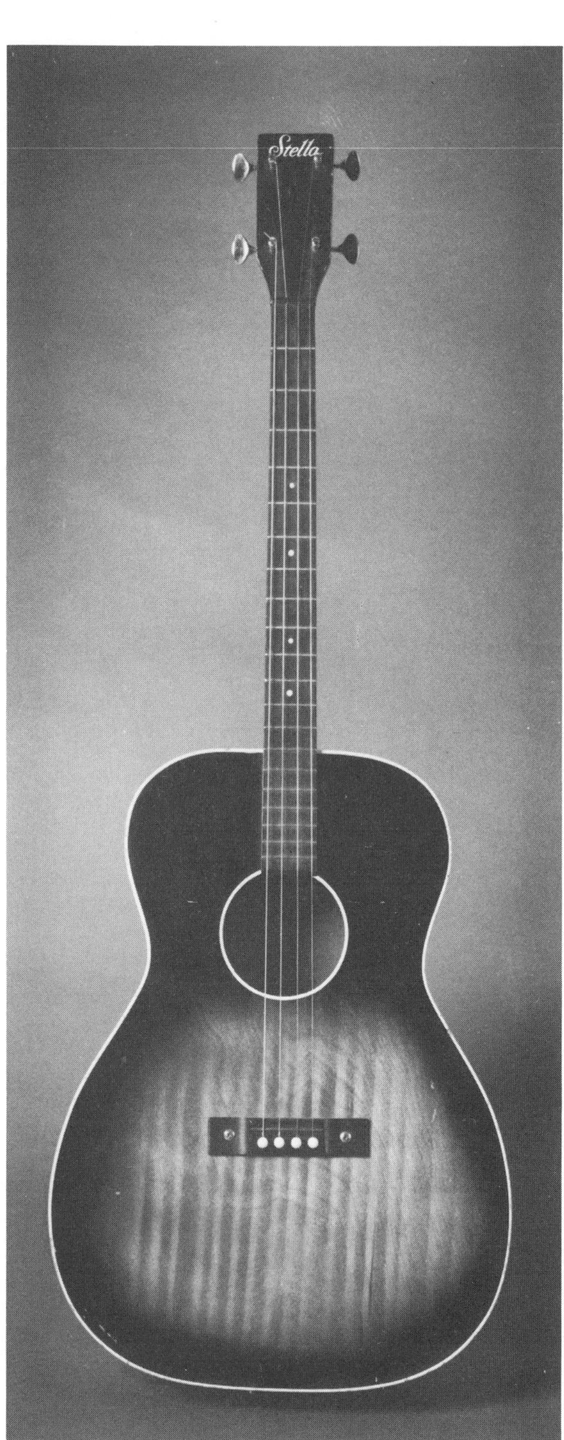

Stella 4-string tenor flat-top. The bridge is screwed into the top, a rather prompt indicator of a budget model. ***Doug Thorstenson/Tom Erlewine***

Harmony HG510; note segmented soundholes. *Wagener/Beaty*

Stella 12-string by Harmony. *Dan Lambert*

Harmony's Super Sovereign, 1970, a nine-foot playable guitar. *Guitar Player*

Near right: **Harmony H-62, late 1950s.** ***Music Shop/Madsen*** ***Far right:*** **Guitar star Roy Smeck with his Harmony Roy Smeck arch-top electric. Gibson also issued Roy Smeck signature guitars.**

One version of the Harmony Stratotone, concentric knobs. *Third Eye*

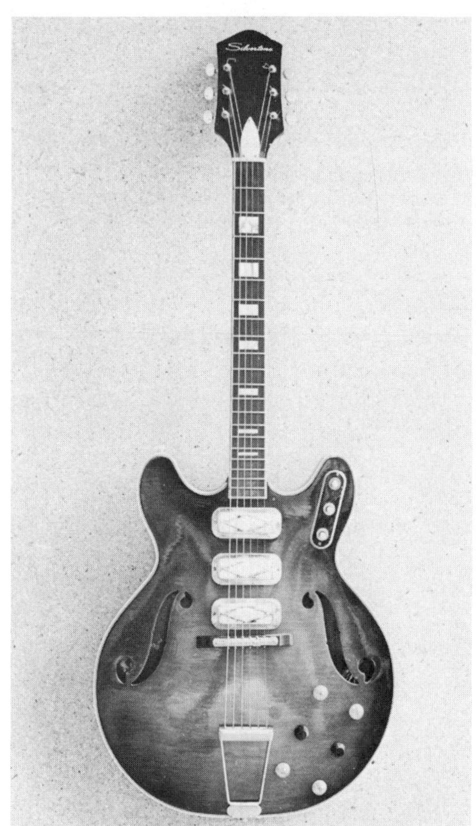
Silvertone, circa 1965, made by Harmony as a variation on its H75 and H77 models. *Third Eye*

brand guitars for Montgomery Ward, but we'd get a little bit of that business during the Christmas rush. We were buying parts from National for our resonator guitars. We were making the Silvertones for Sears, which had owned Harmony since 1916. In the 1930s probably 35 or 40 percent of Harmony guitars were sold to Sears, and during the boom of the middle 1960s it may have been as high as 45 or 50 percent.

1941 wasn't a good year, and that summer Sears had a plan to liquidate the Harmony Company. They sort of froze out Jay and brought in their own man, but we bought the company for ourselves and went on our own. Jay got some cash from Max Adler, and since we didn't want to run the machine shop anyway we sold it to Kluson for $5,000. Kluson agreed to make all our metal parts. We gave that $5,000 to Sears as a down payment along with several notes [loans], and they let us have Harmony.

There were 12 of us original employee/investors. We sold our Sears stock, bought Harmony stock, and hired some workers. Sears encouraged it and let us keep $50,000 as working capital so we could get set up. Jay was president of our new corporation. He appointed me vice-president and gave me a $15-a-week raise, which was a lot at the time. Our first guitar was made in the Racine Avenue plant, and in our first year of operation we got our capitalization back.

Before the war we had made 57 private brands, and it was all very very complicated. There were guitars with many different names on them coming out of the Harmony plant, and we sold only to jobbers [wholesalers]. See, the wholesalers all had their own private brands and we had over 25 wholesalers in the early 1940s—big distributors, catalogue houses, and so on. After the war we cut out almost all of the other names and told the wholesalers they'd be selling guitars with the Harmony name on them.

After the war we mushroomed like Topsy. Our attorney's son-in-law, Sid Katz [see Kay], came with us and left in 1955 or 1956. He was replaced by Jerome King as vice-president. Then there was Catherine Drnochod, known to everyone in the industry as Miss Kay, who was treasurer and controller. We ran the company—Jay Kraus, Jerry King, Miss Kay, and me.

Our peak was 1964–1965. We had as many as 600 employees. I think our gross in 1965 was 11 million dollars. In one year we sold 350,000 instruments—that's a thousand a day. Once we sold 5,963 guitars in one week. I was in GAMA [Guitar and Accessories Manufacturers Association], and all the companies reported their figures, and at one time Harmony made half of the industry's guitars, three-quarters of the ukuleles, and a major share of the other instruments like banjos and mandolins. We produced more than all the other companies combined.

With only a couple of exceptions we were a very close industry. Bob Keyworth [see Kay] was the buyer for Sears in the 1930s and I sold him guitars. We go way back together. We knew Fender out on the coast, too. Don Randall owned Fender Sales, and by coincidence I was in New York when he got his check for several million dollars from the CBS deal, and boy, we had some party that night, making the joints in town. We were friends.

Mr. Kraus died of a heart attack in 1968 and I became president. Profit-wise, it wasn't a good year even though we probably made a majority of the 575,000 guitars produced in America that year. Jay left controlling stock with a trust, and I left the company over a business disagreement with certain people in the trust. They brought in a guy who ran it from 1971 through 1974. The trust decided to become sort of a conglomerate. They bought [Chicago dis-

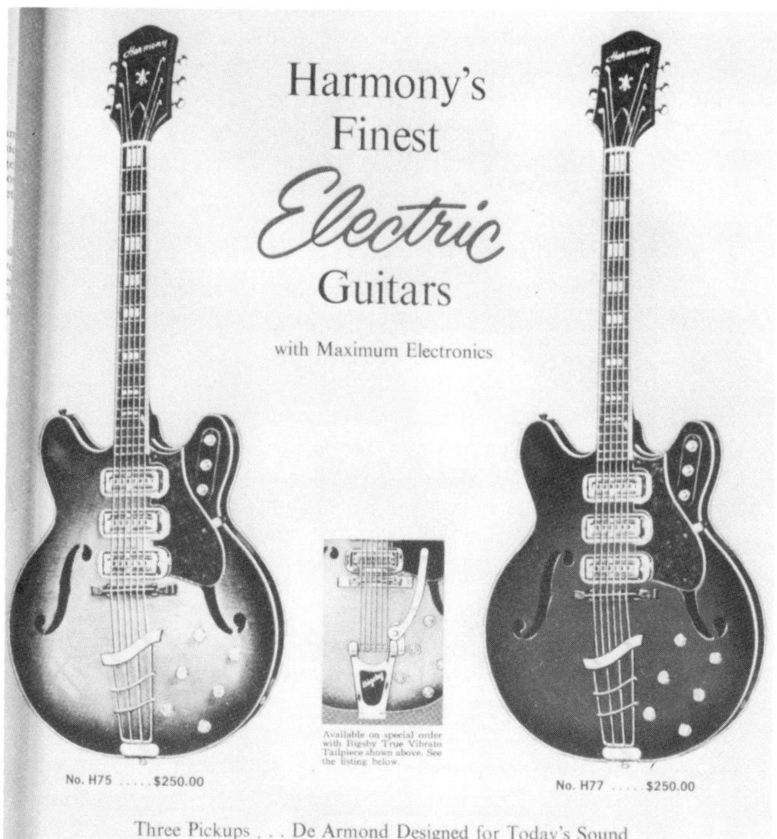

Harmony's
Finest
Electric
Guitars
with Maximum Electronics
Available on special order with Bigsby True Vibrato Tailpiece shown above. See the listing below.
No. H75 ..... $250.00
No. H77 ..... $250.00
Three Pickups . . . De Armond Designed for Today's Sound

Many Harmony electrics were equipped with DeArmond pickups, such as these three-pickup models from 1965.

tributor] Targ & Dinner and some other companies. There was terrible indebtedness. The factory equipment and other assets were sold at auction to satisfy the creditors and they finally liquidated, paying off ten cents on the dollar.

One reason Harmony folded was the Japanese competition. I always said it was my fault they came into the industry [*laughs*], because if we had put up five factories in the U.S., we never would've needed the Japanese. We had the know-how, but we didn't have the guts. We were too conservative. We were very successful, so we didn't want to do more, and as a result the Japanese began to get a bigger and bigger share of the market. We were 10 to 50 times oversold all the time and didn't always realize it. We tripled our production and thought we were doing a great job. We weren't even scratching the surface.

JACKSON/CHARVEL

Grover Jackson arrived in California from Tennessee in the mid-1970s. In 1977 he affiliated with Wayne Charvel, who had just left Schecter and established Charvel Guitar Repair in San Dimas. Jackson and Charvel made bodies and replacement parts, and performed repairs. Occasionally they put together a

The proud Heritage Super Eagle arch-top, with five-piece curly maple neck, 18-inch carved maple body and spruce top. Fingerboard inlays are patterned after the Gibson Super 400.

HERITAGE

A trio of former Gibson employees with decades of guitar-building experience, Jim Deurloo, Marvin Lamb, and J.P. Moats, established Heritage Guitar Inc. in 1985. Bill Paige, another Gibson veteran, later became a partner.

Occupying Gibson's old plant at 225 Parsons Street in Kalamazoo, Michigan—the very building where Lloyd Loar worked his magic in the 1920s and Ted McCarty's crew built Gibson's Golden Age electrics—Heritage today builds 180 to 200 instruments each month with a work force of 18. Most of the arch-tops, semisolidbodies, and solidbodies are clearly inspired by Gibsons of the 1950s and 1960s. Yet they are readily distinguishable. The several Heritage refinements include reconfigured pickups, curly maple pickguards, and peghead veneers.

Jackson Archtop Soloist, serial no. 0002, one of four prototypes built for the 1986 Chicago NAMM show.
James Pennebaker

complete instrument, usually with a Boogie Bodies neck. On November 10, 1978, 29-year-old Grover Jackson bought the company and its assets for about $40,000.

"In 1978 Fender and Gibson were still king," Jackson told *Guitar Player*'s Jon Sievert. "Most of my customers would buy new instruments and bring them to me so I could tear them apart. I installed hotter pickups, bigger frets, wider nuts, and better tuners. Players asked me to flatten the fingerboard radius, oil the back of the neck, and shield the internal cavities. By the time I was done, the instruments were rebuilt."

Soliciting input from individual customers became the foundation of Jackson's guitar-building enterprise. In 1980 he exhibited his own Charvels at the NAMM trade show in Anaheim, California. A few completed guitars, perhaps a dozen or so, had been built from Charvel parts prior to the Anaheim debut. One went to a gifted young hotshot from Pasadena named Eddie Van Halen.

Van Halen's special Charvel had a single rewound Gibson patent-applied-for humbucker; a tremolo from a '58 Strat; a wide, unfinished neck with big Gibson frets; and a black and white paint job of crisscrossing stripes—no subtle Old World sunburst on this axe, thank you. The custom-built guitar also featured low-tech, or even anti-tech, electronics. Said Van Halen: "Give me one knob. That's it."

That guitar was succeeded by another Charvel, a yellow and black hotrod with a "rear-loaded" pickup and no pickguard. Like Van Halen's jaw-dropping pyrotechnics, these built-to-burn machines exploded various conventions. Suggesting a cross between a Stratocaster and a homemade Uzi machine gun, they gave incalculable publicity to the Charvel name and spawned a kamikaze-chainsaw guitar aesthetic that became a 1980s hallmark.

At Christmas 1980, Jackson met an obscure but promising guitarist named Randy Rhoads. "He and I designed the first Rhoads guitar during our initial meeting, December 23, 1980, at an all-night conference," recalled Jackson in 1990. "It was different from what we'd been doing, and I didn't want to dilute what progress I'd made publicizing Charvel, so I gave it a different name, just in case it flopped. It was the first 'Jackson.' "

Generally patterned after Gibson's Flying V, the white solidbody Jackson was hardly a flop.

"Later, Randy came to me and said he wanted something more radical, more shark-finny," said Jackson. "By March 1981, he had it."

Rhoads rocketed to guitar stardom that year, and Jackson benefited substantially. More orders for Jacksons came in, and soon he had 18 employees, still in San Dimas. The distinction between the brands was in the neck: Charvel necks were bolt-ons; Jacksons were neck-through.

These trend-setting instruments were among the most influential guitars of the decade. Whereas Gibson electrics boasted a proud jazz-pop heritage, and early Fenders were embraced by country twangers, Charvels came off the launching pad ready to rip, rock, and roll. Often sporting defiantly unconventional and splashy graphics, these glossy beauties were heavy-duty shred machines for heavy-duty music—built for 1980s-style speedblasting. In other words, they were exactly what the market craved, and the company blossomed.

In 1985, Charvel entered into a complex agreement with Texas-based IMC. Now the nomenclature was based not on neck type, but on location of manufacture. Charvels are made exclusively by Chu Shin Gakki of Matsumoto, Japan, which now produces 3,000 or even 4,000 Charvels a month. Korean-made imports sport the Charvette name. The Jackson plant, in Ontario, California, builds 250 to 300 Jacksons a month—all of which are crafted to individual customers' specifications. In early 1990, Grover Jackson relinquished day-to-day control of Jackson to IMC.

KAY

During the middle third of this century Chicago was the guitar capital of the world, and one of the foremost members of the manufacturing community was Kay Musical Instruments. The firm was officially founded in 1931, but its actual history reaches back to the Groehsl Company. Groehsl, founded in 1890, was renamed the Stromberg-Voisinet Company, which incorporated in 1921 with $50,000 capital stock. Stromberg-Voisinet made the Mayflower line of mandolins and guitars under the direction of vice-president C. G. Stromberg (not to be confused with luthier Elmer Stromberg). Kay's namesake was one of the titans of guitar commerce, Henry Kay "Hank" Kuhrmeyer, who was secretary, treasurer, and later president of Stromberg-Voisinet. Contrary to popular belief, his company was christened after his middle name—Kay—and not his surname's first initial.

Stromberg-Voisinet's three-floor, 18,000 square foot factory was located at 316 Union Park Court in Chicago. Kuhrmeyer lent his middle name to their most popular line, Kay-Kraft, which included three guitars (priced in December 1930 from $25–45), and several tenor guitars, jumbo guitars, mandolins, and banjos. By 1931 Kuhrmeyer was Stromberg-Voisinet's president, and also in that year the company evolved into the Kay Musical Instrument Company, with offices and factories at the same address as its predecessor. Kuhrmeyer's new firm continued to use the Kay-Kraft brand name.

The company announced Kay Wood Amplifying Guitars (probably resophonic) in April 1934 and an adjustable bridge in November 1934. In April of the following year it moved into expanded quarters at 1640 West Walnut Street. Other new products included a Kay electric guitar ($95 with amp, January 1936), Kay-Kraft pickup (March 1936), Kay Kraft string bass (January 1938; *Kay Kraft* was sometimes hyphenated but not always), several cellos (February 1938), and a new line of Kay guitars (to be "sold to a limited number of musical merchandise wholesalers"; April 1941). Kay was also one of America's major manufacturers of bass fiddles.

Kay Kraft Model A, mid-1930s (tailpiece unoriginal).
Bernie Pearl/Danny Norrie

KeyKord baritone, probably made by Kay. The neck entails an ingenious system of push rods and bell cranks underneath the fretboard. When the player presses a button, little metal fingers fret the appropriate strings. Owner David Colburn commented, "It's one of the most complicated things I've ever seen in my life. Someone paid a lot of money back in the late 1920s in order to avoid learning how to play the thing." ***Vintage Fret Shop/A. Caswell***

During the late 1940s Kay's production crew ranged from about 100 to 120 workers, and in terms of price the instruments placed roughly between Harmony and Gibson. Bob Keyworth was a Kay executive who spent 23 years with the company, eventually rising to the presidency. As he put it, "Harmony made the Fords, we made the Buicks, and Gibson made the Cadillacs." Except for the hardware, the guitars were manufactured and assembled in the Kay plant, where production during this period peaked at about 300 instruments a day.

In 1955 Mr. Kuhrmeyer sold Kay to a group of investors headed by the late Sidney Katz, former manager of Harmony's service department. Katz' father and father-in-law both put up money for the purchase; Katz' wife's uncle was Albert Pick of the Pick Hotels conglomerate, and he contributed heavily. Mr. Keyworth recalled: "When we went with Katz we became much more aggressive, much more competitive with Harmony. We moved into the lower price bracket in the late 1950s. We started to grow, and from 1955 to 1965 we increased our dollar volume tenfold. Some of that was inflation, but the main reason was our going into more price brackets and into new markets such as amplifiers. We were selling a lot of instruments to Sears at that time. A lot of their Silvertone guitars were made in the Kay plant."

Kay's heyday was the late 1950s and early 1960s, a time when America's hunger for guitars was voracious. Kay didn't revolutionize guitar design, but it made maple-body arch-tops available to players who couldn't afford an Epiphone, and multi-pickup solidbodies available to beginners whose parents weren't ready to spring for a Telecaster.

In 1957 Kay offered three stringed instrument lines, two of which—the Professional and Recreational—included guitars. Also in that year, the firm introduced its Kay/Kessel Gold Kay series of three guitars: the Pro ($170; small body, no f-holes), the Artist (larger body, solid markers), and the Jazz Special ($400, split markers). All were available in single- and double-pickup versions, and all featured enlarged headstocks. In 1960 the Kay line ran from $24.50 to $400.

In early 1964 Kay moved into a 100,000 square foot plant in the Centex Industrial Park, located near O'Hare Airport in Chicago's Elk Grove Village. The million-dollar facility housed 500 workers who, at their peak, reportedly produced 1,500 guitars a day. The company reached 7,000 retailers in the United States and Canada through a network of 45 distributors. "It was the guitar boom," Mr. Keyworth explained. "With the Beatles and all that, we just couldn't make enough. Most were averaging $100–150 retail price at that time, and many were electric guitars. When I joined in 1944 we were already making

Kay arch-top with fancy trim, sculptured bridge. The same tailpiece was used on Gibson's late-1950s ES-175. ***Wagener/Beaty***

Wagener/Beaty

A World War II era Kay electric hollowbody, with unusually placed knobs. ***Jerry Gauld/Tom Erlewine***

1941 Kay K-155; note amp with wooden cabinet. *Gruhn*

some electrics but not too many. Really nobody did very much in solidbodies until Fender came into the picture, but as the popularity of electrics grew, of course we moved along with it. The boom peaked in about 1964, though 1965 was also a very good year."

In 1963 and 1964 Kay began to suffer quality problems due in part to the company's exploding growth. Also, the guitar boom of 1963 to 1965 began to taper off fairly rapidly, and the whole industry, now overextended, felt the squeeze. In September of 1965 Sidney Katz sold the still-thriving Kay Company to Seeburg, the huge Chicago-based jukebox manufacturer. At the time, Kay's annual sales were reportedly in the millions. Katz became head of Seeburg's music division and negotiated the purchase of several other outfits, including the Gulbransen piano company and King Band Instruments. Bob Keyworth became executive vice-president in charge of the Kay division, which operated independently of the Seeburg organization.

Seeburg owned Kay for less than two years. On June 1, 1967, Seeburg sold Kay to the late Robert Engelhardt, then owner of Valco, in a transaction discussed by former Valco executive Al Frost in the National/Dobro/Valco section. Here is Mr. Keyworth's account: "The guitar business was going down and we were losing money along with Gibson, Harmony, and the whole industry. Seeburg decided that we should acquire Valco so that we could make our own amplifiers and go more heavily into electric guitars. I was against it because I didn't think

Late-1940s or early-1950s Kay electric. *Jacksonville*

Sherwood Standard, an early-1950s electric made for Montgomery Ward by Kay. *Wagener/Beaty*

An early Kay electric bass, probably late 1950s. *Doug Thorstenson/Tom Erlewine*

Valco would bring in enough expertise on the acoustic side, so I suggested that Seeburg *sell* our company to Valco instead of buying Valco, and that's what happened.

"I gather that Engelhardt had gained control of Valco through a deal with [Valco co-owner] Louis Dopyera's widow. I was president of Kay by then, and the day Engelhardt walked in I walked out. There wasn't room for two presidents. Kay and Valco went along for another two years. Valco moved into the Kay plant. At that time Al Frost was out of the picture and the whole thing was in Engelhardt's hands. He didn't have the cash to float the thing, and he didn't have the wherewithal to run the company or adequate knowledge of acoustic guitars. Mainly he was short on cash.

"Some deals had been made through a financial company or a group of investors. Engelhardt couldn't meet his bills, and one day they just came in and changed the locks. And that was the end of the Kay company."

The Kay trade name, like Washburn, Epiphone, and Vega, was later acquired by a distributor of imported guitars.

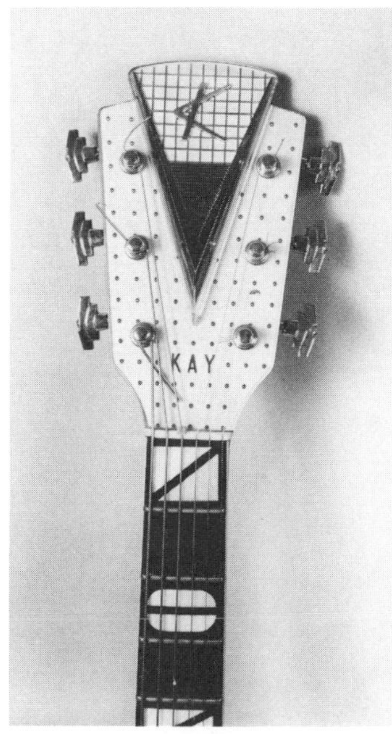

The Barney Kessel's plastic-faced headstock with raised gold dots suggests a late-1950s luncheonette motif. For a full-length view, see color photo 75. *Spitzer's/Sievert*

Segovia called the electric guitar "an abomination," and many clergymen, educators, and civic leaders were no less contemptuous, as if all who played it were juvenile delinquents right out of *High School Confidential.* With ads like this one (Kay, 1965), manufacturers suggested that electric guitars and "rock 'n' roll" were for nice kids too. This preppy fellow is playing a C chord on a K310, one of the budget solidbodies that Kay, Harmony, National, and Danelectro cranked out by the truckload during the 1960s.

1965 Kay Galaxie I amp.

Sam Koontz displays one of his radical electrics, featuring a built-in amp and speakers. *Jack Poley*

KOONTZ

Linden, New Jersey's Sam Koontz has no qualms about loading a whole pedalboard worth of sound effects into an impeccably crafted hollowbody guitar, thus combining elements usually associated with either a rocker's gadget-laden solidbody or a purist's acoustic/electric jazz model. His innovations include a guitar with a self-contained amp and tape recorder, side-mounted electronics (permitting the back to remain uncut), and a hinged internal f-hole cover. Also see Standel and Harptone.

KRAMER

Though the Kramer guitar's namesake was Gary Kramer (a Southern Californian and former partner of Travis Bean, a pioneer of the aluminum-necked guitar), it was Dennis Berardi and Peter J. LaPlaca who made the brand an international contender. Berardi spent a dozen years as a retailer before turning to design, and LaPlaca had worked his way up through the Norlin organization to vice-president.

Berardi and Kramer founded the firm in October 1975, and LaPlaca joined them the following April. They named their company after their initials—BKL—and opened a factory on

Kramer's top-of-the-line instruments in 1978, the 650 bass and 650 guitar.

July 1, 1976. The first Kramer guitars were codesigned by luthier Phil Petillo, Berardi, and Kramer, and the first production run was completed on November 15, 1976. Gary Kramer left the company a month later. By early 1980 the line included 14 guitars and basses from $649 to $1,418.

The central characteristic of a Kramer guitar is its detachable neck, which differs from the all-aluminum Travis Bean design. The forged aluminum Kramer neck is T-shaped in cross section, with full-length wood inlays intended to give it a more natural feel. A more recent feature is a nut assembly with six individual rollers designed to eliminate string drag. Woods include black burl walnut and bird's-eye maple. The guitars also feature Schaller tuners, wooden pickup rings, 25-inch scale lengths, and aluminum dot inlays on most models.

LANGE, PARAMOUNT, AND ORPHEUM

William L. Lange was a senior partner in Rettberg & Lange, a major banjo distributor established circa 1897 at 225 East 24th Street in New York City. Mr. Rettberg and Mr. Lange succeeded their former employer's company, the Buckbee organization, a large maker of moderately priced banjos during the late 1800s. By the early 1920s the William L. Lange Company had succeeded Rettberg & Lange and was selling the Paramount and Orpheum banjo lines through its exclusive distributor, C. Bruno & Son of New York. Late-1920s products included banjos, banjo mandolins, and guitar banjos, but, according to the literature, no guitars.

In 1934, however, Lange formally announced its Paramount guitar series, at least part of which was made by Martin. The Orpheum name, a banjo brand that dates to the turn of the century, was also applied to some of Lange's guitars.

The 1939 Paramounts included six arch-tops, and the flagship of the fleet was christened with a title that would have pleased a Victorian-era rajah: The Free Tone Artist Supreme Grand Auditorium. This unusual guitar had an interior tone chamber, an Indian rosewood body and neck, three-segment soundholes, a ring of grommets (small extra soundholes) along the top's periphery, and a $300 price tag. The 17¼-inch-wide Artist Leader ($240) also had grommets, but the remaining models did not. This latter group included the black, 16-inch Model B; the 16-inch maple Model C; the 17¼-inch mahogany Model D; and the 17¼-inch Model E, available in either rosewood or maple.

Lange went out of business in 1941 or 1942, and in February 1944 New York wholesaler Maurice Lipsky announced a resumption of Orpheum's distribution, which continued at least

Orpheum round-hole with one-piece back, one-piece top, and unusual shading and body trim. The Orpheum name had changed hands, perhaps more than once, by the time this guitar was made; it may be an import. Some Orpheums were made by Kay. ***Len Kapushion/Bill Gunter***

as late as 1962. During the late 1940s, Gretsch & Brenner (see Gretsch) also marketed the Paramount line, which at the time included a few electrics.

LoPrinzi model LR-25. Note diamond inlays, herringbone trim.

LoPRINZI

Thomas R. LoPrinzi and his brother Augie incorporated LoPrinzi Guitars in 1972, opening the original plant—once a chicken hatchery—in Rosemont, New Jersey. (Augie later left to start his own company, Augustino Guitars.) The two LoPrinzis and one helper worked long hours to produce ten guitars each month. By 1974 a staff of 18 was employed. Due to a modernization of production, the company was able to cut back on its staff in 1975 and again in 1977, when with seven employees it produced 60 to 80 instruments each month.

In October 1975 the factory was moved from the 1800 square foot plant in Rosemont to a new facility in Plainsboro, and in August 1979 it moved again to an old schoolhouse in Hopewell, New Jersey; Thomas LoPrinzi converted the brick building into a 5,000 square foot plant.

Early LoPrinzi guitar bodies were made only from Brazilian rosewood with maple binding; later, Indian rosewood, flamed maple, and Honduras mahogany were all used. Early tops were German silver spruce; subsequently, both Canadian and Alaskan spruce were also used.

All LoPrinzi guitars are steel-strings, with spruce tops, Honduras or Amazon mahogany necks, adjustable truss rods, ebony fingerboards, rosewood bridges, pearl or abalone markers, 12 coats of nitrocellulose-based lacquer, 20 frets (14 frets clear), white binding, and 25½-inch scales. There are three sizes—standard, folk, and 12-string; options include left-handed models and scalloped bracing.

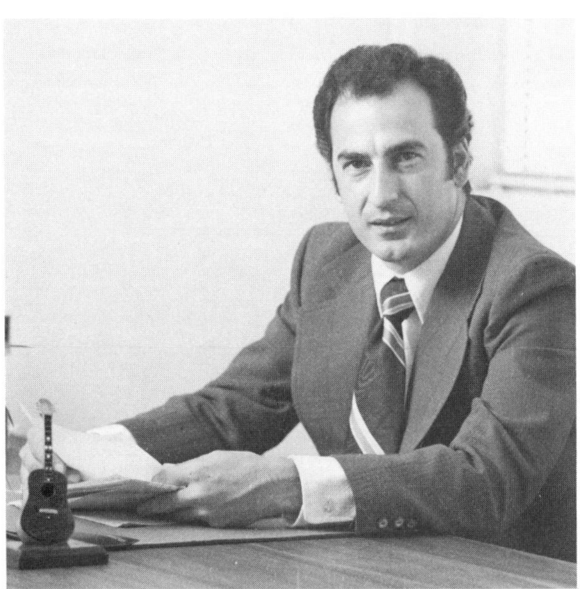

Thomas R. LoPrinzi.

LYON & HEALY

See Washburn

MAGNATONE

Magnatone of West Hempstead, New York, and Torrance, California, is best remembered for its early-1960s amplifiers. The seven models ($69.50 to $499.95) were covered with somber but classy brown and gold material, and several had a most distinctive onboard chorus effect. But the company also built a few guitars. The 1962 line was designed by Paul Barth of National and Rickenbacker (also see Mosrite) and included four models priced from $99.95 to $299.50: an electric-acoustic, a twin-pickup deluxe electric, a single-pickup deluxe electric, and a three-quarter size electric made primarily for the teaching studio trade.

Magnatone's guitars were completely redesigned in 1965 and renamed the Starstream series ($350 to $420). The two 6-strings and the 12-string all had double-cutaways, acoustic-electric bodies, two pickups, ebony fingerboards, spruce tops, and maple backs. The solidbody Starstreams ($170 to $290) consisted of two standard guitars, a three-quarter guitar, and a bass.

The Magnatone name was owned at various times by Estey Electronics, Estey Musical Instrument Corporation, and Magna Electronics. Showrooms were maintained both in Torrance and West Hempstead. The 1966 Magnatones ($119–249) were called the Mark Series and included the single-cutaway, single-pickup Mark III Standard; the single-cutaway, two-pickup Mark III Deluxe; the double-cutaway Mark IV; and the double-cutaway Mark V with Bigsby. The latter two models were designed by Paul Bigsby, of Bigsby vibrato fame.

Magnatone resophonic, built by National Dobro for Montgomery Ward circa 1937. The upper soundhole array was also used on the post-1931 Dobro "Cyclops." ***John Quarterman***

MARTIN

In 1833 Congress enacted Henry Clay's Compromise Tariff Act, Mendelssohn debuted his Fourth Symphony, and Christian Friedrich Martin emigrated from Germany to the New World, there to establish the first family of the American guitar. The Martins had lived in the hillside village of Markneukirchen, Saxony, near the Elbe River, which divides the present city of Dresden. In the early 1800s this hamlet was the home of a guild of violin makers, and Johann Georg Martin, Christian's father, worked as a carpenter, sometimes constructing the wooden packing boxes that were used by guild members to ship their fine violins. Martin was so impressed with the guitar upon its arrival in Northern Europe that he constructed a few models and sold them, thus infuriating his violin-making employers.

Johann's son, Christian Friedrich (or Frederick), became the shop foreman for Viennese violin and guitar maker Johann Georg Stauffer. The junior and senior Martins then worked together, posing a professional challenge so serious to the local guild that its members threatened the father and son team with political pressure. Christian finally decided to move to New York, where in 1833 he opened a guitar shop at 196 Hudson Street and founded CF Martin & Company. The big city proved to be an alien, impersonal place to the guitar maker from Saxony, so after much urging from his fellow immigrant Henry Schatz, Christian decided in 1839 to move to the tiny Moravian town of Cherry Hill, located outside Nazareth in the Lehigh Valley of eastern Pennsylvania. Martin guitars have been made in the Nazareth area ever since.

The following additional details are excerpted from the April 20, 1933, issue of *The Nazareth Item.* It is part of a speech delivered by Frank Martin, the founder's grandson, commemorating his company's one-hundredth year:

1930 00-42, an especially rare and beautiful Martin. Note inlay on fingerboard, top, soundhole rings, and bridgepins. ***Eldon Whitford/Tom Erlewine***

C. F. Martin, Sr. (1796–1873), the patriarch of American guitar manufacturing, founder of Martin, and developer of X bracing. *Martin Guitars*

The Martin factory in 1933. *Longworth*

THE BETTER CONQUEST

THE NAZARETH ITEM

AN INDEPENDENT FAMILY NEWSPAPER DEVOTED TO LITERATURE, LOCAL AND GENERAL INTELLIGENCE

VOL. XLII — NAZARETH, PA., THURSDAY MORNING, APRIL 20, 1933 — No. 21

Baseball To Make Bow Here On Saturday

Nazareth Service Clubs Fete C. F. Martin & Co., Inc. Officials Commemorating the 100th Anniversary of Successful Business

Pioneers In The Manufacture of Mandolins and Guitars Are Honored For Long Career; Frank H. Martin, Senior Member of Firm, Relates History of Company; Handsome Engraved Loving Cup, Baskets of Cut Flowers Presented; Artists Render Musical Selections

MATERIALS FOR MANUFACTURE OBTAINED FROM MANY COUNTRIES

Churchmen Meet In St. John's Reformed

A 1933 newspaper marks the celebration of Martin's first 100 years. *Jon Lundberg*

Except for its strip of wood marquetry around the center of the sides and a shield-shaped wooden plate attached to the neckblock's lower surface, this Martin (circa 1840) is similar to the Style 1. Its body is 19 by $12\frac{5}{16}$ inches—small by today's standards but large for its time. The guitar belonged to a union colonel, John Darragh Wilkins, who kept it at his side during Second Bull Run, Antietam, Chancellorsville, and other Civil War battles. *Michael Cockram*

Martin & Coupa, circa 1850. *Smithsonian*

C.F. "Chris" Martin IV was promoted to vice president of marketing in 1985. Following the death of his father, C.F. Martin III, on June 15, 1986, this sixth-generation Martin became chairman of the board and chief executive officer.

1992 Update

Martin production figures can be calculated from the serial numbers. The last serial number for each of several recent years: 1983 (446,101), 1984 (453,300), 1985 (460,575), 1986 (468,175), 1987 (476,216), 1988 (483,952), and 1989 (493,279). Of the 7,736 guitars built in 1988, 1,546 were Shenandoahs, which are assembled in Nazareth from parts made in Japan. Martin's 1989 output of 9,327 instruments includes over 200 basses. Nearly 300 employees now produce 54 models—including regular guitars (D, M, and J models, among others) and special-order guitars (O, OO, OOO, OM, S, and others), but not including the Shenandoah, Stinger, or Sigma guitars. Additionally, various limited-edition instruments are offered each fall under the Guitar of the Month program.

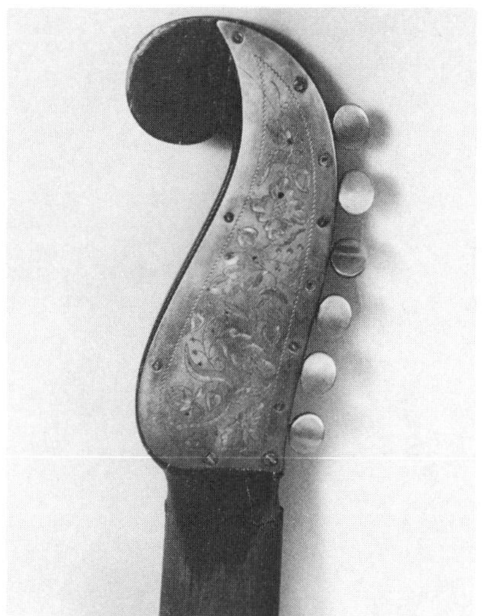

This is not a Martin guitar, but its design was likely derived from the work of Johann Stauffer, the major influence of C. F. Martin's early period. Its bridge is almost identical to one Stauffer-influenced Martin (circa 1834) on display at the factory, and its small, slope-shouldered body is in Martin's "Renaissance" style of the early 1840s. The almost Telecaster-like peghead (note engraved back plate) and clock key neck adjustment are further Stauffer hallmarks. Note the pearl rosette inlay and intricate top trim of colored woods. *Spitzer's/Sievert*

On May 1, 1838, Martin formed a partnership with Charles Bruno, founder of the present importing house of C. Bruno & Son, New York. We recall that there was a panic in 1837 which may have formed a link in the chain of destiny [perhaps encouraging Martin to move]. On May 29, 1839, Martin sold his stock of goods to Ludecus & Wolter of New York, and on December 21, 1839, he bought from Philip Deringer and wife a lot of eight acres in the Bushkill Township. New York was left behind.

About the same time another factor developed. Christian Frederick Martin, Jr., born 1825, who had crossed the ocean with his father in 1833, gradually took over the business management. In 1849 he bought a property to the north of his father's home which he occupied for a time, and in August 1857 he took title to the block on North Main Street between North and High Streets, buying from the Nazareth Moravian Congregation. The following year he built the residence standing at the corner of Main and North Streets with a workshop directly behind it, and in July of 1859 the business was moved from Cherry Hill to the new location.

The guitar factory, being now finally settled, kept on, enjoying prosperity and suffering depression as the business cycle moved. The books show that several years before the Civil War business was bad, but during the war it increased very much. After that there was a general tightening of credit which culminated in the panic of 1873. Recovery came about six years later. Then a new era began, and meantime other changes had come. Christian Frederick Martin died in 1873 at the age of 77. In 1867 the weight of years already showed and he formed a co-partnership with his son Frederick and a nephew, Christian Frederick Hartman, also a skilled worker from the home town who had followed at an early day. About 1885, C.F. Martin, Jr., became sole owner and in 1887 built the first addition to the factory, but his health failed and he died in November, 1888, at the age of 63.

Nearly 30 years of success in the new plant allowed C.F. Martin, Jr. (1825–1888), to double its size in 1887 and, except for

One of the earliest Martins known to exist, a Martin & Coupa. John Coupa was a New York music teacher who was apparently a salesman or distributor for Martin. The guitar was most probably made in the early 1840s, shortly after the factory moved to Nazareth, Pennsylvania. The very rare Martin & Coupas were crucial turning points in the evolution of C. F. Martin's designs, manifesting Stauffer's influence in the peghead as well as a departure from the pinch-waisted Stauffer style bodies. ***Acuff***

C. F. Martin, Jr. (1825–1888). ***Martin Guitars***

Frank Henry Martin (1866–1948). *Martin Guitars*

C. F. Martin III; the guitar at far left is a "Renaissance" style Martin, circa 1840. Note body shape.

1930 Octa-Chorda, a one-of-a-kind 8-string Martin lap guitar. *Martin Guitars/Stull*

Style 1-34, circa 1860, New York Martin with spruce-lined back, ivory bridge, ivory trim, and abalone soundhole purfling. The main difference between Styles 30 and 34 is the latter's ivory bridge. Style 34 was no longer listed after 1898. *Don's Guitar Shop/Don E. Teeter*

that remodeling, the 1858 North Street shop remains intact. The next generation of the family and business was headed by Frank Henry Martin (1866–1948), an astute businessman who capitalized on the booming interest in the banjo, ukulele, and mandolin, greatly expanding his company's reputation for quality. By 1890, the number of Martin craftsmen had grown to 15.

To meet the consistently increasing demand for instruments, Frank enlarged the factory in 1917, 1924, and 1925. The number of employees soon jumped to 75, the yearly instrument production to 3,000. By 1960 the production of 5,000 instruments a year warranted an additional facility, also in Nazareth. It was operating in 1964, though it, too, had to be expanded in 1970 to its present size of 62,000 square feet, which accommodates about 250 people. In only five years or so, the volume of sales went up more than 70 percent under the leadership of Frank Martin, current president, and his father, C.F. Martin III, chairman of the board.

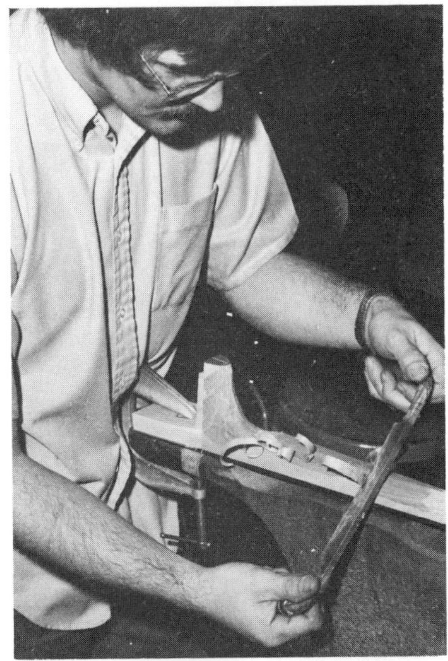

THE MARTIN GUITARS

Influenced by the work of Johann Stauffer, the earliest guitars by Johann and Christian Martin were dramatically pinched at the waist, in an almost figure-8 shape, with all of the tuning keys on one side of the rounded peghead.

Martin's 1898 catalogue reflected the family's pride and confidence in its guitars: "We can afford to warrant them, not for a year or a number of years, but for all time." The book goes on to say that: "The sizes are recommended as follows: No. 2½ for young beginners; No. 2 for ladies or wherever a clear, even tone of moderate loudness is wanted; No. 1, being both strong and well-balanced, for general purposes; No. 0 for concert playing and club use; No. 00 for exceptional power."

There were six styles in 1898: Style 18 (available in sizes 2½, 2, 1, 0, and 00; $22.50–32.50); Style 21 (Sizes 2, 1, 0, 00), Style 27 (2, 1); Style 28 (1, 0, 00); Style 34 (2, 1, 0, 00); and Style 42 (2, 1, 0, 00; $65–80).

The 1917 catalogue listed the six styles plus a special-order 15-inch-wide auditorium model. Prices of the concert guitars ranged from $25 for the 0-18 to $110 for the 0-45. The first 12-fret D-18 and D-28 models appeared in 1931. The 14-fret D-28 came out in 1934; in that same year the first "T-bar" neck rod was installed in guitar No. 57305.

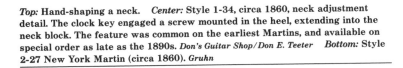

Top:* Hand-shaping a neck. *Center:* Style 1-34, circa 1860, neck adjustment detail. The clock key engaged a screw mounted in the heel, extending into the neck block. The feature was common on the earliest Martins, and available on special order as late as the 1890s. *Don's Guitar Shop/Don E. Teeter* *Bottom:* Style 2-27 New York Martin (circa 1860). *Gruhn

Mid-1800s Style 26, an unusual experiment with body trim featuring a top border of alternating dark and light blocks. ***Music Shop/Madsen***

2½-17, circa 1885. ***Spitzer's/Sievert***

1888 2-27, pearl rosette, multicolored wood top border. ***Spitzer's/Sievert***

Compare relative body sizes, from left: 1921 0-21, 1936 00-42, 1937 000-18, 1954 D-28, 1937 D-45 with custom twelfth-fret neck joint. ***Gruhn***

An Outline of Guitar Body Development

Martin's sizes 1, 2, 2½, and 3 were listed in 1852, sizes 0 and 5 in 1854, size 4 in 1857, 00 ("double-oh") in 1877, the Grand Concert 00 in the 1890s, the size 000 in 1902, and the Ditson dreadnoughts in 1916. While these records may not pinpoint actual first appearances, they provide an outline of early body size evolution. Brazilian rosewood was used for all of the standard styles until Style 17 (in 1909) and Style 18 (in 1917) switched to mahogany bodies.

Martin production totals are drawn from annual records. Descriptions of changes in model specifications—bridges, finishes, inlays, and the like—are based on catalogues and are thus likely to precede by at least a year or so the dates given here. Most of these figures were taken from Mike Longworth's fine book, *Martin Guitars: A History.*

Labels and Stamps

The oldest Martins have paper labels affixed to the inside of the back. The stamp, or brand, is also quite old, sometimes appearing concurrently with the paper label. On early guitars the stamp is usually found in three locations: the neckblock (occasionally upside down), the rear of the peghead, and the back's interior center strip.

A particularly rare 0-45 with ivory bridge. This is one of three made in 1907. Only 60 were made before 1924, and 97 from 1924 through 1930. *Gruhn*

1938 dark-top 00-18. Style 18's early evolution in brief: 1857, first documentation; 1917, body changes from rosewood to mahogany, and mahogany neck replaces cedar; 1920, change from 19 to 20 frets; 1934, change from 12 frets clear to 14 frets clear (12-fret still available). The pointed ebony bridge changed to a flattened-point type by 1917, back to points by 1923, no points by 1929, belly bridge by 1930. *Vintage Fret Shop/A. Caswell*

Martin plectrum guitars like this 1928 1-28P have necks joining the body at fret 15, while the other 4-string models, or tenor guitars, join at fret 14. *Spitzer's/Sievert*

5-18. Size 5 appeared in 1854 (along with Size 0). Sizes 3, 4, and 5 were occasionally called "Terz" instruments in reference to their tuning—initially a third higher than standard. The 5-18 appeared in 1912, and its heyday was from 1949 to 1958, when the annual production averaged 162.

The 0-18, a Martin mainstay since before the turn of the century.

Beginning in the 1830s, the stamp said *C.F. Martin, New York.* In 1867 C.F. Martin, Jr., and his cousin, C.F. Hartman, became partners in the company, and the brand on the interior strip was lengthened to reflect the change, reading *C.F. Martin & Co., New York.* (The other stamps often remained on the peghead and neckblock with the older wording.)

In 1898, over half a century after the move to Nazareth, a new brand was adopted. It distinguished all subsequent guitars from the earlier "New York" Martins. The new wording was *C.F. Martin & Co., Nazareth, Pa.* The words *Made in U.S.A.* were added during the 1960s.

Ivory

On Martins constructed prior to April 1, 1918, elephant ivory was used for bridges (on Style 34 and up), bindings, and certain trim. Ivory supplies dwindled, and about 1919 synthetic binding had replaced the ivory type, and the bridges switched from ivory to ebony. Ivory was used for bridge saddles and string nuts until the 1960s.

Strings and Bridges

Except for a few special-order instruments, all Martin guitars made before the early 1920s were gut-string models. The 2-17

00-18. After 1934, the model went to the fourteenth-fret neck joint shown here. Production *totals:* 1898–1916, 158; 1917–1925, 627; 1926–1939, 2,621. Average *yearly* production figures: during the 1940s, 434; during the 1950s, 608; during the 1960s, 564.

The mahogany D-18. 64 were made in the 12-fret type prior to the conversion to the 14-fret design in 1934 (12-fret and 14-fret refer to the neck/body joint's location). Because of the extra tension of heavy-gauge strings, the braces were changed from the scalloped type (peaked, like a suspension bridge in profile) to nonscalloped, heavier braces in 1944. The D-19 is a fancy D-18, with D-28 type soundhole trim, stained top, extra binding, and white-dot bridge pins.

The first 000-18 was built in 1906 and was a maple-body guitar. Standard versions were made in very limited quantities—only 22 prior to 1923—before taking off in the mid-1920s.

was redesigned to accommodate steel strings in 1922, and by 1928 most Martins were steel-strings. The Stauffer-influenced bridges were replaced during the mid 1800s by rectangular bridges that have "pyramids" on the ends. The "belly" bridge, still in use, replaced the rectangular type in 1929.

STYLE 18

Style 18 is a cornerstone of the Martin line, a regular member since 1857. Its 1898 specifications included gut strings, a spruce top, a twelfth-fret neck joint, an ebony fingerboard without position markers, an ebony pyramid bridge, brass tuners with ivory buttons, and top binding only.

Fingerboard inlays were documented in 1909, and by 1917 the rosewood body and cedar neck had both changed to mahogany. In 1920 a 20-fret fingerboard replaced the 19-fret version, and in 1923 steel strings *officially* became standard, although gut strings were still available (and were apparently more common for four or five more years). The belly bridge appeared in 1929, the fourteenth-fret neck joint in 1934 (earlier on OM-18s; the twelfth-fret joint was still available through 1935), the 12-fret D-18 in 1931, and the 14-fret D-18 in 1934.

STYLE 21

The rosewood Style 21 appeared in the 1860s or early 1870s. By 1898 it resembled the Style 18 except for the 21's herringbone rosette and backstrip. In about 1923 the fingerboard changed from 19 to 20 frets. Other catalogue specs—1927: steel strings standard; 1930: belly bridge; 1939: 000-21 listed as 14-fret model, 0-21 and 00-21 still 12-fret; 1956: D-21 formally introduced; 1961: 00-21NY introduced (it stayed in the line until 1965); 1969: last year of production for D-21.

THE DREADNOUGHT

The large dreadnought was named after a class of battleships ("dread nought," or "fear nothing") and was co-designed by F.H. Martin (1866–1948) and Harry L. Hunt. Mr. Hunt managed the guitar department of the Charles H. Ditson Company, a major New York retailer. Hunt and Martin collaborated on the design of three Ditson Spanish Models. Two were similar to Martin's sizes 1 and 00; the third was the extra-large Dreadnought.

The earliest dreadnought was a member of the three-guitar, Martin-built Ditson line. The marketing organization was the House of Ditson, and the series was labeled *Oliver Ditson & Co., Boston, New York.* That company's address was 179 Tremont Street, Boston. Its president, Charles H. Ditson, died on May 14, 1929, leaving an estate of nearly seven million dollars. The company sold its musical instruments department in April 1931, and by that time Martin was planning its own series of dreadnoughts.

There were two D-1s, which evolved into the D-18, and seven D-2s, which effectively became the herringbone D-28. Early

1959 000-21. From 1902 until the mid-1930s, the 000-21 was made in extremely limited quantities, only 24 in all. Production stepped up in 1938 with 92 guitars. A total of 2,043 were made from 1938 to 1959, when the model was dropped. ***Mandolin Bros./Eyeflex***

1932 D-2, one of seven. It belonged to Luther Ossenbrink, also known as "Arkie." ***Country Music Hall of Fame***

1938 D-45, with rare factory sunburst top. Only nine D-45s were made that year. *Don's Guitar Shop/Don E. Teeter*

1938 D-45 headstock. Note the fingerboard's purfling (similar to the F-9's) and Grover Statite tuners with *"M"* engravings. *Don's Guitar Shop/Don E. Teeter*

1939 D-18. *Don Erlewine/Tom Erlewine*

Sunburst herringbone D-28, 1939. *Eldon Whitford/Tom Erlewine*

Martin Hawaiian models, particularly the K (koa) series, enjoyed popularity during the 1920s and 1930s. This is Norman Blake's D-18H. It is among the rarest of all Martins, and a total of only four were made—this one in 1934, two in 1936, and one in 1966. *Gruhn*

The D-28 is Martin's most popular rosewood guitar. From 1963 to 1973, nearly 32,000 were produced.

Martin dreadnoughts, like the Ditsons, had elongated bodies and twelfth-fret joints. The dreadnought incorporated the fourteenth-fret joint by 1934. In 1967 it became available on three standard slot-head models, the D-18S, D-28S, and D-35S. From 1967 to 1971 Martin made 20 times as many standard D-28s as D-28S's. The D-21, essentially a no-frills D-28, joined in 1955 (only six samples were made that year) and was produced until 1969.

STYLE 28, HERRINGBONE

The date of the Style 28's introduction to the Martin gut-string line has been lost, though it preceded the 1874 price list. An 1870 document simply mentions a pearl inlay, and the 1898 specs included a rosewood body with ivory binding, a spruce top, a cedar neck, a rectangular ebony bridge, a 19-fret ebony fingerboard joining at fret 12 (no inlays), and herringbone trim.

In 1901 the Style 28 was specified to have inlay positions at frets 5, 7, and 9. Other historical developments (dates are catalogue listings and thus approximate) include: a 20-fret fingerboard (1917); celluloid bindings replace ivory (1918–1919); mahogany neck listed, gut strings still standard (1923); white ivory celluloid bridge pins with black dots (1927); steel strings standard, belly bridge standard (1929); 14-fret model listed, 12-fret still available (1934; also see OM-28); D-28 first catalogued (1935); last year for the diamond inlays (1944); back strip changed (1947); D-28S introduced (late 1967).

Prewar D-28s are nicknamed herringbones, and since they are among Martin's most admired guitars ever, "herringbone"

A winning combination: Gene Autry, Martin's first D-45, and a horse. ***Doug Green***

By popular demand, the D-45 was reissued in 1968. There were 230 made with Brazilian rosewood, but export embargoes caused a switch to Indian rosewood, which became standard after guitar no. 256266 in early 1970.

The D-41 is most easily distinguished from the D-45 by its lack of inlay on the first fret and around the portion of the fretboard that overlaps the top. The D-41 was unveiled in 1969, and 31 Brazilian rosewood guitars were made before the switch to Indian rosewood.

In recent years Martin has expanded its use of alternative woods, such as ash, maple, walnut, and koa. The 1989 D-60 shown here is Martin's first bird's-eye maple guitar.

Near right: A general depletion of rosewood sources caused a scarcity of boards wide enough to yield two-piece backs. The D-35, introduced in 1965, features a three-piece back with a center wedge bordered by bookmatched, contrasting pieces. This particular guitar was built after Martin changed to Indian rosewood in 1969. *Far right:* D12-20; note slotted headstock. Other 12-strings include the 14-fret D12-28, introduced in 1970; like the D-28 it has a diamond-shaped protuberance in the neck/peghead joint in the back. The D12-35 was introduced in 1965. Whereas the D12-28 is essentially a 12-string D-28, the D12-35 differs from the D-35 in its slotted head, longer body, and 12-fret neck.

Near right: Martin Bicentennial model D-76, the first one made. *Hollywood Music* *Far right:* As *American Guitars* goes to press, the HD-35 is one of Martin's latest models, a herringbone with a three-piece back.

Left: **1924 koa wood 0-28K. *Right:* 1929 0-28K. By 1930 the pyramid bridge had been fully supplanted by the belly bridge shown here. On the 1924 model, note backstrip and rear V-shaped peghead volute. Martin made three Size 0 koa guitars, all from 1917 to 1935. They were the 0-18K (by far the most common), the rare 0-21K, and 0-28K.**

has become a very potent word leading many people to consider herringbone trim some sort of option. In fact, herringbone goes back well into the last century and was a *standard* feature on all Style 28s until early 1947. The spacing and size of the herringbone have varied slightly, though otherwise the pattern hasn't changed much.

According to author Mike Longworth, all early Martins had imported European marquetry. The domestic industry that provided Martin's later marquetry was small, the quality of its output inconsistent. The company discontinued herringbone after 1946 because the quality was inadequate and because plastics had improved. The change to plain plastic occurred with Martin guitar No. 98233, a D-28; the event wasn't even considered important enough to merit official documentation.

STYLE 42

Style 42 was the top of the line until the Style 45 appeared. Like the Style 40, the 42 had abalone soundhole and top trim, but it also had an additional connecting link along the end of the fretboard. Here's a rough historical sketch—1874: pearl inlay, ivory bridge, Stauffer-type screw neck on some models, rosewood body; 1898: cedar neck, 19 frets total, inlays at frets 5, 7, and 9; 1901: additional inlays at frets 12 and 15; 1918: 000-42 first listed; 1918 or 1919: ivory binding replaced by celluloid, ivory bridge replaced by ebony; 1923: mahogany neck, 20 frets, gut strings still standard; 1927: steel strings; by 1934: 000-42 specified in 14-fret version. Discontinued in 1942.

1946 000-28 herringbone. There were 95 000-28s built between 1902 and 1927, and 1,011 between 1927 and 1943. Production averaged 139 each year for the next decade but only 44 each year for the decade after that. Between 1965 and 1973 (the last year of available records) annual production averaged 173. *Mandolin Bros./Eyeflex*

1926 00-28 herringbone. ***Tut Campbell***

Herringbone trim, detail.

1939 000-42. This model is quite rare. It appeared in 1918 and only 15 were made before 1938. From 1938 until the model's discontinuation in 1943, another 106 were made. ***Mark Huth/Sacha***

Far left: **Martin's reissue herringbone, introduced in late 1976, has several features of the original (1933–1946), including herringbone top trim, scalloped bracing, and zipper back strip.** ***Near left:*** **Style 42, like Style 40, had an abalone border around the top, plus additional abalone top trim around the end of the fingerboard. Style 42, which dates to 1874, was the top of the line until the introduction of the Style 45 in 1904 (the 000 version of the Style 42 appeared in 1918).** ***Glen Quan***

STYLE 45

Style 45 evolved from some 1902 vine-inlaid, extra fancy Style 42s. The first 45s appeared in 1904 in 0 and 00 sizes. Details included a 19-fret neck, ornate scroll-head designs, an ivory-bound ebony fingerboard inlaid at frets 5, 7, 9, 12, and 15, an ivory bridge, and lavish pearl and ivory trim.

Inlays were added at frets 1, 3, and 17 by 1914, and during 1918 and 1919 the ebony bridge replaced the ivory type. The ivory binding was replaced with celluloid by 1923, and steel strings became stock in 1928 (gut strings were still available). The belly bridge appeared in 1929, the OM-45 the following year. In 1934 a 14-fret 000-45 was listed, and in 1938 the D-45—built since 1933—was formally introduced. The 45s were discontinued in 1942 and didn't reappear until 1968 when the D-45 was reissued. The 00-45 and 000-45 reappeared in 1970.

The D-45 is the king of Martins. First made in a 12-fret version for Gene Autry in 1933, the D-45 was discontinued on October 9, 1942, and only 91 prewar models were manufactured. They are among American guitar's irreplaceable treasures.

In 1968, Martin reissued the D-45. There were 230 made with Brazilian rosewood, but because of trade restrictions on that material Martin officially switched to Indian rosewood in 1970.

The first D12-45 was made in 1969 of Brazilian rosewood; all subsequent D12-45s are Indian rosewood.

This is the first Style 45 prototype, actually a 00-42 with special pearl trim. Note the bowl mandolin type pickguard between the soundhole and bridge, and the ornate fingerboard and peghead inlays. ***Lester Davidson/Martin Guitars***

Tut Campbell

Gruhn

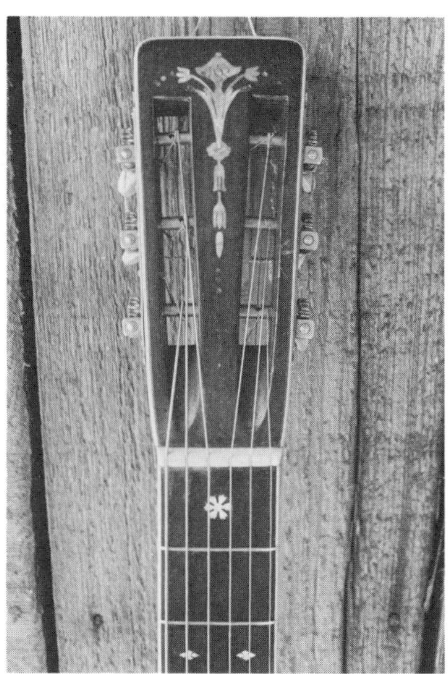

Style 45 "torch" or "flowerpot" peghead inlay. This design appeared shortly after 1904 and featured a three-piece bulb at top center.

0-45 models made in 1907 (*left*) and 1923 (*right*). The extra markers were added by 1914. The ivory bridge (*left*) was replaced by ebony (*right*) in 1918 or 1919.

00-45 peghead. This later torch pattern was first catalogued in 1930, though it appeared at least as early as 1929. It had a two-piece bulb at top center (no longer a separate piece, the circular tip was part of the bulb's top half).

00-45, belly bridge. *Tut Campbell*

1930 0-45T tenor, 4 strings, special inlay on the pickguard and bridge, built by a Martin employee at the factory. It is even fancier than a standard Style 45, though it does not bear the Martin name. *Tut's Guitars./Tut Campbell*

00-45, introduced in 1904. This is a 1970s model.

The D12-45: twelfth-fret joint, long body, slotted head with abalone pearl inlay. The first one was made in 1969 of Brazilian rosewood; all subsequent D12-45s are Indian rosewood. A fairly rare guitar, 52 were made from 1969 to 1973.

This is the only 00-45K ever built. It dates to 1919 and remains in mint condition. The abalone trim against the rich reddish-brown koa makes it one of the most distinctive instruments in Martin history. *Norm's*

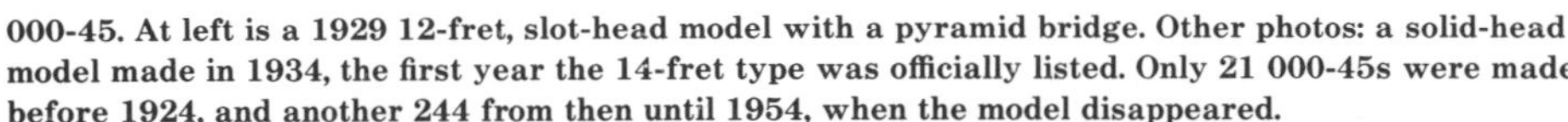

000-45. At left is a 1929 12-fret, slot-head model with a pyramid bridge. Other photos: a solid-head model made in 1934, the first year the 14-fret type was officially listed. Only 21 000-45s were made before 1924, and another 244 from then until 1954, when the model disappeared.

Mandolin Bros./Eyeflex

Tut Campbell

1989 basses, among Martin's most unusual new models. Essentially a Jumbo M body with a 34-inch scale bass neck, the instrument is available with either an Indian rosewood body and white binding (*left*, B-40) or a maple body with tortoise binding (*right*, B-65). Either is available with a pickup, active electronics, or fretless neck.

Bad guy (black hat), 000-45, Tex Ritter. *Doug Green*

1930 OM-28. *Music Shop/Madsen*

THE OM MODEL

In October 1929 an Atlanta banjoist named Perry Bechtel visited Martin and expressed his desire for an instrument that would allow banjo players to more easily convert from their banjos—fading in popularity—to the up-and-coming guitar. Specifically he suggested a neck that would join the body at the fourteenth fret rather than the twelfth. (Note: today such guitars are routinely called "14-fret" and "12-fret" models, referring not to the total number of frets, which is usually 19 or 20, but rather to the neck/body joint location. Gibson L-5s had had 14-fret necks since 1923.)

Martin made a 000-28 with a 14-fret neck, christened it the OM-28 (Orchestra Model), and went into production. Eleven OM-28s were made in 1929, and 476 more over the next four years. The company dropped the OM designation in 1933 and returned to the 000 name. According to *Martin Guitars:* "The only real difference between the OM series and the succeeding 14-fret 000 guitars was the scale length. The OM had a 25.4-inch scale, whereas the 000 had the 24.9-inch "as did the 0 and 00 sizes." But there were other differences as well. The OMs had no name on the front of the peghead, and were built and braced lighter. Their necks were more slender and somewhat V-shaped, and their pickguards were smaller. *[Note: the 12-fret 000 was built through 1933, overlapping the OM.]*

Martin went whole-hog into production of OM guitars from 1930 to 1933, producing 765 OM-18s, 487 OM-28s, only 2 OM-42s (both in 1930), 40 top-of-the-line OM-45s, 14 OM-45 DLXs (snowflake bridge inlays, pearl-inlaid pickguard, gold-plated banjo tuners with pearl knobs), only one OM-18T tenor, and a fair number of plectrum versions. Six special-order S OM-28s were built in 1969.

MARTIN ARCH-TOPS

Martin entered the world of arch-top construction during 1931–1941, that uncertain decade that followed the stock market crash and preceded the Second World War. The first model was the C-1, a roundhole guitar. There were 139 roundhole C-1s made in 1931, 285 more in 1932, and a final 25 in 1933. That was it. Martin made two *f-hole* C-1s in 1932.

In 1933 the number of f-hole C-1s jumped to 78, then to 262 in 1934. Due to wartime shortages of men and materials, Martin discontinued the line, having built a total of 1,236 C-1s, including a single 12-string in 1932. Martin's Style R guitars followed the C-1 and also came in both f-hole and roundhole designs. There were eight models in the F line of 1935–1942: the F-1, a 12-string F-1, the F-2, a *maple* F-2 (only one was made), the F-5, an f-hole F-7, a roundhole F-7, and the F-9.

The F-9 pictured here is truly a collector's guitar. Only 72 were made: 28 in 1935, 19 in 1936, 6 in 1937, another 6 the following year, 7 in 1939, none during 1940 and 1941, and a final 6 in 1942.

The F-9 has rather imposing proportions. Its 16 by 20 inch body has the stately mass, the dignified bulge, of a grand Packard touring car from the same era. It was the cream of Martin's arch-top crop, spiffed up accordingly with a center backstrip similar to the Style 45 but with added black/white markings on either side, an extra border around the elevated pickguard, a bound peghead inlaid with *C. F. Martin* in pearl veneer, and hexagonal pearl fingerboard inlays. The fingerboard sported a pair of white/black/white lines about ¼ inch from the edges of the bound neck. Other details included a rosewood body, a spruce top, an ebony bridge, and a brown sunburst. The F-9 on page 269 belongs to Roy Acuff. As the *Country Music Encyclopedia* puts it, he is "the closest thing country music has to a father figure." He is also a very serious guitar collector, having built a multimillion-dollar museum at the Grand Ole Opry to house his instruments. George Gruhn and Doug Green have written a book on the Acuff collection; it is untitled at this writing. Also see the F-7 pictured in the Introduction.

The vertical *Martin* headstock logo and the hexagonal fingerboard inlays were developed for the arch-top series. Both features later graced certain Style 45s.

MARTIN ELECTRICS

To some, the very thought of Martin electric guitars had all the propriety of The Sons of the Pioneers singing "I Am The Walrus," but in 1958 the Nazareth luthiers introduced the D-18E prototype, which entered production the following year along with the 00-18E and D-28E. The D-18E fizzled after 1959, but the other two stuck it out through 1964. Custom-order electrics

OM-45, circa 1929. ***Martin Guitars***

The rosewood C2, generally an arch-top Style 28, was introduced in a roundhole version during 1931, and the conversion to f-holes occurred shortly thereafter. By 1939, hexagon inlays had replaced the diamond inlays shown here. There were 269 roundhole C2s (1931–1933), and 439 f-hole models (1932–1942).

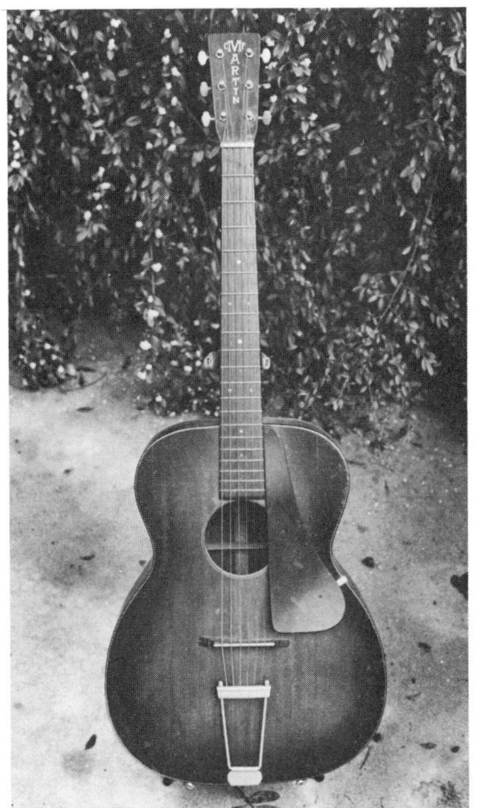

Martin C-1. 449 of these unusual arched-top instruments were made from 1931 to 1933, when the roundhole design was replaced by f-holes. *Acuff*

1935 R-17. Note segmented f-holes. *Vintage Fret Shop/A. Caswell*

Only two Martin F-5s were made, and here's one of them. Note the all blonde body and peghead. The guitar dates to 1940. *Martin Guitars*

1938 Martin F-9, a deluxe rosewood model with carved top, ebony fingerboard, and pearl inlays. Only 72 were made, from 1935 to 1942. *Acuff*

Early-1960s D-18E. *Jacksonville*

Combining Grand Auditorium body width and Dreadnought depth, the powerful J-40M of the late 1980s is an extraordinary guitar, even for Martin. (The hexagon inlays are scaled 1/5 smaller than standard.)

1962 F-65, with Martin's model 700 portable amp (on chair). *Mike Longworth/Herb Kynor*

1966–1968 style GT-75. *Spitzer's/Sievert*

made through 1971 included the 00-28E, 0-18TE, 000-28E, D-41E, D-41SE, and D-12-20E.

In 1961 Martin introduced its F series of arch-top electrics equipped with DeArmond pickups: the single-cutaway F-50 (one pickup), single-cutaway F-55 (two pickups), and double-cutaway F-65. This trio was terminated in 1965 and replaced with the short-lived GT-70 and GT-75. Martin production totals for arch-top electrics are: 519 F-50s, 665 F-55s, 566 F-65s, 453 GT-70s, and 751 GT-75s.

MARTINS MADE FOR OTHER COMPANIES

Martin made guitars with various brand names for about two dozen retailers, teachers, and musical instrument distributors. These people, companies, and labels include: the Bacon Banjo Company (circa 1924), Vahdah Olcott-Bickford (Style 44, or Soloist), Bitting Special (Bethlehem, Pennsylvania), Oliver Ditson (many instruments of several types), Carl Fischer (New York, some special 0-18T guitars in 1929), William Foden (Foden Specials), J. A. Handley (a Lowell, Massachusetts, instructor), Montgomery Ward (circa 1932, several mahogany instruments), Paramount (a few guitars with small soundholes in a ledge that was flush with the sides of the body), Rolando (for J. J. Milligan Music, extremely rare), Rudick's (Akron, 00-17 guitars labeled 0-55; 1935), Southern California Music Company (a retail chain; Martin made a line of Hawaiian guitars, circa 1917–1920), S. S. Stewart (made for Buegeleisen & Jacobson of New York, 1923–1925), John Wanamaker (Philadelphia, circa 1909), H. A. Weymann & Son (ukuleles and taropatch 8-string ukes, circa 1925), Wurlitzer (1922–1924), and Wolverine (made for Grinnell Brothers of Detroit).

MARTIN GUITAR SERIAL NUMBERS, 1898–1979

Year	*Last No.*	*Year*	*Last No.*
1898	8348	1940	76734
1899	8716	1941	80013
1900	9128	1942	83107
1901	9310	1943	86724
1902	9528	1944	90149
1903	9810	1945	93623
1904	9988	1946	98158
1905	10120	1947	103468
1906	10329	1948	108269
1907	10727	1949	112961
1908	10883	1950	117961
1909	11018	1951	122799
1910	11203	1952	128436
1911	11413	1953	134501
1912	11565	1954	141345
1913	11821	1955	147328
1914	12047	1956	152775
1915	12209	1957	159061
1916	12390	1958	165576
1917	12988	1959	171047
1918	13450	1960	175689
1919	14512	1961	181297
1920	15848	1962	187384
1921	16758	1963	193327
1922	17839	1964	199626
1923	19891	1965	207030
1924	22008	1966	217215
1925	24116	1967	230095
1926	28689	1968	241925
1927	34435	1969	256003
1928	37568	1970	271633
1929	40843	1971	294270
1930	45317	1972	313302
1931	49589	1973	333873
1932	52590	1974	353387
1933	55084	1975	371828
1934	58679	1976	388800
1935	61947	1977	399625
1936	65176	1978	407800
1937	68865	1979	419900
1938	71866	1980	430300
1939	74061		

Introduced in the late 1970s, the M-38 is a flat-top version of Martin's F series of arch-tops (1935–1942). Details: rosewood Grand Auditorium body, two-piece back, binding at the heel/rim joint, abalone rosette, bound headstock, and a unique (to Martin) combination of ebony fingerboard and rosewood bridge. The M-36 is similar, although it has a D-35 type three-piece back and lacks the M-38's abalone rosette and binding on the headstock and neck/body joint.

MAURER, PRAIRIE STATE, AND EUPHONON

Mr. and Mrs. Carl Larson. *Hartman*

Maurer steel-string, detail (unoriginal bridge). *William C. Reed*

Carl Johan Ferdinand Larson and his brother, Peter August Larson, were eminent Chicago luthiers during the first half of the twentieth century, building guitars under several brand names including Maurer, Euphonon, Prairie State, Stahl, and Larson; sometimes a single guitar style would be marketed under several of the brands. Chicago Historical Society records show that as early as 1886 Robert Maurer was established as a music teacher, with a studio on Huron Street. Two years later his address was 425 Division, and the listing specified *Robert Maurer, Musical Instruments.* Maurer occupied another shop on Division from 1894 to 1897, and for 1898 the entry reads *Robt. Maurer, Manufacturer Maurer Mandolins & Guitars;* the factory's location was 29-39 East Erie. In 1899 Maurer had moved again, this time to 284 North Avenue.

Carl Larson (born December 31, 1867) and August (born April 24, 1873) were natives of the Småland ("small land") region of Sweden, and as boys they began to learn the skills of cabinetmaking and carpentry. Robert C. Hartman, Carl's grandson, recounted that Carl came to America during the 1880s, settling in Chicago. Soon he had earned enough money to send for his younger brother. The date when August Larson went to work for Maurer has been lost, but records show that in 1900 he was secretary of Maurer & Company, and Robert Maurer was president. By the following year Maurer had left the company, and August had become president, a position held until he died in June 1944.

The Larsons moved into a factory on Elm Street in 1906. It was a three-story barn or loft, with August's living quarters in the shop itself on the second floor, connected to the main level by a crude stairway. Carl worked in the front of the shop, August in the back. Carl was known as Pop or Dad, and he was an expert on tone quality. August, who was married only briefly and spent all of his years working and living in the shop, did the finishing. Carl retired in about 1940 and died on September 4, 1946 at the age of 78, at which time the business was dissolved.

Although the combined output of Robert Maurer and the Larson brothers was presumably modest, their instruments manifested considerable variety in quality and styles, from small, 12-fret "parlor" guitars to some of the hugest steel-strings ever made—behemoths measuring up to 21 inches across the lower bout.

The Larsons' guitars ("the most scientifically constructed in the world") were among the first true steel-strings, heavily braced and clearly not intended for gut strings. Many of the better models under the various brand names were fitted with laminated sandwich braces consisting of sidepieces of spruce and a center strip of rosewood, a most unusual feature. Many, particularly Prairie States, were equipped with a pair of longitudinal interior rods running from headblock to tailblock. According to a mid-1930s catalogue, "the tube near the top withstands the strain of the strings, leaving the soundboard free and resilient," while "the straining rod near the back restrains the neck from bending forward." Some guitars featured adjustable saddles with removable inserts of varying contour that permitted a choice of action. The purchaser could also order an optional tilt-neck mechanism that entailed two screws near the neck/body joint: one in the fretboard and one in the heel.

The mid-1930s Maurer guitars all had slotted pegheads, mahogany necks, and ebony fingerboards. They may be divided into three groups. In the first, all guitars had pearl dot markers and either plain or slightly fancy trim. The eight styles were—

487: oak body, single inlaid backstrip, \$25; 489 was the mahogany version. 491: Grand Concert body (19⅛ inches long) of mahogany, soundhole inlaid with colored wood, extra inlaid backstrips, \$28; 493 was the Auditorium (20 inches long) version, \$30.

494: rosewood body, soundhole inlay of colored wood and celluloid, \$30; 525 was the three-quarter version. 498: rosewood body, soundhole inlaid with colored wood (no celluloid), celluloid binding on top and back, \$35; Style 495 was the maple version.

In the second group the pearl fret markers were a mixture of dots and fancier shapes, and the pegheads featured three similar inlays. The 18⅞-inch long Concert Style 541 (\$45) was a rosewood guitar with colored wood inlays around the soundhole and the top's edge; Style 551 was the Auditorium version. The fancier Style 562 (\$53) was a Standard size Maurer (18 inches long) whose soundhole and top were inlaid with alternating pearl and colored woods; 562½ was the Concert model; and 564 was the Auditorium version.

The models in the third group (\$85–102) all had extremely elaborate tree-of-life fingerboard and peghead inlays, of which there were several variations. They were Styles 585 Grand Concert; 587, a 585 with pearl tuner buttons; 590, an Auditorium-sized 585; and 593, a 590 with pearl buttons. The mid-1930s Prairie States of this period were simply Maurers (from the second and third groups just discussed) with the twin steel reinforcement rods described above.

Certain Larson soundboards were quite unusual, almost a cross between conventional arched tops and flat tops. They were not carved, and yet some of them did bow upwards in the center. Some people consider these to be flat-tops even though many are equipped with f-holes.

Top: This Maurer is representative of the second group of models described in the text. Note the mixture of pearl dots and fancier fingerboard inlays. _Mike Osgaard/Mike Sabatino_ _Bottom:_ Prairie State flat-top: huge rosewood body, laminated spruce/ebony/spruce top braces, abalone binding. Visible through the soundhole is a nickel-plated reinforcement strut, common among Prairie States and Euphonons. _Intermountain/Leonard Coulson_

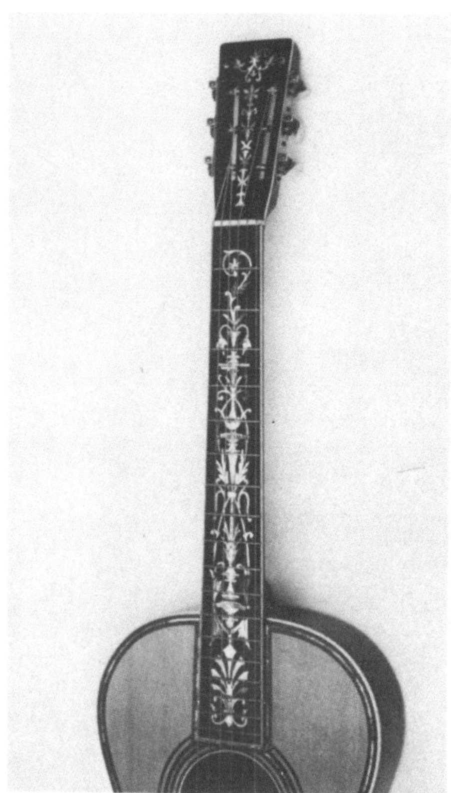
The best of the early Maurers were known for their tree-of-life inlays. *Guitar Trader*

A Mr. Stahl, of Milwaukee, was a music teacher and author of method books. He ordered guitars from the Maurer Company with his own name on them, and their maple X-braces differed from the basic Maurer style rosewood-strip laminations. Although Stahl claimed to be a manufacturer, most or all of his merchandise was made by the Maurer organization. Maurer's WLS guitars were named after the Chicago radio station that hosted the influential *National Barn Dance* program. Dyer Bros. ordered harp guitars from Maurer in several degrees of quality. All were built out of mahogany, including some with extravagant pearl work.

Among the various Maurer/Larson guitars, the Maurers appear to be the oldest, while the other names seem to be from the 1920s and later. Euphonons in particular are later, and most of the guitars with that brand name are 14-fret, generally modern flat-tops. Euphonons and Prairie States came both ways—in smaller 12-fret styles and in the larger and later 14-fret types. Maurers span the greatest time period, their earliest models often sporting very fancy abalone inlays and extremely meticulous detail work. Euphonons appear to be the latest guitars in the group, made through the late 1930s and right up until the early 1940s, recent enough that some are generally Martin-type dreadnoughts, though only about 15 inches across. Other Larson-made instruments are similar to Gibson J-185s in shape. Stahl, WLS, and Larson brand guitars are the rarest of the Maurer/Larson group. (Incidentally, the Larsons also constructed a trio of guitars for Les Paul.)

Maurer guitars were particularly well built, and those that survive show remarkable stability and freedom from warped

An unusual Euphonon dreadnought with a rosewood body and laminated top braces (unoriginal bridge). *Intermountain/Leonard Coulson*

Dyer Bros. harp guitar. *Bob Coward*

This rosewood Euphonon is similar in size to Gibson's Everly Brothers model. *Gruhn*

necks, cracked bodies, and other problems. Although it would be difficult to find a manufacturer who entered the twentieth century with the nineteenth-century quality that Martin continued, the Larson guitars nevertheless make a respectable showing. Because they are basically handmade instruments, variations from guitar to guitar are common. Still, their overall quality is consistently fine. The Larsons built their guitars to last.

Happy customer Roy Clark with a Melobar Powerslide 88. Released in 1987 at a list price of $529, the 88 features a solid alder centerpiece and the patented W.E.S. sustaining bridge.

The company, now called Smith Melobar Guitars, Inc., has relocated from Weiser, Idaho, to larger facilities in Boise. Another new model is the Melobar I. Founder Walt Smith died in 1990.

MELOBAR

Fascinated by the steel guitar, cattle rancher Walter Smith purchased Kenneth H. Clark's 1930s patent for the Harmolin, a guitar with a knee-operated pitch changer. Smith later patented his own knee-lever device, abandoned the concept, and then developed the slant-neck Melobar, which he conceived of as a "stand-up steel."

Ed and Rudy Dopera (see National) produced a few solid-color Melobars for Smith in about 1970 at the Dobro factory in Long Beach, California, and Mosrite built several hundred sunburst models with chrome control panels and white pickguards. Later, former Mosrite employees built sunburst Melobars with tortoise-shell panels, and some of these (like the one pictured here) had replaceable fingerboards labeled with instructional guidelines.

Walter Smith returned to full-time ranching, but in 1981 he and his sons reintroduced the Melobar in a variety of tunings.

MERRILL

Merrill aluminum-body guitars were manufactured by the Aluminum Musical Instrument Company of 142 West 23rd Street and later 127 Fifth Avenue in New York City. Company president Neil Merrill began experimenting with aluminum in 1886 and first displayed his instruments to the public around 1894. Though he built guitars, mandolins, banjos, fiddles, zithers, and even double basses, only guitars and mandolins were offered in the first catalogue, in which Merrill claimed, "With the discovery of aluminum comes a new era to the musical instrument." The Merrill Style AA ($40) flat-top had a plain aluminum body and spruce top. On the Style A ($55) the back was hand engraved, while on the Style B ($75) both the back and sides were engraved. Merrill called his concept "The Greatest Musical Invention of the Age."

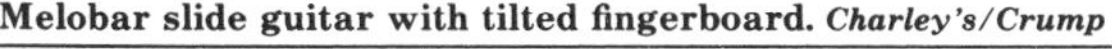

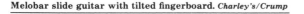

Melobar slide guitar with tilted fingerboard. ***Charley's/Crump***

Elbert Walker *Woody/Baxendale*

Messenger guitar (*left*) and bass, with metal alloy necks.

MESSENGER

In the late 1960s Messenger guitars were built by Musicraft, Incorporated, of 156 Montgomery Street, San Francisco. There were three 6-strings, distinguished by their model designations and finishes: ME-10 Morning Sunburst, ME-11 Midnight Sunburst, and ME-12 Rojo Red. The ME-22 12-string was available in all three finishes. The Messenger design was one of the first to combine peghead, neck, and full-length body extension into a single-piece alloy structure (also see Travis Bean and Kramer). The Messenger also featured distinctive f-holes, a thin body, and stereo output.

MICRO-FRETS

Micro-Frets was a small company whose guitars manifested an appealing eccentricity. It was located at 100 Grove Road in Frederick, Maryland, and was in production from about 1965 to at least 1972. Mid-sixties officers included R. S. Jones, president and treasurer; F. M. Huggins, vice-president and general manager (later president); and A. R. Hubbard, secretary.

Made of solid woods rather than veneers, the Micro-Frets guitars were innovative if not particularly successful, and demonstrated a fierce commitment to space-age newness. All were double-cutaways, and most had only one unusually shaped soundhole. The two most radical features were the Micro-Nut (standard on all models) and the Calibrato vibrato tailpiece. The Micro-Nut supposedly guaranteed perfect intonation by offering string length adjustments at the peghead, while the patented Calibrato entailed individually calibrated string cams to keep the notes in relative tune even when lowered by the bar, an idea that's been kicked around factories and home workshops for at least 20 years. At one time, the Micro-Frets line encompassed three basses and six guitars. The company also produced an instrument with a wireless transmitter way back in 1968. Of all things, it was called the Telecaster, later Teleguitar. Micro-Frets also manufactured a few resonator guitars.

The Orbiter by Micro-Frets. Note the Calibrato tailpiece and pickguard-mounted knobs. ***James Hilligoss***

Micro-Frets Signature. ***Gruhn***

MONROE

Monroe Guitar was founded in 1988 by Robert Monroe Turner, a graduate of the Roberto-Venn School of Luthiery in Phoenix. Turner had apprenticed to *Guitar Player* columnist Dan Erlewine, from whom he learned a fretting method that employs a custom-built neck tension simulation device. The line was introduced at the June 1989 NAMM trade show in Chicago.

Monroe's 20,000-square-foot plant is in Fabens, Texas, about 20 miles east of El Paso. As we go to press, a work force of 20 is building approximately 180 guitars a month, all with a definite rock-and-roll attitude. Every guitar in the catalog is radically shaped and Kahler-equipped. Options include a Floyd Rose, custom graphics, pearl inlays, flamed maple top, and extra pickups. Prices run from about $1,000 to $2,000.

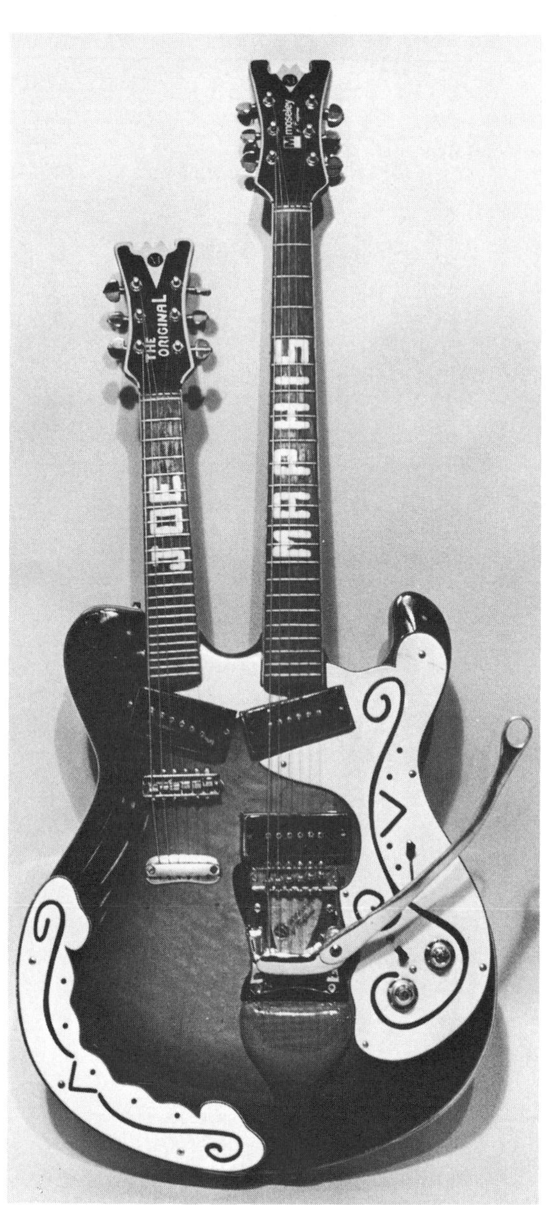

This doubleneck was built for country superpicker Joe Maphis by Semie Moseley. Joe used it from 1954 until the mid-1970s, and its exposure helped launch Mosrite (the short neck is an octave guitar). *Country Music Hall of Fame*

MOSRITE

Semie Moseley just wanted to build guitars and make some money, but the ins and outs of high-dollar industry finance were his downfall—temporarily, anyway. He owed his initial fame to the Ventures, who in the early 1960s were rock and roll's most successful instrumental group. They played Fenders, and their sweet midrange twang helped sell thousands of Jazzmasters and Stratocasters. Ventures and Fender went together like champagne and caviar, like fatback and hogbelly.

But a new kind of guitar began appearing all over Ventures album covers, and to the legions of self-taught players who had cut their teeth on "Shanghied" and worn out their copies of "Mr. Moto," the sight was almost shocking. Such albums bore the words *The Ventures play only the Mosrite guitar.* (People called them *Moss-rites* and *Mōze-rites;* the latter is correct.) In small print were listed the Hollywood addresses for both Mosrite and the Ventures Fan Club: 1213 North Highland Avenue, and 1215 North Highland Avenue. They were next-door neighbors.

Rumors percolated through music stores and rehearsal garages that the Ventures had started a guitar company, and the conclusions were well founded. The group had in fact financed an obscure, small-potatoes guitar builder and part-time gospel musician from the central California town of Bakersfield, home of Buck Owens. His name was Semie Moseley, and his low-action, flat-fretted, oddly shaped guitars enjoyed a rage in the mid 1960s. His Mosrite company prospered, folded, and was resurrected with remarkable consistency during the 1960s and 1970s.

The Hallmark Swept-Wing guitar (wedge-shaped, wide at the top) was made in the late 1960s in very small numbers by a friend of Moseley's named Joe Hall, from Arvin, California. Hall went into business with former Ventures guitarist Bob Bogle. "They used some of my Mosrite parts on those Hallmarks," Semie said, "but I sure didn't build 'em myself. They really didn't go anywhere. The Mosrites, though, that's another story."

Collector George Gruhn detailed five Mosrite solidbodies of some interest, listed here in chronological order. Type 1 had a glued-in neck, Vibramute tailpiece, triple binding on top of the body, side-mounted output jack, and no name on the pickups. Type 2 had a screwed-on neck (as did all subsequent types), a truss rod adjustment at the body end of the neck, a pickguard-mounted jack, and again, a Vibramute and unmarked pickups. Type 3 was like type 2 but with *Mosrite* on the pickups, while type 4 was like type 3 but with a *Moseley* tailpiece. Finally, type 5 was similar to type 4, but it had a headstock-mounted truss rod adjustment.

When Semie Moseley wasn't manufacturing guitars, he tooled around the West in a Greyhound bus or a motor home, played music for evangelists, and geared up for another crack at guitar building. Here is his story in his own words.

An early top-of-the-line Ventures model with body binding. The neck adjustment is visible between the fingerboard and front pickup. On a Mosrite solidbody, a rim-mounted output jack indicates a very early model.

A HISTORY OF MOSRITE BY SEMIE MOSELEY*

I was born on June 13, 1935, in Durant, Oklahoma. My parents moved to Bakersfield when I was nine, and I began taking guitar lessons. I left school when I was in the seventh grade, traveling with an evangelistic group and playing guitar for them.

Traveling with the evangelists didn't work out financially, so I decided that I needed to get a job. I thought maybe it would be possible for me to make guitars. I was living in Los Angeles by this time, and Paul Barth [see National, Magnatone, Rickenbacker] hired me at one dollar an hour to work for Rickenbacker. This was about 1953. I redesigned some of Rickenbacker's guitar necks. I was working for almost two years for a dollar an hour, and Paul finally fired me because I had built my own guitar there.

One of the preachers that I traveled with was Ray Boatright, and he suggested that I go into business for myself. I was 18 at the time. Ray Boatright took me to Sears and cosigned for my first tools, and he let me use his garage for a workshop. This was out in Norwalk, in the Los Angeles area. I went around to all the music stores and told 'em how good I was [*laughs*], and I gave away most of my early work just so I could get a reputation.

I decided to build something that would attract a lot of attention and cause people to have some questions, so I designed a three-neck guitar with mandolin, guitar, and octave guitar necks. Les Paul was my hero, and I loved the way he played so high and so fast, and I thought that having the octave guitar tuned up one octave higher than a standard neck would allow me to get a sound like that, and it worked. Well, the tripleneck did the job and created quite a stir.

If it weren't for Boatright I probably never would've gotten started. I named my company after myself and after Ray Boatright. Ray also suggested that I build a guitar for somebody who was very famous in order to get some publicity. There was a guitarist by the name of Joe Maphis who had a very popular show called *Town Hall*

Early custom Mosrite with high-relief pickguard, concealed pickup (note protruding polepieces), pickguard-mounted output jack, and lower bout body trim. ***Dick Allen***

*From an interview with the author, April 1980.

A Ventures model Mosrite. After the Moseley/ Ventures split, it was replaced by the Mark I (also known as V-I). *Anthony Manfredi*

Ventures 12-string. *Gruhn*

Party. Joe saw my three-neck and asked me if I could build him a doubleneck. So I built him his guitar, and he became the first professional to play a Mosrite instrument. This was about 1955. [*Note: Joe Maphis recalled, "Reverend Boatright come to this club where I was playing one night and said, 'Joe, I very seldom come into these places, but I had to get hold of you. I have a young fellow in the parking lot who's too young to come in but he wants to meet you so bad.' He showed me a guitar, and it was a beautiful thing. I'd go over to the garage and he'd be working in dirty old overalls with the few tools he could scrape up. He put over 300 hours into this guitar. Everything on it he made by hand. I still play the first one." Several of its features became standard in the Mosrite line years after its construction, including the M-carved peghead, zero fret, and slanted pickups. In the photo on page 278, note the body sculpting behind the vibrato, and the octave-neck pickup's curving row of polepieces.*]

The second artist was Larry Collins, who was only about 12 years old at the time, and then I started making custom guitars for quite a few of the local musicians. I was also making quite a few necks for Paul Bigsby's guitars, although I've never revealed this in public before. I also did a lot of the inlays in Bigsby's pickguards. This was after he built the guitar for Merle Travis.

I was building about one custom guitar a month and then I moved into the San Fernando Valley outside Los Angeles in 1956 or 1957. I used to get together with Ernie Ball in those days, and we'd have these jam sessions on Sundays. I had just gone through a divorce and I decided to pack up everything and move back to Bakersfield, where my mother lived.

I moved in with Mom and moved my equipment into her little garage on Kentucky Street. I traveled for a few months with an evangelistic group, returned to Bakersfield, and moved out to this little barn in the country where this friend of mine kept all his tractors. I set up a shop there and pretty soon I met Nokie Edwards of the Ventures. I hadn't even heard of the Ventures, even though they were one of the biggest groups in the world.

When Nokie came over, I showed him a guitar that I had just built for Bob Crooks over at Standel. Crooks had asked me to design a guitar that would be as close to a Fender as possible, so all I did [*laughs*] was to take a Fender, flop it over and trace around it. That was the basic idea for what became the Ventures model guitar. It was just an upside-down Fender. I built about 20 guitars for Bob, but Bob had some independent investors and so he and I never got together on a large commercial scale.

Mosrite was famous for its feather-light vibrato. Note "Moseley" at base. Strings were supported by individual rollers.

Nokie Edwards borrowed a guitar from me to take to Hollywood to make a record with the Ventures. He came back and said that they all loved it. He bought that guitar for $200. A few months later I got a call from Stan Wagner, the Ventures' manager. So there I was, this little country boy working out in the barn, and I get a call from the Ventures' manager, and he proposed that we go into business together. I thought he was kidding at first, but when I realized that he was serious, I proposed that the Ventures' organization become the worldwide distributor for Mosrite guitars. They advanced me some money and I went back to Bakersfield and moved into a new location at 1500 P Street. That's where the original Mosrite production factory was. Over the next few months the Ventures advanced me $75,000.

Mosrite was a very big success right off the bat. I went back to Bakersfield and had all this demand for Ventures model Mosrite guitars. We went from 35 instruments a month to 50 to 300. At our peak we had over 100 employees, most or all of them from the Bakersfield area. We leased another factory at 1424 P Street because we had run out of room in our original location. Eventually we moved everything to the second place because it was much bigger.

Around 1963 or 1964, the investors who had bought the Dobro company sold it to me. Dobro was out in Gardena, outside of Los Angeles, at the time. There were a lot of necks and bodies and resonators in the Gardena plant, and we shipped them all to Bakersfield and assembled about 100 or 150 guitars from those old parts. After that we began to make our own Dobro guitars in Bakersfield. The ones from Bakersfield have the serial numbers imprinted on the fingerboard up around the last fret. After we used up the existing stock of resonators we started to spin our own, but the cover plates that we used all the way through our production were left over from the original Gardena stock. I would say that only about ten percent or less of our efforts at the factory were devoted to making resonator guitars.

Celebrity III, circa 1970. ***Gruhn***

CO Mark I Model 300. ***Wild West Music***

After the success of the Ventures models there was a demand for acoustic-electric guitars, so we designed the double-cutaway hollowbody Celebrity series. Other interesting guitars were the Combo and the Joe Maphis; for them we took a solid slab of walnut and routed out the body from behind, and then affixed a flat back after the electronics were installed.

My designs were influenced by Paul Barth, who had a guitar with a carved top and a flat back, and even more so by Roger Rossmeisl [see Fender and Rickenbacker]. The contour on some of my Mosrite guitars might be called a German carve, and this is a technique that I learned from Roger. The top of the guitar is indented a little bit just inside the edge, and then it comes back up to form a carved crest that parallels the shape of the body.

You'll notice a similarity between Acoustic's Black Widow and my Combo. The man who designed Acoustic's Black Widow—I can't recall his name—came up to me one time and said, "Well, I guess you can see where we got the design." He had taken the idea from the Combo. Later on Acoustic asked me to make some of the Black Widows, and I made about 200 of them. These guitars were among the last Black Widows that Acoustic sold.

The Ventures had someone design an amplifier and they asked me to come down and take a look at it. The one that I saw was really good. The Ventures gave me a $5,000 check and I gave them the right to put Mosrite's name on the Mosrite Award amplifier. I did not participate any further in the amplifier production. Almost

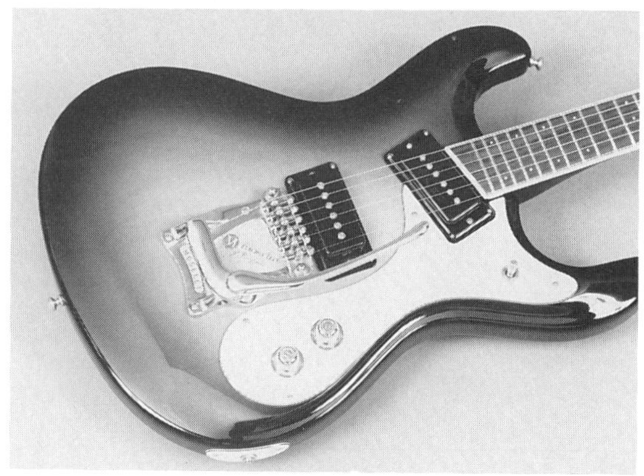

1989 list prices started at $1,898 for this V-89.

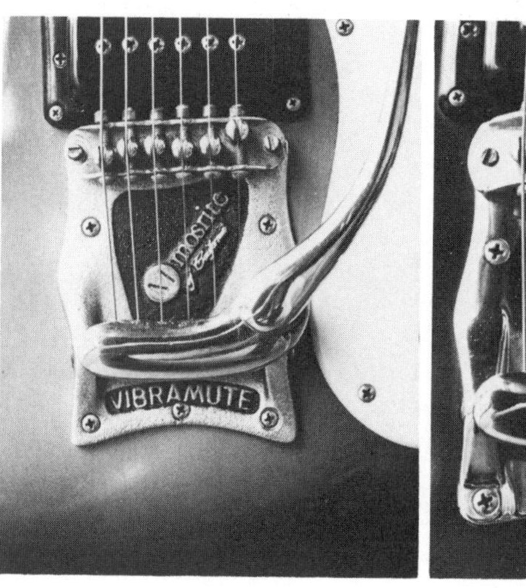

Vibramute (*left*) and Moseley vibrato tailpieces.

every dealer bought from one to a dozen amplifiers, and not one of the amps was any good. That tied up thousands of dollars. The Ventures had a $500,000 line of credit from Crocker National. Their credit was used up, so Crocker shut the Ventures down, and Mosrite Distributing folded. This all took place in the last part of 1968 and the early part of 1969.

I made a very short-lived deal with Vox to be my distributor. They advanced some money and I hung in there for a little while, but it didn't work out. I was getting in deeper and deeper financial trouble, and in 1969 Uncle Sam called me, and I owed him $45,000 in taxes. I was finally shut down on Valentine's Day in 1969 by the factoring agent [one who purchases a company's accounts receivable and assumes the risks of collection in exchange for some discount].

Buck Owens called me about a month later, and he asked me if we should go into business together. We ended up forming the Moseley Musical International company. I designed a red, white, and blue guitar for him, and later he decided that he'd rather have someone else build it. When that Buck Owens deal fell through I went back into gospel concert work, traveling around in a motor home and doing concerts all over the country.

[Note: At about this time, the Dobro name was transferred from Mr. Moseley to OMI, the successor to the Dobro company, through a series of negotiations, the facts of which were later disputed by the principal parties.]

I got together with Bud Ross of Kustom, and a few months later he set me up in business with a $35,000 check. He was going to be the distributor. He ultimately advanced me $100,000 and I set out to build him 200 guitars a month back in the 1424 P Street building. I signed a note to turn over all my work in progress, assets, patents, and trade names in exchange for the advance, but the whole thing didn't work out. The Kustom company was finally taken over by Bud's former sales manager and the note that I had signed was transferred to the new outfit. They wanted the money and I didn't have it, so I was out of business again. I had no operating capital and no place to sell my guitars.

This guitar was built just after the Moseley/Ventures split. *Dennis Maness*

Pacific Music Supply contacted me about this time because they had just lost their Guild account. After the deal with Bud fell

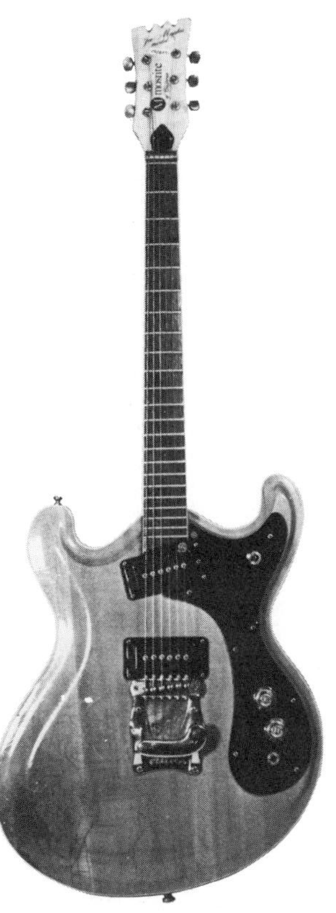

Rick Nielsen's Joe Maphis Mark I. Mosrite also made bass and 12-string versions. *Bob Alford*

The Mark V Model 101, a short-scale size Mosrite with nonadjustable pickups. *Gruhn*

Semie with his late-1980s top of the line, a recreation of his famous Maphis doubleneck ($3,000 to $5,000).

through I went with Pacific in sort of a desperation move to keep some cash flow going, but working through a distributor like that can involve some tragic discounts, so it turned out to be just sort of a tread-water deal and I never did get enough money to really set up for production.

I got me a Greyhound bus, converted it to a motor home, went to Oklahoma, and started touring again. I moved back to Bakersfield in 1976. A number of new guitars had come out and sustain was very important, and I decided to start building again. But again I could not get enough operating capital to really put it into production on a large scale. My new guitar was called the Brass Rail. While I was taking it around to show to people I came across a music store called Hollywood Music down in Los Angeles, and when the owner, Hiro, found out that Semie Moseley was still alive he came up to Bakersfield and said, *"I must have the original Ventures model Mosrite guitar!"* So he fronted me the money to build 12 of them. He sent those to Japan, and then he wanted 50 a month on a regular basis. So I started building the original Ventures models again and sold them all to Hiro, and they all go to Japan, where the Mosrite guitar is incredibly popular. About this time I got very sick, so I moved to Arizona to recuperate. I did a few concerts there and lived in Phoenix for a while. This was 1977.

Hiro specifically requested the Vibra-Mute tailpiece that I'd had on the early Mosrites. I told him that I had carved the mold out of wood and had sandcasted those Vibra-Mutes, but he said that's the kind they wanted in Japan, so I went to a foundry in Bakersfield and we made some molds off of the original Vibra-Mute, and we reproduced 100 of them for Hiro. See, back in the 1960s we had changed from sandcasting to diecasting after we'd gotten some money and got the patents applied for. The new tailpieces said *Moseley,* and the original sandcastings were *Vibra-Mutes.*

1967 D-100 Californian, a short-lived experiment that combined a resonator with a 335-type body. The upper-bout screens were common to all Mosrite/Dobro guitars. *Guitar Player*

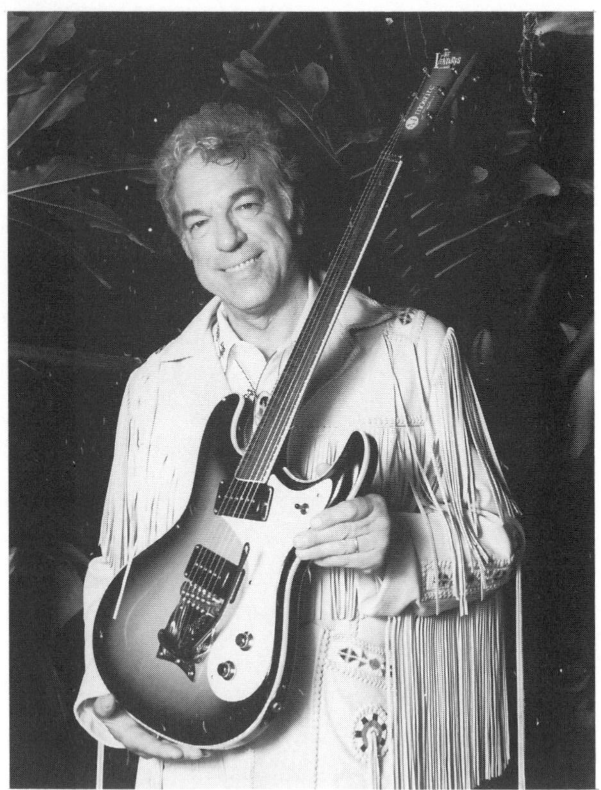

Semie in late 1991 with his latest creation, a sunburst Ventures model with binding.

Well, I had decided that I would never go back into guitar building again, but the people at the foundry were sculptors, and they liked my designs and encouraged me to keep building. All this work turned out to be good therapy for me and I got well. I moved to Carson City, Nevada, and at the present time [1980] we're building about 35 guitars a month for Hiro. But I'm planning to move back to California, either to Bakersfield or to Los Angeles, because Mosrite belongs in California.

1992 Mosrite Update

Semie weathered many storms early in his career, many more in recent years—a car accident that took his leg (it was reattached), persistent colitis, surgery, the forgery of Mosrite guitars by a former employee, and a disastrous factory fire in the abandoned schoolhouse in Jonas Ridge, North Carolina, where Mosrite had relocated in 1982.

But with faith unbroken and against all odds, he persevered. Mosrite now has about a dozen employees producing approximately 20 instruments each month; the half-dozen models include the recent Nokie model, named after Nokie Edwards. Semie reported in 1989 that he looks forward to moving into a new factory that will accommodate an increasing demand, particularly from Japan (where the Ventures and Nokie models are especially popular) and other foreign countries.

MOSSMAN

Stuart Mossman built guitars in his Winfield, Kansas, garage from 1964 to 1969. He then founded the S.L. Mossman Company. After 1,400 guitars had left the factory, a disastrous fire on February 28, 1975, destroyed the entire production line along with most of the work in progress. Local businessmen helped out, and Mossman rallied. The company closed its doors in August 1977 after a disagreement with its distributors. Stuart Mossman then opened a private shop. As of this writing total Mossman production is over 5,000 guitars.

Shown here is one of several incarnations of the Golden Era Custom, with fingerboard inlay pattern inspired by Maurer. The label reveals that it was the 521st Mossman made in 1973, as well as the initials of all the 21 craftsmen who worked on it. *Vintage Fret Shop/A. Caswell*

MUSIC MAN

In March of 1972 Forrest White and Tom Walker founded Music Man, a Southern California company located in Orange County, the original home of K&F, Fender, Rickenbacker, National, and Dobro. Both men were longtime Fender executives, Forrest a vice-president and general manager, Tom a chief salesman. In fact, during the mid 1970s, the Music Man factory much more closely resembled the pre-CBS Fender plant than the CBS/Fender facility, with many seasoned Fender employees working together on the modest production line as they had a decade or two before.

Music Man broke into the instrument market with an immediately successful line of amps, and later introduced a series of solidbody guitars and basses. Leo Fender's company, CLF Research, had an exclusive agreement to build the Music Man instruments. Though several of these feature recent innovations such as internal preamps and phase switches, the classic Fender touch is evident from tuners to tailpiece. For more details, see Leo Fender's interview in the Fender section.

Music Man Sabre II, 1980. Leo Fender's CLF Research company ceased production of Music Man guitars in late 1980.

The Ernie Ball company (see page 40) purchased Music Man's trademarks and designs in 1984, and set up production in the former Earthwood factory in San Luis Obispo, California. While the new owners immediately set about redesigning Music Man guitars, actual production was at first focused exclusively on the basses—not surprising, given those instruments' quality and commercial success. Vice President Sterling Ball explained in late 1989, "We set our quality standards high. Our whole philosophy was, when we can make one model consistently, then we'll make two. So it's taken five and a half years to put together a line of several instruments.

"With the guitars, our objective was to make a lighter model, with a 25½" scale, a shorter string length and a straight string pull on a smaller, 4&2 peghead. We wanted to make it easy to change the pickup without routing out your guitar, and we also designed a better adjusting truss rod." The company reported in 1989 that guitars—the Steve Morse models and the Silhouettes—now accounted for about 40% of the total production. The basses include the Sabre, StingRay, and StingRay 5-string. As we go to press, about 45 employees are working at the San Luis Obispo factory.

In *Guitar Player*'s Dec. 1989 issue, Keith Richards said of the Silhouette, shown here: "It has the opportunity to become . . . one of the classic electric guitars." Its modular pickup assembly and Molex connectors allow a pickup change, without soldering or string removal. Other details: 4&2 headstock (with straight string pull and shorter nut-to-post length), six-bolt neck attachment, 25½-inch scale, and two-octave fingerboard.

Style 4 National Silver guitar, or Chrysanthemum. ***Spitzer's/Sievert***

NATIONAL, DOBRO, AND VALCO

The history of National, Dobro, and Valco is a labyrinthine saga so convoluted and rife with skeletons leaping out of closets that Dickens could have used it for a plot-twisting novel. A tale of two cities, it begins in Los Angeles, where John Dopyera and his associates established the National String Instrument Corporation in late 1925. Dopyera left in late 1927 or 1928 and founded the offshoot Dobro Corporation, Limited. National's company officers the following year included Ted E. Kleinmeyer, president; George Beauchamp (pronounced *Bee-chum*), secretary/general manager; Adolph Rickenbacker, engineer; and Paul M. Barth, vice-president.

Dobro's electric Spanish model was one of America's first production electric guitars, perhaps *the* first, and it was soon followed by cast aluminum lap steels (just who built the first production electric is a matter of dispute; see Rickenbacker). National and Dobro merged in 1931 or 1932, becoming National Dobro, and in the harsh winter of 1936 they moved to Chicago, America's musical instrument manufacturing capital.

John Dopyera.

JOHN DOPYERA AND THE BIRTH OF NATIONAL AND DOBRO

John Dopyera is a Czechoslovakian immigrant who conceived the ampliphonic, or resophonic, guitar, which incorporates one or more stamped or spun metal resonators. He was a cofounder of National and the founder of Dobro, the best known resophonic guitar companies and originators of the models that have set all standards in the field.

Dopyera, his four brothers, and his associates were involved in complicated company histories that were strengthened by family ties but occasionally blemished by distrust and behind-the-back financial maneuvering. National employees would go on during the next half-century to design or to profoundly influence some of the guitars of Rickenbacker, Mosrite, Barth, Magnatone, Supro, Regal, Dobro, Sho-Bro (Gretsch), Mobro (Mosrite), Hound Dog, Dopyera Original, and Original Musical Instruments (OMI).

Rudolph Dopyera. ***John Quarterman***

Other designers have perhaps touched more people with certain phenomenally popular instruments, but few have seen their direct influence filtered through a wider variety of models or more brand names than John Dopyera, the Abraham of the ampliphonic guitar's family tree. Here is Mr. Dopyera's first-person account of the origins of National and Dobro, from an interview with the author, November 1979.

I came to America on the 8th of October, 1908, when I was 15 years and four months old. There were ten of us children all together. The whole family came from Czechoslovakia right straight to Los Angeles.

I had four brothers: Robert, Rudolph [who died in June 1978], Louis, and Emil. Brother Robert and I are the only ones alive now. He was in the guitar business financially, but not as a designer. Rudolph and I, we were the mechanics, and Louis and Robert put money into it. Emil was more on the business side as a salesman and bookkeeper, though later he learned how to make necks and other things. We called him "Ed" for short because he had worked in a place where they had three Emils, and they called him Ed, and we've called him that ever since. *[Note: Emil was born on March 25, 1903, and died on November 24, 1977, in Indio, California, after a long illness.]*

I moved up to Taft, California, where I got the idea for the resonator guitar. I was working on it for years in my mind, but once I started to experiment it took about six weeks to complete the first one. I probably made a couple of barrels of resonators before I made a good one. I tried tin, copper, brass, and various things, but I found that 98 percent pure aluminum gave you the best tone.

I came down to Los Angeles and started the National company with George Beauchamp after meeting him in 1925, I would guess—I can't tell you the date exactly. There has been a lot of arguing and controversy over the last 50 years about Beauchamp and National and me. Let me tell you how we met.

I was repairing instruments [in a shop in Orange County, Southern California], and George came in and wanted a guitar, something like an ampliphonic system, but he really didn't know what that was. He just knew that he wanted something that was louder, and he had seen some kind of ampliphonic violin. He wanted to show that violin to me, but I had already been working on it and had my own ideas and didn't want to see his violin.

Another person who was important was my nephew, Paul Barth [see Rickenbacker, Mosrite, and Magnatone]. I knew that I was going to have to spin resonators out of some kind of metal for the ampliphonic guitars. I didn't know much about spinning, but we had an old lathe in our banjo shop that my brothers and I used to make banjo hoops, and I turned it into a spinning lathe. I was strictly on my own, but I asked Paul Barth to learn how to spin. I had been to three experienced spinners already, and they told me that

Emil (Ed) Dopyera with a stencil used in finishing the Model 60. ***Guitar Player***

what I wanted couldn't be done, and that the metal I wanted to use was too thin. So I kept it in my own family. Paul was only 17 years old when I took him in.

I called in Beauchamp and Barth one day and said, "Boys, she's finished now." Beauchamp played it and couldn't get over it. He just went to pieces loving it. I took him in as a partner because by marriage he had close connections to a lot of money, and we needed an investor to get us going. He had a distant cousin named Ted Kleinmeyer, and Kleinmeyer was very wealthy. I never really learned much about him, but he was the partner with the money. Paul Barth was the fourth partner, so there was Barth, myself, Beauchamp, and Kleinmeyer. Paul was supposed to be a spinner, but he ended up doing a lot of other things, too. I knew how to do it all, but you can't do everything yourself. You've got to have help.

We hired Adolph Rickenbacker right at the beginning. He wasn't a partner or anything; he did the work and got paid for it. Beauchamp and Kleinmeyer knew him for some reason or another. We had about $94,000 worth of dies, and Rickenbacker made most of them. He wasn't a guitar maker. He was a tool and die man there in Los Angeles, located about two blocks down the street from that first National factory. He stamped out the bodies, the tailpieces, and things like that for the metal Nationals. Our first production model was National's Tri-Plate nickel silver ampliphonic guitar. We made about 25 of them by ourselves before Rickenbacker came along.

At the first National factory we had at least 25 men, and after a month or so we were up to 37 men. We started big right away, putting out 50 guitars every day—that was building resonator guitars, and they are more complicated than conventional guitars. Brother Rudy and two helpers were finishing 50 fingerboards a day. We didn't have as many men as some of the big factories but we were building more instruments, so—who knows production? My brother and me.

Louis Dopyera, circa 1930. ***Victor Smith***

Part of the Dopyera clan, circa 1930. (*Front row*) John's parents at right, Louis at far left. Paul Barth third from left. The elder Mr. Barth is seated just behind and to the side of Mrs. Dopyera. *Victor Smith*

I established a basic price of $125 for the plain National. The Chrysanthemum [Style 4] was Beauchamp's idea, and it had too much engraving and cost too much to do, and all that engraving hurt the tone. My wife and I designed the Lily of the Valley [Style 3]. It only cost us $25 or $30 to engrave, but it sold for about $160 compared to the Chrysanthemum, which was $185.

Some of those very big companies almost went broke on account of me. The Depression was at its worst. The country was at its lowest ebb, and the other guitar companies couldn't do anything. Jazz was coming in. Players wanted a louder sound, and my silver guitar was seven times louder than anything else, and we couldn't make them fast enough. Guy Hart [*Gibson's general manager*] came to see us twice. We took him out to dinner—15 dollars a plate—and he wanted to see our factory. He asked us to come to Gibson. He was going to give us a whole floor, but we were already selling everything we could make, so we stayed where we were.

George and I split up. Somebody was telling a lot of people that he was the inventor, and that was ridiculous. There were some financial things, too—fights about spending our money on inventions that were never going to be built. This is all water under the bridge. Let's just say that George and I disagreed about everything—business, money, patents.

I finally told George that I was going to quit if he didn't change, but he just laughed. Well, it got worse, so I left. [*Note: Adolph Rickenbacker painted a very different picture of Mr. Beauchamp in his interview; see Rickenbacker.*]

I split off and started the Dobro company in 1928. At the time I left National I already had the Dobro plate [*resonator*] in mind. Rudolph helped me along with that too. According to the papers and patents, Rudolph was the inventor, but he really wasn't. I was still legally with National and didn't want the new ideas to go to them, because I could see that things were getting worse. If I put my patents in my own name, National would get the rights to them, so I put them in Rudolph's name. There's a thing called *shop rights,* and they say that your company gets your ideas. I didn't design the Dobro at National—I made it at home—but I was afraid that someone might say that I had made it at National. It's been over 50 years since I designed it, and no one's improved on it yet.

Dobro electric guitar and amp, circa 1930. *John Quarterman*

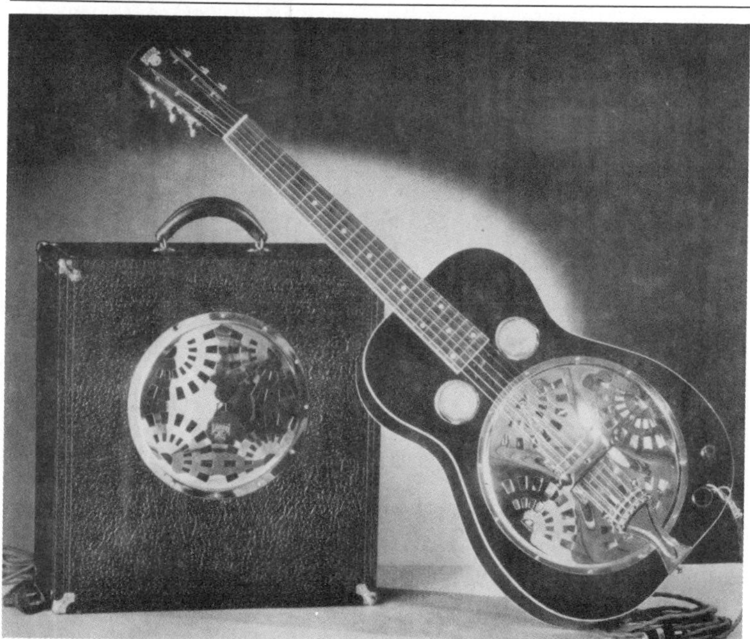

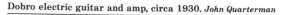

After I left National and started Dobro, Beauchamp, Paul, and Paul's father ran the National company. They were having some trouble until Paul's father stepped in. They had some fights about the stock, and some of the stockholders wanted to get Beauchamp out, and they sold National stock to my brother Louis. Then George was sort of ousted. When brother Louis had a majority of the stock, Dobro and National merged. The brothers were together again.

When National and Dobro merged in around 1932 I left the company. I was still there helping out but no longer in the partnership. I wanted to work on my ampliphonic violin, and I spent 20 months on it. I also had a little store on 59th and Hoover in Los Angeles, doing some repairs. We sold Regal some parts while I was still there at Dobro, so the connection between Regal and Dobro goes back to at least 1931 or so.

Paul Barth and George Beauchamp worked on this little electric Hawaiian guitar that was called the Frying Pan later on because of its shape. Paul and George owed Mr. Rickenbacker several thousand dollars for his work for National, and they took their guitar to him to see if he would build it, and he said, "Well, I'll build it, but it's going to be called the Rickenbacker guitar." Paul and George designed that Frying Pan, and I really can't tell you more than that. I don't know who had the first idea for that guitar, because I was already out of National by that time. It may have been Beauchamp and Paul and Rickenbacker all together; I don't know.

Me, I'm always thinking of these new things. I have a new patent right now for a double-resonator Hawaiian guitar. You should hear it. It's brand new, and it supersedes all the others. This new Hawaiian guitar of mine flows like a river.

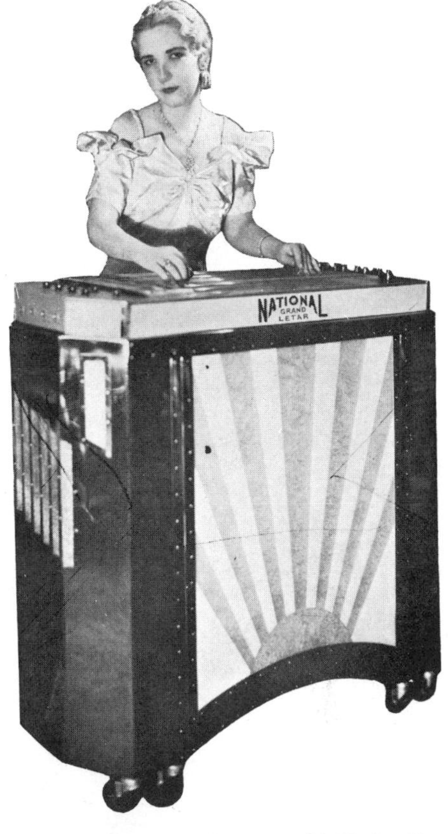

Teacher Letritia Kandle poses with National's Grand Letar console steel.

Left: **cast-aluminum Dobro Electric Hawaiian Guitar (no other model name), one of America's first electric guitars. The 7-string version (*center*) was available for an extra $5. These models were followed by the 26-fret guitar (*right*).**

John Quarterman

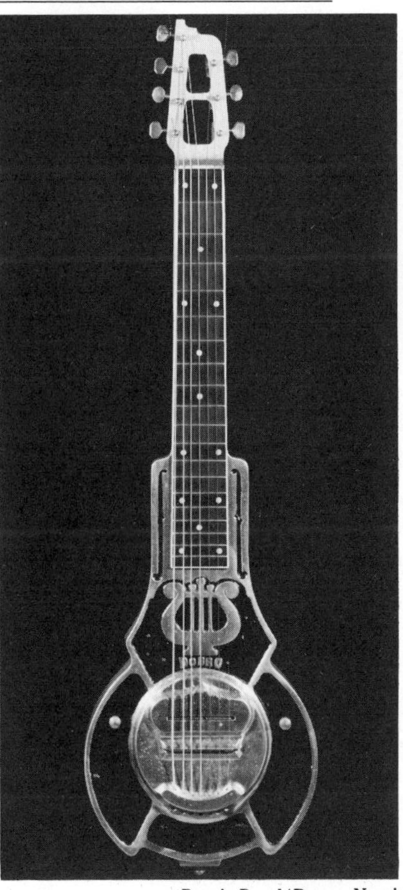

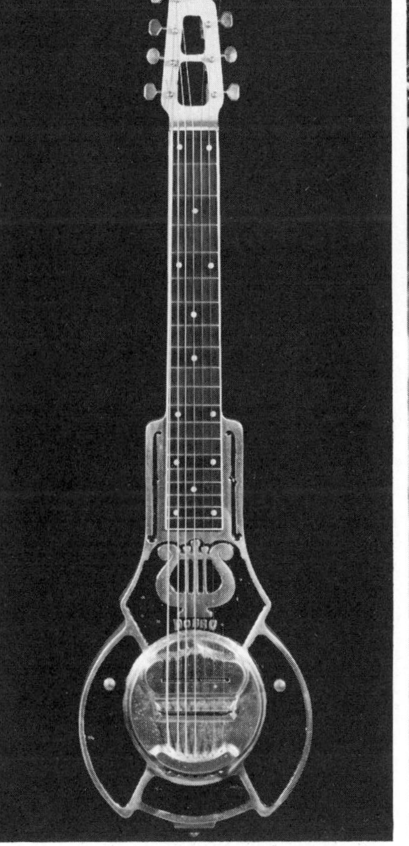

Bernie Pearl/Danny Norrie

Acuff

SOME IMPORTANT DATES, 1930–1944

The following is a list of formal announcements distributed to the industry through trade periodicals; the dates are approximate, often following the actual event by a year or so.

April 1930: CMI becomes National's exclusive central states distributor.
March 1935: National Dobro publicizes its recent move into new, enlarged facilities at 6920 McKinley, Los Angeles.
June 1935: Dobro's dissolution—for some time a fait accompli—is formally announced: "All products to be manufactured henceforth by the National Dobro Corp."
January 1936: Chicago branch office opens.
February 1936: the move to Chicago accelerates.
March 1936: new Supro electric guitar and amp announced.
March 1937: National Dobro, still legally based in Los Angeles, wins a patent infringement suit against Schireson Bros., Los Angeles, makers of Schibro resonator guitars.
July 1937: in this transition period "Chicago & Los Angeles" is sometimes given as the address; "VioLectric" electric violin of 1936 is formally introduced.
August 1937: Regal gains exclusive rights to manufacture Dobros; the Letar Hawaiian guitars are announced.
August 1941: CMI becomes exclusive nationwide distributor for National.
October 1943: the change to the Valco name is formally announced.
May 1944: Valco moves to new quarters at 4700 West Walton Street, Chicago.
June 1944: CMI takes over Dobro distribution.

NATIONAL RESONATOR GUITARS: GENERAL

When one is trying to get a grip on the sometimes confusing National line, it helps to keep in mind four categories of features: body (either metal or wood), neck shape (squared Hawaiian, or rounded Spanish), the ampliphonic system (either single-plate or Tri-Plate), and the neck/body joint (twelfth or fourteenth; 12-fret bodies look more bell-like, with rounded, sloping shoulders). Among Tri-Plates, square-neck Hawaiian lap models are more common, while among single-resonator guitars, round-neck models are more common. Most squarenecks had metal bodies extending all the way along the neck in back, although a few of the last ones actually had squared, wooden necks. Most or all Spanish Tri-Plates were 12-fret models.

NATIONAL TRI-PLATES

The first Nationals were called Triple Resonator guitars, National Silver guitars, or Tri-Plates and were available in either Hawaiian or Spanish models. Made of German silver (also called nickel silver, a silver-white alloy of copper, zinc, and nickel), the Tri-Plates could be ordered in any of four styles differentiated by their ornamentation. Style 1 was plain without much trim. Style 2 was known as the Wild Rose or Wild Irish Rose, while the fancier Style 3 was unofficially termed

Music Shop/Madsen

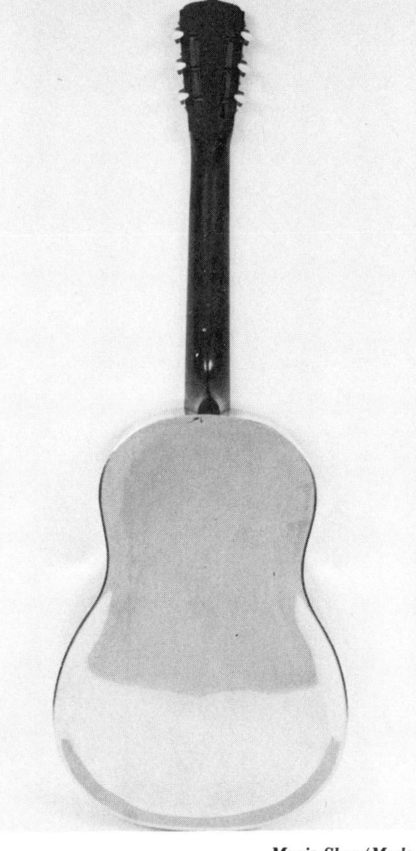

Music Shop/Madsen

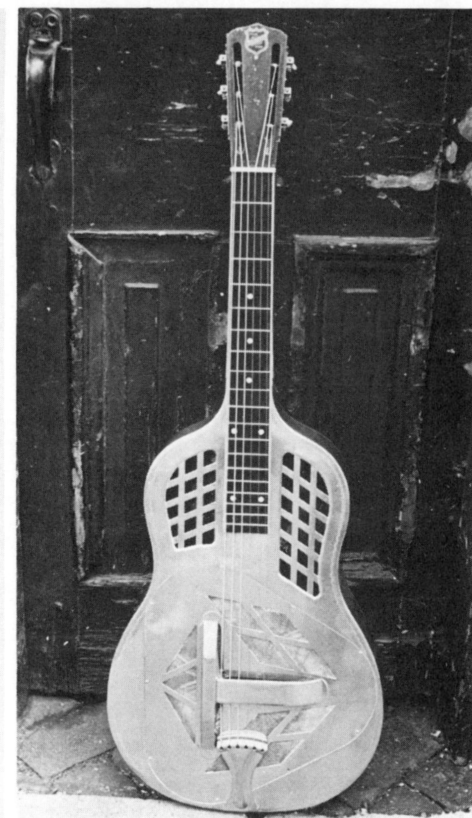

Fred's Music/Fred Bernardo

National Style 1 Spanish (*left* and *center*) and Hawaiian guitars. Note plain, unengraved bodies.

Lily of the Valley. The most ornate member of the line was the heavily engraved Style 4, or Chrysanthemum. The Tri-Plate's three interior resonators were 6-inch spun cones arranged in a triangle, two on the bass side, one on the treble. Their peaks were joined by a T-shaped bridge support.

Mid-thirties Tri-Plates included Style 4 ($195; the last remnant of the original line), Model 35 ($135; nickel silver body with an etching of a Renaissance musician under a willow tree), and the Style 97 (a budget model at $97.50; surf rider etching on a nickel-plated body of brass alloy).

SINGLE-RESONATOR NATIONALS

National's single-cone design came out about two years after the initial Tri-Plates. Instead of three small resonators it had one large one with a circular wooden bridge support, or "biscuit," mounted at the peak; the biscuit can be seen beneath the cover plate.

Style O and Triolian were National's first 6-string guitars with the new design. The Triolian ($47.50) was essentially a Duolian (see below) with a better quality neck and a bound fingerboard. The stock color was brown sunburst, though models with stencilled tropical motifs also appeared (see the photo on page 296, a light-colored Triolian). Like the Duolian, the Triolian evolved into a solid-peghead, 14-fret version. A popular trim package included a simulated wood grain, or "piano finish."

The late-1930s Triolian had a pickguard decorated with wide diagonal stripes and the National *N*, a motif also used on the

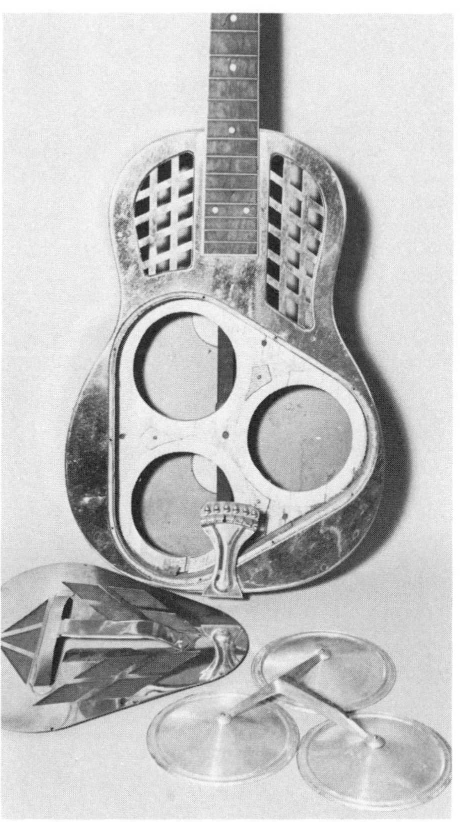

Disassembled Tri-Plate.

Style 2 had a rose motif.

Mid-1930s Style O, 12-fret neck. This type of cover plate was used through the early 1940s. ***Honest Ron's***

Early-1930s Style O. ***Chris Kondrath/Jeff Purcell***

Triolian mandolins, electric Spanish arch-tops, tenors, electric tenors, and electric mandolins.

The late-1920s Style O, a companion to the Triolian, was a very plain, $85 12-fret guitar with a single 10-inch resonator. The early-1930s version ($65) is much better known, with its Hawaiian lagoon, palm trees, clouds, volcanoes, and stars. (Supposedly etchings, these designs were actually sandblasted. The scenery varied, as the photos show.) The Style O had a brass alloy body available in round-neck and square-neck versions. Details of the late-1930s Style O included a 14-fret mahogany neck, an ebony fingerboard bound with celluloid, thin rectangular markers, a solid peghead, and upper f-holes.

The Duolian (circa 1930, $35), National's next single-cone model, had a 12-fret neck and a GI type galvanized look that ranged from light gray to dark greenish black (a few were walnut colored). The peghead was slotted, and the upper bouts had f-holes. The cover plate sometimes had four ribs running from center to rim.

Style O, 12-fret (*left* and *center*) and 14-fret (*right pair*). Compare pegheads, neck/body joints, markers, bodies, coverplates, and decoration. [*Note: 12-fret and 14-fret refer to the neck/body joint's location.*]

An unusual 1928 wood-body Triolian with a yellow paint job and blue- and red-tinged decals. Note that the Triolian is a single-resonator guitar and not a Tri-Plate. *Mike Smith*

An updated version appeared circa 1934 with a 14-fret neck, restyled f-holes, a more square-shouldered body, and a solid peghead. Note that the cover plates on both models had nine diamond shaped clusters of small holes, although at least some late-1930s models had five larger clusters and black pickguards. Available in both Hawaiian and Spanish necks, the Duolian became one of National's most popular instruments.

The wood-body National Trojan was an unusual guitar, an exception to the rule that most Nationals have metal bodies and most Dobros have wooden ones. (To keep the categories sufficiently confusing, there are also metal Dobros.) The Trojan and the less expensive Rosita (also a wooden National) appeared in 1933 to compete with the Dobros. Costing $37.50 in 1936, the Trojan was similar in appearance to the Triolian, with a celluloid-bound mahogany neck (Spanish or Hawaiian), a mahogany-colored body, and a nickel-plated resonator cover plate.

The 1936 catalogue of the National Dobro Corporation (400 South Peoria Street, Chicago) offered the following resophonic instruments: Style 4, Model 35, Style 97, Style O, Triolian, Trojan, Duolian, four tenor guitars (Style 3, Model 97, Style O,

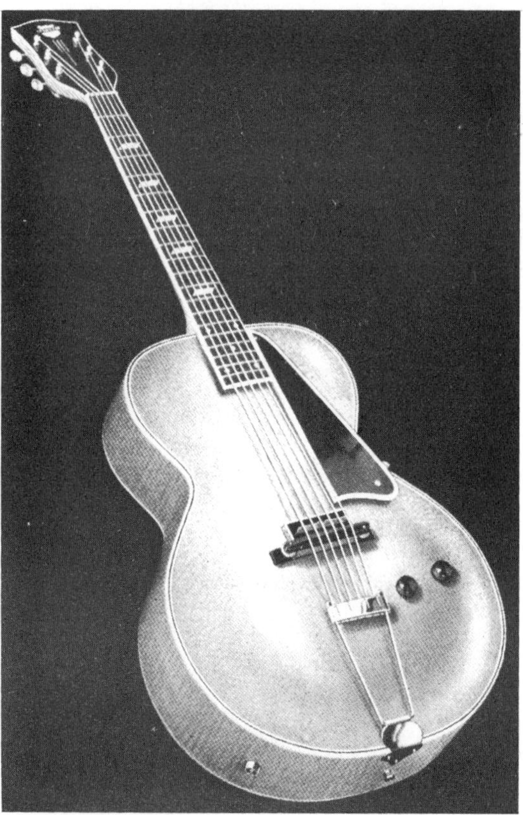

Early-1940s National New Yorker—no f-holes.

Dario Bonetti's guitar is an early-1940s National Sonora. Note clear pickguard. *Al Frost*

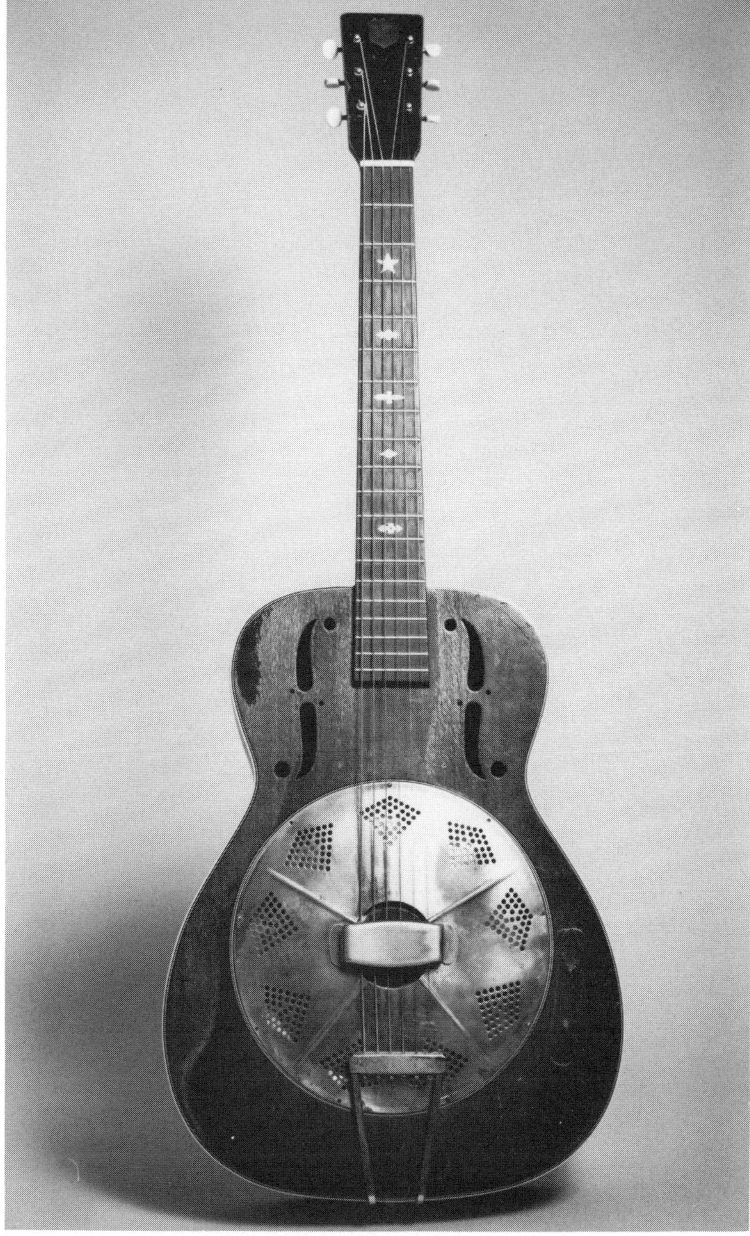

National Estrelita, serial no. 041. *Charley's/Crump*

National El Trovador. *Spitzer's/Sievert*

Triolian), four mandolins (Style 3, Model 97, Style O, Triolian), three ukuleles (Style 3, Triolian, Style O), the VioLectric violin, the New Yorker Hawaiian lap steel (in 6-, 7-, and 8-string models), the $75 Electric Spanish arch-top (with a giant pickup, an oversized peghead, f-holes, a striped pickguard, a maple back, a spruce top, and a seven-ply neck), an electric mandolin, and an electric tenor arch-top. A 15-watt amp with a 12-inch speaker was also depicted.

National's 1938–1939 catalogue listed 15 models of Spanish and Hawaiian guitars, including: Havana, Style O, Marino, Artist Model No. 3, Aragon, New Yorker Spanish, New Yorker Hawaiian, Sonora, Grand Console, and several Supro models—the Arcadia, Collegian, Avalon Spanish, Avalon Hawaiian, No. 60, and No. 70. The company began to emphasize electric arch-tops and Hawaiian lap steels more and more, and the 1940 cat-

Late-1940s National Aristocrat. Note cord.

Gruhn/Baxendale

Music Shop/Madsen

Duolians. From left: 1932 type, 1932–1933 type, post-1933 model. Compare pegheads, neck/body joints, and bodies. The slotted peghead is generally older than the solid type, though slotted heads appear on both 12- and 14-fret models. Note that the model on the right has no ribs on its cover plate.

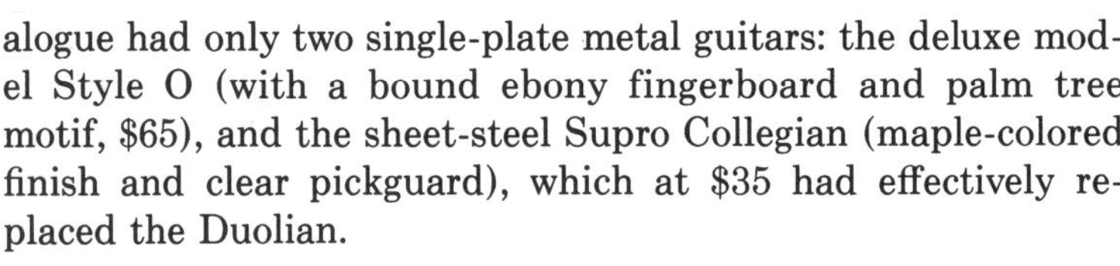

alogue had only two single-plate metal guitars: the deluxe model Style O (with a bound ebony fingerboard and palm tree motif, $65), and the sheet-steel Supro Collegian (maple-colored finish and clear pickguard), which at $35 had effectively replaced the Duolian.

Most Nationals had metal bodies, but this wooden Trojan was an exception. It cost $37.50 in 1936.

DOBRO RESOPHONIC GUITARS

The Dobro is a single-resonator ampliphonic guitar that is easily confused at first glance with single-plate Nationals, but in fact there are fundamental differences in construction theory. The Dobro resonator is dish-shaped (almost the opposite of the volcano-shaped National cone), though its center portion sticks up. The result is something like a sailor's hat, dipping down around the sides and coming back up in the center. The Dobro spider is an eight-legged bridge support that spans the dish and conducts string vibrations (compare the National biscuit).

The pages from Dobro's first illustrated catalogue of 1928–1929 depict a nine-member line of resonator instruments: a uke, two mandolins, three tenor guitars, and three 6-strings. The model designations were sensibly assigned. For example, the 45T tenor and 45G guitar were similarly appointed, and both cost $45. The other two guitars were the Model 37G and the 27G.

A later Dobro flyer includes artist endorsement photos that show off an expanded line of resonator guitars, ukes, tenors,

Aug. 16, 1932 R. DOPYERA 1,872,633

STRINGED MUSICAL INSTRUMENT

Filed June 29, 1929 2 Sheets-Sheet 2

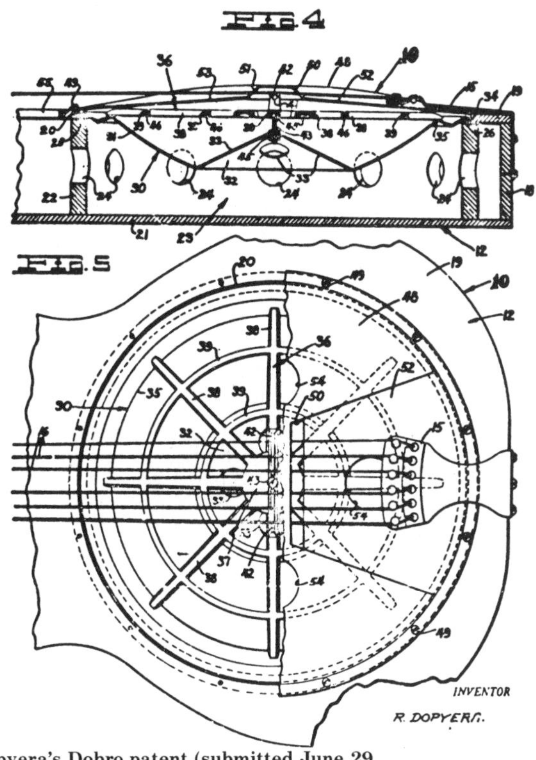

John Dopyera's Dobro patent (submitted June 29, 1929) was filed in his brother Rudy's name.

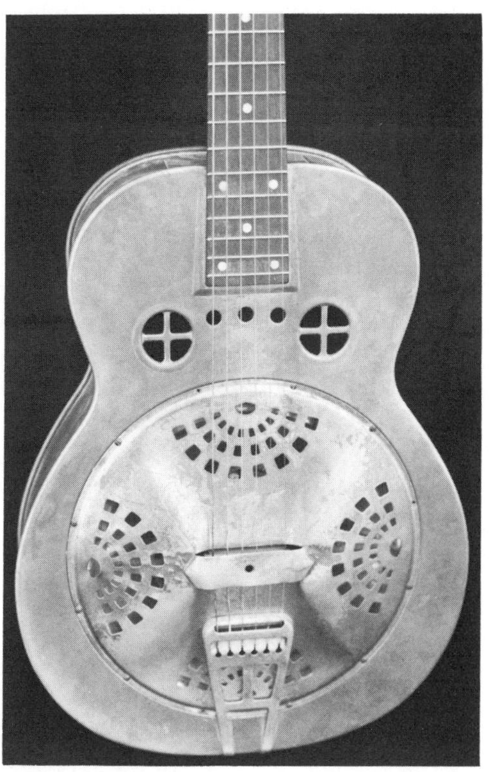

Dobro Model M 14.

mandolins, and banjos. Also shown is the astounding Dobro stand-up bass, a huge, guitar-shaped contraption with three circular soundholes on each upper bout and a resonator as big as a manhole cover—a veritable brontosaurus in American guitar's La Brea tar pits.

Most Dobros had wooden bodies, but there were exceptions. The tops and backs of metal-body Dobros were fastened to the sides with a unique method that required no soldering. The resulting lip around the edges gave rise to the name Violin Edge or, as it was known around the factory, "fiddle edge." The midthirties fiddle edge came in several styles, all with distinctive window-like soundholes in the upper bouts; the M 14 (brass alloy body, very little engraving, rosewood fingerboard, pearl-inlaid Dobro name on headstock, $67.50); M 15 (like the M 14 but with engraved German silver body, $95); M 16 (like the M 15 but with ebony fingerboard and more elaborate engraving, including a large Dobro crest on the back, $135) and No. 62 (plated brass, etched and engraved Spanish dancer/garden scene, $62.50). There were two budget models, No. 32 (sheet metal painted with yellowish brown sunburst, no engraving, $32.50) and No. 46, an all-aluminum guitar known as a Dobrolite or Luma-lite, $45.

The original Dobro Angelus, circa 1928, was a budget guitar ($22.50) made of three-ply birch finished in two-tone walnut. It had a spun cone, real binding, a cover plate with 12 holes arranged in a circle, f-holes on the upper bout, a long-pronged

The Angelus, or Model 19, was a resophonic guitar built by both Dobro and Regal. *John Quarterman*

spider, a slotted headstock, and a neck that joined the body at fret 12. Regal's version, shown here, was constructed with Dobro parts. It appeared in 1934 and continued in the line for six years. It was distinguished from Dobro's Angelus by its stamped (rather than spun) cone, short-pronged bridge, orange and brown finish, and painted, simulated binding. Regal made both 12- and 14-fret models.

Mid-1930s National arch-top electric. Note split-bar pickup and odd f-holes. *Levon Willis*

A pair of very early cast-aluminum lap steels by National. *Ax-In-Hand*

NATIONAL, DOBRO, AND VALCO
by Victor Smith and Al Frost

Victor Smith and Al Frost go way back. To them, Leo Fender was a newcomer. Victor joined the Dobro Company at its inception, and Al followed in 1934. Along with Louis Dopyera they bought out Dobro's successor (the National Dobro Corporation) and formed the Valco Company. Valco, named after the initials of its founders' first names—Victor, Al, and Louis—continued to make Nationals, Dobros, and several other brands. Victor claims to have made the first commercial electric Spanish guitar—a Dobro—and also to have invented the string-driven pickup (as opposed to the wrap-around horseshoe magnet type).

In the following first-person accounts, Victor discusses his first electric guitar, the mechanical differences between Nationals and Dobros, and details concerning the very early cast aluminum lap steels. Both men explain how their instruments were built and recount the history of National and Dobro—the split, the merger, the move to Chicago, the transformation into Valco, and the war years. With remarkable detail they illuminate the Chicago-based American guitar manufacturing community of the 1930s and 1940s, of which they were prominent members (Al was president of NAMM, the National Association of Music Merchants). They discuss the dizzying commercial intersections of many companies and brand names, including Valco, National, Dobro, Supro, Gibson, Harmony, Kay, Regal, Stella, Silvertone, CMI, Sears, and others.

Victor: When I first met Emil Dopyera, he had a music store up around Porterville in California, not too far from Bakersfield. Louis and Bob were in Taft. They had an auto parts place. Rudolph and John were in Los Angeles. Several of the brothers made great contributions, but the whole thing really goes back to John. He was the chief designer. He was responsible for the stock in trade of both National and Dobro. John and Rudy were making resonator banjos before the Depression and they got together one day and said, "If this'll work on a banjo, why can't we make it work on a guitar?" A banjo resonator is a dish, but their idea was to turn the thing over and make sort of a cone out of it. In the banjo resonator, everything works from the bottom up; now they were working from the top down. This idea was the basis of their first guitar designs, which led to the formation of National in Los Angeles.

I met John when we were both taking degree work in the Masonic Lodge. I was a cabinet maker, working in a furniture plant. I was 21. John told me, "We've had this disagreement with some of the people in National, so three of us—Emil, Rudy, and myself—are pulling out to go on our own." See, 50 years ago, people worked together. Today there's jealousy and competition, but back in the old days you stuck by your family, and everything was out in the open. You had to stick together to get by. That's what made America great. It really was.

But a split came, not between the brothers—they stayed close all along, though they did divide up from a financial viewpoint. Here's what happened. George Beauchamp and some of the sales people tried to take over the company. I heard about it many times from all of the brothers. Two of them, Louis and Robert, kept up their financial interest in National. Louis had a controlling interest, and he kept it all the way through; he was the main businessman in both companies.

The new company was called Dobro. That word is short for Dopyera Brothers, *Do-Bro,* but it also means "good" in Czech, so they were making "good" guitars. I joined the company right then. That was in late 1928 or early 1929.

Dobro started in the back room of the Russell Plating Company on Flower Street in Los Angeles. Mr. Russell did all the plating work on the metal guitars. We got to know him because he had been doing the German silver for National, and he kept doing it for both companies. Russell rented a little room back there to us. It was probably 50 by 60 feet, just a little place. We built the wooden bodies and necks for the Dobros in that room—fingerboards, too. National was over there about seven miles from our first plant, and there was always plenty of communication between the two companies. They thrived, and we thrived.

In order to get the company going John had to come up with a new product that would sustain another patent claim, and the Dobro was entirely different from the National. On the Dobro, since it was a dish, John needed something to straddle the space and to support the bridge, and this was done with an eight-legged piece he called the spider. The top of the guitar was machined out. Rickenbacker did that. He was a very sharp boy. He could really roll that metal around. A wooden bridge went in a groove in the spider to give it a nice mellow tone.

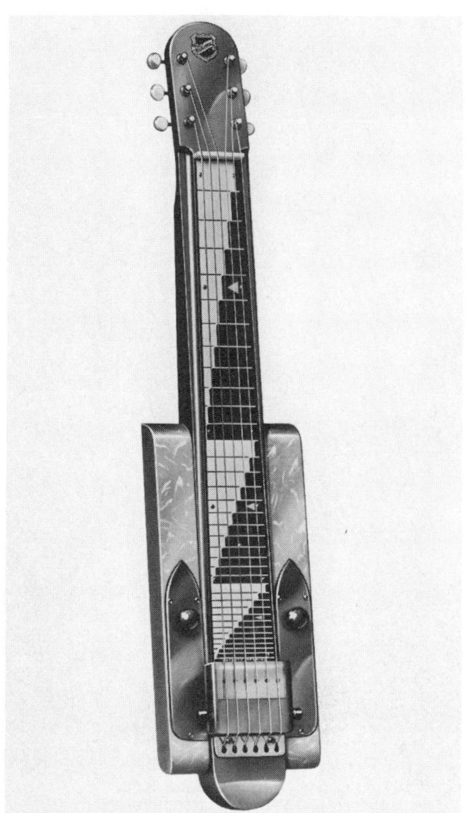

National Dynamic, 1949, "Focused Power" pickup. ***Victor Smith***

National aluminum lap steel, amp, and electric Spanish guitar. The amp employs a resonator coverplate for a speaker grille. ***Gruhn***

Silvertone resophonic model, made by National and sold by Sears; brass body. ***Music Shop/Madsen***

Hawaiian guitar star Sol Hoopii gave National (and later Rickenbacker) valuable exposure.

John Quarterman

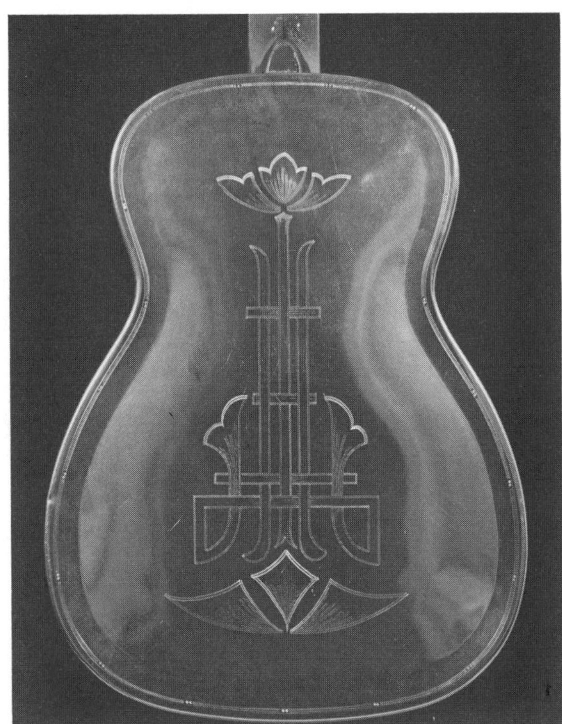

Custom-engraved metal resonator guitar made by National, rear detail. *Bernie Pearl/Danny Norrie*

In the National the supporting well floats, so to speak, and the resonator is supported from the top panel only. The Dobro soundwell, or ring, attaches to both the top and the back, and the cone sits inside this ring. The ring looks sort of like a deep tambourine and has round holes all around it to distribute the sound. *[Note: Many or most f-hole Dobros and some Regal Dobros do not have soundwells.]*

The Dobro resonators were made out of spun aluminum. We would get the blank disks from Rickenbacker or from a mill, and then John would do the spinning. He experimented for months on different ways to do it, and I did some myself. Later on, Rickenbacker stamped out the resonators, but in the early years John did the spinning for both National and Dobro. He'd have a wooden cone that screwed right into a lathe. He would get the center of the blank disk and punch a hole there. A pin would hold it in place, and then the lathe would spin it. John used a special tool for every little crease in the resonator, and he would make the aluminum follow the wooden form. By using these hand tools and the lathe, he'd turn that flat disk into a cone. Basically the idea was like a speaker—that resonating cone had to be flexible so that it could move frontwards and backwards, creating sound waves.

Rudolph made just about all the equipment. You couldn't buy those machines. There was a shaper machine that you could get—it would cut out a groove for the celluloid binding—but Rudolph made the sanders and all the rest. Emil had had experience selling Nationals, so he knew all the jobbers from coast to coast. As a rule, in a small town you only had one National distributor and then one Dobro distributor.

Pretty soon we outgrew that little room behind Russell's, so the three brothers got a man to build a new factory on 62nd Place, also in southern Los Angeles, just north of the Goodyear plant. We moved out there and had about five times the room. Everything looked great. We hired more people. We liked the new factory. And then the crash came, the Great Depression. This was late 1929.

You have to understand what the Depression was like. When I think of it, it still scares the pants off me, and it was 50 years ago. Believe me, if you go through something like that, you don't forget it. You had to work a couple of jobs just to get by, and jobs were hard to get. Times were so tough that the brothers didn't have money for the payroll. They asked if anyone would take stock in the corporation rather than the paycheck. I was the only one who took stock in Dobro, so this put me in a little different position. Now I had a real stake in the future of the company.

I began to work on electronics in my spare time. When I joined up they were making only resonator guitars—no electrics—but people still wanted a louder sound and everybody knew that electric guitars were going to be the thing of the future. Trouble was, nobody knew how to build one.

There were electric guitars before mine, but they didn't work. Most of them were based on using units from telephones, phonographs, or microphones. The pickups before mine were based on the idea that a *polepiece* would break the magnetic flux, just like in a telephone. The polepiece would stick right through the bridge. But I thought—you didn't talk into this thing like a telephone; the string had to be free to vibrate and to distort the magnetic flux.

Many times in 1930 and 1931 we would take a piece of paper and some filings from the grinder and put a magnet under there and watch those filings dance around like they do. We'd study the flux patterns. They'd flare out and in some spots actually *stand up.* So I thought, why not go up there, *above* the pickup, above the magnet, and break that flux with the string itself? This was different from the Rickenbacker pickup, which wrapped around the strings on both the top and bottom. You don't see that kind today.

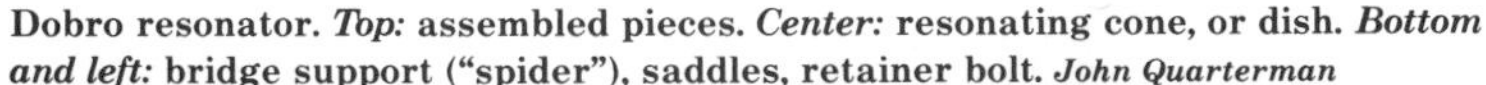

Dobro resonator. *Top:* assembled pieces. *Center:* resonating cone, or dish. *Bottom and left:* bridge support ("spider"), saddles, retainer bolt. ***John Quarterman***

Attaching the bridge saddle to supporting spokes, or "spider."

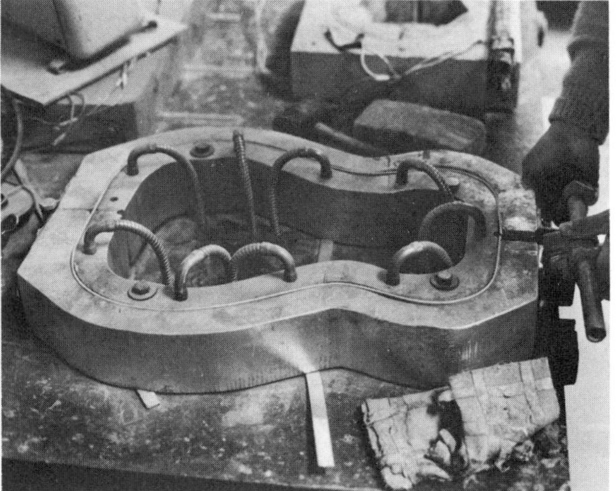

Bending sides in a body mold at the Dobro plant. The metal hoses attach to heating elements.

Dobro bodies await installation of resonators; note placement of sound rings.

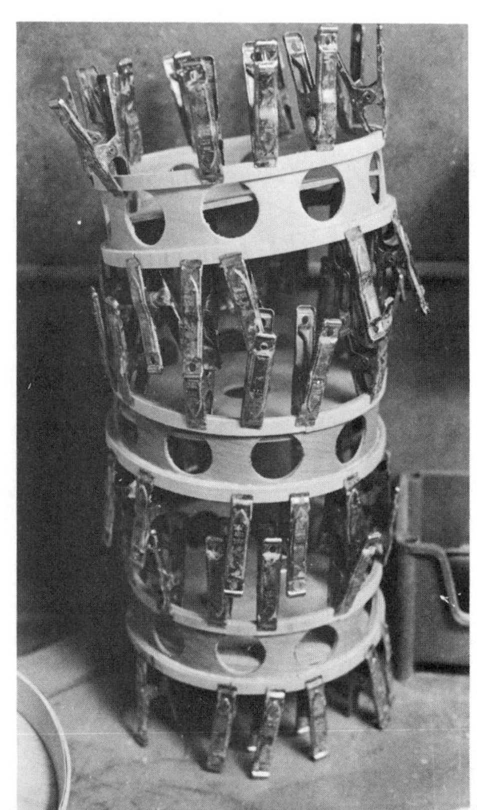

Now here's a problem: This little bitty treble E isn't going to get heard compared to the heavy, wrapped bass string. Well, we got around that by having individual polepieces, one for each string. *[Note: Herb Sunshine claims credit for developing the first pickup with individually adjustable polepieces; see Epiphone. Also see the Leo Fender interview.]*

There were no other electric guitars on the market when the first electric Dobro came out, although people were doing things like sticking a microphone in front of a guitar or sticking one inside it. Now, you're going to hear that Rickenbacker was the first, or at least I've heard it, but we were there first. I don't know when their patent was done, but we were on the market first. The patent doesn't really matter all that much anyway. We had many ideas that we never patented. There's some things about National that I don't know, and I don't mind saying so, but I do know what was on the market, and I know that my guitar was built before the Frying Pan. That I know, because I was there. Another confusing thing is that Paul Barth, who worked on that first Rickenbacker Frying Pan, was also tied up with National.

Well, with Beauchamp gone, and with the Depression having really hurt both companies, the brothers decided to get back together and pool their resources. The companies merged in 1931 or 1932. We had to buy another building, and we'd only been in that enlarged Dobro plant on 62nd Place for a couple of years. Our new place was on McKinley Street. Louis and Bob Dopyera bought it for us.

The first guitar that had my pickup on it was a Dobro Spanish guitar. We put the electric unit in with the resonator so that a musician could have a combination. *[Note: Rudy Dopyera told researcher John Quarterman on numerous occasions that he was working on the aluminum lap steels in 1930. Quarterman reports that the aluminum bodies were definitely not made in the Rickenbacker metal shop; rather they were the product of a method called slush-casting, and were made by a Los Angeles machinist.]* My pickup was patented in Rudy's name—they called it shop rights—but I didn't mind, because I was in the corporation. I had a piece of it, and I had a good job. It was still plenty hard to get jobs in those days, so we all worked together and we didn't care whose name the patent was in.

There were no electric Nationals before the merger, but after the companies joined back up, everybody thought it would be a good idea to make National electrics as well as Dobro electrics. Rudy designed the cast aluminum lap steel Hawaiian guitars, and I designed the others. The National electrics had my pickups in them.

When we merged I became vice-president, and the company became known as the National Dobro Corporation. I would say we had about 15 or 20 people. We were making resonator guitars under both the National and Dobro names, and electrics—both Hawaiian and Spanish—under both names. After the merger we were in that McKinley Street plant for a couple more years, and then we moved to Chicago.

Al: After my mother died my dad married Valeria Dopyera, one of the sisters. I joined Dobro in 1934, when they were called National Dobro. There was some friction between the original National and

A stack of sound rings, held together with clips while the glue dries. Early Dobro sound rings had smaller holes. Some were made with parallelogram-shaped holes, but the dies were lost circa 1939.

Dobro crews. There always is in that kind of situation—who's the fastest worker in a certain kind of assembly operation, and so on.

Victor: We moved to Chicago for two reasons. We were heavily into electronics, and all the tubes and transformers were made back East. We knew we'd save a lot of money if we could be closer to the raw materials source. The other reason was that Chicago was the center of the music industry. Gibson was nearby, and Chicago had the big distributors, like Chicago Musical [CMI], Targ & Dinner, Tonk Bros., and the rest. Most of the guitar factories were located there—Regal, Kay, Harmony, and others. There were some accessory manufacturers like John Kluson, and also the big mail-order houses like Sears and Montgomery Ward.

Al: The move to Chicago—I remember it very well. It was February of 1936, that awful winter when Lake Michigan almost froze completely over. We all piled into a Graham Paige. We came across at Texarkana, and the Mississippi River was frozen. Oh, that was a winter. Vic Smith and his wife and Emil and a fellow by the name of Harry Gersten—he was sales manager at the time—we all piled into that wonderful car and set out for Chicago.

Victor: When we moved, the Dopyera brothers were still active in the company, but they didn't all go back to Chicago. Louis and Bob were still involved in the financial end, and Louis did take some trips back there in the beginning. Emil went back and rented some space on Peoria and Van Buren. That was the old Addressograph building, well known in Chicago. He rented space on the third or fourth floor, and we set up an assembly line. Then I went out and hired all my technicians in Chicago.

The only one I brought with me from Los Angeles was Al Frost, a young boy out of junior college in Pasadena. Emil stayed there in Chicago, got an apartment, and hired a salesman to help him out. John stayed in California. Rudy made a few trips but stayed in California as well.

1930 Dobro 45G with spruce top. ***John Quarterman***

The unusual upper soundholes gave rise to the nickname "Cyclops" for these Dobros. All were built in 1931 or 1932, the switch from the original (*left*) to the oval, twin-hole design occurring in late 1931.

Late-1930s Regal-Dobro Artist model. The Professional had a similar peghead and less body engraving, while the Leader had a very plain peghead, dot markers, and an unengraved body. Note the ribs in the upper soundholes. ***Gruhn/Baxendale***

Al: When we got to Chicago the kingpins of the industry were Freddie Martin [of Martin], Jay Kraus [Harmony], Guy Hart [Gibson], and Hank Kuhrmeyer [Kay]. We gradually moved more and more of our operation from California, and I'd say by 1939 the whole thing was in Chicago.

Victor: We moved from upstairs in the Addressograph building on Peoria Street down to the main floor, and put in a lot of heavy equipment. When we outgrew that place, we went out and bought a new building. Louis found the building and bought it for us—he was always the money man. The new facility was on the West Side of Chicago, and we moved over there to 4700 West Walton Street; we were on Normandy Street for a while, too.

This was a community, you understand. These manufacturers were the people that we buddied with and ran around with and had dinner and drinks with. We were in and out of each other's factories all the time. We exchanged things. I bought a *lot* of Harmony bodies and put resonators in them. Regal, Kay, Gibson—we all worked together. That's manufacturing for you, and that's what built the United States. We were pioneers and we pooled our resources. Over there at National Dobro we used bodies from various companies, but we made all our own necks and all our own electrical parts.

Some of the best business was from the big mail-order houses. Several of them carried Nationals and Dobros. Harmony was one of the biggest companies in the country at that time, and they were owned by Sears. So they made the Sears acoustic guitars and put the name "Silvertone" on them. We made the electric guitars for Sears before the war, and those guitars were also called Silvertones. For as long as I was in Chicago, up until 1948, no one else made Silvertone electric guitars or amplifiers. We made all of them. *[Note: Danelectro, Harmony, and other companies made Silvertone electrics after the war.]* Another line we made was called Kraftsman, which went to Montgomery Ward. We made electrics for the Spiegel catalogue, too. Mail-order houses would put their stuff out on bid. We were the lowest bidder because we'd been in electronics longer and knew our business. We could underbid all the other factories. We really didn't have much competition for that kind of work before the war.

Al: It wasn't just the manufacturers who were competing; the jobbers had a hell of a lot of competition among themselves as well. Harmony was pretty much the low end of the market. In general, Kay was located between Harmony and Gibson. Kay at one time had very fine quality, and both Regal and Kay were a step up from Harmony. In the industry, Martin was generally recognized as the premier flat-top, and Epiphone was regarded as being right at the top of the arch-tops.

Before we moved to Chicago we just sold resonators to Regal, but after we moved, there was a reciprocity. We could get bodies from them because they were better set up to build wooden guitar bodies. When we came to Chicago, instead of setting up the additional plant facility to make the bodies, we started getting wooden ones from Regal for the Dobros. So a Chicago-made Dobro might very well have a Regal body.

Victor: Regal also made many resonator guitars with their bodies and our parts. Several companies made electric guitars using our pickup units, which included the tone and volume controls. We produced guitars under several names right up until World War II. Back in Los Angeles, Rickenbacker and the people in the McKinley

Far left: Model 37G, mid-1930s. *McPeake's/Robt. Foust* *Near left:* Regal-Dobro Model 19. *John Quarterman*

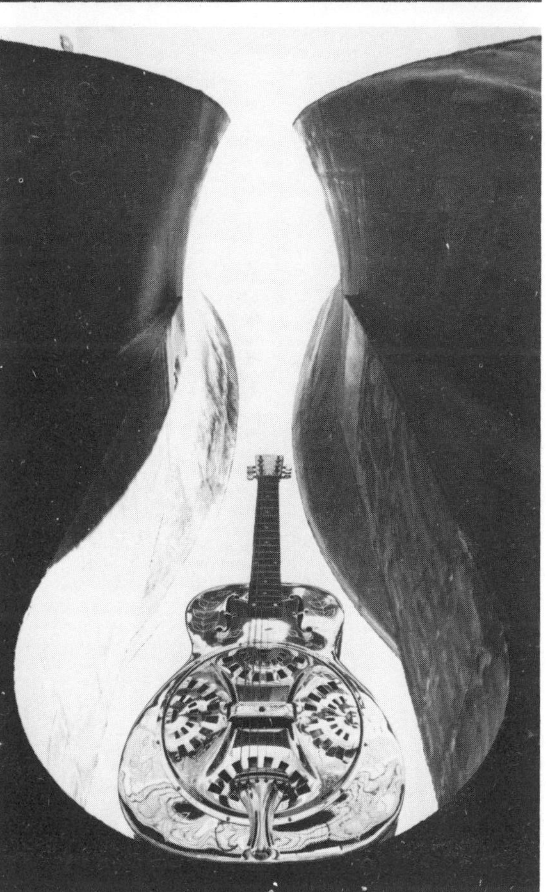

Far left: Dobro Model 27G, circa 1930. *Music Shop/Madsen* *Near left:* Dobro Model 36.

Formerly National Dobro Corporation

ANNOUNCEMENT

We, of VALCO MANUFACTURING COMPANY, are pleased to announce the moving of our Plant and Office as of May 1st, 1944, from the old location at 400 South Peoria Street to our modern New Home at

4700 West Walton Street
CHICAGO 51, ILL.
New Phone MANsfield 7574

Kindly Mark Your Records Accordingly—THANK YOU

VIC SMITH AL FROST LOUIS DOPYERA

Manufacturers of Renown "National" Electronic Guitars

Victor Smith

The Valco plant in Chicago. ***Victor Smith***

Al Frost at his desk in the National Dobro factory, late 1930s. ***Victor Smith***

Street plant were still making the resonator parts. They would ship them to Chicago, and we would assemble them there with bodies we bought from various Chicago guitar makers. See, you could ship parts for about one fourth the cost of shipping an instrument. So we'd assemble them in Chicago and send them on out. From the time that we moved, the *electric* guitars were made from scratch in Chicago. We were buying bodies from Harmony, Regal, Kay, and Gibson. In exchange, we would sell them resonators or electric parts.

One time I received a postcard from New York with a picture of the Empire State Building on it, and I thought that the peak and those step-downs on the sides would make a nice looking, modern Hawaiian guitar. That thought struck me one Sunday afternoon. I went in Monday and built a guitar that was shaped sort of like the Empire State Building. We called it the New Yorker, and it was very popular—everybody copied that thing. At the beginning, most of the electrics we made were steel guitars, by far.

We started another brand name, which was Supro, and this was our line of slightly lower-budget instruments. We planned to distribute them to schools. It was very successful, and quite a few of the catalogues got into Supro guitars and amplifiers. We made Supros both before and after World War II. Most of the Supro acoustic guitars were made with either Kay or Regal bodies and then we made the electrics from scratch.

Al: When we sold our main lines—National, Supro, and Dobro—the distributor had to keep our names on them, but they could come in and order up names of their own, and we would change the models around a little bit. The distributor would just buy some decals, and we'd put them on there and spray over them with lacquer.

Victor: Our company, like the whole industry, was turned upside down when World War II came. We all got letters from the President telling us to halt production. They needed the aluminum, steel, and other materials for the war. We went to Washington, started bidding on war production work, and picked up our blueprints. The McKinley Street plant back in Los Angeles had been making our resonator parts until the war started. Then we shut it down.

People were saying that we had to get ready for the war. It was no secret that it was coming. So we had the McKinley Street plant ship

The National Dobro crew poses outside the Los Angeles factory on the day of the Chicago move in the winter of 1936. Several people made the trip in the Graham Paige auto on the left. ***Victor Smith***

The Valco crew, April 1946. Victor Smith is standing third from left.

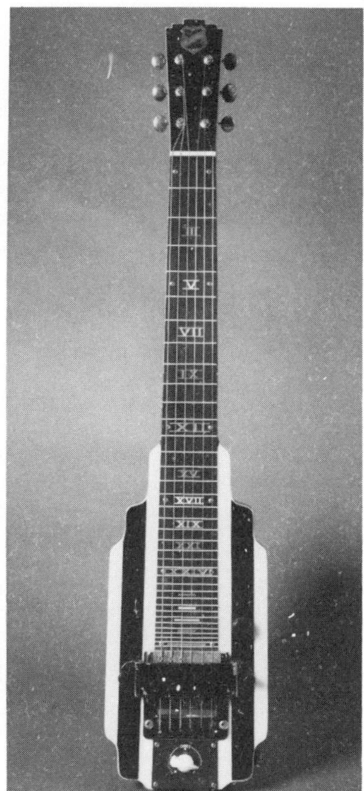

National Electric Hawaiian Guitar (no other model name), circa 1941. Also available in 7- and 8-string versions. *Doug Thorstenson/Tom Erlewine*

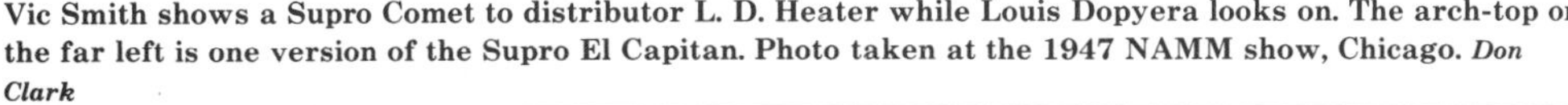

Vic Smith shows a Supro Comet to distributor L. D. Heater while Louis Dopyera looks on. The arch-top on the far left is one version of the Supro El Capitan. Photo taken at the 1947 NAMM show, Chicago. *Don Clark*

National flat-top, circa early 1950s, made with a Gibson body. CMI distributed both Gibson and National in the 1950s, which accounts for certain Nationals with Gibson bodies, and at least one Gibson resophonic (see photo, page 139). *Dan Lambert*

Supro nameplate.

Early cast-aluminum Supro 6-string lap steel.
John Quarterman

us everything they had, and Rickenbacker shipped his dies and tooling. We did only war work—no guitars. When the war started, three of us—myself, Al Frost, and Louis Dopyera—bought out the others. We took the first letters of our first names—V, A, and L—and named our new company Valco. Ed was at that time the president of National Dobro, but he really never stayed in Chicago too much after that first year. The National Dobro Corporation was dissolved, and all of the war work was done under the name Valco.

Al: When the limitation order came down, Louis bought up all the old parts and stock from the other brothers. He became the sole proprietor just as a liquidation method. This was for a very short period in 1942, and they called it the National Dobro *Company*. It was just on paper. It was later on in 1942 when we formed Valco. I was managing sales, and distribution; Vic had the shop management; and Louis was president. I'd get up at four or five in the morning and come home at eight or nine at night. We made parts for probably every plane in the air. It was a fascinating period, but it gives me the creeps to even think about it.

Victor: The minute the war was over we all said, "Oh boy, now we can get back to work." But you couldn't buy any parts. I was out there trying to buy magnets, wire, anything, but it took quite a while. It was rough because we depended on metal much more than the other guitar companies. Fortunately, we did have stacks of stuff stored all during the war, and we were able to make some Tri-Plates and other resonator guitars. But it was probably six months or a year before we got it going again at full speed. After the war, we really didn't make too many resonator guitars, except for the ones we had put together from leftover parts. We shipped the Dobro dies and everything back. Our main focus was electrics.

At first all of the original amps were made in the Dobro plant, and then we farmed out the work on the chassis. Jim Lansing's speaker company [later JBL] was right next door to us on McKinley Street, and he made all the speakers for the first talking pictures studios. He liked us. His regular speakers were too expensive to put into a guitar amp, so he made us a special line. The first Dobro amplifiers had Lansing speakers.

When we moved to Chicago, a company called Chicago Electric made our amps—Nationals, Dobros, and Supros. Sometimes we would hire a guitar case company to make the amplifier cases. And then we would farm out the chassis work and buy tubes and speakers and assemble them in our Chicago plant.

Al: Shortly after the move to Chicago we started using plastic more and more. On the less expensive solidbodies they'd go right from the sander into the finishing room to be sprayed. Then we'd take plastic, which was just like a rubber glove, and cement it to the guitars and trim it off. We found that with the electrics you didn't need all that resonance, so we tried making the bodies out of polyester resin and fiberglass. We would take a mold, spray the finish in, then the fiberglass, pull it out of there, and the finish would already be on it. Oh, it was beautiful. The dies themselves were made out of fiberglass. We made Res-O-Glas guitars in reds and blues and whites and all sorts of colors. They were really something. The Res-O-Glas guitars date to about 1961 and we were still making them as late as 1964, but they were really just a fad.

The demise of Valco involved the Kay company. In 1962 we changed the name from Valco Manufacturing to Valco Guitars, Inc. I was president of the corporation. Robert Engelhardt [now de-

Far left: National used many Harmony and Kay bodies for its arch-tops. The squared shoulders suggest that this body is likely a Kay, such as the kind used on Kay's K-39, K-42, K-44, and K-46 models of the late 1940s. *Spitzer's/Sievert* *Near left:* Supro Folk Star resonator guitar with plastic body, circa 1964. *Reid Scudder*

Far left: National Debonaire. *Wagener/Beaty* *Near left:* Early-1950s National model 1155 with stock Gibson-built J-50 style body. The polepieces of the factory-installed pickup are visible near the last fret. *Gruhn*

1956 Supro Dual-Tone. Supro had only two other solidbody Spanish models at the time—the single-pickup Belmont and the budget model Supro Sixty. At $135 the Dual-Tone was a remarkable value in a two-pickup solidbody. *Aeolian Music*

ceased] had come in as our accountant, and he bought into the company. I sold out to him in 1964, and he became president for three or four years. Sidney Katz [now deceased] was Hank Kuhrmeyer's successor. Kay's next owner was Seeburg, the juke box company.

Louis died. It must have been 1963, because it was about a year before I left in 1964. The young partner, Engelhardt, was extremely ambitious. He was out raising money when we were out burying Louis. After Katz left Kay, Seeburg called me up and said, "Hey, where can we get some guitar management?" I said, "I know some guys who are running a pretty good little plant." I was talking about the people at Valco. I thought that they would sell out to Seeburg. But they went out and *bought* Kay, and that was the demise of it. Valco and Kay got tied up together, and when Kay sank, Valco sank. *[Note: See Robert Keyworth's account of all this—in the Kay chapter.]* It was never officially announced, and I never could figure it out. After I left, Engelhardt moved Valco into the Kay plant, which was a much bigger facility. He borrowed a lot of money and went in deeper and deeper. I don't know the total, but I know that I lost a hell of a lot of money in it. Whoever had the loans just came into the factory and closed the doors. I talked to a few of the workers and they said it was as simple as that. They just locked the doors. God knows where all the money went. In fact, to this day I've not received official notice. It just disappeared into thin air.

THE RESURRECTION OF DOBRO: OMI

World War II had ended. The victorious American people, united in war, united again in an orgy of unprecedented commercial consumption. Yet it looked like it was all over for the resonator guitar. The Allies' demands for aluminum, brass, copper, nickel, and steel were death knells to many metal enter-

1990 Update

Chester and Betty Lizak, OMI's auditors and accountants, bought the company in October 1985 from Gabriela Lazar, sister of John Dopyera and mother of Ron Lazar, both now deceased. About a dozen people at the Huntington Beach, California, factory build up to 200 Dobros a month, which are sold directly to retailers in the United States and through distributors in Japan, Australia, and Europe. Chester reported in 1989: "You know, I'm 70 years old. If I were 30, I'd take this thing and really run with it. There are so many opportunities out there, it's a wonder more people don't go after them. All of the help here have input, and suggestions are always welcome from players. We intend to keep on doing what we're doing, building Dobros the way they've always been built."

Late-1950s National "Reso-Phonic" Model 1133, with a wood body covered in sheet plastic. The cover plate is similar to that of an early-1930s Duolian. This was a student model. *Music Shop/Madsen*

Late 1950s National Town & Country, thick white plastic overlay on back. The Avalon was a less fancy two-pickup guitar; the Bolero had one pickup. *Wagener/Beaty*

1958 Bel-Aire: three-way pickup selector with individual volume knobs for each position plus a master tone control; Gibson ES-175 body. The fancier 1959 model had three pickups. *Gruhn/Baxendale*

1959 National Model 1102 Stylist, $159.50. *Terry Smith*

Rick Nielsen's 1964 National Glenwood 98. *Bob Alford*

1570 BELMONT
FIBERGLAS BEAUTY—WITH OR WITHOUT EXCLUSIVE 2-WAY VIBRATO
This value guitar has exceptionally fine tone. Playing action of the 24¾" scale is excellent.
The neat 13½" x 18" body is all new Fiberglas in beautiful cherry red. This permanent polyester finish will not stain, fade or check. Rosewood fingerboard—fully adjustable unit and bridge.
Instrument has separate volume and tone controls. Exclusive Kord-King neck.
1570R Glas Hollow Body Guitar (less Vibrato), Strap and Cord .... $99.50 B
1570V Glas Hollow Body Guitar (with Vibrato), Strap and Cord .... $124.50 B
715-32 Case (Plush-Shaped Hard Shell) .... $45.00 B
715-34 Case (Flannel-Square Hard Shell) .... $19.50 B
715-40 Case (Soft Shell-Single Ply) .... $10.50 B

1540T BERMUDA
BUILT IN ELECTRONIC TREMOLO
Attractive body is styled in durable glass-fiber—finished in brilliant polyester cherry—Two tone ranges—Selector Switch—Tone and Volume controls.
Units are fully adjustable for perfect string balance. Neck is of the super Kord-King design with arched rosewood fingerboard. Scale is popular 24¾".
The special reinforced hollow body construction provides a soft yet full resonate tone response—clean—clear—sustaining Body measures 15¼" wide x 19" long x 1¾" deep.
1540T Tremolo Guitar, Cord and Strap .... $127.50 B
715-52 Case, Soft Shell .... $12.50 B
715-57 Case — (Plush-Shaped—Hard Shell) .... $45.00 B
FINGER TIP CONTROL
INSTANT TREMOLO AT ARTISTS COMMAND

Supro guitars from Valco's 1963–1964 catalogue.

tainment products that couldn't be replaced with plastic substitutes, and resophonic guitars were no exception.

John Dopyera had long since left large-scale manufacturing. Victor Smith retired to California in 1948. Louis and Robert Dopyera were never mechanics and were unable or not inclined to resurrect the family business. It appeared that if any of the Dopyera brothers were going to get back into guitar production, it would have to be Emil.

Despite the postwar economic boom, metalwork had come to entail much higher production costs. (To this day National Tri-Plates can't be profitably manufactured, because it would cost too much to reconstruct the dies.) Sales dropped to a trickle and were mostly of guitars assembled from leftover parts. Nationals and Dobros, at one time the loudest thing anyone had ever heard, were generally drowned out in the oncoming tide of electric guitars.

In the late 1950s and early 1960s popular interest in folk music and related ethnic genres increased, and Dobros and Nationals were being pulled out of attics, dusted off, and tuned up. The name *Dobro* evolved into a generic term applied to any resophonic guitar, and the value of the originals soared. During this period certain Nationals and Dobros were selling for several times their original list price.

In about 1959, Emil returned from an extended Alaskan vacation and began building resophonics in El Monte, California. Louis Dopyera arranged for the return of the equipment and the transfer of the Dobro trade name from Valco to Emil. (Emil and Rudy built some resophonics for Standel at this time.) In 1961, Emil's son (also named Emil) and his partners bought out most of Emil's and Rudy's shares in the company. They relocated the factory to 1908 West 135th Street, Gardena, California, offering wooden 12-fret Dobros and later some 14-fret models in limited quantities.

In 1966 or 1967 the company was sold to Semie Moseley, founder of Mosrite, through a deal that caused some bad blood among the Dopyeras; certain family members hardly spoke to each other for years. The first of the Mosrite Dobros were made in the Gardena plant, though later Moseley moved the operation up to his central California home in Bakersfield. He started assembling Gardena-made parts and building his own Mobro instruments from scratch. Mosrite collapsed, but Semie Moseley still owned the Dobro trade name under his early-1960s agreement with Emil Dopyera's partners. Emil began

Top: **1964 National 85 bass. Note bridge pickup's connecting wire and "quadrant" markers. Note that the right-hand cutaway is somewhat pointed rather than rounded. National had three similarly shaped 6-strings: the Newport 82 (one standard pickup), the Newport 84 (standard pickup plus bridge pickup), and Newport 88 (two standard pickups plus bridge pickup).** ***Third Eye*** ***Bottom:*** **1964 National Westwood 72. The Westwood 75 looked almost identical but had a bridge mounted pickup, while the Westwood 77 had two standard pickups and a bridge unit.** ***Frank Lucido***

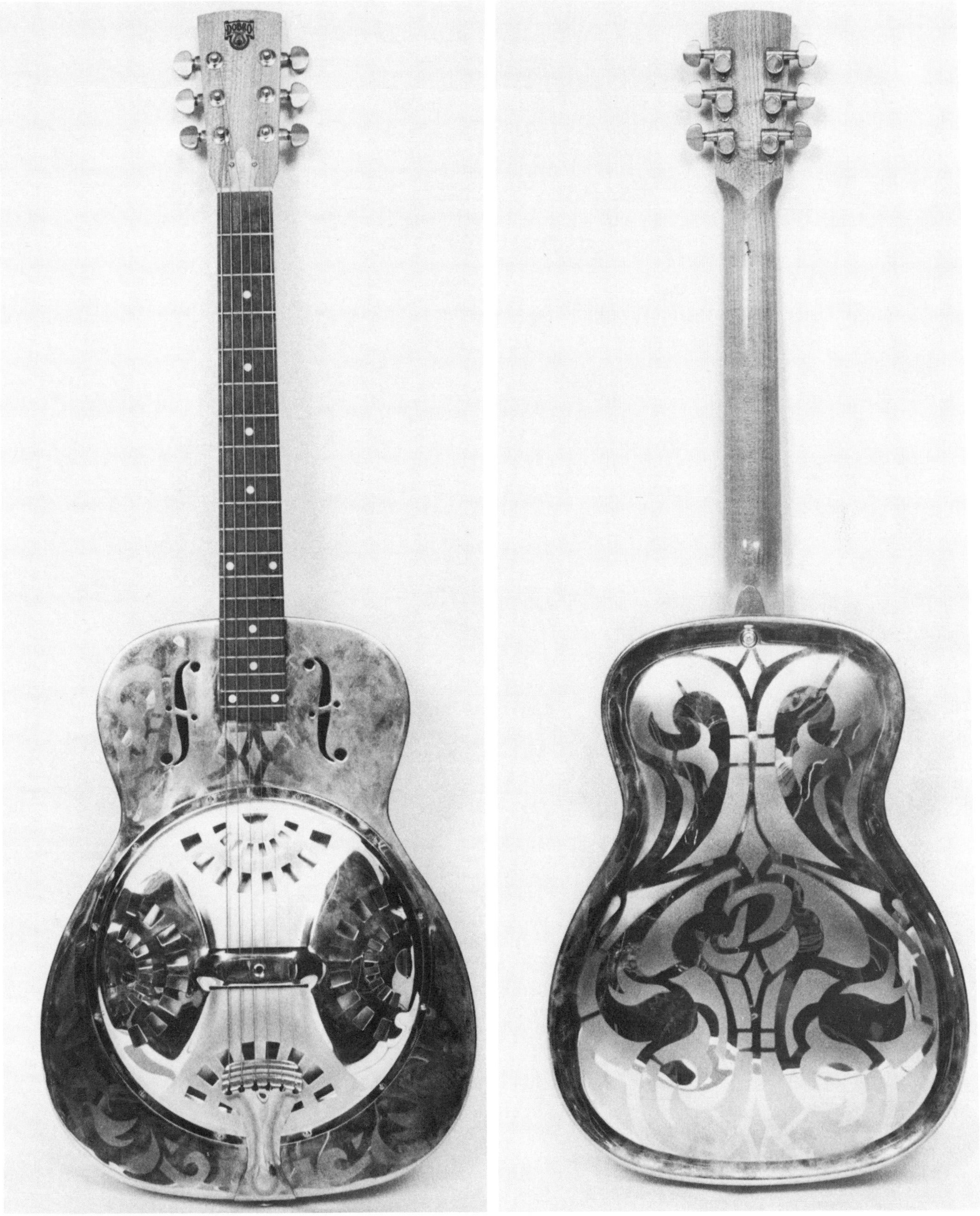

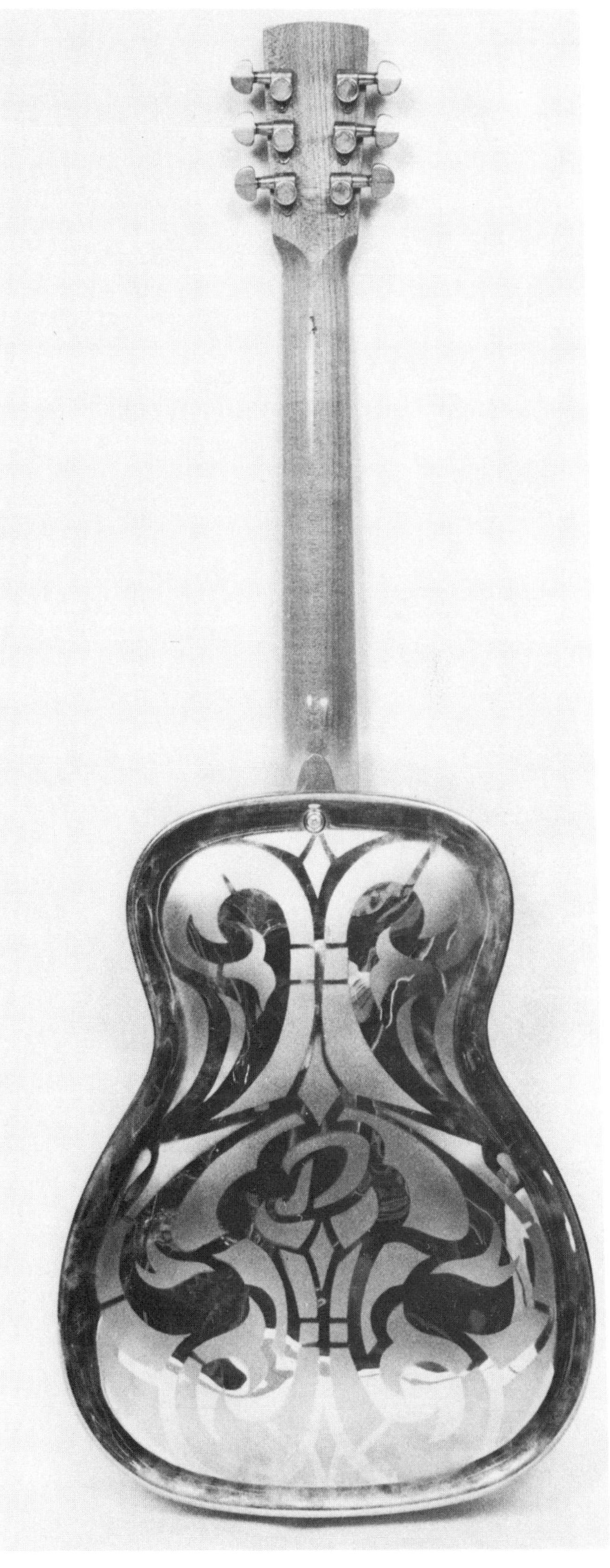

Late-1960s Dobro 33D. *Music Shop/Madsen*

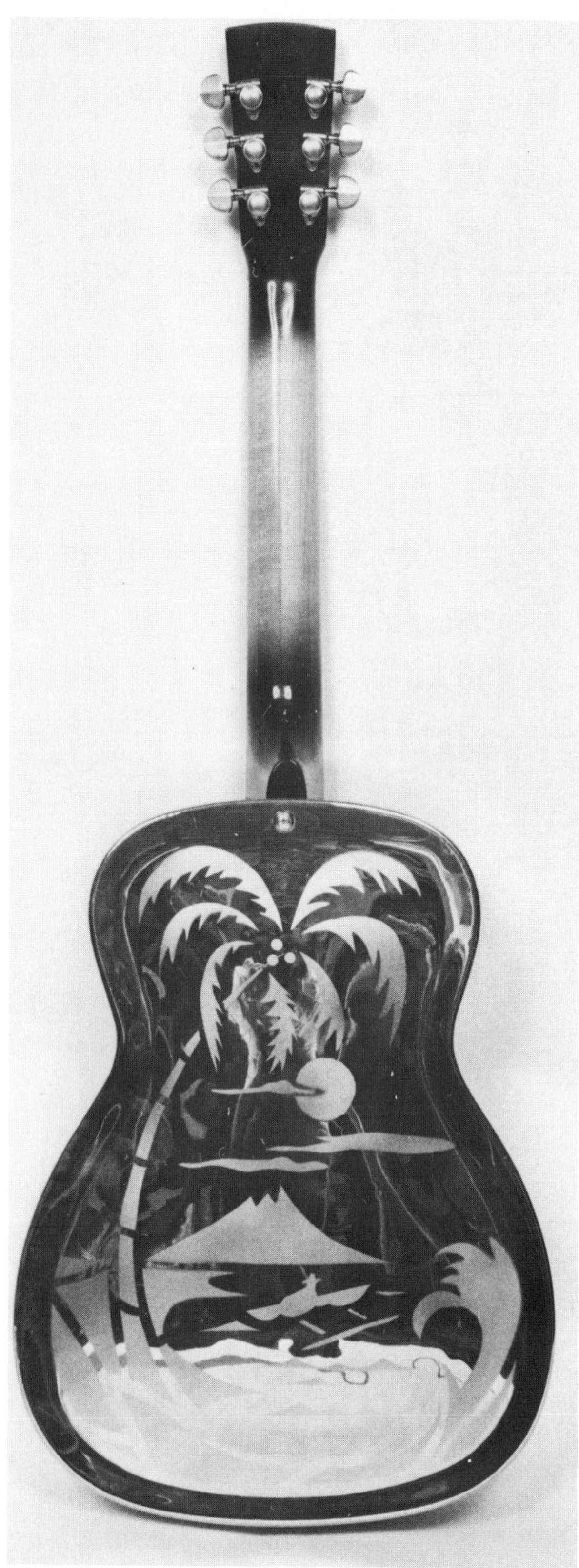

1970s Dobro 33H, carrying on the Hawaiian motif of Style O.
Music Shop/Madsen

Dobro Model 66, recent issue.

calling his own guitars Hound Dogs and Dopera Originals (*Dopera* was an Americanization of *Dopyera*).

In 1970 or 1971 the Dobro name again became available. Emil and new associates opened a factory at 1404 Gaylord Street in Long Beach. Their new company was called the Original Musical Instrument Company, Incorporated, or OMI. Under the gradually increasing business guidance of Ron Lazar, the Dopyeras' nephew, OMI began to tap the market for authentic resophonics, a market that had existed since the folk boom of the early 1960s. A hardwood body model was offered, as were several metal guitars with bodies (but not resonators) built along the lines of the single-plate Nationals. The latter included the sheet steel Model 30, the chrome-plated sheet steel Model 33 (with a diamond etching on the back), and the chrome-plated bell brass Model 36.

More recent *metal*-body Dobros come in two categories. The first is factory-equipped with the Dobro-type resonator and spider bridge, though the National-style cone is optional at no extra cost. This category includes the maple-neck Model 36, with its chrome-plated bell brass body, floral engraving, 14-fret neck, and 24½-inch scale.

The other metal guitars in this category (Dobro type resonator) share most of their features with the Model 36, differing in cosmetic details. The second kind of late model metal Dobro is

The last photo of the Dopyera brothers together: Emil, John (with the first Dobro ever made), and Rudy. *John Quarterman*

the Model 90 Duolian. It has the National-type cone resonator with biscuit, a chrome-plated bell brass body, and a palm tree/lagoon motif. Recent *maple*-body Dobros have rosewood fingerboards and include the Model 60 and several variations.

ORPHEUM

See Lange

OSCAR SCHMIDT; STELLA

The Oscar Schmidt Company was established in the late 1800s (published accounts specify both 1879 and 1893) and was incorporated under the state laws of New Jersey for $125,000 in 1911. Founder Oscar Schmidt was president, and his son Walter was vice-president. Their factory was a four-story brick building with 40,000 square feet, located at 87 Ferry Street, Jersey City. It produced an extremely wide variety of stringed instruments. Among its trade names were Stella, Sovereign, (both acquired by Harmony), and La Scala. The company was later known as Oscar Schmidt International, and was succeeded in 1935 or 1936 by Fretted Instrument Manufacturers, headquartered at the Ferry Street facility.

Pre–World War I Stella Sovereign. Stellas, especially 12-strings, found great favor among early blues artists and manifested impressive quality for moderately priced, mass-produced guitars. *Spitzer's/Sievert*

Charles Kaman, founder of Ovation. *Deford Dechert*

Stellas, though inexpensive and not particularly durable, were often of good quality, and they became favorites among blues artists of the late 1920s and 1930s. Their 12-strings were especially good. Leadbelly, Blind Blake, and Blind Willie McTell all played them. While the interior finishing work was often crude and hastily completed, the exteriors looked exceptionally good, particularly considering the cost. Also see Harmony.

OVATION

Charles Huron Kaman restructured some long-standing equations of musical instrument commerce by proving that one could establish a major name in guitars in a surprisingly short time provided he or she had a good product, marketing experience, and plenty of money. Charles Kaman had all three.

A native of Washington D.C., Mr. Kaman (like *command* without the *d*) was born in 1919, the son of a construction supervisor. Like his father, young Charlie was an avid guitar picker, playing with radio station WJSV's Originality Boys in high school, and earning an offer in 1937 to join Tommy Dorsey's band at $90 a week. Preferring to play guitar as a hobby rather than a profession, he declined. After graduating from Catholic University in 1940 he went to work for United Aircraft. Having designed a helicopter rotor blade, Kaman raised $2,000 from family members and friends and founded his own company in 1945.

The Kaman Corporation, now a conglomerate of about 30 companies, was earning millions of dollars each year in aerospace before it entered the music business. After being turned down in his bids to buy both Martin and Harmony, Mr. Kaman established his own company, Ovation Instruments, Incorporated, in 1967. The fledgling firm, which later employed some 300 guitar craftsmen, was inaugurated to apply its parent corporation's sophisticated technological know-how to the manufacture of instruments. Before Ovation's success it was assumed that no serious acoustic guitarist would be caught dead playing an instrument made out of synthetics, and that there was no more room for giants in the acoustic guitar's domestic marketplace. Ovation dismantled these maxims in fairly short order.

After intensive analysis with some of the world's most sophisticated sonic equipment, Kaman's engineers settled on a one-piece parabolic body shell pressed from synthetic fibers similar to the covering the company used for helicopter rotor blades. Given the diminishing sources of various guitar woods, the acceptance of Ovation may well foreshadow a general and perhaps inevitable trend toward the use of synthetics throughout

1990 Update

In 1985 William "Bill" Kaman II, Charles H. Kaman's son, took over day-to-day operations of Kaman Music Corp., which now claims to be America's largest producer of acoustic guitars and which also distributes the Japanese-made Takamine guitars. In June 1988, Kaman acquired Hamer.

Since the mid-1980s, Ovation's Elite models (with Adamas-like top styling, but in spruce) have been very successful; in 1990 they comprised 25 percent of total production. Other distinctive Ovations during the 1980s: the Thunderbolt acoustic/electric with lightning-bolt-shaped soundholes, and an acoustic/electric that also serves as a MIDI controller.

Ovation offers nine families of guitars—Balladeer, Legend, Custom Legend, Elite, Thunderbolt, Collectors' Series, Classic, Adamas, and Adamas II; most are available in 6- or 12-string versions. As of 1990 Ovation has manufactured approximately 600,000 guitars, including 400,000 U.S.-made Ovation-brand roundbacks and 200,000 other roundbacks and solidbodies; Kaman has also manufactured nearly 300,000 roundbacks in Korea and Japan. In 1990, 450 people were working for Ovation, Kaman Musical String, Hamer, and the distributors C. Bruno and Coast Wholesale (Kaman Corp. employs 6,500 people).

The worker at this station is drilling holes in an Ovation body for the neck attachment and strap knobs.

An Applause body bowl mounted in an outer ring bond fixture.

The oldest Ovation, prototype No. 6 (1–5 were bowl assemblies).

Deluxe Balladeer steel-string.

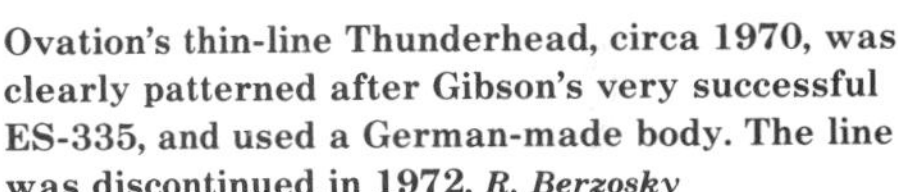

Ovation's thin-line Thunderhead, circa 1970, was clearly patterned after Gibson's very successful ES-335, and used a German-made body. The line was discontinued in 1972. *R. Berzosky*

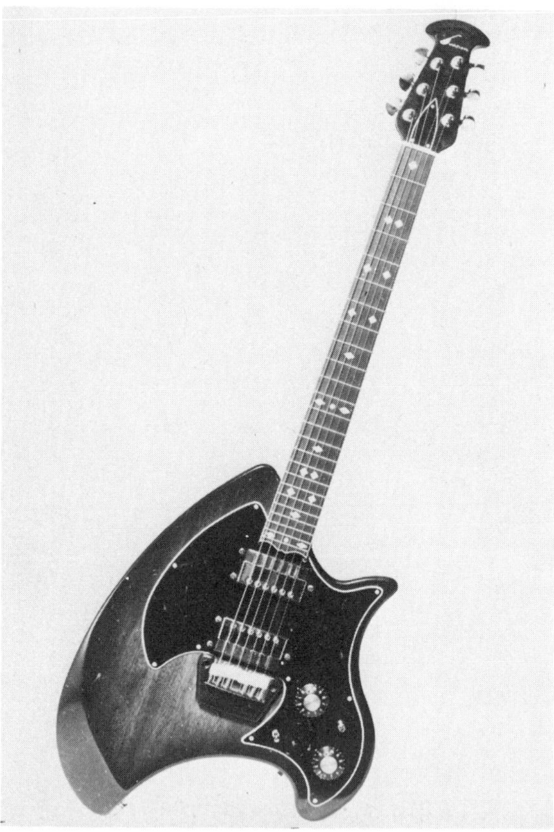

Ovation Deacon.

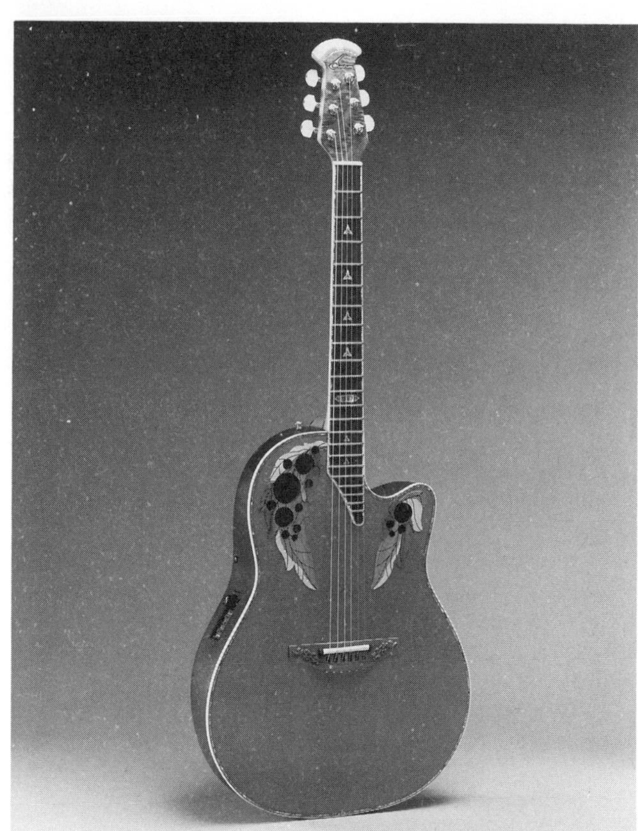

1987 Collectors' Series: deep bowl, Sitka spruce top, abalone inlay, piezo pickup with three-band active EQ, figured walnut facing on the headstock.

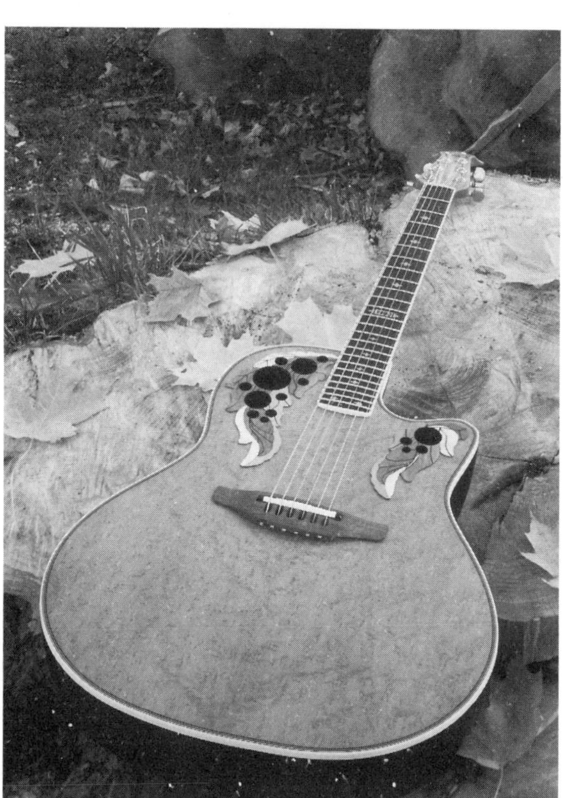

Every year since 1982, Ovation has introduced a new Collectors' Series model, each with unique features. There are 1,000 to 2,000 guitars per series. Examples include a supershallow-bowl guitar in 1983, the first supershallow 12-string in 1986, the first 16-frets-to-the-body neck in 1987, and this 1990 acoustic/electric with a highly figured bird's-eye maple top.

the industry. The Lyrachord bowl's dense surface is more reflective than wood, and the parabolic dish (like radar reflectors, amphitheaters, and the human ear) focuses the sound waves, directing them through the soundhole; Ovations are well known for their bright sound and projection.

Kaman's Bloomfield, Connecticut, corporate offices were the site of the design and testing of Ovation's early instruments, and the prototypes were constructed in the former Fuller Brush factory where Kaman's helicopter rotor blade plant was located. John Ringso, a Norwegian woodcarver who had become Kaman's fourth employee in 1945, built most of the prototypes. After the completion of less than 100 instruments, the shop was moved on the first weekend of February 1967 to New Hartford, Connecticut, home of one of Ovation's two factories. The production facilities overflowed from a wing of a five-story brick building (a former textile mill, built in the 1800s) to another Kaman plant 93 miles away in Moosup, Connecticut.

Of Ovation's early days, managing engineer Jim Rickard said: "We were a small group of people trying to make a good quality guitar, the concept of which many thought was a joke. It was uphill. In September of 1966 we needed a name for the first production guitars. A local group of folksingers called the Balladeers had bought some of our very first instruments. They were performing at the Eastern States Exposition, a large agricultural fair. They got a standing ovation, and about two weeks later it was decided that the guitars would be called Ovations and that we would have four models: a Standard Balladeer, a Deluxe Balladeer, a Classic, and a Josh White."

Each Adamas guitar is tested in this chamber, and its fundamental frequency is included in the serial number; for example, 495-91 had a fundamental frequency of 91 Hz.

Adamas. Note the radical soundhole array.

With his enormous resources, Mr. Kaman could have launched a titanic advertising campaign, but instead he chose a moderate course, personally exhibiting his guitar first to Charlie Byrd and then Glen Campbell. "I needed to know the truth," he said in *Guitar Player* magazine, "whether this guitar was something that could make it. We started in a modest way, and it was an uphill battle, but that's the key to succeeding in business—go slowly."

By trying to go slowly he went fairly fast, scoring a crucial endorsement from Glen Campbell (previously a Mosrite endorser) in the early 1970s. The battleaxe shape of the Deacon, one of Ovation's first two solidbodies, was intended to provide a right leg support (lower body scoop) for the sitting player. Other details included a mahogany body and neck, a midrange filter switch, volume trim controls for each pickup, a phase switch, master volume, FET preamp, three-point bridge mount, and Schaller tuners with a 12:1 gear ratio. Like its companion, the similarly shaped dot-neck Breadwinner, the Deacon never really caught on. The Breadwinner was introduced in the summer of 1971, the Deacon in January 1972.

The Magnum 1 Stereo bass. Its front pickup has a separate coil wrapped around each polepiece, and each polepiece has its own volume control. The rear pickup has two side-by-side coils and large U-shaped polepieces. Magnum 2 has a graphic equalizer.

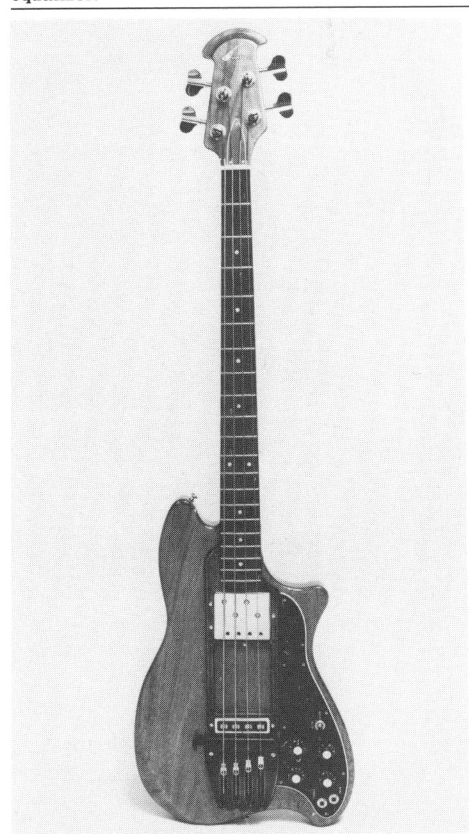

Generally patterned after Richie Sambora's custom guitar, Ovation's $8,000 doubleneck Elite became available on custom order in 1989. *Right:* 1989 limited-production acoustic/electric Elite Bass.

Ovation Adamas prototype. Note the upper fretboard configuration and unusual soundholes.

The Adamas, top of the Ovation line, went into production in late 1975 and represents a particularly radical departure from traditional guitar design theory. The top is a laminate of two 0.005-inch plies of carbon graphite with a 0.035-inch birch veneer sandwiched between them. Initially developed for supersonic aircraft, carbon graphite is strong enough to permit a much thinner top than usual. The most readily apparent innovation is the use of multiple soundholes and their relocation to the upper bouts, which in the words of Mr. Kaman "enhances the integrity of the top as a vibrating membrane while permitting us to use our newest brace system to transmit sound rather than support the weakness of the soundhole." For several years the company grew at the almost explosive rate of approximately 50 percent a year.

When he first made the decision to manufacture guitars, Charles Huron Kaman, one of the wealthiest men in American guitar history, found himself an underdog. Ovation's success against considerable odds is likely due in part to the fact that Mr. Kaman is a lifelong guitarist, one who can communicate with and learn from other players. (His son, C. W. Kaman II, carries on the tradition of the guitarist/engineer/executive.) At first his company was written off by some self-styled experts as just another black-ink venture for a high-tech corporate heavyweight. While it may have been tempting for some to view Kaman as a Lear jet exec competing with leather-aproned old-timers steeped in guitar heritage, the fact is that several of those other major companies are now run by managers with far less guitar background than Charles Kaman's. The round-back Ovation guitar is both a probable indicator of things to come and an instrument in the proud tradition of American guitar building and innovation.

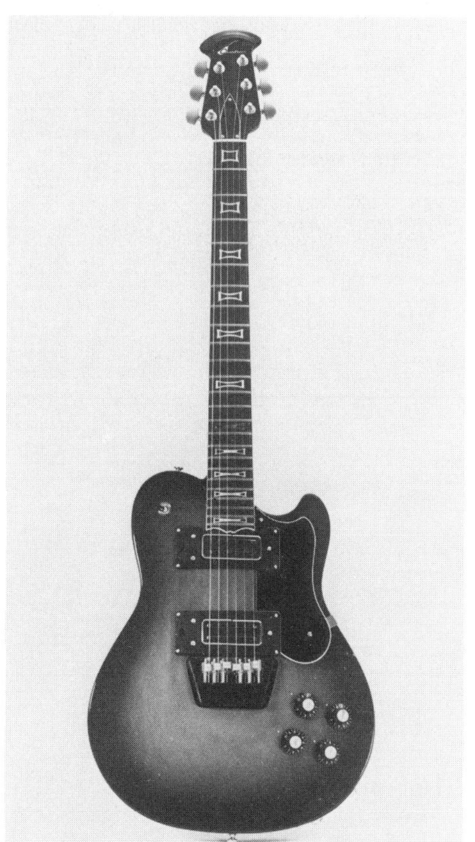

UK (Ultra Kaman) II, introduced January 1979. The UK II has a Urelite body molded over a cast-aluminum frame, and series/parallel pickup selectors.

PARAMOUNT

See Lange

PAUL REED SMITH

Combining painstaking craftsmanship, a variety of sparkling tones, exceptional playability, often spectacular curly maple tops, and dazzling finishes, Paul Reed Smith's guitars are some of the most sought-after instruments in the world. Even vintage purists sometimes speak of them with a reverence usually reserved for rare classics, and in fact Smith's own passion for vintage Fenders and Gibsons fueled his desire to build guitars and inspired some of his designs. His success in blending elements from Stratocasters and Les Pauls has been remarkable.

Smith began making guitars and basses in his Annapolis, Maryland shop in 1976. By 1985, his company had grown to 40 employees, and his instruments had become well known, due in part to the support of Carlos Santana and Al Di Meola. In 1990, the 55-employee company was producing about 325 PRS instruments per month.

The Classic Electric has an alder body, 3-position toggle, and bolt-on neck. Three models have one-piece mahogany bodies: the Standard (PRS Standard pickups and "sweet switch" tone circuit); the Studio (two single-coils and one Hot Vintage humbucker); and the Special (wide-thin neck, HFS Treble pickup, Vintage Bass pickup, and pull-up tremolo routing). The choicest PRS guitars are designated the Custom class and have flamed curly maple tops. Within that group, the top-of-the-line Signature Series (an example is shown here) sports PRS' finest maple and Smith's personal signature. Due to available options, some guitars mix features from these models.

The bodies are carved with the 3-D tracer, one of several machines developed by Smith and his co-inventor and mentor Eric Pritchard. Such machines and techniques provide the meticulous quality control of a small shop as well as the efficiency of a manufacturing operation, permitting the guitars to be retailed for about $1,000 to nearly $3,000—impressively reasonable, considering their artistry and versatility.

These uniquely carved and contoured guitars are also known for their ability to produce generally Strat-like tones from humbuckers; locking quick-change tuners; a self-lubricating string nut; a 5-position rotary selector; a refined, Fender-derived vibrato (the smoothest, most controllable device the author has encountered); and an unusual 25-inch scale length—in between those of a Strat and a Les Paul. In reviewing the PRS for *Guitar Player,* esteemed designer/builder Rick Turner commented, "It has what good antiques, great cars, and fine art objects have: an effortless sense of being just right for what they are.... I've not played an electric guitar I've liked better." Indeed, for many, the Paul Reed Smith is nothing less than the finest solidbody of its era.

PEAVEY

Hartley Peavey with a Peavey T-60 electric.

Meridian, Mississippi's Hartley Peavey is something of a renegade, sort of the Waylon Jennings of guitar manufacturers. He thought that, from a consumer's point of view, industry trends during the 1960s and 1970s were ridiculous: prices were too high and imports too cheap, and as far as he was concerned the whole thing was one big corporate ripoff. "Now, *gentlemen,*" he would say to his dealers, "I submit to you that this situation is pure bull manure" (or words to that effect). The tape recorder industry and others had been begun by Americans but taken over by foreigners, and Mr. Peavey thought that guitars could go the same way unless someone stepped in to turn the tide—he also reckoned that that someone was Hartley Peavey.

Born December 30, 1941, Hartley is a third-generation music businessman. He studied electronics, sheet metal work, and machinery and at age 16 began working on radios and record changers. (His teenage idol, Leo Fender, had similar experience.) Peavey took up guitar and began building amps, discovering that the mechanical and electronic aspects of instruments captivated him much more than the music itself. At Mississippi State University, he became what he called a music business "horse trader"—booking groups, dealing in guitars and amps, refinishing instruments, and winding pickups.

Hartley graduated in 1965 and founded Peavey Electronics the following year. Against the initial advice of his experienced father, he made the first in a string of decisions that evidenced a respect for the self-made man, the underdog: as a manufacturer of amplifiers, he would take on "the big guys," "the fat cats," and give them a run for their money. Superficially at least, his strategy was simple—work more efficiently and offer the customer more for his dollar. He succeeded. He built a "vertical" corporation (with much in-house component production or, as Hartley put it, "no corporate sugar daddies") and offered an extensive catalogue of P.A. gear, sound reinforcement equipment, and amplifiers. By 1981 Peavey claimed to be the largest guitar/amp company in the United States, employing 900 people.

Peavey's Unity Series bass.

Peavey launched a modern guitar and bass manufacturing operation, based in large measure on the input of head designer Chip Todd. The instruments were the products of computer testing and the monitoring of various vibrational and electronic properties—body mass, tensile strength, and so forth. By mid 1979, the Meridian plant had shipped more than 40,000 guitars.

The standard T-60 guitar's ash body is completely shaped and carved by numerically controlled machines originally designed for contouring metal aircraft subassemblies. The bolt-on, tilt-adjustable maple neck is of an unusual, two-piece construction. Each pickup gradually changes from a humbucking (two-coil) mode to single-coil as its tone control is turned up, and the circuitry, while simple, is exceptionally versatile.

The T-25 is a comparatively low-priced electric guitar and also an achievement of which Peavey is especially proud. The results of VMA (vibrational mode analysis) convinced company engineers that a good solidbody need not be perfectly solid, and that certain parts of the body could or should have controlled, varying densities. Thus, the solid core of the T-25 is surrounded by a shaped shell of foamed polymers. The deep cutaway body is arched on the top and back and barely wider than the output jack at its narrowest. Other details include two epoxy-potted, high-output dual-coil pickups with ferrite magnets, a die-cast bridge with a three-point anchor, and a pickup switch. Peavey's T-15 solidbody features a short 23½-inch scale (like Gibson's Byrdland). Most remarkably, it was priced in 1981 at under $200, with case. It's a decidedly simple but functional instrument. As Hartley Peavey would say, "Just because a guitar ain't covered with gingerbread doesn't mean it won't do the job."

1992 Update

Peavey's original 45,000-square-foot facility was supplemented with a 30,000-square-foot woodworking plant in the mid-1980s—making it probably the largest guitar plant in the United States. There were nearly 1,900 employees by late 1989, of whom just under 200 were working in the two guitar facilities.

All Peavey guitars feature the patented bilaminated neck. The truss rod is installed before the neck is carved. In the pickup winding operation, the bobbin is stationary and the wire is precision-layered with a constant tension—as opposed to the conventional method of spinning the bobbin at high speeds while the wire wraps around it.

Hartley Peavey laments the current situation in guitar manufacturing: "The present state is unfortunate," he said. "The original pioneers have, for the most part, departed. By the '70s, conglomerates had taken over most of the U.S. production. Since 1975, most of them have departed, to be replaced by ownership that is essentially distribution-minded rather than manufacturing-minded. [There are some exceptions, but] most of the American-based companies have become largely distributors of foreign-made instruments."

In contrast, Peavey notes that his company manufactures all its guitars in the U.S. "And," he adds proudly, "we are among the oldest companies in continuous electric guitar production under the same management."

Peavey prides itself on producing good guitars at reasonable prices, and the Generation Series 1 (above, listing at $799 in 1989) is a prime example. The Peavey TL-Six 6-string bass (below) is handcrafted on a special-order basis. It is shipped with a low B to high C tuning. The TL-Six features a graphite-reinforced, through-body neck, Kahler bridge, and active EQ with low-impedance output.

Mike Pedulla founded M.V. Pedulla in 1975. He shares ownership with his brother Theodore.

PEDULLA

At M.V. Pedulla in Rockland, Massachusetts, ten workers produce 50 to 60 basses each month, and craftsmanship is paramount.

"Our manufacturing includes much handwork," said Mike Pedulla. "Our craftsmen work on instruments from beginning to end, rather than on a production line where people specialize in separate parts."

Pedulla's exceptional MVP and Buzz instruments feature contoured, figured maple bodies, neck-through construction, 34-inch scale lengths, Schaller hardware, and special-design Bartolini pickups and preamps. The stunning fretless Buzz bass has inlaid white "fret" markers and a "Diamondkote" fretboard finish. Series II models are less expensive, yet very well made and versatile.

Pedulla's exceptionally fine basses are noted for their clear, punchy sound. Beautiful finishes range from subtle solid colors to knockout sunbursts.

PENSA-SUHR

Peter Frampton, Mark Knopfler, and Victor Bailey are some of the discriminating musicians who have been entranced by the exceptional quality and artistry of Pensa-Suhr guitars.

Rudy Pensa founded Rudy's Music Stop, a New York City retail store, in 1978. John Suhr added a repair department in 1983, and two years later the pair began producing guitars and basses. Built by Suhr and Mas Hino, the guitars came in the "dinky" size (a smaller Strat style) and a dish-carved-top model. Exotic woods, different fret sizes, and various electronics were among the options. The guitars listed from $1,900 to $2,600 in 1990 and were available direct from Rudy's.

PETILLO

Phil Petillo builds about a dozen acoustic guitars and several electrics each year in his Ocean, New Jersey, workshop. His guitars are distinguished by their exquisite inlays and marquetry; a single ornament may require 70 pieces of wood, individually cut and inlaid. Phil built the first four prototypes of the Kramer aluminum-necked guitars, though he later severed his association with that company.

PRAIRIE STATE

See Maurer

REGAL

Established in 1908, the Regal Musical Instrument Company was the senior member of the Chicago powerhouses of the 1930s, 1940s, and 1950s, with factory and general offices on Grand Avenue at Sawyer Street. Though the company had been making tenor guitars for some time, it was not until April of 1927 that it officially announced its first concert guitar. A carved-top auditorium model ($45) debuted in May of 1932, and in the following January Regal announced its ampliphonic instrument, which featured a Dobro resonator [see National]. In 1937 it acquired exclusive rights to manufacture and sell Dobros, formerly made by National Dobro of Los Angeles and Chicago.

In July 1938 Regal inaugurated a direct-to-dealer policy, and in July 1940 it introduced a ukulele assembly kit, one of its scores of bargain-basement products. Two years later its $8 Victory model guitars appeared; they "contained 1 percent critical materials," a reference to government-imposed restrictions on supplies needed for the World War II effort. Regal later leased a large new building at 372 South First Street, San Jose, California.

During the late 1930s Regal was under the guidance of company president Frank Kordick. In May of 1941 Al Hunter was promoted from vice-president to president, and he became one of the kingpins of the Chicago guitar scene. During this period the firm built guitars under various brand names for several distributors.

Regal discontinued business in February of 1954, selling much of its equipment and work in progress at a huge auction. The trade names and "good will" were acquired by Harmony. In 1959 Harmony entered into an agreement to build Regal-brand acoustic guitars for Fender and continued to do so at least as late as 1966, after Fender had established its own acoustic guitar plant in Southern California.

Genuine Regal-made Regals vary widely in quality, for although the facility was one of the world's major plants and produced thousands of student-grade guitars, it also entailed a custom shop whose craftsmen were capable of impeccable work. Some Regals are quite ornate, not unlike the fancier Washburns.

A mid-1930s Regal, made with Dobro parts for Montgomery Ward. ***David Vinopal/Tom Erlewine***

Early-1940s demonstrators strike a classic pose. From left: Armstrong Dansant guitar, Rick 10-string, shaded Model 59, De Luxe amp, three NS Silver guitars (*top center*), Model B, Model S-59 Spanish with screw-on pickup, NS Silver model. Note the quotes around "electric" on poster.

RICKENBACKER

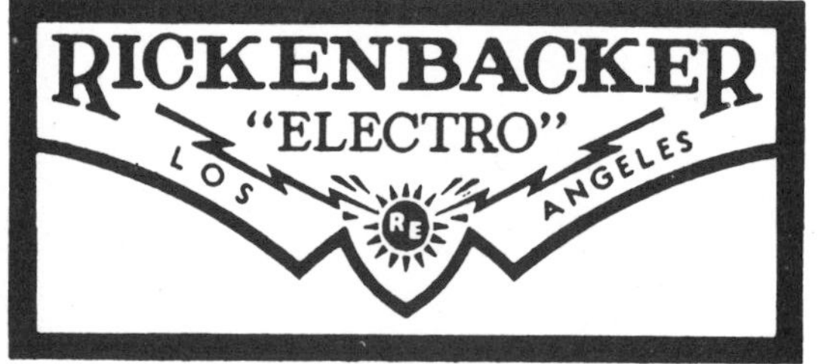

The late Adolph Rickenbacker, a Swiss tool-and-die maker and relative of air ace Eddie Rickenbacker, was a founder of Electro String Instrument Corporation and a charter member of the Los Angeles guitar-building community of the 1930s. For decades the company that now bears his name claimed credit for inventing the electric guitar—the "Frying Pan" Hawaiian lap steel—and aside from Vivi-Tone it was the first significant manufacturer of a solidbody electric Spanish model (in about 1935).

For the first 25 or 30 years of its existence, Electro's bread-and-butter products were its pickups (some of which were sold to other manufacturers), its lap steels, and its amplifiers, all manufactured under the Rickenbacker brand. The company's modern guitar heyday followed unofficial mid-sixties endorsements by Jim McGuinn of the Byrds, John Lennon and George Harrison of the Beatles, and others, and ultimately resulted in some of American guitar's most distinctive and unusual products: the 6/12 converter, Rick-O-Sound stereo, an electric 12-string with an immediately recognizable tone, the radical and influential 4001 bass, and slanted frets.

Except where noted, all photos courtesy of Rickenbacker.

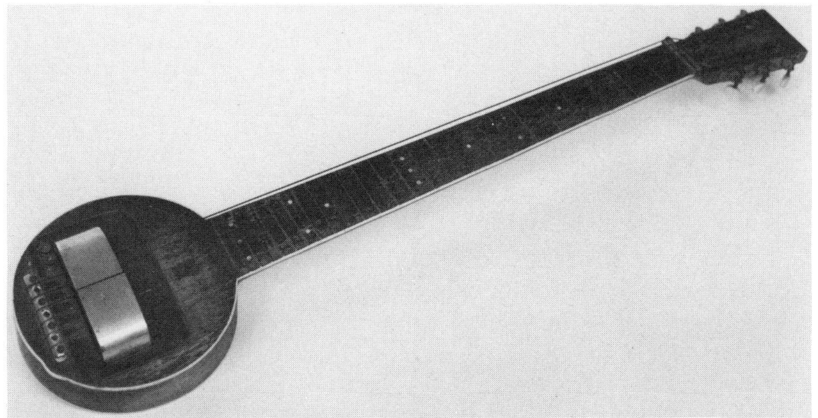

The wooden Frying Pan prototype. The huge horseshoe magnet would be an essential Rickenbacker feature until the late 1950s.

ADOLPH RICKENBACKER AND GEORGE BEAUCHAMP

All accounts of Adolph Rickenbacker's entry into guitar manufacture are tied to the Dopyera brothers [see National]. The personal relationship between Rickenbacker and the Dopyeras was, to say the least, never warm. It was marred by distrust and occasional ridicule, finally deteriorating into the verbal equivalent of switchblades and garbage can lids in the alley. The National and Rickenbacker partisans began feuding like Hatfields and McCoys over a half-century ago, and the arguments still linger (see the interviews with Victor Smith and John Dopyera in the National chapter, and Adolph Rickenbacker's account below).

The late George Beauchamp (pronounced *Bee-chum*) was right at the heart of it all. As far as the Dopyeras and their commercial heirs were concerned, Beauchamp was a troublemaker who came to John Dopyera in 1925, with an idea for a resonator guitar. Beauchamp knew little about instruments, the story goes, and Dopyera had already designed a resonator of his

1990 Update

In 1984 John C. and Cindalee P. Hall acquired the company from John's father, Francis (F. C.), and Catherine Hall. Rickenbacker International Corp. (RIC) was formed as a new company to purchase the guitar-making operations of Rickenbacker, Inc., and Electro String, which still exist as nonmusic enterprises; this consolidation reflected an emphasis on the firm's international commerce (Rickenbacker won the president's coveted "E" award for excellence in exports).

During 1989 the company invested in new equipment and moved into a new 37,000-square-foot facility in the Southern California city of Santa Ana, while resolutely maintaining many of its decades-old construction techniques. As we go to press, Rickenbacker offers 14 production guitar models, seven basses, eight vintage reissues, and five limited editions.

The model designation 381/12V69 indicates this is a reissue of 1969's Model 381 12-string; it was reintroduced in 1987.

Adolph Rickenbacker holding the first Frying Pan. His successor, F. C. Hall, is on the right.

Extremely early Rick with a solid wood body, either a prototype or a very limited production item. ***Dale Fortune***

The Rickenbacker Western Avenue factory in the 1930s.

own. Still, Dopyera took Beauchamp in as a National partner because of the latter's financial connections. Beauchamp was allegedly a wild party-goer and squanderer who took credit for the ideas of others and corrupted the stockholders, finally causing enough dissension to necessitate or encourage Dobro's split from National. It was only when he was forced out—and, the Dopyeras claimed, he had it coming—that the brothers and their companies were able to reunite. As for Rickenbacker, he wasn't a guitar maker, merely a tool-and-die man contracted to make bodies and parts for National. That's the Dopyeras' side of the story.

Adolph Rickenbacker's opinions and recollections of all this were precisely the opposite. Sure, George Beauchamp may have been an extravagant spender—much of his money was spent on others, and he was merely generous. But he was also a sensitive musician and a fine inventor. If it hadn't been for him, National never would have gotten off the ground. Those Dopyeras could repair fiddles, but that was about it. They knew nothing about building anything. They stole Beauchamp's design. It was Beauchamp who had the idea and Rickenbacker who built the guitars, at least the metal ones. The Dopyeras cruelly fired Beauchamp without sympathy for his problems or his family. That was Rickenbacker's view.

Having already designed the Frying Pan (discussed below) with Paul Barth [see National and Mosrite], Beauchamp needed someone to manufacture it for him; for whatever the reason, he left National, apparently in 1929 or 1930, and allied himself with Adolph Rickenbacker. The result of that alliance was the Electro String Instrument Corporation, manufacturer of Rickenbacker guitars.

It is at this point in our story where the plot thickens and virtually petrifies. Who done it? The relative contributions of John Dopyera and George Beauchamp to the resonator guitar

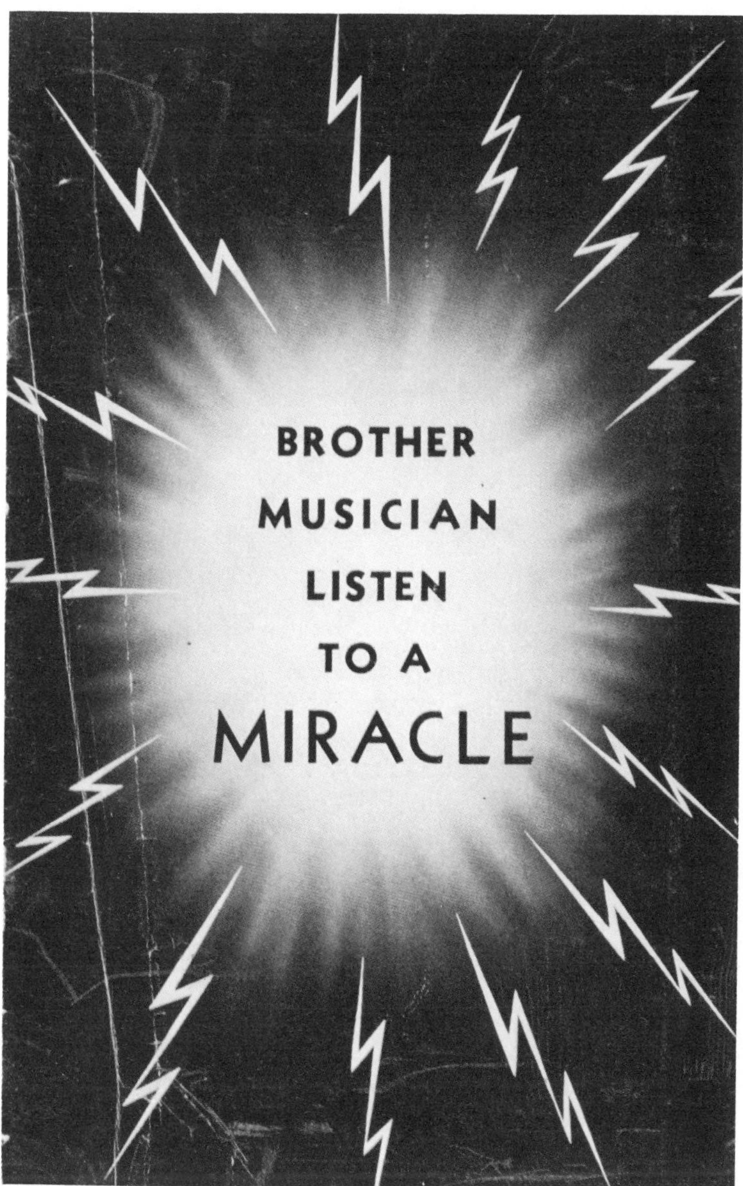

Early catalogue, circa 1936.

This photo of The Sweethearts of the Air, circa 1935, is the earliest published picture known to the author of an artist with a production model solidbody Spanish guitar (*at right*), the mid-1930s Rickenbacker.

Rickenbacker Electro Violin and amp, mid-1930s.

are unclear. The roles of Paul Barth, George Beauchamp, and Adolph Rickenbacker (who died in March 1976) in the invention of the Frying Pan electric lap steel are somewhat less hazy. More than once Mr. Rickenbacker referred to the Frying Pan's cardinal electrical principle as "the idea that *I* had" [emphasis added], though on several occasions he freely credited Beauchamp. It is the author's opinion that John Dopyera, working virtually alone, was the originator of the resophonic guitar, and that George Beauchamp was an important contributor to National's early success and chief designer of Rickenbacker's Frying Pan.

The views of John Dopyera and Victor Smith are included in the National/Dobro/Valco section, and Adolph Rickenbacker's opinions are expressed here in a first-person account taken

During the 1980s Rickenbacker marketed several limited-edition signature models, including those associated with Pete Townshend (shown here), Roger McGuinn, John Kay, Susanna Hoffs, and John Lennon.

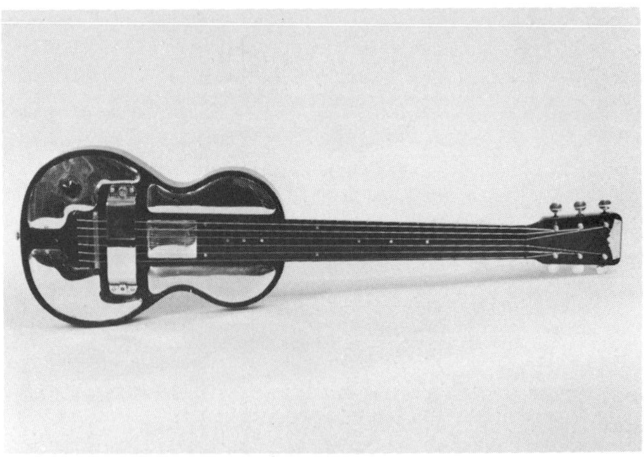

Electro electric solidbody, probably the first commercial guitar of its type. Few were made (some with vibratos), and the idea didn't catch on until Fender's Broadcaster more than a decade later. Note spelling: Rickenbacher. *Art Risk/Tom Devlin*

from a March 1972 interview with John Hall, son of F. C. Hall (see below) and himself a key company employee. It is interspersed with a couple of sentences from a written company history dated June 17, 1969 and compiled by Adolph Rickenbacker. Mr. Rickenbacker recalled:

George Beauchamp was a cotton picker for his dad down in Texas. The only thing he could make a living on was the guitar. I'll tell you, he could make you cry, a beautiful player. He was the fellow who strapped one of those big phonograph horns on the body of the sounding board to make more music. George had the idea of mounting a radio speaker diaphragm inside the guitar and mounting a bridge on top of it. Then when picking the strings it would vibrate the diaphragm, and to his surprise it worked and increased the volume about twice.

He came into my shop and told me that his guitar wasn't loud enough. He knew that I would develop patents, see, and he asked if there was anything I could do about it to make it louder. So I was telling him about the idea that I had for the [lap steel pickup].

The Dobros [Dopyera brothers] didn't know nothing. They could repair a fiddle, but I don't think they ever had an idea of making another thing. Everything they did, they ruined. None of them had any idea of making anything. I made the things. They were selling them [National guitars], lots of them, too. The Dopyeras never had no money [but see the National section]. Teddy Kleinmeyer [see National] was the fellow that had the money to put in it. Teddy had an income from an oil well. He was buying everybody big automobiles. Kleinmeyer got short of money and sold his stock to the Dopyera brothers in the company that was making the National diaphragm guitar. The first thing they did, they fired my friend George Beauchamp. George also spent everything as fast as he made it, you know. They came over and told him he was out of work, and he had a family to feed, and they fired him out.

George came over to the shop crying about it and I said, well, George, I've got an idea that I've had a long time. I said we'd build up some kind of magnetic field where the strings vibrated between. That's the reason my design [wrap-around horseshoe magnet] is better than the little points [standard polepieces], because my way you've got them vibrating over one point. I said to George, if this one works, we'll all make a lot of money, and we'll put the Dopyera brothers out of business, that stole the [National design] from you.

And the darned thing is, the first one we made worked, but we couldn't sell one. Nobody'd buy them. For a year or so nobody bought one. All of a sudden everybody started to infringe on our electric guitar [Model A-22, or Frying Pan]. I sent an attorney to Chicago but he came back after five days with a bill for $5,000 so I said the heck with this musical instrument business. I just let everybody make them, and when everybody started to make them, everybody started to buy them. We made thousands and thousands of the darned things just as fast as we could. We sold them all over the world.

We stamped the Frying Pan guitars out of sheet metal and soldered the top in and found it didn't have much tone to it, so we had to stuff the hollow aluminum neck with newspaper just as tight as we could stuff it. Couldn't have that air in there. It was hollow, though, to keep it light. We made some wooden ones, too, and we molded some out of Bakelite. *[Note: Bakelite is a dense synthetic material used in bowling balls.]*

All the head guys, the Hawaiians, played our guitars. They wouldn't buy anything but a Rickenbacker in Hawaii. The old guitars are the best ones because they're the heaviest. We used to have a set of dies where we would mold the bodies, the aluminum ones, but the factory burnt down, burnt up our dies, our patterns, see, so instead of having new patterns made we made dies to stamp them out of sheet metal.

My good friend George Beauchamp passed on, and if there is a heaven, which I know there is, he surely has a grandstand seat playing a Grand Harp amplified with a Rickenbacker pickup unit, which I still think is the best in the world. As I go to sleep listening to some good Hawaiian music I feel proud of George and myself that we did not let the guitar players down.

Ken Roberts model, middle or late 1930s, unusual seventeenth-fret neck/body joint, sideways vibrato. *Dick Allen*

Adolph Rickenbacker passed control of his company to F. C. Hall, a prominent figure in Southern California manufacturing circles for 40 years. (Hall and his wife had founded Radio-Tel, an early Fender distributor.) In 1980 Mr. Hall remembered: "My wife and I bought out the interests of Mr. Rickenbacker and his two partners in Electro String in 1953 or 1954. The original factory had been over on Western, in Los Angeles, while Radio-Tel was on Oak, in Santa Ana. Electro moved to 2118 South Main in about 1954, and in 1965 we moved to 201 East Stevens. In about 1978 we relocated to our current address at the corner of South Main and Stevens.

"Mr. Rickenbacker was very good with business. So was his wife; she was working with him. He was also a very intelligent tool-and-die maker and guitar designer. After the sale he didn't retain any financial ties, but he was still interested in the products. My wife and I formed Rickenbacker in 1965, although it didn't really change the factory. It was an organizational change. Electro is the manufacturer, and Rickenbacker is the sales company. They are separate corporations at arm's length. I became president of Rickenbacker right at the beginning."

RICKENBACKER GUITARS

The first and by far the most famous of the early Ricks is the cast aluminum A-25 lap steel guitar, much better known by its "Frying Pan" or "Fry Pan" nickname. It was designed by George Beauchamp with the assistance of Paul Barth. In the April 1974 *Guitar Player,* guitar historian Robb Lawrence quoted Barth's recollections that the two men worked on Beauchamp's kitchen table and in Paul's father's garage, laboring long hours and winding coils on a sewing machine. (Barth also built a handful of guitars under the Bartel brand, 1965–1970.) George's son Nolan was quoted as saying that Beauchamp removed the pickup from a Brunswick phonograph and mounted it on a two-by-four fitted with a single string.

The first Frying Pan, on display at Rickenbacker in Santa Ana, was actually built of maple by Harry Watson, formerly National's factory superintendent. The body is 31¾ inches long, 7 inches wide, and 1⅝ inches thick, and it features 25 frets, celluloid binding, and a phenolic (molded synthetic) plate surrounding its heavy tungsten horseshoe magnet. The com-

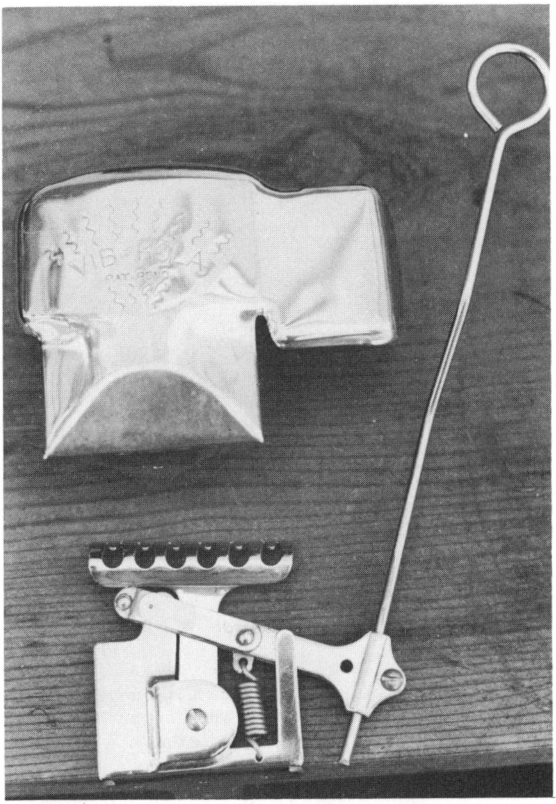

Rickenbacker Vibrola, designed by Doc Kauffman, patent filed August 19, 1929.

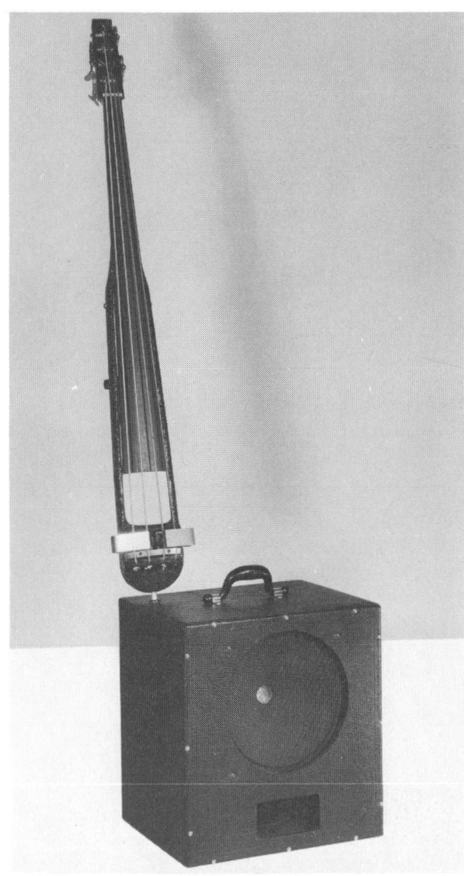

It came from California—the extremely scarce Rickenbacker all-electric bass with amp, announced November 1936.

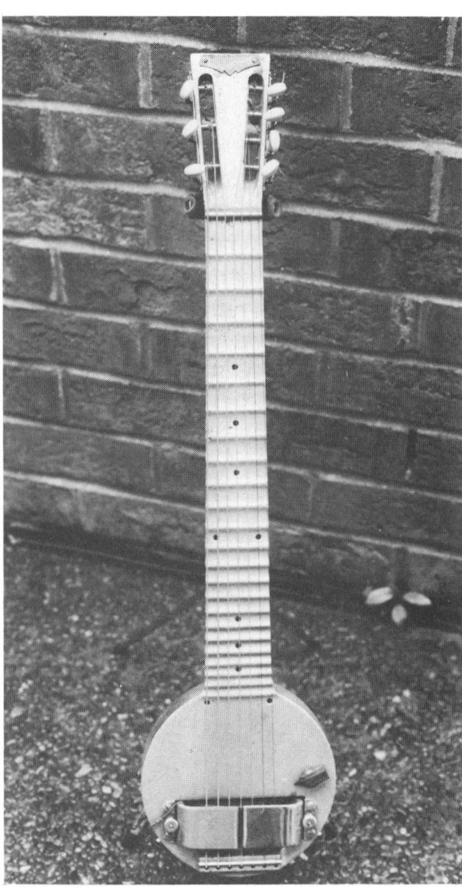

Frying Pan, 7-string version. *Acuff*

1940s Model SP Spanish electric with maple body, arched spruce top, and f-holes on the upper bouts. The tailpiece may be unoriginal. *Levon Willis/Jim Scott*

Radio star Perry Botkin demonstrating the Electro Vibrola Spanish guitar. Designed by Doc Kauffman, it had a motorized device that moved the tailpiece for a vibrato effect. The amplifier stand held it in playing position. Circa 1940.

mercial A-25 debuted in 1932 and had a small, eight-sided volume knob and a 22½-inch scale. The very similar model A-25 had a 25-inch scale. According to Dirk Vogel, a longtime and trusted Rickenbacker enthusiast, tone controls did not appear on Frying Pans until 1935. Contrary to a common belief, the Frying Pan was available off and on until the late 1950s. In the late 1970s, Sho-Bud manufactured an 8-string A-22 lookalike labeled "Fry Pan." According to Hawaiian steel great Jerry Byrd, 300 were made: 150 of the Series A short-scale models, and 150 Series B long-scale models.

As explained in the Fender chapter of this book, the problem of who invented the electric guitar is inherently insoluble in the author's view, due to simultaneous efforts of independent inventors, the conflicting recollections of principal parties, and even disagreements over what constitutes an electric Spanish guitar. Is it an arch-top with a microphone stuck inside, or a lap steel with frets? Is it a guitar-shaped Hawaiian model? Could it be a 4 by 4 board with frets and strings? There are several contenders. Whether the Frying Pan predated Vic Smith's electric Dobro is a matter of dispute. Perhaps it did. Still, at the very *least* the Frying Pan was the first electric to be built on a major scale for more than a few years, and thus the roles of Beauchamp, Barth, and Rickenbacker in guitar history are substantial indeed.

A Rickenbacker catalogue from the 1930s listed several electric instruments with horseshoe pickups: a flat-backed, oval-hole mahogany mandolin; 6- and 7-string aluminum Frying Pans; a hollow Spanish guitar with a single knob, slotted peghead, and a National-type mahogany body (perhaps a Trojan, with unmistakable National-style f-holes on the upper bouts); and a tenor guitar (4-string version of the Spanish).

One of the world's first commercial solidbody *Spanish* models (perhaps *the* first, depending on your definition; see Vivi-Tone) was Rickenbacker's Electro Spanish Guitar, a modification of the black, guitar-shaped Hawaiian model that succeeded the Frying Pan. (Early literature specified no model names other than Electro Spanish Guitar, and so on; both the black Hawaiian and Spanish models were soon designated Model B.) The exact date of the solidbody's appearance is lost, but it was about 1935. It had a fourteenth-fret neck joint, a 24-fret fingerboard, and a black and silver body. It cost $125 with the amp, and a tenor version was also available.

The Ken Roberts Electro Spanish model was an electric with a hollow, three-ply mahogany body, a seventeenth-fret neck/body joint, and a sideways vibrato designed by Doc Kauffman, the "K" of K&F [see Fender]. Electro also made a bizarre violin with no peghead and nothing resembling an acoustical chamber. It was simply a neck with a pickup, strings, bridge, and chin rest.

By 1941 or 1942 the line's size required some model names so that dealers and players (and readers half a century later) could keep things straight. The black guitar-shaped lap steel became

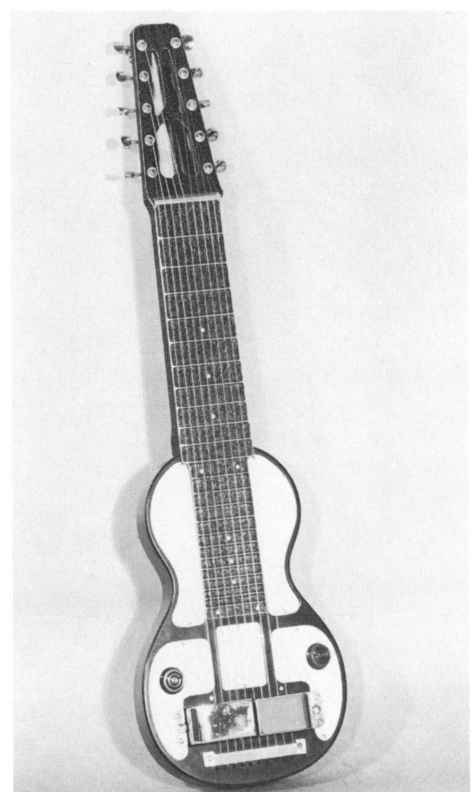

A very rare 10-string Model B. All indications are that the original version (chrome cover plates instead of white-painted) was sold as early as 1937 or 1938.

Model BD lap steel. Note peghead cover with vertical logo.

Product demonstrator with a tulip-body Combo 400, circa 1956. Standard Combo models in rear. Note pointed peghead centerpieces.

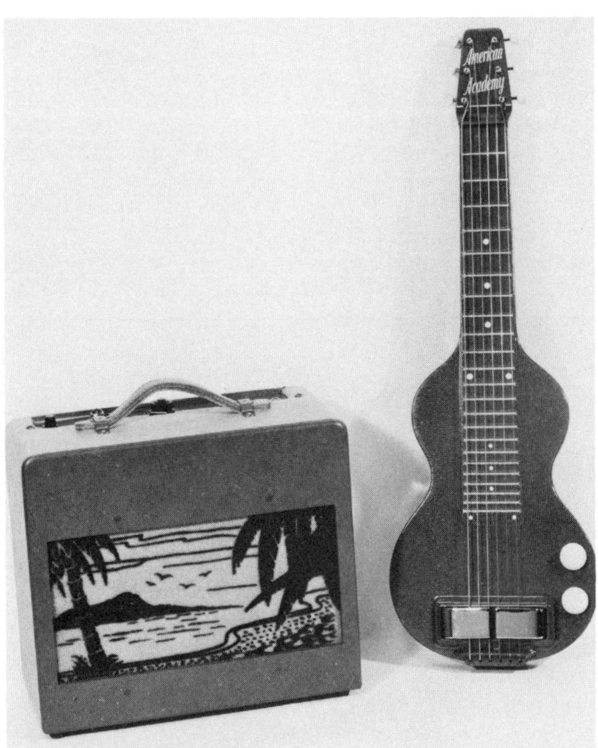

Electro's American Academy student lap steel and amp. The amp is very similar to the Ace model, which depicts a surf rider.

Model B and now had both tone and volume knobs and white fret markers; it came in 6- and 8-string versions (7- and 10-string models were available shortly thereafter).

The nameplates on these guitars were positioned horizontally; late-1940s Model Bs had enlarged T-shaped nameplates (horizontal *Rickenbacker,* vertical *Electro*). The original brand name—Rickenbacher—was Americanized to its familiar spelling in the 1930s. However, leftover nameplates with the old spelling were sometimes used in the early 1940s, a few in the late 1940s.

The S-59 ($59.50) was an electric Spanish guitar with a screw-on Electro pickup attachment, and a hollow body probably made by Kay. Electro also marketed the *Bakelite* model Spanish guitar, a very early solidbody ($65) with Kauffman's vibrato.

Other early Ricks included some doubleneck lap steels, a maple hollowbody Spanish guitar with *upper*-bout f-holes, and the Vibrola Spanish Guitar ($175 with amplifier). Electro also manufactured lap steels with brand names other than Rickenbacker, including Ace and American Academy.

Except for the Frying Pan it is the post-1950s Rickenbackers that are of substantial interest to most guitar buffs, simply because the great majority of earlier instruments were Hawaiian lap steels. The black Bakelite Spanish electric of the mid-1930s

1957's new Combo 850 had deeper cutaways than its predecessor.

A snapshot of Ricky Nelson, circa 1957, with a Rickenbacker jumbo steel-string. Nelson's bass player is at right; at left, a very young James Burton.

Three-quarter size Combo Model 1000, circa 1958, 18 frets. *Ax-In-Hand*

and early 1940s never caught on; in some company literature of the 1940s it's not even pictured. Early-1950s catalogues still depicted the amps and Hawaiian guitars that had been company mainstays since the mid 1930s.

Rickenbacker's first modern electric Spanish guitars were the two-pickup Combo 800 and one-pickup 600 solidbodies of the mid 1950s. In about 1955 two Combos, still the only electric Spanish guitars in the line, received enlarged asymmetrical pegheads that foreshadowed the distinctive look of instruments to come; the new peghead had a plastic centerpiece that looked almost like an extension of the fretboard and tapered downward into a sharp "horn."

The year 1956 brought a new look and new guitars. Pickguards on the 800 and 600 were now substantially larger. The new Combo 400 had an extremely early (perhaps the first) full-length neck centerpiece with glued-on body parts, as well as one of Rick's first "conventional" (nonhorseshoe) pickups. The body's two convex cutaways gave it sort of a tulip shape. It came in blue-green, golden brown, and black. The Combo 600 and 400 single-pickup guitars had tone selector switches; the 800 was similarly equipped and also had a pickup selector.

The Combo line expanded again about 1957, this time considerably. While the 800 and 600 were cut away on the left (bass) side between the fifteenth and sixteenth frets, the new one-pickup 650 and two-pickup 850 were cut away near the twentieth fret to increase fretboard accessibility. The new Combo 450 was a dual-pickup version of the 400. A trio of three-quarter, short-scale tulip-body guitars was added: the 900 with one pickup and 21 frets, the two-pickup 950, and the 1000 with one pickup and 18 frets. Finally, 1957 also saw the debut of Rickenbacker's first solidbody bass, Model 4000.

Ricky Nelson, circa 1958, with a Model 390 designed by Roger Rossmeisl. Note radical soundholes. James Burton on pedal steel.

The July 1958 price list specified all the 1957 Combo models plus two categories of Capri guitars, thin-body and thick-body. The *thin* Capris had flat tops recessed at the tailpiece and very distinctive, sweeping double cutaways with sharp points. Some of their features would become company hallmarks of the 1960s: triangular fretboard markers, split-level pickguards, diamond knobs (on some models), and soundholes that were bold slashes instead of traditional f-holes. The following table lists specifications of thin-body Capris; the abbreviations are: S (for Standard, referring to the trim, type of tailpiece, and scale length), ¾ (three-quarter scale length), D (Deluxe trim, including contrasting body and neck binding and large fingerboard inlays), and V (Vibrato).

Model	*Trim*	*Tailpiece*	*Scale*	*Pickups*
310	S	S	¾	2
315	S	V	¾	2
320	S	S	¾	3
325	S	V	¾	3
330	S	S	S	2
335	S	V	S	2
340	S	S	S	3
345	S	V	S	3
360	D	S	S	2
365*	D	V	S	2
370	D	S	S	3
375	D	V	S	3

* Some 365s had an extra long soundhole and two knobs instead of four.

The *thick*-body Capris of 1958 included some of Rickenbacker's most distinctive guitars ever. Model 390, for example, was a nonelectric designed by Roger Rossmeisl, later of Fender. It was a single-cutaway with a hand-carved, arched top; its dramatic soundholes were long, curving slits reminiscent of Gretsch's Synchromatics from the 1940s. Electric versions included the two-pickup Model 391, the two-pickup 392 with vibrato, the three-pickup 393, and the three-pickup 394 with vibrato. Another intriguing late-1950s thick-body Capri was Model 381, sometimes called the Western Concerto. It had sweeping, pointed double cutaways; triangular markers; a single, slit-shaped soundhole; two pickups; two switches; two small metal knobs; and a one-piece pickguard shaped like the later split-level type.

Other thick-body Capris from 1958 were the nonelectric Model 380, the 382 with vibrato, the three-pickup 383, the three-pickup 384 with vibrato, the flat-top 385 steel-string with a V-shaped headstock, the two-pickup 386, the 387 with vibrato, the three-pickup 388, and the three-pickup 389 with vibrato. Models 330F to 375F were *single*-cutaway thin Capris from 1959 with triangular markers, diamond knobs, and split-level pickguards.

Model 450 solidbody, circa 1958. The high, cresting wave-shaped cutaway first appeared on this guitar circa 1958 and became a long-lasting Rick hallmark. (Model 425 was the single-pickup version.) During the 1960s, Model 450's peghead logo plate was replaced with the sharp, horn-shaped piece, and the metal pickguard was replaced with plastic. ***Soest/Rountree***

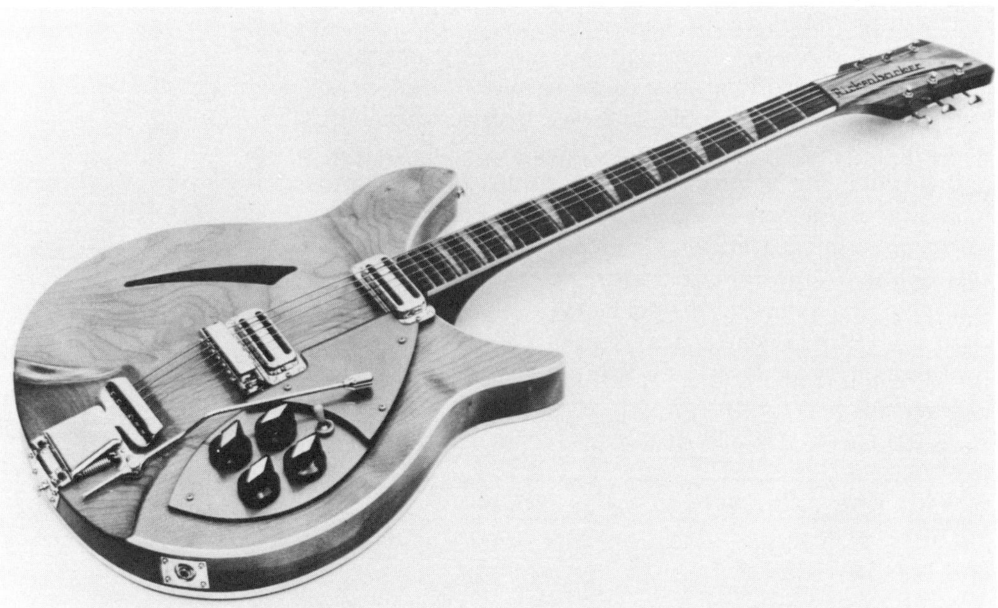

Model 365, circa 1959, recessed body (at tailpiece), triangular markers, diamond knobs, original style vibrato.

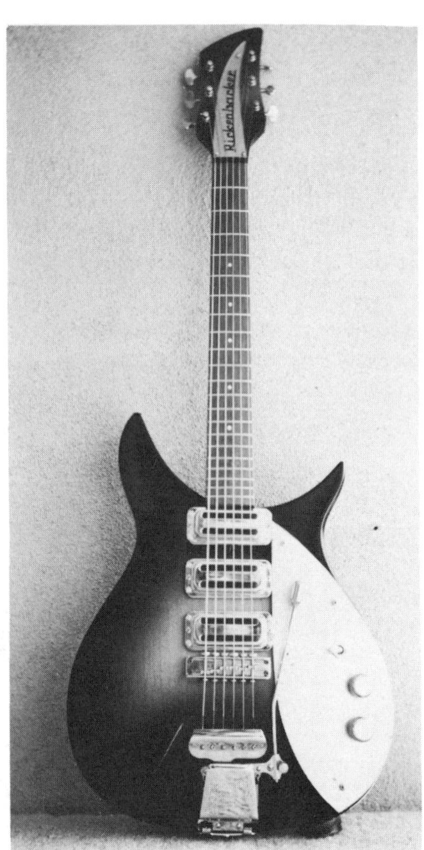

1958 Model 325. Later versions had a standard f-hole.

1959–1960 365F: single-cutaway, diamond knobs, split-level pickguard. Late-1960s versions had double-cutaways, smaller knobs, and new vibratos.

Capri thin-body Model 360, circa 1958. *Ax-In-Hand*

The July 1964 price list specified four categories of guitars. The first was the Combo series, with its cresting wave-shaped cutaways: the one-pickup Model 425 with vibrato, the two-pickup 450 with no binding, the two-pickup 460 with deluxe white binding, the 600, the two-pickup 615 with vibrato, the 625 with Rick-O-Sound Stereo, the 800, the 850, the three-quarter size 900, and the three-quarter size 950.

The *thin* hollowbody series included four three-quarter guitars: the 310, the 315 with vibrato, the three-pickup 320, and the three-pickup 325 with vibrato. The four standard 6-strings were the 330, the 335 with vibrato, the three-pickup 340, and the three-pickup 345 with vibrato. Finally, there were five deluxe models ($434–550) with triangle inlays, white binding, and stereo; these were the Model 360, the 360-12 12-string, the vibrato-equipped 365, the three-pickup 370, and the three-pickup 375 with vibrato.

The F (Full body) Series standard electric hollowbodies of mid 1964 were the 330F, the 335F with vibrato, the three-pick-

1964 Rose, Morris export Rickenbacker Model 1993. The first Rick 12-string came out in mid-1963. George Harrison's was the second (December 1963).

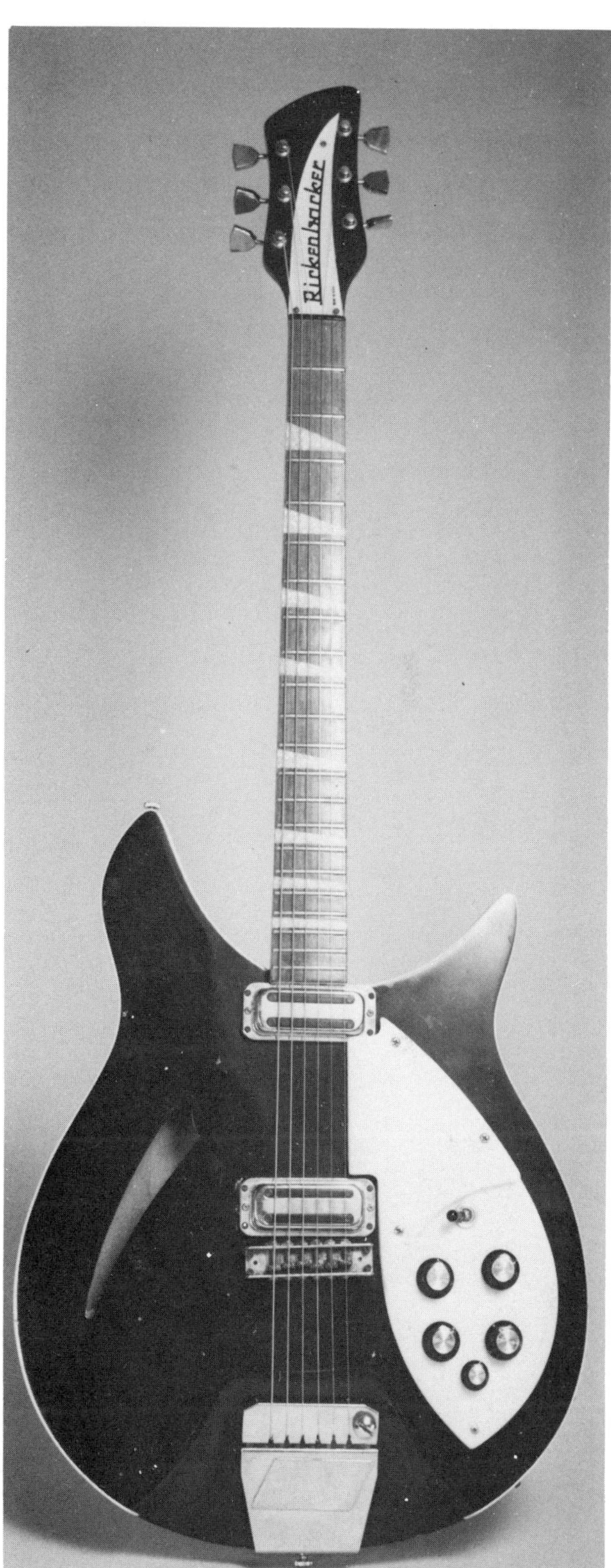

One of the very distinctive Capris: swept wing body, cat's-eye soundhole, triangular markers, split-level pickguard. ***Charley's/ Crump***

Model 335, circa 1960: fretboard dots, no binding.

Famed banjo showman Eddie Peabody with a Banjoline; the six strings constitute two pairs and two singles, and it's played like a 4-string plectrum instrument.

up 340F, and the three-pickup 345F with vibrato. The Deluxe-trim models were the 360F, 365F with vibrato, three-pickup 370F, and three-pickup 375F with vibrato.

The 1964 *thick*-body nonelectric (n) and electric guitars were the 380 (n), 381, 385 (n, roundhole), 386 (electric, roundhole), 390 (n, carved top and back), 391 (electric, carved), and 392 (carved top, two pickups, vibrato, $859).

Two basses were listed in 1964, the 4000 and 4001. The year 1965 saw three new guitars, the budget Combo Model 420 (one pickup, $179.50), plus a pair of 12-strings: the 450-12 solidbody and the 330-12 thin hollowbody.

Seldom can the origin of a musical genre be traced to a single recording, but when the Byrds released their electrified version of Bob Dylan's "Mr. Tambourine Man" in June 1965, folk-rock was seemingly born on the spot. Along with the choir-like harmonies, the most identifiable element of the Byrds' early sound was the crystalline chime of a Rickenbacker electric 12-string. The company's various 12-strings enjoyed an intense if short-lived popularity, and collectively they were perhaps Rickenbacker's most important late-1960s guitars, just as the 4001 bass would become its most significant instrument of the 1970s. John Lennon and Pete Townshend also favored Rickenbackers, and their unofficial endorsements helped make the mid and late 1960s a time of unprecedented popularity for the company.

Comparing the 1968 catalogue to the 1965 price list reveals several additions by 1968: Model 1000 (a reappearance, ¾, 18 frets), and three 6/12 converter models: the 336-12, 366-12, and 456-12. There were also several deletions: Models 600, 800, 850, and 950. By 1964 the big diamond knobs that had distinguished earlier hollowbodies were replaced with smaller, faceted round knobs with silver-dish tops.

Models 360 to 375 (1968) were fancier hollowbody guitars, all with bound bodies and necks, stereo outputs, rounded cutaways, and triangular markers. The 360 ($429) had two pickups; the 360-12, 366-12, and 365 were, respectively, 12-string, converter, and vibrato versions. The 370 had three pickups, as did the vibrato-equipped 375 ($515).

Rickenbacker guitars numbered 360F to 370F ($439–515) had minimal single cutaways and bound semiacoustic maple bodies, single soundholes, stereo outputs, triangular markers, and five knobs arranged in a crescent. The two-pickup 360F and 365F were, respectively, standard and vibrato guitars, while the 370F and 375F (vibrato) were three-pickup versions.

Models 380 to 394 all had deep bodies and included the 380, a very rare double-cutaway *non*electric guitar. The 381 ($498) had two pickups, triangular markers, a split-level pickguard, and extensive top sculpting that included raised ridges following the body's outline. The 385 was a jumbo flat-top with a V-shaped peghead; the 386 was similar but had two pickups. The 390 was very similar to its 1958 predecessor; 391 and 392 ($859) were two-pickup standard and vibrato versions, respectively.

Other members of the late-1960s line included the Banjoline (guitar shape, 6 strings, banjo neck, standard and deluxe ver-

Model 325, a mid-1960s three-quarter size semiacoustic. ***Allen Woody***

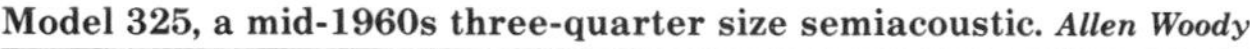

1968 Model 375. Note pointed vibrato handle.

sions), the Bantar (banjo shape, 5 strings), and several basses—the original 4000, the 4001, 4005 hollowbody, and 4005-6 6-string bass.

The 4001, with its extreme cutaways and black and white block binding, became Rickenbacker's most distinctive instrument of the late 1960s and 1970s. Its radical looks, thin neck, and especially its twangy tone made it a popular alternative to the Fender Precision.

Models 330 to 345 ($365–449) were maple hollowbodies with fairly sharp double cutaways and dot markers: the 330 and 330-12 had two pickups; the 335 was vibrato-equipped; the 336-12 had a 6-12 converter; and the 340 and 345 were, respectively, nonvibrato and vibrato-equipped three-pickup models.

There were no announced model changes in 1969. Comparing the June 1971 price list to the 1969 catalogue reveals several additions: Models 331 (frequency modulated, internally lighted body), 430, 470 (Deluxe trim, 24 frets), and 480 (styled like the 4000 bass, 24 frets). There were also several deletions: Models 310, 391, 392, and 1000.

Rickenbacker's glossy, lacquered fingerboards have long been a distinguishing feature. In about 1971 another unusual characteristic appeared—optional slanted frets, designed to more naturally accommodate the player's hand. Most guitars could be factory-equipped with slanted frets for an extra $100, and within four years all guitars were eligible for the option. On Model 481 the feature was standard. The modified fingerboards required slanted nuts, pickups, and bridges.

The Rickenbackers of the mid-1970s included a few late-1960s holdovers like the 420, 450, 450/12, 456/12, 460, and the 950 (its old tulip body restyled with the wave-shaped cutaway). The 620 was a nonvibrato version of the 1968 Model 625, and the 430 was an all new guitar with 24 frets and all-black pickups. The late-1960s Rickenbacker pickups had chrome borders and a pair of horizontal dark strips in the center, while on all mid-1970s models except the 320 the entire center portion was black. The late-1960s triangular markers extended to the edge of the fretboards, in contrast to the smaller markers of the mid-1970s.

Other mid-1970s models included the 320 (one traditional f-hole, three-quarter body, three pickups). The two-pickup 330, 330/12 12-string, 336/12 converter, and three-pickup 340 were all thin, sharp-cutaway semiacoustics with dot markers. The 360, 360/12, 366/12, and three-pickup 370 were all deluxe, rounded-cutaway thin hollowbodies with stereo, bound soundholes, and triangle markers. The 362/12 was a hollow 6/12 doubleneck, and the 4080 was a solidbody bass/guitar doubleneck. Like the dot-neck 480, the 481 (triangles, phase switch) was a solidbody shaped like the 4001 bass. Mid-1970s basses included the 4000, 4001, 4005, and the 4005/6 6-string bass. Model 490 was advertised to have 24 frets and a phase switch, but the guitar never went into production; in fact, the one illustrated in brochures was the only one ever made.

Comparing the June 1976 price list to the 1975 catalogue reveals several deletions: 490, 900, and 456/12 were gone. Comparing the January 1977 price list to the June 1976 list reveals two new models—the 4080/12 bass/12-string doubleneck, and the 4002 bass (high- and low-impedance). The deletions were Models 331, 336/12, 365, and 366/12.

RIPLEY

Steve Ripley was a guitarist for Bob Dylan and a recording engineer for Leon Russell before establishing Ripley Guitars, Inc. At the January 1983 NAMM trade show, his stereo guitars were big news. Their patent-pending circuitry uses one or more multi-channel pickups, plus a pan pot (balance control) for each string. Ripley explained that he had "a vision of the guitar as a multi-channel system, with each string being its own entity, to be processed and mixed much like I would mix instruments in the studio."

Early clients included Eddie Van Halen, whose support led to a licensing agreement with Kramer. A single-pickup guitar and a 5-string bass were marketed.

Meanwhile, Ripley developed more elaborate systems. Options now include: stereo gating, or triggering from an external source such as a drum machine; stereo tremolo; effects sends for each string, with multi-effect returns; individual distortion for each string; and more.

Ripley's most successful instrument is the 5-string bass. "Neck-through-body basses are popular, but a lot of us love bolt-ons," said Ripley. "I think we have the best 5-string for the guy who's played a Precision or Jazz Bass all his life."

Ripley favors light woods, rather than expensive hardwoods. "As a rule, with the exception of swamp ash, the prettier the wood, the worse it sounds," he said. "The greatest of the old Fenders feel like feathers compared to most instruments today. Lighter woods feel more alive to me."

In 1986, Ripley moved to his "mad scientist's lab" in Tulsa, Oklahoma. In 1988, he and Kramer ended their association. His newest product is the "D Neck," which can, without modifications, turn any bolt-on neck guitar into a long-scale (28.62-inch) instrument with two extra frets on the low end.

Steve Ripley's personal guitar, with panning, compression, tremolo, hex distortion, 6-channel gating, and breath controller.

Long-scale Tele-style guitar with the Ripley "D Neck."

ROBIN

Robin Guitars of Houston was founded by David Wintz, a repairman, designer, builder, and vintage retailer. From 1982 through 1986 his guitars were produced in Japan. They had reversed Explorer-style headstocks; later in the decade, other manufacturers adopted this feature.

Wintz brought the production to the States and introduced his first U.S.-made model, the Medley Custom TX (for Texas), at the Anaheim, California NAMM trade show in 1987. It featured a mahogany neck-through-body design and curly maple arched top. The line soon expanded to include bolt-on neck guitars and basses in both conventional and unconventional styles. Robin produces 40 to 50 instruments a month, some of which are exported.

Dave Wintz is shown here with the first Robin (1982) and a 1989 layered-body Machete with a split 4 × 2 headstock.

Richard Hoover, co-founder of Santa Cruz Guitar Co.

SANTA CRUZ

With their avowed intent to "apply the values of custom luthiery to a limited production setting," builder Richard Hoover and repairmen William Davis and Bruce Ross founded the Santa Cruz Guitar Co. in 1976. By the mid-1980s over 400 custom and standard model flat-tops, classicals, and arch-tops had been crafted.

Davis left the California company in 1978, and Hoover bought Ross' interests in 1989. Today, Hoover, Jeff Traugott, and Bill Hardin, with employees Fred Latt and Steve Swan, are crafting about 20 instruments a month, and the focus remains the same as when the company was founded. Models include the FS (Finger Style), with blue wooden purfling and rosewood binding; and the small-body (yet deep) Model H, inspired by Gibson's 1930s Nick Lucas Special.

Santa Cruz guitars are known for their elegant simplicity. The Model D dreadnought, for example, has neither fingerboard markers nor pickguard. List prices, including case, run from about $1,700 for the D and H up to about $4,000 for the FJZ arch-top, for which elaborate inlay work is available.

Detail of custom FTC Cutaway.

258

GUITARS AT PRICES BEYOND COMPARE.

22330 $3.85

22326 $2.70

22336 $9.60

22328 $3.60

22335 $8.20

LIBERAL TERMS Any guitar sent C.O.D., subject to examination when $1.00 is sent with order. FIVE DAYS' TRIAL FREE When cash in full accompanies order the guitar may be returned at any time within five days, if not found exactly as represented and entirely satisfactory, and money will be cheerfully refunded in full. WE GIVE WITH EVERY GUITAR A VALUABLE INSTRUCTION BOOK AND FULL SET OF SUPERIOR STEEL STRINGS.

We pack these instruments as carefully as possible in a light, strong box, which insures their reaching you in perfect condition. When boxed for shipment package weighs about 12 pounds.

THE TROUBADOUR.

No. 22326 An instrument of surprising quality and tone. Neat inlaying around sound hole. Fingerboard accurately fretted with raised frets, inlaid position dots, metal tailpiece, highly polished, mahogany finish so near like the genuine wood that most people readily believe it to be the real wood. Genuine American patent head. A complete and desirable outfit, such as no other concern can possibly give at anything like our price.
Our special price, standard size........ $2.70

ThE ENCORE.

No. 22328 A genuine American made instrument of great beauty and immensely popular with every purchaser. Made of the best solid birch, in imitation of rosewood, highly polished. Fingerboard is perfect in scale, accurately fretted with raised frets, inlaid position dots, American patent head, metal tailpiece, celluloid bound top edge, beautiful inlaid strip in back. A regular $8.00 guitar.
Our special price, standard size........ $3.60

THE OAKWOOD.

No. 22330 This beautiful guitar is made of selected quarter sawed oak, highly finished. The top is handsomely finished in orange color, offering a pleasing contrast with the oak back and sides. Beautiful inlaid strip in back. Fancy inlaying around sound hole. Rosewood fingerboard with position dots and raised frets perfect in scale. American screw patent head, metal tailpiece.
Our special price, standard size........ $3.85

THE MARLOWE.

No. 22331 Our special solid mahogany guitar, mahogany neck, rosewood fingerboard, accurately fitted with raised frets and inlaid position dots, orange colored top, handsome inlaying around sound hole, and strip down the back. Best American made brass patent head.
Our special price........ $5.95

Our "20th Century" Bargain.

THE GREATEST VALUE EVER OFFERED.
$16.00 ACME PROFESSIONAL GUITAR FOR $8.20.

No. 22335 is made of selected bird's eye maple, with black edges, beautiful inlaid strip in back; selected cedar front, with beautiful inlaid strip around sound hole. Mahogany neck, with ebony fingerboard, inlaid with three pearl position dots; brass patent head and patent nickel plated tailpiece. Standard size.
Our special price........ $8.20

THE KENMORE.

No. 22336 For $9.60 we offer a solid rosewood guitar of highest merit and retailed at $15.00 to $18.00. A beautifully modeled instrument, with the finest French polish. Popular orange colored front. Best selected cedar neck. Fingerboard absolutely correct in scale with raised frets and inlaid position dots. Genuine American screw patent head. Inlaid around sound hole and beautiful inlaid strip in back. In every respect a superior instrument.
Our special price, standard size........ $9.60

No. 22338 Same guitar as No. 22336, but large concert size.
Our special price........ $10.80

GUITAR CASES AND FURNISHINGS OF ALL KINDS LISTED ON PAGE 281

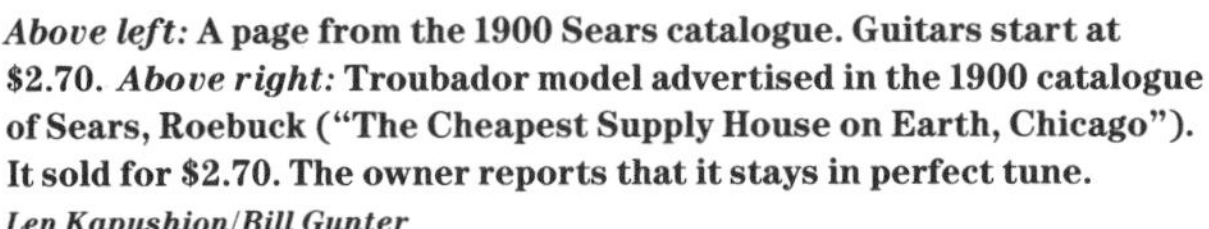

Above left: A page from the 1900 Sears catalogue. Guitars start at $2.70. *Above right:* Troubador model advertised in the 1900 catalogue of Sears, Roebuck ("The Cheapest Supply House on Earth, Chicago"). It sold for $2.70. The owner reports that it stays in perfect tune. *Len Kapushion/Bill Gunter*

The Santa Cruz Tony Rice model is a rosewood dreadnought with an extra-stiff spruce top and enlarged 4¼-inch soundhole. *Paul Schraub*

SEARS AND SILVERTONE

Sears catalogues were the Dick & Jane primers of popular guitar literature during the 1950s and 1960s. Far more widely distributed than any manufacturer's brochure, they introduced thousands of players to the guitar's basic vocabulary: arch-top, machine head, Bigsby, reverb. Sears' brand name was Silvertone, and many youngsters no doubt pictured some Silvertone factory, perhaps not too different from that of Gibson or Martin.

Of course, there was no Silvertone factory as such, or even a Silvertone company. Like many of the brands appearing in the mammoth catalogue, the name was owned by Sears and applied to products made by various manufacturers, in this case Harmony (which Sears owned), Valco, Danelectro, and to a lesser extent, Kay. For details, see the sections on those companies.

Flat-top by Geo. Bauer of Philadelphia. Note fleur-de-lis peghead inlay. *Spitzer's/Sievert*

SLINGERLAND

The Slingerland Banjo and Drum Company of Chicago, best known for its drums, was established in 1916 and incorporated under the laws of Illinois. H. H. Slingerland was president and general manager, and his offices and a 25,000 square foot factory were located at 1815 Orchard Street. In September 1936 the company announced its Marvel line of carved-top guitars. One catalogue depicts a line of Slingerland models sold under various brand names, from the $7.80 Songster and $8.50 College Pal through several May-Bell flat-tops (some with painted tops) and May-Bell Violin Craft f-hole models (starting at $10) up to the $45 Slingerland Nite Hawk arch-top.

S. S. STEWART; BAUER

The reportedly eccentric S. S. Stewart (221–223 Church Street, Philadelphia) was a leading banjo manufacturer who during the late 1800s became one of the first to demonstrate that mass-production techniques could be applied to instrument building with good results. Mr. Stewart entered into a partnership with a fellow Philadelphian and well-known guitar maker in his own right, George Bauer, and the two established a new company, Stewart & Bauer, also in Philadelphia.

The very rare first-generation S. S. Stewart guitars are similar enough to Bauer's own models to suggest that Bauer was already building for Stewart when the partnership was formed. Pehr Anderberg [see Ditson] supervised the Stewart & Bauer operation for a period during the early 1900s.

When Stewart died, Bauer continued to market guitars, many of which bore the S&B logo and carried the Monogram brand name. After Mr. Bauer took ill, the company was dissolved. Stewart's family put out some instruments labeled S. S. Stewart's Sons, and in the late 1930s or early 1940s the Stewart name began appearing on all sorts of low- and moderate-grade guitars, including Harmonys, some of which were distributed through Weymann. These later guitars were related to the early Stewarts, Bauers, and Stewart & Bauers in name only.

Steinberger XL2: headless design for improved balance, double ball string system, and body-mounted micrometer tuners. The body and neck are constructed from a proprietary blend of carbon and other fibers, molded with a specially modified thermoset resin.

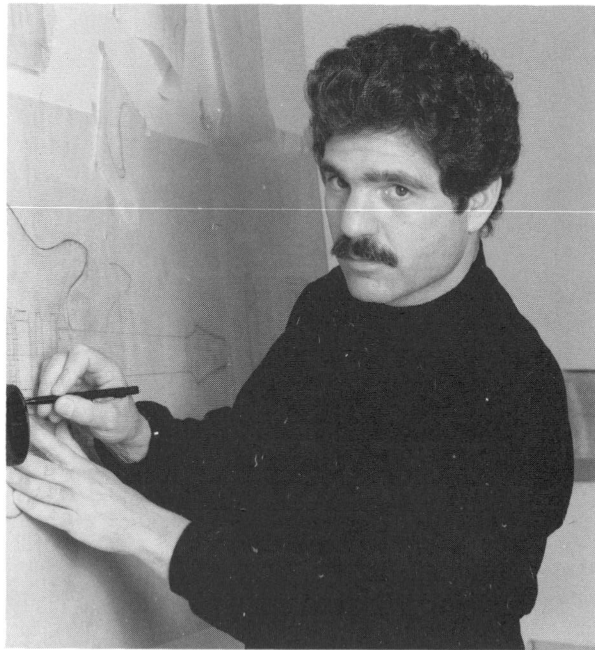

Ned Steinberger, an award-winning industrial designer in the form-follows-function tradition of Leo Fender.

Introduced in 1987, Steinberger's GM4 has a somewhat conventionally shaped body and EMG pickups.

STANDEL

Standel was founded circa 1960 by Bob Crooks, a southern California electronics engineer. Located at 4983 Double Drive, Temple City, California, it gained prominence as a major manufacturer of solid-state amplifiers, particularly in the mid 1960s. In 1966 or 1967, Sam Koontz [see Koontz, also Harptone], designed a series of basses and acoustic and electric guitars that were manufactured in the Harptone plant in Newark, New Jersey, and marketed by Standel under the Standel name. According to Mr. Koontz, only a few hundred Standel instruments were produced. Bob Crooks was indirectly responsible for the shape of the Mosrite Ventures model [see Mosrite].

STEINBERGER

It's unlikely that we'll ever again see a designer as influential as Leo Fender, but if anyone can be called the Leo Fender of the 1980s, Ned Steinberger is a credible contender in some respects. Neither man took up guitar. Like Fender, Steinberger brought his radical designs to a stubborn, tradition-bound industry, and like Fender, he revolutionized American guitars. During the 1960s and 1970s, guitar players, for all their interest in radical sounds, were quite traditional in their tastes in instruments. Guitars and basses were supposed to look a certain way, and any that didn't, well, they were usually ignored, ridiculed, or both.

Enter Ned Steinberger. His bass looked wrong in every way, at least by conventional standards: tiny body, no tuners on the headstock—in fact, no headstock. It wasn't even made of wood. Yet starting from the ground up, Steinberger had created one of the purest examples of form following function since the Telecaster.

In December 1979 he started his company, using his personal 1,500-square-foot work space at the Brooklyn Woodworkers Co-op, where he was a member. The co-founders were Stanley Jay and Hap Kuffner, both of the Mandolin Bros. music store, and plastics engineer Bob Young. In 1983 Steinberger moved into a 12,000-square-foot facility in Newburgh, New York. In 1986 Gibson acquired 10 percent of the firm, and a year later it acquired the remaining 90 percent. As we go to press, Steinberger has 35 employees in all, and is producing approximately 350 guitars and basses per month. The vast majority of Steinberger production occurs at the Newburgh facility, although some of the wooden bodies come from Gibson's factories in Tennessee and Montana. The only exceptions are the XM basses, which have bodies made by Guitabec in Canada. Some older GM and XM bodies were also made there.

Among Steinberger's many notable achievements is the precision-crafted TransTrem transposing tremolo, which permits the user to shift the instrument's pitch up or down to any of several positions (and then to actually play in tune—it works!). Steinberger produces its composite-neck instruments under a license from Modulus Graphite, and in turn Steinberger licenses Hohner and Cort to make instruments with the double-ball string system. Hohner has an exclusive license to build guitars with the Steinberger shape, which itself is a registered trademark [also see Spector].

STELLA

See Oscar Schmidt

STROMBERG

Charles A. Stromberg was a Swedish cabinetmaker who immigrated to Boston in 1887. He spent 18 years at the Thompson & Odell firm supervising the production of some 3,500 guitars, banjos, and mandolins. In about 1905 he went into business for himself, building special-order orchestra and band instruments, drums, banjos, and a few guitars. He also worked for Vega as a repairman, specializing in harps and violins.

Charles Stromberg had two sons. Elmer was born in Chelsea, Massachusetts, on July 14, 1895. In 1910 he joined his father in the shop, and later became his only partner. Though his name never appeared on the Stromberg label, it was Elmer who built the guitars that made the company famous among the East Coast's jazz artists of the 1930s, 1940s, and 1950s.

According to researcher Jeff Tripp, Elmer served as an ambulance driver during World War I. Except when his temper got the best of him, he was by all accounts a very pleasant gentleman. He, his wife Mary, and his father lived in an apartment in Somerville's Ten Hills district. Elmer and Mary had no children.

An early Stromberg shop was located at 19 Washington Street, Boston, but the best-known guitars were built on the fourth floor of 40 Hanover Street, where the two men moved in about late 1927. This 250 square foot facility was near the Casino Burlesque theatre, just off Scollay Square, currently the site of Boston's Government Center. The shop became a mecca for visiting jazz guitarists, who would congregate there to talk, play, and give advice to Charles and Elmer. Distinguished Stromberg endorsers included Mundell Lowe, Irving Ashby, Barry Galbraith, Laurindo Almeida, and Freddie Green.

Collector/retailer Louis Catello of Berlin, New Hampshire, knew Charles and Elmer Stromberg. He recalled: "Elmer was the typical starving craftsman. He made a living, but that was it. Sometimes he would take wood home from the shop to burn in order to save money on coal. *[Note: Elmer salvaged excellent woods for his guitars from torn-down houses. According to former Vega president Bill Nelson, the Strombergs also ac-*

The massive but elegant Stromberg 400. *Spitzer's/Sievert*

quired woods from Vega.] Elmer had an awful old car. Seems to me it was a '37 Pontiac that he drove up until the 1950s. His father was an octogenarian and when he died, Elmer didn't last much longer, just a few months. The place closed up. The whole section was torn down years ago.

"They were both exceptionally fine repairmen. Charlie was a wonderful old man who looked like a characterization of Saint Nick, with a bald head, round spectacles, and little tufts of hair. He was a hale and hearty man.

"Elmer attached pickups only on special order, and on some of the later models he had a detachable neck with a truss rod adjustment located underneath the string nut. There was a knack to getting the neck out because it wasn't glued; you just sort of gave it a karate chop at a certain angle, and it popped right out. Elmer's pickguards looked a lot like John D'Angelico's. There was always a lot of talk about who copied whom."

Stromberg arch-tops were produced in limited quantities, reportedly about 640 in all, and guaranteed for life. The earlier guitars were generally smaller, often had three-segment soundholes and nonadjustable necks, and were of mediocre quality. It was the larger and later guitars that established Stromberg's reputation for excellence, and the finest of these rivaled the best of Gibson, Epiphone, and D'Angelico. They typically had conventional f-holes and a single diagonal top brace. The latter feature, essentially one half of an X brace, was most unusual.

Elmer Stromberg in his Boston shop.

Elmer's crowning glory, the Master 400, was among the widest of the East Coast's distinguished arch-tops. At 19 inches across, its lower bout was even greater than Gibson's Super 400, D'Angelico's New Yorker, and Epiphone's Emperor. The Master 400 had a comparatively thick spruce top, ivoroid-bound f-holes, and a slim and comfortable maple neck. The Master 300 had the same size body, solid block markers, and less fancy trim. Other Strombergs included the G-100, G-3 (17⅜ inches wide, standard pickguard, standard Klusons, split rectangle markers), G-1, and Deluxe (17⅜ inches wide, stairstep pickguard, and Seal Fast Klusons). Most were available in cutaway models.

According to Jeff Tripp, the Strombergs simply used their business cards for labels during the early years, and the telephone numbers can help determine when a particular model was made. Here are some phone numbers, all with *Bowdoin* prefixes, and their corresponding dates: 1728R or 1728M (1920), 6559W or 1242W (1927), and 1878R (1929). A later number was CA 3174 (1932–1945). By 1949, the number had been changed to CA 7–3174.

Elmer Stromberg, who died December 11, 1955, had definite ideas about the relationships among bracing, body size, and tone. To this day guitarists argue about the merits and the suitability of his guitars for various applications, but the fact that many Stromberg enthusiasts were former users of Gibsons, D'Angelicos, or Epiphones is strong testimony to the quality of Stromberg instruments. As collector George Gruhn said, "Whereas the D'Angelicos were sort of like super Gibsons—beautiful sounding and very versatile—the better Strombergs were like super Epiphones, with an awful lot of cutting power. If you wanted a pretty sound for the studio you might not pick a Stromberg, because its tone wouldn't come into its own until you played it really hard. But if you played rhythm in a big band with horns and you wanted to be heard, one of the later, big-body Strombergs would deliver. They were the loudest guitars in creation."

TAYLOR

Bob Taylor lives and builds guitars in Lemon Grove, California, a community near San Diego. He worked with Kurt Listug and Steve Schemmer at the American Dream guitar repair shop in Lemon Grove, and when that enterprise folded in October of 1974, Taylor and his two friends bought it. They became partners and converted the old repair shop into a guitar factory, soon producing 12 instruments each month. By 1978 monthly production was up to 50 guitars—each taking about 35 hours of work—and five full-time craftsmen were employed.

1992 Taylor Update
Bob Taylor and Kurt Listug bought out Steve Schemmer in 1983 and the new partners incorporated later that year. The company's smaller-size Grand Concert guitar, introduced in early 1984, caught on, and by 1989 accounted for 20 percent of the firm's sales. In 1985 Taylor unveiled its first signature guitar, the Dan Crary Signature Model.

In 1987, Taylor moved to a new 5,000-square-foot facility in Santee, California. By 1989, production was up to about 10 guitars—and 12 cases, built in a separate 2,500-square-foot area—per day. As we go to press, Taylor employs 32 people.

TILTON

See Ditson

Kurt Listug (left) and Bob Taylor.

Taylor 855 12-string. By late 1981 Taylor had shrunk to a three-man operation, although the crew claimed that its output of 30 guitars a month ranked fourth among U.S. acoustic guitar manufacturers.

Travis Bean Artist 1000.

Travis Bean, making final adjustments on one of his guitars.

TRAVIS BEAN

Guitars with aluminum necks? A sensible innovation, or just a bozo notion from some California motorcycle racer? Despite all the advertising fireworks about the latest and the newest, guitar design is often surprisingly conservative. Truly radical departures generally have a tough go of it.

Travis Bean grew up in San Fernando, near Los Angeles. A Lockheed employee named Kenneth Soule had a home shop, and from him Travis learned the fundamentals of metal machine work.

Bean's first career was motorcycle racing. At one time he ranked 19th out of 4,500 California Motorsport Club members. But he had another passion, metal sculpting. After having broken one too many bones, Travis Bean abandoned motorcycling and took up guitar building.

As far as Travis was concerned, not much had happened in guitar design since the introduction of the classic Fenders and Gibsons in the Golden Decade of the 1950s. Travis became friends with guitar repairman Marc McElwee. Watching Marc work, he became convinced of the inefficiency of tuning systems and instability of wooden necks, which required constant adjustments. These observations led to the aluminum neck, the essential feature in Travis Bean guitars. It was strictly an experiment in maintenance improvement that also happened to work well on other counts.

The Bean prototype had Gibson humbuckers, a body shaped like a Melody Maker, a Fender bridge and tailpiece, and a neck carved from solid aluminum. For extra support, a 3/16-inch plate was installed under the neck, extending back to the tailpiece. This neck/plate assembly evolved into the Bean receiver, a one-piece unit that anchors the strings at both ends (peghead and bridge) and serves as the neck and pickup mounting frame as well. This unitary construction enabled Bean almost literally to mount the pickups in the neck, and have the wood body surround the pickups flush, without mounting rings.

Bean got a job at a sports car dealership through Gary Kramer, later the namesake of Kramer guitars, the only other major manufacturer of aluminum-necked guitars. With money saved from that job, Bean and McElwee went into business in 1974. Kramer soon joined.

The company moved into an industrial complex in Sun Valley, California, opened a large factory, cranked up the lathes, and began manufacturing aluminum-necked instruments with Hawaiian koawood bodies. The necks were fashioned from Reynolds 6061-T6 aluminum, and players who didn't like the cold metal feel could order a neck coating of duPont Emron.

Travis Bean had his share of financial hassles. Tensions mounted between Bean and Gary Kramer, who decided to go on his own. Further conflicts arose between Bean and his financial backers. The company founder felt he was being pressured to compromise on quality, and he simply decided to leave the guitar business. The last Travis Bean was made on July 31, 1979.

VEGA; BACON & DAY

Boston's Julius Nelson was a Swedish immigrant and a fine cabinet maker who, along with several other men, founded the predecessor to the Vega Company in 1881. Early partners included two veterans from Pehr Anderberg's shop [see Ditson], C.F. Sundberg and a Mr. Swenson. Julius was the foreman of the crew, which numbered about two dozen men; during the mid-1920s banjo boom the total number of employees peaked at about 130. Julius and his brother Carl gradually bought out the interests of the other founders, who continued as workers. Carl served as sales director, office manager, and later president. The Nelsons renamed their company Vega, which means *star*—their logo was a star pattern—and incorporated it in 1903.

According to Carl Nelson's son, William W. Nelson (himself later president of Vega), the original factory was located on Commercial Street in Boston. After three fires it moved to 62 Sudbury Street, and in June 1917 it moved again to expanded quarters at 155 Columbus Avenue, where it stayed for at least another three decades. The Nelson brothers acquired banjo manufacturer A.C. Fairbanks & Company after that firm suffered a ruinous fire in March of 1904. Fairbanks veteran David L. Day became Vega's general manager.

Frederick J. Bacon of Vermont was a very popular banjo artist who lent his name to Vega-made banjos. In 1921 he set up his own 60,000-square-foot plant in Connecticut. In September 1922 David Day left Vega to become Bacon's vice-president and general manager. The company, now called Bacon & Day, marketed a few guitars, though according to collector George Gruhn they had no guitar-making facility of their own. Many Bacons were apparently made by Regal.

In September 1925 Vega announced the Vegaphone model. During 1929 and 1930 the company, profoundly affected by the Depression, began to concentrate less on banjos and more on guitars. In September 1933 the Vegaphone model was expanded into the Vegaphone carved-top line with steel-reinforced necks. During the mid 1930s Vega advertised Señorita and Super 400-size Sultana Grande arch-top models, both made by Regal. (Regal also made the latter type guitar under its own name.) Gretsch acquired the Bacon name about 1940.

In February 1936 Vega announced its Electrovox electric guitar with Dual-Tone pickup and amplifier. In November of that same year Carl Fischer Musical Instruments Company became Vega's sole national distributor. In May of 1937 Vega announced its Vibra electric footpedal, a volume control for electric guitars, and in June of that year it marketed a $100 six-tube amplifier and AC/DC electric guitar outfit. Two years later it announced its electric violin. It also manufactured electric Hawaiian guitars and electric mandolins, their pickups designed by company president William W. Nelson. Vega also made some of the guitars for Weymann & Son. During the 1930s Vega was reported to have produced over 40,000 guitars.

A lovely Vega with a very unusually arched top and back, unique f-holes, and a delicate inlay. *Ax-In-Hand*

Vega C-66 Advanced Model, late-1930s type; two-pieced carved spruce top, single-piece bird's-eye maple back, one-piece mahogany neck, 17-inch body, 25-inch scale, gold-foil sticker; the serial no. 39117 is stamped on the end of the peghead. *Ed Britt*

GROSSMAN MUSIC CO.
KLEARTONE
CLEVELAND, OHIO
VEGA
Famous Vegaphone Guitars
Made by Vega
A Name Renowned the World Over
VEGA
No. C-60
$125.00
Illustration of Double Steel Reinforced Neck
No. C-70
$200.00
No. C-80
$285.00

1935 Grossman catalogue, Vega models (*left to right*) C-60, C-80, C-70.

Vega Duo-Tron, circa 1948: orange see-through tuning machine buttons, screw-in jack attachment, tailpiece-mounted knobs, and a spectacular one-piece curly maple back.

Nelson took a leave of absence in September of 1942 to do war work and was temporarily replaced by John A. Allen. In October 1947 Vega unveiled its Duo-Tron Spanish guitar, and at about this time another model, the Supertron, was also introduced. In November 1949 a new line of cutaway guitars was announced. Vega was by then a major wholesaler as well as a manufacturer, and it bought bodies from Harmony in addition to making its own. By 1950 John Allen had become general manager and William Nelson was treasurer. Vega moved in 1961 to 40 Leon Street in Boston and again in September 1966 to 155 Reservoir Street in nearby Needham Heights.

On May 17, 1970, Vega was acquired by Martin, who moved the operation to Nazareth, Pennsylvania. At the time, Vega was a small operation of only about 18 people including office staff and production crew, and they built flat-top guitars and banjos. Martin soon laid off the crew, folded the guitar operation, and applied the Vega brand name to an imported line. A decade later William Nelson recalled: "We had a lot of labor disputes and union problems, and we really weren't doing all that well. Martin wanted to acquire a banjo operation. I was the sole owner at the time and my helpers were getting on in years, so it seemed like a good time to sell." In 1980 Martin sold Vega to Sun Pyo Hong, president of Korea's Galaxie Trading Corporation.

Harvey Citron (*left*) and Joe Veillette. ***Elliott Landy***

VEILLETTE-CITRON

Joe Veillette (a former student of Michael Gurian's) and Harvey Citron met in 1966 while attending City College of New York's school of architecture. After years of experimentation, small-scale construction, and repairs, they founded their company in 1974, collaborating the following year on designs for an electric guitar and bass. They soon outgrew their first shop, a converted storefront owned by Tom Vinci of Vinci Strings, and the pair relocated in Brooklyn's Marine Park. In February 1979 they moved again, to Kingston, New York. After exhibiting their prototypes at the June 1976 National Association of Music Merchants (NAMM) show, they hired two employees and began production. Over the next few years Veillette-Citron became fairly well-known for its elegant, expensive electrics.

Veillette-Citron 8-string bass (*left*) and laminated-body electric guitar. ***Elliott Landy***

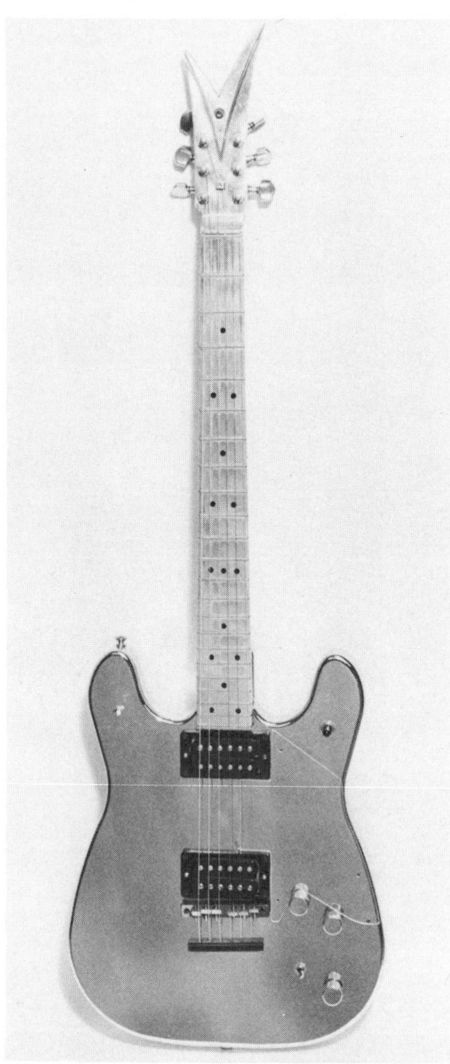

Veleno aluminum electric guitar, mirror finish.
Dan Kronemann/Jon Bartlett

VELENO

John Veleno of St. Petersburg, Florida, was a machinist and a guitar teacher with an idea: in order to attract more students to his guitar studio and to circumvent a municipal ordinance restricting the size of business signs, he would construct a shiny aluminum guitar-shaped mailbox. In 1968 or 1969 Veleno's raw materials supplier suggested that he build a real guitar instead, and that's just what he did.

The top and back halves of the double-cutaway symmetrical Veleno body were machined out of a solid aluminum block in such a way as to leave supporting struts and ⅛-inch-thick rims. The neck was cast from an aluminum/magnesium compound, shaped like a Telecaster neck, and contoured on the fretting surface to resemble a Les Paul Standard fingerboard. There was no fingerboard as such; the Veleno's fret slots were cut directly into the neck. Several brands of pickups were used. The mirror finish consisted of layers of zinc, then copper, then chrome. John's wife designed the V-shaped peghead, which was ornamented with a replica of her birthstone, the ruby.

VIVI-TONE

Among the grand gaggle of rare birds, the early-1930s Vivi-Tone is a virtual pterodactyl, as goofy looking and extinct as a trilobite. But its inventor was Lloyd Loar, Gibson's most revered instrument designer, and the Vivi-Tone manifests several of his most radical principles. In fact, Loar was ultimately too radical for Gibson; he left the company in part because of its

Vivi-Tone acoustic-electric, detail: drawer-mounted pickup, twin bridges, adjustment levers.
Rich Masterson

This Vivi-Tone has soundholes in its back, or "secondary soundboard."

reluctance to accept his designs for electric instruments. A list of one Vivi-Tone's features, to cite an example, looks like a string of typographical errors: one soundhole is located under the bridge, and the back is carved from spruce and has two f-holes, like a top.

Loar conceived several fine Gibsons (and perhaps the Heavens and the Earth, if early company accounts are to be believed). Lewis A. Williams and Walter Moon, who became Vivi-Tone's president, formed a partnership with Loar and incorporated their new company on November 1, 1933, in Gibson's hometown of Kalamazoo, Michigan; executive offices were at 6330 Gratiot Avenue in Detroit.

Their basic instrument departed from traditional guitar theory in several respects. For the back, Loar chose spruce for precisely the same reasons (resonant qualities, straightness of grain) that most luthiers select it for tops. He perforated the back with soundholes, then extended the rims outward so that the player's body would not come into contact with the back. All of this was to convert the back from a generally inert refractive surface to an active vibrating tone source. Loar called it the *secondary soundboard.*

The Vivi-Tone's top, or *primary soundboard,* is also unconventional, with a single soundhole located directly under the bridge. In the patent document of this guitar, No. 2,020,557, filed May 14, 1934, and granted November 12, 1935, Loar explained, "I make the primary soundboard continuous, or imperforate, from each foot of the bridge to all edges of the board, so that there is no interruption in the travel of vibration from the feet of the bridge to the edges of the board." An internal framework of bars and blocks connects the headblock, tailblock, and two "tops" so that the body vibrates as an integrated system. Brochures solemnly affirmed that the sound chamber was "manufactured under stethoscope testing."

Though slightly crowned for added strength, the twin bound sunburst soundboards are generally flat. Company literature challenged prospective buyers to compare Vivi-Tone's vibration to a conventional arch-top, asserting that on the former "the finger so placed will be made numb from the high intensity of vibration even at the rim." Other features of the $59 Vivi-Tone acoustic include Grover tuners, "Fairy Action High Frets," a manganese tailpiece, a steel-reinforced mahogany neck with a dovetail joint, and a 20-fret fingerboard inlaid with mother-of-pearl. Options included a high string nut and a reversible bridge with straight-line notches for Hawaiian playing.

In line with advertising practices common during the period, the Vivi-Tone was touted as being so superior to competing products ("it will carry 125 feet farther than any guitar made") that comparisons were supposedly laughable. In line with ad-

Mid-1930s Vivi-Tone plank-body electric, one of the very earliest solidbody guitars. ***Stu Cohen/Steve Gallo***

Lloyd Loar's homely duckling, the acoustic-electric Vivi-Tone, with Vivi-Tone Type 2 amp (note speaker cover plate). *Rich Masterson*

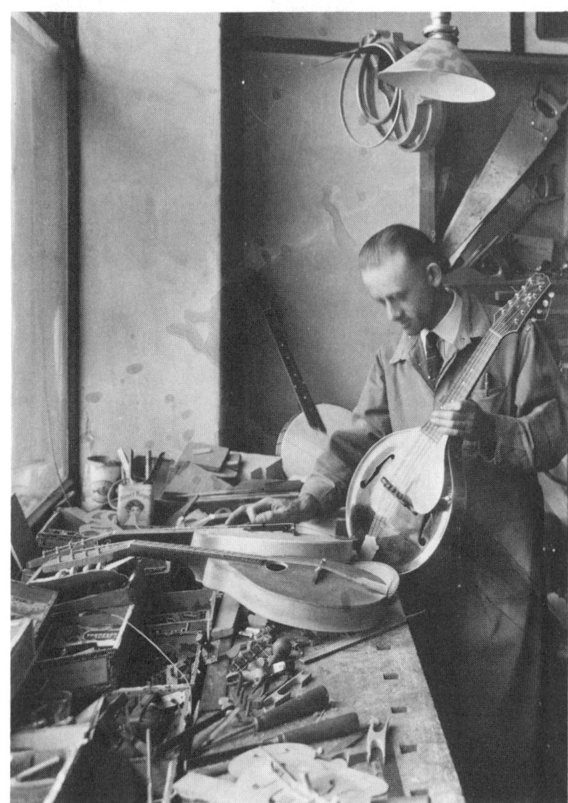

Lloyd Loar with a 10-string mando-viola in his workshop. *Julius Bellson*

vertising practices that, for better or worse, continue to this day, the guitar was practically guaranteed to make one a better player: "Beginners play well in a short time—hold interest in practice and playing; players improve unbelievably—many become virtuosi."

Lloyd Loar's early-1930s acoustic-electric models were even more strange, one type built out of solid wood (perhaps America's first solidbody, though never produced on a significant scale), and another, a hollowbody, with a pickup attached to a rim-mounted drawer that slid in and out of the instrument's body. The latter is a standout in American guitar's noble heritage of bizarre designs. As Loar expert Roger H. Siminoff said in *Frets* magazine, "Basically, Loar's approach to designing double basses and violins was to do away with just about everything but the pickup and strings." Loar's hollowbody electric evidenced a similar approach to isolate the instrument's purely electric qualities. In one of his patents (No. 2,025,875, filed January 27, 1934; granted December 31, 1935), he specified that his guitar could be used "either as a generator, *or a musical instrument,* or both" (emphasis added).

Loar's hollow electric instrument was one of the most unusual guitar designs of all time. It incorporated two bridges, and its pickup was mounted on a drawer which slid into a hole in the body's left side. The base of the standard bridge, or "string bridge," was attached to a support plate. One end of this plate was magnetized, and it was suspended over the pickup inside the body. The top of the bridge poked through a hole in the soundboard and supported the strings. When the strings were struck, the vibrating, magnetized bridge support activated the interior pickup.

The guitar's back, or secondary soundboard, had its own bridge, a flat wooden board that attached to the back's interior surface and extended through the top just ahead of, and parallel to, the string bridge. This back bridge served as the pivot point for a pair of rocker-arm levers (one for treble, one for bass), positioned parallel to the strings and just underneath them. Ahead of the back bridge/pivot point (i.e., toward the neck) the levers attached to top-mounted adjustment bolts. The other end of each lever attached to the string bridge. By raising the bolts and rocking the levers over the back bridge, the player could transfer the string vibrations through the regular bridge/pickup assembly, activating the guitar's electric mode. By tightening them, he could transfer the vibrations through the back bridge/pivot point to the back, or secondary soundboard, engaging the acoustic mode. A mix of electric and acoustic modes could also be effected by adjusting the bolts accordingly. A medley of odd features, the multimode guitar is but a single chapter in Lloyd's lore. For details, see the Gibson section.

WASHBURN; LYON & HEALY

Its history reaching back into the last century, Lyon & Healy is one of America's oldest music companies. Though now known primarily for its harps, it was at one time one of the world's largest guitar makers, servicing Montgomery Ward, other mail-order houses, and several distributors. The firm was founded in 1864 by Oliver Ditson [see Ditson] as his Chicago distributor. It was named after Ditson associates George Washburn Lyon, who lent his middle name to the fretted instruments, and P. J. Healy, a guitar maker who got his start in the music business as an errand boy for the G. P. Reed retail store on Boston's Tremont Row. Aside from manufacturing highly regarded flat-tops, the company also took credit for inventing the tenor guitar and for bringing the tiple from South America to the United States.

During the late 1800s Lyon & Healy's huge factory was located at Randolph Street and Ogden Avenue, Chicago, with the salesrooms at State and Monroe Streets. (By the late 1920s, the address was Wabash Avenue at Jackson Boulevard.) The 1899 catalogue boasted that 20,000 Washburns were then in use, and later literature claimed that the annual production was an astounding 100,000 instruments. Whereas Martin and Gibson had begun as one-man operations and grew to larger shops and factories only as demand exceeded supply, Lyon & Healy started big, with clear intentions of mass production and with only a few pretenses of extensive individual craftsmanship. In their own way the Washburn brochures were manifestoes of the Industrial Revolution, marking a decided shift away from the traditional emphasis on handwork. One proclamation (suggestive of Gibson's purple prose of the 1920s) was that: "The scale on every Washburn is guaranteed to be *absolutely correct,* the tone unequaled, the workmanship unapproachable. The guitars . . . so graceful that competitors constantly endeavor to copy them but never succeed. With special machinery . . . it is possible for the manufacturers of Washburns to more accurately duplicate their instruments than for other makers, the others depending to a large extent on their workmen, more or less at their mercy, never certain of the result, and often making dismal failures."

Another departure was Lyon & Healy's contention that, for guitar making, mahogany ("an honest wood, trustworthy") is superior to rosewood, the latter alleged—at least in one catalogue—to be "very unsatisfactory, unreliable, so porous and so coarse that it never can be depended on to withstand time's destroying touch; it deteriorates in appearance, continually, from the day it is finished." This argument is particularly odd, considering that the brochure that contained it also offered a

Washburn's Models 156, 256, and 356 of 1897 varied in body size, but all were ornamented and trimmed like this one. ***Acuff***

Near right: Number 4 Auditorium size Washburn, the company's largest model (14½ inches across). Similar to an early Martin, it has "new model" marked on the interior, and X bracing. Nonoriginal bridge. *Don's Guitar Shop/Don E. Teeter* *Far right:* Type 1 Washburn, 1897, $20–25. *Dick Gray/Tom Erlewine*

whole line of gut-string flat-tops, all of rosewood. The explanation: Lyon & Healy felt that "the public demand for this material should be recognized, but any of these instruments may also be had in Mahogany" (which the brochure went on to recommend).

Lyon & Healy's famed 1897 catalogue included two lines. The budget series cost from $5.63 to $22.50, comprised both gut-strings and steel-strings, and included the Jupiter, Columbus, Marquette, Lakeside (oak body), Arion (mahogany), and American Conservatory (rosewood). The official Washburn line embraced nine slot-head flat-tops, their four sizes paralleling those of the 1899 models detailed below. The decorative appointments for 1897 were—type 1: top edge and soundhole trimmed with plain stripes, unbound fingerboard; type 2: diagonal-stripe soundhole and body trim, unbound fingerboard with dots; type 3: bound board, decorative markers at frets 7, 9, and 12; type 4: added marker at fret 5, bridge inlaid with pearl, unbound peghead; type 5: bound peghead, inlaid bridge, markers starting at fret 5; type 6: markers beginning at fret 1, rectangular bridge; type 7: ornate, bridge carved and fan-shaped at either end, ebony board; type 8: extremely ornate, solid pearl fingerboard, silver-plated tuners with pearl buttons; and type 9: top-of-the-line ($220 in Grand Concert size), entire length of fingerboard inlaid with urns and twisting vines, sometimes called the tree-of-life pattern.

Washburn, gut strings, Brazilian rosewood body, banjo-type mechanical friction pegs. *Vintage Fret Shop/A. Caswell*

The 1899 Washburn bodies may be classified in four sizes (all dimensions approximate, length by width in inches): No. 3/4 (15 by 10), No. 1 (Standard, 18 by 12½), No. 2 (Concert, 18¾ by 13¼), No. 3 (Grand Concert, 19 by 14), and No. 4 (Auditorium, 19½ by 14½).

The styles of ornamentation for 1899 may be organized as follows: type 1, plain edge between top and rim (no trim); type

2, simple inlay around top edge, no bridge inlays; type 3, bridge inlays, unbound fingerboard and peghead, body trimmed with alternating black/white block purfling; type 4, bound board and head, dot neck; type 5, star peghead inlay, more elaborate position markers and trim; type 6, fan-shaped peghead inlay, carved bridge (fan-shaped at either end); and type 8, very wide top trim with a lyre ornament on the soundboard's lower center edge. There was no type 7.

The 1899 model designations consisted of the size number, then a zero, and then the ornamentation number. Thus, Model 203 was a Concert sized guitar (No. 2) with trim package No. 3, while 308 was a Grand Concert with top-of-the-line appointments. Prices ranged from the $20 No. 101 3/4 to the $100 No. 308. The most expensive models cost only about half of their 1897 counterparts, and there was nothing in the 1899 line to compare to the tree of life or solid pearl fingerboard of 1897.

But the 1913 line again offered a wide range of guitars, all of them slot-head rosewood flat-tops with twelfth-fret neck/body joints. The astonishingly fancy model 3150—virtually encrusted with pearl, abalone, and celluloid trim—cost $237.50, an extraordinary sum for the time.

Lyon & Healy's plant suffered a major fire not long after the turn of the century, and most or all of their later guitars were built by other manufacturers: Vega and especially Regal.

In 1928 or 1929, control of the Washburn name passed from Lyon & Healy to the Tonk Bros., a large distributor that figured prominently in the histories of several Chicago manufacturers. Regal continued to build Washburns after the Tonk acquisition. (Collector Jon Lundberg reported an oval-hole carved-top whose headstock was mistakenly labeled Washburn in front, Regal in back.) Some "Tonk Washburns" were built by W. R. Stewart.

During the 1970s the Washburn name was acquired by an importer of guitars made in the Orient.

WEYMANN & SON (W&S)

H. A. Weymann & Son, Incorporated, later the Weymann Company, was established in 1864 at 1108 Chestnut Street in Philadelphia. Later Philadelphia addresses included 10th and Filbert, and 1613 Chestnut Street. It incorporated in 1904 and marketed guitars and other instruments under several names, including Weymann, Keystone State, W&S, and later, Varsity, their quality ranging from student-grade to very fine. Some were manufactured by Vega, and others were likely made by Regal. A catalogue from about 1914 depicts four guitar styles priced from $35 to $60. The company's label said: *Weymann Highest Grade, H. A. Weymann & Son, Phila, PA, Makers of The Keystone State, W&S.*

A W&S (Weymann & Son) flat-top: rosewood body, spruce top, mahogany neck, pyramid bridge, and multicolored wood inlays around the soundhole and top. Note the unusually shaped, half-slotted peghead. Very similar guitars with identical pegheads were labeled "Regal" and "Bruno," which suggests that Regal made them all and sold them through various distributors. Weymann was best known for its Jimmie Rodgers–endorsed flat-top. ***Fred Isenor/Charles Fullerton***

ZION

After nearly ten years of repair and customizing experience, Ken Hoover founded Zion Guitar Technology in 1980. Zion gained considerable notice in 1983 when its one-of-a-kind Silverbird appeared on the cover of *Guitar Player.* The Silverbird sported a dazzling custom finish by Wayne Jarrett, the firm's custom paint whiz.

In 1987, Hoover developed the Radicaster, which is reminiscent of a Strat, but with ultra-deep cutaways, a 22-fret ebony fretboard, basswood body, and Floyd Rose. Shown here is the Radicaster/ Classic Maple Series, with EMG pickups and a bird's-eye maple top.

While earlier Zion guitars were built entirely in the U.S., more recent models feature bodies and necks milled in Canada. All other work is performed at Zion's Greensboro, North Carolina plant by about a half-dozen craftsmen, who produce 40 to 50 guitars a month.

In this photo Carl holds a 4-string curly maple fretless bass. In the foreground, he is flanked by two of his 6-string basses. Note their starkly original body-bridge extensions. In the rear, an early maple scroll-body 6-string and a maple left-handed 8-string.

CARL THOMPSON

Every Carl Thompson instrument is unique; there are no models, per se. Carl builds about five or six of these uncompromisingly personal, custom-order instruments each year, most of them 6-string basses.

Carl moved from Pitcairn, Pennsylvania to New York City in 1967. To supplement his income as a musician, he worked in Dan Armstrong's guitar shop, where he learned repairs from Eddie Diehl. After Armstrong closed his doors, Carl teamed with Charles LoBue to form the Guitar Lab. The pair split up, and in 1971 Carl set up a new shop with fellow guitarist Joel Frutkin. The first Carl Thompson bass was made in 1974. Soon, noted players such as Anthony Jackson and Rick Laird placed orders.

Carl gained considerable notice after designing and building a bass for Stanley Clarke. Shortly after that Carl and Graig Bennett built a 36-inch scale, twin truss rod mahogany 6-string bass for Anthony Jackson. The carved heel block is a distinctive feature of every Carl Thompson instrument.

The early layout work (cutting neck blanks, roughing out bodies, etc.) is performed in Carl's small shop in Stahlstown, Pennsylvania, while the final carving, electronics, and finishing is done in Thompson's apartment workshop in Brooklyn. Carl generally works alone, although Michael Parisi helps with layout work and Thompson's early influence, Eddie Diehl, helps with detailing.

FODERA

Fodera Guitars was founded in 1983 by luthiers Vincent Fodera (*right*) and Joseph Lauricella (*left*), shown here with virtuoso performer Anthony Jackson and a 1988 Jackson Signature Fodera Contrabass guitar.

Located in Brooklyn, the Fodera shop produces four to ten stunning solidbody guitars and basses each month. The superbly crafted instruments are among the finest available. The line includes the 4-string Monarch Deluxe bass with 24 frets and a 34-inch scale length; the Emperor Elite 5-string bass, with neck-through-body construction and custom active circuitry; and the 6-string Jackson Contrabass.

Foderas are distinguished by special-design Bartolini pickups, active/passive circuitry, a unique solid brass adjustable locking bridge, and domestic and exotic woods such as shedua, bubinga, zebrawood, koa, and spalted beech.

Bill Collings with a Clarence White model.
Paul Bardagjy

COLLINGS

In 1975, Ohio native Bill Collings moved to Texas, where he built his first instruments. Eleven years later he opened Collings Guitars in Austin. *Frets* magazine called him one of the luthiers who has "raised the art dramatically in the last two decades."

Patterned after Clarence White's modified Martin D-28, Collings' own limited production Clarence White model, shown here, has an enlarged soundhole and elongated fretboard. Collings built the late-1980s Gruhn acoustic line, co-designed by George Gruhn. Collings also crafts arch-tops, and they are simply breathtaking.

Jerry Jones' Guitarlin extended-range 6-string is a companion to his longhorn basses and guitars.

JERRY JONES

Jerry Jones began practicing his craft in 1978 at Nashville's Old Time Pickin' Parlour, and two years later he opened his own shop. A request from Merle Haggard for a lighter version of Jerry's neck-through Telecaster-style guitar resulted in the development of a distinctive semi-hollow guitar. Several models, including the Fat Cat, were based on this design.

Long intrigued by the simplicity of Danelectros and recognizing a growing demand for vintage-style instruments, Jerry introduced several Danelectro-type models, including the "long horn" shown here. As we go to press, Jones employs five craftsmen and manufactures about 300 guitars a year.

KEN SMITH

New York's Ken Smith helped pioneer the concept of the high-tech custom bass, and he remains at the forefront of the craft. He was a professional studio musician who needed a better instrument, so he built one.

Smith began in the early 1970s to research the intricacies of luthiery; in 1978 he started his business. "I studied and played some of the basses by the Italian masters," he says. "After all, the art is centuries old, and there must be something useful we can adapt to improve the electric." In 1980 the first Smiths appeared, including the memorable IIG, which had a maple body with rosewood trimmings, a multi-lam graphite-inlaid neck, rosewood-encased custom Bill Lawrence pickups, metal disc peghead logo, and a massive 24-karat gold-plated control panel.

As we go to press, Ken Smith offers the B.T. Customs, early versions of which appeared in 1981. There are three models, all with a neck-through design and heelless cutaway, a feature as beautiful as it is functional. The models include the Standard Custom (3-piece neck), the Custom (5-piece neck), and Custom G with graphite supports inlaid on both sides of the truss rod under the fingerboard, to combine the strength and tone of graphite with the feel of wood. Smith offers 4-, 5- (high C or low B), and 6-string models; the 6-string appeared in 1981 and was designed with Anthony Jackson's input. Several exquisite body woods are available—bubinga, figured oak, flamed ebony, and others.

Each month, Smith and eight employees produce about 24 basses. Today's models are streamlined, with sculpted bodies, sleek black pickup covers, and fewer knobs and switches. Details include a "coat of arms" carving behind the headstock, scalloped string nut, and a pearl logo. Shown here: cover photo, 1988 catalogue.

MODULUS GRAPHITE

At an aerospace company, Geoff Gould worked on projects such as the Voyager Jupiter/Saturn probe. In the late 1970s he and several associates formed Modulus Graphite, whose instruments and necks are produced using the same processes and materials used in the manufacture of satellite antennae.

A prototype was developed in 1976; the first commercial bass with a Modulus molded graphite neck (U.S. patent No. 4,145,948) was premiered by Alembic at a January 1977 trade show. Since then Modulus has made legal agreements with Steinberger, Kawai, Tokai, Status, and Cort/Westheimer (Hohner), allowing them to manufacture their own molded graphite necks. Other companies using completed necks built by Modulus, or Modulus-made neck shells, include Alembic, Moonstone, Music Man, Ibanez, Aria, and Zon.

While the company's initial products were Fender-style replacement necks, Modulus soon began to market complete instruments. In the early 1980s, 5- and 6-string basses were introduced. The Quantum 5 SPX, Modulus' best seller in the late 1980s, has a 35-inch scale length that according to Gould increases the response and definition of the notes below low E. Many well-known artists have used Modulus necks or instruments, including Jack Casady, John Entwistle, Phil Lesh, Adam Clayton, The Edge, and Andy West. Geoff Gould is shown here with his triple-pickup 6-string bass. *Photo: Jon Sievert*

NOVA

John Buscarino of Largo, Florida apprenticed with Augustine Lo Prinzi and Robert Benedetto, and then in 1981 went into business for himself. Today his Nova Guitar Co. builds about 10 to 12 instruments each month, including rock and roll oriented solidbodies, cutaway acoustics, and basses. Nova's "deadbolt" locking neck joint permits a smaller, more comfortable heel. Shown here is Earl Klugh's electric classical.

FRITZ BROTHERS

In 1987 Nashville luthier/repairman Roger Fritz joined Marc Fisher and blues/rock/country guitarist Roy Buchanan in forming Fritz Brothers Guitars. The company relocated to Mobile, Alabama in 1988 and began building the Roy Buchanan Bluesmaster, as well as three other handsome models. Buchanan died later that year, but the Bluesmaster is still available, with a portion of the proceeds going to the late virtuoso's estate. Roger Fritz is shown here with a completed semi-hollow Buchanan Deluxe.

Tobias workshop; Mike Tobias in right rear corner.

SCHOENBERG

Schoenberg Guitars was founded in 1986 by fingerstyle guitarist Eric Schoenberg and self-taught luthier Dana Bourgeois, and for a long time they were the company's only employees. During the early years, Schoenberg and C.F. Martin formed a unique alliance intended to combine the accuracy and efficiency of Martin's superb production capabilities with the skill and personal touch of the luthier. Given the status, beautiful sound, and impeccable quality of the guitars, the alliance succeeded.

Bourgeois left in 1990 and was replaced by longtime Schoenberg associate T.J. Thompson, who performs more handwork on the instruments than his predecessor. "T.J. braces and voices the tops himself in his Lansing, Michigan shop," says Schoenberg. "We're aiming for higher quality and lower quantity, and doing more reproductions, such as a dead-ringer OM-28 that we call the Concert Model."

Schoenberg's standard model is the Soloist, patterned after Martin's revered 1929–1933 OM, or Orchestra Model. Shown here is a Martin-style OM-45 DLX, one of Schoenberg's reissues. Features include wooden purflings, ebony neck-reinforcement bar, bar frets, and gold-engraved banjo tuners with pearl buttons. *Photo: David Etnier*

TOBIAS

Michael Tobias belongs to a handful of uncompromising builders who represent the highest standards of the art and craft of contemporary guitar making. In 1977, after a three-year stint repairing instruments at The Guitar Shop in Washington, D.C., he established his own business, also called The Guitar Shop, in Orlando, Florida. The first electric he built was a 4-string bass (serial no. 0178, for January 1978). By 1981, The Guitar Shop had produced about 40 Tobias instruments, mostly basses. Tobias moved to San Francisco in 1981, then to the Los Angeles area in 1982. Since then, his company has acquired seven employees and now produces about 24 instruments each month, most of them 5-string basses and all of them with a multi-laminated neck-through design.

Tobias basses feature stunning woods such as figured maple, purpleheart, koa, bubinga, zebrawood, flamed or bird's-eye maple, and cocobolo.

Michael Tobias added: "Aside from accommodating the different numbers of strings, we use the same special-design Bartolini electronics for all our basses; these are 'transparent' circuits that allow the lamination and combination of woods to determine the sound. The neck is carved asymmetrically, and all detailing is performed to maintain a comfortable playing position."

Tobias Basic 5 Flame + bass.

PREMIER

Premier guitars were made in New York City (some of them, anyway). Collector Skip Henderson told Teisco Del Rey in *Guitar World* magazine that some early plywood-top arch-tops can be positively identified as American-made due to their Waverly tuners. Still, the best-known Premiers are the flashy solidbodies from the 1960s and, apparently, the late 1950s—at least some of which were assembled from Italian bodies and other foreign parts. Distributed by Sorkin, many of these guitars featured Premier's hallmark, an upper-body scroll/curlicue. Associated brand names include Royce, Strad-o-lin (flat-tops and budget solidbodies), Bell-tone (cheap, pseudo-resophonic guitars), and Marvel.

SPECTOR

Spector Guitars was founded in August 1976 by repairman Stuart Spector and cabinet maker Alan Charney, members of the Brooklyn Woodworkers Cooperative. Their early SB-1 basses and G-1 guitars had neck-through-body construction, black walnut bodies, and DiMarzio pickups.

By 1976 the soon-to-be-revolutionary Ned Steinberger had joined the co-op, and as Spector recalls, "he became interested in our instruments and offered to design a new one, resulting in the NS-1 bass." The novel body curvature provided comfort and balance, as well as Spector's immediately recognizable hallmark. By 1978 Spector had five employees and had expanded to a 5,000-square-foot shop. In 1982, the EMG pickup-equipped NS-1B and NS-2J bolt-on neck basses were added. "They introduced a much-copied, deep-inset neck joint," asserts Spector.

The year 1984 saw the introduction of the Steinberger-designed NSX bass, with a flat body and bolt-on neck. Kramer purchased Spector in December of 1985 and relocated the equipment to Kramer's 40,000-square-foot facility in Neptune, New Jersey, where Spector and Charney continue to supervise production. The latest instruments are the NS-5 5-string bass and NS-6T guitar. Some of the original U.S.-made models later became imports. Shown here are Stuart Spector at left with an NS-2 bass, and Alan Charney with an NS-6T guitar. *Photo: Gerard Sea*

HARPTONE

Harptone, of 127 South 15th Street in Newark, New Jersey, was established in 1893 as the commercial successor to the Felsberg Company (established 1886). During the 1930s, president Morris Brooks guided Harptone to prominence as a manufacturer of accessories—most notably its Bull's Head cases. A few guitars were made between 1924 and 1942 (and some electric models and amps in the late 1940s), but it wasn't until 1966 that Harptone began making the instruments for which it is remembered today: arched-back acoustic models.

The company's chief designer during the 1960s was Sam Koontz, whose pegheads were one of Harptone's chief identifying features. The line included dreadnoughts, jumbos, 12-strings, the cutaway Sultan, and a guitar-like acoustic bass. In 1973, a line of cutaway electric-acoustics was listed ($720–$1,600) along with the 17-inch-wide George Harrison/Ringo Starr model.

In the mid-1970s Harptone's trade name for guitars and guitar manufacturing equipment was sold to the Diamond-S Musical Instrument Corporation of East Main Street, Independence, Virginia, who continued to manufacture arched-back Harptone guitars on a limited basis. Their models were the D-10 (mahogany), D-20 (maple), and D-30 (rosewood) dreadnoughts; C-20 maple cutaway jumbo; B-4 acoustic bass; and T-20 thin-body steel-string.

Harptone Sultan.

SCHECTER

The whole consciousness of assembling custom instruments through mix and match combinations of neck woods, body woods, pickup configurations, and hardware owes a lot to David Schecter's pioneering work.

In the early 1970s Schecter began a repair/modification business, generally working with Fender-style guitars. International Sales Associates (ISA) was formed to market his products, which included tapped pickup assemblies, Tele-style bridges with individual string pieces and bodies and necks made of exotic woods. ISA also offered completed Schecter instruments. The staff grew to include such luminaries as Dan Armstrong and Tom Anderson.

By the late 1970s the company seemed well established, but too-rapid growth caused problems with overhead and cash flow. To keep afloat, distribution rights were sold to a Dallas food wholesaler. But the California manufacturing plant could not keep up with the orders taken in Texas. At that time, said a Schecter source, "the Texas faction found alternate sources for their instruments [suggesting the Orient instead of California]."

Through legal action, the California group regained rights to the Schecter name in 1988. In 1990, Schecter Guitar Research maintained a limited production shop in Van Nuys, California. Shown here: a pair of 1989 limited-edition Strat-style Schecters.

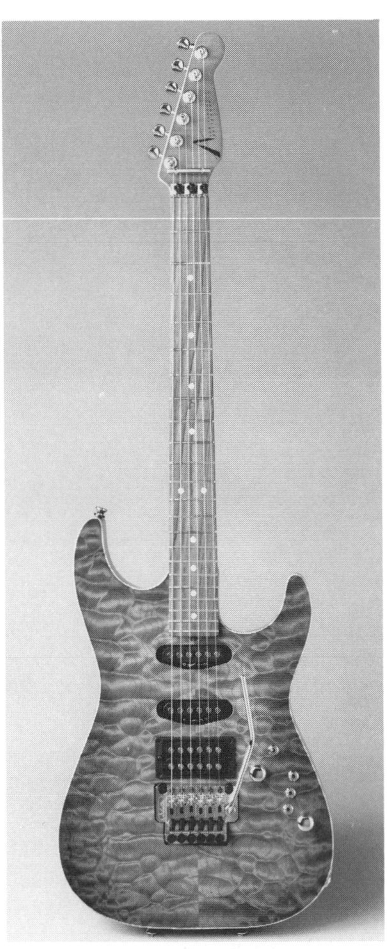

TOM ANDERSON

Tom Anderson worked for Schecter from 1977 until mid-1984, when he started his own business. Since then he has been acclaimed for his fine Strat-style guitars as well as his own designs. "We've tried to take existing concepts and then refine them," he says. "We've installed sunken tremolos, refined our pickups and electronic switching, and also contoured the heel block to make the neck more accessible—mostly just making guitars that work right."

Anderson favors basswood for bodies. "It's very light, as light as the lightest alder. I like the way it sounds. It's very harmonic and rich, and slightly compressed sounding—when you hit it real hard it doesn't hurt your ears. At loud volumes it really sings, and you can feel it vibrating against your body. There are some wonderful alder guitars out there, but out of ten pieces of alder, three might be bad. But basswood is amazingly consistent."

As we go to press, sole owner Tom Anderson and his workforce of ten are producing about 25 guitars a month in their Newbury Park, California plant. Luthier Steve Ripley has known Anderson since the days when they worked together at Schecter, and Tom now makes bodies and necks for Ripley's unique stereo guitars. Ripley credits Anderson as simply "the best Fender-style body and neck maker in the world." *Photo: Gerry Wilson Studios*

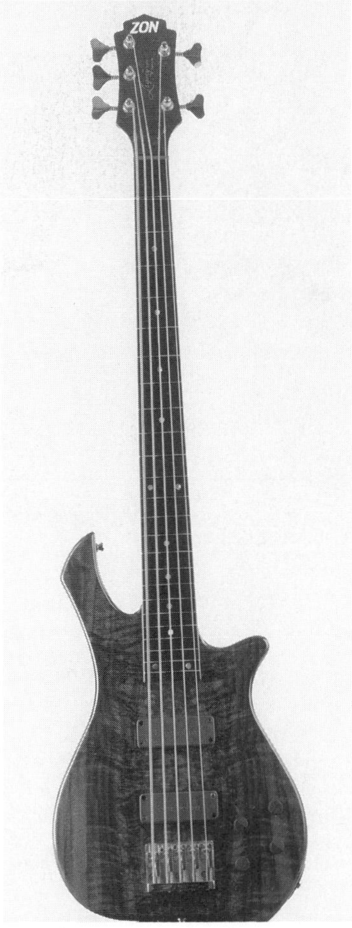

ZON

Musician/luthier Joseph Zon founded Zon Guitars in 1982, and four years later moved his company from Buffalo, New York, to Redwood City, California, expanding the facility to accommodate an increasing demand.

The hollow, no-truss-rod Zon neck is fashioned from 100 percent carbon graphite fibers. Graphite's density and stiffness help increase sustain and harmonics, promote an even response throughout the fingerboard's range, and eliminate the sympathetic vibrations that can cause dead spots. The bolt-on neck models have Zon's unique deep-inset/extended heel design, which provides more contact surface between the neck and body for better stability and sustain; other models feature a set-in neck, which has very much of a neck-through-body feel and stability. The lightweight hand-shaped bodies are constructed of maple and alder.

The Legacy Elite V 5-string shown here was introduced in 1986. Like all Zon basses, it has active electronics, a phenolic fingerboard with 24 frets, a Schaller bridge, and custom-wound Bartolini pickups. *Guitar Player* reviewer Roger Sadowsky, himself a distinguished builder, commented that there was no standard neck width among makers of 5-strings, but that "Zon has used the string spacing (1⅞ inch at the nut) that may ultimately become the standard." Sadowsky described the interior circuit board, custom made to Zon's specs by Polyfusion Electronics, as "the most beautiful I have ever seen in a guitar or bass."

A Legacy 6-string was unveiled in 1988, expanding the line to eight basses and six guitars, all available in a variety of colors or with a laminated book-matched top of any of several gorgeous woods. Given their extraordinary craftsmanship, strength, tone, and beauty, it's not surprising that Zon instruments have been embraced by musicians in some of the world's most prominent bands.

VALLEY ARTS

Valley Arts began as a teaching studio in North Hollywood, California in 1963, relocated to Studio City, became a respected retail store specializing in pro-oriented services, and finally expanded into a production facility. In March 1989 the production was moved to a larger shop in North Hollywood. Designer/luthier/co-owner Michael McGuire supervises a workforce of over 15 employees who build about 75 guitars per month.

A long list of options (two scale lengths, eight body woods, twelve neck options, virtually any electronics package, etc.) permits almost endless personalizing. Many Valley Arts guitars are "ultimate Strat" type instruments, with generally Fender styling but significant refinements and innovations, including exotic woods, eye-popping finishes, a slightly scaled down body size, sophisticated electronics, and the "interlock" neck joint. Patented in 1987, the interlock neck joint is designed to facilitate fingerboard accessibility, a solid transfer of sound, and easy neck removal. These stunning instruments have been embraced by some of L.A.'s most esteemed and discriminating players, including Larry Carlton and Steve Lukather.

INDEX

Note: Italic page numbers refer to illustrations